Police powers
A practitioner's guide

THIRD EDITION

Howard Levenson, SOLICITOR,
Fiona Fairweather, SOLICITOR
and
Ed Cape, SOLICITOR

LAG Legal Action Group
1996

Third edition published in Great Britain 1996
by LAG Education and Service Trust Limited
242 Pentonville Road, London N1 9UN
First edition (as *A Practitioner's Guide to the Police and Criminal Evidence Act 1984*) 1985
Second edtion 1990

© Howard Levenson, Fiona Fairweather and Ed Cape 1996

British Library Cataloguing in Publication Data
A CIP catalogue record for this book is available from the British Library

ISBN 0 905099 62 1

The Codes of Practice (appendix 2) are Crown copyright and reprinted with the sanction
of the Controller of HMSO.

Phototypeset by Datix International Limited, Bungay, Suffolk
Printed in Great Britain by Bell & Bain Ltd, Glasgow

Preface and Acknowledgements

This book is the third edition of a book originally published by the Legal Action Group in January 1985 under the title *A Practitioner's Guide to the Police and Criminal Evidence Act 1984*.

The original authors are delighted to have been joined by Ed Cape for this edition and to have the advantage of his expertise and experience.

This is a subject that is never closed. The years since the second edition was published have seen the passage of much legislation on criminal law and police powers, in particular the Criminal Justice and Public Order Act 1994, as well as a thorough revision of the Codes of Practice and numerous new authoritative court rulings. As we go to press the Home Office is considering bringing in changes to the law on offensive weapons as a response to recent tragic events, and no doubt the run-up to the next general election will bring fevered political debate on the subject of police powers.

However, our task has not been to engage in political controversy but to set out as clearly as we can for the help of practitioners a statement of the law and a discussion of its meaning and ambiguities, endeavouring to state the law as it is on 1 January 1996.

We would like to acknowledge the forbearance, support and assistance of our families, Brian Bracegirdle, colleagues at our respective places of work, and of the Legal Action Group, with whom we have all been associated for many years, in particular its publishing staff, whose enthusiasm and efficiency in the preparation of this edition has been particularly welcome.

Contents

APPENDICES

Table of cases

xviii   *Table of cases*

Table of statutes

Table of statutory instruments

CHAPTER 1

General issues

This chapter contains a discussion of concepts which are essential to the operation of many of the police powers and duties referred to in the following chapters and which are mentioned repeatedly throughout the text. Consideration is given to the application of the Codes of Practice, the meaning of 'serious arrestable offence' and 'reasonable grounds', the definition of 'constable', the use of discretionary power and the validity of police actions. The application of the Police and Criminal Evidence Act 1984 to the armed forces is also discussed. The powers of customs and excise officers are dealt with separately. The 1984 Act forms the core of police powers but they are, in addition, found in many other statutes and in the common law. In this chapter, unless otherwise stated, section references are to the 1984 Act.

Codes of practice

The 1984 Act is supplemented by five Codes of Practice issued by the Secretary of State under ss60 and 66 of the Act. These codes cover:

- the exercise by police officers of statutory powers of stop and search (Code A)
- the searching of premises by police officers and the seizure of property found by police officers on persons or premises (Code B)
- the detention, treatment and questioning of persons by police officers (Code C)
- the identification of persons by police officers (Code D) and
- the tape recording of police interviews (Code E).

References in this book to the Codes are, unless otherwise indi-   1 cated, to the third edition, which came into effect in April 1995. In places, the codes restate the provisions of the Act (see appendix 2 for the text of the codes).

The Secretary of State may revise the whole or any part of a code at any time, in which case a draft should be published, representations considered and modifications made if necessary. The draft should then be laid before both Houses of Parliament, before being brought into operation by order made by statutory instrument.

Although the provisions of the codes most directly affect the conduct of police officers, the Act extends their ambit to all persons charged with the duty of investigating offences or charging suspects s67(9). While the codes clearly cover those under a statutory duty to investigate offences, for instance immigration and customs officers,[1] it has been held that others, such as commercial investigators and store detectives, who have contractual obligations involving investigation of crime, are also bound by the codes.[2] In *R v. Bayliss*[3] the Court of Appeal held that whether or not a person is subject to s67(9) is a question of fact in each case, although a question of law may arise if the duty involved the construction of a statute or other document. It might be that only part of an interview is covered.[4] It is undecided whether electricity officials are subject to the codes[5] while the RSPCA considers that its officers should be bound to comply with them.[6]

The codes contain, in places, 'Notes for Guidance'. These are not provisions of the codes, but are guidance only to police officers and others about their interpretation. There are also annexes to the codes which *are* provisions of the codes (see, eg, Code C para 1.3).

The Codes of Practice must be readily available at all police stations for consultation by police officers, detained persons and members of the public.[7] Specific provisions of the codes are described below in the relevant chapters.

---

1 See, eg, *R v Okafor* [1994] 3 All ER 741 and see further Chapter 9; see also *R v Director of Serious Fraud Office ex p Saunders* [1988] Crim LR 837.
2 See *R v Twaites and Brown* [1990] Crim LR 863; *Joy v The Federation Against Copyright Theft Ltd* [1993] Crim LR 588 and *R v Bayliss* [1994] Crim LR 687; but see *R v Seelig and Spens* (1991) 94 Cr App R 17, where DTI inspectors were held not to be investigating officers.
3 Above, n2.
4 Even if it is found that a person is not subject to the Codes, any evidence obtained in circumstances where there would have been a breach if s67(9) had been applicable, may still be excluded under ss76 or 78 (see chapter 11).
5 *R v Stewart* [1995] Crim LR 500.
6 *RSPCA v Eager* [1995] Crim LR 59.
7 In the case of Code E, in appropriate police stations (see Code E para 1.1).

The custody officer and the custody record

The role of the custody officer in relation to the keeping of custody records is described in detail in Code C para 2. The main safeguards in the Act relating to the detention, treatment and questioning of suspects in police detention, are the role of the custody officer (see below p148) and the records which are required to be kept for all persons in detention. The custody officer is under a duty to ensure that all persons in police detention at the police station are treated in accordance with the 1984 Act and any code issued under it (s39(1)). Defence lawyers should obtain copies of custody records as soon as possible; if there has been any breach of the provisions of the codes it will have the consequences described below.

When a person is brought to a police station under arrest or is arrested at a police station, the custody officer must clearly inform the person of his/her right to consult the Codes of Practice, as well as informing him/her of his/her other rights (Code C para 3.1, and see below p185).

A separate custody record must be opened as soon as practicable for each person detained at a police station. All information which has to be recorded under Code C must be recorded as soon as practicable, in the custody record, unless otherwise specified. Where any conduct towards the detainee requires the authorisation of an officer of a specified rank, the name of the officer must be entered into the custody record. This does not apply to terrorist investigations, when the warrant number and duty station of the officer will suffice. All entries in the custody record must be timed and signed by the person making them. Warrant or other identification numbers should be used in cases of detention under terrorism provisions, and, in the case of a record entered on a computer, this should be timed and contain the operator's identification (Code C para 2.6).

The custody officer is responsible for the accuracy and completeness of all entries in the custody record. The custody officer must also ensure that the record or a copy of the record accompanies a detained person who is transferred to another police station. The record should show the time and the reason for the transfer and the time a person is released from detention. A solicitor[8] or appropriate adult must be permitted to consult the custody record as soon as

8 Defined for the purposes of the codes as 'a solicitor who holds a current practising certificate, a trainee solicitor, a duty solicitor representative or an accredited representative [clerk] included on the register maintained by the Legal Aid Board' (Code C para 6.12).

practicable after their arrival at the police station (Code C para 2.4). On leaving police detention or appearing before a court, either the detainee, a legal representative or the appropriate adult should be supplied on request with a copy of the custody record as soon as practicable. This entitlement lasts for 12 months after release. Also, if any of the above named gives reasonable notice of a desire to see the original record, once the detainee is out of detention, this should be allowed (para 2.5).

Complaints

Code C also provides that if a complaint is made by or on behalf of a detained person about treatment after arrest, or if it comes to the notice of any officer that the detainee may have been treated improperly, a report must be made as soon as practicable to an officer of the rank of inspector or above who is not connected with the investigation. If the matter concerns a possible assault or the unnecessary or unreasonable use of force, then the police surgeon must also be called as soon as practicable. A record must be made of any arrangements made for an examination by a police surgeon consequently carried out and also of any such complaint reported, together with any relevant comments by the custody officer (para 9.1 and 9.7).

The status of the codes and the effect of breach

Police officers are no longer statutorily liable to disciplinary proceedings for failure to observe the codes.[9]

The Act provides that a police officer, or any other person subject to the provisions of the codes who fails to observe them, will not automatically be liable to any criminal or civil proceedings (s67(10)). However, the breach is admissible in evidence in all criminal and civil proceedings and if any provision of a code appears to the court or tribunal conducting the proceedings to be relevant to any question arising in the proceedings it must be taken into account in determining that question (s67(11)). 'Criminal proceedings' for the purpose of s67 has the extended definition given to it in s67(12) and includes proceedings before a court martial. In *R v Kenny*[10] the Court of Appeal held that s67(11) is not limited in its application to questions of law for the judge to decide, for instance on the admissibility of a

9   The Police and Magistrates' Courts Act 1994 has repealed PACE s67(8). It is anticipated by the Home Office that the disciplinary code, presently under discussion, will deal with the situation directly.

10   [1992] Crim LR 801.

confession, but is also applicable to questions of fact for the jury. For instance knowledge of breaches of the codes may be relevant to the jury's assessment of weight to be attached to evidence.

Evidence obtained after a breach of the codes is not necessarily inadmissible.[11] Every case will turn on its facts and the court will take into account, for instance, whether the breach was deliberate[12] and the number and significance of the breaches, if more than one.[13] It has also been held that a court may have regard to current codes of practice when considering the fairness of something done before the code came into force.[14] For a more detailed discussion of exclusion of evidence and confessions see Chapter 11.

It may be possible to argue that police officers who fail to observe the provisions of the code are not acting in the execution of their duty.[15]

Definition of 'serious arrestable offence'

The definition of 'serious arrestable offence' is vital to the operation of the 1984 Act. If the definition is satisfied, the police are entitled to exercise some of their more draconian powers: for instance, a person suspected of such an offence may be detained in some cases for 96 hours, access to a solicitor and notification of detention to a friend or relative may be denied for up to 36 hours and magistrates have power to issue search warrants for evidence.[16] The definition is contained in s116, as amended,[17] supplemented by Sch 5.

The arrestable offences (whether at common law or statutory) listed in Sch 5 Pt I and the statutory offences listed in Sch 5 Pt II are always serious arrestable offences. 'Arrestable offence' is defined in s24 (see below p114).

Schedule 5 Pt I, as amended, lists treason, murder, manslaughter,

11 *R v Stewart* (above, n5).
12 Eg, *R v Wright* [1994] Crim LR 55; *R v Hassan* [1995] Crim LR 405.
13 *RSPCA v Eager* (above, n6).
14 *R v Ward* [1993] 2 All ER 577; (1993) *Times* 29 August, CA.
15 In *Collins v Wilcock* [1984] 3 All ER 374 the High Court held that a police officer who was administering a caution to a suspected prostitute in accordance with established practice at the time (Home Office Circular 109/59) was not acting in the execution of her duty when she wrongly interpreted the Circular and detained the suspect in order to administer the caution.
16 These powers and others are described in detail in the relevant chapters.
17 Amended by the Prevention of Terrorism (Temporary Provisions) Act 1989, the Criminal Justice Act 1993 and the Drug Trafficking Act 1994.

rape, kidnapping, incest with a girl under the age of 13, buggery with a person under the age of 16, and an indecent assault which constitutes an act of gross indecency. For gross indecency between men see p126 and Sexual Offences Act 1956 s13. However, many such acts do not constitute indecent assaults because there is consent and so do not amount to serious arrestable offences. This category of serious arrestable offence applies mainly to offences by an adult on a child under 14.[18]

Arrestable offences under the following statutes listed in Sch 5 Pt II, as amended, are also classified as serious:

- Explosive Substances Act 1883 s2 (causing an explosion likely to endanger life or property);
- Sexual Offences Act 1956 s5 (intercourse with a girl under the age of 13);
- Firearms Act 1968 ss16, 17(1) and 18;
- Taking of Hostages Act 1982 s1 (taking of hostages);
- Aviation Security Act 1982 s1 (hijacking);
- Road Traffic Act 1988 s1 (causing death by dangerous driving) and s3A (causing death by careless driving when under the influence of drink or drugs);
- Aviation and Maritime Security Act 1990 s1 (endangering security at aerodromes), s9 (hijacking of ships) and s10 (seizing or exercising control of fixed platforms);
- Channel Tunnel (Security) Order 1994 No 570 article 4 (hijacking of Channel Tunnel trains), and article 5 (seizing or exercising control of the tunnel system);
- Protection of Children Act 1978 s1 (indecent photographs of children);
- Obscene Publications Act 1959 s2 (publication of obscene matter).
- Criminal Justice Act 1988 s134 (torture).

Offences listed in the Drug Trafficking Act 1994 s1(3)(a)-(f) are also serious arrestable offences.

Offences under the Prevention of Terrorism (Temporary Provisions) Act 1989 ss2, 8, 9, 10 or 11 (see chapter 8) (and conspiracies and attempts to commit such offences, but not incitement) are always classified as serious arrestable offences for the purposes of ss56 and 58 (notification of detention and access to legal advice, see below pp196–207). This does not preclude their classification as such so far as the other provisions of the Act are concerned, but the classification

18 Indecency with Children Act 1960 and R v R (J) [1993] Crim LR 971.

is not automatic in those cases: the offence would have to satisfy the criteria described below, as would other arrestable offences (s116(5)).

Threatening, conspiring and attempting offences

An arrestable offence which consists of making a threat is serious if carrying out the threat would be likely to lead to any of the consequences detailed below (an example of such an offence is making a threat to kill under the Offences Against the Person Act 1861 s16 as amended).

Other arrestable offences are serious only if their commission either has led to any of the consequences specified below or is intended or is likely to lead to any such consequences (s116(3)). The phrases 'is intended to' and 'is likely to' mean that incitements, conspiracies and attempts are included.

The actual, intended or likely consequences of an arrestable offence must be any of the following, in order to convert the offence into a serious arrestable offence:

a) serious harm to the security of the State or to public order. This is clearly far-reaching. The phrase 'serious harm . . . to public order' is open to wide interpretation;
b) serious interference with the administration of justice or with the investigation of offences or of a particular offence;
c) the death of any person;
d) serious injury to any person. 'Injury' includes any disease and any impairment of a person's physical or mental condition;
e) substantial financial gain to any person. 'Substantial' is again open to differing interpretations; the Act does not specify to whom the gain must be substantial; and
f) serious financial loss to any person. Loss is serious for these purposes if, having regard to all the circumstances, it is serious for the person who suffers it. This definition causes exceptional difficulties and is a fertile ground for argument. In the first place it clearly means that the loss of a small sum to a poor person is 'serious' and it may mean that the loss of a small sum to a miserly person is serious, thus depending not only on the financial status but also on the character of the victim. When something is primarily of sentimental value, it is certainly some financial loss and presumably serious to the victim, but it could be argued that it is outside this category, because

'serious' qualifies 'financial loss' and not merely 'loss'.

Another problem with both (e) and (f) is whether or not an offence which on its own is insignificant, but is in fact part of a series of offences, should be considered individually or as part of the whole.

The courts have in several cases, for instance *R v Eric Smith*[19] and *R v Neil McIvor*,[20] shown a willingness to substitute their own interpretations of (e) and (f) for those of the police.

In ss56 and 58 of the Act (authorisation of delay in notification of a friend or relative and access to legal advice) the suspect must (inter alia) be detained in connection with a serious arrestable offence (see below pp196–207). If therefore, the courts subsequently rule that the police were wrong in their view of the offence, any action taken under those sections will be unlawful.[21] In the case of other actions by the police which hinge on the definition (for instance, the issue of warrants by magistrates under s8 (below, p52) their actions will be lawful if there existed 'reasonable grounds' for their belief that the offence fell within this category.

Constables

Definition of 'constable'

Many of the powers conferred on the police, especially by the 1984 Act, are stated to be exercisable by a 'constable', but the Act does not define what is meant by this term. The meaning of constable is thus to be determined by the general law.

The word refers to somebody holding the office of constable, not to a police officer holding the rank of constable. Thus, all police officers of whatever rank are constables.[22]

The 'hallmark of the present-day constable remains, as in the seventeenth century, his attestation'.[23] Constables are 'officers to whom the law commits the duty of maintaining the peace and bringing to justice those by whom it is infringed'.[24] To be a constable, a

---

19 [1987] Crim LR 579.
20 [1987] Crim LR 409.
21 See, eg, *R v McIvor* (n20 above).
22 See, eg, *Lewis v Cattle* [1938] 2 KB 454; *Yates v Lancashire County Council* [1974] 10 ITR 20.
23 Halsbury's Laws of England vol 36 (Butterworth, 4th edn) para 204.
24 Jowitt, *Dictionary of English Law* (Sweet & Maxwell, 2nd edn, 1977) p429.

person must have been appointed as such and be attested as a constable making the appropriate declaration. Until such attestation, the person does not hold the office of constable. In the Metropolitan Police the attestation is made before the Commissioner or an Assistant Commissioner. In other cases it is made before a justice of the peace or other authority nominated by statute.[25]

These rules apply to ordinary police officers, special constables, and constables appointed for particular purposes (see below). However, a constable who is a member of a police force[26] has all the powers and privileges of a constable throughout England and Wales and the adjacent United Kingdom waters as well as some other offshore areas.[27] Constables appointed for areas on either side of the Anglo-Scottish border have a limited jurisdiction across the border.[28] (See p114 for cross-border powers of arrest.)

Special constables are appointed by the chief officer of police for their area, and have all the powers and privileges of a constable within their own area and any contiguous police area. A City of London constable also has powers within areas contiguous to the Metropolitan Police District.[29]

Other bodies of constables may be appointed for particular limited purposes, with powers limited geographically or in some other way. When acting within their jurisdiction they are acting as constables, but not otherwise. Thus, when an Act confers a power on a constable, it must be referring to such constables (and special constables) when they are acting as such, as well as to members of ordinary police forces. Such bodies include the United Kingdom Atomic Energy Authority Police, British Transport Police,[30] Canal Police, Harbour Police, Civil Aviation and Airport Police, Parks Police and University (Oxford or Cambridge) Police.[31] The

25 Police Act 1964 s18.
26 That is, a police force for the City of London police area, or the Metropolitan Police District, or maintained by a police authority listed in the Police Act 1964 Sch 1A as substituted by the Police and Magistrates' Courts Act 1994 s1.
27 Police Act 1964 s19(1); Continental Shelf Act 1964 s11(3); Mineral Workings (Offshore Installations) Act 1971 s9(5).
28 Halsbury's Laws of England vol 36 para 319.
29 Ibid paras 208–210. See also *Sheikh v Chief Constable of Greater Manchester Police* [1989] 2 All ER 684, CA.
30 British Transport Commission Act 1949 s53, Transport Police (Jurisdiction) Act 1994. The 1994 Act deals with the problems of jurisdiction arising from proposals for rail privatisation. The jurisdiction of the British Transport Police extends to London Underground and the Docklands Light Railway.
31 Halsbury's Laws of England vol 36 paras 211–219.

armed forces also maintain bodies of constables with limited powers.

A police cadet is neither a member of a police force nor a constable.[32]

Section 6 of the 1984 Act gives special powers of search to constables employed by statutory undertakers (defined in s7(3))(see chapter 2).

Certain people have statutory authority to act as constables in certain circumstances but do not hold the office of constable. These include water bailiffs,[33] fishery officers[34] and prison officers acting as such.[35] Within their limited jurisdictions it seems that such people can exercise powers conferred by the 1984 Act on a constable.

Ministry of Defence police

A new civilian police force was set up under the Ministry of Defence Police Act 1987 consisting of former Defence Council special constables, and new members nominated by the Secretary of State and attested before a JP. The Secretary of State appoints the chief constable, and an advisory police committee.

Ministry of Defence police have 'all the powers and privileges of constables'[36] in certain places, and also with respect to certain matters and persons in all places. The places mainly relate to 'land, vehicles, vessels, aircraft and hovercraft' used for defence or ordnance purposes, including those of a dockyard contractor. The other matters include defence contracts; Crown, defence, ordnance and dockyard property; and in particular 'for the purpose of securing unimpeded passage of any such property'.[37] They also have jurisdiction in respect of any person subject to the control of, or employed by or for the purposes of, the Defence Council or subject to service courts under the Visiting Forces Act 1952.

The powers of the Ministry of Defence police, especially in relation to the free movement of goods or the investigation of crime, overlap considerably with those of the ordinary police. Home Office guidelines reserve to the local police the investigation of serious offences and those outside military establishments. The exercise of

---

32 Police Act 1964 s17(1); *Wiltshire Police Authority v Wynn* [1980] 3 WLR 445, CA.
33 Salmon and Freshwater Fisheries Act 1975 s36(1).
34 Sea Fisheries Regulation Act 1966 s10(3).
35 Prison Act 1952 s8.
36 Ministry of Defence Act 1987 s2(1) and (3).
37 Ibid s2(3)(d).

powers outside such establishments must be notified to the local chief constable in advance except in cases of extreme urgency.[38] When the Ministry of Defence police are acting as constables, then they will be subject to any restrictions or safeguards in the 1984 Act or other legislation relating to constables.

The Ministry of Defence police are different from the service police (see below).

Constables in uniform

In some cases a power may only be exercised by a constable in uniform (for example under the road traffic legislation). Again this is left undefined in the 1984 Act. In cases under the road traffic legislation the test has been said to be whether the constable was easily identifiable as a police constable. Thus a constable not wearing a helmet and emerging from a marked police car was held to be in uniform,[39] although it has been left open whether a police officer wearing a raincoat over the uniform is in uniform.[40]

Use of force by a constable

A constable who is given a power under the Act is given a reserve power to use force in its exercise. The force must be reasonable and must be used only if necessary. The reserve power is inapplicable if the initial power can be exercised only with the consent of some person other than a police officer (s117).

Several sections of the Act give the police power to take action in the absence of a person's consent, for example, their power to enter and search premises, to search persons at a police station and to take fingerprints. If force is used in the exercise of such power, two questions have to be answered: first whether the use of force was necessary and second, if it was necessary, whether the amount of force used was reasonable. If the officer's belief that force is necessary is in fact mistaken, the use of force is unlawful as s117 does not contain any reference to the officer's mental state; the lawfulness of the use of force must be judged objectively. Similarly the reasonableness of the degree of force must be objectively assessed. The question of whether force used is reasonable depends on an objective assessment of the facts. Constables who use force when it is unnecessary or

38 *Independent* 4 November 1987.
39 *Wallwork v Giles* [1970] RTR 118; (1969) 114 SJ 36.
40 *Taylor v Baldwin* [1976] RTR 265; [1976] Crim LR 137.

use excessive force are not acting in the execution of their duty and anyone lawfully resisting should not be convicted of an offence under the Police Act 1964 s51.[41] The force must be more than trivial; in *Collins v Wilcock* it was said that there was a distinction between a touch to gain a man's attention which was acceptable and a physical restraint which was not (in those circumstances).[42]

For the right of an individual to resist police power by force see p324 below.

The exercise of discretion

Many of the powers in the 1984 Act and other statutes concerning policing grant a wide measure of discretion. An example is the power of the Secretary of State to make an exclusion order under the prevention of terrorism legislation (see chapter 8). Often the power is subject to certain conditions, such as the existence of reasonable grounds for suspicion, which is discussed in more detail below. One leading writer has pointed out that:

> It is a cardinal axiom . . . that every power has legal limits, however wide the language of the empowering Act. If the court finds that the power has been exercised oppressively or unreasonably . . . the action may be condemned as unlawful.[43]

Lord Denning has summarised the grounds on which the courts may intervene as follows:

> . . . the courts will not themselves take the place of the body to whom Parliament has entrusted the decision. The courts will not themselves make the original findings of fact. They will not themselves embark on a rehearing of the matter. But nevertheless, the courts will, if called upon, act in a supervisory capacity. They will see that the decision-making body acts fairly. The courts will ensure that the body acts in accordance with the law. If a question arises on the interpretation of words, the courts will decide it by declaring what is the correct interpretation . . . If the decision-making body is influenced by considerations which ought not to influence it; or fails to take into account matters which it ought to take into account, the court will interfere. If the decision-making body comes to its decision on no evidence or comes to an unreasonable finding – so unreasonable that a reasonable court would not have come to it – then again the courts will interfere. If the decison-making body goes outside its powers or misconstrues the extent

41   See *Collins v Wilcock* [1984] 3 All ER 374.
42   See also *Donnelly v Jackman* [1970] 1 All ER 987.
43   Wade, *Administrative Law* (Oxford University Press, 6th edn, 1988) p39.

of its powers, then, too, courts can interfere. And, of course, if the body acts in bad faith or for an ulterior object which is not authorised by law, its decision will be set aside. In exercising these powers, the courts will take into account any reasons which the body may give for its decisions. If it gives no reasons – in a case when it may reasonably be expected to do so, the courts may infer that it has no good reason for reaching its conclusion and act accordingly.[44]

The control exercised by the courts over the use of discretionary powers is a developing area and in many cases it is not possible to predict with any certainty the approach that the courts will adopt. Hitherto they have been reluctant to interfere with the manner in which the police exercise their discretion, although most of the leading cases have involved policy decisions of the Metropolitan Police Commissioner rather than decisions in respect of individual cases. In 1968 the Court of Appeal said:

> Although the chief officers of police are answerable to the law, there are many fields in which they have a discretion with which the law would not interfere.[45]

This was affirmed in 1973 when Lord Denning indicated that the courts would only interfere in 'extreme cases'.[46] However, the question of control over the way in which discretion is exercised is separate from the legal issue of whether the power or discretion exists. The courts will not hesitate to intervene on a question of whether a legal power exists.

It is theoretically possible, but in practice unlikely, for the courts to find that reasonable grounds exist which confer a power, but the power has been exercised for an improper purpose.[47] In any event, when issues of national security are concerned, which might sometimes be the case in the exercise of police powers, especially under the prevention of terrorism legislation, the courts are extremely reluctant to interfere with the exercise of discretion.[48]

44 *GEC v Price Commission* [1975] ICR 1 at 12.
45 Per Lord Denning MR in *R v Metropolitan Police Commissioner ex Blackburn* [1968] 1 All ER 763 at 769.
46 *R v Metropolitan Police Commissioner ex Blackburn* (No 3) [1973] 1 All ER 324, CA. See also *R v Chief Constable of Devon and Cornwall ex p CEGB* [1981] 3 All ER 826 and *R v Oxford ex p Levey* (1986) *Independent* 30 October, CA.
47 *Mohammed-Holgate v Duke* [1984] 1 All ER 1054, HL.
48 *Liversidge v Anderson* [1942] AC 206; *R v Secretary of State for Home Department ex p Hosenball* [1977] 3 All ER 452, CA; *Council of Civil Service Unions v Minister for Civil Service* [1984] 3 All ER 935, HL, but cf *R v Secretary of State for Home Department ex p Ruddock* [1987] 2 All ER 518.

Reasonable grounds

Many of the powers conferred by the 1984 Act can be exercised only if there are reasonable grounds, for example, for suspicion. This can be seen in the powers of search under Pts I and II and arrest under Pt III, and the applicability of this concept to specific powers is discussed in the following chapters. The meaning of 'reasonable grounds' is not defined in the Act, but the concept is a familiar one in the law. The use of the word 'reasonable' indicates that the *court* must be satisfied that the grounds were reasonable; it is not a matter for the subjective judgment of the constable. The constable must be able to justify the suspicions; a genuine suspicion is not enough if it is not based on reasonable grounds.[49]

Suspicion can be based on reasonable grounds although those grounds would not justify conviction, amount to prima facie evidence of guilt, nor be admissible in evidence.[50] In a slightly different context, Lord Hailsham has said:[51]

> . . . unreasonableness can include anything which can objectively be judged to be unreasonable. It is not confined to culpability or callous indifference. It can include, where carried to excess, sentimentality, romanticism, bigotry, wild prejudice, caprice, fatuousness, or excessive lack of common sense.

Lord Hailsham went on to point out that the court is not entitled simply to substitute its own view of the matter, and two reasonable people can perfectly reasonably come to opposite conclusions on the same set of facts without forfeiting their entitlement to be regarded as reasonable.[52] In deciding whether there are reasonable grounds for the exercise of police powers the court should taken into account any relevant provision of the Codes of Practice (s67(11)).

Validity of police action and directions to the police

Many powers conferred on the police by the 1984 Act can be exercised only if certain conditions are fulfilled. In a number of places the Act

---

49 See, eg, *Re W (An Infant)* [1971] 2 All ER 49, HL per Lord Hailsham at 56 and cf *McKee v Chief Constable of Northern Ireland* [1985] 1 All ER 1, CA, where the police power did not rest on reasonable grounds.
50 Halsbury's Laws of England vol 11 (Butterworth, 4th edn) para 101.
51 *Re W (An Infant)* n49.
52 See also *Secretary of State for Education and Science v Tameside MBC* [1977] AC 1014.

makes clear that the exercise of the power is unlawful or invalid if the condition is not fulfilled. Examples are the need for reasonable grounds for suspicion before a search without arrest may be made (s1(3)) or the duty to inform arrested persons that they are under arrest (s28(1)).

In some places a direction is given but the Act does not state that the action is unlawful unless the direction is complied with. This is the case in connection with search without arrest, when a constable must give certain information to the person to be searched (s2(2)). It is provided that a search may not be commenced until this duty has been performed, but the lawfulness of a search in breach of the duty is not spelt out.

In a number of places the Act requires a document to be completed after a power has been exercised, such as a notice that a vehicle has been searched (s2(6)) or a record of a personal search (s3(1)). The Act does not specify whether a subsequent failure to complete the record renders the search unlawful.

In addition, there are many requirements in the Codes of Practice. The Act provides that a breach of the codes, does not give rise to criminal or civil liability on its own (s67(10)), but does not state the effect of such a breach on the lawfulness of any action taken. Where an Act is not explicit, then according to the common law:

'. . . the court must determine the question. This the court does by weighing the inconvenience of holding the condition ineffective against the inconvenience of insisting upon it rigidly. It is a question of construction, to be settled by looking at the whole scheme and purpose of the Act and by weighing the importance of the conditon, the prejudice to private rights and the claim of the public interest.'[53]

It is not possible to be certain whether a requirement is mandatory (that is, a condition of legality) or merely directory (that is, giving directions but not a condition of legality) in the absence of a court ruling, and it is difficult to extract clear rules from the existing case-law. For example, the Prison Rules have been treated in some cases as merely directory and in other cases as creating enforceable rights.[54]

53 Wade op cit n43 p246.
54 Ibid p247.

Application of the Act to the armed forces

The Secretary of State may by order direct that any provisions of the 1984 Act relating to the investigation of offences conducted by police officers or to persons detained by the police will apply, subject to any modifications considered necessary, to any investigations of offences conducted under the Army Act 1955, the Air Force Act 1955 or the Naval Discipline Act 1957 or to any person arrested under those Acts (s113(1)). This has been done with effect from 1 January 1986.[55]

Section 67 requires persons investigating offences to have regard to the codes issued under the Act even if they are not police officers. This does not apply to service police investigations (s113(2)). Instead the Act requires the Secretary of State to issue a Code or a number of Codes of Practice which may contain provisions relating to:

a) the tape recording of interviews;
b) searches of persons and premises; and
c) seizure of material found during searches.

The Secretary of State has the same powers to modify these codes as the codes regulating police behaviour and they have the same status as the latter codes and the effects of breach are the same, with appropriate modifications (s113(8)-(11)).

The rules of evidence contained in the Act apply to proceedings before any army or air force court martial and before a standing civilian court, subject to such modifications as the Secretary of State may direct (s113(12)).

55 Police and Criminal Evidence Act 1984 (Application to Armed Forces) Order 1985 SI No 1882, as amended by 1990 SI No 1448.

CHAPTER 2

Stop and search without arrest

The police have several statutory powers to stop, detain and search persons or vehicles without first making an arrest. Many of these powers are specific or limited (see below, p44–47 and 443–445). However, the 1984 Act as amended creates a general power and also (together with the Code of Practice[1]) provides certain safeguards for nearly all such searches.

Searches which take place in breach of the legislation or code may render the police liable to civil action, prosecution, or disciplinary proceedings (see chapters 12 and 13).

General power under the 1984 Act

The 1984 Act s1(2) empowers any constable acting on reasonable grounds for suspicion to stop, detain and search persons or vehicles or anything in or on a vehicle, for certain items which may be seized.

Stolen or prohibited articles etc

Searches under s1 must be for stolen or prohibited articles or certain articles with a blade or sharp point (s1(2)(a)).

1 Code of Practice for the Exercise by Police Officers of Statutory Powers of Stop and Search, Code A in the Codes of Practice 3rd revised edition (effective 10 April 1995) issued under the Police and Criminal Evidence Act 1984, HMSO 1995. The Codes are reproduced in Appendix 2 and Code A applies to any search by a police officer which commenced after midnight on 9 April 1995. Searches which commenced before then are governed by earlier versions of the Code (reproduced in previous editions of this book).

'Stolen' is not defined in the Act. Presumably it means obtained in contravention of the Theft Act 1968 s1 (theft). It is unclear whether the meaning of 'stolen' includes things obtained in contravention of sections of the 1968 Act relating to fraud (s15), blackmail (s21) or collections on display to the public (s11). The proceeds of blackmail or fraud, and other types of goods, are stated by the 1968 Act to be included in the definition of handling 'stolen' goods (ss21 and 24) but only for the purposes of the 1968 Act. The general rule of interpretation is that penal statutes are to be interpreted restrictively and therefore 'stolen' in the 1984 Act should have the narrower meaning. Accordingly there must be reasonable grounds for suspecting that an offence of theft has been committed, though not necessarily by the person to be searched.

There are two categories of prohibited articles defined in the Act: (a) an offensive weapon and (b) an article to be used in connection with certain offences of dishonesty.

Offensive weapon

An offensive weapon is further defined (s1(9)) to mean one of two things, considered in turn below. An offensive weapon is a prohibited article for these purposes even if the person has lawful authority or reasonable excuse to have it and is therefore not committing an offence under the Prevention of Crime Act 1953 or the Criminal Justice Act 1988.

'*Any article made or adapted for use for causing injury to persons*'   This relates to the nature of the article itself and not to the intention of the person who has it, though it does relate to the intention of the person who made or adapted it. There must be evidence of such intention (which might be implied); otherwise there would be no reasonable grounds to search for the item.

Articles made for this use would include a cosh, sword-stick, knuckleduster, revolver, police truncheon and flick knife.[2] However, not all knives will be included since knives have many other uses, as does a machette.[3] The same would be true of explosives. However some knives which are not offensive weapons within the

---

2 *R v Butler* [1988] Crim LR 695; *R v Petrie* [1961] 1 All ER 466; *Gibson v Wales* [1983] 1 All ER 869; *R v Simpson (Calvin)* [1983] 3 All ER 789; *Houghton v Chief Constable of Greater Manchester* (1987) 84 Cr App R 319.

3 *R v Williamson* (1977) 67 Cr App R 35; *Green v McCoy* (1983) 21 June, unreported, DC.

1984 Act definition will be caught by the blade or sharp point provision. Rice flails seem to be treated as made for causing injury.[4]

To be adapted, an object must be altered.[5] Articles adapted for this use could include razor blades inserted into something which could be held, or a piece of wood studded with nails (which could be covered both by this provision and by the blade or sharp point provision).

'Any article intended by the person having it for use by anyone for causing injury to persons.' This could include any item at all: not only obvious possibilities such as knives and heavy implements, but also a comb, coin, bunch of keys, torch, screwdriver, pencil, or ruler.[6]

The required intention must be present and must already be formulated by the time of the search and must relate to the future.[7] The Act requires that the person having the article must intend its use by him or herself or 'some other person' (s1(9)(b)). Conceivably this could mean some other particular person, but the courts are more likely to interpret this as meaning any other person.

The Act does not say that the intended use must be unlawful, so the item would be included even if intended for use in self-defence or to effect a lawful arrest. Although persons with a lawful authority or reasonable excuse would not be guilty of the offence of possessing an offensive weapon under the Prevention of Crime Act 1953, they would still be liable to the stop and search powers under the 1984 Act.

'Injury to persons' is not defined in the 1984 Act. In another context this phrase has been held to include intimidation capable of producing injury through the operation of shock.[8] Since 'injury' is an ordinary word of the English language, the courts will have to decide in each case whether the word has been used appropriately.

Article for use in connection with certain other offences
An article is prohibited for the purposes of the stop and search power if it is made, or adapted, for use in the course of, or in

---

4 *Copus v DPP* [1989] Crim LR 577; *R v Malnik* [1989] Crim LR 451. But see the commentaries on those decisions and also Smith and Hogan *Criminal Law* (7th edition Butterworths 1992) at p444.
5 *R v Formosa, R v Upton* [1990] Crim LR 868 CA. See also Smith and Hogan op cit and cases cited in their note 20.
6 A piece of broken glass was treated as an 'article' for similar purposes in *Wood v Commissioner of Police of the Metropolis* [1986] 2 All ER 570.
7 See, eg, *R v Allamby* [1974] 3 All ER 126.
8 *R v Edmonds* [1963] 2 QB 142, interpreting the Prevention of Crime Act 1953 s1(4).

connection with, certain offences, or if it is intended by the person having it for such use by him or herself or some other person (s1(7)(b)).

The relevant offences are all defined in the Theft Act 1968, and are burglary (s9), theft (s1), taking a conveyance without authority (s12) and obtaining property by deception (s15). Offences under s12 include being a passenger in a conveyance taken without authority, and taking a bicycle. In most cases it will be impossible to say whether an article was made or adapted for such a purpose, unless there is evidence of the use of the article, or of the intention of the person making, adapting or carrying it. Such intention must exist by the time of the search. Clearly, such articles as jemmies, car keys and ladders could be included, but credit cards, cheque books, means of identification, gloves to conceal fingerprints, and any other items to be used in deception, would also be covered.

The power relates to articles for use in the course of or in connection with certain offences. This is a very wide formulation and is based on the formulation in the offence of 'going equipped' in the Theft Act 1968 s25. It seems to cover items to be used in preparation for a crime or for escaping after it has been committed, though in the cases under s25 there must be a direct connection between the offence and the use of the item. Possession of a driving licence to obtain a job which would give an opportunity to steal was regarded as too remote to be 'in connection with' theft.[9] The requirement 'for use in the course of or in connection with' relates to future use, though not necessarily with a particular offence in mind.[10] Thus an item which has been used in the past in connection with theft but which is not intended for such use again is not prohibited within the 1984 Act, and cannot be searched for in the absence of arrest. Neither can an item which a person is carrying but has not decided to use.[11]

The power of stop and search under the 1984 Act does not include search for drugs, firearms or explosives (except as offensive weapons) or other items but there are powers under other statutes which are referred to on p46 and 443–445.

Blades or sharp points

One category of items for which a constable can exercise the stop and search power is any article to which s1(8A) applies, that is any

9   *R v Mansfield* (1975) Crim LR 101.
10   *R v Ellames* (1974) 60 Cr App R 7.
11   *R v Hargreaves* [1985] Crim LR 243.

article in relation to which a person has committed or is committing or is going to commit an offence under the Criminal Justice Act 1988 s139. The constable must have reasonable grounds for suspecting that such an article will be found (s1(3)). It will rarely be possible to prove that a person 'is going to commit an offence' and if this cannot be proved, then the wording of s1(8A) requires that the offence must actually have been committed or be in the process of being committed. This means that the search will turn out to have been unlawful (unless justified by the article being included in some other category) if there is a defence under CJA 1988 s139 or if the article turns out not to be included within s139.

The s139 offence is to have in a public place an article to which the section applies. This is any article (other than a folding pocketknife) which has a blade or is sharply pointed, or a folding pocketknife if the cutting edge of the blade exceeds three inches.[12] Of course an article not within s139 can still be an offensive weapon for the purposes of the stop and search power, but many articles which are not offensive weapons can still come within the s139 offence. It is a defence for the person charged to prove that there was good reason or lawful authority for having the article in a public place, or that the person had the article for use at work, for religious reasons or as part of any national costume. These defences will apply to the s139 offence even if the item is an offensive weapon, although the stop and search power would be exercisable in such a case.

Where the public has access

The general power of stop and search under the 1984 Act may be exercised only in places where the public has access.

Legal right of access or permission

A person may be stopped and searched if in a place to which, at the time of the proposed search, the public (or any section of the public) has access as a matter of legal right, or because there is permission.

A place may be included even if the permission is implied and even if access has to be paid for (s1(1)(a)). This covers various places, including many which are actually private property (provided there

---

12 A folding lockknife which is capable of being locked in an open position so that it can only be folded back after activating a trigger mechanism is not a folding pocketknife for these purposes: *Harris v DPP, Fehmi v DPP* [1993] 1 All ER 562, QBD.

is a legal right or permission). Included would be private car parks, pub and garage forecourts, cinemas, grounds in housing estates, many publicly owned buildings and so on. Any question of whether the public has access in a particular case will have to be decided by the court.[13] A constable who wrongly believes that the public has access will not be protected by this provision even if his or her belief is reasonable.

The access must be available at the time of the proposed stop and search, so the power would not be available, for example, once the cinema had closed.[14] However a place which does not come within this provision might come within the next paragraph.

Ready access

The stop and search powers may also be exercised in a place to which people have ready access at the time of the proposed stop and search, which is not a dwelling (s1(1)(b)).

The power cannot be exercised in a dwelling unless the legal right of access above applies. Apart from that restriction, virtually anywhere can be covered: any areas of open ground, or fenced ground with an open gate, any building with an unlocked and unattended door which is not a dwelling, and so on. The question here is whether there is ready access in fact, not whether there is a right of access. Again this is a question for the courts to decide and a constable who wrongly thinks that people have ready access to a place and carries out a stop and search there, will be acting unlawfully. Under this paragraph ready access must be available to 'people'. This could make it wider than 'the public' or 'section of the public' in that 'people' might have access but not amount to a definable 'section of the public'. It is not clear how many individuals need have access to amount to 'people'. Conversely it could be argued that 'people' means 'all people' and that the definition is narrower than 'section of the public' although the same as 'the public'.

If the place in question is private property, it seems that the owner of the property can expel a constable from the property even when the power of stop and search is being exercised.[15]

---

13 The front garden of a house is probably not a public place for these purposes: *R v Llewellyn Edwards* (1978) 67 Cr App R 228; *Fellowes v DPP* 28 January, QED, unreported

14 In *Marsh v Arscott* (1982) 75 Cr App R 211, it was held that a shop car park is not a public place at 11.30pm on a Saturday night.

15 Douglas Hurd, then Minister of State at the Home Office, HC Standing Committee E, col 123, 29 November 1983.

Who may be searched and protection for occupiers

The general rule is that any person or vehicle may be searched, provided that the power is exercised for the proper purpose in an appropriate place (s1(2)(a)). However, there is protection from search in certain circumstances.

If a person or vehicle is on any garden, yard or land 'occupied with and used for the purposes of a dwelling', a constable may not search the person or the vehicle (or anything in or on it) without reasonable grounds for believing that the person, or the person in charge of the vehicle, does not reside in the dwelling and that the person or vehicle to be searched is not there with the express or implied permission of a person who resides in the dwelling (s1(4) and (5)).

Whether the area in question is 'occupied with and used for the purposes of a dwelling' is a question of fact for the courts, and a police officer who mistakenly believes that an area is not so occupied would, subject to the following paragraph, have no power to stop and search under s1 even if the belief is reasonable. Enclosed spaces within a housing estate would be included, though public roads would probably not be.[16]

However, constables will have such a power if they reasonably believe that the person or vehicle is there without the consent of the occupier. Although such a belief may be wrong in fact it may be reasonable. It is for the court to say whether the grounds of the belief were reasonable. The belief must exist before the stop and search is carried out. Thus a constable merely seeing people or a vehicle in a garden or yard attached to a house or block of flats would have no power to stop and search without forming the belief that they were there without the permission of the owner. This might be based on their conduct or on information received, for example. Casual visitors and people such as milk and post deliverers and window cleaners would clearly be protected, as in practice should all people behaving normally.

Reasonable grounds for suspecting

The power of stop and search under s1 can be exercised only if the constable has reasonable grounds for suspecting that stolen or prohibited articles will be found (s1(3)).

16 A block of flats is not a public place if access is exclusively by way of key, security code, intercom or caretaker although it might be different if stairways and landings are open to the public: *Williams (Richard) v DPP* [1992] Crim LR 503, QBD, distinguishing *Knox v Anderton* (1983) 76 Cr App R 156, QBD.

Presumably this means that articles will be found as a result of the search. Suspicion of anything else, eg, that an offence not involving possession of such articles has been committed, would not justify a search. 'Reasonable grounds for suspecting' is not defined in the Act but the concept is dealt with in Code of Practice A para 1.6 and Note for Guidance 1A. In particular, the code points out that there must be some objective basis for the reasonable suspicion which would lead a careful officer to form it, and that the use of the power may have to be justified to the court or a superior officer.

The use of the word 'reasonable' means that the suspicion must be such that a reasonable person would have had that suspicion in those circumstances. If the point is at issue in court proceedings, the court or jury would say what is reasonable. There must be something which gives rise to the suspicion; this might relate to the article itself being visible, the time and place, information received, or to the behaviour of the suspected person.[17] A person's age, colour, style of dress or hairstyle or previous conviction for possessing an unlawful article are insufficient factors on which to base suspicion. Nor may it be founded on the basis of stereotyped images.[18] In one case involving a search for drugs the court pointed out that the mere fact that someone in the middle of the night strolls aimlessly, especially in a popular area like Soho, does not provide reasonable grounds to stop and search, even if there is ample opportunity for criminal activity.[19]

Clearly the constable must suspect that the person has, or the vehicle contains, a stolen or prohibited article, and the reasonableness of the suspicion relates to whether the article in question was stolen or prohibited, as well as to whether the person had it. If the suspicion relates to a prohibited article (other than a s139 article (see p24) or an offensive weapon made or adapted for causing injury), the suspicion must be that the article will be used, not merely that it has been used (see above). However, presumably such suspicion can be based only on manifestation of intention − either the use has been threatened in some way, or there is a fear that a use to which the article has been put will be repeated. The fact that a person is suspected of carrying a steel comb, or that a car is suspected of containing a wheel brace, could not of itself justify a search.

The person who is searched need not be the person who has stolen the goods or who will use the item. In the case of offensive weapons not made or adapted for causing injury, or an article not

17 Code A para 1.6.
18 Ibid para 1.7.
19 *Tomlinson v DPP* May 1992 *Legal Action* 21, QBD.

made or adapted for use in connection with one of the listed offences, the person searched must be suspected of intending that the item will be used by someone unless it is a s139 article.

Routine searching, eg, of everyone entering a football or other sports ground, would be difficult to justify under the s1 power, since suspicion must relate to the particular individual searched and be based on reasonable criteria. The Code of Practice points out that such routine searches by consent or as a condition of entry are unaffected by the code.[20] This would only be the case if the search is not conducted under the s1 power. There is a separate statutory power of search inside sports grounds under the Sporting Events etc Act 1985 (see p46), but this is subject to the Code of Practice and statutory safeguards in the same way as the s1 power.

Code A itself states (in Note for Guidance 1Db) that it does not affect the ability of the police to search a person in the street on a voluntary basis, but the police must make it clear that 'co-operation' is being sought. However, there may be cases where it is not clear whether a search was by consent or under a statutory power. Juveniles, persons suffering from mental handicap or disorder and others who appear incapable of giving an informed consent should not be subject to a voluntary search (Note for Guidance 1E).

Where a police officer has reasonable grounds to suspect that person is in innocent possession of an item for which there is power to stop and search (whether under the 1984 Act or any other power governed by Code of Practice A – see below p46) then that power of stop and search exists even though there would be no power of arrest. However every effort must be made to secure the person's co-operation in producing the article before resorting to the use of force.[21] However, in some cases there is no power to stop and search where innocent possession is the issue – for example, under the blade or sharp point provision (see above p20–21). In this latter case, the power to stop and search derives from suspicion that the person is or will be guilty of an offence under the Criminal Justice Act 1988 s139.

Stopping and detaining

Any constable can conduct a search of a person or a vehicle and does not have to be on duty or in uniform, except actually to stop a vehicle.

20 See also HC Debs Vol 78 col 570, 2 May 1985; Code A Note for Guidance 1Da.
21 Code of Practice A para 1.7A.

In order to exercise the power under s1 a constable may detain a person or vehicle (s1(2)(b)). A detention under s1 may be only for the purposes of a search. A stop or detention for any other purpose would be unlawful unless based on some other legal authority. The reasonable suspicion must already exist before the stop or detention takes place.

There is no power to stop or detain a person against his or her will in order to find grounds for a search. A person who has been stopped with a view to a search may be questioned about the behaviour or circumstances which gave rise to the suspicion. If the answers are satisfactory and there cease to be reasonable grounds for suspicion for the search, no search may take place. Although the existence of reasonable grounds may be confirmed or eliminated as a result of such questioning, they must exist to begin with and cannot arise merely from the questioning or from any refusal to answer.[22]

The Act does not provide an express power to 'stop' persons or vehicles (but see p35 for road checks and pp40–44 and pp250–252 for the power of stop and search under written authorisation provided by Criminal Justice and Public Order Act 1994 s60 and Prevention of Terrorism (Temporary Provisions Act) 1989 s13A); it is possible that the power to 'detain' necessarily includes a power to stop. It is also possible that the power of detention can be exercised only if a person has already been stopped for some other purpose or a vehicle is stationary or has been stopped under the Road Traffic Act 1988 s163 (see below p35). The Act expressly states that s1 does not authorise a constable not in uniform to stop a vehicle (s2(9)(b)).

The Act imposes certain duties on a constable who proposes to detain and search (ss2 and 3) (see below pp31–34).

Searching persons and vehicles

The power to search a vehicle includes a power to search anything (but not any person) in or on it (s1(2)). If the suspicion is that stolen or prohibited goods are in a bag in the vehicle, it is unclear whether that justifies a search of the whole car.

If a constable suspects that the goods are in the car and there is also a person in the car, it seems that there must be separate suspicion relating to that person before the person can be searched as well.

22 Code A paras 2.1 to 2.3.

Limitations on the power

If a person is carrying a bag, there is nothing in the Act which specifically allows a search of the bag as well as or instead of a search of the person. The Metropolitan Police Act 1839 s66 (repealed by the 1984 Act) referred to any person 'having or conveying' in 'any manner', but similar words do not appear in the 1984 Act. The Code of Practice assumes that a bag may be searched.[23] The wording of the 1984 Act may be contrasted with the wording of the powers of search under written authorisation contained in Criminal Justice and Public Order Act 1994 s60 and Prevention of Terrorism (Temporary Provisions Act) 1989 s13A (discussed on pp40–44 and pp250–252 below). The 1989 and 1994 Acts use the specific wording '. . . search him *or anything carried by him* . . .' (s13A(3)(b) and s60(4)(b) respectively). This strengthens the argument that the absence of such words means that the power in the 1984 Act does not extend that far.

A constable may use reasonable force, if necessary, in the conduct of the search (and in the detention) (s117). Reasonable force is not defined in the Act, but it is an objective test for the court or jury to apply. The concept of reasonable force has been discussed above on pp11–12. The Code of Practice provides that force 'may only be used as a last resort' and only if it has been established that a person is not willing to co-operate.[24]

The thoroughness and extent of the search that is justifiable depends on what is suspected of being carried. The requirement of reasonable grounds for suspicion implies that the search is limited in extent and matter to what is justified by the original reasonable suspicion.

The power conferred by the 1984 Act s1 is to detain and search without making an arrest. A constable who wishes to search a person but has no power to do so might be able to arrest under a different provision and then search after arrest (s32) (see pp144–146).

It has been suggested that since stop and search powers are hedged about with more safeguards than arrest, police officers are more likely to make an arrest, conduct a post-arrest search for evidence, and then release the suspect if nothing is found.[25] There are no reliable statistics on this point. The official statistics[26] show that in

23 Code A para 3.2.
24 Code A para 3.2. It seems that a person may cooperate in a search which is not carried out voluntarily.
25 (1984) 134 NLJ 616.
26 Home Office Statistical Bulletin 16/95 on the Operation of Certain Police Powers Under PACE, 29 June 1995. See also an analysis of these statistics in *Statewatch* July 1995 at pp18–21.

1994 the police recorded 576,000 stops and searches in England and Wales (of which 291,895 were by the Metropolitan Police). There has been a steady increase in number from 109,800 in 1986. Twelve per cent of stops and searches in 1994 resulted in an arrest.

Seizure

If a constable discovers, during the course of a search under s1, an article for which there are reasonable grounds for suspecting it to be a stolen or prohibited article, the constable may seize it (s1(6)). If the grounds for such suspicion are unreasonable, the seizure is unlawful. If the search is for a stolen article, but a prohibited article is found, it seems that the latter may be seized, and vice versa.

There is a procedure under the Police (Property) Act 1897 for the recovery of property seized by the police (see p326). The power of the police in relation to seized items is governed by s22 and is discussed in chapter 4 below.

Provisions governing all stop and search powers

Introduction

Sections 2 and 3 of the 1984 Act and the Code of Practice apply to virtually all powers of constables to search a person who has not been arrested, or to search a vehicle without making an arrest. Their applicability is not limited to the stop and search power under s1. The only exceptions are powers of search under the Aviation Security Act 1982 s27(2) and the 1984 Act s6(1). The latter power relates to statutory undertakers and is discussed on p44–45. Other powers are dealt with on pp45–47. Powers under the Aviation Security Act 1982 s27(1) are not exempted from these provisions.

General

A person or vehicle may be detained for a search only for such time as is 'reasonably required' to permit a search to be carried out either at the place where first detained or nearby (s2(8)). Implicit in the phrase 'reasonably required' must be the idea that it is required by the reasonable suspicion.

An early draft of the Code of Practice stated that 'it is an unusual search that cannot be completed within a minute or so'. The existing code limits this guidance to searches which involve only superficial examination of outer clothing in public.[27] Nevertheless it is, for example, unlikely that a car could be fully stripped down in order to exercise the search power under the 1984 Act s1.

There is no definition of the word 'nearby'. Cases under the roadside breath test legislation (now Road Traffic Act 1988 s6(3)), which allow a test to be administered 'at or near' the relevant place have held that what is meant by 'near' is to be judged in a purely geographical sense and is a question of degree and fact for the court or the jury. The High Court refused to interfere with decisions that a mile-and-a-half away in a police car was not nearby[28] and that 160 yards away on foot was not nearby.[29] On general principles, the higher courts would interfere only with a decision on the facts that was so unreasonable that no reasonable court or jury could have reached it.

For the purposes of the search power, vessels, aircraft and hovercraft are treated as vehicles (s2(1)). It is not provided that persons in or with a car which is being searched may be subjected to reasonable force in order to make them wait until the search of the car is completed.

A constable who detains a person or vehicle in order to search need not actually conduct the search if it appears consequently that no search is required (eg, if what the constable mistakenly thought to be an offensive weapon was a harmless object on a second look) or that a search is impracticable (s2(1)).

Extent of search of a person

A constable can only require a person to remove in public an outer coat, jacket or gloves (s2(9)(a)). There is no provision empowering the removal of hats (or turbans) or footwear in public for the purposes of a search. This restriction applies only to a search in public. This is not defined but presumably refers to the actual or potential presence of other people not involved in the search. The code provides that a search in the street should be regarded as being in public even though the street may be empty at the time a search begins.[30] A person may voluntarily agree to a more thorough search in public but this would

---

27 Code A Note for Guidance 3B.
28 *Arnold v Kingston upon Hull Chief Constable* [1969] 1 WLR 1499.
29 *Donegani v Ward* [1969] 1 WLR 1502.
30 Code A Note for Guidance 3A.

be subject to the rules providing for the avoidance of embarrassment and exclusion of members of the other sex (see below).

A nearby place under s2(8) could be a place not in public, but where a more thorough search could be carried out, eg, a police van or a nearby police station.[31] However, there is no power to carry out an intimate search on a person who has not been arrested (s53). Intimate search is defined in s118(1) and dealt with on pp192–196, and can be carried out only in the circumstances discussed there. Even a non-intimate search may be acutely or sexually embarrassing but there are no explicit restrictions on such searches, or on strip searches, taking place, provided there is a suitable private place near the place of stopping.

The restriction in s2(9) applies only to the removal of clothing. It does not explicitly prevent a constable feeling inside or under clothing, even in public. The Code of Practice states that any search involving the removal of more than an outer coat, jacket, gloves, headgear or footwear may be made only by an officer of the same sex as the person searched and may not be made in the presence of anyone of the other sex.[32] This does not explicitly apply to feeling inside or under clothing, but the code also provides that every reasonable effort must be made to reduce to the minimum the embarrassment that a person being searched may experience.[33]

According to the code, the thoroughness and extent of the search must depend on what is suspected of being carried. If the suspicion relates to a particular article seen to be slipped into a pocket, the search must be confined to that pocket. If an item can be readily concealed, a more thorough search might be necessary.[34] This provision of the code does not apply to the powers of search under written authorisation contained in Criminal Justice and Public Order Act 1994 s60 and Prevention of Terrorism (Temporary Provisions) Act 1989 s13A, as those powers do not depend on reasonable suspicion about the person being searched (see pp40 and 250–252 below).

Unattended vehicles

If any unattended vehicle is searched (or anything in or on it), a notice to this effect must be left behind stating the police station to

---

31 Code A para 3.5.
32 Code A para 3.5.
33 Ibid para 3.1.
34 Ibid para 3.3.

which the constable is attached, and stating that claims for compensation should be made to that police station and that the owner or person in charge of the vehicle at the time of the search is entitled to a copy of the search record if requested within 12 months of the search (s2(6)). The notice must be left inside the vehicle unless it is not reasonably practicable to do so without damaging the vehicle (s2(7)).

If the damage caused by the search is unreasonable in relation to the constable's suspicion (eg, if the suspicion relates to a large object but the car has been damaged by a minute search) there is a civil right of action. Otherwise, damage is compensated under an ex gratia scheme. The Under-Secretary of State told the House of Commons[35] that:

> In the Metropolitan Police the rules are broadly that the police will pay compensation regardless of whether the search proved to be justified in the sense that a prohibited article of some kind was found, unless it is clear that the damage was the fault of the person being searched.

The vehicle must, if practicable, be left secure.[36]

Information to be given by constable

Before starting a search a constable must take reasonable steps to bring certain information to the attention of the person to be searched, or the person in charge of the vehicle to be searched (s2(2) and (5)). The search must not begin until this has been done. However, the duty to give the information does not apply:

– to a search of an unattended vehicle (but see above);
– to a search by a statutory undertaker in a goods area (see p45); nor
– to a search under the Aviation Security Act 1982 s27(2) (searching vehicles and inspecting goods leaving airport security areas).

The meaning of 'reasonable steps' is a question of fact for the court or jury to decide. If there is a search of large numbers of people (eg, in a queue for admission to a football match), then the information should still be given to each person searched but the reasonable steps which must be taken might be different from the steps if only one

35 HC Standing Committee E, col 293, 8 December 1983.
36 Code A para 4.10.

person were to be searched, eg, if there is too much noise to make communication easy. If the person will not listen, or is hostile or struggles, the constable must take reasonable steps, bearing in mind the circumstances.[37] At a football match, the search could be by consent as a condition of the club allowing entry rather than under the Act, in which case the courts might take the view that no information need be given (see above p25).

Bringing information to a person's attention

The duty is to bring the information to the person's attention, not necessarily to give it to him/her directly. If it is clear that the person is deaf or does not speak English, presumably it would be reasonable to give the information to somebody with him/her who could interpret or write it down. If such a person is alone, it might be that there are no reasonable steps that could be taken. If the constable is not in uniform, reasonable steps must be taken to bring to the person's attention documentary evidence of being a constable. The code provides that this must be by showing the constable's warrant card.[38] The other information to be given is:

- the constable's name and police station;
- the object of the proposed search;
- the constable's grounds for proposing to search; and
- the availability of the search record (see p33–34), unless it will not be practicable to make such a record (s2(3) and (4)).

If a constable detains someone in order to search, but then decides not to, the information must still be given, since the duty arises on the contemplation of a search. There is no duty to give any warning that the police have the power to use force to effect a search, but if such a warning is not given, the police will find it difficult to show that the force used was reasonable.

The information must be given even if it is not requested. The amount of detail to be given is unclear. Is it sufficient to say that the purpose of the search is to look for 'stolen or prohibited articles', or must the constable specify which category of prohibited article, or must the actual article suspected be identified? Can the constable search for articles not specified? Similarly, is it enough to say 'I

---

37 See, eg, the situation in the pre-Act cases of *R v Hamilton* [1986] Crim LR 187 and *Pedro v Diss* (1980) 72 Cr App R 193.
38 Code A para 2.5.

suspect you have the articles', or must the constable say 'Your appearance, the time of night, and the place where I find you cause me to suspect'?

The fact that the Act specifies the object of the search and the grounds as separate items seems to imply that the fullest information should be given. One case has suggested that the purpose of giving information is to enable the suspect to provide an explanation.[39]

Duty to make records

A constable who has carried out a search must make a written record unless it is not practicable to do so (s3(1)). If it is practicable to make a record, but not on the spot, it must be made as soon as is practicable after the completion of the search (s3(2)). An example might be where the search is followed by a struggle, or perhaps where the search is in the open air and it starts to rain heavily. Examples of where it is not practicable to make a record at all are a quick search for weapons of numbers of people at a football match, where each search might only take seconds, or in cases of public disorder in seaside areas during Bank Holiday weekends.[40] The duty under s3(1) arises only where a search has actually been carried out. There is no duty to record a detention which does not in fact lead to a search.

Contents of the record

If the constable knows the name of a person who has been searched, the record must include a note of the name. However, a constable may not detain a person to find out his or her name (s3(3)). If the constable does not know the name of the searched person, the record must describe the person in some other way (s3(4)). The search record must include a note of the person's ethnic origin and a description must be noted of any person whose name is not known.[41] If a vehicle has been searched, the record must describe the vehicle (s3(5)).

Failure to provide a name might lead to an arrest where an offence is suspected (see pp122–123). The constable is under no duty to show the suspect the record or serve a copy of it there and then, and there is no power to detain a person (or a vehicle) once a search has been completed. (Of course, detention could take place under some other power, eg, to arrest.)

39 R v *Edward Fennelley* [1989] Crim LR 142.
40 Code A para 4.1.
41 Code A para 4.5.

The record of a search of a person or vehicle (or vessel, aircraft or hovercraft) must identify the constable making it and state the following:

– the object of the search;
– the grounds for making it (which must explain briefly but informatively the reason for suspecting the person concerned, whether by reference to behaviour or other circumstances);
– the date and time when it was made;
– the place where it was made;
– whether anything, and if so what, was found; and
– whether any, and if so what, injury to a person or damage to property appears to the constable to have resulted from the search (s3(6)).

A person who has been searched, or the owner or the person in charge of a vehicle at the time of the search, may obtain a copy of any record made, on request, within 12 months of the date of the search (s3(7)-(9)). The record is made after the search and there is no guarantee that what is entered on the record actually corresponds to what the searched person was initially told under s2(2).

Failure to make a record

If a record should have been made but was not, it is unlikely that this renders the search unlawful, since the search will already have taken place. The constable will be liable to disciplinary proceedings and perhaps prosecution (see chapters 12 and 13). However, it is argued that a search made without the information being given that is required by s2(2) would be unlawful, since that would strike at the very nature of the power being given (see chapter 1). If an arrest is made as a result of the search, it will always be practicable to make a record.

It might be possible to persuade a court that in a civil action or prosecution the police cannot rely on any grounds for search not stated in the search record. If the court will not accept this as a matter of law, it would certainly cast doubt on the police account as a matter of fact if they sought to rely on information not mentioned in the search record.

Clearly, if a person wishes to complain about the stop or search, or if the results of any search are relevant to court proceedings, a solicitor or any other adviser must obtain a copy of the search record as soon as possible.

Annual reports

The 1984 Act provides that every annual report of a chief officer of police must contain information about searches recorded under s3 (see above p33) and about road checks set up under s4 (see below) (s5(1)). The information about road checks must include information about the reason for authorising each road check and the result of each one (s5(3)).

The information about searches must not include information about individual searches but must include, in respect of each month it covers, the total number of searches, broken down into searches for stolen articles, offensive weapons, and other prohibited articles, and the number of persons arrested in each category as a result of such searches (s5(2)). Information need not be provided about the number of vehicles stopped by each road block, or the number of charges or convictions resulting from a search.

The information provided can be useful in monitoring police activity in general, and constables know that at some stage each individual search must be allocated to a category. This should prompt them to think initially about ensuring that the search is justified by the Act.

Road blocks

Generally

Contrary to a widely held but mistaken view, the 1984 Act does not create any new power to set up road blocks (referred to in the Act as road checks). The power to set these up has other sources. The police have a general power under the Road Traffic Act 1988 s163 to require anybody driving a motor vehicle or riding a bicycle on a road to stop. The requirement must be made by a constable in uniform, and it is an offence to fail to stop when so required. The power under s163 is only to stop, not to search or do anything else. Any search or other action must be justified by some other provision, such as the search powers discussed in this chapter, except that a constable who reasonably suspects that a stopped vehicle is stolen may detain it for a reasonable time to enable an arrest to be made.[42]

---

42 *Lodwick v Saunders* [1985] 1 All ER 577; *Sanders v DPP* [1988] Crim LR 605.

The police also have powers at common law to set up road blocks in connection with their duty to prevent breaches of the peace[43] and to make reasonable enquiries in connection with their duty to detect crime, so long as there is no 'malpractice, caprice, or opprobrious' behaviour. The power could be used if necessary to protect property from criminal damage, prevent crime, or bring an offender to justice.[44] However, when such powers are used for certain purposes relating to escaped prisoners, or serious arrestable offences, the procedure set out in the 1984 Act s4 must be followed.

It seems that the motorist must stop when required to do so by a constable in uniform, even if the requirement is not made on reasonable grounds or is unlawful. A remedy against an unlawful stop must be established subsequently. The remedy cannot be to refuse to stop.[45]

There are new and distinct powers under the Criminal Justice and Public Order Act 1994 s60 and Prevention of Terrorism (Temporary Provisions Act) 1989 s13A to stop and search on written authorisation. These powers are discussed in detail on pp40 and 250–252 below. The exercise of these powers is not subject to the safeguards in 1984 Act s4, but carry their own safeguards and are also subject to the provisions of Code of Practice A.

Under the 1984 Act the power is limited for the purposes discussed below, but its exercise for other purposes (eg, to keep the peace, or for road traffic or vehicle excise purposes) is unaffected (s4(16)).

The 1984 Act s4 applies when the road check is carried out in such a way as to stop, in a locality, for a period, all vehicles or vehicles selected by any criterion (s4(2)). This is rightly very wide, since the procedures under s4 are tighter than the general procedures under the 1988 Act s163. The criterion might relate to an occupant of the vehicle (eg, skin colour, clothing etc) or the vehicle (eg, colour, type etc). A road check aimed at finding a particular identified vehicle would also be covered by s4. Indeed it is difficult to envisage a check which does not come within this category. However, the s4 procedure applies only when a road check is carried out for the purposes of

43 *Moss v McLachlan (Charles)* (1985) 149 JP 167, which concerned the establishment of road blocks to stop miners' pickets driving along motorways towards pits.
44 *Chief Constable of Gwent v Dash* [1985] Crim LR 674. See also *Rice v Connolly* [1966] 2 QB 414, and cases in n45.
45 *Steel v Goacher* [1982] Crim LR 689; *Beard v Wood* [1980] Crim LR 384.

ascertaining whether a vehicle is carrying a person who is unlawfully at large (see p85) or a person who has committed or is intending to commit, or has witnessed, an offence other than a road traffic or vehicle excise offence (s4(1)).

The road check need not involve a physical barrier; it could consist of police officers waving down motorists. The police officer requiring the stop must be in uniform, but non-uniformed officers may be present and may speak to the occupants of the car.

Authorisation for road checks

If a road check is governed by the s4 procedure, then there are two ways in which it can be authorised: by senior officers normally, or by any officer if required as a matter of urgency. If it is not authorised in either of these ways, then it is unlawful.

Senior officers
Subject to the provisions on urgency (see below), a road check for s4 purposes may be established only if authorised in writing by a police officer not below the rank of superintendent (s4(3)). The authorisation must specify the locality in which vehicles are to be stopped (s4(1)), the name of the authorising officer and the purpose of the check including any relevant serious arrestable offence (s4(13) and (14)). The authorisation must specify a period not exceeding seven days, during which the road check may continue, and may direct that the road check shall be continuous or conducted at specified times during that period (s4(11)).

If any of the required information is missing from the authorisation, the court will have to decide whether that renders the road check unlawful (since this is not specified in the Act). If the authorisation does not specify the name of the officer giving it, it is probably invalid, since it would not be possible to tell whether the authoriser's rank was sufficient. If it does not specify a period, then it can be argued that it means no period at all. If it does not specify a locality, it is difficult to see how it can be called an authorisation.

The grounds on which an authorisation can be given depend on the purpose for which it is given. If the purpose is to check whether a vehicle is carrying a person who is unlawfully at large, the officer must have reasonable grounds for suspecting that the person is, or is about to be, in the locality (though not necessarily in a vehicle) in which vehicles would be stopped if the road check were authorised (s4(4)(d)). Grounds are reasonable if a court or jury would regard them as such. In this case it would usually be based on a sighting, information received, or some trace of the person. If the locality of the road checks is wider than the locality in which the person is believed to be, then the check is unlawful even within the locality where the person is believed to be.

If the purpose relates to a person who has committed, or intends to commit, or has witnessed an offence, the officer must have reasonable grounds for believing that the offence is a serious arrestable offence. The meaning of this phrase is defined in s116 and discussed on pp5–8. If the purpose is to check whether a vehicle is carrying a witness, then this requirement is sufficent (s4(4)(b)). However, the witness, if found, need not co-operate and cannot be searched or arrested. If the purpose is to check for a person who has committed an offence, the officer must have reasonable grounds for suspecting that the person is, or is about to be, in the locality (though not necessarily in a vehicle) in which vehicles would be stopped if the road block were authorised (s4(4)(a)).

If the purpose is to ascertain whether the vehicle is carrying a person intending to commit a criminal offence, the officer authorising the block must have reasonable grounds to believe that the offence (if committed) would be a serious arrestable offence (s4(4)(c)(i)) and for suspecting that the person is, or is about to be in the locality (s4(4)(c)(ii)). Whether there are reasonable grounds to believe all this is an objective question for the court or jury to decide. If, as a result of a road block, the police do find someone *intending* to commit an offence, they still cannot arrest that person unless the arrest is authorised under Part III of the Act (see chapter 5), for example because the police reasonably believe that the person is about to commit an arrestable offence.

Since the authorisation must specify the purpose and locality of the road check (s4(13)) and any relevant serious arrestable offence (s4(14)), in any contest over the lawfulness of the check, it can be seen whether the grounds for belief related to the purpose (although the grounds for belief are not noted on the authorisation). A check for any purpose not allowed under other powers and not specified in the authorisation would be unlawful. A stop and search for a prohibited article would have to be justified in relation to the particular vehicle under the 1984 Act s1. Once the road check is made and a vehicle stopped, any search or arrest must be justified under other powers and of course need not be limited to the purpose specified in the authorisation.

'Locality' is not defined or limited except that the road check must be in the locality where the person being sought is reasonably suspected to be.

The authorisation under s4(4) may be given only for a period not exceeding seven days (s4(11)(a)) but is renewable indefinitely (in writing) for periods of up to seven days at a time (s4(12)). Presumably the renewal must be founded on the same grounds as the initial authorisation although the Act does not explicitly say this. It is the authorisation that lasts for up to seven days; the road check cannot last beyond the end of the period of authorisation. If the authorisation directs the check to be conducted at specific times, it would be unlawful to conduct it at other times.

Urgency and all officers
Any other police officer (ie, of rank below superintendent) may authorise a road check for one of the prescribed purposes if it appears to him/her that a road check is required as a matter of urgency. The grounds to justify the check are the same as discussed above but the question of urgency is not defined and is a purely subjective test on the part of the officer involved (s4(5)). The Act does not expressly limit the period of time during which such an authorisation may last (although it could be argued that it must end when the officer believes that it is no longer required as a matter of urgency). The authorisation must be recorded in writing at the time it is given (s4(6)), specifying the locality in which vehicles are to be stopped (s4(1)), the name of the officer and purpose of the check (s4(13)), and any relevant serious arrestable offence (s4(14)). It must be reported as soon as practicable to an officer of at least the rank of superintendent (s4(6) and (7)). The officer to whom it is reported may give a written authorisation for the check to continue (s4(8)). The authorisation is in the same form as the ordinary senior officer authorisation, and the time limits apply. Presumably the grounds are the same as for the senior officer authorisation. Once the issue is with such senior officer, the question of urgency is no longer relevant (the urgency power being given only to officers of lower rank).

If the officer to whom the urgent check is reported considers that the road check should not continue, that officer must record in writing the fact that it took place and the purpose for which it took place (s4(9)). The Act does not specifically require that the road check must end if the senior officer decides that it should, and in the unlikely event of it continuing it is not clear that it would be unlawful while the urgency continued.

Right to a statement and remedies

Where a vehicle is stopped in a road check, the person in charge of the vehicle is entitled to obtain a written statement of the purpose of the check on application within 12 months from the stop (s4(15)). It is not handed over at the time. This is a very limited right, since the statement need not include details of the ground for or the duration of the stop, but would certainly help to prove the fact of the stop and show what grounds would have to be proved in any subsequent proceedings. The police would not really be able to prove the lawfulness of the stop without producing the authorisation and details of the grounds on which it was based. If a s1 search takes place, a s3 search record can also be obtained (p33). The general question of remedies is dealt with in chapter 13. If it is suspected that a particular road check is unlawful it might be possible to obtain an injunction to prevent its continuation.

Powers under Criminal Justice and Public Order Act 1994 s60

Generally

Constables in uniform may stop and search pedestrians and vehicles for offensive weapons and dangerous instruments, when a senior police officer who reasonably believes that incidents involving serious violence may take place has issued a written authorisation.[46] The exercise of this power is subject to Code of Practice A[47] but, like most legislation on police powers, its introduction was politically and legally controversial. It is an additional power and does not derogate from any other power.[48]

Who may issue the authorisation

The authorisation may be issued by any police officer of the rank of superintendent or above (s60(1)) but may also be issued by a chief

---

46 For a full analysis of this provision and the background to it see Card and Ward, *The Criminal Justice and Public Order Act 1994* (Jordans 1994) pp9–20, although it should be noted that these authors did not have access to the final version of the revised Codes of Practice and do not seem to appreciate the full extent of the applicability of the 1984 Act to the s60 power.

47 Code of Practice A para 1.5(b).

48 Criminal Justice and Public Order Act 1994 s60(12).

inspector or inspector on the basis of the same criteria if he also reasonably believes that incidents involving serious violence are imminent and no superintendent is available (s60(2)). This is a narrower power than that given to a superintendent (see below) in that the belief must relate to the imminence of serious violence. 'Imminent' is not defined but seems to convey some sense of immediacy and urgency. The reasonable belief required probably does not qualify the question of the availability of a superintendent, which seems to be a question of fact. 'Available' is not defined but presumably refers to availability sufficiently prior to the expected violence to issue the authorisation. It would be rare for a superintendent not to be available in a metropolitan area and this provision might be of more relevance in small towns or rural areas.

The basis for issuing the authorisation

A police officer of the rank of superintendent or above may issue the authorisation if he reasonably believes that incidents involving serious violence may take place in any locality in his area and that it is expedient to do so to prevent their occurrence (s60(1)). Reasonable belief is an objective test subject to the considerations discussed on pp12–14 above. On normal principles of interpretation, anticipation of a single incident will suffice. 'Serious violence' is not defined but is probably limited to personal violence. 'Locality' is not defined but must be within the area for which the authorising officer has responsibility. The officer must also reasonably believe that actions under the authorisation may help to prevent the incident(s).[49] The authorisation must be justified by what is anticipated, not by what has happened, unless that affects what is anticipated.

Duration of the authorisation

The period of the authorisation may not exceed 24 hours (s60(1)) but should be the minimum period that the authorising officer considers necessary to prevent or try to prevent or deal with the risk of violence.[50] The period may be extended once for a further six hours

---

49 Criminal Justice and Public Order Act 1994 s60(1)(b) and Code of Practice A para 1.8.
50 Code of Practice A para 1.8 and Notes for Guidance 1F.

beyond the original time limit (not up to 30 hours unless the original time limit was 24 hours) if it appears to either the original authorising officer or a superintendent that it is expedient to do so having regard to offences which have or are reasonably suspected to have been committed in connection with any incident falling within the authorisation (s60(3)). However, this extension must still be justified by what is anticipated, not only by what has happened. There can be no further extension, but a completely fresh authorisation may be issued.[51]

The authorisation and the locality

The authorisation must be in writing and signed by the authorising officer and must specify the period during which and the locality in which the powers under it are exercisable. An extension must also be in writing, unless that is not practicable, in which case it must be recorded in writing as soon as possible (s60(9)). An initial authorisation must always be in writing from the outset.

It is for the authorising officer to determine the geographical area in which the use of the powers is to be authorised and the officer should take into account factors such as the nature and venue of the anticipated incident, the numbers of people who may be in the immediate vicinity of any possible incident, their access to surrounding areas and the anticipated level of violence. The officer should not set a wider area than that s/he believes necessary for the purpose of preventing the anticipated violence.[52]

What is authorised

Where an authorisation has been issued, any *constable in uniform* may stop and search any pedestrian or anything carried by the pedestrian, or any vehicle, its driver and any passenger, for offensive weapons and dangerous instruments (s60(4)) and seize any dangerous instrument or any article which the constable has reasonable grounds for believing to be an offensive weapon (s60(6)). Vehicle includes caravan (s60(11)) and the same power applies (with any necessary modifications) to ships, aircraft and hovercraft (s60(7)). 'Pedestrian' is not defined. It has been pointed out that if its meaning is limited to

51 Ibid.
52 Code of Practice A Note for Guidance 1G.

a person on foot, there would be no power to stop a person on horseback.[53]

A dangerous instrument is an instrument which has a blade or is sharply pointed (s60(11)). This definition is clearly influenced by the wording of the offence in Criminal Justice Act 1988 s139 (see above p21), but for the purposes of s60 a dangerous instrument includes a folding pocketknife, even if the cutting edge of the blade does not exceed three inches. 'Offensive weapon' has the same meaning as in the 1984 Act s1(9) (see above p21). There need be no suspicion that any person to be searched has committed or is committing or will commit an offence.

Any person or vehicle may be stopped and searched, whether or not the constable suspects or has any grounds for suspecting that the person or vehicle is carrying offensive weapons or dangerous articles, and the constable may make any search that s/he thinks fit (s60(5)). However, such stops and searches are subject to the safeguards in the 1984 Act ss2 and 3 (p28–35 above) concerning information to be given, the nature of the search and record keeping. They are also subject to the provisions of Code of Practice A (except where the code deals with reasonable grounds for suspicion). In particular, the code aims at restricting the degree of embarrassment that may be experienced, reserving force as a last resort, and limiting the nature of any search in public (see above pp29–30). On general principles the nature of the search must be limited to what is appropriate to search for offensive weapons or dangerous items.

Section 60 is silent on where the power to stop may be exercised. The context suggests that it applies on the highway and not on private premises but on this aspect the drafting is very sloppy and in due course this issue will have to be settled by the courts or by further legislation.

Failure to stop

A person who fails to stop when required to do so by a constable in the exercise of powers under s60 commits an offence and is liable on summary conviction to imprisonment for a term not exceeding one month or to fine not exceeding level 3 on the standard scale or to

53 Card and Ward, op cit n46 at p15. Presumably the same consideration would apply eg, to circus performers on elephants. How would the power apply to people who are not moving at all, perhaps sitting on a park bench? Presumably until they started walking they would have to be treated in the same way as a person watching the street from a window.

both (s60(8)). This is not an arrestable offence and any arrest would have to be justified under s25 of the 1984 Act (see below pp119–126), although if a person does not stop at all, the general arrest conditions would in any case be satisfied. A search would then have to be justified either by s60 or by the 1984 Act s32 (see pp144–146).

The creation of this offence seems odd since it is clear that by virtue of having the power to stop, a constable may use force to exercise this power. Resisting a lawful stop could then amount to an offence of obstructing or assaulting a constable in the exercise of duty. The same would be true if, having stopped, a person resisted a lawful search, a situation to which the new offence does not apply.

Written statements

Where a vehicle is stopped by a constable under s60 (whether or not a search takes place) the driver is entitled to obtain a written statement that the vehicle was stopped under that section if an application for such a statement is made within twelve months of the stop (s60(10)). A similar right is conferred on a pedestrian who is stopped and searched under s60 (s60(10)). These rights are in addition to those conferred by the 1984 Act s3 (see above pp33–34).

Powers under specific provisions

Stop and search by statutory undertakers

Special powers to stop and search vehicles are given to constables employed by statutory undertakers. 'Statutory undertakers' is defined in s7(3) and means bodies authorised by statute to carry on a railway, transport, dock or harbour undertaking. The larger of such bodies employ their own police forces, whose members have the powers of constables within a geographically limited area (see pp8–11). Any such constable may stop, detain and search any vehicle before it leaves any part of the undertaker's premises used wholly or mainly for the storage or handling of goods (s6(1) and (2)). Such stops are carried out routinely and there is no legal need for reasonable suspicion in relation to any particular vehicle, nor any duty to make records of such stops. There is no statutory limitation on what may be searched for.

There is no power under this provision to search individuals, only vehicles. There is no power of seizure, although the undertaker has the legal right to seize its own property. There is a power to use reasonable force to enforce the stop and search (s117). Powers under the provisions of s6 cannot be exercised by members of the ordinary police forces to which the Police Act 1964 applies.

To the extent that other legislation authorises the search of individuals by constables employed by statutory undertakers, such searches must be recorded under the provisions of s3 and are subject to the duties set out in s2 of the 1984 Act.

Many statutes authorise statutory undertakers to search for unlawfully obtained goods but there is no comprehensive list of such powers in the 1984 Act or the Code of Practice. The Act does remove any need for periodic renewal of such powers (s7(2)(b)).

Powers under pre-1984 Act statutes

The 1984 Act repealed all powers of search for stolen or unlawfully obtained goods conferred by local Acts (including the County of Merseyside Act 1980 s33 and the West Midlands County Council Act 1980 s42). It also repealed powers of stop and search under the Metropolitan Police Act 1839 s66, the Vagrancy Act 1824 s8, the Canals (Offences) Act 1840 s11, and the Pedlars Act 1871 s19. Any stop and search which might have taken place under these provisions now has to be justified under the 1984 Act s1 (s7).

The same is true of all such powers under private Acts other than those relating to statutory undertakers. However, other pre-1984 Act powers are preserved (see pp443–445).

Public stores and the United Kingdom Atomic Energy Authority Constabulary

Under the Public Stores Act 1875 s6, a constable may stop, search and detain any vessel, boat or vehicle in or on which there is reason to suspect that any of Her Majesty's stores, stolen or unlawfully obtained may be found, or any person reasonably suspected of having or conveying in any manner any of Her Majesty's stores, stolen or unlawfully obtained. The 1984 Act s6(3) brings within these powers any person appointed as a special constable on premises controlled by British Nuclear Fuels Limited and deems any goods belonging to that company to be Her Majesty's stores for these purposes. Such special constables are in fact organised in the UK Atomic Energy Authority Constabulary.

Sports grounds

Reference has been made above to police searching people routinely as they enter sports grounds. Insofar as this is with their consent, possibly as a condition of entry, the search is not conducted under the 1984 Act, and the provisions of the Act and the Code do not apply. There might well be problems in proving whether a particular search was voluntary. If it was not, it must be justified by either the general power in the 1984 Act or some other statutory power.

The Sporting Events (Control of Alcohol etc) Act 1985 creates a number of offences and s7(2) empowers a constable to search (and presumably stop and detain for such a purpose) a person whom the constable has reasonable grounds to suspect is committing or has committed an offence under the Act.

A constable may also stop and search a public service vehicle (such as a bus) or a railway passenger vehicle if the constable has reasonable grounds to suspect that a person on the vehicle possesses intoxicating liquor or is drunk and the vehicle is being used principally to carry passengers to or from a designated sporting event (s7(3)). Other offences under the Act include possession of intoxicating liquor or a portable drink container (such as a bottle or can) which is capable of causing injury to a person struck by it, during a designated sporting event while in a designated sports ground, or while entering or trying to enter such. It is also an offence to be drunk at or while entering or trying to enter such an event (s2). The power to search is not limited to the items listed above, although the constable must have reasonable grounds to suspect an offence under the Act. Nevertheless the search might reveal other items (such as stolen goods) which would justify an arrest or other action.

The powers under the 1985 Act s7 are subject to the provisions of the 1984 Act ss2 and 3 and to the Code of Practice.

Provisons annexed to the code

Annex A to the Code of Practice lists and summarises the main powers of stop and search to which the code and the appropriate provisions of the 1984 Act apply. The annex is reproduced on pp443–445. However, the summary is very brief and sometimes misleading (eg, on the applicability to the Sporting Events (Control of Alcohol etc) Act 1985) and reference should be made to the wording of the provisions listed. The list in the annex to the code is not an exhaustive list and the safeguards will apply to any power to search a person or a vehicle without making an arrest (except those given by the 1984 Act s6 or the Aviation Security Act 1982 s27(2)).

CHAPTER 3

Entry and search of premises

Introduction

The powers of the police to enter and search premises are derived not only from the 1984 Act as amended, but also from many other statutes and the common law. The 1984 Act gave the police new powers to search for evidence, but in some cases limited existing statutory and common law powers. The Code of Practice for the Searching of Premises and the Seizure of Property (Code B) applies to all searches under warrant, including those issued under the 1984 Act Sch 1 and ss17, 18 and 32 (see below). The Code also applies to all searches undertaken for the purposes of an investigation into an alleged offence with the occupier's consent. This is not the case, however, where it is a routine scene-of-crime search or a call to a fire or burglary made by or on behalf of an occupier or searches following the activation of alarms or bomb threat calls. Furthermore Code B does not apply where the police do not have to obtain consent because doing so would cause disproportionate inconvenience to the person concerned (see below p92) or where the police are exercising powers of entry unconnected to the investigation of crime (Code B paras 1.3, 4.4 and Note for Guidance 1.3B; see appendix 2).

Neither the Act nor the Code defines 'search' but in *Dudley Metropolitan Borough Council v Debenhams plc*,[1] deciding that trading standards officers were bound by the Code, it was said in the Divisional Court that a search took place when a person entered and looked about. There was no need for physical interference with goods.

A broad outline of police powers to enter and search under the

1 (1994) *Times* 16 August.

1984 Act, the classifications of evidence, and the effect of the Act on other search powers, is given below. The classifications of evidence, and the procedure which the police must adopt in order to enter and search for them, are then considered in turn. Those sections are followed by detailed explanations of how applications for search warrants and production orders should be made, how searches (whether with or without a warrant, under other statutory or common law powers, or by consent) should be executed, and the action to be taken after a search is made.

Police powers under the prevention of terrorism legislation are described in chapter 8; under the Criminal Justice Act 1988 and the Drug Trafficking Act 1994; and under the Criminal Justice Act 1987 in relation to the investigation of fraud, below (pp94–98). For the powers of the security services to enter property, see p98.

The scheme of the 1984 Act

In this section, the scheme of powers of entry and search under the 1984 Act is outlined. The provisions and the procedures to be followed are considered in detail below.

The Act and Code B provide certain procedures which the police must follow where they want to enter premises to search for evidence of an offence, or in connection with making an arrest.

Only a partial definition of 'premises' is provided by the Act (in s23). 'Premises' includes any place, which is not defined, but must include land: in s1(4) and (5) 'place' clearly includes land. In *Palmer v Bugler*,[2] a field used regularly for a car boot sale was capable of being a 'place' for the purposes of Shops Act 1950 s58 (now repealed). 'Premises' also includes any vehicle, vessel (see s118), aircraft or hovercraft, and offshore installation (see Mineral Workings (Offshore Installations) Act 1971 s1) and any tent or moveable structure.

Entry and search by warrant, order or on other written authority

Where the police want to enter premises to search for evidence of an offence, the procedure that must be followed under the 1984 Act will depend initially on whether the owner or occupier has consented in writing to the search. If the police have the owner or occupier's

2 (1988) *Times* 28 November.

written consent, they may enter and search premises provided that the owner gave an informed consent (see p92 below). Lack of written consent will cast doubts on police claims of consent.

Where the police do not have the consent of the owner or occupier, the procedure to be followed will depend on the nature of the evidence sought. 'Evidence' is referred to throughout the 1984 Act as 'material', and might consist of anything, for instance bullets, clothes, human tissue, cheque books, accounts or fingerprints. The nature of the evidence is important because the Act provides special safeguards to protect evidence which could be described in general terms as being of a confidential nature; that is, it is held in confidence by the person possessing it.

In the vast majority of cases where the police want to search for evidence, but cannot obtain consent to do so, the evidence that they are seeking will not be subject to any special safeguards; the police will simply apply to a magistrate for a search warrant.

However, the Act provides safeguards where the police are seeking:

– some categories of personal records, human tissue or tissue fluid, or journalistic material, which are held by a person in confidence – 'excluded material';
– certain other evidence held by a person in confidence, such as company accounts – 'special procedure material'; and
– items subject to legal privilege.

It is essential to establish how the evidence in question is classified, as different safeguards apply to each category.

If the police are seeking excluded or special procedure material, in most cases they will have to apply to a circuit judge for a production order (rather than to a magistrate for a search warrant). A production order requires the person in possession of the evidence either to produce it to a constable to take away, or to give a constable access to it, so the person is not subjected to a search of premises. When the police apply for such an order, the person possessing the evidence is served with a notice to that effect. Once the notice is served, the person is, effectively, prohibited from concealing or disposing of the evidence. Unlike an application for a search warrant, an application for a production order is made inter partes.

In exceptional cases the circuit judge may issue a search warrant in addition to, or instead of, a production order. (For the detailed provisions on access to special procedure and excluded material, see below pp60–79.)

Legally privileged material is exempt from any powers to search (except under written authority other than a warrant, see below).

Where the police have the power to apply for a search warrant under another statute, the classifications of evidence, as above, are effective, and the procedures in the 1984 Act and Code B apply. Thus, statutes (including local Acts) passed before the Act which give the police powers to obtain search warrants from magistrates are ineffective so far as excluded material is concerned (s9(2)(b)). In such a case, an application to a circuit judge would have to be made in accordance with the provisions of the 1984 Act.

However, statutes which enable the police to gain access under written authority other than a warrant are unaffected, because the 1984 Act refers only to warrants. The Official Secrets Act 1911 s9(2), for example, gives a superintendent the power to give a written order to search in a case of great emergency and in the interests of the State. A superintendent may still exercise that power (provided that the criteria in the 1911 Act are met) in relation to any evidence, no matter how that evidence might be classified under the 1984 Act. Thus, even legally privileged material, which is otherwise exempt from any powers of search, would be subject to search under such written authority (for restrictions on seizure powers see chapter 4). For a list of statutory police powers to enter and search premises on written authority other than a warrant, see appendix 6.

Where the police have the power to apply for a search warrant under any statute, the application for the warrant and the conduct of the search are subject to the provisions of ss15 and 16 and the Code of Practice (below p79).

Entry without a warrant

All police powers to enter premises without a warrant for the purposes of, or in connection with, making an arrest are contained in the 1984 Act (see ss17 (entry for arrest and other purposes), 18 (entry after arrest) and 32 (entry on arrest)). Existing statutory powers of entry without a warrant for other purposes (for example the powers of entry without warrant under the Gaming Act 1968 as amended) were unaffected by the Act. All common law powers of entry without warrant were abolished, except the powers of entry to deal with or prevent a breach of the peace.

Applications to a magistrate for a search warrant under the 1984 Act

Where the police want to enter premises to search for evidence of a serious arrestable offence, and there are no powers under other statutes to obtain a warrant from a magistrate and that evidence is not subject to special safeguards (see above), they may make an application ex parte (s15(3)) to a magistrate for a search warrant. Such applications are governed by s8.

A magistrate should issue a search warrant only in the last resort: if the police can gain entry by consent they should do so (see s8(3) below). A warrant may be issued to search any premises, not only those whose occupier is under suspicion.

Conditions governing issue of a warrant

The magistrate must be satisfied that there are reasonable grounds for believing that the evidence does not consist of or include material which is subject to special safeguards (s8(1)(d)), and that the warrant is absolutely necessary to gain entry (s8(3), below). In addition, the magistrate must be satisfied that there are reasonable grounds for believing that:

– a serious arrestable offence has been committed (s8(1)(a)); and
– there is evidence on the premises which is likely to be of substantial value (whether by itself or together with other evidence) to the investigation of the offence (s8(1)(b)); and
– the evidence is likely to be relevant evidence (s8(1)(c)).

These conditions are considered in turn below.

'Reasonable grounds for believing'

The magistrate must be satisfied that there are 'reasonable grounds for believing' that all the conditions are met. Many statutes use similar language, for example the Misuse of Drugs Act 1971 s23(3), and it has been held that the magistrate must exercise a judicial discretion.[3] (See above p12 for the control of discretion and below p339 for judicial review.)

3 *Hope v Evered* (1886) 17 QBD 338.

Evidence not subject to special safeguards

Detailed definitions of 'excluded', 'special procedure' and 'legally privileged' material, which are subject to special safeguards, are given below on pp60, 66 and 56 respectively. A magistrate should not issue a warrant under s8 if there are reasonable grounds for believing that the material includes material subject to special safeguards. In the case of 'excluded' or 'special procedure' material the police should apply to a circuit judge for a production order or, in exceptional circumstances, a warrant.

It should be noted that in certain situations the police may apply to a magistrate for a warrant to obtain special procedure material which does not consist of documents or records other than documents, but under some other statutory power, not under s8 (see p68 below).

Issue of the warrant must be necessary

Section 8(3) makes it clear that a magistrate should not issue a search warrant if the police could gain access to the evidence with the consent of the relevant person. Thus, the magistrate must be satisfied that there are reasonable grounds for believing that:

a) it is not practicable to communicate with any person entitled to grant entry to the premises (s8(3)(a)); or

b) it is practicable to communicate with a person entitled to grant entry to the premises but it is not practicable to communicate with any person entitled to grant access to the evidence (s8(3)(b)); or

c) entry to the premises will not be granted unless a warrant is produced (s8(3)(c)); or

d) the purpose of a search warrant may be frustrated or seriously prejudiced unless a constable arriving at the premises can secure immediate entry to them (s8(3)(d)).

'Practicable' in s8(3)(a) and (b) above is not defined. The conditions in s8(3)(c) and (d) cover situations where entry is likely to be refused or the investigation hampered, so s8(3)(a) and (b) ought to cover, by implication, other circumstances, such as where the owner of the premises or the material which is believed to be evidence is untraceable. In relation to Sch 1 para 14(a) (below p77), which uses exactly the same wording, the Divisional Court has given a wide interpretation to 'practicable', which encompasses para 14(d) and in this case would encompass s8(3)(d).[4] In this case solicitors argued

4 *R v Leeds Crown Court ex p Switalski* [1991] Crim LR 559.

that para 14(a) was inapplicable because one of them was available to grant access to the documents. The Court held, however, that 'practicable' was not limited to 'feasible' or 'physically possible' but included consideration of all the circumstances, including the nature of the enquiries and the persons against whom they were directed. There is no indication in the Act of who is entitled to grant entry to premises.

Unlike the position in relation to applications for excluded and special procedure material under Sch 1 (see below), there is no requirement that other methods of obtaining the material have been tried without success or have not been tried because they are bound to fail.[5]

'Serious arrestable offence'

'Serious arrestable offence' is defined in s116, see p5.

Evidence 'likely to be of substantial value'

The evidence sought need be only 'likely to be' of substantial value to the investigation of the offence; therefore if it turns out to be otherwise the warrant will not be invalid on that ground alone.

The application for a search warrant must be supported by an information in writing, which must give (inter alia) an indication of how the evidence relates to the investigation (Code B para 2(6)(iii)). The magistrate must have reasonable grounds for believing that the material is likely to be of substantial value or the warrant may be invalid (s8(1)) (see further chapter 13 for the liability of magistrates).

'Relevant evidence'

'Relevant evidence' means anything that would be admissible at a trial for the offence (s8(4)). Again, the phrase 'is likely to be' in s8(1)(c) means that if the evidence turns out be inadmissible as evidence or if it is simply not used at the trial, the warrant will still be valid.

Procedure governing applications

Code B sets out the action to be taken by police officers before an application for a search warrant is made. Section 15, which is consid-

---

5 R v Billericay JJ and Dobbyn, ex p Frank Harris (Coaches) Ltd [1991] Crim LR 472; cf R v Lewes Crown Court, ex p Hill [1991] Crim LR 376, below p69.

ered in detail below on p80, states how the application must be made. Breaches of the Code may be relevant in any civil or criminal proceedings (s67(11)). Section 15 and the code apply not only to applications for search warrants under the 1984 Act, but to those under all other statutes giving the police power to apply for a search warrant.

Appeals against the issue of a warrant

There is no appeal to the Crown Court from the issue of a warrant under s8, but obviously there is a right to make an application to the High Court for judicial review or for an injunction. In reality, however, such an application is unlikely to be made before the search has taken place and the appropriate remedy must be sought afterwards (see chapter 13).

Access to legally privileged material

The definition of items subject to legal privilege is contained in s10 (see below) and is intended to reflect the common law definition.[6] The definition is crucial, since such items are exempt from any powers of search under the 1984 Act and any powers to issue a warrant to search for such material contained in other statutes enacted before the 1984 Act are of no effect (s9(2)(a)). Whether this prohibition applies so far as legislation passed after the 1984 Act is concerned depends on the contents of each statute. The Divisional Court has held[7] that the police should never apply ex parte to a magistrate under s8 when seeking a warrant to enter premises in order to search for material which may consist of or include items prima facie subject to legal privilege. (In *Primlaks Holdings* the argument centred on whether or not the material sought was held with the intention of furthering a criminal purpose under s10(2) and thus was no longer privileged.) Since this will almost always be excluded or special procedure material, the police should use the procedure set out in Sch 1

---

6 See the majority view of the House of Lords in *Francis and Francis* (*a firm*) *v Central Criminal Court* [1988] 3 All ER 775 (this case is considered further on p60 below).

7 *R v Guildhall Magistrates' Court ex p Primlaks Holdings Co* [1989] 2 WLR 841. See also *R v Secretary of State for Home Department ex p Propend Finance Property Ltd* (1994) *Times* 5 April, where a warrant was wrongly issued under the Criminal Justice (International Co-operation) Act 1990 s7(4).

instead.[8] It has also been held that circuit judges must be extremely cautious about issuing warrants under Sch 1 (see below p78) where there is any chance that any of the material may be legally privileged. The police should draw the judge's attention to such material and provide sufficient information for the judge to reach a conclusion. Where there is any doubt legal advice should be obtained to assist the judge.[9] It has also been suggested that any warrant issued under Sch 1 should contain some express provision excluding items subject to legal privilege. A circuit judge has a very heavy responsibility when it comes to making an order which may contain legally privileged material and such orders should be rare. The police have a responsibility to ensure that any legally privileged information obtained under such a 'blanket order' should not be misused and in some cases it may be appropriate to require them to give an express undertaking to that effect.[10] (For the position in the case of statutes giving the police power to obtain evidence under written authority other than a warrant see above p51 and below p66.) If such material is found during a search for other material, it should not be seized (see chapter 4).

Since it is neither excluded nor special procedure material, there is no power to apply to a circuit judge for a production order in respect of it. Legally privileged items may not be sought after arrest (see s18) and although a search for such material seems permissible upon arrest for an offence (s32) such material should not be seized (s19 and see chapter 4). (See further pp89 and 91.)

'Legally privileged material'

For the purposes of the 1984 Act, there are three categories of evidence subject to legal privilege. The categories are considered in turn below. In each category, the definition hinges on who can be called a profes-

8 This ruling did not apply in *R v Leeds Magistrates' Court ex p Dumbleton* [1993] Crim LR 866 apparently because there was evidence from which the justices could be satisfied that there were reasonable grounds for believing that the material for which the warrant was sought did not include items subject to legal privilege or special procedure material. This was either because they were not within the statutory definition or because they were held with the intention of furthering a criminal purpose (see below p59). Access was properly applied for under the Forgery and Counterfeiting Act 1981.

9 *R v Southampton Crown Court ex p J and P* [1993] Crim LR 962.

10 *R v Leeds Crown Court ex p Switalski* [1991] Crim LR 559. In this case a 'blanket order' was justified. The circumstances were unusual because the firm of solicitors itself was under investigation.

sional legal adviser. The term clearly includes barristers and solicitors. Solicitors' clerks would also be included because they are acting on behalf of solicitors and therefore come under their professional responsibility. It is also clear from the section that the adviser does not have to come from a firm of solicitors; it is the status of the adviser which is at issue. Therefore the adviser may work from a law centre or advice centre. Although the advice of unqualified persons would not be privileged, it would still be excluded material in most cases (see below). This position would not of course protect it from seizure (see chapter 4). If the unqualified adviser were acting as agent for a solicitor or barrister, then it might be possible to claim that communications are legally privileged. If however the adviser is acting for someone else, then that would not be possible.

Section 10(1)(a)

In the first category of legally privileged communications are those between a professional legal adviser and a client or someone representing the client, made in connection with the giving of legal advice to the client (s10(1)(a)).

Communications can be written or oral, so that, for example, a tape recording of an interview between a solicitor and client concerned with legal advice would be privileged, as would a note of the interview, and the term must be taken to include drafts, notes and other documents incidental to the obtaining and giving of advice. The Divisional Court stated in 1995 that the correct approach is to look at the 'substance and reality of the document, the circumstances in which it came into existence and its purpose'.[11] It has also been held that a solicitor's professional duty is not limited to the provision of advice on legal matters per se but extends to advice relating to the commercial wisdom or entering transactions in respect of which legal advice is also sought. Therefore communications between the adviser and the client relating to such a transaction would be privileged, provided they pertained directly to the performance of the solicitor's function as legal adviser.[12]

The material has to have been made in connection with the

11 *IBM Corporation v Phoenix International (Computers) Ltd* [1995] 1 All ER 413 at 429c-d.
12 *Nederlandse Reassurantie Groep Holding NV v Bacon and Woodrow (a firm) and Others* [1995] 1 All ER 976; and see *R v Crown Court at Inner London Sessions ex p Baines and Baines* [1987] 3 All ER 1025 (and see below, nn18 and 46). See also *Barclays Bank v Eustace* [1995] 4 All ER 511, where discovery of documents relating to advice in a commercial transaction was ordered despite a claim of legal professional privilege.

provision of legal advice and it is not sufficient that material which was already in existence has become available to the adviser.[13] Similarly privilege cannot be claimed in respect of copies of material taken for the purpose of legal advice where the original document is not privileged.[14] It has been held, however, that where a selection of documents has been copied or assembled by a solicitor which 'betrays the trend of advice' given to the client then the pre-existing documents and the copies become privileged.[15]

Section 10(1)(b)

The second category is that of communications between a professional legal adviser and a client or someone representing a client, or between such an adviser or a client or any such representative and any other person made in connection with or in contemplation of legal proceedings and for the purposes of such proceedings (s10(1)(b)).

Letters from a psychiatrist to a client prescribing treatment would not be privileged even if the illness were to be a defence in a trial because they would not have been written in connection with or in contemplation of legal proceedings. Reports specifically obtained for the purposes of legal proceedings by a solicitor, however, would be privileged. Unlike the position at common law, if there is more than one purpose, it does not appear to be necessary for legal proceedings to be the dominant one in order for the communications to be privileged.

Section 10(1)(c)

Thirdly, items enclosed with or referred to in such communications and made either in connection with the giving of legal advice or in connection with or in contemplation of legal proceedings and for the purpose of such proceedings are also privileged, but other items would not be (s10(1)(c)). It is important to note the limits on the items for which legal privilege can be claimed in this category. Legal privilege would not attach, for instance, to documents submitted to either an expert witness for an opinion, or a legal adviser by a client for the adviser's advice, if they have not been 'made' (s10(1)(c)) in connection with the giving of legal advice or in connection with legal proceedings.

A blood sample provided to a doctor by a defendant at the request

13 *Ventouris v Mountain* [1991] 3 All ER 472.
14 *Dubai Bank Ltd v Galadari* [1989] 3 All ER 769.
15 *Dubai Bank Ltd v Galadari (No 7)* [1992] 1 All ER 658.

of his solicitors in order to conduct his defence in a trial for sexual offences has been held to be legally privileged. It was an item 'made' for the purposes of legal proceedings.[16] 'Made' means lawfully made and does not extend to forged documents.[17]

In *R v Crown Court at Inner London Sessions ex p Baines & Baines*,[18] the Divisional Court considered an application for judicial review of a production order concerning records and correspondence relating to the purchase of a property. Clearly such material cannot be described as being 'made in connection with or in contemplation of legal proceedings' (s10(1)(b)) but the Court indicated, obiter, that advice, for instance on factors 'serving to assist towards a completion, the wisdom or otherwise of proceeding with it, the arranging of a mortgage and so on'[19] would be privileged within s10(1)(a) as communications made in connection with the giving of legal advice. The Court was not prepared to hold, however, that the conveyancing matter itself would be privileged. It did not refer to the possibility of such records being privileged within s10(1)(c)(i) as items 'enclosed with or referred to in such communications and made in connection with the giving of legal advice'. Solicitors are advised to keep records of documents and items enclosed with communications if it is conceivable they could come within the definition.[20]

All the items referred to above must be in the possession of someone entitled to possession or they lose their protected status (s10(1)).

Intention of furthering a criminal purpose

According to s10(2), items held with the intention of furthering a criminal purpose are not subject to legal privilege. A letter from a solicitor advising a client of criminal liability if a particular course of conduct were pursued would be privileged, as it is not produced with the intention of furthering a criminal purpose.[21] Similar considerations would apply to a letter from a solicitor inducing a breach of contract, which is a tort, not a crime.[22]

16 *R v R* [1994] 4 All ER 260, CA.
17 *R v Leeds Magistrates' Court ex p Dumbleton* (above, n8).
18 [1987] 3 All ER 1025.
19 Ibid at 1030.
20 See E Hiley 'Production Orders under the Police and Criminal Evidence Act' (1987) 84 LS Gaz 3088.
21 *Butler v Board of Trade* [1971] Ch 680.
22 *Crescent Farm (Sidcup) Sports v Sterling Offices* [1972] Ch 553.

The courts have had difficulty with the question of whose purpose is relevant in s10(2).[23]

In *Francis & Francis v Central Criminal Court*[24] the House of Lords clarified the position. This case concerned an application for files relating to a conveyancing transaction under Drug Trafficking Offences Act 1986 s27 and the person under suspicion was not the conveyancing client but a member of her family. The House of Lords held that the relevant intention was certainly not limited to that of the solicitors, nor indeed their clients, but may include that of a third party. In this case therefore, the conveyancing documents which were to be used by a third party to further the criminal purpose of laundering the proceeds of illegal drug trafficking and which were held innocently by a solicitor, were not subject to legal privilege. This has been followed where forged documents have been in a solicitor's possession. The documents were also denied the status of special procedure material.[25]

Access to excluded material

Where the police want to obtain access to evidence classified as 'excluded material', they must apply to a circuit judge for a production order if they are unable to obtain access with the owner's consent. (In exceptional circumstances, see p75, a judge may issue a warrant in addition to, or instead of, a production order.)

'Excluded material'

Excluded material is evidence held by a person in confidence, which falls into one of three categories: personal records, human tissue or tissue fluid, and journalistic material.

All three categories of evidence must be held in confidence to come within the definition, that is, the evidence must be held subject to:

23 See, eg, *R v Crown Court at Snaresbrook ex p DPP and Akhoonjee* [1988] 1 All ER 315 (disapproved by the House of Lords in *Francis & Francis*, below).
24 [1988] 3 All ER 775, HL. In *R v Governor of Pentonville Prison ex p Osman (No 3)* [1989] 3 All ER 701, the Divisional Court held that where it is alleged that a communication is not privileged because its purpose was the furtherance of crime, the court is entitled to look at the material in question without requiring the party seeking production to prove the purpose of the document by independent evidence.
25 *R v Leeds Magistrates' Court ex p Dumbleton* [1993] Crim LR 866.

a) an express or implied undertaking to hold it in confidence; or
b) a restriction on disclosure or an obligation of secrecy contained in any statute, including an Act passed after the 1984 Act (s11(2)).

The law on confidentiality is complex and uncertain.[26] It is clear that s11(2) is broadly drafted (an 'implied' undertaking to hold material in confidence is included), and therefore there is considerable room for argument that particular evidence falls within the classification. It has been held that the following elements are essential to found a duty of confidentiality:[27]

– the information itself must have the necessary quality of confidence about it; and
– it must have been imparted in circumstances importing an obligation of confidence.

The first element will not normally be present where the information is in the public domain, and information may lose its original confidential character if it subsequently enters the public domain. An example of a statute imposing restrictions on disclosure and obligations of secrecy is the Official Secrets Act 1911.

Personal records
Personal records constitute excluded material if a person has acquired or created them in the course of any trade, business, profession or other occupation or for the purposes of any paid or unpaid office and holds them in confidence (s11(1)(a)).

Personal records (for the purposes of this Part of the Act) consist of documentary and other records concerning an individual, living or dead, who can be identified from them and which relate to three broadly defined spheres of activity (s12). First, personal records may relate to physical and mental health. Thus medical and psychiatric records would clearly be excluded material (provided the above requirement relating to their being held in confidence were met). Dental records and a study mould of a person's teeth have fallen within this category,[28] as have hospital records of a patient's admission and discharge.[29] In the latter case the court said that the words 'relating

---

26 See D Capper 'Damages for breach of the equitable duty of confidence' (1994) 14 LS 313.
27 Megarry J in *Coco v A N Clark (Engineers)* [1969] RPC 41 at 47, approved in *AG v Guardian Newspapers Ltd (No 2)* [1988] 3 All ER 545, HL.
28 *R v Singleton* [1995] Crim LR 236.
29 *R v Cardiff Crown Court ex p Kellam* (1993) *Times* 3 May.

to' in s12 were to be given a broad meaning and that the essence of the definition is the identifiability of the patient.

Second, personal records relating to spiritual counselling or assistance given or to be given may constitute excluded material, again if the requirement relating to their being held in confidence were met. There are no definitions of records relating to spiritual counselling or assistance, although they are clearly meant to include any records kept, for example, by priests, and there is no reason why any members of agencies such as the Samaritans, or even religious sects, should not be able to shelter behind this provision.

The third and final category concerns personal records relating to counselling or assistance given or to be given to a person for the purposes of personal welfare, by any voluntary organisation or by any individual who must either have:

a) responsibilities for someone's welfare by reason of their office or occupation; or

b) responsibilities for a person's supervision by reason of a court order.

Head (a) presumably includes school, college and careers advice records, provided they identify the relevant person; records of advice given by law centres, social workers, advice centres such as citizens advice bureaux, and so on.

Head (b) was inserted expressly to protect the records of probation officers, but is not of course restricted to such records.

Personal records held by a parent or guardian would not be 'excluded material' because the records have not been acquired or created within the confines of s11(1)(a).

Human tissue or tissue fluid

Human tissue or tissue fluid is excluded material if it has been taken for the purposes of diagnosis or medical treatment and a person holds it in confidence (s11(1)(b)), for example a blood sample.

There may not be any circumstances where human tissue or tissue fluid is not held in confidence, but it

> . . . is better that the phrase [held in confidence] appear so that things are made clear. After all, we are talking about one of the most sensitive aspects of a relationship.[30]

30 Minister, HC Standing Committee E, Col 620, 19 January 1984.

Journalistic material

Journalisitic material is excluded material if it it comprises documents or records other than documents, which are held in confidence. However, in addition to the requirements of confidentiality under s11(2) that all three categories of excluded material must meet (p61 above), journalistic material must have been continuously held subject to an express or implied undertaking to hold it in confidence or to a statutory restriction on disclosure or obligation of secrecy since it was first acquired or created for the purposes of journalism (s11(3)).

'Documents' has the extended meaning given to it in the Civil Evidence Act 1968 Pt I s10 and includes, in addition to a document in writing:

a) any map, plan, graph or drawing;
b) any photograph;
c) any disc, tape, sound track or other device in which sounds or other data (not being visual images) are embodied so as to be capable (with or without the aid of some other equipment) of being reproduced therefrom; and
d) any film, negative, tape or other device in which one or more visual images are embodied so as to be capable (as in (c)) of being reproduced therefrom. ('Film' includes a microfilm.)

'Records' are not defined in the 1984 Act.

'Journalistic material' is defined exceptionally broadly (see s13). The definition is unhelpful and circular, defining the material in terms of whether or not it is acquired for the purposes of 'journalism' (s13(1)). The great fear of journalists at the time of the Act was that inevitably the courts would have to define this term. It is extremely important to note that the definition relates to the purpose for which the material is held (see below) and not the status of the person holding the material. It is immaterial whether or not a person is a professional journalist, or indeed engaged in journalism at all. The definition clearly covers broadcasting and includes, for instance, a film of a demonstration for possible use in a news item. This would not, however, be excluded material because it is not held in confidence. (It would be special procedure material, see below.) The question remains whether or not film made for entertainment, for example a view of an audience at a cricket match, would constitute journalistic material. It was stated that not all broadcast entertainment is journalistic and that it would depend on the facts of the case.[31]

31 HC Standing Committee E, Col 677, 24 January 1984.

Another vexed question arises over material in the hands of the myriads of people who publish group or local newsletters. Until there is guidance from the courts, it is impossible to state categorically that they would fall within the definition, although in arguing for protection, the breadth of s13 is very helpful. Similarly, there is no indication and therefore no limitation in s13 that the material should be intended for publication. Research material for a film or article for instance should fall, therefore, within this category.

Material can be journalistic matter only if it is in the possession of a person who acquired or created it for the purposes of journalism (s13(2)). Where material acquired or created for those purposes passes into someone's possession for other purposes it ceases to be journalistic material. The protection is no longer deemed necessary in such cases as it is then irrelevant to the free and active operation of the press and broadcasting media.

Unsolicited material sent to someone for the purposes of journalism is journalistic material, irrespective of the intentions of the recipient or their status (s13(3)). There is no need for the person holding the material for the purpose of any paid or unpaid office to be the actual worker in that position.

The comments on confidentiality on p61 above will be particularly important in assessing whether journalistic material is also excluded material. In committee the minister stated:

> Journalistic material is objectively . . . to be considered by the Court, perhaps at the point of application by a magistrate or circuit judge or, if a real issue arises, by the jury, and would simply be a matter of fact for them, just as the concept of 'in confidence' would be.[32]

Conditions governing issue of a production order or warrant

The essential difference between the procedure where the police are seeking excluded material, and where they are seeking evidence of a general nature not subject to special safeguards, is that, for excluded material, the application is to a circuit judge for a production order or a warrant and the application is inter partes in the case of a production order (Sch 1 para 7). (In exceptional circumstances a judge may issue a warrant to search for excluded material, see below p75.)

As stated on p51 above, s9(2) provides that statutes passed before

32 HC Standing Committee E, Col 617, 19 January 1984.

the Act (including local Acts) which give the police powers to obtain warrants from magistrates are ineffective so far as excluded material is concerned. (Legislation since 1984 sometimes specifies that s9 is applicable, eg, Cinemas Act 1985 s13(8).) Before issuing a production order or warrant, a circuit judge must be satisfied:

a) that there is material which consists of or includes excluded material on the specified premises; and

b) that, but for s9(2), there would have been a power under another Act to issue a warrant for the evidence; and

c) that the issue of such a warrant would have been appropriate (Sch 1 para 3).

Effectively, therefore, even if the excluded material sought is evidence of a serious arrestable offence, it may not be the subject of a production order (nor a warrant (below)) made under Sch 1, unless the police could have obtained, prior to the Act, a search warrant in respect of it.[33] A circuit judge may make a production order (or issue a warrant) even if the application relates to evidence which is additional to the excluded material, provided a magistrate would have had power to issue a warrant under another statute or under s8 of the 1984 Act (thus avoiding the necessity for the police to make separate applications to a magistrate and to a circuit judge, where the evidence sought is both excluded and other material).

The effect of the 1984 Act can be seen in the following example. If a secret military plan were passed to a journalist by a confidential source, the plan would be excluded material (see definition, above). Prior to the 1984 Act, a warrant could have been issued by a magistrate under the Official Secrets Act 1911 s9(1) to search for the plan, but, by virtue of the 1984 Act s9(2)(b), the police may no longer make an ex parte application to a magistrate in respect of excluded material. They could, however, apply to a circuit judge inter partes for a production order (or ex parte for a warrant), because the condition in (b) above is met.

Nothing in the 1984 Act prevents the holder of excluded material from disclosing it voluntarily to the police. This applies even if the police would not have been successful in a Sch 1 application.[34] The

---

33 For a case where an order was made in error see *R v Central Criminal Court ex p Brown* (1992) *Times* 7 September. The offence under investigation was murder and the order should not have been made because, before enactment of s9(2), no enactment would have authorised the issue of a warrant to seize the material.

34 *R v Singleton* [1995]Crim LR 236.

suspect's remedy, if any, would lie against the holder of the material in an action for breach of confidence.[35]

However, statutes which enable the police to gain access to such material under written authority other than a warrant are unaffected by the Act (s9(2)). (See appendix 6 for a list of such statutes.) In the above example, therefore, it would still be possible for a superintendent to give a written order to search in a case of great emergency if it were in the interests of the State to do so (Official Secrets Act 1911 s9(2)).

The procedures governing applications to circuit judges for production orders and warrants are dealt with below, p71.

Access to special procedure material

Where the police want to obtain access to evidence that is classified as special procedure material and are unable to do so by consent, they may be able to apply to a magistrate for a search warrant, or to a circuit judge for a production order, depending on the nature of the evidence. (In exceptional circumstances, a judge may issue a search warrant in addition to, or instead of, a production order, see below p75).

Special procedure material

Special procedure material is:

a) evidence which is held on a confidential basis by a person who has acquired or created it in the course of any trade, business, profession or other occupation or for the purpose of any paid or unpaid office (s14(2)); and

b) journalistic material which does not fall to be classified as excluded material, either because it is not documentary or because it is documentary but does not meet the stringent confidentiality requirement for excluded material (for example a film or photograph of a demonstration, see above), will be special procedure material (s14(1)(b)).

The provisons are widely drafted. As in s11 (definition of excluded material), anything held by voluntary workers, provided it meets the criteria described below, would be included. 'Other occupation' is not defined and it is so broad as to include almost any activity, for

---

35 See D Capper at (1994) 14 LS 313 (above n26).

instance being employed in a left luggage department at a station. As in s11, there is no need for the person holding the material for the purpose of any paid or unpaid office to be the actual worker in that position. The provisions defining special procedure material (s14), unlike those defining journalistic material (s13), do not contain any partial definition of 'acquired'. Thus it is not clear, as it is in s13, that unsolicited material is included. On a general definition of 'acquired' it would seem to be included and it can be argued that since, at the time the Act was in Parliament, there had been much controversy over the status of unsolicited material received by journalists, the provision was included in s13 only to make the position absolutely clear. Again provisions relating to confidentiality in s14 are vague and give much scope for argument. The person holding the material must hold it subject to an express or implied undertaking to hold it in confidence or to a statutory restriction or obligation as is referred to in s11(2)(b) (p61) (s14(2)(b)). That subsection refers to statutory restrictions on disclosures.

Examples of special procedure material other than journalistic material are company accounts or stock records held on behalf of a client by a bank, solicitor or accountant. Material which falls outside the definition cannot be converted into special procedure material by being passed on to an employee by employers, or to an associated company by an associate, subject to an undertaking to hold it in confidence, unless it was special procedure material prior to such an action (s14(3)).

Similarly, where material is created by an employee or an associated company subject to an instruction from an employer or associated company to hold it in confidence, it does not become special procedure material, unless it would have been so if created by the employer or first company (s14(4) and (5)). The purpose of these provisions is clearly to prevent artificial conversion into special procedure material, but nothing in them prevents material originally classified as such from losing that classification merely by being passed to an employee or associated company. An associated company for the purposes of s14 is as defined in the Income and Corporation Taxes Act 1988 s416 (s14(6)).

Conditions governing issue of a production order or warrant

Where the police are seeking access to special procedure material (see definition above) whether they apply ex parte to a magistrate for a search warrant, or inter partes to a circuit judge for a production order (or warrant), will depend on whether the material consists of documents or records other than documents, and, if it does not, on whether they have the power under an existing statute to apply to a magistrate for a warrant in respect of it. 'Documents' are defined above on p63.

If the special procedure material does not consist of documents or other records, and there is power under another statute to apply to a magistrate for a search warrant in respect of it, the police should do so. That is, s9(2) (above) does not affect police powers to obtain warrants from magistrates in respect of special procedure material which does not consist of documents or records other than documents. So, for example, if stolen clothing were given to a dry cleaner with intructions to clean it secretly, the police could apply to a magistrate for a warrant to search for it; since the clothing is not documentary, they have the power to do so under the Theft Act 1968, and that power is not affected by the 1984 Act. The application to a magistrate would be made under the existing statutory provision and not, of course, under the 1984 Act s8, because s8 does not apply to special procedure material and its use would be unnecessary in any event.

However, police powers to obtain warrants from magistrates in respect of special procedure material which consists of documents or records other than documents *are* affected by s9(2). Therefore, if the police are seeking special procedure material which consists of documents or other records (whether or not they have power under another statute to apply for a warrant), or non-documentary special procedure material where they do not have such a power to apply to a magistrate for a warrant (see below), they must apply to a circuit judge for a production order. (In exceptional circumstances, a judge may issue a warrant in addition to, or instead of, a production order, see below p75).

In order for a production order to be made, the police must satisfy either of two sets of conditions.

Search warrant unavailable under any other statute

The first set of conditions, set out in Sch 1 para 2, should be used when a search warrant cannot be, or could not have been, obtained under any other statute. This set of conditions gave the police a new power to gain access to evidence. It is applicable only to special procedure material (not to excluded material, which is more sensitive) which is reasonably believed to be evidence of a serious arrestable offence. The new power is additional to powers in other statutes which, in the case of special procedure material consisting of documents or other records, are subject to the safeguards in the 1984 Act. (The power corresponds to the power in s8 of the 1984 Act to obtain a warrant from a magistrate to search for evidence of a serious arrestable offence, where the evidence is not subject to special safeguards.)

The judge must be satisfied that there are reasonable grounds for believing that:

a) a serious arrestable offence has been committed; and
b) there is material which consists of or includes special procedure material and does not also include excluded material on the specified premises; and
c) the material is likely to be of substantial value (whether by itself or together with other material) to the investigation of the offence; and
d) the material is likely to be relevant evidence, that is, likely to be admissible at a trial for the offence.

In addition to the above grounds the judge must be satisfied that it is in the public interest that a production order should be made, having regard to the benefit likely to accrue to the investigation if the evidence is obtained and to the circumstances under which the person in possession of the evidence holds it. The judge must also be satisfied that other methods of obtaining the material have been tried without success or have not been tried because it appeared that they would be bound to fail (Sch 1 para 2). The Divisional Court has held that the plain intention of the Schedule is that the application is 'substantially the last resort'.[36] The applicant for the order should seek the consent

---

36 *R v Lewes Crown Court ex p Hill* [1991] Crim LR 376. Cf the situation in relation to applications under s8 (above p54). For a case in which it was argued unsuccessfully that the s9 and Sch 1 procedure had not been 'the last resort', see *R v Central Criminal Court and BRB ex p AJD Holdings Ltd* [1992] Crim LR 669 and below pp79 and 81.

of the holder of the material first. In this case the applicant should have shown that proceedings under s7 of the Bankers' Books Evidence Act 1879 had been exhausted before the application, or if it had not, there should be evidence before the court to show that if it had been used it would have been bound to fail.[37] The tests in (a), (c) and (d) above are identical to those set out in s8 (conditions governing applications to a magistrate for a search warrant). The comments relating to the meaning of 'reasonable grounds for believing', 'serious arrestable offence', evidence 'likely to be of substantial value' and 'relevant evidence' on p54 therefore apply equally here. It has been confirmed, with reference to Sch 1 para 2(a)(ii), that an order can be made in respect of 'mixed material', that is special procedure material and other material,[38] so long as the other material could be obtained by an application to a magistrate.

In *R v Bristol Crown Court ex p Bristol Press and Picture Agency Ltd*[39] the Divisional Court had to consider whether the judge had correctly applied the tests relating to 'public interest'. The police wanted access to photographs of violent disturbances and thus, by virtue of journalistic material being special procedure material and, in this case, possibly evidence of a serious arrestable offence, they had to apply to a judge for an order under s9 and Sch 1. The court however, refused to protect the material from disclosure, ruling that 'there is a very great public interest that those guilty of crime, and particularly of serious crime involving widespread public disorder, should be brought to justice'. In *R v Northampton Magistrates' Court ex p DPP*[40] the court held that where a judge found that a serious arrestable offence had been committed and that the special procedure material sought would be of substantial value to the investigation, an application for an order could not be refused. It was inconsistent to find anything other than that it was in the public interest to make such an order.

---

37 For a criticism of this requirement see [1991] Crim LR at 379.
38 *R v Preston Crown Court ex p McGrath* (1992) *Times* 27 October.
39 [1987] Crim LR 329. See also *Re an Application under s.9 of the Police and Criminal Evidence Act 1984* (1988) *Independent* 27 May and a decision by Mota Singh J in Southwark Crown Court (1989) 18 August, unreported, denying police access on the ground that the unscreened BBC footage sought would not help the police.
40 (1991) *Times* 18 April.

Search warrant previously available

The second set of conditions is contained in Sch 1 para 3 and should be used where the police are seeking special procedure material which consists of documents or records other than documents for which they could have obtained a warrant to search prior to the Act. The same provision governs applications for production orders in relation to excluded material (see comments on p65 above), and it is not necessary that the material be evidence of a serious arrestable offence.

As in the case of excluded material, the judge may, under both sets of access conditions, make a production order (or issue a warrant) even if the application relates to evidence which is additional to the special procedure material, unless the application is under the first set of conditions (relating to evidence of a serious arrestable offence for which there were no existing powers to obtain a warrant) and the extra material is excluded material. Again a circuit judge has this power to avoid the necessity for the police to make applications to both a magistrate and a circuit judge where the evidence consists of special procedure and other material.

Applications to a circuit judge for a production order

Introduction

The procedure governing an application for a production order is set out in Sch 1 of the Act and in Code B. A production order is an order requiring the person in possession of the evidence either to produce it to a constable to take away, or to give a constable access to it. The application is made inter partes to a circuit judge.

A production order will be made only if certain conditions are met. These conditions are set out, with regard to excluded material, on p64, and, with regard to special procedure material, on p68 above.

In exceptional circumstances, the judge may issue a search warrant in addition to or instead of, a production order when the order is not complied with, or compliance is impracticable (see p75 below.) Circumstances may arise in which the police are seeking both excluded material and special procedure material in the possession of the same person. In such a case, a production order may be made which covers both classifications of evidence.

When the police apply for a production order, the person

possessing the evidence is served with a notice that such an application has been made. Once the notice is served the person is prohibited from concealing or destroying the evidence. The effect of service of such a notice is considered in detail below.

The application

There is no longer a requirement that an application for a production order must be authorised by an officer of at least the rank of superintendent, except in cases under the Prevention of Terrorism (Temporary Provisions) Act 1989.[41] In fact there is no indication in the Code that any authorisation is required for the application. Where information is received which appears to justify an application, the officer concerned must take reasonable steps to check that the information is accurate, recent and has not been provided maliciously or irresponsibly. An application should not be made on the basis of information from an anonymous source unless corroboration has been sought (Code B para 2.1). The officer should have ascertained as specifically as possible the nature of the articles concerned and their location and should also have made enquiries to establish what, if anything, is known about the likely occupier and the nature of the premises. The officer should also have tried to establish whether the premises have been previously searched and if so how recently, and should have tried to obtain any other information relevant to the application (Code B paras 2.2 and 2.3).

If satisfied that all the conditions (see above) are met and that an order should be made, the judge will make an order under Sch 1 para 4 that the person who appears to be in possession of the evidence should either produce it to a constable to take away or give a constable access to it. The person in possession must comply with the order within seven days from the date of the order or within such longer period as may be specified in the order (Sch 1 para 4).

Where the evidence is information stored in a computer, an order under para 4 has effect as an order to produce the evidence in a form in which it can be taken away, and in which it is legible (a computer disc would not suffice for example) (Sch1 para 5).

A judge hearing an application for production of documents has jurisdiction to decide whether the application should be heard in open court or in chambers.[42]

---

41 Code B para 2.4; see below p256 for a discussion of the terrorism provisions.
42 *R v Central Criminal Court ex p DPP* (1988) *Independent* 31 March.

Service of notice of an application

Notice of an application for a production order may be served on a person in one of the four following ways:

a) by delivering it;
b) by leaving it at the proper address;
c) by posting it in a registered letter; or
d) by the recorded delivery service (Sch 1 para 8).

The notice may be served on a body corporate by serving it on the secretary or clerk or other similar officer and, in the case of a partnership, on one of the partners (para 9). The 'proper address' for the purposes of Sch 1 is, in the case of a corporate body, that of the registered or principal office of the firm; and in any other case the last known address of the person to be served (para 10).

The schedule does not deal with the position of an unincorporated body. In *R v Central Criminal Court ex p Adegbesan and Others*[43] Watkins LJ alluded to this point but could not say on whom such a notice should be served without hearing further argument. In the meantime he advised the police that it would be wise, when proceeding against such a body, to name an officer of that body, chair or secretary as the case may be.[44]

If the requirements in paras 8, 9 and 10 (above) have not been complied with, then presumably the addressee would, if feasible, ask for a postponement of the hearing of the application, or, if it were too late, the order should be challenged in the High Court as invalid.

It has been confirmed that where an application for an order is made, the only parties concerned are the police who made the application and the person or institution in whose possession the material is thought to be. The police are not required to give notice of the application to any person suspected of or charged with the offence or to serve a copy of the application on him or her.[45]

Contents of notice of an application

What exactly the contents of this notice must be has caused problems. The combined effect of the Divisional Court's decisions in four

---

43 [1986] 3 All ER 113.
44 Ibid at 118b-e.
45 *R v Crown Court at Leicester ex p DPP* [1987] 3 All ER 654 and *R v Lewes Crown Court ex p Hill* [1991] Crim LR 376.

cases[46] is that the party in possession of the material must be given a description of all the material which is sought to be produced and the nature of the offence under investigation.[47] Although it is preferable for both matters to be set out in documentary form, it is not essential, so long as it can be proved that the information was given orally before service of the notice.[48] The notice of application need not contain a recital of the evidence upon which the police intend to rely, as disclosure of their case too early may lead to destruction of the material. However, it has been held that whatever is served on the court must also be served on the other side. This means that where the application is not accompanied by evidence in support, then the party allegedly in possession of the material should be provided with the evidence at the hearing. There should then be an opportunity to seek an adjournment if the evidence cannot be adequately responded to there and then.[49] What is now clear is that the applicant has a duty to set out all the material in his/her possession relevant to the application, even if it is prejudicial to the application.[50]

If the prosecution does not disclose all such material however, the respondent to the application cannot later complain if they were in possession of the material but chose not to disclose it.[51] It has also been held that, in applications for orders, absolute compliance with strict rules of evidence cannot be expected, but that any statements which have no substance, to the prejudice of the party against whom the order is sought, should be ruled out by the judge.[52]

Effect of receipt of notice of an application

Restrictions are placed on the behaviour of the person possessing the evidence sought from the moment the notice has been served. The evidence must not be concealed, destroyed, altered, or disposed of until the application has been dismissed or abandoned or until any production order has been complied with (Sch 1 para 11).

---

46 *Adegbesan* (above n43); *R v Crown Court at Inner London ex p Baines and Baines* [1987] 3 All ER 1025; *R v Central Criminal Court ex p Carr* (1987) *Independent* 5 March; *R v Manchester Crown Court ex p Taylor* [1988] Crim LR 386.
47 *Adegbesan* (above n43) and *Carr* (above n46).
48 *Taylor* (above n46).
49 *Baines and Baines* (above, n46).
50 *R v Lewes Crown Court ex p Hill* [1991] Crim LR 376.
51 *R v Acton Crown Court ex p Layton* [1993] Crim LR 458.
52 *Baines and Baines* (above, n46).

In effect the material is frozen. The Act does not specify any purpose for which the material may not be concealed and so on, but surely it must be argued that if material is hidden not in order to thwart the application but in order for a person to meet professional obligations, for example to maintain confidentiality, that must fall outside the prohibition, since penal statutes are construed restrictively. No sanction is provided in the Act for such behaviour before an order is made (Sch 1 para 15 (below) only applies to failure to comply with an order and so can take effect only after an order has been made); but the recipient of a notice may be in contempt of court. There is no restriction on copying the material before producing it or giving the police access to it.

If, however, the recipient obtains leave of a judge or written permission of a constable before the application is dismissed or abandoned or complies with the production order, any of those activities otherwise prohibited may be performed (Sch 1 para 11).

The hearing

As indicated above (p73) a suspect or defendant has no right to be notified of an application for an order and therefore will not normally be aware of the hearing. In addition the Court of Appeal has ruled, in *Barclays Bank v Taylor*,[53] that the person in possession of the material, in this case the bank, is not under any duty to notify the suspect or defendant of the application or indeed to oppose it.[54] In some circumstances (see eg, below p95) notification may even be an offence. It appears that a judge may decide, however, to hear representations from such a person where appropriate. This would not be the case where to do so might hinder the investigation but it may be appropriate where it was very unlikely that the suspect's conduct would adversely affect the proceedings.[55]

Failure to comply with a production order

If a production order is not complied with, the judge may, in certain circumstances, issue a warrant authorising a search for the evidence,

53 [1989] 3 All ER 363.
54 For a thorough criticism of this situation see Zuckerman, 'The Weakness of PACE Special Procedure for Protecting Confidential information' [1990] Crim LR 472.
55 *R v Lewes Crown Court ex p Hill* [1991] Crim LR 376.

but in other cases the person possessing the evidence will be liable only for contempt (see below).

If the issue of a production order is challenged in the Divisional Court, appeals from that Court do not lie to the Court of Appeal but to the House of Lords.[56]

A warrant may be issued if a judge is satisfied that a production order has not been complied with, and the evidence specified in the order is excluded material or special procedure material consisting of documents or records other than documents for which a search warrant could have been obtained prior to the Act (Sch 1 para 12). Anyone who fails to produce such evidence risks therefore being subjected to a search of premises and may, in addition, be in contempt of court (Sch 1 para 15). The justification for giving a power to search premises lies in the fact that such evidence would have been subject to search warrants issued by magistrates prior to the Act. The Act provides the safeguard that access to such evidence must now be authorised by a circuit judge, often after argument in court. Compliance with a production order would make a search unnecessary.

Applications to a circuit judge for a search warrant are considered below.

Anyone who fails to produce other evidence (that is special procedure material which is likely to be admissible in evidence at a trial of a serious arrestable offence, which was not obtainable by the police prior to the Act) will risk only being in contempt of court. A search warrant could be issued in respect of such material only where compliance with a production order is impracticable (see below).

Where a production order would be impracticable

In exceptional circumstances, a judge may issue a search warrant on the application of a constable, effectively where the making of a production order would be impracticable.

The Divisional Court has stated on several occasions that the special procedure under s9 and Sch 1 of the Act is a serious inroad upon the liberty of the subject and that circuit judges bear a heavy responsibility to ensure that the procedure is not abused.[57] This was

56 *Carr v Atkins* [1987] 3 All ER 684, CA.
57 R v *Maidstone Crown Court ex p Waitt* [1988] Crim LR 384; R v *Lewes Crown Court ex p Hill* (above), and R v *Southampton Crown Court ex p J and P* [1993] Crim LR 962. See also R v *Secretary of State for the Home Department ex p Propend Finance Property Ltd* (1994)*Times* 5 April.

particularly so when dealing with ex parte applications by the police for warrants under Sch 1 para 12. The preferred method of obtaining access to evidence should be by way of an inter partes order; the issue of warrants under para 12 should never become a matter of common form. That judicial review is the correct way to challenge an ex parte order, rather than by re-application to the circuit judge to review it inter partes, has also been confirmed.[58]

It might be appropriate in some cases to issue a warrant in respect of part of the material only, leaving the rest to be sought through an inter partes application. Also although the Act does not require a judge to give reasons for making an order, there may well be a need to do so.[59] For the particular need for caution where legally privileged material may be involved see above p56.

The judge must be satisfied that a production order could be made in respect of the evidence, and that either:

a) it is not practicable to communicate with any person entitled to grant entry to the premises; or

b) if it is practicable to communicate with a person entitled to grant entry to the premises, it is not practicable to communicate with someone who is entitled to grant access to the evidence; or

c) where someone holds evidence subject to a restriction on disclosure or an obligation of secrecy contained in any statute, including an Act passed after the 1984 Act, and the evidence is likely to be disclosed in breach of such a restriction or obligation (for example, where a document is subject to the official secrets legislation and may be disclosed unless the police act quickly); or

d) service of a notice of application for an order (under Sch 1 para 4, above) may seriously prejudice the investigation (Sch 1 paras 12 and 14).

Heads (a) and (b) above are identical to the conditions in s8 relating to applications to magistrates for search warrants, and the comments on p53 above therefore apply equally here.

Costs

The costs of any application under Sch 1 and of anything done or to be done in pursuance of an order made under it are in the discretion of the judge (Sch 1 para 16).

---

58 *R v Liverpool Crown Court ex p Wimpey plc* [1991] Crim LR 635.
59 *R v Southampton Crown Court ex p J and P* [1993] Crim LR 962.

Applications to a circuit judge for a search warrant

The application

A constable may make an ex parte application to a circuit judge for a search warrant under Sch 1 in certain circumstances where a person has failed to comply with a production order or where compliance would be impracticable for one of a number of reasons (see above).

If relevant, the application under Sch 1 should indicate why it is believed that service of a notice of application for a production order may seriously prejudice the investigation (Code B para 2.7). In other respects an application for a search warrant under Sch 1 is treated by the Act and the Code of Practice in exactly the same way as an application for a search warrant under any other statute (see s15 and Code B para 2). Indeed there is no longer any need for an application for a warrant under Sch 1 to be authorised by an officer of superintendent's rank or above.[60] Presumably authorisation is to be the same as for other search warrants (see below p79).

Conduct of the search

A search of premises under a warrant issued by a circuit judge is subject to special safeguards in the Code of Practice, because the search will usually be through private documents and files. Such a search is subject to other search warrant safeguards in the Code of Practice (where applicable) and the Act (see s16 and Code B para 5 and p81). An officer of at least the rank of inspector must take charge of such a search and as indicated by the other requirements of Code B, must be present at the search. The officer is responsible for ensuring that the search is conducted with discretion and in such a manner as to cause the least possible disruption to any business or other activities carried on in the premises (Code B para 5.13).

The officer in charge should ensure that the evidence cannot be taken from the premises secretly and should then ask a person who is in authority and has responsibility for the documents, to produce them. This must be done before a search is instigated. The clear intention of the Code is that a search should be the last resort. If this is not done, there may be consequences for later proceedings (see p4).

The officer in charge also has the right to see the index, if any, to files held on the premises. Only files which, according to the index,

---

60   See the revision to Code B para 2.4 (referred to above p72).

appear to contain any of the material sought can be searched. A more extensive search of the premises should only be made in defined circumstances:

a) if the person responsible refuses to produce the material sought or refuses to allow access to the index;
b) if it appears the index is inaccurate or incomplete (clearly a vague ground); or
c) if for any other reason the officer in charge has reasonable grounds to believe that such a search is necessary in order to find the material sought. The belief must be 'on reasonable grounds' and is therefore subject to review by the courts (and see above p14).

For other safeguards in relation to searches see p81.

Searches under warrant

The 1984 Act governs *all* applications for search warrants under any statute, whether in existence prior to the Act or passed afterwards and all searches under those warrants. It applies equally to applications and searches under the 1984 Act, whether the warrant is obtainable from a magistrate or a circuit judge. The Act is supplemented by Code B. Any breach of the provisions of the Act (ss15 and 16), renders the entry and search unlawful (s15(1))[61] (see chapter 13 for remedies and see below p81), while any breach of the Code, as previously stated, may be used as evidence in any civil or criminal proceedings (s67(11)).[62]

Requirements for a valid search warrant

Code B specifies certain action to be taken before an application for a warrant is made (para 2). No one below the rank of inspector can authorise an application unless the matter is urgent and there is not

---

61 For criticism of the obscure drafting of this section see *R v Longman* [1988] Crim LR 53 and *R v Central Criminal Court and BRB ex p AJD Holdings Ltd* and commentary at [1992] Crim LR 669. For a case where a declaration that a warrant was invalid and null was granted and substantial exemplary damages awarded for the search and seizure which were held to be unlawful, see *R v Reading Justices and Others ex p South West Meat Ltd* [1992] Crim LR 672, (1991) *Times* 18 November. See also *R v Chief Constable of Lancashire, ex p Parker and McGrath* [1993] Crim LR 204, where owing to breaches of s16 the seizure of the documents was unlawful (see below p82).
62 See particularly *R v Stewart* [1995] Crim LR 500.

an inspector available: in that case the senior officer on duty has authority. In all cases, where a search is likely to have an adverse effect on relations between the police and community the local police community liaison officer must be consulted, except where the matter is urgent. Where it is urgent, the officer should be informed of the search as soon as practicable after it has been made (Code B Note for Guidance 2B). In *Bayliss v Hill*,[63] Mr Justice Hirst said:

> The institution of [the search warrant] procedure was very important as it secured a right of entry into a person's home. Consequently, it behoved the senior ranks of the police force to proceed with special care before invoking the procedure, in particular to ensure that reliable evidence was available to support an application for a warrant. It behoved junior officers executing a warrant to perform their duty with consideration and care.

The information

An application for a warrant can be made by any constable (except where otherwise specified), is ex parte and must be supported by an information in writing (s15(3)). Code B states the contents of the information, which are:

a) the enactment under which the application is made;
b) the premises to be searched and the object of the search; and
c) the grounds on which the application is made, including, where the purpose of the proposed search is to find evidence of an alleged offence, an indication of how the evidence relates to the investigation.

The Act requires the constable to state the grounds for making the application and the statutory authority for the issue of a warrant; the premises must also be specified. The constable must also identify, so far as is practicable, the articles or persons to be sought (s15(2)) and in addition, the constable must be prepared to answer any questions on oath (s15(4)). The magistrate or judge issuing the warrant must exercise a judicial discretion[64] (see above p52).

The warrant

The warrant itself must specify, in addition to the premises, the name of the applicant, date of issue and statutory authority and must identify, so far as is practicable, the articles or persons to be sought

63 (1984) *Times* 17 April.
64 *Hope v Evered* (1886) 17 QBD 338.

(s15(6)). It has been held that the articles detailed in the warrant should be those identified in the information.[65] A warrant authorises entry on one occasion only (s15(5)). There is, of course, nothing to prevent a further application so long as there are additional grounds. (Code B para 2.8). Two copies, clearly certified as copies, must be made of every warrant (s15(7) and (8)). A warrant may authorise persons to accompany any constable who is executing it, eg, an expert witness (s16(2)). The Act does not say that the persons must be named and therefore it would seem that a general authorisation could validly be included. It has been held, however, that the warrant must limit the number of people who can accompany the police, it is wrong to leave it open.[66] For the liability of those issuing a defective warrant see below p339.

Execution of a search under a warrant

Any constable may execute a search warrant (s16(1)). The 1984 Act repealed sections in statutes which provided for only named constables to execute warrants, for instance the Biological Weapons Act 1975 s4, as it did those providing for constables only in a specific area to execute warrants, for instance the Immigration Act 1971 Sch 2 para 17. Entry and search must take place within one month (that is, one calendar month (Interpretation Act 1978)) of issue of the warrant (s16(3)), otherwise it will be unlawful unless there is consent. A warrant must be executed at a reasonable hour, unless it appears to the constable executing it that there are grounds for suspecting that the purpose of a search may be frustrated by an entry at a reasonable hour (s16(4)). It appears that an honest, even if unreasonable, belief on the part of the constable will suffice to make the search lawful. What is a reasonable hour will depend on the nature of the premises concerned, for example whether they are business or domestic premises, and on the occupier. In determining at what time to make a search, the officer in charge should have regard, among other considerations, to the times of day at which the occupier of the premises is likely to be present, and should not search at a time when any person on the premises is likely to be asleep, unless it is unavoidable (Code B para 5A).

The Act specifies that the identity of the constable executing the

65 *R v Central Criminal Court and BRB ex p AJD Holdings* [1992] Crim LR 669. In this case, where the warrant was found to be invalid, it was also held that the articles sought had not been identified 'so far as practicable'.
66 *R v Reading Justices and Others ex p South West Meats Ltd* (above n61).

warrant must be made known to the occupier of the premises if present or if not, to someone who appears to be in charge of the premises. A constable who is not in uniform should produce identification. The search warrant should also be produced and the occupier or person in charge should be supplied with a copy (s16(5)).[67] The code contains similar provisions, with the additional requirement that the constable should explain to the occupier (or person who appears to be in charge) that there is authority to enter the premises and should ask the occupier to allow this. Consent obtained in these circumstances does not need to be written (Code B Note for Guidance 4B and see below p92). The code waives these requirements if:

i) the premises are known to be unoccupied;
ii) the occupier or other person is known to be absent; or
iii) there are reasonable grounds to believe that to alert the occupier or any other person entitled to grant access by attempting to communicate with them would frustrate the object of the search or endanger the officers concerned or other persons (para 5.4).

In *R v Longman*[68] the Court of Appeal confirmed that the police could enter premises in the circumstances mentioned above (in this case under para 5.4 (iii)) before there was any requirement for the constable to produce identification or a search warrant.

Notice of powers and rights
The police are required, unless it is impracticable to do so, to provide the occupier of premises to be searched with a copy notice in standard format setting out police powers and the occupier's rights (for the contents of the notice see Code B para 5.7).

If present, the occupier should be given copies of the notice and the warrant before the search begins if this is practicable, unless the officer in charge reasonably believes that this would frustrate the object of the search or endanger the officers concerned or other persons.

If the occupier is not present, copies of the warrant and the notice setting out police powers and occupiers' rights must be left in a prominent place on the premises or appropriate part of the premises. The notice of powers and rights must be endorsed with the name of

---

67 In *R v Chief Constable of Lancashire ex p Parker and McGrath* [1993] Crim LR 204 breaches of s16 meant that evidence was found to be seized unlawfully.
68 [1988] Crim LR 534 and commentary thereon. The first edition of the Codes, containing the same provision, was in force.

the officer in charge, the name of the station to which the officer is attached and the date and time of the search. The warrant itself should be endorsed to show that this has been done (Code B para 5.8).

A search under a warrant may be only to the extent that is required for the purpose for which the warrant was issued (s16(8)). Any further search would be unlawful and an action for trespass may lie. Code B provides in addition that a search under a warrant may not continue under the authority of that warrant once all the items specified in it have been found, or the officer in charge is satisfied that they are not on the premises (Code B para 5.9). Where other officials accompany the police to execute a search warrant it is important that they do not exceed their authority and that the police do not overly defer to their experience. The police must be very wary of 'delegating their powers in an unacceptable manner'.[69] For the liability of those executing a defective search warrant see below p335. For further safeguards, applicable to all searches, see pp92–93 below.

Procedure following a search

The warrant must be endorsed with certain information specified in the Act and Code B. The Act states that the endorsements must state whether articles or persons sought were found (no endorsements are required indicating their seizure), and whether any *other* articles were seized (s16(9)). Neither the Act nor the code requires any articles to be specified. Code B also requires endorsement of the date and time of execution, and the names of the executing officers except where the investigations are linked to terrorism, where warrant numbers and duty stations should be shown. In addition the warrant must be endorsed to show whether a copy of the warrant together with a copy notice of powers and rights was handed to the occupier or left on the premises, or whether a copy was endorsed (as above) and left on the premises together with the copy notice, and if so where on them (para 7.2).

The police must return an executed warrant or one which has not been used within a month, either to the clerk to the justices if it was issued by a magistrate or to the appropriate officer of the court if it was issued by a judge. Neither the Act nor the code places any time limits on the return, but the clerk or appropriate officer is obliged to

69 R v *Reading Justices and Others ex p South West Meats Ltd* (1991) *Times* 18 November.

keep the warrant for 12 months from the date of its return, so that it can be inspected by the occupier of the premises to which it relates (s16(10)-(12)).

For the duty to compile records of searches see below p94.

Entry and search without a warrant

Statutory powers to enter without a warrant

Many statutes empower the police to enter premises without a warrant, other than for the purposes of making an arrest. Often these are directed towards the enforcement of a statutory scheme for the regulation of a specified activity (for example the Gaming Act 1968 s43(2)); these powers were unaffected by the Act. (For a full list of the powers see appendix 6.)

In *Foster v Attard*,[70] the Divisional Court held that once a police officer was lawfully on any premises, no matter what power placed him or her in that position, the officer was lawfully there for all purposes. In this case, police entered an unlicensed night café at night time for the sole purpose of detecting offences under the Misuse of Drugs Act 1971. It was held that they were there lawfully because of their powers of entry under the Greater London Council (General Powers) Act 1968 and the Gaming Act 1945 even though their entry had been made without a warrant issued under the 1971 Act.

The police have only one common law power of entry: to deal with or prevent a breach of the peace (1984 Act s17(5) and (6)). With the exception of the aforementioned powers, all police powers to enter premises without a warrant are contained in ss17 (entry for arrest and other purposes), 18 and 32 (entry after arrest) (see below). These three sections also contain limited powers of search. The police do not have any power to enter premises against the wishes of the occupier for the purpose of pursuing enquiries into an alleged offence.

Section 17 powers

A constable may enter and search any premises for the many purposes set out in s17. This permits entry and search for the purpose of ~~~uting an arrest warrant issued in connection with or arising out ~~~al proceedings or a warrant of commitment issued under

,6] Crim LR 627.

the Magistrates' Courts Act 1980 s76 (s17(1)(a)). The latter are warrants issued for failure to pay a sum adjudged to be paid on conviction (for example a fine or compensation order) or by an order of the magistrates' court (for example a maintenance order). Civilian enforcement officers, employed by a number of magistrates' courts' committees, do not have this right of entry. A constable may enter and search premises in order to arrest someone for an arrestable offence (see s24 and p114) or for offences specified under some sections of the Public Order Acts of 1936 and 1986 and under the Criminal Justice and Public Order Act 1994 s76 (s17(1)(b) and (c)).[71]

A constable may enter and search premises for the purpose of arresting a person for offences under the Criminal Law Act 1977 ss6–8 and 10, offences of entering and remaining on property (s17(1)(c)(ii)). There are still anomalies in the law; for instance there is still no power to enter diplomatic, consular or inviolable premises to effect an arrest under the Criminal Law Act 1977 s9, without the authority of the lawful occupier. There is also no power to enter premises without a warrant for the arrest of a person who has been driving while disqualified contrary to the Road Traffic Act 1988 s103, as amended even though there is a power of arrest. That offence does not come within the definition of 'arrestable offence' and there is no specific power to enter in either Act. This means that a constable in pursuit of such a driver could effect an arrest at any time before the driver reached any premises, but if the driver enters them the constable must either obtain a warrant (to fall within s17(1)(a) above), obtain entry with consent, serve a summons, or wait for the driver to emerge.

A constable in pursuit of a person unlawfully at large may enter and search premises for the purpose of recapturing that person (s17(1)(d)). This subsection has been considered by the House of Lords in *D'Souza v DPP*[72] where it was held that the expression 'unlawfully at large' within the section does not have a technical or special meaning. It would include someone who has escaped from lawful arrest or from lawful detention and in some cases from mental institutions. In this particular case it was held that a person who escapes lawful detention in a hospital under the Mental Health Act 1983 s6(2) without leave and who is liable to be taken into custody and returned to hospital is unlawfully at large within s17. In order for the power of entry under the section to arise the police must,

71 S17(1)(c) as amended by the Public Order Act 1986 and the Criminal Justice and Public Order Act 1994.
72 [1992] 4 All ER 545.

according to *D'Souza*, be in the act of pursuing. It seems that there has to be a chase so that the pursuit is almost contemporaneous with the entry. An intention to arrest per se is insufficient to justify the phrase 'hot pursuit'. If the police merely have information that such a person is at a certain address, then, unless they obtain the occupier's consent to enter, they require an arrest warrant to secure entry unless there are reasonable grounds for suspecting the person of the commission of an arrestable offence, in which case the provisions of s17(1)(b) apply.

A constable may also enter premises without a warrant or consent for the purpose of saving life or limb or preventing serious damage to property (s17(1)(e)). A police constable must, in all the above cases under s17 (except s17(1)(e)—saving life and limb), have a reasonable belief that the person sought is on the premises (s17(2)(a)). This means that the lawfulness of the entry must be judged objectively. An honest but unreasonable belief would mean that the entry and search would be unlawful and there may then be grounds for an action for trespass or criminal damage (see chapter 13). In *Chapman v DPP*,[73] the Divisional Court held, interpreting the same phrase in s24, that the constable must not only have reasonable grounds for believing but must in fact so believe.

In *Kynaston v DPP* and *Heron v DPP*,[74] the Divisional Court was prepared to hold that a search was lawful on the basis that the police had 'reasonable grounds to suspect' that the person whom they wanted to arrest was on the premises. This involves a much lower test than the Act specifies and in this respect the decision is unsatisfactory.

A constable must be in uniform in order to exercise the powers of entry to effect an arrest under the Criminal Law Act 1977 and under the Criminal Justice and Public Order Act 1994 (s17(1)(c)(ii) and (iv)). If the officer is not in uniform, there is no right of entry. Uniform is not required in order to exercise the other powers of entry under s17 (s17(3)).

The Code of Practice applies to both the entry and the search (Code B para 1.3). A constable is entitled to use reasonable force if necessary to effect an entry or search under this section (Code B para 5.6 and s117), but only when access has been requested and denied unless one of the following provisions applies:

73 [1988] Crim LR 482.
74 (1987) *Times* 4 November.

- it is impossible to communicate with the occupier or other person entitled to grant access;
- the premises are known to be unoccupied;
- the occupier is known to be absent; or
- the occupier or other person entitled to grant entry has refused entry to the premises; or
- it is possible that such communication would frustrate the object of the search or endanger the officers concerned or other persons (Code B paras 5.4–5.6).

If force is applied unnecessarily or excessively, the police may be liable to a criminal or civil action for assault or prosecution for criminal damage (see chapter 13).

Limitations on s17 searches

The police are permitted only a very limited form of search under s17. They can search only to the extent that is reasonably required for the purpose for which the power of entry is exercised (s17(3)). Since it is a search for a person, a search through drawers, for instance, would not be authorised by the Act and would be unlawful. The police may be held liable for trespass.

In *Murray v Ministry of Defence*,[75] the House of Lords stated, obiter, that under Northern Ireland (Emergency Provisions) Act 1978 s14 (now repealed), which gave the armed forces a similar power of search,[76] in view of the risks of forcible resistance to arrest where the person sought was suspected of involvement with the IRA, the forces had a more extensive power of search. It was army procedure to enter premises and search every room for occupants, who were then directed to assemble in one room. The reason for the procedure was to avoid soldiers being distracted by the activities of occupants in other parts of the premises and perhaps thereby to prevent a shooting incident. Lord Griffiths said:[77]

> The search cannot be limited solely to looking for the person to be arrested and must also embrace a search whose object is to secure that the arrest should be peaceable. I also regard it as an entirely reasonable precaution that all the occupants of the house should be asked to assemble in one room.

In principle there seems to be no reason why such powers should not be given to the police under the 1984 Act s17, but only if it were

75 [1988] 2 All ER 521.
76 'for the purposes of arresting a person under this section a member of Her Majesty's forces may enter and search any premises ...' (s14(3)).
77 [1988] 2 All ER 521 at 527e.

thought likely that an arrest would be forcibly resisted, giving rise to a similar situation of great tension.

In the case of a building containing two or more separate dwellings, the search is limited to the dwelling in which it is reasonably believed the person sought may be, and any communal parts (s17(2)(b)).

Common law powers to enter without a warrant

Legal authority for the power of entry to deal with a breach of the peace was established in the nineteenth century, whereas a power of entry to *prevent* a breach of the peace was not established until 1935 in *Thomas v Sawkins*.[78] It is clear that the police have power to enter public or private premises to prevent a breach of the peace occurring.[79] A breach of the peace has been defined as 'an act done or threatened to be done which either actually harms a person, or, in his presence, his property, or is likely to cause such harm or which puts someone in fear of such harm being done'.[80] In *McLeod v Commissioner of Police of the Metropolis*[81] the Court of Appeal stressed that the police must have a genuine and reasonable belief that a breach of the peace is about to take place. The apprehension must relate to the near future and it may be necessary in a future case to consider how far in advance of a possible breach the right arises, which will depend on the facts of the case. The police must act with great 'care and discretion', particularly where the entry is on private premises without the consent of the owner or occupier. The officer must be satisfied that there is a real and imminent risk of such a breach. These are the only common law powers of entry to survive the 1984 Act.

Entry to search for evidence after an arrest

The 1984 Act provides the police with clear statutory authority to enter premises occupied or controlled by a person whom they have arrested for an arrestable offence (see p114) in order to search for and seize evidence of that offence, or some other arrestable offence which is connected with or similar to that offence (s18). There is provision for a more limited search of premises when a person is arrested but

78 [1935] 2 KB 249.
79 *McLeod v Commissioner of Police of the Metropolis* [1994] 4 All ER 553.
80 *R v Howell* [1982] QB 416 at 426. See also *McConnell v Chief Constable of Greater Manchester Police* [1990] 1 All ER 423.
81 [1994] 4 All ER 553 per Neill LJ at 560f-j.

not for an arrestable offence (s32, below p91). The provisions for entry and search on arrest for an arrestable offence (s18) are also activated where a person who is already under arrest at a police station is rearrested at the police station by a constable in the lawful exercise of the powers under s31 (a section which prevents abuse of detention powers by a series of rearrests after release, see below p143). The extent of the search permitted on the rearrest will depend on the reason for the arrest.

The search which takes place after arrest for an arrestable offence (authorised by s18) should not be for items subject to legal privilege (s18(1)), but there is no such restriction on excluded or special procedure material. It is possible of course that legally privileged items might be seized, but it would be unlawful.[82]

Written authority

The search should not take place without written authorisation by an officer of at least the rank of inspector (s18(4)). The authorisation should (unless wholly impracticable) be given on the notice of powers and rights (Code B para 3.3 and see p93 below).[83]

A constable may conduct such a search without written authorisation and without first taking the person to a police station only if the presence of that person at a place other than a police station is necessary for the effective investigation of the offence, for instance, if it were necessary to obtain evidence which is in imminent danger of being destroyed and taking the person to a police station would facilitate the destruction (s18(5)). There is no scope for reasonable belief on the part of the constable here; the search must in fact be necessary for the effective investigation of the offence and if challenged later and found unnecessary, an action for unlawful imprisonment may lie, inter alia (see chapter 13). The constable is in all events constrained in that the premises should be searched only if there are reasonable grounds to suspect that there is evidence (other than legally privileged items) relating to that offence or another *arrestable* offence (s24, below p114), connected with or similar to that offence (s18(1)). There must actually be reasonable grounds for suspicion and if in later proceedings it were found as a matter of fact that there were not, an action for trespass might be brought and any seizure

---

82 See chapters 4 on seizure, 11 on exclusion of evidence and 13 on remedies.
83 See also *R v Badham* [1987] Crim LR 202. The Crown Court decided, before the existence of the present para 3.3 of Code B that the authorisation must be on an independent document. A note in the policeman's notebook was not sufficient.

might be unlawful (see chapter 13). The question of similar offences may cause problems, but on general principles should be construed restrictively.

If the search was conducted without written authority, the constable must inform someone who could have authorised the search as soon as practicable afterwards (s18(6)). That officer must then record the grounds of the search and the nature of evidence sought, as should also be done where the search is under written authority (s18(7)). This is in addition to the duty of the constable in charge of the search to make a record under Code B (see below). If any person wishes to complain about the exercise of the powers, or to bring court proceedings, or if the results of any search are relevant to court proceedings, a copy of the records should be obtained promptly.

Limitations on s18 searches

If a person who occupies or controls premises which are searched under s18 is in police detention after an arrest, the record of the search should be made in the custody record. This must be done even if the search was not made in connection with the detainee's arrest (s18(8)).[84]

The police are entitled to search only premises occupied or controlled by the person under arrest. The premises must be occupied or controlled by the person; there is no scope for 'reasonable belief'. 'Controlled' is not defined, and there is considerable room for argument. It may, for instance, include ownership without occupation as well as management without either. Where premises are let to a tenant it would be possible to argue that they should not be searched on the arrest of the landlord because they are not controlled by the landlord.

The search must be only to the extent that is reasonably required for the purpose of discovering evidence relating to the arrestable offence (s18(3)). Any further search would be unlawful. Code B also governs searches under s18 (see below pp92–93). The police are entitled to use reasonable force if necessary to secure entry and search (see s117 and above, p11). Where the police suspect that evidence of unconnected offences or of connected offences which are not arrestable is to be found on premises, it would be necessary for them to apply for a warrant, to obtain other written authority or to obtain consent.

84 In *R v Wright* [1994] Crim LR 55 there was a breach, inter alia, of this provision, but it did not affect the admissibility of evidence obtained in the search.

Searches under s32

Where a person is arrested in a place other than a police station and the arrest is for an offence, the police have supplementary powers of entry and search under s32 (see also p144). The police have power to enter any premises in which the person was at the time of, or immediately prior to, the arrest, and may search those premises provided that they have reasonable grounds for believing that there is evidence on the premises relating to the offence (s32(2) and (6)). What are reasonable grounds for belief is a question of fact for the courts, as is the interpretation of 'immediately'. The premises need not be owned, controlled or occupied by the person arrested. The power to search is limited; the police may only search to the extent that is reasonably required for the purpose of discovering evidence, and any further search will be unlawful (s32(3)). Again the police may use reasonable force to effect entry and search (s117) and Code B also covers searches under this section (see pp92–93).

In *R v Badham*[85] the Court held that, although the Act did not specify a time limit, this, in contrast to the powers in s18, was an immediate power, and the police should not use it to return to premises several hours after the arrest. This distinction is obviously welcome although difficult to sustain in the light of the differing circumstances pertaining to each section.

The Court of Appeal considered s32 in *R v Beckford*[86] and confirmed that the police must have a genuine belief that there is evidence of the offence for which they have made the arrest on the premises. The section must not be used to validate general fishing expeditions. It is for the jury and not the judge to decide whether the police entered lawfully for the reasons stated by them.

If the premises consist of separate dwellings, for instance a block of flats or perhaps separate lockable bedsits, the power of search is limited to that dwelling in which the arrest took place or in which the person arrested was immediately before the arrest and any parts of the premises that are used in common with others (s32(7)). In *Beckford* (above) the defendant emerged from a house which was divided into three flats with a common entrance. The police entered the ground floor flat because they had prior knowledge that the flat had been used for drug dealing and therefore they thought that this was where it was likely that the defendant had been before the arrest. The suggestion that it is a question of the police's belief which is relevant

85 [1987] Crim LR 202.
86 [1991] Crim LR 918.

to the lawfulness of the entry conflicts with the section, which infers that the arrested person must *actually have been* on the premises.

Searches with consent of person entitled to grant entry

Code B provides that consent must, if practicable, be given in writing on the notice of powers and rights before the search takes place. Before seeking consent the officer in charge must make enquiries in order to be satisfied that the person is in a position to give consent and the officer must state the purpose of the proposed search, inform the person concerned of the right to refuse consent, and that anything seized may be produced in evidence. When the police state the purpose of the search they should, if it is the case, state that the person is not under suspicion. In the case of lodgings or similar accommodation, a search should not be made on the basis of the landlord's consent alone unless the lodger, tenant or occupier is unavailable and the matter is urgent.

If consent was given under duress or is withdrawn, the police do not have the right to enter and search unless they have alternative authority.

The code provides that it is unnecessary to seek consent where to do so would cause disproportionate inconvenience to the person concerned, for instance where the police need to make a brief check of gardens for stolen goods when they have been pursuing someone along that route.

Where the police have powers to enter premises without consent they are still obliged to seek co-operation (in most cases – see above p87) before entry, if practicable. If they do obtain consent there is no need in these circumstances for it to be in writing (Code B para 4).

General safeguards for searches

Code B provides safeguards for all searches covered by the code (see Code B para 1.3). Some of the safeguards applicable to searches under warrant are also applicable to other searches. This is the case with the requirement that all searches should be made at a reasonable hour, unless this would frustrate the object of the search (Code B para 5.2) and that the officer in charge should attempt communication and identification in some cases (Code B paras 5.4 and 5.5 and above p86).

Similarly, the occupier of any premises which have been searched is entitled to a notice of powers and rights as described in Code B para 5.7 and above p82. This must be given to the occupier, or left on the premises if the occupier is not present, in the same way as in a search under warrant.

In the case of all searches, a constable may use reasonable force, if necessary, to enter and search premises (s117 and above p11). Code B provides that before reasonable force is used a request for access must have been made to the occupier or person entitled to grant access, and the request must have been refused. Exceptions to this rule are made if it is impossible to communicate with the occupier or any other person entitled to grant access, or if any of the provisions in para 5.4 above, apply (Code B para 5.6). The code provides that reasonable force should be used to effect a search only where this is necessary because the co-operation of the occupier cannot be obtained or is insufficient for the purpose (Code B para 5.10). Where force is subsequently alleged to have been excessive or unnecessary, an action for assault or criminal damage may lie (see further chapter 13). What is unreasonable or excessive force is a question of fact for the courts.

Code B provides that searches must be conducted with due consideration for the property and privacy of the occupier, and with no more disturbance than is necessary. Any search may be only to the extent necessary to achieve the object of the search, having regard to the size and nature of whatever is sought. If the occupier wishes to ask a friend or other person to witness the search, then this must be allowed, unless the officer in charge has reasonable grounds to believe that it would seriously hinder the investigation. A search need not be delayed unreasonably for the purpose (paras 5.9–5.11). Code B provides that if premises have been entered by force the officer in charge must, before leaving, be satisfied that they are secure either by arranging for the presence of the occupier or an agent or by any other appropriate means (para 5.12). The latter provison may mean that in some cases the police would be under an obligation to leave premises in a better state than they were before the entry, but it is very unlikely that the paragraph would be construed in such a way in the event of a complaint.

Action to be taken after searches

For all searches covered by the code, the officer in charge of the search is under a duty to make or have made a record of the search. The police record must include:

a) the address of the premises searched;
b) the date and time of the search;
c) the authority under which the search was made. Where the search was made in the exercise of a statutory power to search premises without warrant the record must include the power under which the search was made, and where the search was made under warrant, or with written consent, a copy of the warrant or consent must be appended to the record or kept in a place identified in the record;
d) the names of the officers who conducted the search (unless the enquiries are linked to terrorism, in which case only the warrant number and duty station of each officer need to be included);
e) the names of any persons on the premises if they are known;
f) either a list of any articles seized or a note of where such a list is kept and, if not covered by a warrant, the reason for their seizure;
g) whether force was used and, if so, the reason why it was used; and
h) a list of any damage caused during the search, and the circumstances in which it was caused (Code B para 7).

Where premises have been searched under warrant, the warrant must be endorsed as described on p83 above.

Each subdivisional police station must maintain a search register and all records which are required to be made by the Code of Practice must be made, copied or referred to in the register (Code B para 7).

Investigations into drug trafficking

Police powers to investigate drug trafficking are contained in the 1984 Act and the Drug Trafficking Act 1994. A circuit judge has power to make an order for the production of material which may be relevant to an investigation into drug trafficking on the application of a constable or customs and excise officer (s55 of the 1994 Act). The judge must be satisfied that there are reasonable grounds for suspecting that a specified person has carried on or has benefited from drug trafficking; that there are reasonable grounds for suspecting that the material to which the application relates is likely to be of substantial value (whether by itself or together with other material) to the investigation for the purpose of which the application is made, and does not consist of or include items subject to legal privilege or excluded material; and that there are reasonable grounds for believing it is in the public interest (having regard to the possible benefits to the investigation and the circumstances under which the person in possession holds it) that the material should be produced or access given to it (s55(4)). A judge who makes such an order may also order any person who appears to be entitled to grant entry to the premises to allow a constable to enter to obtain access to the material (s55(5)). An application under s55(1) or (5) may be made ex parte to a judge in chambers (s55(6)). The Act does not specify when this should be the case, but presumably it would be in cases of urgency or where an inter partes hearing might prejudice the investigation (s55(6)).[87]

The order is against the person in possession of the material, who may not necessarily be implicated in the drug trafficking at all. The application may be made at any time in relation to the criminal proceedings against the person suspected of drug trafficking (before or during the proceedings, or after the conviction) for the purposes of establishing any of the matters necessary to the making or enforcement of a confiscation order.

Apart from the exceptions covering legally privileged and excluded material (see above p56 and p60 for definitions), the order can override any other obligations of confidentiality or secrecy, including statutory obligations, and may apply to a government department (s55(9)).

There are provisions for the judge to issue a search warrant if an order under s55 has not been complied with or it is inappropriate or impractical to make an order.

The grounds listed in 1994 Act s56 are similar to those in the 1984 Act Sch 1 (see above p76) which empower the judge to issue a warrant. The issue of a warrant and its execution are of course governed by ss15 and 16 of the 1984 Act and Code B (see above pp79–83). For a description of what may be seized see below p109. The provisions of ss21 and 22 of the 1984 Act, regarding access to material and police powers of retention are also applicable (see pp107–109).

Where an order under s55 of the 1994 Act has been applied for or made, or a warrant has been issued under s56, it is an offence[88] for a person knowing or suspecting the investigation is taking place to make any disclosure likely to prejudice the investigation (s58). The accused does not have to know or suspect that an application

---

87 The predecessor of s55(6) was not enacted in the Drug Trafficking Offences Act 1986, but was introduced by the Criminal Justice Act 1993.

88 On summary conviction the maximum sentence is six months or a fine of the statutory maximum or both and on indictment the maximum sentence is five years or a fine or both.

for an order has been made, only that the investigation is taking place. It is a defence to prove that the accused did not know or suspect that the disclosure was likely to prejudice the investigation or that there was lawful authority or reasonable excuse for making the disclosure. By virtue of s58(3) it is not an offence for a professional legal adviser to disclose any information or other matter to a client or a representative of the client in connection with the giving of legal advice, or to anyone in consequence of, or in connection with, legal proceedings and for the purpose of those proceedings. This protection does not apply, however, in relation to any information or other matter disclosed with a view to furthering any criminal purpose (s58(4)).

Investigation of serious fraud

The Director of the Serious Fraud Office has power to investigate any suspected offence which appears to him or her on reasonable grounds to involve serious or complex fraud (Criminal Justice Act 1987 s1(3)). To this end the Director can exercise very wide powers under s2 to investigate the affairs or any aspect of the affairs of any person (s2(1)). The Director may by written notice require any person whom he has reason to believe has relevant information to attend before him and answer questions or otherwise furnish information with respect to any matter relevant to the investigation. Similarly any person may be required to produce relevant documents (s2(2) and (3)). 'Documents' include information recorded in any form (s2(18)).

The Director can take copies or extracts from the documents and require explanations. Failure to comply with such requirements without reasonable excuse is a summary offence (s2(13)). These powers continue after charge and since this is the case the defence of reasonable excuse in s2(13) apparently cannot arise.[89] In *Re an Inquiry under the Company Securities (Insider Dealing) Act 1985*,[90] the House of Lords held that a journalist who refused to disclose his source did not have a reasonable excuse under the similar offence of refusing to give information, contained in the Financial Services Act 1986 s178. Any person who knowingly or recklessly makes a statement which is

---

89 *R v Serious Fraud Office ex p Smith* [1993] AC 1 HL and *R v Metropolitan Stipendiary Magistrate* (1994) *Independent* 24 June.
90 [1988] 1 All ER 203.

false or misleading is also guilty of an offence, as is anyone who knowing or suspecting that an investigation is being carried out falsifies, conceals, destroys or otherwise disposes of documents or causes or permits any of the above, knowing or suspecting them to be relevant. In this case the burden of proof shifts to the defendant to show that there was no intention to conceal the facts from the investigation (s2(14)–(17)).

In addition, if documents are not produced, the Director can require the person who was required to produce the documents to state where they are (s2(3)). Finally, if a magistrate is satisfied in relation to any of the documents, that there are reasonable grounds for believing that:

a) a person has failed to comply with an obligation under s2 to produce them; or
b) it is not practicable to serve a notice as above; or
c) the service of such a notice might seriously prejudice the investigation; and
d) that they are on premises specified in the information,

the magistrate may issue a warrant (s2(4)). There is no protection in this section for 'excluded' or 'special procedure' material with the limited exception of certain information held by bankers (see s2(10)). Legally privileged documents are, however, exempt from production. 'Legally privileged' is not defined here and the definition in the 1984 Act does not apply. The general law on the subject will therefore be applicable. A lawyer may, however, be required to disclose the name and address of a client (s2(9)).

The warrant authorises any constable to enter (using reasonable force if necessary) and search premises and to seize the specified documents or take any steps necessary to preserve and prevent interference with them. Sections 15 and 16 of the 1984 Act (see pp79–83 above) of course apply to the execution of such warrants and ss19–22 of the 1984 Act apply to the seizure.

Unless it is not practicable, a constable executing such a warrant must be accompanied by either a member of the Serious Fraud Office or someone else whom the Director has authorised (s2(6) and (7)).

Although these powers are very wide, the uses to which the information received may be put are limited. Any statements made in response to requirements under the section may be used only in evidence against the maker of the statement in a prosecution for an offence under s2(14) (above) or in a prosecution for some other offence, where in giving evidence an inconsistent statement is made (s2(8)). In addition, the Serious Fraud Office may disclose the information only to specified persons (see Criminal Justice Act 1987 s3).[91]

Confiscation of proceeds of crime

By virtue of the Criminal Justice Act 1988, as amended by the Proceeds of Crime Act 1995, any criminal court has power in relation to all indictable offences and specified summary offences to make a confiscation order (see further chapter 10). For the purposes of an investigation into whether any person has benefited from criminal conduct or to the extent or whereabouts of any proceeds, a constable may apply ex parte to a circuit judge in chambers for an order for the production of a particular material, not consisting of excluded or legally privileged material. In the event of non-compliance with an order, or where it is impracticable to make such an order, the judge may issue a warrant (1988 Act s93H).

Entry and search of premises by the security services

Any entry on, or interference with, property is lawful if it is authorised by a warrant issued by the Secretary of State under the Intelligence Services Act 1994 s5.[92] On application by the relevant security service, the Secretary of State may issue a warrant if he thinks it necessary to do so on the ground that it is likely to be of substantial value in assisting the applying organisation in carrying out any of its functions and is satisfied that what the action seeks to achieve cannot reasonably be achieved by other means (s5(2)). In addition, the Secretary of State must be satisfied that satisfactory arrangements are in force with respect to limitations on disclosure of information obtained (s5(2)(c)).

The function of the Security Service (MI5) is the protection of national security, in particular against threats from espionage terror-

---

91 These powers have been criticised and have been subject to review by the ECHR, for example, in the case of Ernest Saunders (*Guardian* 19 September 1994); see Frommel: 'The Right to Silence and the Serious Fraud Office'. *Company Lawyer* Vol 15 No 8 p227.

92 For an analysis of the 1994 Act see the note by John Wadham at (1994) 57 MLR 916–927. The Security Service Act 1989 deals with MI5, the 1994 Act with MI6 and GCHQ, but the 1994 Act s6 repeals 1989 Act s3. The result is that the rules for obtaining warrants by all security services are now governed by the 1994 Act ss5 and 6.

ism and sabotage, from the activities of agents of foreign powers and from actions intended to overthrow or undermine parliamentary democracy by political, industrial or violent means. It also has the function of safeguarding the economic well-being of the United Kingdom against threats posed by the actions or intentions of persons outside the British Islands.[93]

The functions of the Intelligence Service (MI6) are to obtain and provide information and to perform other tasks relating to the actions or intentions of persons outside the British Islands, but only in the interests of national security with particular reference to the defence and foreign policies of the government, or in the interests of the economic well-being of the United Kingdom, or in support of the prevention or detection of serious crime.[94]

The functions of the Government Communication Headquarters (GCHQ) are to monitor or interfere with emissions and equipment, obtain and provide information derived from or related to these (but only in the interests of national security with particular reference to the defence and foreign policies of the government, or in the interests of the economic well-being of the United Kingdom, or in support of the prevention or detection of serious crime) and to provide to the government and armed forces advice and assistance about languages, terminology, cryptography and similar matters.[95]

A warrant authorising the taking of action in support of the prevention or detection of serious crime may not relate to property in the British Islands (s5(3)) but this restriction does not extend to warrants issued for other legitimate purposes. There are special provisions in s7 dealing with authorisation of acts outside the British Islands, but they are not within the scope of this book.

The warrant authorises the taking of any action which it specifies in respect of any specified property. There are no limits to what may be specified. The type of interference authorised could include 'forcible surreptitious entry, search, copying and removal of papers, installation of bugging or surveillance equipment or equipment to monitor vehicle movements'.[96] However, the only action authorised by the Act is that specified in the warrant.

The Act gives no further details of what must be in an application

---

93 Security Service Act 1989 s1.
94 Intelligence Services Act 1994 s1.
95 Ibid s3.
96 'The Security Service Act 1989' by Leigh and Lustgarten (1989) 52 MLR 801–836 at 825, commenting on the predecessor provision in 1989 Act s3.

for a warrant but in practice the application contains a description of the case, the name of the person or organisation, the property involved and details of the operational plan.[97]

Only the Secretary of State can issue a warrant, unless the matter is urgent, in which case an official in the department, of Grade 3 or Diplomatic Service Senior Grade or above, may issue the warrant, provided that the Secretary of State has expressly authorised its issue and that fact is endorsed on the warrant.

A warrant issued by the Secretary of State expires at the end of six months beginning on the day on which it was issued, but if it was issued by anyone else it expires at the end of the period ending with the second working day following that day. (Working day is defined as any day other than a Saturday, Sunday, Christmas Day, Good Friday or a Bank Holiday in any part of the United Kingdom). However before a warrant expires it may be renewed by the Secretary of State for a further six months if it is still needed for the purpose for which it was issued. The Secretary of State must cancel a warrant if satisfied that it is no longer necessary.

The Tribunals and the Commissioners

The Security Service Act 1989 (in ss4 and 5) and the Intelligence Services Act 1994 (in ss8 and 9) each establishes a tribunal and a commissioner, the former in respect of the Security Service and the latter in respect of the Intelligence Service and GCHQ. References to 'service', 'Tribunal' or 'Commissioner' below refer to all three institutions and both tribunals and both commissioners.

Any person (which includes any organisation and any association or combination of persons) who is aggrieved by anything the service has done may complain to the Tribunal. Unless the Tribunal considers that the complaint is frivolous or vexatious, it must investigate it. If the complaint relates to property, the Tribunal must refer it to the Commissioner. The latter should then investigate whether a warrant was issued in respect of the property, and if so, shall apply the principles applied by a court on an application for judicial review, to determine whether the Secretary of State was acting properly in issuing or renewing the warrant. The Tribunal must give the complainant notice of any determination in his or her favour. If no such determination is made by the Tribunal or Commissioner, the Tribu-

97 Report of the Commissioner for 1990, Cm 1480 para 4.

nal must give the complainant notice of this. If the complainant receives a determination as above, the Tribunal may:

a) quash any warrant in respect of any property of the complainant which the Commissioner found to be improperly issued or renewed and which the Commissioner considers should be quashed; and

b) direct the Secretary of State to pay any compensation to the complainant which the Commissioner considers to be appropriate (Sch 1 para 6(2)).

If the Tribunal concludes that no determination in the complainant's favour should be made, but that it is appropriate to investigate whether the Service has acted unreasonably in any other respect in relation to the complainant or his or her property, it must refer the matter to the Commissioner. The latter may then refer any such matter to the Secretary of State who can take any action he or she considers fit, including any action which the Tribunal could have taken. The decisions of the Tribunal and the Commissioner are not subject to appeal nor liable to be questioned in any court.[98]

If the Service's activities were not authorised by a warrant and were performed without consent, they are of course unlawful and the ordinary remedies may be sought.

98 Security Service Act 1989 s5(4); Intelligence Services Act 1994 s9(4).

CHAPTER 4

Seizure of evidence

The police have powers to seize property under many statutes. They have power under the Theft Act 1968 (s26), for instance, to search premises for stolen goods and to seize any goods believed to be stolen. (For a list of such statutes see appendix 6.) The 1984 Act gave the police additional specific powers to seize evidence (see below) and further confirmed their powers of general seizure.

A police officer may use reasonable force, if necessary, when exercising any power to seize property (s117). For police powers of entry and search, see chapter 3 above.

Powers of seizure under the 1984 Act: introduction

Under the 1984 Act the police have the following specific powers to seize property:

a) to seize any article which they have reasonable grounds for suspecting to be stolen or prohibited which is discovered in the exercise of a search under s1 (s1(6)) (see above chapter 2);

b) to seize and retain anything for which a search was authorised under s8 (magistrate's power to issue a search warrant for evidence of a serious arrestable offence) (s8(2)) (see above chapter 3);

c) to seize property for which a circuit judge has issued a search warrant under Sch 1 (Sch 1 para 13) (see above chapter 3);

d) to seize and retain anything for which they may search when a person is under arrest for an arrestable offence (s18(2)) (see above chapter 3);

e) to seize and retain anything found during a search of a person after arrest, where the arrest takes place other than at a police station (s32(8) and (9)) (see below chapter 5); and

f) to seize and retain anything discovered during a search at a police station or whilst in police detention (ss54(3) and 55(12)) (see below chapter 7).

However, in addition to these specific powers, the police, provided that they are lawfully on any premises, are given extensive powers to seize anything (except items subject to legal privilege) regardless of whether they had authority to search for it (s19). For the restrictions on police powers to seize legally privileged material see below (p104).

General power of seizure

Where a police officer is lawfully on any premises there exist the general powers of seizure described below. An officer is lawfully on any premises if:

a) pursuant to written authority;

b) pursuant to a valid[1] search warrant issued under 1984 Act or any other statute;

c) under s17 (entry to effect arrest, to recapture a person unlawfully at large, or to save life or limb, see p84 above);

d) under s18 (entry after arrest, see p88 above);

e) under s32 (entry and search of premises in which a person was arrested or in which a person was immediately prior to arrest, see p91 above);

f) to deal with or prevent a breach of the peace; or

g) with the consent of the occupier.

A police officer may seize anything if there are reasonable grounds for believing:

– that it has been obtained in consequence of the commission of an offence (s19(2)(a)); or

---

1 Where the warrant in invalid seizure is unlawful: see *R v Reading Justices and Others, ex p South West Meat* [1992] Crim LR 672 and *R v Central Criminal Court and BRB ex p AJD Holdings Ltd* [1992] Crim LR 669 and see above p79. Similarly, where the warrant is improperly executed under s16 seizure of material will be unlawful: *R v Chief Constable of Lancashire Constabulary ex p Parker* [1993] 2 All ER 56.

– that it is evidence in relation to an offence which the officer is investigating (not necessarily the offence in connection with which the officer is on the premises) or any other offence (s19(3)(a));[2] and
– in either of the above cases, that it is necessary to seize the property in order to prevent it being concealed, lost, altered or destroyed (s19(2)(b) and (3)(b)).

It is important to note that there is nothing to prevent special procedure or excluded material being seized under these provisions: only legally privileged material is protected (s19(6)). The effect of these provisions is that if, for example, a police officer were in an accountant's office with the accountant's consent, not to carry out a search but to conduct an interview, and noticed a set of accounts which there were reasonable grounds to suspect constituted evidence of a fraud offence, the oficer might seize them. If an occupier consents to an entry but the officer has an undisclosed intention to seize or surreptitiously scrutinise property (for example documents), then this may constitute trespass, as the entry is outside the police officer's authority. There are of course problems of proof.[3]

Where an officer has reasonable grounds for believing that property has been obtained in consequence of the commission of an offence, but decides that it is inappropriate to seize it owing to an explanation given by the person holding it, the officer must inform the holder of his/her suspicions and explain that disposal of the property may give rise to civil or criminal proceedings (Code B para 6.3).

Items subject to legal privilege

For the definition of such items see p56 above. A constable should not seize any item which there are reasonable grounds for believing to be legally privileged. This restriction applies whatever the authority for the entry or search (s19(6)). If privileged material is seized, the lawfulness of the seizure must be assessed by gauging the constable's belief objectively: an honest but unreasonable belief will not validate a seizure. The reasonableness of a constable's belief must be

2 'Other offence' has been held to relate only to domestic offences and not to offences allegedly committed outside the UK. See *R v Southwark Crown Court ex p Sorsky Defries* (1995) *Times* 21 July.

3 For a discussion of this point in connection with burglary, see E Griew, *The Theft Acts* (Sweet and Maxwell, 7th edn 1995).

gauged at the time of the seizure and not in the light of anything that happens afterwards.

When a person is arrested somewhere other than in a police station, the police have power, inter alia, (see above p114):

a) to search the arrested person if they have reasonable grounds for believing that the person may present a danger to him or herself or others (s32(1)); and

b) to search for anything which might be used to assist the person to escape from lawful custody; and to search for anything which might be evidence relating to an offence (s32(2)(a)).

In the case of a search under s32(1), the restrictions on police powers to seize legally privileged material are limited by s19(6), but in the case of s32(2)(a) the restrictions on seizure of legally privileged material are absolute (s32(9)).[4]

Restrictions on seizure

Although the powers of seizure are clearly wide, the powers to search are strictly limited. Under a warrant or other written authority, only a search for the purposes of execution is lawful; anything further would be trespass. Entry under s17 to effect arrest, recapture or save life or limb (see above), or entry to deal with or prevent a breach of the peace, is for those strictly limited purposes. Similarly under s18 (entry and search after arrest), the power to search is strictly limited to only the extent that is reasonably required for the purpose of discovering such evidence (s18(3)). Under s32 (search on arrest) there is again only a limited power of search (s32(3) and (6)). Code B also states that searches should be strictly limited (para 5.9 and above p93).

The police are not entitled to seize large numbers of documents, without giving thought to whether each file or bundle might reasonably constitute evidence (unless they have the consent of the occupier, of course). In *Reynolds and Another v Commisioner of Police of the Metropolis*, Slade LJ stated:[5]

> It is not correct in law for the judge to direct the jury that the reasonableness (or otherwise) of the police in executing the search warrant was the only criterion. The jury should have been asked

4 See also the restriction on the seizure of legally privileged material in Code B para 6.2.

5 [1984] 3 All ER 649, CA at 660.

whether in regard to each file, book, bundle or separate document, the officer in question, at the time of the removal, had reasonable cause to believe that it might contain either forged material or evidence showing that the plaintiff was guilty of some other crime.

Unlawful seizure

Documents or other items seized unlawfully may still constitute admissible evidence (see further chapter 12). The police have no right to retain unlawfully seized evidence however.[6] For civil actions for the return of property and for the procedures under the Police Property Act 1897, see below chapter 13.

Computerised information

A police officer, in the exercise of certain powers of seizure (see below) may require information stored in a computer to be produced in a form in which it can be taken away and in which it is visible and legible – for instance, as a printout rather than a floppy disc.

This facility relates to the following powers of seizure:

a) powers of seizure contained in any statutes passed before or after the 1984 Act;

b) powers of seizure contained in s8 (warrants issued by magistrates for evidence of serious arrestable offences), s18 (entry and search after arrest) and Sch 1 para 13 (search for excluded or special procedure material) of the 1984 Act; and

c) the power to seize evidence discovered although not actually the object of a search while a police officer is lawfully on any premises (s19). In this case the police officer must have reasonable grounds for believing either:

– that it is evidence relating to an offence which s/he is investigating or any other offence; or

– that it has been obtained in consequence of the commission of an offence; *and*

– in either case, that it is necessary to seize the evidence to prevent it being concealed, lost, tampered with or destroyed (s19(4)).

6 See R *v Chief Constable of Lancashire Constabulary ex p Parker* [1993] 2 All ER 56.

As before, there is no power to seize information which a police officer has reasonable grounds for believing to be subject to legal privilege (s19(6) and Code B para 6.2).

Access to seized items and the taking and provision of copies

If it can be shown that a person who is either the occupier of premises from which the property was seized, or someone who had custody or control of the property immediately before its seizure has asked for a record of seized items, a police officer must provide it within a reasonable time of the request (s21(1) and (2)).

The police may in theory have to present at least three records to different people. That is, it would be possible for custody and control to be vested in separate persons, for instance an accountant may hold documents on behalf of a client and therefore have custody, while the secretary typing the documents may have control. There is no provision requiring the police to provide a record to anyone acting on behalf of a person in one of the categories above. What is a reasonable time will depend on the number and nature of the items seized and is bound to cause problems, particularly in cases where a large number of documents is removed, for instance in fraud investigations.

Unless the officer in charge of the investigation for the purposes of which the items were seized has reasonable grounds for believing that access to the items or the supply of a photograph or copy of the articles would prejudice the investigation of that offence or any other offence, or any criminal proceedings which may be brought as a result of any investigation, access must be allowed, or a copy or photograph of the articles must be provided, to the person who had custody or control of the articles immediately before seizure or to that person's representative, at their own expense. Access will be under the supervision of a police officer and, unless the articles are photographed or copied by someone else, the applicant will be supervised in this process. If the photograph or copy is made by someone else it must be supplied to the person who made the request within a reasonable time of the request (s21(3)–(8)).

In deciding whether or not the owners of documents have a right to receive copies from the police where the documents have been lawfully seized, the court must weigh carefully the competing interests. In *Arias v Commissioner of Police of the Metropolis* May LJ stated:[7]

> where there were two conflicting public interests involved it was a question of a balancing exercise, setting off one public interest against the other. The most important consideration was that the documents belonged to the plaintiffs.

In that case, the police had sworn an affidavit that the supply of copies might seriously hamper the investigation, but this was held to be mere speculation and in fact might be said in any case where documents were incriminating. If access or a copy is refused on the above grounds, a record of the grounds must be made (Code B para 6.9). The Court of Appeal has ruled that when complainants seek to challenge a chief constable's refusal to permit copies to be made of documents seized from them by the police, they should do so by judicial review.[8]

Use and retention of seized items

The police have power to photograph or copy, or have photographed or copied, any seized items, irrespective of a request for a copy under s21 above. Indeed the police should not retain anything if a photograph or copy would be sufficient for their purposes (s22(4)). However the police may retain anything seized by a police officer, or taken away in the case of information stored on a computer, so long as it is necessary in all the circumstances (s22(1)).[9] This provides the police with a certain leeway; for instance, it may be necessary for them to keep evidence for an appeal, or they may not be under any obligation to return the evidence at all, as in the case of unlawfully possessed controlled drugs. The Act provides specifically that anything which has been seized for the purposes of a criminal investigation may be retained (except where a photograph or copy would suffice) for use as evidence at a trial, or for forensic examination or for investigation in connection with any offence.

---

7   (1984) *Times* 1 August, CA.
8   *Allen and Others v Chief Constable of Cheshire Constabulary* (1988) *Times* 16 July.
9   In *Chief Constable of West Midlands Police v White* (1992) *Times* 25 March, the police were not permitted to retain money seized from a person who later pleaded guilty to a charge of selling intoxicating liquor without a licence. They were also unable to obtain an order for its retention under the Police (Property) Act 1897.

Similarly if there are reasonable grounds for believing that something has been obtained in consequence of the commission of an offence, it may be retained in order to establish its lawful owner.

Anything which was taken from a person in police detention or custody on the grounds that it might be used to:

a) cause physical injury to any person;
b) damage property;
c) interfere with evidence; or
d) assist in escape from police detention or lawful custody (see further p191)

should be returned when that person is no longer in police detention or the custody of a court, or is in the custody of a court but has been released on bail (s22(3)).

As bailees of seized property the police are under a duty to take reasonable care of the property.[10]

Where documents have been seized lawfully by the police, they may be produced by the police following a subpoena in civil proceedings without the consent of the person from whom the documents were seized. This would be the case if their production were necessary for a full and fair trial. Before disclosure of the documents, however, the police should give the owner a reasonable opportunity to raise objections.[11]

Nothing in the Act affects the power of a magistrates' court to make an order for the return of the property under the Police (Property) Act 1897 (s22(5)). Code B provides that a person claiming property seized by the police should be informed 'where appropriate' of the procedure under the 1897 Act (Note for Guidance 6A).

For specific powers of seizure in relation to cases of suspected serious fraud which must be read in conjunction with the above powers see above p97.

Powers of seizure under the Drug Trafficking Act 1994

A police officer who has entered any premises in pursuance of a warrant may seize any material, other than items subject to legal

---

10 *Sutcliffe v Chief Constable of West Yorkshire* (1995) *Times* 5 June. Here the police were not in fact held liable for damage to a car caused by vandals. The Chief Constable had discharged the burden on him of proving that he had taken reasonable care of the vehicle.

11 *Marcel v Commissioner of Police of the Metropolis* [1992] 1 All ER 72.

privilege and excluded material, which is likely to be of substantial value (whether by itself or together with other material) to the investigation for the purpose of which the warrant was issued (1994 Act s56(5)).

If the police seize legally privileged items or excluded material the seizure will be unlawful even if there were reasonable grounds for believing that the material was not in those categories. Once on the premises in pursuance of the warrant, the police have the general powers of seizure contained in 1984 Act s19 (see above).

Customs officers and police also have power under the Drug Trafficking Act 1994 s42 to seize cash above prescribed amounts, where the money is reasonably suspected of being the proceeds of, or intended for use in, drug trafficking and is being imported into or exported from the UK.

CHAPTER 5

Arrest

Before the passage of the Police and Criminal Evidence Act, there were numerous statutory powers of arrest,[1] as well as certain powers at common law. The 1984 Act rationalised the position and set out comprehensive provisions empowering a constable or civilian to arrest for an offence without a warrant. It also placed certain duties on constables who make an arrest, whether with or without a warrant, and whether under their statutory or common law powers.[2]

It has been pointed out in the Court of Appeal that the Act was not a codifying Act in the sense that it merely codified the law that existed at the time. It did make substantial changes in the law governing arrest, although some aspects of the previous law were left unaffected.[3]

All the previous police powers of arrest without warrant[4] were incorporated into the scheme of the Act, and, apart from powers preserved in Sch 2, all other statutory provisions, except one, were repealed by s26 of the Act. However, many new statutory powers of arrest have been created since the passage of the 1984 Act, especially by public order legislation, and it is a matter for regret that they were not also incorporated into the scheme created by the Act.

The powers of arrest without warrant that now exist can be grouped as follows:

1 Over one hundred powers of arrest without warrant were identified by the Royal Commission on Criminal Procedure. See 'Law and Procedure' vol (Cmnd 8092–1, HMSO 1981) Appendix 9.
2 See chapter 1 p8–11 on who can exercise such powers.
3 *Lewis and Another v Chief Constable of the South Wales Constabulary* [1991] 1 All ER 206 at 208 per Balcombe J.
4 For a discussion of the meaning of arrest and a statement of the old law, see H Levenson 'The concept of arrest' March 1981 *LAG Bulletin* 58–62.

a) at common law for breach of the peace;
b) for an arrestable offence under s24 of the Act;
c) for a non-arrestable offence in certain circumstances under s25 of the Act;
d) under an enactment specified in Sch 2 of the Act (where there is power to arrest without warrant in certain circumstances where the offence is not an arrestable offence);
e) for being guilty, in a public place, while drunk, of disorderly behaviour;[5]
f) to be fingerprinted under s27 of the Act;
g) for failure to answer to police bail under s46A of the Act;[6]
h) to provide a sample under s63A of the Act;[7]
i) of a young person for breaking conditions of remand;[8]
j) created by statute after the passage of the 1984 Act.

Unless an offence is an arrestable offence under s24 it cannot be a serious arrestable offence,[9] in respect of which the police are given enhanced powers. In particular, an offence for which a person can be arrested under s25 or one of the Sch 2 powers is not capable of being a serious arrestable offence.

An arrest for which there is no authority in law is an unlawful imprisonment.[10]

The 1984 Act does not say anything about what constitutes an arrest, but the common law rules are unchanged.[11] Persons are under arrest if it is made clear to them, by what is said and done, that they are not free to go.[12] In one case an arrest took place when a suspect was trapped by the automatic activation of door locks inside a motor vehicle especially adapted by the police.[13] There is no special form of words that must be used.[14] Whether an arrest has taken place is a

---

5 *DPP v Kitching* [1990] Crim LR 394.
6 Inserted by Criminal Justice and Public Order Act 1994 s29.
7 Inserted by Criminal Justice and Public Order Act 1994 s56.
8 Children and Young Persons Act 1969 s23A, inserted by Criminal Justice and Public Order Act 1994 s23.
9 Defined in s116 and further discussed on pp5–8.
10 See chapter 13 for remedies for this.
11 *Murray v Ministry of Defence* [1988] 2 All ER 521; *Lewis and Another v Chief Constable of South Wales Constabulary* [1991] 1 All ER 206.
12 *R v Inwood* [1973] 1 WLR 647, CA.
13 *Dawes v DPP* [1994] Crim LR 604.
14 *R v Brosch* [1988] Crim LR 743.

question of fact. It is not a legal concept.[15] The validity of the arrest is a separate matter.[16]

An arrest will usually occur by the constable touching the person being arrested, but this is not crucial to an arrest if the person submits to the arrest and goes with the police officer.[17]

Arrest under warrant

The Act does not create any new powers of arrest under a warrant. There are many statutory provisions enabling arrest warrants to be issued but the most significant is the Magistrates' Courts Act 1980 s1. The warrant is issued by a magistrate in respect of a person, aged at least 18, who is suspected of an offence which is indictable or punishable with imprisonment or where the address is insufficiently established for a summons to be served. (There are special provisions for those under the age of 18.) There must first be an information in writing, substantiated on oath.

Under the 1980 Act s117, the magistrate has a discretion whether to endorse the warrant for bail. If the warrant is so endorsed, the suspect must be released on bail as specified. The warrant remains in force until it is executed or withdrawn.[18] It may be executed anywhere in England and Wales by any constable of the police force to which it is directed or by any constable acting within his or her own police area.[19] Warrants to arrest for an offence and certain other warrants (listed in the 1984 Act s33) need not be in the possession of the constable at the time of the arrest but must be shown on demand to the person arrested as soon as practicable.[20] The provision in the 1984 Act s28(3) (see below pp135–137) seems to require that an arrested person is entitled to know whether the arrest is by warrant or otherwise.[21]

If a warrant has been endorsed for bail without sureties it is not necessary for the arrested person to be taken to the police station. A

---

15 *Spicer v Holt* [1976] 3 All ER 71; *Lewis and Another v Chief Constable of South Wales Constabulary* [1991] 1 All ER 206.
16 *R v Brosch* [1988] Crim LR 743.
17 *Alderson v Booth* [1969] 2 All ER 271.
18 Magistrates' Courts Act 1980 s125(1).
19 Ibid s125(2). For cross-border enforcement in Scotland or Northern Ireland see Criminal Justice and Public Order Act 1994 ss136 and 139.
20 Ibid s125(3) and (4) as amended by 1984 Act s33. Cf *DPP v Peacock* (1988) *Times* 10 November on warrant of arrest for non-payment of fine.
21 Cf Parker LJ in *R v Kulynycz* [1971] 1 QB 367; [1970] 3 All ER 881, CA.

person who is taken to the police station must be released as specified.[22]

A warrant issued in Scotland or Northern Ireland for the arrest of a person charged with an offence may be executed in England or Wales by any constable of any police force of the country of issue or of the country of execution as well as by any other persons within the directions in the warrant.[23]

Summary arrest for an arrestable offence

The 1984 Act uses the phrase 'summary arrest' in s24 to mean arrest without warrant and s24(1)–(3) lists the arrestable offences.

Arrestable offences

The following are arrestable offences under s24:

a) any offence for which the sentence is fixed by law. The only such offences at present are murder and treason[24] and possibly piracy;[25]
b) any offence for which a person aged 21 or over, not previously convicted, may be sentenced to a term of imprisonment for five years or more. This includes those offences of criminal damage of value not exceeding £5,000[26] which are triable and punishable summarily only. This category includes indecent assault,[27] and all offences of theft, including petty shoplifting. Certain additional firearms offences have recently become arrestable offences by virtue of an increase in the maximum penalty;[28]
c) any offence for which a person may be arrested under the customs and excise legislation listed in the Customs and Excise Manage-

---

22 Magistrates' Courts Act 1980 s117(3) as amended by 1984 Act s47(8).
23 Criminal Justice and Public Order Act 1994 s136(2). See s136(5) for the power to use reasonable force and s139 for the power to search on arrest.
24 Murder (Abolition of Death Penalty) Act 1965; Treason Act 1814 s1.
25 See discussion of Offences at Sea Act 1799 and Piracy Act 1837 in Smith and Hogan, *Criminal Law* (Butterworth, 7th edn, 1992).
26 Figure substituted in Magistrates' Courts Act 1980 s22(1) by Criminal Justice and Public Order Act 1994 s46. The provisions of 1980 Act s33 are ignored for the purposes of the arrest powers in 1984 Act.
27 Since the passage of Sexual Offences Act 1985 s3(3).
28 Penalties increased by the Criminal Justice and Public Order Act 1994 s157 and Sch 8 Part III.

ment Act 1979 s1(1). This provision gives the police powers to assist customs officers, who have separate powers of arrest;

d) offences under the Official Secrets Acts 1920 and 1989 which do not carry a penalty of imprisonment for five years or more. This does not apply to certain summary offences under the 1989 Act s8;

e) causing prostitution of women contrary to the Sexual Offences Act 1956 s22;

f) procuration of a girl under 21 contrary to the Sexual Offences Act 1956 s23;

g) taking a motor vehicle or conveyance without authority or driving or being carried on such a vehicle contrary to the Theft Act 1968 s12;[29]

h) going equipped for burglary, theft or cheat contrary to the Theft Act 1968 s25(1);

i) throwing missiles, indecent or racialist chanting, or going onto the playing area at a designated football match contrary to the Football (Offences) Act 1991;

j) publishing obscene matter contrary to the Obscene Publications Act 1959 s2;

k) taking, permitting, distributing, showing, possessing or advertising any indecent photograph of a child contrary to the Protection of Children Act 1978 s1;

l) unauthorised selling or offering a ticket for a designated football match[30] contrary to the Criminal Justice and Public Order Act 1994 s166;

m) publishing material likely to stir up racial hatred contrary to the Public Order Act 1986 s19;

n) touting in a public place for certain hire car services contrary to the Criminal Justice and Public Order Act 1994 s167;

o) an attempt to commit any of the above offences except (g); [31]

---

29 This extends to the aggravated offence under Theft Act 1968 s12A inserted by the Aggravated Vehicle-Taking Act 1992.

30 This offence may be extended by statutory instrument to certain other sporting events pursuant to the Criminal Justice and Public Order Act 1994 s166(6).

31 Attempt is defined in Criminal Attempts Act 1981 s1. By virtue of Criminal Justice Act 1988 s37, when read in conjunction with the 1981 Act, there is no longer any such offence as an attempt to commit an offence under Theft Act 1968 s12. There is probably no offence of attempting to commit the aggravated offence contrary to the Theft Act 1968 s12A. (See the discussion by JN Spencer in [1992] Crim LR 699–705 at 701–2.' Also, this seems to come within the 'state of affairs' exception to attempt identified by Smith and Hogan in their *Criminal Law* 7th edition, Butterworths 1992 at p315).

p) conspiracy to commit any of the offences in (a) to (n) above. Conspiracy to defraud is an arrestable offence by virtue of the maximum penalty it carries.[32] Statutory conspiracy contrary to the Criminal Law Act 1977 s1 carries the same maximum penalty as the substantive offence.[33] Common law conspiracy to corrupt public morals[34] or outrage public decency[35] carries a maximum penalty of life imprisonment and accordingly is an arrestable offence;

q) inciting, aiding, abetting, counselling or procuring the commission of any of the offences in (a) to (n) above.

Many police powers are exercisable only in relation to an arrestable offence and it is therefore important to be able to identify easily which offences are arrestable.

The powers of arrest granted by s24 are not subject to the restrictions set out in s25 (see below) and can be exercised even when it would be practicable to proceed by way of summons.

Summary arrest by any person

Any person may arrest without warrant anyone who is, or whom that person has reasonable grounds for suspecting to be, committing an arrestable offence.[36]

This and the following power are most likely to be exercised by constables and store detectives but are available to anyone. If the person arrested was not in fact committing an arrestable offence, then reasonable grounds for suspicion must have existed at the time of arrest for it to be lawful. The meaning of 'reasonable grounds for suspicion' is discussed below.[37] The requirement for reasonable

---

32 Ten years' imprisonment under the Criminal Justice Act 1987 s12(3).
33 Criminal Law Act 1977 s1 as amended defines statutory conspiracy and s3 of that Act provides for penalties.
34 See *Shaw v DPP* [1962] AC 220, HL.
35 See *Knuller v DPP* [1973] AC 435, HL.
36 1984 Act s24(4). There is a similar power under Theft Act 1978 s3(4) governing arrest for committing or attempting the offence of making off without payment. This power has been removed from constables by virtue of 1984 Act s26 but seems to remain for non-constables, eg, store detectives, shopkeepers, taxi-drivers. Thus, in this context constables have fewer powers of arrest than other people.
37 See the discussion and cases cited in Clayton and Tomlinson: *Civil Actions against the Police*, (Sweet & Maxwell 1992) p171–178.

grounds applies to all the powers of summary arrest under s24, but under s24(4) the suspicion must be that the offence is being committed at the moment of arrest. For many offences it is unclear whether the offence consists of a single or continuing act. This can cause difficulties with, eg, shoplifting. If theft is a single act, an arrest could not be justified under s24(4) unless it took place at the moment of dishonest appropriation – and this is notoriously difficult to pinpoint.[38] However, most arrests by store detectives would probably come under s24(5).

Section 24(5) provides that where an arrestable offence has been committed, any person may arrest without warrant anyone who is, or whom they have reasonable grounds for suspecting to be, guilty of the offence. Hence an offence must actually have been committed. Thus, for example, if a store detective sees someone take some goods and subsequently leave the shop without paying for them, and on reasonable grounds arrests him or her for theft, and that person is acquitted because of lack of necessary intention, then the arrest will have been unlawful.[39] If an offence has been committed by someone else, the arrest is lawful if there are reasonable grounds to suspect the person arrested.[40]

Summary arrest by constables

A constable with reasonable grounds for suspecting that an arrestable offence has been committed, may arrest without warrant anyone whom that constable has reasonable grounds for suspecting to be guilty of the offence (s24(6)). The extra power given to a constable here over other people under s24(4) is that the constable need only suspect that an arrestable offence has been committed; it need not actually have been committed.

A constable may arrest without warrant any person who is, or whom the constable has reasonable grounds for suspecting to be, about to commit an arrestable offence (s24(7)). The additional power given to police constables in this subsection, over other persons under s24(4), is that it relates to the future. The arrested person must be about to commit an offence or the constable must have reasonable grounds to suspect that that is so. It should be noted that no offence will have been committed here (not even an attempt, for attempts are

38 *R v Morris, Anderton v Burnside* [1984] AC 320; [1983] 3 All ER 288, HL.
39 *R v Self* [1992] 3 All ER 476, CA.
40 *Walters v WH Smith and Sons Ltd* [1914] KB 595.

governed by the power of arrest in s24(6)). Therefore, the arrest cannot be followed by a charge. However, the person arrested could be brought before a court with a view to the court binding over that person to be of good behaviour, which the court has power to do 'in circumstances where there is apprehension that the defendant may do anything contrary to law'.[41] Such an arrest will not be subject to the provisions of s25 and it is not an arrest 'for an offence' (see pp151–152 for the consequences of this).

Not only must there be reasonable grounds for suspicion; the constable must also actually suspect (though not necessarily believe) that the person to be arrested is guilty and must believe that the reasonable grounds for suspicion exist.[42]

A constable who restrains a person in the the mistaken belief that the person is under arrest is not acting in the execution of duty.[43]

An arrest by a constable is unlawful if it is based on reasonable suspicion of having committed an arrestable offence, but the arrested person can prove that there is no possibility of a charge being made.[44]

A constable does not have a duty to arrest a person suspected in connection with arrestable offences. It is always open to proceed by way of summons but, unlike arrests under s25, there is no assumption that the summons procedure will or should be adopted.

Reasonable grounds for suspicion

The meaning of 'reasonable grounds for suspicion' has been discussed more generally above at p14.

Lord Devlin has stated that:

> suspicion in its ordinary meaning is a state of conjecture or surmise where proof is lacking; 'I suspect but I cannot prove' . . . suspicion can take into account matters that could not be put in evidence at all . . . previous convictions . . . .[45]

41 *R v Sandbach ex p Williams* [1935] All ER Rep 680. See generally B Harris and B Gibson, *Criminal Jurisdiction of Magistrates* (Longman, 11th edn, 1988).

42 *R v Redman* [1994] Crim LR 914; *Chapman v DPP* (1988) 89 Cr App R 190, CA (relying in part on the pre-1984 Act case of *Castorina v Chief Constable of Surrey* (1988) *Times* 15 June, CA); *Siddiqui v Swain* [1979] RTR 454; but cf *Kynaston v DPP* (1987) 87 Cr App R 200. See also the analysis of *Redman* by Jo Cooper in February 1995 *Legal Action* 17.

43 *Kerr v DPP* [1995] Crim LR 394, QBD.

44 *Plange v Chief Constable of South Humberside Police* [1992] *Times* 23 March, CA.

45 *Shaaban Bin Hussein v Chong Fook Kam* [1970] AC 942; [1969] 3 All ER 1626, PC.

The general idea is that the circumstances are such that a reasonable, unprejudiced, dispassionate person would consider that there were grounds for suspicion.

The belief in the existence of reasonable grounds need not be based on anything that the constable has witnessed personally and can, for example, be based on information from another constable, from the police computer or from a member of the public, but the information itself must be based on reasonable grounds for suspicion.[46]

The belief could be based on information from an informer who is known to be trustworthy, but such information should be treated with very considerable reserve and the constable should hesitate before regarding such information by itself as the basis of the reasonable grounds for suspicion.[47]

It is irrelevant that the constable does not personally believe a person to be guilty. The extent to which the police might be obliged to make further inquiries once a constable believes that there are reasonable grounds for suspicion is unclear. However, there is a discretion whether an arrest should be made (as opposed to ignoring the matter, making further enquiries, or proceeding by way of summons) and this discretion must be exercised on the same basis as the exercise of any administrative discretion.[48]

Arrest for breach of the peace at common law

Section 26 of the 1984 Act repealed all statutory powers of arrest which were not expressly preserved by the Act. Section 24(1)(b) brought common law offences within the definition of an arrestable offence. The remaining pre-Act power of arrest which is not mentioned in the Act is the common law power of a constable to arrest for breach of the peace.[49] Such arrests are subject to the provisions of s28 but, unless amounting to an arrest for an offence (see below), are not subject to the restrictions in s25 (see below). The Act specifically provides that the s25 restrictions apply only to the power of arrest

---

46 *Moss v Jenkins* [1975] RTR 25; *McKee v Chief Constable of Northern Ireland* [1984] 1 WLR 1358; *Siddiqui v Swain* [1979] RTR 454.
47 *Jones v Chief Constable of South Wales* (1991) *Independent* 29 April, CA.
48 See the discussion on p12–13 in chapter 1 and see further Clayton and Tomlinson op cit pp174–178.
49 This power is preserved by Public Order Act 1986 s40(4).

conferred by s25 (s25(6)). The power of arrest for breach of the peace conferred by common law is unaffected by s25.[50]

Professor Leigh summarises the power of arrest as follows:

A constable has power at common law to arrest without warrant any person whom he sees breaking the peace or who so conducts himself that he causes a breach of the peace to be reasonably apprehended. If no breach of the peace is imminent the most that a constable can do is to admonish the persons concerned to keep the peace. A constable cannot justify an arrest after the breach of the peace has terminated unless he is in fresh pursuit of the offenders or reasonably apprehends a renewal of the breach of the peace.[51]

These powers are also possessed by a private citizen and according to the Court of Appeal:

. . . there is a breach of the peace whenever harm is actually done or is likely to be done to a person or in his presence to his property or a person is in fear of being so harmed through an assault, an affray, a riot, an unlawful assembly or other disturbance . . . .[52]

In a civil action against the police for wrongful arrest, where the arrest was to prevent an imminent breach of the peace, it is for the judge and not for any jury in the case to decide whether the conduct of the defendant was reasonable, although it is for the jury to resolve any conflict of fact.[53]

A constable trying to speak to a person in pursuance of the preservation of the peace or the prevention of or investigation into a crime is acting in the execution of duty even if the power to arrest has not arisen.[54]

Statutory powers of arrest for breach of the peace are dealt with on pp133–134. In a prosecution where the lawfulness of an arrest is in issue it is important to identify clearly the power of arrest on which a constable was relying.[55]

---

50 *Albert v Lavin* [1983] 3 All ER 878, HL. See also *McConnell v Chief Constable of Greater Manchester Police* [1990] 1 All ER 423, CA re private premises.

51 L Leigh, *Police Powers in England and Wales* (Butterworth, 2nd edn 1985) p184 and cases cited therein.

52 *R v Howell* [1981] 3 All ER 383 at 388–389. There is no power of arrest at common law for abusing a constable: *Nawrot and Shaler v DPP* [1988] Crim LR 107. Cf Public Order Act 1986 s5(4).

53 *Kelly v Chief Constable of Hampshire and Another* (1993) *Independent* 25 March, CA, applying *Dallison v Cafferey* [1965] 1 QB 348.

54 *Weight v Long* [1986] Crim LR 746.

55 *R v Redman* [1994] Crim LR 914, CA.

Arrest subject to conditions

Power of arrest

A general power of arrest for offences is provided by s25 of the 1984 Act.[56] The only exceptions from the restrictions associated with this power are the powers of arrest:

a) for arrestable offences;
b) at common law for breach of the peace;
c) for those offences listed in the 1984 Act Sch 2; and
d) created by some post-1984 provisions.

Section 25 gives the police a general power to arrest for any non-arrestable criminal offence no matter how petty or minor (other than those listed above) but only if at least one of the general arrest conditions listed in s25(3) is satisfied, and it appears therefore that service of a summons is impracticable or inappropriate. There is no power to arrest if none of the arrest conditions is satisfied and any purported arrest would be unlawful (see chapter 13 on remedies for unlawful arrest).

The assumption in s25 is that the police should proceed by way of summons rather than arrest, and if they do so the person will not be taken into custody but will in due course be given a time and date on which to appear at a particular court. A constable can exercise the power of arrest under s25 only if:

a) the constable has reasonable grounds for suspecting that an offence has been, or is being, committed or attempted; and
b) the constable has reasonable grounds to suspect a person of having committed or attempted, or of being in the course of committing or attempting to commit that offence; and
c) it appears to the constable that service of a summons is impracticable or inappropriate; and
d) the impracticability or inappropriateness is because one of the general arrest conditions is satisfied (s25(1) and (2)).

These headings are considered in detail below.

'Reasonable grounds'

The meaning of 'reasonable grounds to suspect' has been discussed generally (p14) and in relation to arrest specifically (pp118–119).

---

56 See *Anna Lawson* 'Whither the General Arrest Conditions?' [1993] Crim LR 567.

The test of reasonable grounds is an objective one and can be challenged in the courts. However, the test of 'appears to him' in (c) above is a subjective one. It depends on the constable's own perceptions and cannot be challenged unless it is alleged that the constable has acted in bad faith or (possibly) taken into account irrelevant considerations.[57]

It is not sufficient that the offence is or has actually been committed or attempted or that service of the summons is impractical or inappropriate. The constable must actually have the state of mind required by the wording of s25.[58]

'Has been, or is being, committed or attempted'

The power of arrest under s25 clearly does not arise if the constable suspects that an offence will be committed in the future even if one of the general arrest conditions is satisfied. The constable must have reasonable grounds for suspicion that an offence has been, or is being, committed or attempted ((a) above). There must be at least an attempt as defined in the Criminal Attempts Act 1981 s1 and not merely some action or contemplation that falls short of an attempt.

An attempt to commit a summary offence (ie, an offence not triable before a jury) is not itself an offence under the 1981 Act. There could still be an arrest under s25 of the 1984 Act (since there is an attempt to commit an offence) but this would not be an arrest for an offence. See pp151–152 for the consequences of this.

'Constable'

An arrest under s25 can be carried out only by a constable (see (a), (b) and (c) above). A non-constable may arrest only for an arrestable offence under s24 or in pursuance of a specific statutory power. See pp8–11 for the meaning of constable.

General arrest conditions

The general arrest conditions ((d) above) are as follows.

Name unknown (s25(3)(a))

This covers the case where someone refuses to give a name, but only

---

57 See eg, *Smith v East Elloe RDC* [1956] AC 736, HL.
58 *Edwards v DPP* (1993) 88 Cr App R 166; [1993] Crim LR 854, QBD. This case involved the arrest of person B for intervening in the arrest of A, who was in turn intervening in a police search of three others. The arrest of A was unlawful because there was no power to arrest for the reason given by the police at the time of the arrest. This rendered unlawful the arrest of B.

where it cannot be readily ascertained by the constable. 'Readily' is not defined in the Act. It is a question of fact to be decided by the court whether or not a name can be readily ascertained. There is no power to search without arrest in order to establish identity[59] and there is no power to detain a person refusing to give a name, without making a formal arrest. In practice, an arrest would usually follow a refusal to give a name, but the arrested person would have to be told for what offence s/he was being arrested, not just that it was because s/he had failed to give a name.[60]

Name doubted (s25(3)(b))

The power to arrest arises where the constable has reasonable grounds for doubting that the name given is the person's real name. This is an objective test – the grounds must appear reasonable to a reasonable person. They must be grounded in something concrete – an inconsistent document, recognition by the constable, an unlikely name (eg, Mickey Mouse) and so on. It is insufficient for a constable to base an arrest on the experience of offenders generally giving false details of name and address.[61] The Act does not list any criteria for deciding whether the name is real. Certainly it would appear unreasonable to doubt a name merely because it is foreign or unusual.

There is no power to detain a person giving a false name, short of making a formal arrest.

Failure to furnish a satisfactory address for service of a summons (s25(3)(c))

The power to arrest arises if the person fails to furnish an address (this is a straight question of fact) or if the constable has reasonable grounds for doubting whether an address furnished is a satisfactory address for service.

'Reasonable grounds' is an objective test and must be based on something concrete, eg, the officer believing that the address is non-existent. An address is a satisfactory address for service if it appears to the constable that the relevant person will be at it for a sufficiently long period for it to be possible (not merely practicable) to serve him

---

59 *R v Eeet* [1983] Crim LR 806.
60 *Nicholas v Parsonage* [1987] RTR 199, sub nom *Nicholas v DPP* [1987] Crim LR 474.
61 *G v DPP* [1989] Crim LR 150. The court seems to have reached the correct decision in the case but by faulty reasoning. See the commentaries by Professor Birch at [1989] Crim LR 150 and in the article by Anna Lawson op cit.

or her with a summons, or that some other person specified by the suspect will accept service (s25(4)).

Clearly the address given need not be the suspect's own address. It could be that of a friend, relative, solicitor, women's refuge, social worker, probation officer, or place of employment or study. Obviously, some people will find it difficult to satisfy the police on this basis, eg, squatters, homeless people, tramps, gypsies and travellers. A constable's decision that an address is not a satisfactory address for service must be reasonable (s25(3)(c)(ii)). It is difficult to see how a constable can establish whether an address given is satisfactory. There is no power to detain while it is being checked, although possibly the suspect will wait voluntarily, knowing that arrest might be the alternative. Would the suspect's inability to provide proof of address justify an arrest? It seems that the onus is on the constable to show reason to doubt that it is satisfactory. Since 1 July 1991 it has been possible to serve process in a foreign state under the provisions of the Criminal Justice (International Co-operation) Act 1990. This provides some protection from unnecessary arrest to those who reside outside the jurisdiction.[62]

Detention without arrest

There is no power in the Act enabling constables to detain a person without arrest in order to investigate an offence. The touching of a person in order to engage attention is lawful, although the degree of physical contact must be no greater than is reasonably necessary in the circumstances; physical restraint for these purposes is not lawful.[63] If a person whose attention has been obtained then refuses to speak, or runs away, the constable would be able to arrest the suspect under s25 provided that the name and address of the suspect were unknown to the constable, or another arrest condition were satisfied. Technically, anybody who waits without being arrested is doing so voluntarily and may go at any time unless arrested.

The conditions dealt with so far relate to the impracticability of serving a summons. The remaining conditions relate to its inappropriateness because of the need to prevent some consequence.

---

62 See D Birch 'Powers of arrest and detention' [1985] Crim LR 545, where she suggests 'as rather a long shot' (pp549–550) that an arrested person must be told that it is possible to give another person's address for service.
63 *Collins v Wilcock* [1984] 3 All ER 374.

Preventative arrest

Like the other general arrest conditions, the conditions for preventative arrest apply only once conditions (a) to (d) on p121 are satisfied. An arrest cannot take place under this power unless it is reasonably suspected that the arrested person is committing or attempting or has committed or attempted an offence.

The constable must have reasonable grounds for believing that the arrest is necessary to prevent one of the consequences discussed below. This is an objective test, and a court can decide whether the constable has acted reasonably. Other steps to prevent the consequences must be tried first, if practicable, such as giving the suspect an opportunity to stop the behaviour, otherwise the arrest cannot be said to be necessary. The consequences to be prevented are as follows:

Causing physical injury to self or another (s25(3)(d)(i))

Physical injury is not defined in the Act, and must await the attention of the courts before it is clear what is covered by this provision. The injury need not be serious, and the other on whom it is to be inflicted could be the arresting officer. This should be seen in the light of the right to use reasonable force to resist an unlawful arrest (see p325). Nevertheless, an aggressive response to a police enquiry could justify a police belief that arrest is necessary. A suspect threatening to injure him or herself can also be arrested, even if the injury threatened is minor.

Suspect suffering physical injury (s25(3)(d)(ii))

This condition is to protect the suspect from injury by another, perhaps in revenge for the offence (or where the suspect is, eg, drunk on the road in the path of oncoming traffic). Presumably physical injury has the same meaning here as in the previous paragraph.

Causing loss of or damage to property (s25(3)(d)(iii))

Again this may be trivial. The property under threat could even belong to the person arrested. 'Loss or damage' is not further defined and is not linked to definitions under the Criminal Damage Act 1971. Writing on walls could be regarded as damage to property. Property is not defined in the Act, although earlier drafts of the Bill gave it the same meaning as in the Theft Act 1968 s4.

Committing an offence against public decency (s25(3)(d)(iv))

Many such offences carry a power of arrest unrestricted by s25 and these are summarised on p115 above. The Act does not define what is meant by an offence against public decency. Clearly the anticipated behaviour must constitute a criminal offence and it must be expected to occur in public – at least in the presence of others. It is unlikely that the provision could justify an arrest on private premises unless there is a display visible to the public. Offences against public decency presumably include indecent exposure, soliciting by female prostitutes and male homosexual importuning.[64] It would clearly include overt sexual activity such as intercourse or genital contact, and could include gross indecency between men. Gross indecency does not require physical contact; it is enough if it can be said that two men put themselves in such a position that it could be said that a grossly indecent exhibition is going on.[65] It has been suggested that if two males kissed each other in a way that was 'immoral and unnatural' that might be indecent but it would not be grossly indecent.[66] If it is not grossly indecent it is not an offence and the power of arrest cannot be invoked. Lesbian sexual activity does not constitute an offence (unless it involves a child or the absence of consent) and cannot be the occasion of an arrest under this provision. It might be said to constitute a breach of the peace offence and in such a case any arrest would have to be under the breach of the peace provisions. If behaviour between two or more people went so far as to outrage public decency or corrupt public morals[67] it could constitute an arrestable offence under s24, in which case the s25 restrictions would not apply.[68]

It must be emphasised that an arrest cannot take place under s25

64 In *DPP v Bull* [1994] 4 All ER 411 the Divisional Court confirmed that soliciting contrary to the Street Offences Act 1956 s1 can only be committed by a female, and importuning contrary to s32 of that Act is a near-equivalent offence that can be committed by a male. Section 41 of that Act confers on anyone a power to arrest without warrant a person found committing an offence contrary to s32. However, by virtue of s26 and Sch 6 para 9 of the 1984 Act, a constable can only exercise this power in accordance with s25 of the 1984 Act. Thus non-constables (such as shopping precinct security guards or park attendants) have a wider power of arrest in these circumstances than do police officers.

65 *R v Hunt* [1950] 2 All ER 291, CA.

66 See generally Smith and Hogan, op cit n25.

67 *Shaw v DPP* [1962] AC 220, HL, and *Knuller v DDP* [1973] AC 435, HL.

68 For this reason the authors cannot accept the view put forward in Halsbury's Statutes that the meaning of 'offence against public decency' relates only to outraging public decency – see 1994 Re-issue Vol 12 p875.

unless an offence is already suspected. There cannot be an arrest under this provision merely for anticipated behaviour, nor if there is a way of preventing it other than by arrest, nor if there is no chance of the offence recurring. The power to arrest on this basis is limited by the requirement that the conduct must take place:

in circumstances where members of the public going about their normal business cannot readily avoid the person to be arrested (s25(5)).

This test is not further defined in the Act.

Causing an unlawful obstruction of the highway (s25(3)(d)(v))

This power replaces and restricts the power of arrest for obstruction given by the Highways Act 1980 s137(2) (repealed by s26(1) of the Act) which did not require that arrest be necessary to remove the obstruction.

Because of the requirement of necessity to prevent further obstruction, it is unlikely that an arrest could take place unless a constable believes on reasonable grounds that the person has refused to move the obstruction and that the arrest will remove it. Thus, someone holding a public meeting on the highway who refuses to move could be arrested but not someone who had parked illegally or left a barrow in the highway, because the arrest would not prevent the continuation of the obstruction.[69]

'Obstruction' is not defined in the 1984 Act but its meaning under the highways legislation has been discussed in a number of cases.[70]

The obstruction prevented must be of the highway. Whether a place is part of the highway is a question of law. It has been held, for example, that the subways of Piccadilly Circus Underground station in London are not part of the highway.[71]

The obstruction must be unlawful. Anybody who had a licence to trade on the highway, or whose obstruction was not wilful (eg, because they were unconscious) would not be causing an unlawful obstruction.[72]

To protect a child or other vulnerable person (s25(3)(e))

The protection must be from the person who is to be arrested. The harm to be protected against is not specified. It is presumably wider than just physical injury (otherwise the power would add nothing to

69 *Arrowsmith v Jenkins* [1963] 2 QB 561.
70 See, eg, *Mounsey v Campbell* [1983] RTR 36; *Cooper v Metropolitan Police Commissioner* (1986) 82 Cr App R 238, DC.
71 (1976) 126 NLJ 50 (letter).
72 Highways Act 1980 s137.

s25(3)(d)) and could include danger of exploitation for sexual purposes. The power is additional to the arrest powers preserved under children's and mental health legislation (Sch 2).

'Vulnerable' is not defined in the Act. In the Commons committee the minister said:[73]

> It means someone who is particularly susceptible to injury, somebody who is at risk and particularly at risk. In other words, it is someone who is in need of protection.

This circular definition does not help very much. Since the constable must have reasonable grounds for believing that the arrest is necessary, in the first place the constable will have to decide whether someone is vulnerable (or is a child), and must be able to justify this decision to a court.

Preserved statutory powers of arrest without warrant

Apart from the powers contained in or expressly preserved by the Act all other statutory powers of arrest by constables without warrant or court order are abolished by s26. This includes powers under local Acts, and covers arrest for an offence and arrest other than for an offence. Of course this does not include powers created after the passage of the Act (31 October 1984).

The repeal does not apply to powers of arrest given to non-constables by specific legislation, eg, to gamekeepers under the Night Poaching Act 1828 s2 or to railway officers under the Regulation of Railways Act 1889.[74] Schedule 2 of the 1984 Act (reproduced in appendix 1) lists a number of statutory powers of arrest which remain in existence although they pre-date the 1984 Act. They deal mainly with persons unlawfully at large, immigration offences and offences relating to animals. There is also a special provision which preserves the power of arrest under Representation of the People Act 1983 Sch 1 r36.[75]

The Sch 2 powers are not subject to the conditions set out in s25, but many of them carry other conditions. For example, the powers of arrest for trespass under the Criminal Law Act 1977 can be exercised only by a constable in uniform.

The Sch 2 offences are not necessarily arrestable offences within s24, and if they do not relate to offences punishable by five years'

73 HC Standing Committee J, col 574, 8 February 1983.
74 *Moberly v Alsop* (1992) *Guardian* 8 January, QBD.
75 Representation of the People Act 1985 s25(1).

imprisonment they cannot be exercised by a civilian, and they do not attract the wider powers available only in the case of a serious arrestable offence.

Powers of arrest under the prevention of terrorism legislation are considered in chapter 8.

Arrest without warrant for fingerprinting (s27)

The circumstances in which fingerprints may be taken at a police station are set out in s61 (see pp228–230). Section 27 is aimed at those people who appeared on a summons and were not taken to a police station.

A constable may arrest someone without warrant in order to have his/her fingerprints taken at a police station in certain circumstances:

a) the person must have been convicted of a recordable offence (s27(1)(a)). Recordable offences are specified in regulations approved by Parliament (s27(4) and (5)). They include all offences punishable with imprisonment, loitering or soliciting for the purposes of prostitution, improper use of a public telecommunications system and tampering with motor vehicles;[76]

b) the person must not at any time have been in police detention for the offence (s27(1)(b)). 'Police detention' is defined in s118(2) (see p151);

c) the person must not have had fingerprints taken either in the course of the investigation of *that* offence by the police, or since the conviction in connection with any matter (s27(1)(c)); and

d) the person has failed to comply with a s27 requirement (s27(3)). Such a requirement may be made by any constable (not just a constable who dealt with the offence) and must be made within one month of the date of conviction (s27(1)). It is the date of conviction that is relevant, not the date of sentence if that is different.[77] Thus the requirement can be made before sentence but not before conviction (in some cases the month will have passed before sentence is imposed).

A s27 requirement is that the person attend a police station in order to have fingerprints taken. The requirement must give the

---

76 National Police Records (Recordable Offences) Regulations 1985 SI No 1941. See also Code D Note for Guidance 3A.

77 *R v Drew* [1985] 2 All ER 1061, CA.

person a period of at least seven days within which to attend but may specify a time of day on which to attend (although not which particular day)(s27(2)). It is not clear whether the seven days specified in the requirement must all be within the one-month period.

There is no provision for the request to be in writing, nor for any reason to be given for the request. However, the arrest will be subject to the requirements of s28 (pp135–137) concerning reasons for the arrest.

A person arrested under s27 must be taken to a police station. The fingerprints may be taken without consent (s61(6)). There is no power to detain a person whose fingerprints have been taken.

An arrest for fingerprinting which does not comply with the conditions set out in s27 is unlawful and the arrested person will have the appropriate remedies (see chapters 12 and 13).

Arrest without warrant for failure to answer police bail (s46A)

This power of arrest was inserted into the 1984 Act by Criminal Justice and Public Order Act 1994 s29. A constable may arrest without warrant any person who, having been released on bail under Part IV of the 1984 Act subject to a duty to attend at a police station, fails to attend at the appointed time (s46A(1)). This applies whether the release was before or after the commencement of the new power (s29(5) of the 1994 Act). The person arrested must actually have been released and have failed to surrender. It is not sufficient for a constable merely to believe or suspect that this has happened or that the person arrested was the person released on bail.

As soon as practicable after the arrest a person who is so arrested must be taken to the police station to which the surrender should have been made (s46A(2)). Such an arrest is then treated as an arrest for the offence for which bail had been granted (s46A(3) of the 1984 Act and s 29(4) of the 1994 Act). Thus, for example, the provisions of s30 of the 1984 Act (see p138–142) and s 31 (see p143) apply. The application of s30 is subject to s46A(2) above. The legislation does not specify what should happen if the police station to which the surrender should have been made is closed.

Arrest without warrant to have a sample taken (s63A)

This power of arrest was inserted into the 1984 Act by Criminal Justice and Public Order Act 1994 s 56.

The circumstances in which samples may be taken are set out in ss62 and 63 of the 1984 Act (see p230–236). The power of arrest without warrant in s63A arises when there is a failure to comply with a requirement to attend a police station to have a sample taken. This power is aimed at the following three groups of people during the time when they are neither in police detention nor held in custody by the police on the authority of a court:

a) those who have been charged with a recordable offence or informed that they might be reported for such an offence and have not had a sample taken in the course of the investigation of the offence by the police, or if they have had a sample taken, it was either unsuitable or insufficient for 'the same means of analysis', and

b) those who have been convicted of a recordable offence and have not had a sample taken since conviction, and

c) those who have had a sample taken before or since conviction but it was either unsuitable or insufficient for 'the same means of analysis'.

The meaning of 'the same means of analysis' is not specified but presumably refers to the means of analysis that is now being proposed. The meaning of 'conviction' and of 'recordable offence' has been explained in the discussion of arrest for fingerprinting (see p129 above).

Any constable may, within the allowed period, require a person who is in one of the above categories, and is neither in police detention nor in custody on the authority of a court, to attend a police station in order to have a sample taken (s63A(4)). The allowed period for those in category (a) is one month beginning with the date of charge, or one month beginning with the date on which the officer investigating the offence is informed of the unsuitability or insufficiency of the sample (s63A(5)(a)). Whether or not intended by the drafting of this power, this provision seems to allow an indefinite period where someone has been informed that he will be reported for an arrestable offence but has not been charged. Once he has been charged, the police have one month in which to make the requirement. The allowed period in categories (b) and (c) is one month beginning with the date of conviction or one month beginning with the date on which the officer in charge of the police station from which the investigation was conducted is informed of the unsuitability or insufficiency of the sample (s63A(5)(b)). Again, this seems to leave an open-ended power so that in principle a person who has been convicted of a recordable offence is at indefinite risk of being subject to a requirement whenever it is realised that further analysis is desirable.

However, section 63A does not create any power to take samples, so that in practice the exercise of the power to require attendance is limited by the constraints on the power to take samples which are found in Part V of the 1984 Act (see pp230–236).

The requirement to attend must give the person at least seven days within which to attend and may direct attendance at a specified time of day or between specified times of day (although not on a particular day) (s63A(6)). There is no provision for the request to be in writing nor for any reason to be given for the request.

Any constable may arrest without warrant a person who has failed to comply with a s63A(4) requirement (s63A(7)). The arrest will be subject to the requirements of s28 concerning the giving of reasons for the arrest (see p135–137). There is no power to detain further pursuant to this arrest once the sample has been taken, and an arrest to have a sample taken which does not comply with the conditions set out in s 63A is unlawful and the person arrested will have the appropriate remedies (see chapter 13).

Arrest of a young person for breaking conditions of remand

A person who has been remanded or committed to local authority care, and in respect of whom conditions under the Children and Young Persons Act 1969 s23(7) or (10) have been imposed, may be arrested without warrant by a constable who has reasonable grounds for suspecting that that person has broken any of those conditions.[78] If such a person is arrested within 24 hours of the time when s/he is due to be brought before the court, then no special steps need be taken in connection with arranging a court hearing. In other cases the person must be brought as soon as practicable before a JP for the area in which the arrest took place, and in any event within 24 hours (discounting Christmas Day, Good Friday, or any Sunday).[79]

78 Children and Young Persons Act 1969 s23A, inserted by the Criminal Justice and Public Order Act 1994 s23.
79 Ibid s23(2).

It is important to note that the initial requirement is to bring the person before a court as soon as practicable (not as soon as *reasonably* practicable). If it is practicable to do this before 24 hours have elapsed, or on a Sunday or bank holiday, then this must be done. If necessary, special hearings will have to be convened. The 24-hour rule provides a safety net and can only be relied on if it has not been practicable to bring the person before a JP at an earlier stage.

The JP must determine whether any condition has been broken. If no condition has been broken, then the remand or committal continues subject to the same conditions as previously. If a condition has been broken, the JP must remand the person and s23 of the 1969 Act applies as though the person were charged with or convicted of the offence for which the original remand or committal had been made.[80]

Post-1984 statutory powers of arrest

General

Many new powers of arrest have been created since the passage of the 1984 Act, especially in the field of public order. The extent of each of these powers is defined by the relevant statutory provision, each of which sets out the circumstances in which the power is to be exercised.[81] New powers of arrest under the Criminal Justice and Public Order Act 1994 and powers under road traffic legislation are set out below.

The Criminal Justice and Public Order Act 1994

a) A constable in uniform who reasonably suspects that a person is in the process of committing an offence under any of the following sections of the 1994 Act may arrest that person without a warrant:

s61 trespass in connection with intending residence (power to arrest in s61(5))

s63 trespass in connection with a rave (power in s63(8))

s65 breach of direction not to proceed to a rave (power in s 65(5))

s68 aggravated trespass (power in s68(4))

---

80 Ibid s23(3).
81 See Sporting Events (Control of Alcohol etc) Act 1985 s7 and Public Order Act 1986 ss3, 4, 5, 12, 13, 14, 18(1) and 39(2) and Sch 2 para 1(2).

s69 breach of direction to leave an aggravated trespass (power in s69(5))

s76 trespass during an interim possession order (power in s76(7))

b) A constable in uniform may arrest without warrant anyone who is or whom s/he reasonably suspects to be guilty of committing an offence of trespass during the currency of an interim possession order contrary to s76 (s76(7)).

c) Section 70 of the 1994 Act inserts new sections 14A, 14B and 14C into the Public Order Act 1986. These deal with powers and offences in relation to trespassory assemblies. By virtue of s14B(4) and 14C(4) a constable in uniform may arrest without warrant anyone he reasonably suspects to be in the process of committing an offence under s14B or s14(C).

d) Section 73 of the 1994 Act inserts a substitute s7 into the Criminal Law Act 1977. This creates an offence relating to adverse occupation of residential premises. A constable in uniform may arrest without warrant anyone who is, or whom he with reasonable cause suspects to be guilty of this offence (s7(6) as amended).

Road traffic offences

The law relating to road traffic offences was largely consolidated in the Road Traffic Act 1988 and the Road Traffic Offenders Act 1988 as amended by the Road Traffic Act 1991.

The only offences which are arrestable by virtue of the sentences they carry are:

a) causing death by dangerous driving contrary to s1 of the Road Traffic Act 1988 as replaced by s1 of the 1991 Act;

b) causing death by careless driving when under the influence of drink or drugs contrary to the Road Traffic Act 1988 s3A as inserted by s3 of the 1991 Act;

c) causing danger to other road users contrary to s22A of the Road Traffic Act 1988 as inserted by s6 of the 1991 Act.

The maximum sentence for (a) and (b) offences is five years' imprisonment and for (c) is seven years' imprisonment, in each case together with an unlimited fine.[82]

---

82 Road Traffic Offenders Act s33 and Sch 2 and Road Traffic Act 1991 s26 and Sch 2.

The Road Traffic Act 1988 confers certain specific powers of arrest without warrant as set out below, but the offences involved are not arrestable offences.

Section	Who may arrest	Power of arrest
4(6)	Any constable	Reasonable cause to suspect commission of offence of driving or being in charge when under the influence of drink or drugs.
6(5)	Any constable	Reasonable cause to suspect excess alcohol as a result of a breath test or person has failed to provide a specimen of breath under s6 and reasonable cause to suspect alcohol in body.
103(3)	Constable in uniform	Any person driving on a road where reasonable cause to suspect that person of being disqualified.

No other road traffic offences carry a specific power of arrest but all are subject to arrest under 1984 Act s25 (above pp121–128). In particular, there are various offences relating to failure to provide a correct name and address. These could occasion arrest in accordance with 1984 Act s25(3)(a)–(c) (above pp121–124).

Information to be given on arrest (s28)

A person who is being arrested must be informed of the fact of, and the ground for, the arrest, either at the time or as soon as is practicable after the arrest (s28(1) and (3)).[83] This applies irrespective of who is making the arrest (constable, store detective, civilian), but if it is a constable, the information must be given, regardless of whether the fact of, or the ground for, the arrest is obvious (s28(2) and (4)).

There is no express requirement that a non-constable must give the information if the facts are obvious. This is to prevent non-constables incurring liability as a consequence of arrests in which they might not be aware of all the technicalities. However, the facts must

[83] Cf the rule in Northern Ireland: *Murray v Ministry of Defence* [1988] 2 All ER 521, HL.

be so obvious as to amount to the conveying of information, otherwise the arrest will not be lawful.

The requirements apply whether the arrest is with or without warrant, under a statutory power or at common law, for an offence or otherwise.

The arrest is unlawful if the ground given does not in fact justify the arrest.[84]

After arrest

If not given on arrest, the information must be given as soon as practicable. This is an objective question of fact and a fairly high test. It means as soon as at all practicable, not merely as soon as is reasonably practicable. Examples might be when a drunk sobers up, when an armed person is disarmed, or when a violent suspect calms down or is subdued.[85] It might never be practicable to tell a person who is incapable of understanding.

If the person arrested escapes from arrest before the information can be given, and therefore it is not reasonably practicable to give it, then the information need not be given (s28(5)). Of course, the requirements will apply afresh on any rearrest. In all other cases the information must be given at some stage – either on arrest or as soon after as is practicable.

Breach of the s28 requirements renders the arrest unlawful, and the person making the arrest could be liable to civil penalties.[86]

A police officer who makes an arrest where it is impracticable to give a reason immediately, is under a duty to maintain the arrest until it is practicable to inform the arrested person of the ground, and an assault on the officer during this period will be an assault on a police officer in the execution of duty under the Police Act 1964 s51.[87] However, a constable who should give a reason and does not, is not acting in the execution of duty.[88] Since arrest is not a legal concept but a matter of fact arising out of the deprivation of a person's liberty, and is a continuing act, an arrest which is unlawful

---

84 *Edwards v DPP* (1993) 88 Cr App R 166. See also *Nicholas v DPP* [1987] Crim LR 474.

85 See eg, *DPP v Hawkins* [1988] 3 All ER 673. See also the facts of *Dawes v DPP* [1994] Crim LR 604.

86 Eg, £2,000 damages awarded in *Murphy v Oxford* (1985) CAT No 56; [1985] CLY 140.

87 *DPP v Hawkins* n85 above.

88 See, eg, *R v JD Lowe* [1986] Crim LR 49.

because no reason for it has been given can become lawful as soon as a reason is given.[89]

Content of the information

The information which must be given need not include the information on which the suspicion must be based, but one reason for the requirement is to give the person an opportunity to present a convincing denial.[90] A person arrested in Liverpool for burglary on a particular date at a hotel in Newquay was held to be entitled to be told more than that he was being arrested for burglary in Newquay.[91]

If a person is arrested under s25 for not giving a name and address, there is no duty to explain why they are needed (eg, to serve a summons) but the person must be told what offence is involved and that the arrest is because the particulars have not been given.[92]

The reason given for an arrest need not be in technical terms and need not relate to the charge on which the arrested person is eventually prosecuted.[93] As to informing someone that they are under arrest, the Court of Appeal has held that on arrest there is a duty to make plain to the suspect by what is said and done that they are no longer free.[94]

Voluntary attendance at a police station etc (s29)

A person who, for the purposes of assisting with an investigation, attends voluntarily at a police station or any other place with a constable without having been arrested is entitled to leave at will unless placed under arrest (s29(a)). If placed under arrest, the person must be informed as soon as the decision is taken by the constable. The constable cannot wait until it is practicable to give the information concerning the fact of arrest (s29(b)). Once the arrest is made, the rule under s28 (above) concerning the ground of arrest applies.

The Act does not specifically state that a breach of s29(b) renders an arrest unlawful, but that can be inferred from the general policy of s28.

89 *Lewis and Another v Chief Constable of South Wales Constabulary* [1991] 1 All ER 206, CA.
90 *Christie v Leachinsky* [1947] AC 573, HL.
91 *Murphy v Oxford* [1985] CLY 140.
92 *Nicholas v Parsonage* [1987] RTR 199.
93 *Christie v Leachinsky* n90. See also *Abbassy v Commissioner of Police of the Metropolis* [1990] 1 All ER 193, CA.
94 *R v Inwood* [1973] 1 WLR 647, CA.

Section 29 does not create a new power of arrest. The arrest must still be justified by the common law or statute, and is subject to other provisions of the Act concerning the treatment of arrested persons.

There seems to be no requirement that persons attending a police station voluntarily be told that they are free to leave, unless they are cautioned but not arrested (see p218). In this case, Code C provides that they must be informed that they are not under arrest but are free to leave and to obtain legal advice if they decide to remain at the police station.[95]

There is no limit on the length of time that a person may be at a police station voluntarily. The Act defines police detention as requiring an arrest (s118(2)) and therefore the limits on the length of police detention in Pt IV of the Act do not apply (see chapter 6).

If a person is at the station voluntarily and is prevented from leaving but not informed that s/he is being arrested, that would appear to be an unlawful arrest because there is a purported arrest but the requirements of ss28 and 29 have been ignored.

Because a person who is attending at the police station voluntarily is not in police detention within the meaning of the Act, many of the provisions of the Code of Practice do not apply (see chapter 7), although the Code advises the police to treat such people with no less consideration than those in detention. In particular, they should enjoy an absolute right to obtain legal advice or communicate with anyone outside the police station.[96]

A person attending the police station voluntarily who asks about entitlement to legal advice must be given a copy of the notice available to detained persons which explains the arrangements for obtaining legal advice.[97] There is no obligation on the police to volunteer this information or to supply a copy of the notice if the question of entitlement is not raised.

Arrest elsewhere than at a police station (s30)

Generally

Subject to the exception dealt with below, the general rule is that a person arrested for an offence by a constable, or taken into custody

95 Code C paras 3.15 and 10.2. See appendix 2.
96 Ibid Note for Guidance 1A
97 Code C para 3.16.

by a constable after being arrested by someone else, shall be taken to a police station (see below) as soon as practicable after arrest (s30(1)). In practice, the majority of arrests take place other than at a police station, and this provision is of great importance. It is unlikely that the original arrest is rendered unlawful if this provision is breached, but a continued detention in breach of the provision would be both a criminal offence and a civil wrong[98] and the officer would not be acting in the execution of duty (see chapter 13 on remedies). There is no definition of what is meant by practicable. This is a question of fact for the courts to decide.

If a person is arrested by a person other than a constable (eg, a store detective), the common law rule is that the arrested person must either be taken before a magistrate as soon as reasonably practicable or be handed over to the police without unreasonable delay, although a store detective can first take the arrested person to a superior in the store. A person who arrests a child may not lawfully deliver the child to its parents rather than to the police or a magistrate.[99] This has not been changed by the Act and still applies. Once the arrested person is handed over to the police, the provisions of s30 apply.

Usually a constable will be called and informed of the situation. At this stage the suspect must be allowed to leave unless the constable makes an arrest (usually under s24), at which point the safeguards relating to arrest apply (s28, see pp135–137). The private citizen has no power to detain the suspect further.

If persons are arrested by a constable at a place other than a police station, and the constable is satisfied before reaching the police station that there are no grounds for keeping them under arrest, they must be released (s30(7)). A constable who releases a person under this provision must record the fact of the release as soon as is practicable after the release (s30(8) and (9)). Again, continued detention would be unlawful in those circumstances. It is up to the constable to be satisfied. This is a subjective test, but once the constable is satisfied, then the prisoner must be released. If the original grounds of arrest are no longer valid, but there are new grounds of arrest then s30(7) does not require the release of the prisoner.

The provision in s30(7) is particularly important where there has been an arrest under s25 (see pp121–128). If the person's name or

98 See, eg, *Middleweek v Chief Constable of Merseyside* (1985) *Times* 1 August, [1990] 3 All ER 662, CA.
99 *John Lewis & Co Ltd v Tims* [1952] AC 676, HL; *R v Brewin* [1976] Crim LR 742.

address becomes known on the way to the police station, or if there is no longer any danger of injury to person or property, or of an offence being committed, then the person must be released unless one of the other general arrest conditions applies.

Juveniles should not be arrested at their place of education unless this is unavoidable, in which case the principal or the principal's nominee must be informed.[100]

Taken to a designated police station

The arrested person must be taken to a designated police station, subject to the exceptions dealt with below (s30(2)). This is a police station designated under s35 as having enough accommodation for detaining arrested persons (see p148).

A constable who is working in a locality covered by a non-designated police station, or who is not a police authority constable (see pp8–10), may take an arrested person to any police station unless it appears to the constable that it may be necessary to keep the arrested person in police detention for more than six hours (s30(3) and (4)).

In certain circumstances, any constable may take an arrested person to any police station. This can be done if the constable has arrested the person, or taken the person into custody from a non-constable, without assistance from any other constable and no other constable is available to assist, and it appears that it will not be possible to take the arrested person to a designated police station without the arrested person injuring him or herself, the constable or some other person (s30(5)).

An arrested person cannot be held at a non-designated police station for more than six hours, and by the end of that time must have been released or have been taken to a designated police station (s30(6)).

If a person is detained in breach of the provision, eg, by being taken to a non-designated police station when s30(4) and (5) do not apply, or by being held at a non-designated police station for more than six hours, there will be an unlawful detention. See chapter 13 for a discussion of the available remedies.

Delay in taking to the police station (s30(10))

The requirement in s30(1) that an arrested person be taken to a

---

100 Code C Note for Guidance 11C.

police station as soon as practicable after arrest does not prevent a constable delaying if:

a) it is reasonable to carry out certain investigations immediately; and
b) the presence of the arrested person is necessary in order to carry out those investigations (s30(10)).

Where there is a delay in taking an arrested person to the police station after arrest, the reasons for the delay must be recorded on first arrival at a police station (s30(11)). This provision is based on the common law principle set out by Lord Denning MR in *Dallison v Caffery*:[101]

> when a constable has taken into custody a person reasonably suspected of felony he can do what is reasonable to investigate the matter, and to see whether the suspicions are supported or not by further evidence. He can, for instance, take the person suspected to his own house to see whether any of the stolen property is there; else it may be removed and valuable evidence lost. He can take the person suspected to the place where he says that he was working, for there he may find persons to confirm or refute his alibi . . . .

It must be reasonable to carry out the investigations immediately. What is reasonable is a question of fact for the court (not the police) to decide. The actual presence of the person must be necessary, possibly to identify persons or items. If the offence can be equally efficiently investigated without the person's actual presence, for instance because the person can give the relevant evidence without being taken elsewhere, then s30(10) does not justify delay in taking the person to a police station.

This provision applies equally to customs officers taking arrested people to customs offices. The Court of Appeal has ruled in two such cases that any questioning during this period must be in relation to issues which require immediate investigation and must not be in the nature of a cross-examination or amount to an interrogation of the kind which ought properly be reserved for the police station with the full protection of the legislation and the codes of practice. Evidence obtained by using s30(10) to circumvent the rules could be excluded by the judge under s78.[102]

---

101 [1965] 1 QB 348, CA.
102 *R v Kerawalla* [1991] Crim LR 451; *R v Khan* [1993] Crim LR 54. In neither of these cases was the evidence actually excluded under s78. For a similar Court of Appeal case involving police officers see *R v Keane* [1992] Crim LR 306. There are now more restrictive rules governing the conduct of interviews away from the police station: Code of Practice C para 11 in the 1995 revised edition.

There is no statutory limit on the length of the delay, but it may only last for as long as the person's presence is necessary elsewhere. However, the time limits on detention without charge (s41, see pp162–164) do not take account of any delay under s30(10) when the arrest is in the same police area as the police station.

The provision concerning recording the delay under s30(11) is explained as follows:

> This requirement is designed to ensure that the discretion not to take a person directly to a police station is properly and responsibly used, and subject to scrutiny by supervisory officers.[102a]

The power under s30(10) applies only where a person is arrested otherwise than at a police station, and does not apply once the person has arrived at a police station – although there is nothing to prevent the detained person being taken from the police station to help in investigations.

Section 32 authorises the search of premises of someone who has been arrested (see p91) but this does not limit the necessity requirement of s30(10).

Exceptions (s30(12))

The requirement in s30(1) that an arrested person be taken to a police station as soon as practicable does not affect:

a) the power to authorise detention at a port or on board a ship or aircraft or elsewhere under the prevention of terrorism legislation or the Immigration Act 1971 (s30(12)(a) and (c)); nor

b) the power to take someone found drunk and disorderly or incapable to a detoxification centre, under the Criminal Justice Act 1972 s34 (s30(12)(b)).

If a person has been detained under the Immigration Act 1971 Sch 2 para 16, there is an additional power under para 18(3) of that schedule for a detained person to be taken to any place where attendance is required for the purpose of ascertaining nationality or citizenship or of making arrangements for admission to another country, or for any other purpose connected with the operation of the 1971 Act. This power is unaffected by s30(10) of the 1984 Act (s30(13)).

102a Notes on clauses produced by Home Office for passage of Police and Criminal Evidence Bill through the House of Lords.

Arrest for a further offence (s31)

Where a person has been arrested for an offence and is at a police station in consequence of that arrest and it appears to a constable that the person is also liable to arrest for any other offence, the person must be arrested for that other offence (s31). The arrested person must then be informed of the new arrest and the grounds for it under the provisions of s28 (see pp135–137). The time limits on detention under s41 (see pp162–164) apply from the time of the first arrest (s41(4)). The aim of this provision is to exclude the possibility that a person may be released on bail, having been charged with the offence for which first arrested, and then immediately rearrested for another offence, so turning the detention clock back to zero.[103]

The provision applies only when each arrest is for an offence, not when it is an arrest to prevent a breach of the peace, or to prevent an offence under s24(7)(pp117–118). The section confers no discretion. If it appears to a constable that the person is liable to arrest for another offence then 'he shall be arrested', and there is no discretion not to arrest for an outstanding arrestable offence.

However, some matters are left unclear by the wording of the section. Does it apply if any constable anywhere in the country thinks there is liability to further arrest? The section says 'if it appears to a constable'. If it does not mean this, to which constables does it refer?

If a person is arrested, and it does not appear to a constable that there is liability for a further arrest, and the person is released, then clearly any subsequent arrest will not be covered by s31. However, if arrest for a further offence is required by s31 but does not take place, does this render unlawful a subsequent arrest that should have been made while the suspect was already in custody? The Act does not say that this is unlawful, but if it is not unlawful it is difficult to see how s31 can be enforced.

It does not seem to make any difference whether the further arrest is for an offence arising out of the same facts as the first offence, or on a totally separate matter.

The further arrest need not take place immediately. 'We see nothing in the section which would prevent the constable delaying arresting . . . until the time (if it ever arrived) when . . . release was imminent.'[104] When the arrest does take place, the person must be reminded of his or her rights and might then ask for a solicitor.

103 Ibid.
104 *R v Samuel* [1988] 2 All ER 135, CA, 141 per Hodgson J; cf *R v Davison* [1988] Crim LR 442. See also *R v Mason and Stevens* [1992] 24 March, CA Case No 90/3987/74.

Search on arrest other than at a police station (s32)

Section 32 gives certain powers of search to a constable when someone has been arrested elsewhere than at a police station. They are
separate from powers to search a person without arrest (see chapter
2) or to search property without an arrest (see chapter 3). Where the
arrest is at a police station, powers of search are governed by Pt V of
the Act (see chapter 7).

Powers to search premises when an arrest has been made are
given by s32(2)(b), (6) and (7), and these are discussed in chapter 3.

The following discussion deals only with the power to search
persons. The power to search under s32 applies whether the arrest is
for an offence or otherwise, so long as the arrest is not at a police
station. The Act does not specify where and when the search may
take place. Presumably it may take place at any time and place
between arrest and arrival at the police station.

Grounds for the search

A constable may search an arrested person on reasonable grounds
for believing that the arrested person may present a danger to him or
herself or others (s32(1)). The constable's belief must be based on
reasonable grounds. This is an objective test and it would be up to a
court to decide whether reasonable grounds existed. It is difficult to
imagine such grounds being based on anything other than overt
behaviour, threats, past activities such as suicide attempts or violence,
or something such as a tell-tale bulge of a weapon. However there is
no need to suspect the presence of any particular type of danger.

A constable who has reasonable grounds for believing that an
arrested person may have concealed on him or her anything which
might be used to escape from lawful custody or which might be
evidence of an offence, may search that person for such a thing
(s32(2)(a) and (b)). Again, the constable's belief must be based on
reasonable grounds, such as those indicated above, which would be
evaluated by a court.

Nature of the search

The nature of the articles for which a search may be made is very
wide, since virtually anything can constitute evidence of an offence
(which need not be the offence for which the arrest was made) or be

used to facilitate an escape.[105] This particular power is separate from the power of search of a person believed to present a danger.

In effect, virtually anyone arrested will be subject to search under these powers, although the reasonable grounds must be identifiable in each case. It is not lawful to search an arrested person under s32 in order to establish identity.[106]

However, the search may be only to the extent reasonably required for the purpose of discovering the article (s32(3)). This must be related to the nature of the article suspected to be concealed. For example, if the suspected article is a stolen video recorder, this could not justify a more thorough search than to look under an overcoat or jacket.

Since the article must be suspected to be concealed 'on him', on the face of it there is no power under this section to search eg, a vehicle or a bag. A search of a vehicle could be separately justified under s1 (pp26ff) and a search of other property at the police station is dealt with in chapter 7.

Intimate searches (see pp192–196) may not be carried out under s32 (ss53 and 55). There are restrictions on searching in public similar to those on a search under s1 (see pp29–30) (s32(4)). The Code of Practice would apply to strip searches, as discussed on p30 and pp189–190.[107]

The comments on the use of reasonable force by police to search under s1 (p27) also apply to searches under s32 (s117).

At common law a personal search is unlawful unless a reason is given or is obvious or it is impracticable to give reasons.[108] This rule continues to apply[109] although there is no express statutory requirement to this effect in s32 (cf s2(2)).

Property found by the search

The property found by the search should be recorded under the provisions of s54 (see pp188ff) although there is no requirement in the Act to record the grounds for the search.

A constable conducting a search of a person believed to be a danger, may seize and retain anything found if there are reasonable grounds for believing that it might be used to cause personal injury to him or herself or to any other person (s32(8)); this is subject to the

105 But see *R v Churchill* [1989] Crim LR 226, CA.
106 *R v Eeet* [1983] Crim LR 806.
107 Code C para 4.1 and Annex A.
108 *Brazil v Chief Constable of Surrey* [1983] 3 All ER 537.
109 *Sheehan v Metropolitan Police Commissioner* (1990) July *Legal Action* 23.

objective test of reasonable grounds. Under s32(9), a constable may search for anything for use to assist escape or for evidence, and may seize and retain anything found if there are reasonable grounds for believing that it is to assist escape or has been obtained in consequence of an offence.

Anything seized under the above provisions because it might be used to cause physical injury or to assist in an escape must be returned to the person it was taken from as soon as that person is released (by the police or a court), and must be returned earlier if retention is no longer necessary in all the circumstances (s22). If, for example, a person is in a police cell, it cannot be necessary to retain car keys on the ground that the car might have been used to assist an escape.

For the position concerning items subject to legal privilege see chapter 4. The powers of search under s32 do not limit the power conferred by the prevention of terrorism legislation, which is discussed in chapter 8. The power of the police to retain seized items, and the provisions for access and copying governed by ss21 and 22, are discussed in chapter 4.

CHAPTER 6

Detention by the police

The scheme

Introduction

The Police and Criminal Evidence Act 1984 Pt IV creates a scheme involving a number of stages during a suspect's detention by the police at which the continuation of custody must be authorised. The authorisations are by police officers in the earlier stages (of increasing rank at each stage) and by magistrates in the later stages. The maximum period for which detention without charge can be authorised is 96 hours in the case of a serious arrestable offence and 24 hours in other cases, but in practice a suspect might be in police custody for a number of hours before the detention clock starts to run. The detention is supervised by a custody officer.

This chapter examines in detail the detention procedure outlined above. Detention in breach of the provisions might give rise to criminal, civil or disciplinary liability on the part of police officers. Chapters 12 and 13 deal with the remedies if such liability is established. For the treatment of detained persons, see chapter 7. A detention which is initially lawful can become unlawful if the circumstances change.[1] The Code of Practice for the Detention, Treatment and Questioning of Persons by Police Officers (Code C) referred to in this chapter is reproduced in appendix 2.

Section 45(2) provides that any references in Pt IV to a period of time or a time of day are to be treated as 'approximate only'. The Act gives no further guidance on what is meant by this and it will be

---

1 *Middleweek v Chief Constable of Merseyside* [1990] 3 All ER 662 and *Furber v Kratter* (1988) *Times* 21 July; [1988] 8 CL 290. But see also *Hague v Deputy Governor of Parkhurst Prison* [1991] 3 All ER 733.

for the courts to decide what margin of variation is tolerable.[2] This proviso is to 'reflect the unpredictability of police work and the pressures on police station staff'.[3] In *Bellott v Chequers Development Ltd*,[4] it was held that 36 feet is 'approximately' 35 feet but 40 feet is not. In *Louis Dreyfus Cie v Parnaso Cia Naviera SA*,[5] 10,069 tons was held to 'approximate' to 10,400 tons. It is a question of fact for the court to decide in each case.

Designated police stations

A person arrested for an offence must normally be taken to a police station[6] as soon as practicable after the arrest (s30 and see p138). If the arrested person is to be detained for more than six hours, s/he must be taken to a designated police station before six hours has elapsed (s30). A breach of this requirement would render continued detention unlawful.[7]

Section 35 requires the chief officer of police for each area to designate police stations appearing to provide enough accommodation for the purpose of detaining arrested persons. At designated police stations, custody officers are appointed, but at other stations the functions of the custody officer can be performed by any officer (s36, see below). A chief officer who fails to designate sufficient or adequate police stations can be compelled to do so by an order of mandamus if such failure is unreasonable or in bad faith.

Custody officers

One or more custody officers must be appointed for each designated police station.[8] The appointment is made by the chief officer of police or by a police officer directed to so do by the chief officer. Nobody can be appointed a custody officer unless of at least the rank

2 Note, however, the strict interpretation of the time within which an application for a warrant of further detention under s43 must be made. See p165.
3 Notes on clauses supplied by the Home Office during the passage of the Bill through Parliament.
4 [1936] 1 All ER 89.
5 [1960] 2 QB 49, CA.
6 Normally it must be a designated police station. For exceptions, see p140.
7 Not all commentators would agree with this proposition and it is not in D Birch's list of mandatory requirements, [1985] Crim LR 545 at 554.
8 It was held in *Vince and Another v Chief Constable of the Dorset Police* [1993] All ER 321, CA that a chief constable has a duty to appoint one custody officer for each designated police station and a discretion, which must be reasonably exercised, to appoint more than one.

of sergeant (s36(1)–(3)). There is no requirement that the custody officer be in the uniformed branch, but that was the Home Office's intention and is the general practice.

If a custody officer at a designated police station is not readily available to act as such, the functions may be performed by an officer of any rank (s36(4)). At a non-designated police station the same functions should be performed by an officer not involved in the investigation of the offence for which the suspect is in police detention, but if such an officer is not readily available the functions are to be performed by the officer who took the suspect to the station or by any other officer (s36(7)). If it does fall to the officer who took the suspect to the police station to perform the custody officer's functions, this officer must as soon as practicable inform an officer of at least the rank of inspector, who is attached to a designated police station, that this is the case (s36(9) and (10)). There is no such requirement if the functions are performed by any other officer.

The phrase 'readily available' is not further defined and it is a question of fact for the court to decide in any particular case whether somebody was 'readily available'. Apart from the special case above, none of the functions of a custody officer can be performed by an officer who at that time is involved in the investigation of the offence for which the person is in police detention (s36(5)).[9] This will always apply in the case of a designated police station. However, the Act does not prevent the functions being performed by an officer who has previously been involved in the investigation. Note that Code C para 3.4 prohibits the custody officer from putting specific questions to a detained person about his or her involvement in any offence.

The above provision does not prevent the custody officer from performing any function assigned by the Act or codes or doing anything in connection with the identification of a suspect or the provision of specimens for analysis under the Road Traffic Act 1988 ss7 and 8 (s36(6)).

References to the duties of a custody officer also apply where those duties are carried out by an officer performing the functions of a custody officer (s36(8)).

Some custody officers will be full-time with no other police responsibilities, especially at busier police stations, but this will not always be the case.

9 Although in *R v Bailey and Smith* (1993) 97 Cr App R 365; the Court of Appeal did not find s36(5) to have been breached where the custody officer co-operated with the investigating officers in placing the defendants in a bugged cell.

If a function of a custody officer is performed by another officer in circumstances not permitted by the Act (for example by the investigating officer at a designated police station) this is unlawful and, if as a result the suspect is detained longer or suffers some other detriment, the suspect will have the appropriate remedies.

Duties of the custody officer

The Act makes the custody officer responsible for ensuring that all persons in detention at the police station are treated in accordance with the Act and the Codes of Practice, and that all matters required to be recorded are recorded in custody records relating to such persons (s39(1)).

The treatment of persons at the police station and the Codes of Practice are dealt with in chapter 7, and the importance of custody records is dealt with in chapter 1.

If the custody officer permits the transfer of someone in police detention to the custody of the investigating officer or an officer who has charge of that person outside the police station, the responsibilities under s39(1) pass to that officer, who, on returning the person to the custody of the custody officer, must report to the latter on the manner in which these responsibilities have been carried out (s39(2) and (3)).

If an officer of a higher rank than the custody officer gives directions relating to a person in police detention which are at variance with a decision which the custody officer has made or would have made, the custody officer must refer the matter at once to an officer of the rank of superintendent or above who is responsible for the police station (s39(6)).

The provisions relating to custody officers and custody records are of crucial importance to such safeguards for suspects as are in the Act, and in each case defence lawyers should check that the provisions have been complied with. However, the custody officer is not responsible for what happens before a suspect arrives at the police station.

Police detention

The Act sets out various grounds and conditions on which an arrested person may be detained (see further below). There is a general provision that a person arrested for an offence must not be kept in police detention except in accordance with those grounds and conditions (s34(1)).

Police detention is defined in s118(2) and means being detained at a police station having been arrested for an offence (or having been arrested under the Prevention of Terrorism (Temporary Provisions) Act 1989 s14 or Sch 5 para 6)[10] and taken to the police station; or having been arrested at the police station (even if not for an offence) after attending voluntarily or accompanying a constable to it. It also includes being detained elsewhere in the charge of a constable (for example at a hospital) having been at the police station under arrest. However it does not include being at court after being charged, although it does include being en route to and from court if in the charge of a constable.

A person who has been arrested and is on the way to the police station is not in police detention, and neither is a person who has been arrested and who is not taken immediately to the police station under the provision of s30(10) (eg, where, having been arrested, s/he accompanies the arresting officer while s/he conducts a search under s32 before going to the police station). Nor is a person who is detained, having been arrested for other than a criminal offence (eg, under the authority of a warrant, under a power of arrest attached to a matrimonial injunction, or for breach of the peace), nor a person who attends at a police station and who has not been arrested, in police detention.

Note that a number of police powers and obligations under PACE apply only where the person is in police detention (eg, reviews under s40). The right of intimation (s56) and the right to legal advice (s58), however, apply to all those who are held in custody in a police station or elsewhere. Generally, Code C applies to all people in police custody, whether arrested for an offence or not, and including people removed to a police station as a place of safety under the Mental Health Act 1983 ss135 and 136,[11] although this is subject to certain exceptions.[12]

Interpretation

There are two particular problems of interpretation here. First, it seems that if a person has been the subject of an arrest which is in fact unlawful, then there is no power to keep him or her in police detention, the person does not count as an arrested person,[13] and the detention provisions do not apply. Second, a person who has been

10 But see p254.
11 Code C paras 1.10 and 1.11.
12 See Code C paras 1.10 and 1.12.
13 By analogy with *Spicer v Holt* [1977] AC 987; [1976] 3 All ER 71, HL.

arrested under s24 for being about to commit an arrestable offence, or under s25 for attempting to commit a summary offence, has not been arrested 'for an offence' and on the face of it many of the detention provisions of the Act do not apply. The courts have yet to decide whether the common law continues to apply to them, whether the 1984 Act is to be interpreted so as to include them, or whether there is some other solution.[14]

A person who has been arrested under the Road Traffic Act 1988 s6(5) (suspicion of excess alcohol or failure to provide a specimen) is treated under the 1984 Act as having been arrested for an offence (s34(6)). There is a special concurrent power to detain such a person until sober (1988 Act s10). A person who returns to a police station to answer bail or is arrested under s46A (failure to return to the police station to answer bail) is treated as having been arrested for the offence in connection with which s/he was granted bail (s34(7)).

Mandatory release

If at any time the custody officer at the police station where a person's detention was last authorised becomes aware that the grounds for detention have ceased to apply, the custody officer must order that person's immediate release from custody unless the person appears to the custody officer to have been 'unlawfully at large' at the time of arrest (s34(2)–(4)).

The above requirement depends on the subjective test of the custody officer's own knowledge. Thus it is important for suspects or their advisers or relatives to inform the custody officer of anything which might show that grounds for detention no longer exist. If the custody officer is not aware that the grounds no longer exist, it seems that continued detention will not be unlawful.

The duty to order release applies even if the person is not at the police station at the time but is, for example, under police guard at a hospital or elsewhere. It would also seem to apply, in principle, when the suspect is en route to court, having been charged.

The release must be unconditional, unless it appears to the custody officer that proceedings may be taken against the suspect for, or there is need for further investigation of, any matter in connection with which the suspect was detained at any stage. In such a case the release must be on bail to return to the police station at some later

14 See H Levenson 'Powers of arrest since the 1984 Act' December 1988 *Legal Action* 22 and the discussion of arrest for attempt at p23.

date (s34(5)).[15] This provision is very wide and the phrase 'further investigation of any matter in connection with which' is not limited to criminal offences, nor to investigation of the person released. It seems to apply also to a person who has been released without charge under s37(7)(b).[16]

On arrival at the police station

Unless a suspect is actually at a police station, the Act provides that a person must usually be taken to a police station as soon as practicable after arrest (s30(1)). The exception to this and the rules concerning which police station should be used are discussed on pp138–142.

A separate custody record must be opened as soon as practicable for each person brought to a police station under arrest or arrested at the police station having attended voluntarily.[17] Such a record must include a note of all the possessions the person has on arrival at the police station or on arrest after attending voluntarily (s54(1)).

If a person is arrested on a warrant endorsed for bail[18] and is taken to a police station, the person must be released from custody on entering into any personal recognizance required, (which may only be required in the case of bail in non-criminal proceedings) or after complying with any directions in the endorsement. If a surety is required, it is a matter for the custody officer whether any particular surety is acceptable. There is no provision for delay in the perform-ance of these duties.[19]

Deciding whether to charge

As soon as practicable after arrival at any police station of a person

15 Note that conditions cannot be attached to bail under s34(5). In principle it would seem that the person could be required to provide a surety or security before release, although it is difficult to see what sanction could be applied if s/he refused to do so (s47(1A) and Bail Act 1976 ss3 and 3A).
16 D Birch disagrees with this point. See [1986] Crim LR 74–75 (letters).
17 Code C para 2.1. Strictly the requirement applies whether or not detention is then authorised. In practice, custody records are not opened unless detention is authorised, although there are very few cases when the custody officer does not authorise detention. See I McKenzie, R Morgan and R Reiner, 'Helping the Police with Their Inquiries: the Necessity Principle and Voluntary Attend-ance at the Police Station' [1990] Crim LR 22.
18 Under Magistrates' Courts Act 1980 s117.
19 Ibid as amended by 1984 Act s47(8)(b).

answering to bail[20] or having been arrested for an offence (except on a warrant backed for bail) or after arrest for an offence (if arrest is at the police station) the custody officer must determine whether there is sufficient evidence to charge the person with the offence for which s/he was arrested. This must be done at each police station to which the person is taken before charge. The person may be detained at the police station for as long as is necessary for the custody officer to make such a determination (s37(1), (10)). By Code C para 1.1 all persons in custody must be dealt with expeditiously and must be released as soon as the need for detention has ceased to apply.

This duty must be carried out 'as soon as practicable' which is a very stringent requirement. This will be a question of fact for the court to decide. The minister told the House of Commons committee:

> A custody officer must get on with his job unless there are persuasive reasons to the contrary that will satisfy other people.[21]

Earlier the minister suggested an example of where the requirement might be met, by drawing a distinction between an officer who delayed doing the job to drink a cup of tea, and one who had been on duty for 12 hours with nothing to eat and needed a break while in the middle of booking in a large number of people arrested after a riot.

Consideration could also validly be delayed by the behaviour of anybody present or the illness of anyone involved (for example the arresting officer). Detention for this purpose must be for no longer than is 'necessary'. Since the custody officer has to go on the evidence that is 'before him' all that is necessary in most cases is time to read the file, listen to the arresting officer, hear any comment by the detained person, consult any documents and reach a decision.

If the custody officer decides that there is sufficient evidence to charge, the person must be:

a) charged; or
b) released without charge unconditionally; or
c) released without charge on bail (s37(7)).

If no decision has yet been taken on whether a person released without charge should be prosecuted, the custody officer must inform the person of that fact (s37(8)).

The meaning of 'sufficient evidence to charge' is not defined. It

---

20 A person returning to a police station to answer to bail, or arrested under s46A (failure to surrender), is treated as arrested for the offence in connection with which s/he was originally granted bail (s34(7)).
21 HC Standing Committee E, col 1077, 9 February 1984.

can be argued that it means evidence amounting to a prima facie case. This is a higher standard than that required for an arrest[22] but is arguably lower than a belief that there is sufficient evidence for a prosecution to succeed. Code C para 16, which deals with the stage at which an officer must take a suspect before a custody officer with a view to charge, refers to there being 'sufficient evidence to prosecute' and 'sufficient evidence for a prosecution to succeed'. Such a distinction would not be necessary if 'sufficient evidence to charge' (or prosecute)[23] meant sufficient evidence for a prosecution to succeed. The significance of this is that in many cases the custody officer will be in possession of sufficient evidence to charge when the person is first brought into the police station and therefore has no power to detain for the purpose of gathering further evidence under s37(2). This is particularly so in the case of persons arrested for offences that have little or no guilty intent and/or where the primary prosecution evidence comes from the officers who carried out the arrest.

Release

If the person is charged, the custody officer must decide whether to release him or her, either on bail or without bail, or to keep him or her in detention (see further p172). If the custody officer decides that there is sufficient evidence to charge, but decides not to do so, the suspect should normally be released without bail unless s34(5) applies (see p152). For the position where the custody officer decides that there is insufficient evidence to charge at this stage, see below. However, an arrested person who is not in a fit state to be charged or released under s37(7) may be kept in police detention until fit (s37(9)). The person may not be kept in police detention without charge for more than 24 hours even if still unfit (s41(1), (7)). The person would have to be released then since there would be no grounds for continued detention (s41(8)).

The Act does not define what is meant by a 'fit state'. The Code of Practice deals with any need for medical treatment (see Code C para 9). The Home Office gave as an example a person who is drunk or under the influence of drugs and who would not understand the terms of charges.[24] An officer of the rank of inspector or above must

---

22 Since, in any event, reasonable suspicion for an arrest does not have to be based upon admissible evidence.
23 Presuming, as would seem likely, that 'charge' and 'prosecute' mean the same thing in this context.
24 Notes on clauses, n3.

review the matter periodically to decide whether the person is in a fit state yet to be charged (s40(9)). If a person becomes fit within 24 hours then the normal procedure must be resumed.

A person detained in breach of the above requirements will have disciplinary, civil and criminal remedies (chapters 12 and 13). The position after release on bail is dealt with on p177 and after charge on p172.

Detention without charge

Insufficient evidence to charge

If the custody officer decides that there is insufficient evidence to charge, then the arrested person must be released unconditionally or on bail[25] (see p177) except in the following circumstances.

Release is not obligatory when the custody officer has reasonable grounds for believing that detention without charge is necessary:

a) to secure or preserve evidence relating to an offence for which the person is under arrest; or

b) to obtain such evidence by questioning of the person (s37(2)).

In such a case the custody officer may authorise the keeping of the person in police detention (s37(3)) and must make a written record of the grounds as soon as is practicable (s37(4)). The custody officer must, at the time, inform the suspect of the grounds for detention (s37(5)) unless s/he is incapable of understanding what is said, or is violent or likely to become violent, or is in urgent need of medical attention (s37(6)).

– This decision must be based on reasonable grounds. It would be for a court to say whether there were reasonable grounds.
– The detention must relate only to evidence or questioning; thus it cannot be justified in the interests of the suspect or to prevent the repetition or continuation of an offence.
– The detention must be necessary for the purpose of securing, preserving or obtaining evidence and is unlawful if the purpose can be achieved without it, for example if someone else can provide the

25 But see research reported in McKenzie, Morgan and Reiner 'Helping the police with their inquiries' [1990] Crim LR 22 (n17), which concluded that authorisation of detention by custody officers 'has become a de facto rubber-stamping decision'.

evidence or information, or if there is sufficient evidence to charge the person anyway (see discussion below).

Detention for questioning

The provision legalises detention for questioning. It could be argued that if a suspect can be questioned at home, then it is not 'necessary' for there to be detention for questioning at a police station, but a similar argument was rejected under the pre-1984 law.[26] Similarly, it could be argued that detention is not necessary if the police are seeking to secure or preserve evidence that does not require the involvement of the suspect. In practice, suspects are frequently detained out of convenience rather than necessity. Somewhat surprisingly, this matter does not appear to have been considered by the courts since PACE was introduced.

However, the questioning must relate to an offence for which the person is under arrest, and there is no power to arrest just for questioning. Thus, these provisions do not authorise police 'fishing trips'. The conduct of questioning is dealt with in chapter 7 as is the question of searching for evidence.

It has been argued in previous editions that if the custody officer had reasonable grounds for believing that the person would not answer questions, then detention could not be justified by reference to the need to obtain evidence by questioning. Code C Note for Guidance 1B deals with this in part by providing that a police officer, when trying to discover whether, or by whom, an offence has been committed, is entitled to ask questions of any person, an entitlement not affected by a person's declaration that s/he is unwilling to answer questions. Of greater significance is Criminal Justice and Public Order Act 1994 ss34, 36 and 37, the consequence of which is that, in certain circumstances, a failure to answer police questions can, in effect, amount to evidence.[27]

The test in s37(6) (see p156) of when a person need not be present when the written record of the grounds for the detention is made, is an objective question of fact, not determined solely by the belief of the custody officer. If a person's absence cannot be justified under s37(6), any continued detention authorised at that stage is unlawful. If the absence is justified, the appropriate explanation is required by Code C to be given as soon as practicable.[28]

26 For the old law see *Holgate-Mohammed v Duke* [1984] 1 All ER 1054, HL.
27 For further discussion on this point, see E Cape, *Defending Suspects at Police Stations* (Legal Action Group, 2nd edn 1995) ch 5.
28 Code C para 1.8.

Juveniles

There are special provisions relating to those who are under the age of 17. If they are arrested without a warrant, the provisions of s37 apply. However, if the arrest is in pursuance of a warrant they must not be released unless their parent or guardian enters into a recognizance for such amount as the custody officer considers will secure attendance at the hearing of the charge. In addition the custody officer may make the parents' or guardians' attendance at the hearing a condition of the recognizance.[29]

The minimum age of criminal responsibility is 10[30] and a child under that age cannot be arrested for an offence or be held in police detention within the meaning of the 1984 Act. If such a child were arrested because of a mistake about the child's age, the custody officer would have to release the child as soon as the true facts became known.[31]

The place of safety provisions, set out in the Children and Young Persons Act 1969 s28(2) and the 1984 Act Sch 2, were repealed by the Children Act 1989 Sch 15. The Children Act 1989 s46 established a new scheme for the protection of children and police powers to remove a child in the case of emergency.[32]

The original scheme of the Children and Young Persons Act 1969 was to remove children under the age of 14 from the criminal process.[33] However, that Act has not been brought fully into force and currently the detention rules in Pt IV of the 1984 Act apply to such children.[34] Children under the age of 14 are rebuttably presumed not to be able to commit crime.[35]

For protective provisions relating to juveniles whilst in police detention, see chapter 7.

29 Children and Young Persons Act 1969 s29 substituted by 1984 Act Sch 6 para 19(b).
30 Children and Young Persons Act 1933 s50.
31 1984 Act s34.
32 See appendix 8 below.
33 Children and Young Persons Act 1969 s70(1).
34 1984 Act s37(15). S37(11)-(14) was repealed by the Criminal Justice Act 1991 s72 without ever having been brought into force.
35 See C v DPP [1995] 2 WLR 383.

Review of detention

The Act provides a system of reviews of detention to be carried out periodically in respect of all those who are in police detention (see p151, and see Code C para 1.10). The procedure applies whether the arrest is for an offence or otherwise, whether or not further detention has been authorised (see pp164–165) and whether or not the suspect has been charged. It does not apply in the case of a person who is attending the police station voluntarily and has not been arrested (see p137), nor if the person has been arrested for other than an offence, for example, to take fingerprints (see Code C para 1.10).[36]

The review clock starts running at the time the detention is first authorised under s37 (see p156) (s40(3)). In this respect it is different from the detention clock (see p162). In the case of a person who has been charged, the review is carried out by the custody officer (s40(1)(a)).

In the case of a person who has not been charged, the review is carried out by an officer of at least the rank of inspector who has not at any stage been directly involved with the investigation (s40(1)(b)). This means that for such people the custody officer's initial decision is reviewed by an officer who is independent of the investigation, which might not always be the case with the custody officer. The officer carrying out the review is referred to in the Act as the review officer (s40(2)).

The general rule

The general rule is that the first review must be not later than six hours after the detention was first authorised, and subsequent reviews must take place at intervals of not more than nine hours (s40(3)).

In some cases the review may be postponed, although not cancelled. This may happen if, having regard to all the circumstances prevailing at the review deadline, it is not practicable to carry out the review at that time (s40(4)(a)). The test of impracticability is a strict one for the police, but it is a question of fact for the court to decide. The Act gives two specific examples of impracticability:

a) if the person is being questioned and the review officer is satisfied that an interruption of the questioning would prejudice the investigation (s40(4)(b)(i)); or

b) if, at the time, no review officer is readily available (s40(4)(b)(ii)).

---

36 See 1984 Act s27 and p129 above.

'Readily available' is not defined.

Other examples of impracticability might be where there have been mass arrests, or where there is an emergency requiring the attention of senior officers. A review may be carried out over the telephone rather than postponed, if in the circumstances this is the only practicable way of conducting a review.[37]

The reason for the postponement of review must be recorded in the custody record by the review officer (s40(7)) and any postponed review must take place as soon as practicable (s40(5)). Where detained persons are being interrogated, this means that the review officer must keep him or herself informed of the progress of the interrogation. In any event, Code C provides for regular breaks in interviews[38] and a review could be conducted during such a break. If a review is postponed, subsequent reviews must take place as though the review had not been postponed.[39]

Detainees not charged

The review procedure in respect of a person not yet charged is the same as the procedure followed by the custody officer under s37(1)–(6) (p156) in deciding whether to detain an arrested person (s40(8)). This means that the person must be released unless the grounds for detention under s37(2) still exist. However, if the custody officer did not charge or release the person under s37(7) because the person was unfit under s37(9) (see p155 above), the role of the review officer is to decide whether the person is yet in a fit state to be charged or released (s40(9)). If the person is fit, presumably the custody officer must then apply s40(8), although the Act does not say so specifically. A person who is not so fit continues to be treated as someone who has not been charged.

Charged detainees

If the person has been charged, the post-charge procedure under s38(1)–(7) is applied by the review officer (see p172) (s40(10)). In practice, since the review will be carried out by the custody officer (s40(1)(a)), this provision means that the s38 procedure must be repeated periodically until the suspect is brought to court.

---

37 Code C Note for Guidance 15C, although the Note makes it clear that a review to decide whether to authorise continued detention under s42 must be conducted in person.

38 Code C para 12.7.

39 1984 Act s40(6). The wording of the Act is not altogether clear but this is the generally agreed interpretation.

Representations

Before deciding whether to authorise a person's continued detention, the review officer must give the person, or any solicitor instructed who is available at the time, an opportunity to make oral or written representations (s40(12), (13)). The initiative in contacting them must be taken by the review officer. A suspect who is asleep is not given such an opportunity, and a review officer who considers that the suspect is unfit to make oral representations because of condition or behaviour, may refuse to hear such representations (s40(14)). If the detained person is likely to be asleep at the latest time for a review, the time should be brought forward to enable representations to be made.[40] The solicitor always has the right to make representations, and the review officer must hear them even if they are made over the telephone, and even an unfit suspect may make written representations. The Act does not specifically allow a non-solicitor to carry out this function (although Code C para 6.12 gives an extended meaning to the terms 'solicitor' – see p197), but the Code of Practice gives such a right to an appropriate adult in the case of a juvenile and gives the review officer discretion to hear anyone having an interest in the person's welfare.[41] Representations might deal with:

- whether the police are in possession of sufficient evidence to charge, or whether further detention is necessary to secure or preserve evidence (both relevant to the power to detain without charge under s37(2));
- whether the investigation is being conducted expeditiously (as required by Code C para 1.1); or
- whether a detention limit has expired or is about to expire (see p163).

The duty to hear representations applies even where the person is being held incommunicado and/or is being denied access to legal advice (ss56 and 58, see chapter 7). In such cases there may not be anyone other than the detained person him or herself to make representations. However, it should be noted that the appropriate adult provisions apply even where a person is being held incommunicado under s56. Further, the power to delay access to legal advice under s58 does not, in principle, prevent a solicitor from representing the detained person, and thus making representations at review.

40 Code C Note for Guidance 15A.
41 Code C para 15.1.

The rule in s39(6), that a dispute between a custody officer and a higher ranking officer must be referred to a superintendent or more senior officer responsible for the police station, also applies in the case of a review officer (s40(11)).

When does the detention clock start running?

Limitations on the length of police detention, discussed later in this chapter, are based on the passage of time from a particular point, described as the 'relevant time' (s41(2)).

The general rule is that the time starts on arrival at the first police station to which the suspect is taken after arrest (s41(2)(d)). There might be some delay between arrest and arrival caused by investigation under s30(10) (see p140) but delay caused by travelling should be minimal since the general rule is designed to apply where a person is arrested and taken to a police station within the area of the same constabulary. The Act does not provide a maximum allowable period of delay in such cases.[42]

If a person has attended voluntarily at the police station or accompanied a constable to a police station without having been arrested, and is then arrested at the police station, the time starts with the arrest (s41(2)(c)).

If someone is arrested outside England and Wales, the time starts 24 hours after entry into England and Wales, or on earlier arrival at the first police station to which the person is taken in the police area in which the offence for which the person was arrested is being investigated. This rule applies to arrests in Scotland, both parts of Ireland, and the Channel Islands, as well as the rest of the world (s41(2)(b)). There is no statutory maximum on the delay between arrest and arrival.[43]

If someone is arrested in England Wales but in a police area other than the one in which arrest is sought, then if the person is questioned in the area of arrest to obtain evidence in relation to an offence for which the arrest was made, time starts to run under the general rule in s41(2). If the person is not so questioned, the time starts 24 hours after arrest or on earlier arrival at the first police station to which the person is taken in the police area in which arrest was sought (s41(2)(a), (3)). However, if the person has already been arrested for a different offence and taken to a police station in one area (or has

---

42 But see s30(1).
43 Ibid.

been arrested there) but has not been questioned in order to obtain evidence of an offence for which arrest is sought in another area, the time starts 24 hours after leaving the last place of detention in the first area, or on earlier arrival at the first police station the person is taken to in the area in which arrest is sought (s41(5)).[44] Code C prohibits questioning while in transit 'except in order to clarify any voluntary statement made'.[45]

If a person has been arrested for one offence while already under arrest for another offence (s31), the above references relate to the original arrest (s41(4)) so that the detention period cannot be prolonged by a series of rearrests.

Where a person is released on police bail subject to a duty to return to a police station on a future date under s47(3)(b) and is detained on return, the relevant time is that which relates to the initial detention. This is so even if the person is arrested under s46A for failure to surrender to police bail (s47(6)). However, if the person is re-arrested other than under s46A,[46] the relevant time is that relating to that subsequent arrest (s47(7)).

If a person has been in police detention as defined in s118(2) and is taken to hospital for medical treatment, the detention clock runs during any questioning to obtain evidence relating to any offence (not just the offence for which arrested) but does not otherwise run during transit or at the hospital (s41(6)). The Act makes no provision for the period between arrest and arrival at the police station if somebody is taken directly to hospital after arrest. However, a person who is not too ill can leave hospital voluntarily and thus start the process running. Code C prohibits questioning at hospital without the agreement of a responsible doctor.[47]

Time limits – the general rule

The general rule is that a person may not be kept in police detention for more than 24 hours without being charged; must be released, unconditionally or on bail, at the end of that time if still in detention without having been charged; and cannot be rearrested without a warrant for the same offence(s) unless new evidence justifying a

---

44 For problems in applying this rule, see D Birch [1986] Crim LR 545 at 555–556.
45 Code C para 14.1.
46 Which s/he may be if new evidence justifying a further arrest has come to light since the initial release (s47(2)).
47 Code C para 14.2.

further arrest has come to light since release (s41(1), (7), (9)).[48]

In the case of a serious arrestable offence, a person can be detained for longer if the procedure set out below is followed (s41(8)) but in any other case the 24-hour limit is binding. The definition of serious arrestable offence is discussed on p5.

Authorisation of continued detention

At any time after the second s40 review has been carried out (usually within 15 hours of detention being authorised, see p159) and before the expiry of 24 hours (s42(4)), an authorisation of continued detention can be given, subject to certain conditions.

The authorisation can be given only by an officer of the rank of superintendent or above who is responsible for the police station at which the person is detained (s42(1)). The authorisation may extend the period of detention up to 36 hours from the time when the detention clock started to run. If a lesser period than 36 hours is authorised, the authorisation may be extended for up to the rest of the 36-hour period, but at each extension the conditions set out below must still be satisfied (s42(2)). The procedure set out below must be followed at each extension. The officer must take into account any distance and time required if it is proposed to transfer the person to another police area (s42(3)).

The officer giving the authorisation can do so only where s/he has reasonable grounds for believing that:

- an offence for which the person is under arrest is a serious arrestable offence;
- the investigation is being conducted diligently and expeditiously; and
- continued detention without charge is necessary to secure or preserve evidence or to obtain evidence by questioning the suspect (s42(1)).

The evidence must relate to an offence for which the suspect is under arrest. The need for reasonable grounds for belief is an objective test and the court will determine whether such grounds existed.

Section 42(6)-(8) applies provisions about hearing representations similar to those which apply on a s40 review (s40(12)-(14) see p161) and the same comments apply. The review at which the s42 decision

---

48 Although this does not prevent an arrest for failure to surrender to custody, having been granted police bail (s46A).

is made should be conducted in person, not over the telephone.[49] In addition to possible representations set out on p161, representations under s42 should also deal with:

- the diligence of the investigation;
- whether the person is under arrest for a serious arrestable offence; and
- how long the continued detention should last.

Section 42 does not give the police any power to delay charging someone where the police have sufficient evidence to charge[50] (although see pp170–172).

The requirements of s42(6) and (7) are mandatory and if they are not followed no valid authorisation may be given.[51]

If the authorisation is given, the officer must inform the person of the grounds for continued detention and record the grounds in the custody record (s42(5)). If at the time, the person has not exercised a right under s56 (p206) to have someone informed of his or her arrest, or under s58 (p196) to consult a solicitor, neither of which can be delayed by the police beyond 36 hours, the authorising officer must inform the suspect of the right, decide whether it may be exercised, and record the decision and the grounds of any refusal (s42(9)).

Where continued detention has been authorised then, if still not charged, the person must be released unconditionally or on bail by the end of 36 hours and must not be rearrested without warrant for an offence for which previously arrested unless new evidence justifying a further arrest has come to light since release.[52] This does not apply where a s43 application is made (see below) (s42(10), (11)).

Justices' warrant of further detention before charge

The application

In certain circumstances justices can authorise further detention

---

49 Code C Note for Guidance 15C.
50 *R v Samuel* [1988] 2 All ER 135 at 141.
51 *Police v Mudd and McDonough* (1987) November *Legal Action* 19, reported as *In the matter of an application for a warrant of further detention* [1988] Crim LR 296.
52 Although this does not prevent an arrest for failure to surrender to custody, having been granted police bail (s46A).

before charge even beyond the 36 hours that can be authorised by police officers under s42.

There must be an application on oath made by a constable and supported by an information. A magistrates' court must be satisfied that there are reasonable grounds for believing that the further detention is justified (s43(1)).

The detention is justified only if the offence for which the suspect is under arrest is a serious arrestable offence, the investigation is being conducted diligently and expeditiously, and the detention is necessary to secure or preserve evidence relating to the offence or to obtain such evidence by questioning the suspect (s43(4)). Thus, detention cannot be authorised for the investigation of an offence for which the suspect is not under arrest. The detention must be necessary, which means that the court must be satisfied that its purpose cannot be achieved in any other way, for example by questioning the suspect at home (but see p157).

If it is clear that the suspect does not want to answer further questions, and that release will not hamper police investigations, then continued detention would not normally be justified. However, Code C, Note for Guidance 1B provides that a person's declaration that s/he is unwilling to reply does not alter the police's entitlement to put questions, and CJPOA s34 means that failure to answer questions put by the police in further interviews could be evidentially significant. Nevertheless, unless there are grounds for believing that further evidence will become available that has not previously been put to the detained person, it will be difficult to justify further detention by reference to the need to obtain evidence by questioning. The court may refuse the application if the police have not followed the correct procedure in authorising detention beyond 24 hours.[53]

The information

The information submitted under s43(1) must state the nature of the offence, the general nature of the evidence on which the person was arrested, what enquiries have been made, what further enquiries are proposed, and the reasons for believing the continued detention to be necessary (s43(14)).

The amount of detail that must be disclosed, and what is meant by 'general nature of the evidence' is unclear. However, in such cases

---

53 *Police v Mudd and McDonough* (n51 above). See also *R v Sedgefield Justices ex p Milne* (1987) unreported CO/1318/87 (Lexis transcript).

the defence will have an early opportunity of assessing the likely strength of the prosecution evidence.

The application

The court may not hear the application unless the suspect has been given a copy of the information and has been brought before the court for the hearing (s43(2)). The suspect is entitled to be legally represented and is entitled to an adjournment in order to obtain representation (s43(3)(a)). Such advice and representation may be given under the police station duty solicitor scheme.[54] The police may, but are not obliged to, keep the suspect in custody during the adjournment (s43(3)(b)).

The police officer who makes the application will be available to be cross-examined on oath, and representations can be made to the court. The representations may relate to:

- the lawfulness of the detention;
- whether the investigation is being conducted diligently and expeditiously;
- whether the application process and time limits have been complied with;
- whether the suspect is under arrest for a serious arrestable offence;
- whether detention is necessary for one or more of the specified purposes (see p166);
- whether the suspect should have been charged already because there is sufficient evidence to do so; and
- the period of the warrant if one is to be made.

The application may be made at any time before the expiry of 36 hours from the start of the detention clock. If it is not practicable for the court to sit at the expiry of 36 hours, and it would not have been reasonable to make the application earlier, and the court will sit during the following six hours, the application may be made within the six-hour period when the court will be sitting, during which time the suspect may be kept in police detention (this fact and the reason

---

54 See generally the Duty Solicitor Arrangements 1994. Although the Arrangements do not specifically mention applications for a warrant of further detention, there is provision for enhanced payment of duty solicitors providing representation on such applications in the Legal Advice and Assistance at Police Stations (Remuneration) Regulations 1989.

being noted on the custody record) (s43(5)–(7)).

The application is actually made when a constable gives evidence and makes the application.[55] If it is made later than at the expiry of 36 hours, the court must dismiss it if it appears to the court that it would have been reasonable for the police to have made it before (s43(7)). This is a mandatory requirement.[56]

The police must plan with the time limits in view, so that the officer making the s42 decision after 24 hours (p164) should have considered the question of applying for a warrant of further detention.

An application may be made before the expiry of the 36 hours (s43(5)) and that should also be borne in mind by the police and the court. In such a case, the court may adjourn the application until the expiry of the 36 hours, and the suspect may be detained during the adjournment (s43(8)(b), (9)).

The court hearing an application is a magistrates' court of at least two justices (or a stipendiary magistrate), but the sitting is not open to the public (s45(1)).

Refusal of a warrant of further detention

If, on a s43(1) application, the court is not satisfied that further detention is justified under s43(4), the court may adjourn the hearing until a time not later than the expiry of the 36 hour period (see above), but otherwise it must refuse the application (s43(8)).

If the application is refused, the suspect may still be held until the expiry of 24 hours from detention, or 36 hours if continued detention was authorised under s42 (p164) (s43(16)). However, if on the application the court takes the view that the suspect is not under arrest for an offence which is a serious arrestable offence, then the police cannot have reasonable grounds for believing that the suspect is under arrest for such an offence (see s42(1)(b)) and once 24 hours has elapsed, the custody officer must order the suspect's release (s34(2)) even if continued detention has been authorised under s42.

By the expiry of the 24 or 36 hours, or on the refusal or dismissal of the application (whichever is appropriate), the suspect must be charged or released unconditionally or on bail (s43(15)).

Where an application is refused, no further application may be

---

55 R v Slough Justices ex p Stirling [1987] Crim LR 576.
56 Ibid. In the Milne case (n53), the police acted reasonably but the magistrates' court was criticised for lack of co-operation.

made in respect of that suspect unless supported by evidence which has come to light since the refusal (s43(17)).

Issue of a warrant of further detention

If the magistrates' court decides to issue a warrant of further detention under s43(1), the period of further detention must be stated in the warrant and may be any period up to 36 hours from the time of issue of the warrant that the court thinks fit, having regard to the evidence and any distance and travelling time in a proposal to transfer the suspect to another police area (s43(10)-(13)). The warrant must state its time of issue (s43(10)(a)). If it does not, it is invalid, and any action taken under it will be unlawful.

At the end of the period specified in the warrant, the suspect must, unless the warrant is extended under s44 (below), be charged or released unconditionally or on bail. In these circumstances the suspect may not be rearrested without warrant for the offence for which previously arrested, unless evidence justifying a further arrest has come to light since release (s43(18), (19)).[57]

Extension of a warrant of further detention

On application made on oath by a constable, supported by an information, a magistrates' court may extend a warrant of further detention if it is satisfied that there are reasonable grounds for believing that the further detention is justified on the criteria set out in s43(4) (s44(1); (see also p166)).

Section 44(6) states that the provisions of s43 relating to notification to the suspect (s43(2)) and legal representation (s43(3)) apply in s44 applications, as do those relating to the contents of the information (s43(14)).

The period of extension must be endorsed on the warrant (s44(5)) and must be such period as the court thinks fit, having regard to the evidence before it (s44(2)) but may not be longer than 36 hours, nor expire more than 96 hours after the detention clock began to run (s44(3)). Thus, if a suspect has been in police detention for 36 hours from the time the detention clock began, and a warrant of further detention for 36 hours is issued, the warrant may be extended under s44 only for 24 hours. Furthermore, the 24 hours must be reduced by

---

57 Although this does not prevent an arrest for failure to surrender to custody, having been granted police bail (s46A).

any time spent between the expiry of the first 36 hours and waiting for the court to sit under s43(5)(b).

If the warrant has been extended for a period ending before the 96 hours, it may be further extended (repeatedly) if the court is still satisfied as to the criteria discussed above. Rules relating to the extension of warrants also apply to the further extension of warrants (that is, rules as to the discretion of the court under s44(3), the period of extension under s44(3), the endorsement under s44(5), and the applicability of s43(2), (3) and (14)) (s44(4) and (6)). Where an application for extension or further extension is refused, the person must be charged, or released unconditionally or on bail immediately, or released at the expiry of the period of any earlier extension or further extension (s44(7) and (8)).

If an extension or further extension is granted, at the end of the period specified, the suspect must (unless there is a further extension) be charged or released unconditionally or on bail and may not be rearrested without warrant for the offence for which previously arrested, unless evidence justifying a further arrest has come to light since release (s43(18) and (19)).[58]

Charge

An officer who considers that there is sufficient evidence to prosecute successfully, and that the detained person wishes to say nothing further, must without delay bring that person before the custody officer.[59]

However, Code C para 16.1 provides that where a person is detained in respect of more than one offence the officer may delay taking him or her before the custody officer until these conditions are satisfied in respect of all of the offences (but see below).

If the custody officer decides that s/he has before him/her sufficient evidence to charge the person with the offence for which s/he was arrested, the officer must either charge the suspect, or release him/her without charge (either on bail or without bail) (s37(7)). Section 37 does not deal with the situation where the custody officer believes that there is evidence to charge the person for an offence for which s/he has not been arrested (as opposed to an offence for which s/he has). Section 31 requires that the person be arrested for

58 Although this does not prevent an arrest for failure to surrender to custody, having been granted police bail (s46A).
59 Code C para 16.1.

such an offence if it appears that s/he would be liable to arrest on release. However, if the officer simply charges the person with such an offence, s/he would no longer be liable for arrest on release.

The duty of the custody officer under s37(7) raises two issues. First, whereas the interviewing officer does not have to take the suspect before the custody officer under Code C para 16.1 unless s/he believes that there is sufficient evidence for a prosecution to succeed, the custody officer must make a decision about charge as soon as s/he has before him/her sufficient evidence to charge. The term 'sufficient evidence to charge' is not defined but it is suggested that it means something less than 'sufficient evidence for a prosecution to succeed'. Therefore, if the custody officer becomes aware that there is sufficient evidence to charge, s/he must make a decision about charge even if the investigating officer has not completed his or her enquiries or completed interview(s) with the suspect.

Second, although (as noted above) Code C para 16.1 provides that a suspect arrested for more than one offence need not be taken before the custody officer until the conditions have been satisfied in respect of all offence, a similar provision is not to be found in s37. Therefore, if the custody officer determines that there is sufficient evidence to charge in respect of one offence, s37 requires that the decision about charge is then taken. However, in these circumstances the suspect may be re-arrested on release, since there is no prohibition on re-arrest in these circumstances. If a person is released in circumstances where a decision about prosecution has not yet been taken, the custody officer must inform him/her of this fact (s37(8)). If the person is charged, or informed that s/he may be prosecuted under s37(8), s/he must be cautioned in the following terms:

> You do not have to say anything. But it may harm your defence if you do not mention now something which you later rely on in court. Anything you do say may be given in evidence. (Code C para 16.3)

After being charged or being informed that s/he may be prosecuted, the person should not normally be interviewed in relation to the offence(s) concerned, although there are exceptions (Code C paras 16.4 and 16.5, and see p221).

There is no power in the Act to detain further a person in respect of whom the custody officer has decided that there is sufficent evidence to charge, but who has not in fact been charged (s37(7)(b)).[60]

Where a person has been arrested for an offence otherwise than

<hr>

60 Although note the power to detain an unfit driver under the Road Traffic Act 1988 s10.

on a warrant endorsed for bail, and has been charged, the custody officer must order release from police detention, unconditionally or on bail (which may be conditional or unconditional) unless one of the detention criteria (below) applies (s38(1)). If one or more of the conditions does apply, the custody officer may authorise the suspect to be kept in police detention (s38(2)). This applies to any offence, arrestable or otherwise, but is subject to the Criminal Justice and Public Order Act 1994 s25. This provides that bail cannot be granted to a person charged with murder, attempted murder, manslaughter, rape or attempted rape if s/he has previously been convicted of any of those offences.[61]

These provisions do not apply if arrest is other than for an offence (for example to avoid a breach of the peace).

Detention after charge

The detention criteria (s38(1))

Name and address unknown or doubted

The first criterion is where the name or address of the suspect cannot be ascertained or where the custody officer has reasonable grounds for doubting whether a name or address is correct (s38(1)(a)(i)).

'Cannot be ascertained' is a very strict test. It does not mean 'cannot reasonably' but 'cannot at all'. Any doubt as to the genuineness of a name or address proffered must be based on reasonable grounds. This is an objective test for the court to interpret. The mere failure to provide corroboration could not in itself be a reasonable ground.

Non-appearance

The second criterion is that the custody officer has reasonable grounds for believing that the suspect will fail to appear in court to answer bail (s38(1)(a)(ii)). In considering this ground the custody officer must have regard to the following factors (s38(2A)):

– the nature and seriousness of the offence,
– the character, antecedents, associations and community ties of the suspect,

---

61 Although if the previous offence was manslaughter, the prohibition only applies if the accused was then sentenced to imprisonment or, if then a child or young person, long-term detention.

- the suspect's record in respect of previous grants of bail, and
- the strength of the evidence.

These factors are the same as those that a court must take into account in similar circumstances. The same comments on reasonableness apply as for the above condition.

Prevention of further offences or prevention of injury or damage

With regard to prevention of further offences or prevention of injury or damage, s38 distinguishes between people arrested for imprisonable offences and those arrested for non-imprisonable offences. Note that, somewhat oddly, the relevant factor is the offence for which they were arrested rather than the offence with which they have been charged.

Where the person was arrested for an imprisonable offence, the third criterion is that the custody officer has reasonable grounds for believing that detention is necessary to prevent him/her from committing an offence (s38(1)(iii)). This is similar to the ground under the Bail Act 1976,[62] except that under the Bail Act the court must have substantial grounds, whereas a custody officer needs only *reasonable* grounds, which suggests a lower threshold. However, the custody officer must have grounds for believing that detention is necessary, and detention will not be necessary if adequate protection can be provided by other means, in particular by granting bail subject to conditions (see p177).

Where the person was arrested for a non-imprisonable offence, the third criterion is that the custody officer has reasonable grounds for believing that detention is necessary to prevent him/her from causing physical injury to any other person or from causing loss of or damage to property (s38(1)(a)(iv)). The comments as to reasonable grounds and necessity (above) also apply. This ground is more limited than that relating to imprisonable offences, since a fear that the suspect will commit an offence that does not involve injury, loss or damage would not be sufficient to deny bail.

In considering these criteria, the custody officer must have regard to the same factors as for the non-appearance criterion (see above).

62 Sch 1, Part 1, para 1(2)(b). Note that the Bail Act 1976 Sch 1, Part 1, para 2A, provides that where a person is charged with an indictable or either-way offence, s/he need not be granted bail if it appears that they were on bail on the date of the alleged offence. However, this ground is not repeated in PACE.

Interference with the administration of justice

The fourth criterion is that the custody officer has reasonable grounds for believing that detention is necessary to prevent the person from interfering with the administration of justice or with the investigation of offences or of a particular offence (s38(1)(a)(v)). The comments as to reasonable grounds and necessity (above) also apply. In considering this criterion, the custody officer must have regard to the same factors as for the non-appearance criterion (see above).

Own protection

The fifth criterion applies where the custody officer has reasonable grounds for believing that detention is necessary for the person's own protection (s38(1)(a)(vi)). Again, the comments on reasonable grounds and necessity (above) apply, but the custody officer is not required to have regard to the s38(2A) grounds set out in respect of the non-appearance criterion. This criterion may be relevant because the person is at risk from others, because s/he is vulnerable through age or mental disorder, or because s/he is at risk of self-harm.

Juvenile's own interests

The final criterion is that, in the case of an arrested juvenile (someone who appears to be under the age of 17 – s37(15)) the custody officer has reasonable grounds for believing that the juvenile ought to be detained in his or her own interests (s38(b)(ii)).

The concept of 'own interests' is intended to be wider than 'own protection', although the distinction will not always be easy to draw. This criterion might apply where the juvenile would otherwise be released to vagrancy, homelessness, prostitution or loneliness.

The custody officer must secure that a juvenile who has not been released is moved to local authority accommodation, where a person acting on behalf of the authority may detain the child, unless the custody officer certifies that:

a) it is impracticable to do so; or
b) in the case of an arrested juvenile who has attained the age of 12 years, that no secure accommodation[63] is available and that keeping him/her in other local authority accommodation would not

---

63 'Secure accommodation' means accommodation provided for the purpose of restricting liberty (s38(6A)). See further the Children Act 1989 s25.

be adequate to protect the public from serious harm from him/ her (s38(6)-(6B)).

Any certificate must be produced to the court at the first hearing (s38(7)).

With regard to impracticability, Code C Note for Guidance 16B makes it clear that lack of secure local authority accommodation does not make it impracticable for a juvenile to be transferred. Furthermore, it provides that neither the juvenile's behaviour nor the nature of the offence charged provides grounds for keeping a juvenile in police custody.[64]

With regard to lack of secure accommodation, this only applies to juveniles at least 12 years old where keeping them in other local authority accommodation would not be adequate to protect the public from serious harm from them. If the juvenile is charged with a violent or sexual offence (as defined by the Criminal Justice Act 1991 s31), 'serious harm' means death or serious personal injury, whether physical of psychological, caused by further offences committed by the juvenile (s38(6A)). Serious harm is not defined for other offences but it is suggested that it should be given a similar meaning.

If a juvenile is transferred to local authority accommodation in pursuance of such arrangements, the custody officer ceases to be under the duty imposed by s39(1) in relation to the juvenile (s39(4)).

Recording the detention

A custody officer who has authorised a charged person to be kept in detention must, as soon as practicable, make a written record of the grounds for detention in the presence of the accused, who must be informed of these grounds at the same time (s38(3), (4)). However, an accused who at the time is incapable of understanding what is said, is violent or likely to become violent, or is in urgent need of medical attention need not be present (s38(5)). These are questions of fact, but the responsibility for the decision seems to lie with the custody officer. If the situation changes, the accused must be informed of the grounds for detention as soon as practicable.[65]

---

64 Home Office Circular 78/1992 'Criminal Justice Act 1991: Detention etc. of Juveniles' states that 'impractical' means circumstances where transfer would be physically impossible by reason of, for example, floods, blizzards, or the impossibility, despite repeated efforts, of contacting the local authority. It would probably also include circumstances where the local authority fails or refuses to provide any accommodation.

65 Code C para 1.8.

There is no provision for representations to be made at this stage.

Production at court[66]

Section 46 sets out the procedure for those who have been detained after charge to be brought before a magistrates' court (s46(1)).

If the person is to be brought before a court for the petty sessions area in which the police station is situated (normally the case, especially in urban areas), this must happen as soon as practicable and at any event not later than the first sitting after charge (s46(2)). If no sitting is due on the day of charge or the next day, the custody officer must inform the clerk to the justices of the situation (s46(3)).

If the person is to be brought before a court for a magistrates' court area other than the one in which the police station at which charging took place is situated, the person must be taken to that area as soon as practicable, and brought before the court as soon as is practicable thereafter and in any event not later than the first sitting after arrival in the area (s46(4)). Again, if no sitting is due either on the day of arrival or the following day, the person must be taken to a police station in the area and the custody officer must inform the clerk to the justices of the situation (s46(5)).

If it is practicable to bring the person charged before the court earlier than the first sitting after charge or arrival in the area, this must be done. For example, if somebody is charged or arrives at 11.00am while the court is still sitting, it might be practicable to bring the matter to court before the court rises at 1.00pm rather than wait until the next sitting at 2.00pm or the following morning. Practicability is a question of fact for a court to determine in each case.

When the clerk to the justices has been notified under either s46(3) or (5), the clerk must arrange for a court to sit not later than the day following the day of charge or arrival, unless that day is Christmas Day, Good Friday, or a Sunday, in which case the court must sit on the first day which is not one of those days (s46(6)-(8)).

The above scheme does not, however, require a person who is in hospital to be brought before a court if not well enough (s46(9)).

---

66 Practical problems were discussed in *R v Avon Magistrates' Court Committee ex p Broome* [1988] Crim LR 618. The police decide which court or clerk to notify, but the clerk arranges where the court is to sit.

Total length of police detention

Figure 1 (p178) shows in chart form the time-table provided by Pt IV of the Act. In summary, a person may not be held without charge for longer than 96 hours (24 hours if arrest is not for a serious arrestable offence) not including any time taken to reach the police station after arrest (up to a maximum of 24 hours, if not arrested in the police area in which wanted). Following the charge, the maximum police detention before appearing in court is 48 hours if the suspect is charged shortly after midnight, not including any time taken travelling to the area in which the court is situated, and subject to a further maximum of 48 hours if Christmas Day falls on a Saturday or Monday, or 24 hours if charged on a Saturday. This maximum period of eight or nine days' detention will apply only in an unfortunate combination of circumstances, but six or seven days is certainly possible.

For example, if a suspect is wanted in London for a serious arrestable offence and is arrested in Scotland, the time-table might look as follows:

Monday	00.05 am	arrested in Scotland
Tuesday	00.05 am	detention clock starts
Wednesday	00.01 am	continued detention authorised
	12.01 pm	warrant of further detention
Thursday		warrant extended at special late-night sitting
Friday		warrant in force
Saturday	00.05 am	charged
Sunday		(discounted)
Monday	04.00 pm	appears in court

The suspect will have spent the best part of eight days in police detention.

Bail from the police station

At several stages after arrest, the police have the power or duty to decide whether to release somebody on bail, that is, subject to a duty to attend such court or police station at such time as the custody officer decides (s47(3), (8)). The custody officer can give written notice that attendance at the police station is no longer required

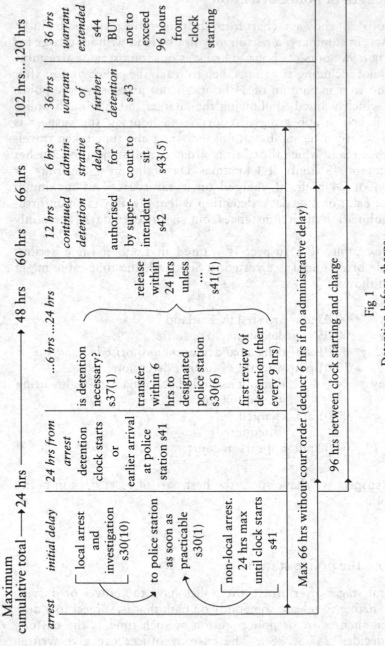

Fig 1
Detention before charge

(s47(4)) but does not have a similar power in respect of attendance at court, although the court itself does have that power.[67]

A release on bail is treated as a release on bail granted in accordance with ss3, 3A, 5 and 5A of the Bail Act 1976 (s47(1)). This means broadly that the custody officer has the same power as a court to require a surety or security or impose conditions and similar duties to make appropriate records of the decision. However, conditions (but not sureties or securities) can only be imposed where the person is being granted bail under s38(1),[68] that is, after charge (s47(1A)). A custody officer can impose any condition a court could impose except a condition to reside in a bail hostel or a condition to co-operate with the making of a report (Bail Act 1976 s3A(2)). A security or surety cannot be required, and conditions cannot be imposed, unless it appears to the custody officer that it is necessary to do so in order to prevent the person from:

a) failing to surrender to custody, or
b) committing an offence while on bail, or
c) interfering with witnesses or otherwise obstructing the course of justice, whether in relation to him/herself or any other person (Bail Act 1976 s3A(5)).

It has been held in respect of a decision by a court that conditions can be imposed provided the court perceives a real, as opposed to a fanciful, risk and it is suggested that a similar principle should apply to custody officers.[69] Where a custody officer grants bail subject to conditions, or varies any conditions imposed (see below), s/he must give reasons for imposing or varying those conditions, and must make a note of the reasons in the custody record and a give a copy of that note to the suspect (Bail Act 1976 s5A(2) and (3)). It is suggested that the requirement to give reasons is more onerous than the requirement to inform a person of the grounds for detention where bail is denied under s38(3) and (4), and requires the custody officer to explain why it is necessary to impose conditions having regard to the Bail Act 1976 s3A(5) (see p175).

If bail is granted subject to conditions under s38(1), that is, after

---

67 Magistrates' Courts Act 1980 s43 as amended.
68 Including s38(1) as applied by s40(10), that is, where bail is considered in respect of a person whose detention is under review at some time following charge.
69 See *R v Mansfield Justices ex p Sharkey* [1985] QB 613.

charge,[70] the suspect may make an application to the same or another custody officer serving at the same station to vary the conditions, who may impose more onerous conditions (Bail Act 1976 s3A(4)). The suspect may also make application to a magistrates' court to vary conditions, whether or not s/he has applied to a custody officer to vary (Magistrates' Courts Act 1980 s43B(1)). The court may, on such an application, impose more onerous conditions or deny bail altogether (Magistrates' Courts Act 1980 s43B(3)).[71] Where conditional or unconditional bail has been granted by a custody officer in respect of an indictable or either-way offence, the prosecution may apply to a magistrates' court to impose or vary conditions or to deny bail, but only if the application is based on information not available to the officer granting bail at the time the decision was taken (Bail Act 1976 s5B(1)-(3)).[72]

Bail granted under PACE is generally enforceable in the same way as bail granted under the Bail Act 1976, although there are some important variations. Failure to surrender to custody at the appointed place and time without reasonable cause is an offence under the Bail Act 1976 s6. This applies whether the person is under a duty to surrender to a court or to a police station. Where the person is bailed to attend a police station, s/he may be arrested without warrant if s/he fails to do so (s46A(1)). Normally, where the person surrenders to bail or is arrested under s46A(1), time spent in police detention before to being granted bail will count in calculating the maximum period of detention (s47(6) and see p163). However, this does not apply, and the detention clock will start again, if the accused is re-arrested other than under s46A(1).[73] Where the defendant is bailed to

70 In fact, Bail Act s3A(4) enables an application to be made where bail has been granted in criminal proceedings which, by the Bail Act 1976 s1(b), is defined to include bail granted to a person under arrest for an offence and would therefore apply to bail granted under other provisions of PACE. However, it is unclear whether the conditions referred to in s3A(4) are confined to conditions as defined in the Bail Act 1976 s3(6) or include sureties and securities provided for by s3(4) and (5). Section 3A(5) implies the latter interpretation is correct. If so, it would be possible for a person granted bail subject to a surety or security under PACE powers other than s38(1) to apply for variation.

71 For the application procedure, see the Magistrates' Courts Rules 1981 r84A(4), as inserted by the Magistrates' Courts (Amendment) Rules 1995 r2(2).

72 The procedure is governed by the Magistrates' Court Rules 1981 r93B, as inserted by the Magistrates' Courts (Amendment) Rules 1995 r2(3). It would seem that this provision applies to bail granted under any provision of PACE, since s5B(1) applies where bail has been granted in criminal proceedings, which are defined by s1. See n70.

73 Which s/he may be if new evidence justifying a further arrest comes to light after release (s47(2)).

attend court, the court may issue a warrant for his/her arrest if s/he fails to surrender, and a police constable may arrest without warrant if s/he has reasonable grounds for believing that the person is not likely to surrender (Bail Act 1976 s7(1) and (3)).

Where a person has been granted bail subject to conditions with a duty to surrender to a court, s/he may be arrested by a constable if s/he breaches those conditions or if the constable has reasonable grounds for believing that s/he is likely to do so (Bail Act 1976 s7(3)). Following arrest, the constable must then take the person before a justice of the peace as soon as practicable and in any event within 24 hours (Bail Act 1976 s7(4)). Breach of conditions does not amount to an offence.

A person who attends at a police station to answer to bail or is arrested under s46A (see p170, n58), may be detained without charge only if the custody officer has reasonable grounds for believing that such detention is necessary to secure or preserve evidence relating to the offence or to obtain such evidence by questioning the person (see p156). This follows from s34(7), which provides that a person who attends at the police station in either of these circumstances is deemed to have been arrested for an offence for the purposes of PACE Part IV. Any period spent in detention before being bailed is counted together with the new period for the purposes of the detention clock (see above).

If there are no such grounds, the custody officer must release or charge the person (in which case the s46 procedure will apply – see p176). A person who has answered bail at a police station may be released again on bail.

Remand by the court to police detention

A magistrates' court has a general power to remand people in police custody in certain circumstances. A remand of not more than three clear days[74] may be in police detention but the person may not be kept in police detention unless there is a need to do so for the purposes of enquiries into other offences and the suspect must be brought back before the court as soon as that need ceases. Meanwhile the person is to be treated as someone in police detention for the purposes of the custody officer's responsibilities under s39 (p150) and periodic reviews under s40 (p159).[75]

74 24 hours in the case of a child or young person (Children and Young Persons Act 1969 s23(14)).
75 Magistrates' Courts Act 1980 s128(7), (8) as amended by 1984 Act s48.

Such remands are often made only with the consent of the person involved.[76] The Act does not specify the need for consent but in many cases if the person is unco-operative it cannot be said that there is a need for a remand in police detention. The distinction is important for a remanded person, since a prison will usually have better facilities (although it might be further from home and family) and at a prison the person will be able to refuse to see police officers.

It should be emphasised that the need for further enquiries after charge is not a ground for the refusal of bail by the court. The power to remand in police custody only arises where a person has been denied bail on the normal grounds under the Bail Act 1976.

Police detention as time towards a custodial sentence

Any time spent in detention under the prevention of terrorism legislation (see chapter 8) or in police detention under the 1984 Act is to count towards any custodial sentence subsequently imposed for an offence in connection with which the person was in police detention.[77]

The phrase 'in connection with which' is very wide, so that the offence for which the sentence is imposed need not be precisely the same as the offence for which the person was arrested or with which the person was charged.

Detention records

Section 50 of the 1984 Act requires each police force to keep records concerning the operation of the detention procedure. The purpose is to allow the use of detention powers to be subject to scrutiny by police authorities and HM Inspectorate of Constabulary.

Powers unaffected by Pt IV of the 1984 Act

Other statutory powers

Certain statutory powers have their own detention schemes providing fewer safeguards for the suspect than the 1984 Act and are preserved (s51).

---

76   But see *R v Feltham Magistrates ex p Cook* (1988) 10 May, unreported, QBD.
77   Criminal Justice Act 1967 s67 as amended by 1984 Act s49.

The preserved powers are:

- powers of immigration officers as to control on entry etc under the Immigration Act 1971 s4 and Sch 2;
- powers of arrest, detention and removal under the prevention of terrorism legislation (see chapter 8); and
- police officers' duties in relation to service personnel under the provisions listed in s51(c).

Habeas corpus etc

People who are in police detention under the Act retain the right to apply for habeas corpus or any other prerogative remedy (s51(d)). These are explained more fully in chapter 12. They provide means whereby the legality of the detention can be challenged and would be available for example if the detention were not based on grounds on which it could be justified under the Act. It is less clear whether a failure to make a written record subsequently would invalidate the legality of detention.

CHAPTER 7

Questioning and treatment of suspects

The questioning and treatment of persons after arrest is governed primarily by the 1984 Act Pt V, but this is supplemented by other statutes, the common law and the Codes of Practice. The Code referred to throughout this chapter unless otherwise specified, is the Code for the Detention, Treatment and Questioning of Persons by Police Officers, Code C. The treatment of persons detained under the Prevention of Terrorism (Temporary Provisions) Act 1989 is discussed on p265.

Procedure on arrival at police station

Code C provides that a custody record must be opened as soon as practicable for each person taken to a police station under arrest or arrested there. All details relating to the treatment of the person while detained must be recorded in it. The custody officer is responsible for the accuracy and completeness of the record and for ensuring that the record or a copy accompanies the person if transferred to another station. When a suspect is taken before a court or leaves police detention, the suspect or legal representative or appropriate adult is entitled to be supplied, on request, with a copy of the record as soon as is practicable. The entitlement lasts for twelve months after release. The suspect's legal representative or appropriate adult is entitled to see the custody record as soon as practicable after their arrival at the police station,[1] although strictly there is no provision for further sight of the custody record during the person's detention. The suspect, legal representative and appropriate adult are entitled

---

1 If they attend the police station more than once, they are presumably entitled to see it every time they attend.

to inspect the original custody record after the suspect has left police detention on giving reasonable notice (Code C para 2).

A person who is taken to a police station under arrest or who is arrested there having attended voluntarily must be informed clearly by the custody officer of the following rights and that they are continuing rights which may be exercised at any stage during the period in custody. They are the rights to:

- have someone informed of the arrest;
- legal advice in private (and that it is available free of charge);
- consult the Codes of Practice (Code C para 3.1).

The custody officer should also provide a written notice setting out these rights, the right to a copy of the custody record and the caution (see below p218). The notice must also explain the arrangements for obtaining legal advice. The suspect should be given another notice setting out his or her rights while in custody. The detainee should be asked to sign the record, acknowledging receipt of these notices; refusal to sign the record should be recorded (Code C para 3.2). Failure to inform the suspect of these rights may result in exclusion of evidence.[2] Any comments made by the suspect in relation to the arresting officer's account or in relation to the decision to detain him/her must be noted in the custody record. The custody officer must not invite comment and must not put specific questions to the suspect regarding such comments or regarding his or her involvement in any offence (Code C para 3.4).

If the custody officer authorises detention, the detainee must be informed of the grounds, which must be recorded, as soon as practicable and in any event before being questioned (Code C para 3.4). The detainee must then be asked to sign the record signifying whether or not legal advice is required at that time. Where such advice is requested previous versions of Code C required the custody officer to act without delay to secure the provision of such advice. This has been omitted from the current version, but in any event s58(4) provides that where requested, the person must be permitted to consult a solicitor as soon as is practicable (except where delay of legal advice is permitted – see p198). If the custody officer does delay

---

2 See for example *R v Williams (Violet)* [1989] Crim LR 66. No authority does more than indicate that a detainee has a right to read the code. Such a right does not, for instance, prevent the intoximeter procedure from continuing: *DPP v Cornell* (1989) *Times* 13 July, QBD and see Code C Note for Guidance 3E.

contacting a solicitor where legal advice has been requested, the fact of and reason for the delay must be noted in the custody record (Code C para 1.1A).

Volunteers[3]

If a suspect is not arrested but is cautioned (see below p217), the officer who gives the caution must at the same time inform the suspect that he or she is not under arrest, and is free to leave at any time, but that if s/he remains at the station there is a right to free legal advice. The officer must point out that the right to legal advice includes a right to speak to a solicitor on the telephone and must ask the volunteer whether s/he wishes to do so (Code C para 3.15). Whether or not s/he is cautioned, a volunteer at the police station who asks about entitlement to legal advice must be given a copy of the notice (above).

Any person attending a police station voluntarily must be allowed to leave at will unless arrested. A person who is not allowed to leave is effectively under arrest and must be informed of this and taken before the custody officer, who is responsible for ensuring that the suspect receives the same information concerning rights as other detainees (Code C para 3.15).

Searches of persons

Generally

The extent to which the search of a person and the seizure of property is permitted depends on the status of the person. If the person has not been arrested the police may search without consent under the powers described in chapter 2. These powers may be exercised at a police station if a person is already there voluntarily, or if a police station is 'nearby' (see pp28–29 above) and the police need, for instance, to remove headgear. If someone is arrested anywhere but at a police station, the police have the powers of search given them by s32 (p144). When someone is brought to the station after being arrested[4] elsewhere or after being committed to custody by an order or sentence of a court or has been arrested at the station or is detained there

---

3 For definition, see p137.
4 Whether for an offence or otherwise.

having surrendered to bail or is arrested having failed to surrender to bail, under s46A (see p177), the police are required to ascertain the property that the person has with him/her and may search the person for that purpose (s54 as amended by the Criminal Justice Act 1988 s147 and the Criminal Justice and Public Order Act 1994 Sch 10). No one should be subjected to an intimate search however, whatever their status, unless the search is within the provisions of s55 (see below p192 for the definition of 'intimate search' and the scope of s55).

Apart from the limited power under s32, the only powers that the police have to search a person who is in police detention at a police station are:

a) under s54;
b) under legislation passed after the 1984 Act, eg, the Prevention of Terrorism (Temporary Provisions) Act 1989; and
c) in limited cases, under s55.

All powers contained in legislation passed before the 1984 Act to search persons in detention at a police station ceased to have effect as a result of s53. However, where a person is in police detention somewhere other than at a police station, for instance in a hospital, the police retain their powers of search (but not of intimate search) under other statutes and also their common law powers (narrower than the s54 power) described by Donaldson LJ in *Lindley v Rutter*.[5] The police also retain powers of search (but again not of intimate search) under other statutes and at common law, in addition to their powers under s54, if a person has been taken to a police station after arrest where the arrest was for other than *an offence*. (The definition of police detention in s118(2) requires careful examination – see p150.)

A decision regarding detention must be made as soon as is practicable (s37(10), see above p153) after an arrested person is taken to a police station, or, where a person is arrested at a police station, after the arrest, but this does not necessarily preclude a prior search. As the requirement of speedy authorisation is stated categorically, a prior search at the police station could be justified only in exceptional circumstances:

. . . there may be circumstances when the power of search should go ahead. One can imagine an affray or violence outside a dance hall or at a football match, where a dozen or more cases are brought into a

5 [1981] QB 128 at 134. The police also have powers of search under s54(6A). See p188.

station. The custody officer will be processing those in detention and it might be inappropriate or even dangerous if other officers were not permitted to carry out searches, under the jurisdiction and control of the custody officer, at the same time as detention was being looked at in relation to other offenders.[6]

Searches under s54

The custody officer is under a duty, by virtue of s54 as amended (see p187), to ascertain the property which suspects have with them at the police station. This duty applies when a person is brought to a police station having been arrested elsewhere or after being committed to custody by an order or sentence of the court or has been arrested at the station or is detained there having surrendered to bail[7] (see p177). The duty also exists where a person is on lodgement at a police station with a view to production in court from such custody or has been transferred from detention at another station or from hospital or has been detained under s135 or 136 of the Mental Health Act 1983.[8] The custody officer is also responsible for ascertaining any property a person may have acquired for an unlawful or harmful purpose while in custody (s54(6A) and Code C para 4.1(a)(ii)). Particulars of the property should be recorded in the custody record which the arrested person should then check and sign. Any refusal to sign should be recorded (s54(2) and Code C paras 2.7 and 4.4). This duty also applies to any property which was removed on arrest. The custody officer is not required, however, to record any property in the custody of the arrested person if by virtue of its nature, quantity or size it is not practicable to remove it to the police station (Code C Note for Guidance 4B).

If the custody officer considers it necessary to search a person in order to perform this duty, the officer may search, or authorise such a search, and reasonable force may be used if necessary to carry it out (ss54(6) and 117). It is not necessary for the officer's belief to be reasonable, so long as it is honest. The custody officer must, however, consider the search necessary and it is therefore unlikely that search on the basis of standing orders would be lawful. The courts have consistently stated that the police must have regard to the circumstances of the particular case (see *Lindley v Rutter* (p187) and *Brazil v*

---

6 Minister, HC Standing Committee E, col 1306–1307, 21 February 1984.
7 Or is arrested having failed to surrender to bail, under s46A.
8 See Code C para 4.1.

Chief Constable of Surrey).[9] *In Middleweek v Chief Constable of Merseyside*,[10] however, the Court of Appeal said that this did not mean that if a standard procedure were followed without consideration being given to the particular case it must follow that the search was unlawful. The existence of standing instructions was in itself not conclusive as to whether the search was unlawful; if its legality were challenged it was for the police to show that the search had been justified in the particular case.

Although the officer is under a duty to ascertain all the property in the person's possession, it appears that there is a power to search only the person and not any baggage (it may be seized however; see below p191).

Anyone in custody (see Code C para 1.10) at a police station or in police detention elsewhere may be searched at any time to ascertain whether s/he is in possession of anything which could be used to:

a) cause physical injury to themselves or any other person;
b) damage property;
c) interfere with evidence; or
d) assist in escape (s54(6A) inserted by Criminal Justice Act 1988 s147).

Neither the Act nor the Code of Practice states that the police should inform the person concerned of the reasons for the search, but the High Court held in *Brazil v Chief Constable of Surrey* (above) that unless circumstances render it unnecessary or impracticable to do so, reasons for the search must be given. If reasons are not given where it would be practicable to do so, then the police are not acting in the execution of their duty; nor are they if they conduct a search without the necessary belief. Such a search may constitute an assault or indecent assault (see further chapter 13).

Searches under s54 may be carried out by any police officer, but only of the same sex as the person searched (s54(8) and (9)).

It is possible for a strip search to be conducted under s54 (but not an intimate search, see p192). A strip search is defined in Code C (Annex A part B) as a search involving the removal of more than outer clothing. Such a search may take place only if the custody officer considers it necessary to remove an article which the detained person would not be allowed to keep and the officer reasonably

---

9 [1983] Crim LR 483. See also *Sheehan v Metropolitan Police Commissioner* (1990) July *Legal Action* 23.
10 [1990] 3 All ER 662 (subsequently overruled, in other respects, by *Hague v Deputy Governor of Parkhurst Prison* [1991] 3 All ER 733, HL).

considers that the person might have concealed such an article (Code C Annex A para 10). It would seem that an article that a person 'would not be allowed to keep' refers to anything in the person's possession subject to s54(3) and (4) (see p191). Note that the custody officer must reasonably consider that the person might have concealed such an article, and para 10 of Annex A specifically provides that strip searches must not be routinely carried out where there is no reason to consider that articles have been concealed.

If a strip search is authorised, the Code states that the reason for the search and its results must be recorded (Code C Annex A para 12), whereas in the case of an ordinary search reasons are not required on the record – only a list of all the person's property. In the case of an arrested person, the record would be part of the custody record. Prior to the Act, the courts recognised that strip searches caused acute embarrassment; in *Lindley v Rutter* (above) Donaldson LJ stated that it was 'the duty of the courts to be ever zealous to protect the personal freedom, privacy and dignity of all . . .' and that searches 'involve an affront to the dignity and privacy of the individual'. In that case, where the police constable tried to remove a brassiere from a suspect in accordance with what she believed to be the chief constable's standing orders, Donaldson LJ said that the removal of a brassiere would require considerable justification.

The conduct of strip searches is now governed by Code C Annex A para 11, which contains provisions regarding privacy and generally requires that no person of the opposite sex should be present other than an appropriate adult specifically requested by the suspect. Further, the paragraph provides that where it is necessary to assist the search, the person may be required to hold his/her arms in the air, or to stand with his legs apart and to bend forward so that a visual examination of the genital and anal area may be made. The latter represents a change of policy on the part of the Home Office, which previously considered that visual examination of intimate parts of the body would amount to an intimate search.[11] In any event, no physical contact must be made with any body orifice during a strip search. Where articles are found in any body orifice (other than the mouth), and the person refuses to hand them over, they cannot be removed unless the conditions for conducting an intimate search are satisfied (see p192).

11 See Home Office Circular 88/1985.

Limitations on s54 searches

The police should not seize any item which there are reasonable grounds for believing is legally privileged (s19(6) above p55). Therefore an honest but unreasonable belief that the items were not legally privileged would not justify the seizure which would be unlawful and an action for trespass to goods might lie (see chapter 13).

The police have power to seize and retain any other property in the person's possession, subject to limitations in regard to clothes or personal effects (s54(3) and (4)). They must, however, give to the person concerned reasons for the seizure unless the person is violent or likely to become so, or is incapable of understanding what is said, eg, because of the effects of alcohol (s54(5)). If this is the case or the person is in need of urgent medical attention, the reasons for seizure must be given as soon as practicable (Code C para 1.8). If the person does not understand English or appears to be deaf and the custody officer cannot communicate the information, then an interpreter called under Code C para 3.6 should communicate the information. There is no requirement for reasons for the seizure to be recorded.

Clothes and personal effects may be seized only in limited circumstances. With the same exceptions as above, the person must be told the reasons for the seizure. Personal effects are those items which a person may lawfully need to use or refer to while in detention, but do not include cash and other items of value (Code C para 4.3). In House of Lords committee it was stated that 'spectacles and watches are pre-eminently personal effects'.[12] If the custody officer believes, not necessarily on reasonable grounds, that the person from whom they are seized may use them to:

a) cause physical injury to themselves or another person;
b) damage property;
c) interfere with evidence; or
d) assist in escape,

such items may be seized (s54(4)(a) and Code C para 4.2). Otherwise a constable may seize clothes or personal effects only if there are reasonable grounds for believing they may be evidence relating to any offence (s54(4)(b)). The lawfulness of seizure by the police on this last ground can therefore be objectively assessed. Unlike other items, reasons for the seizure of clothes and personal effects should be recorded (Code C para 4.5).

The police can retain the property in accordance with s22 (see

12 Lord Trefgarne, HL Standing Committee, 16 July 1984.

above p106), but if it was seized for any purpose other than that it might constitute evidence, it must be returned when the person from whom it was seized is no longer in police detention or the custody of a court or has been released on bail (s22). The custody officer is responsible for the safekeeping of any property which is seized and remains at the police station (Code C para 4.1).

Details of seized property must be given to the magistrates' court when the case comes before it (Magistrates' Courts Act 1980 s48) and the court may order the return of all or part of the property of the accused.

If items are wrongfully seized or retained, an action for trespass to goods may lie (see chapter 13). The goods may still be admissible evidence (see chapter 11).

Intimate searches

An intimate search consists of the physical examination of a person's body orifices, other than the mouth (s65). 'Body orifice' is not defined but would include the ears, nose, anus and vagina. Physical insertion into a body orifice would amount to an intimate search, as would any application of force to an orifice or its immediate surroundings, and would include the removal of something that is in an orifice (Code C Annex A para 11).[13] Note the differences between those parts of the body which are intimate for the purposes of a search, and those parts that are intimate for the purpose of taking a sample (see p230). The police do not have any powers at all to conduct intimate searches without consent or to authorise anyone else (eg, a doctor or nurse) to effect such searches other than under s55 of the Act.[14] Unless a search can be justified under s55, an intimate search without consent would be unlawful and might constitute an assault, indecent or otherwise. (Nothing in the Act, however, affects the powers of customs and excise officers to perform intimate searches, see p276).

An intimate search may be conducted only when a suspect is in police detention (see s118(2) and p150 above) and the search has been authorised by someone of at least the rank of superintendent.

---

13 Para 11 also implies that touching an orifice in these circumstances would amount to an intimate search.

14 Arguably, an intimate search can only be carried out where the s55 conditions are satisfied, even if the suspect does consent. Section 55 makes no mention of consent, and s53 abolishes any common law rule that authorises a search by a constable of a person in police detention at a police station.

This latter authorisation can be written or oral, which of course includes authorisation by telephone, but if it is oral it must be confirmed in writing as soon as practicable (s55(3)).

The search should be carried out only for the purposes stated in the section. There is no general power to conduct an intimate search to look for evidence, even of a serious arrestable offence.

Reasonable grounds for searching

The authorising officer must have reasonable grounds for believing that the suspect has concealed either something which could harm someone or Class A drugs of which the suspect was in possession with the appropriate criminal intent (see below) before arrest (s55(1)). The officer's belief is therefore subject to review by a magistrate or jury, who must be satisfied not only that such a belief was held but that it was reasonable to hold it. In the case of potentially harmful items, the authorising officer must reasonably believe that the suspect has hidden on his or her person an item which both could be used to injure the suspect or others and also might actually be so used while the suspect is in police detention or the custody of a court. Examples of such items are micro-detonators, razor blades, knives, explosives and in some cases drugs.

In the case of Class A drugs (which include heroin but not cannabis) the authorising officer must believe, on reasonable grounds, that a Class A drug is concealed on the suspect who was in possession of it with the appropriate criminal intent before arrest. The 'appropriate criminal intent' means an intent to commit an offence under:

a) the Misuse of Drugs Act 1971 s5(3) (possession of controlled drugs with intent to supply to another); or

b) the Customs and Excise Management Act 1979 s68(2) (exportation etc with intent to evade a prohibition or restriction) (s55(17)).

'Class A drug' has the meaning assigned to it by the Misuse of Drugs Act 1971 s2(1)(b) (s55(17)). An intimate search for such drugs cannot be justified only on the ground that the authorising officer reasonably believed the suspect was a drug-taker or user; the officer must have reasonable grounds for believing that the suspect was going to supply or export such drugs.

In *R v Maginnis*,[15] the House of Lords reviewed the meaning of 'supply' in the Misuse of Drugs Act 1971 s5(3). In attempting to apply its 'ordinary and natural meaning' it held that 'supply' connoted

15 [1987] 1 All ER 907, HL.

more than the mere transfer of physical control of an object from one person to another. It considered that the additional element was that of enabling the recipient to apply the object to purposes for which he or she desired or had a duty to apply it. It was not a necessary element in the concept of supply that the provision should be made out of the personal resources of the person supplying the drugs.[16]

A search should be authorised only if the authorising officer believes on reasonable grounds that the item(s) cannot be found without an intimate search (s55(2)). This is potentially a severe restriction on the use of these searches. Section 55 does not impose any time limit. If the items were likely to be exposed naturally in time, as would be the case with most items, then it could be argued that the search should not be authorised (but see chapter 6 on detention limits).

Medical personnel

A drugs offence search (as searches for Class A drugs are described in the section) should be conducted only by a suitably qualified person, that is, a registered medical practitioner or registered nurse (s55(4)). A search for potentially harmful items should also be carried out by a doctor or nurse, but may be conducted by a police officer, if an officer of at least the rank of superintendent believes that it is not practicable for it to be carried out by a doctor or nurse (s55(5)). In this case there is no need for the belief to be reasonable, but the officer does not have complete freedom of choice in the matter. In order to come to the conclusion that a search by a doctor is impracticable, the officer would have to have reasons, and if these reasons were implausible it is highly unlikely that magistrates or a jury would believe either that the officer honestly thought it was impracticable or that the matter had been considered at all. If such a search is carried out by a police officer, the reasons must be recorded (Code C Annex A para 8).

The Act does not require a doctor or nurse to conduct such a search and they cannot be ordered to do so. The Act merely provides the authority in law to conduct such searches.

If the search is conducted by the police, the police officer must be of the same sex as the person searched (s55(7)) but if the search is carried out by a doctor or nurse there is no such requirement. The Code provides that no one of of the opposite sex (except a doctor or nurse) may be present (but see below), nor should anyone whose presence is unnecessary. Before the search takes place the person

16 Lord Keith of Kinkel at 909g-n.

should be informed why it is considered necessary (Code C Annex A para 2).

The police may use reasonable force if necessary to effect an intimate search (s117). However, there is no provision in the Act for medical practitioners to exercise such force or for any police constable present at such a search to use any force – so any force applied by a doctor, or police officer who is present but not conducting the search, may constitute an assault.

Venue

A drug offence search (see above) should be carried out only at a hospital, a registered medical practitioner's surgery or at some other place used for medical purposes. An intimate search for potentially harmful items, however, may be carried out at any of those places, and also at a police station, but nowhere else (s55(8)). The reason for the distinction is that the latter search is likely to be urgent. Intimate searches which are conducted elsewhere will be unlawful.

The police have the same powers of seizure and retention as under s54, and they must provide reasons in the same circumstances (s55(12) and (13)). Where it is impossible to communicate with the suspect because of the latter's incapability, the information must be given as soon as practicable (Code C para 1.8). Incapability would include drunkenness, but not deafness or inability to understand the language, unless the search takes place before it is practicable to call an interpreter (see above).

Code C Annex A para 5 provides that a search of a juvenile or a person who is mentally disordered or mentally handicapped should take place only in the presence of the appropriate adult (see below pp208 and 210) of the same sex unless the person specifically requests the presence of a particular adult of the opposite sex who is readily available. In the case of a juvenile, the search may take place in the absence of the adult only if the juvenile signifies in the adult's presence that this is what is preferred and the adult agrees. A record of this decision should be made and should be signed by the adult (Code C Annex A5 para 5). These provisions apply only to searches taking place at police stations and it appears therefore that the presence of such an adult is not required when the search is carried out at a hospital for example.

The Act requires that as soon as practicable after the search the parts of the body which were searched and the reasons should be recorded in the custody record (s55(10)). In addition, Code C provides that the custody officer should record who carried out the search, who was present and the results of the search (Code C Annex A para 7).

Access to legal advice

An arrested person who is held in custody by the police in a police station or other premises has the right to consult a solicitor privately at any time (s58)[17]. The right under this section is not restricted to persons who have been arrested for an offence and are in a police station, but extends to anyone who has been arrested whether or not for an offence, including those arrested under the Mental Health Act 1983 s136. (For the rights of a person detained under the Prevention of Terrorism (Temporary Provisions) Act 1989 see chapter 8). Access can be delayed for those in police detention (see s118(2)) in exceptional circumstances, but even then only for 36 hours from the relevant time, that is, the time detention began (ss58(5) and 41(2), and see p162). A volunteer is always entitled to legal advice, and there is no provision for delay (see p186).

A person must be informed of the right to advice when s/he is taken to a police station under arrest, or arrested having attended voluntarily (Code C paras 3.1 and 3.5); immediately before the beginning or re-commencement of any interview at the police station or other authorised place of detention (Code C para 11.2); before a review of detention is conducted (Code C para 15.3); after s/he has been charged or informed that s/he may be prosecuted, if the police wish to bring to his/her attention any statement or the content of an interview, or where they wish to re-interview (Code C para 16.4 and 16.5); before being asked to provide an intimate sample (Code D para 5.2); and before an identification parade, or group or video identification (Code D para 2.15). If the person declines legal advice in any of these circumstances, the police officer must tell him/her that the right to legal advice includes the right to speak to a solicitor on the telephone and must ask him/her if s/he wishes to do so. If the person still declines, the officer must ask them why, and must record any answer. However, once it is clear that the suspect does not wish to speak to a solicitor at all, the officer must cease to ask him/her the reason (Code C para 6.5).

17 This applies equally to juveniles and mentally disordered or handicapped suspects. Code C Note for Guidance 3G provides that a request for legal advice by such a person must be acted upon in the normal way. It has been held that, in effect, the right under s58 does not arise until detention has been authorised under s37: *R v Kerawalla* [1991] Crim LR 451.

Code C para 6.15 provides that, where a solicitor attends at a police station to see a particular client, the person must be informed (unless Annex B applies) of the solicitor's arrival and asked whether s/he would like to see the solicitor. This applies whether or not the person is then being interviewed, and even if s/he has declined advice or, having requested it, subsequently agreed to be interviewed without having received it. The attendance and the suspect's decision should be noted in the custody record. The code also provides that access to a solicitor should not be delayed on the ground that initial instructions were by someone other than the detainee, provided that the latter wants access (Code C Annex B para 3).[18] If the police deny access improperly, a confession obtained in the absence of a solicitor might not be admitted by virtue of ss76 or 78 (see chapter 11).

Availability of legal advice

Section 58 refers only to the right to consult a solicitor, but Code C para 6.12 gives this word an extended meaning throughout all the PACE Codes of Practice. 'Solicitor' in this context means a solicitor who holds a current practising certificate, a trainee solicitor, a duty solicitor's representative,[19] or an accredited representative included on the register of representatives maintained by the Legal Aid Board.[20] If a solicitor sends a non-accredited or probationary representative[21] (hereafter 'clerk') to see a person held in custody, an officer of at least the rank of inspector may give a direction to refuse admission if s/he considers that such a visit will hinder the investigation of crime (Code C para 6.12). Hindering the investigation of crime does not include giving proper legal advice in accordance with Code C Note for Guidance 6D.

In *R v Chief Constable of Avon and Somerset ex p Robinson*,[22] the Divisional Court ruled that this is a decision for the individual police officer, but that there is no reason why his or her seniors cannot advise the officer of the activities and proclivities of clerks. In deciding whether to deny access, the officer must consider whether

---

18 The right of a third party to instruct a solicitor was confirmed in *R v Jones* (*Sally*) [1984] Crim LR 357, CA.
19 See the Legal Aid Board Duty Solicitor Arrangements 1994 Part VI.
20 See the Legal Aid Board Legal Advice and Assistance at Police Stations Register Arrangements 1994.
21 Defined in the Legal Aid Board Legal Advice and Assistance at Police Stations Register Arrangements 1994 para 1 as a person who has registered but who has not passed the relevant tests.
22 [1989] 1 WLR 793, 2 All ER 15.

the identity and status of the clerk has been satisfactorily established, whether s/he is of a suitable character,[23] and any other matter in any written letter of authorisation provided by the employing solicitor (Code C para 6.13).[24] Code C para 6.13 makes no reference to qualifications or experience of the clerk, and the court in *Robinson* did not think that the police would be able to refuse admission on the ground that the quality of advice would be poor. If a clerk is denied access or is not allowed to remain at an interview, the solicitor should be notified forthwith and be given an opportunity to make alternative arrangements. The detainee should also be informed and the custody record noted (Code C para 6.14).

Consultation with a solicitor may be in person, on the telephone or in writing (Code C para 6.1). A request to see a solicitor and the time it was made must be recorded in the custody record, unless it is made at a time when the person is at court (even in a cell) after being charged with an offence, as must a reason for delay in permitting access (s58(2), (3) and (9)). A person who asks for legal advice should be given the opportunity to consult a specific solicitor, or another solicitor from the same firm, or the duty solicitor, and the custody officer must act without delay to secure the advice (Code C Note for Guidance 6B). No attempt should be made to dissuade the suspect from obtaining legal advice (Code C para 6.4). If advice is unavailable from these sources or the person does not want to consult the duty solicitor, the person should be given an opportunity to choose a solicitor from a list of those willing to provide advice. If this solicitor is unavailable two others may be chosen. Further attempts may be permitted at the custody officer's discretion. Apart from carrying out these duties, a police officer must not advise a suspect about any particular firm of solicitors (Code C Note for Guidance 6B). Solicitors may advise more than one client in an investigation, subject to their views on any conflict of interest. Waiting for a solicitor to finish advising another client may mean, however, that a suspect may be interviewed without a solicitor under (b) below (Code C Notes for Guidance 6G).

Postponement of the right to legal advice

A person who requests legal advice must (subject to the provisions below) be permitted to consult a solicitor as soon as is reasonably

23 The Code states that a person who has a criminal record is unlikely to be suitable unless it is for a minor offence and not of recent date.
24 The Law Society requires that a letter of authorisation be carried. See (1989) LS Gaz 17 May p40.

practicable (s58(4)). An interview should not be commenced without legal advice, or continued if it has been requested, except in certain circumstances:

a) delay in obtaining a solicitor has been authorised under s58(6) and Code C Annex B (see p202); or
b) an officer of at least the rank of superintendent has reasonable grounds to believe that –
   – delay will involve an immediate risk of harm to persons or serious loss of or damage to property (in which case questioning must cease as soon as sufficient information to avert the risk has been obtained, unless other grounds for continuing the interview in the absence of legal advice apply (Code C para 6.7)); or
   – awaiting the arrival of a solicitor who has been contacted and has agreed to attend would cause unreasonable delay to the process of investigation; or
c) the solicitor cannot be contacted, has indicated an unwillingness to be contacted or has declined to attend, and the person has been advised of the duty solicitor scheme but has decided not to use it or the duty solicitor is unavailable. In these circumstances the interview may be started or continued without further delay provided that an officer of the rank of inspector or above has given agreement for the interview to proceed; or
d) the person who wanted legal advice changes his or her mind, in which case the interview may be begun or continued without further delay provided that the person has given his or her agreement in writing or on tape to being interviewed without receiving legal advice and that an officer of inspector rank or above has given agreement for the interview to proceed. Before doing so, the officer must enquire into the person's reasons for his/her change of mind, and the reasons given and the name of the authorising officer must be recorded in the interview record.

The second ground ((b) above), based on 'unreasonable delay', is extremely vague. The officer should ask the solicitor how long it is likely to take to come to the station and bear in mind the time for which detention is permitted, the time of day, whether a period of rest is imminent (see below) and the requirements of other investigations in progress. If it appears necessary that the interview will have to begin before the solicitor's arrival, the latter should be told how long the police could wait before the grounds in (b) become applicable. This is so that the solicitor can make arrangements for someone else to attend (Code C Note for Guidance 6A). There must be reasonable grounds for the officer's belief, again a question of fact for the court. Code C provides that access to a solicitor should not be delayed or denied on the ground that the person might be advised not to answer questions (Code C Annex B para 3).

If any interview is commenced in the absence of a solicitor, or the solicitor has been asked to leave an interview, this must be noted in the interview record. There is no need for reasons to be recorded (Code C para 6.17). The police are not obliged to delay taking specimens under Road Traffic Act 1988 s7 until a solicitor arrives.[25]

Keeping the detainee informed

In *R v Vernon*,[26] the defendant was arrested during the night. She requested legal advice but her solicitor was unavailable. She was not informed of the duty solicitor's imminent arrival at the police station to advise her co-defendant and signed the custody record agreeing to be interviewed in the absence of a solicitor. It was held that, as the defendant would probably have chosen to have the duty solicitor present at her interview, had she known of his imminent arrival, there was a duty to inform her of the scheme. The judge excluded the interview. It appears from this case therefore, that a person who has requested legal advice but cannot obtain it and has not been informed of the duty solicitor scheme, has not agreed to be interviewed without a solicitor. This is not expressly stated in the Code.

However in *R v Hughes*,[27] the Court of Appeal was prepared to admit damaging admissions on the basis that the defendant had consented to being interviewed in the absence of a solicitor, even though he had been misinformed about the availablity of a duty solicitor.[28]

The codes do not permit the police to refuse access to a nominated solicitor on the ground that the solicitor has been called to the station

---

25 *DPP v Billington and Others* [1988] 1 All ER 435 and Code C Note for Guidance 3E; or until the detainee has read the codes, see n1. On drink-drivers see further D Tucker, 'Drink-Drivers' PACE Rights: A cause for concern' [1990] Crim LR 177.

26 [1988] Crim LR 445.

27 [1988] Crim LR 519. See further p304 below.

28 See also *R v Williams (Violet)* [1989] Crim LR 66 and *R v Beycan* [1990] Crim LR 185.

to advise a co-accused, even if they fear that the solicitor may pass on information. (Code C Note for Guidance 6G)

What constitutes an 'interview'?

There may be problems over the meaning of 'interview'. This of course affects the above police duties, because information must be given and access to a solicitor granted, if appropriate, before an interview. The police also have certain obligations during a conversation if it amount to an 'interview' (see p212). Code C para 11.1A defines 'interview' as:

> the questioning of a person regarding his involvement or suspected involvement in a criminal offence or offences which, by virtue of paragraph 10.1 of Code C, is required to be carried out under caution. Procedures undertaken under section 7 of the Road Traffic Act 1988 do not constitute interviewing for the purposes of this code.

Code C para 10.1 requires that a person is cautioned before being questioned about his/her involvement or suspected involvement in an offence (or questioned further where the answers given to previous questions provide the grounds for suspicion) if there are grounds to suspect him/her of that offence. It goes on to provide that a caution is not necessary if the questions are put for other purposes, and gives examples such as questions solely to establish identity, and questions put in furtherance of a search.[29]

The definition of interview has, in the past, caused some difficulty and has changed each time the Codes of Practice have been revised. Some cases decided in relation to previous definitions may no longer be valid. However, *R v Foster*,[30] in which it was held that it was the subject–matter of an exchange and not its length that matters, is still good law.[31] An exchange consisting of only one question and answer can amount to an interview.[32] Questioning by a custody officer, where it concerned involvement in an offence, has also been held to amount to an interview.[33] Such questioning by a custody officer is now prohibited by Code C para 3.4. However, for an exchange to amount to an interview there must be one or more questions, so that

---

29 See *R v Langiert* [1991] Crim LR 777.
30 [1987] Crim LR 821.
31 See also *R v Cox* (1992) *Times* 2 December.
32 See *R v Ward* [1993] 2 All ER 577; (1993) *Times* 29 July, CA.
33 *R v Oransaye* [1993] Crim LR 772.

where a suspect makes unprompted admissions, this will not amount to an interview.[34]

Generally, once a decision to arrest a person has been made, s/he must not be interviewed except at a police station (Code C para 11.1).[35] See further p212. In circumstances where an interview can be conducted other than at a police station, the right to legal advice under s58 does not apply.

For the exclusion of evidence obtained when there have been breaches of the code or statute, see further chapter 11.

Grounds for postponement of right to legal advice

If a person has been detained in connection with a serious arrestable offence (see above p5 for problems of definition) and has not been charged, and certain conditions apply (see s58(8) and Code C Annex B), the right to consult a solicitor may be suspended for a maximum of 36 hours from the relevant time (s41(2), see above p162). The Act specifies a 36-hour maximum delay; the Code states that the delay cannot be continued after charge (Annex B para 1). The 36-hour time limit coincides with the time when an application for a warrant of further detention must be made under s43 (above pp165–170). In any event a detained person must be permitted to consult a solicitor for a reasonable time before any court hearing, which includes an application for a warrant of further detention (Code C Annex B para 5). (Although the code does not state here that the consultation must be private, it should be read subject to s58(1) which does so provide.) The police should neither listen to a telephone call to a solicitor nor read letters to solicitors (Code C para 5.7).

Delay in providing access to a solicitor can be authorised only by an officer of at least the rank of superintendent. The authorisation can be oral or in writing, but if oral it must be confirmed in writing as soon as is practicable (s58(7)). Delay may be authorised if the authorising officer believes on reasonable grounds (again, therefore, the court must consider them reasonable) that, at the time the request is made, access to a solicitor would lead to interference with, or harm to, evidence connected with a serious arrestable offence (it need not be the same offence as the one for which the suspect is

---

34 *R v Younis and Ahmed* [1990] Crim LR 425. For further discussion of interviews see E Cape, *Defending Suspects at Police Stations* (Legal Action Group, 2nd edition, 1995), esp. p97.

35 Note that this applies once a *decision* to arrest has been made, as opposed to the arrest itself.

detained), or interference with or physical injury to other persons, or will lead to the alerting of other persons suspected of having committed such an offence but not yet arrested. 'Such an offence' must mean a serious arrestable offence, but it seems that it could mean any such offence. The third ground for postponing access is that the officer reasonably believes that access at the time of the request would hinder the recovery of any property obtained as a result of such an offence; again it seems that it need not be the same offence. An important safeguard is that if delay is authorised under s58(6) the detained person must be told the reason for the delay and the reason must be noted on the custody record. The moment the reason for delaying access ceases to subsist, the suspect must be asked, as soon as practicable, whether access to legal advice is required and must sign the custody record accordingly. The appropriate action should then be taken (Code C Annex B). Where postponement of legal advice is authorised an interview could begin, or be continued, before the suspect actually receives legal advice (see pp198–202). Once the original reason for the delay ceases to subsist the police must not postpone access for another reason (s58(11)). It is not possible to authorise delay simply on the ground that a solicitor may advise the suspect not to answer questions (Code C Annex B para 3).

There have been two significant amendments to s58. The first amendment was made by the Drug Trafficking Offences Act 1986 (s32)[36] which stated that in addition to the grounds above an officer of at least the rank of superintendent may authorise delay (subject to all the conditions stated above) if the serious arrestable offence is a drug trafficking offence and the officer has reasonable grounds for believing that the detained person has benefited from the drug trafficking and that the recovery of that person's proceeds of drug trafficking will be hindered by granting access to a solicitor (s58(8A)). 'Drug trafficking', 'drug trafficking offence' and 'drug trafficking proceeds' have the same meaning as in the Drug Trafficking Act 1994 (1984 Act s65 as amended).

The second amendment was made by the Criminal Justice Act 1988 (s99). This amendment, in principle, considerably widens the grounds on which access to legal advice can be delayed. Delay can be authorised in any case in which the serious arrestable offence is one to which Criminal Justice Act 1988 Pt VI applies and the officer has reasonable grounds for believing that the detainee has benefited from the offence and that the recovery of the value of the property obtained

36 Not repealed by the Drug Trafficking Act 1994 in this respect.

by the detainee will be hindered by the exercise of the right (see s58(8A) for the exact wording). Part VI of the 1988 Act deals with the powers of the courts to make confiscation orders in the case of most indictable offences or those in Sch 4 of the Act.[36A] This schedule consists of certain summary offences under the Local Government (Miscellaneous Provisions) Act 1982 (offences relating to sex establishments); the Video Recordings Act 1984 and the Cinemas Act 1985. The schedule may be altered by statutory instrument. The purpose of this amendment is to allow time for an application to be made for a restraint order together with the necessary freezing of the assets of the arrested person (see 1988 Act s76(2)).

Where a person has been arrested or detained under the terrorism legislation access to legal advice can be postponed for up to 48 hours (see p267).

Guidelines from the courts on postponement

In *R v Samuel*,[37] the Court of Appeal confirmed clearly a number of important points. First that on a straightforward construction of Code C Annex B para 1, the right of a detained person to receive legal advice cannot be delayed once the police have charged the person with any offence, especially not a serious arrestable offence. Second, the right of a detainee to have access to a solicitor is fundamental and a police officer attempting to justify delaying access has to do so by reference to the circumstances of the particular case and the particular solicitor. The officer not only has to believe access to a solicitor 'will' and not merely 'may' lead to the alerting of other suspects, but the officer has also to believe that if a solicitor were allowed access, the latter would then commit the offence of alerting other suspects or would be hoodwinked into doing so inadvertently or unwittingly. Code C now contains the same guidance on this point and states that if access to a solicitor is delayed, the suspect must be offered access to another solicitor who is a member of a duty solicitor scheme (Code C Annex B).

Hodgson J was of the view that police officers should only rarely form this opinion since: 'Solicitors are intelligent professional people; persons detained by the police are frequently not very clever and the expectation that one of the happenings set out in paras (a) to (c) of

---

36A As a result of the Proceeds of Crime Act 1995 s1 (amending 1988 Act s71), the former requirement for the defendant to have benefited by at least £10,000 has been removed. There is now no minimum amount.

37 [1988] 2 All ER 135, CA.

s58(8) will be brought about in this way seems to contemplate a degree of intelligence and sophistication in persons detained, and perhaps a naivety and lack of common sense in solicitors, which we doubt often occurs.'[38] The Court further commented obiter that in the case of duty solicitors it would be very difficult to justify delaying access since he or she would be well known to the police.

In *R v Alladice*,[39] the Court of Appeal, while supporting the decision in the previous case, was reluctant to share the court's scepticism about solicitors being used as unwitting channels of communication. The court stated here that it may be necessary on a voir dire to investigate a number of matters, including the degree of sophistication of the detainee and in some cases the conduct of the solicitor or of any representative. It may also be necessary to discover from the solicitor the advice which would probably have been given to the detainee. In this case, unlike *R v Samuel*, the Court of Appeal upheld the judge's decision to admit statements made by the defendant, on the basis that although there was a clear breach of s58, the interviews had been conducted with propriety and the presence of a solicitor would have added nothing to the knowlege of his rights which the defendant had already. In *R v Samuel* the Court of Appeal was of the view that if the trial judge had held that refusal of access of a solicitor was unjustified and that the relevant interview was unlawful, he may well have decided that admission of the evidence would be so unfair it ought not to be admitted. The conviction was quashed (see further chapter 11). For a case in which denial of access was held to be proper see *R v Governor of Pentonville Prison ex p Walters*.[40]

For Law Society guidance for solicitors and their staff who advise suspects in the police station, see *Advising a suspect in the police station*.[41] The Law Society has also published a training kit, *Police Station Skills for Legal Advisers* (1994).

---

38 [1988] 2 All ER 135 at 144b-d.
39 [1988] Crim LR 608. See also *R v Dunford* (1990) 140 NLJ 517, CA.
40 (1987) *Times* 9 April. See also *R v Walsh* [1989] Crim LR 822, *R v Dunford* [1991] Crim LR 370 and *R v Anderson* [1993] Crim LR 447.
41 The Law Society, 1991.

Duty to notify arrest and protect vulnerable people

Generally

A person who has been arrested and is being held in custody in a police station or elsewhere is entitled at public expense to have one friend or relative or other known person or someone who is likely to take an interest in the suspect's welfare (this would include a solicitor) told of the arrest and where the suspect is being held (s56 and Code C para 5). The right is not limited to those arrested for an offence. The police must allow this notification as soon as is practicable. Code C provides that custody officers must inform the detainee of this right orally and in writing, when they authorise detention (Code C paras 3.1 and 3.2). The duties of the police in relation to juveniles, the blind, the mentally disordered or handicapped and citizens of Commonwealth countries or foreign nationals are described below. Where a friend, relative or person with an interest in the suspect's welfare enquires as to the whereabouts of the suspect, the information must be given, provided the person agrees and provided delay in notification has not been authorised as described below (Code C para 5.5). The suspect is allowed to receive visits at the custody officer's discretion (Code C para 5.4).

Notification can be delayed only in the case of a serious arrestable offence and then for a maximum of 36 hours from the relevant time (see p162) or until the suspect is charged with an offence (see Code C Annex B). The delay can be only for the same reasons as apply in delaying access to a solicitor (see s58 and p202 above), and must be authorised and recorded, and the reason must be given, in exactly the same way. This section was amended in the same way as s58 by the Drug Trafficking Offences Act 1986 and the Criminal Justice Act 1988 (see above p203). Once the grounds for delay cease to apply, the suspect must be asked, as soon as is practicable, if he or she wants to have someone notified. If so the appropriate action must be taken and recorded (Code C Annex B). The right may be denied to persons detained under the Prevention of Terrorism (Temporary Provisions) Act 1989 for slightly different reasons and for a longer period (see below p266).

The person detained must be cautioned that what is said in any letter, call or message may be given in evidence, except that the police should not listen to a call to a solicitor or read a letter to a solicitor (Code C para 5.7).

If the person nominated by the detained person cannot be contacted, two alternatives may be chosen. If they too cannot be contacted the custody officer has discretion to allow further attempts until the information is conveyed. All such contacts or attempts to contact are at public expense. This right may be exercised each time the suspect is moved, subject to the provisions on delay (s56(8)). In addition, the suspect should be supplied with writing materials, if requested, and allowed to speak on the telephone to one other person. These privileges can be denied or delayed, however, if the person is detained in connection with an arrestable or serious arrestable offence and an officer of the rank of inspector or above considers that any of the consequences set out in Annex B para 1 may result from their exercise (Code C para 5.6). The letters may be read however, hence the need for the caution (above). Records should be kept of requests for notification, letters or messages sent, calls made or visits received and also any refusals on the part of the detained person to have information given to an outside enquirer. In the last case the person must be asked to countersign the record accordingly and any refusal to sign should be recorded (Code C para 5.8).

Children and young persons

Under the Act and the code the police have additional responsibilities[42] where children and young persons are concerned. Section 34(2) of the Children and Young Persons Act 1933 is amended by s57 of the 1984 Act and Sch 15 of the Children Act 1989 and references in this paragraph are to that section as amended. Where a child or young person is in police detention (see p150), the police must take all practicable steps to ascertain the identity of the person responsible for a child or young person's welfare (s34(2)). If they can do this, such a person should be informed of the arrest, the reason for the arrest and the place of detention as soon as practicable (s34(3)). A person is responsible for the welfare of a child or young person if he or she is either the parent or guardian (further defined in s34(8), below) or any other person who has for the time being assumed responsibility (s34(5)). A child is a person under the age of 14 years; a young person is someone who has attained the age of 14 but is under 17 (Children and Young Persons Act 1933 s107). If the child or young person appears to be subject to a supervision order (under the Chil-

---

42 That is, in addition to the right of intimation under s56 which, subject to the exceptions noted, applies irrespective of the age of the person arrested and held in custody.

dren and Young Persons Act 1969 s11 or the Children Act 1989 Part IV) the supervisor, that is social worker or probation officer, must also be given the same information as soon as is reasonably practicable (s34(7)). If the child or young person is in the care of a local authority, it should be contacted as the parent or guardian (s34(8)) as should anyone else who has, for the time being, assumed responsibility for the suspect's welfare. Similarly, the authority must be informed if a child or young person is accommodated by or on behalf of a local authority under the Children Act 1989 s20.[43]

The police must comply with these requirements even if delay is authorised under s56 (see p206) or s58 (see p202) or the child or young person is detained under the terrorism provisions.

In addition to the duty to notify set out above, Code C provides that the police should ask the appropriate adult, who may or may not be a person responsible for the juvenile's welfare (above), to attend the police station to see the child or young person (Code C para 3.9). The 'appropriate adult' here means parent or guardian or, if in care,[44] the care authority or voluntary organisation, a social worker, or failing either of these another responsible adult aged 18 or over who is not a police officer nor employed by the police (Code C para 1.7). The police should explain the grounds for detention to the appropriate adult (Code C para 3.9).

Note for Guidance 1C provides that a person should not act as appropriate adult (even if a parent or guardian) if suspected of involvement in the offence or a witness or the victim of it, or in some other way involved in the investigation.[45] The same has applies if s/he has received admissions from the juvenile before attendance at the police station. The estranged parent of a juvenile should not be asked to act as the appropriate adult if the juvenile expressly and specifically objects (see p223).

If a juvenile admits an offence to or in the presence of a social worker other than during the time that the social worker is acting as

43 A local authority has a duty to provide accommodation in certain circumstances, for example, where the person caring for the child is prevented, whether permanently or temporarily, from caring for him/her.

44 Code C para 1.7 defines 'in care' as meaning all circumstances in which a juvenile is 'looked after' by a local authority under the Children Act 1989. This presumably includes both juveniles accommodated under the terms of a care order and those accommodated under s20 of the 1989 Act.

45 In *DPP v Morris* (1990) 8 October, unreported, the Divisional Court held that a social worker who had called the police and who would be seen by the juvenile as being 'on the side of the police' probably should not have acted as appropriate adult.

appropriate adult, that social worker should not then act as appropriate adult (Code C Note for Guidance 1D). A solicitor or a lay visitor present at the police station in that capacity may not act as the appropriate adult (Code C Note for Guidance 1F).

The purpose of the code is clearly to ensure that there is an impartial adult available to safeguard the rights of the child or young person. Thus in *R v Morse and Others*[46] the judge indicated that the suspect's father, who had a low IQ, was virtually illiterate and who was probably incapable of appreciating the gravity of the situation, should not have been asked to act as appropriate adult.[47] If the juvenile is in the care of a local authority or voluntary organisation but is living at home, the parents should normally be informed in addition to the authority or organisation, unless they are suspected of involvement in the offence concerned. Even if the juvenile is not living at home the police should consider informing the parents (Code C Note for Guidance 3C).

The Codes do not specify the role of the appropriate adult in general terms, but in relation to police interviews, the police are to inform such people that they are not expected to act simply as observers, but are there to advise the juvenile, to observe whether the interview is being conducted properly and to facilitate communication with the interviewer. Generally, a juvenile must not be interviewed in the absence of an appropriate adult unless the conditions for conducting an urgent interview outside of the police station (see Code C para 11.1) or at the police station (Code C Annex C) are satisfied. Code C para 3.13 implies that a custody officer must seek to secure legal advice if the appropriate adult requests it, even if the juvenile has not requested, or indeed, does not want it. In the latter circumstances, the lawyer may consider treating the appropriate adult as the client. The appropriate adult would be entitled to legal advice under the police station advice and assistance scheme, since s/he is likely to come within the definition of a volunteer (s29 and see p137).[48]

---

46 [1991] Crim LR 195, a Crown Court case.

47 In *R v W and Another* [1994] Crim LR 130 the suspect's mother, who was psychotic, was accepted as an appropriate adult, but the facts were unusual. See also *R v Palmer* September 1991 *Legal Action* 21, where it was held that a 17-year-old brother of the suspect was not appropriate since he was not 18 or over and was too close in age.

48 See the Legal Advice and Assistance Regulations 1989 reg 6(1)(c).

Mentally disordered or handicapped persons

Where a mentally disordered or handicapped person is arrested and held in custody, the police are under a duty to inform the 'appropriate adult' of the arrest, the reasons for it and the whereabouts of the person (Code C para 3.9). This duty also applies where an officer suspects, or is told in good faith, that a person is mentally disordered or handicapped or is mentally incapable of understanding the significance of questions put to him/her or his/her replies. In fact, Code C Note for Guidance 1G goes further, and states that where the custody officer has any doubt as to the mental state or capacity of a detained person, s/he should contact an appropriate adult. Further, if the person appears to be suffering from mental disorder, the custody officer must immediately call the police surgeon whether or not the suspect has requested medical attention (Code C para 9.2).[49]

The term 'appropriate adult' here means either a relative, guardian or other person responsible for care or custody; someone who has experience of dealing with such people but is not a police officer nor employed by the police; or failing either of these another responsible adult aged 18 or over who is independent of the police (Code C para 1.7). Although Code C suggests that it may be more satisfactory for the appropriate adult to be someone who has appropriate experience or training, if the suspect prefers a relative to a better-qualified stranger, his/her wishes must be respected (Code C Note for Guidance 1E). The provisions regarding the suitability of potential appropriate adults, and the role of the appropriate adult, are generally the same as for a juvenile.

In addition to the normal power of arrest police constables have the power to remove a person from a public place to a place of safety if they consider that the person is suffering from a mental disorder and is in immediate need of care and control (Mental Health Act 1983 s136). This power is available whether or not the person is suspected of a criminal offence. A police station may be a place of safety for these purposes although Home Office Circular 66/1990 (see below) provides that wherever possible the person should be detained in hospital. A person so removed may be detained for up to 72 hours for examination by a doctor and interview by a social worker in order that suitable arrangements for care and treatment can be made. Code C (except for para 15, which relates to reviews and extension of detention) applies to people detained at a police

---

49 Or, in urgent cases, take the person to hospital or call the nearest available medical practitioner.

station under these powers, and Code C para 3.10 provides that they should be assessed as soon as possible and that an approved social worker and a medical practitioner should be called as soon as possible in order to facilitate this.

The Home Office has issued circular 66/1990 'Provision for Mentally Disordered Offenders', supplemented by circular 12/1995 'Mentally Disordered Offenders: Inter-Agency Working', the purpose of which is to encourage diversion from the criminal justice process where possible, and to encourage best practice, especially in terms of inter-agency co-operation.

Deaf persons and those who do not understand English

If a person is deaf, or appears to be so or does not understand English or there is doubt about his or her speaking ability and the custody officer cannot establish effective communication with the person, the officer should call an interpreter as soon as possible to provide all the information required to be given at the police station (Code C paras 1.6 and 3.6). Further provisions relating to interpreters are contained in Code C para 13.

Blind persons

If a person is blind, seriously visually handicapped or is unable to read, or appears to come into any of these categories, the custody officer should ensure that a solicitor, relative, the 'appropriate adult' or some other person likely to take an interest (and not involved in the investigation) is available to help check documentation. Where the code requires written consent or signification, the person assisting may be asked to sign instead, if the detained person wishes (Code C paras 1.6 and 3.14).

In the case of all the above vulnerable groups, any action taken should be recorded (Code C para 3.18). For further provisions relating to their treatment see below p222.

Citizens of independent Commonwealth countries or foreign nationals

Such persons have absolute rights to communicate at any time with their High Commission, Embassy or Consulate and have other rights as set out in Code C para 7.[50] These rights may not be suspended for any reason[51] and are in addition to their rights under the Act and code to obtain legal advice and have someone informed of the arrest. They must be informed of their rights as soon as practicable. Irrespective of the wishes of the suspect, if the suspect is a citizen of a country with which a bilateral consular convention or agreement is in force,[52] the appropriate High Commission, embassy or consulate must be informed as soon as practicable (Code C para 7.2). However, if the person is a political refugee or is seeking political asylum, contact should only be made at the express request of the suspect (Code C para 7.4).

Conduct of interviews

The conduct of police interviews[53] is governed by the Codes of Practice. The overriding principle is that all persons in custody must be dealt with expeditiously and released as soon as the need for detention has ceased to apply (Code C para 1.1). Once a decision to arrest a suspect has been made (not necessarily implemented), the suspect must not be interviewed about the offence except at a police station (or other authorised detention place) unless the subsequent delay would be likely to:

a) lead to interference with or harm to evidence or interference with or physical harm to other persons; or

b) lead to the alerting of other persons not yet arrested in connection with the offence; or

c) hinder the recovery of property obtained in consequence of the commission of the offence (Code C para 11.1).

If an interview is conducted under any of the above exceptions, it must cease once the relevant risk has been averted or the questions necessary to avert the risk have been asked. If a person makes a 'significant statement or silence'[54] before arrival at the police station, whether or not in the context of an interview, such a statement or

---

50 See *R v Van Axel and Wezer* September 1991 *Legal Action* 12.
51 Even if the right of intimation is being postponed under s56. See *R v Bassil and Mouffareg* December 1990 *Legal Action* 23.
52 For a list of such countries, see Code C Annex F.
53 For the definition of 'interview' see p201.
54 Defined by Code C para 11.2A.

silence must be put to that person at the commencement of an interview in the police station (Code C para 11.2A).[55] The suspect must be reminded of the right to free legal advice at the commencement or re-commencement of an interview at a police station or other authorised place.[56] All such reminders should be noted in the interview record (Code C para 11.2).

An accurate record should be made of each interview whether or not it takes place at a police station (Code C para 11.5). The record should be made in the course of the interview, unless in the investigating officer's view this would not be practicable or would interfere with the conduct of the interview, and must constitute a verbatim record or an account of the interview which summarises it accurately and adequately (Code C para 11.5(c)). If the record is not made in the course of the interview it must be made as soon as practicable after the interview's completion (Code C para 11.7). The record must state, inter alia, the place of the interview, the time it begins and ends, any breaks and the names of those present. (The last requirement is waived where the officers are interviewing persons detained under the Prevention of Terrorism (Temporary Provisions) Act 1989; in this case only warrant numbers and duty stations are required.) It must be made on forms provided for the purpose or in the officer's pocket book or in accordance with the Code of Practice for the Tape Recording of Police Interviews (Code E, see appendix 2) (Code C paras 11.5 and 11.6). Written records must be timed and signed by the maker and if an interview record is not made contemporaneously with the interview the reason must be recorded in the officer's pocket book (Code C paras 11.8 and 11.9).

Unless it is impracticable, the person interviewed must be given the opportunity to read a written interview record and to sign it as correct or to indicate the respects in which it is considered inaccurate. Where the interviewee cannot read or refuses to read the record, the senior police officer present must read it out and ask whether the interviewee would like to sign it as correct or to indicate the respects in which it is considered inaccurate. The officer should then certify

---

55 For a discussion of this, and its relationship to the 'right to silence' provisions of the Criminal Justice and Public Order Act 1994, see E Cape, *Defending Suspects at Police Stations*, (Legal Action Group, 2nd edition 1995), especially chapters 5 and 7.

56 See Code C para 6.5 and p196 for the procedure to be followed when a police officer informs or reminds a person about his/her right to legal advice.

on the record itself what has occurred (Code C para 11.10). If the interview is tape-recorded, the provisions in Code E must be followed.

If a suspect makes any comments outside the context of an interview which might be relevant to the offence, a written record should be made which should be timed and signed by the maker. Where practicable, the suspect should be given the opportunity to read it and sign it or indicate any respects in which it is considered inadequate (Code C para 11.13). An 'appropriate adult' or solicitor who has been present throughout the interview must be given the same opportunity to sign the record and any written statement. (Code C para 11.11).

Any refusal to sign interview records or records made under para 11.13 should be recorded (Code C para 11.12). In *R v Matthews*,[57] the Court of Appeal indicated that when a suspect refuses to read or sign a statement, it might be a wise precaution for the police to serve a photocopy on the suspect's solicitor, noting the time and reason on the custody sheet.

In *R v Delaney*[58] the police failed to make a contemporaneous record or a record as soon as it was practicable to do so. The defendant argued that his confessions should not be admitted by virtue of ss76 and 78 of the Act. The Court of Appeal, while of the opinion that it was not the duty of the courts to punish the police for breaches of the Codes and that such breaches did not automatically mean that evidence thus obtained had to be excluded, thought the confessions should have been excluded. It was of the view that the officers concerned had deprived the court of the most cogent evidence as to the contents of the interview and this, coupled with other factors such as the defendant's character, meant that the evidence was inadmissible. A similar view was taken in *R v Keenan*,[59] where the Court of Appeal held that the interview should have been excluded under s78, and also in *R v Canale*.[60] However, failure to comply with the recording requirements has not always led to exclusion, especially where a legal adviser is present at the interview.[61]

---

57 [1990] Crim LR 190.
58 [1989] Crim LR 139, CA. And in *R v Canale* [1990] Crim LR 329, the Court of Appeal said that the rules relating to contemporaneous note-taking could scarcely be overemphasised.
59 [1989] 3 All ER 598, CA.
60 [1990] 2 All ER 187, CA.
61 *R v Dunn* (1990) 91 Cr App R 237 and *R v Waters* [1989] Crim LR 62.

In *R v Saunders (Rosemary)*[62] a more difficult situation arose. In this case the accused was incorrectly cautioned (see below) and then she made it clear that she would not allow her interview to be written down. She answered questions which the police later recorded. No record of dispensing with the requirement, under Code C, of recording the interview contemporaneously was made and the accused was not given a chance to check the written record. This, together with the defective caution, was sufficient to mean that the interview was excluded from the evidence. In such cases the police should presumably inform the interviewee that at some point a record must be made which the latter must then be allowed to check. Note that special provision is made for a person who objects to having their interview tape-recorded (Code E para 4.5).

Solicitor's presence during interview

Unless delay in obtaining access to legal advice has been authorised under s58 (see p202), a person arrested and held in custody in a police station or other premises is entitled to have a solicitor (who is available at the time the interview commences or is in progress)[63] present whilst s/he being interviewed.[64] Code C para 6 implies that this only applies to a person in police detention, that is, where the person has been arrested for an offence (see p150 for definition). However, s58 provides that all people arrested and held in custody (whether or not for an offence) are entitled to legal advice at any time, which should include when an interview is being conducted. Note, however, that the Court of Appeal held in *R v Kerawalla*[65] that a person held other than at a police station before detention has been authorised is not held in custody.[66] A solicitor[67] may be required to leave an interview only if an officer of at least the rank of superintendent, or above (if readily available, otherwise an inspector) considers

62 [1988] Crim LR 521.
63 Code C para 6.8 defines 'available' as being present at the police station or on the way, or easily contactable by telephone.
64 See p198 for the circumstances in which an interview may be started without a solicitor being present even though legal advice has not been delayed under s58.
65 [1991] Crim LR 451; note the critical commentary at p453.
66 It was held in *R v Chief Constable of South Wales ex p Merrick* [1994] Crim LR 852 that a person held in custody at a magistrates' court does not have a right to advice under s58, but does have a common law right.
67 Including a clerk, although note the additional powers to refuse entry to the police station to a clerk on p197.

that the conduct of the solicitor is such that the investigating officer is unable properly to question the suspect (paras 6.9 and 6.10). Code C now takes a positive view of the role of the defence solicitor, providing that his/her only role is to protect and advance the legal rights of his/her client, which may require the solicitor to give advice which has the effect of his/her client avoiding giving evidence which strengthens the prosecution case. As a result, the Code accepts that a solicitor may intervene in order to seek clarification, or to challenge an improper question or the manner in which it is put, or to advise his/her client not to answer a particular question, or in order to give further legal advice. Removal will only be justified if the conduct of the solicitor is such as to prevent or unreasonably obstruct proper questioning, or prevent his/her client from answering police questions. Examples given of such behaviour are answering questions on behalf of the suspect and providing written replies for him/her to quote (Code C Note for Guidance 6D).

The code stresses that the removal of a solicitor is a very serious step; the officer must be in a position to satisfy a court that the decision was properly made and an officer of at least the rank of superintendent should consider whether to report the matter to the Law Society and, in the case of a duty solicitor, to the Legal Aid Board as well. The suspect should be given a chance to consult another solicitor before the interview is continued and a note should be made in the interview record (Code C paras 6.11, 6.16 and 6.17).

Restrictions on interviewing[68]

PACE itself does not directly regulate the conduct of police interviews, although it does so indirectly by providing for the exclusion of confession evidence obtained by oppression or in circumstances likely to render it unreliable (s76) or any prosecution evidence if to admit it would affect the fairness of the proceedings (s78). Code C does contain a number of provisions concerning interviews although they are not directly enforceable (see chapters 11 and 13).

A police officer must not try to obtain answers to questions or to elicit a statement by the use of oppression. Similarly, an officer must not normally indicate, except in answer to a direct question, what action will be taken on the part of the police if the person answers questions, makes a statement or refuses to do either, eg, holding out

---

68 For a discussion of the meaning of 'interview' see p201 and for further detail on what may amount to improper police behaviour, see E Cape, *Defending Suspects at Police Stations* (LAG, 2nd edn 1995) ch 7.

promises of police bail. If the police are asked directly what action may be taken, they may inform the person so long as the proposed action is proper and warranted (Code C para 11.3). Exceptionally, where (having been cautioned) failure to co-operate may have an effect on immediate treatment of a suspect, s/he should be informed of the consequences and the fact that they are not affected by the caution. Code C para 10.5C gives as an example that fact that a person's refusal to provide his/her name and address may render him/her liable to detention after charge.

The Court of Appeal has held[69] that an offer of immunity to an arrested person might on rare occasions be justified, but that the arrested person should be given full opportunity to discuss it with a solicitor before coming to a decision.

A person heavily under the influence of drink or drugs (to the extent of being unable to appreciate the significance of questions (Code C para 12.3)), should not be interviewed in that state unless an officer of at least the rank of superintendent considers that delay will involve an immediate risk of harm to persons or serious loss of or serious damage to property. No other reasons will suffice. The same applies to arrested juveniles or to persons suffering from a mental disorder or handicap when the appropriate adult (see above p210) is absent, or a person with a hearing defect or someone who has difficulty understanding English when an interpreter is absent. The reasons for any decision to begin interviewing in those circumstances must be recorded but there is no need for the reasons to be adequate – the officer need have only a bona fide belief that the interview should begin. However, if the reasons are inadequate it would obviously be more difficult for the officer to satisfy a court of a bona fide belief. Questioning should not continue once enough information has been obtained to avert the risk. It is stressed in the Code that these 'urgent interviews' without the usual safeguards for vulnerable groups should take place only in cases of 'exceptional need' (Code C Annex C).

Cautions

Code C contains a number of provisions requiring a suspect to be cautioned. The primary cautioning requirement is contained in Code C para 10, which provides that a person must be cautioned, if there are grounds to suspect him/her of an offence, before any questions

69 *R v Mathias* (1989) *Times* 24 August, CA.

about the offence (or any further questions if it is answers to previous questions that have given cause for suspicion) are put to the suspect regarding his/her involvement or suspected involvement in that offence. This requirement only applies if his/her answers or failure or refusal to answer[70] may be given in evidence in a trial. Thus a caution is not necessary if the questioning is for other purposes, such as to establish the person's identity or the ownership of a vehicle or in the furtherance of the proper and effective conduct of a search (Code C para 10.1).[71] Clearly a person must be cautioned before being interviewed within the meaning of Code C para 11.1A (see p201), but by Code C para 10.3 the suspect must also be cautioned on arrest unless it is impracticable because of the person's condition or behaviour or unless s/he was cautioned immediately before arrest.[72] Where a person is cautioned, or reminded of the caution, without being arrested, s/he must be told that s/he is not under arrest and need not remain with the officer (Code C para 10.2). If a juvenile or mentally disordered or handicapped person is cautioned in the absence of an appropriate adult, the caution must be repeated in the adult's presence (Code C para 10.6).

The caution to be given in the above circumstances must be in the following terms:

> You do not have to say anything. But it may harm your defence if you do not mention when questioned something which you later rely on in court. Anything you do say may be given in evidence. (Code C para 10.4)

The wording of the caution follows, in particular, from the Criminal Justice and Public Order Act 1994 s34.[73] If a person does not appear to understand the caution, the officer should explain it in his/her own words (Code C Note for Guidance 10C). Minor deviations from the prescribed wording do not constitute a breach of the cautioning requirement (Code C para 10.4). In *R v Saunders*

---

70 Para 10.1 also refers to a failure to answer satisfactorily although the meaning of this is not completely clear.

71 Note *R v Langiert* [1991] Crim LR 777, in which it was held that an officer must not use a search to try to justify an interview about matters unconnected with the conduct of the search.

72 Arguably the wording of the caution is inappropriate at this stage, since it implies that questioning is imminent; see D Wolchover and A Heaton-Armstrong, 'Questioning and Identification: Changes under PACE 95' [1995] Crim LR 356 at p366.

73 For a discussion of the implications of the caution and the right to silence provisions of the 1994 Act see E Cape, *Defending Suspects at Police Stations* (Legal Action Group, 2nd edition, 1995), esp, chapters 5 and 7.

(*Rosemary*)[74] the caution was defective in that it did not remind the suspect of her right to silence, and because of this and other breaches of the Code, the interview was not admitted in evidence.

If there is a break in questioning, the interviewing officer must, on resumption, make sure that the interviewee is still aware that s/he is under caution and, if there is any doubt, give the caution again in full (Code C para 10.5) The same caution must also be given when a person is charged or informed that s/he may be prosecuted (Code C para 16.2) and it must be in the written notice which must be given to a suspect when charged (Code C para 16.3). If a person is questioned after charge or after being informed that s/he may be prosecuted,[75] s/he should not be cautioned in the above terms, but must be told that s/he does not have to say anything but that anything s/he does say may be given in evidence (Code C para 16.5). The reason for this is that a failure to answer questions after charge cannot lead to inferences being drawn at court under the Criminal Justice and Public Order Act 1994 s34.

Code C para 10 contains special provisions which apply where a person is questioned after arrest about matters that might lead to inferences being drawn under the Criminal Justice and Public Order Act 1994 ss36 or 37. Section 36 enables inferences to be drawn from failure or refusal to account for objects, substances or marks found on a suspect's person, in or on his/her clothing or footwear, or otherwise in his/her possession, or in the place where s/he was arrested. Section 37 enables inferences to be drawn from failure or refusal of an arrested person to account for his/her presence at a place at or about the time the offence is alleged to have been committed.[76] Code C para 10.5B provides that before an inference can be drawn under either s36 or s37 the officer must first tell the suspect in ordinary language:

a) what offence s/he is investigating;
b) what fact s/he is asking the suspect to account for;
c) that s/he believes this fact may be due to the suspect's taking part in the commission of the offence in question;
d) that a court may draw a proper inference if the suspect fails or refuses to account for the fact about which s/he is being questioned; and

---

74 [1988] Crim LR 521, a decision on a previous version of the caution.
75 Which should only occur in limited circumstances: see Code C para 16.5.
76 For a detailed discussion of these two sections, see E Cape *Defending Suspects at Police Stations* (Legal Action Group, 2nd edition 1995) ch 5.

e) that a record is being made of the interview and that it may be given in evidence if s/he is brought to trial.

This special warning would have to be given in addition to any caution that may be required under Code C para 10.1 (see above).

Length of interviews and charging of detained persons

The duration of interviews and the treatment of interviewees while being interviewed is contained in Code C para 12. In particular, in any period of 24 hours a detainee must be allowed a continuous period of at least eight hours for rest. This should normally be at night and should not be interrupted or delayed unless there are reasonable grounds for believing that it would:

a) involve a risk of harm to persons or serious loss of or damage to, property;
b) delay unnecessarily the person's release from custody; or
c) otherwise prejudice the outcome of the enquiry.

In addition, breaks from interviewing should be at recognised meal times. There should be short breaks for refreshments approximately every two hours. The interviewing officer has a discretion to delay a break if there are reasonable grounds for believing that the break would have any of the three results set out above. Ground (c) is clearly broad, but the safeguard is that the delay and reason for it must be recorded in the interview record and therefore the reasonableness of the delay could quite easily be challenged in court when considering the admissiblity of evidence (Code C para 12.11). In *R v Trussler*,[77] a confession was held to be inadmissible as being unreliable because the provisions in the code on rest periods had been breached.

As soon as a police officer who is making enquiries of any person about an offence believes that a prosecution should be brought and there is sufficient evidence for it to be successful, the suspect should be asked if s/he has anything else to say. If not, questioning must cease (Code C para 11.4). (This does not prevent revenue officers or officers acting under the confiscation provisions of the Criminal Justice Act 1988 or the Drug Trafficking Offences Act 1986[78] complet-

---

77 [1988] Crim LR 748.
78 Code C para 11.4 still refers to the Drug Trafficking Offences Act 1986 although this has been largely repealed and replaced by the Drug Trafficking Act 1994.

ing formal records. Any further interviewing for these purposes, however, may well be in breach of the codes.) The person should then be taken before the custody officer who is responsible for considering whether or not the suspect should be charged (Code C para 16.1). When a person is detained in respect of more than one offence, Code C para 16.1 provides that the person need not be taken before the custody officer until the above conditions are satisfied for all the offences. It can be argued that this is contrary to the 1984 Act, since s37(7) provides that if the officer has before him/her sufficient evidence to charge,[79] then s/he must proceed to make a decision. There is no provision in the Act for this decision to be delayed. In any event, once the custody officer is informed that there is sufficient evidence to charge in respect of an offence, s/he must take a decision in respect of that offence even if there are other offences outstanding. If the person is a juvenile, mentally disordered or handicapped, any resulting action should be in the presence of the 'appropriate adult' (see above pp207 and 210). A person who is charged should be cautioned and given a written notice setting out particulars. If relevant the notice should be given to the appropriate adult (see Code C para 16.3).

Once a person has been charged or informed of possible prosecution there should be no further questioning in relation to that offence. Questions are only allowed in the limited circumstances set out in para 16.5 and the person should be cautioned before any such questions are put (see p219). Improper questioning may result in the evidence being excluded.[80] These questions and answers should be contemporaneously recorded and the record must be signed by that person or, if they refuse, by the interviewing officer and any third parties present (Code C para 16.8 and Code E). In *R v Woodall*,[81] in a broad interpretation of these provisions, the Crown Court held a statement to be inadmissible. However, in *R v Pall*,[82] although failure to caution in a post-charge interview was held to be a significant and substantial breach, the confession was not excluded.

---

79 Section 37(7) does not require that the custody officer believe that there is sufficient evidence for a prosecution to succeed. See p171.
80 *R v Waters* [1989] Crim LR 62, CA. But contrast *R v Williams* (1992) *Times* 6 February.
81 [1989] Crim LR 288.
82 (1991) *Times* 4 November.

Statements

All written statements made under caution at police stations must be written on forms provided for the purpose (Code C para 12.12), and all written statements under caution, wherever taken, must be taken in accordance with Code C Annex D. Note that Annex D requires that a statement have a caution at the beginning.

Treatment of persons in police custody

Generally

In addition to specific provisions relating to matters such as legal advice and interviews, Code C prescribes conditions for detention which establish minimum requirements concerning a suspect's physical surroundings and the provision of food, clothing and exercise. In addition, they provide that a person in detention must be checked hourly and, if drunk, at least every half hour (Code C para 8). In *Hague v Deputy Governor of Parkhurst Prison*[83] it was held that the conditions in which a person was detained could not render an otherwise lawful detention unlawful, although a person held in extremely poor conditions may have a claim in negligence.

The code also prescribes the medical treatment of detained persons; for instance that if a detained person requests a medical examination the police surgeon must be called as soon as practicable (Code C para 9).

Additional requirements apply to juveniles, foreign nationals, deaf persons, mentally disordered and handicapped persons and those detained in hospital. Juveniles may be interviewed at their place of education only in exceptional circumstances and then only where the principal or a nominee agrees. If such circumstances do exist, every effort should be made to notify the parents or person responsible for the juvenile's welfare and the appropriate adult, if this is a different person, and reasonable time should be allowed to enable the appropriate adult to attend the interview. In some cases the principal or a nominee may act as the appropriate adult. Juveniles should not be arrested at their place of education unless this is unavoidable, in which case the principal or a nominee should be informed (Code C

83 [1991] 3 All ER 733.

para 11.15 and Note for Guidance 11C).[84] It has been held that the police need not obtain leave of the court before interviewing wards of court for the purpose of criminal investigations so long as they comply with the codes in relation to juveniles. It is for the person having charge of the minor to notify the court.[85] A juvenile should not normally be placed in a police cell[86] but if this has to happen, the cell must not be shared with an adult (Code C para 8.8).

In *Kirkham v Chief Constable of Greater Manchester Police*[87] it was held that police officers who are aware that a prisoner has suicidal tendencies are under a duty of care to prevent the prisoner committing sucide. In this case the police were successfully sued for damages for failing to warn the prison service of the prisoner's suicidal tendencies.

Vulnerable groups

Code C recognises that juveniles, the mentally disordered and the mentally handicapped[88] are particularly vulnerable to suggestion and for that reason it is important to obtain corroboration for any facts admitted wherever possible (Note for Guidance 11B).[89] Also for that reason the code provides that such persons, whether under suspicion or not should not be interviewed in the absence of the 'appropriate adult' unless Annex C (see above p217) applies, in other words, because an interview is extremely urgent (see above pp207 and 210 for

---

84 If the juvenile is arrested, s/he should not normally be interviewed except at a police station. See Code C para 11.1 and p212.

85 *Re R, re G (minors)* [1990] 2 All ER 633.

86 But Code C para 8.8 provides that exceptionally a juvenile can be placed in a cell if there is no other available secure accommodation or if a cell provides more comfortable accommodation than other secure accommodation in the police station!

87 [1990] 3 All ER 246, CA.

88 Note that the special provisions relating to mentally disordered and mentally handicapped people extend to those who are mentally incapable of understanding the significance of questions put to them or of their replies, and apply where an officer has any suspicion or is told in good faith that the person comes within the description (Code C para 1.4).

89 Note that s77 provides that a jury must be warned of the special need for caution where a case against a mentally handicapped defendant rests wholly or substantially on a confession made in the absence of an independent person. See, for example, *R v McKenzie* (1992) 96 Cr App R 98, CA, where it was held that in the circumstances the case should have been withdrawn from the jury. See also *R v Bailey* (1995) *Times* 26 January, CA, which concerned a confession made to a person who was not a police officer.

definition of 'appropriate adult'). The provision is applicable wherever the interview takes place – it is not limited to interviews in police stations. Annex C applies only to juveniles who have been arrested. It has been held that a confession made in the presence of an estranged parent whose presence has been specifically objected to by a juvenile should not be admitted.⁹⁰

In *R v Everett*⁹¹ the Court of Appeal ruled that it was the suspect's actual mental state which was important, not what the police officers considered to be his mental state.

If the appropriate adult, when informed of the person's right to legal advice (as should take place under Code C para 3.7), wishes to exercise that right on behalf of the other person, all the provisions of the Code relating to legal advice come into effect (Code C para 3.13). For the people who must be informed on the arrest of a juvenile, mentally disordered or mentally handicapped person, see above pp206–211. The appropriate adult should be informed that s/he is not simply expected to act as an observer but has an active role to play: first to advise the person being questioned and to observe whether or not interviews are being conducted fairly and properly, and second, to facilitate communication with the person being interviewed (Code C para 11.16, and see p209 above).

Where the appropriate adult is present at an interview that is recorded in writing, the police should ask the adult to read the record and sign it. If the adult refuses, this should be recorded by the police (Code C paras 11.11 and 11.12). If the interview is recorded on tape, the appropriate adult must be asked to sign the label sealing the master tape. If s/he refuses, an inspector or above (or if such an officer is not available, the custody officer) must be called into the interview room and asked to sign it (Code E para 4.15).

A person who has difficulty understanding English or appears to be deaf is entitled to have an interpreter present at an interview, unless agreement is given in writing to be interviewed without one, or unless Code C Annex C (see above p217) applies.⁹² The code specifies the duties of the interpreter at the interview (Code C para 13). When interpretation is needed for the purpose of obtaining legal advice, the interpreter should not be a police officer, but in any other

90 *DPP v Blake* [1989] 1 WLR 432; (1988) 89 Cr App R 179; see Code C Note for Guidance 1C and p208 above.
91 [1988] Crim LR 826 (although note that s76 requires that the confession be obtained in consequence of something said or done) and see below pp298. See also *R v Dutton* (1988) 11 November, CA, unreported.
92 *R v Clarke* [1989] Crim LR 892, CA.

case a police officer may interpret provided that the detained person or the appropriate adult agrees (Code C para 13.9).

A person in police detention at a hospital should not be questioned without the agreement of a responsible doctor (Code C para 14.2).

Tape recording of interviews

The tape recording of interviews with suspects at police stations is governed by Code of Practice E, which is reproduced in Appendix 2. Breaches of the code should be dealt with in the same way as breaches of the other codes issued under the Act (see p4).

Code E provides for mandatory tape recording of interviews in the following circumstances:

a) with a person who has been cautioned in accordance with para 10 of Code C in respect of an indictable offence (including an offence triable either way); or

b) after charge, or after a suspect has been informed of possible prosecution, where the police wish (exceptionally)[93] to put further questions about an indictable or either-way offence; or

c) where the police want to bring to the notice of such a person any written statement by another person or the content of an interview with another person.

The police have a discretion to record other interviews on tape, and this is now the normal method of recording all police interviews with suspects. There is no requirement, however, to tape record interviews for certain terrorist offences[94] or for an offence under the Official Secrets Act 1911 s1 (Code E para 3.2). The custody officer has power in other cases to authorise the interview to be recorded in writing rather than on tape if it is not feasible for the interview to be recorded and the interview should not be delayed, and the reasons for such a decision must be recorded (Code E para 3.3). A decision not to tape record an interview for any reason may be the subject of comment in court (Code E Note for Guidance 3K).

---

93 See p221.

94 That is, those of a person arrested under the Prevention of Terrorism (Temporary Provisions) Act 1989 s14(1)(a) or Sch 5 para 6, or interviews with persons being questioned in respect of an offence where there are reasonable grounds for suspecting that it is connected to terrorism or was committed in furtherance of the objectives of an organisation engaged in terrorism. However, the exception does not apply where the suspected terrorism is connected solely

Where the interview is recorded, the whole interview must be recorded on tape, including the taking and reading back of any statement. Whether a conversation amounts to an interview may be a matter of dispute, although there is less scope for this in relation to conversations in police stations. See p201 above.

The code deals with the formalities of the recording and the position where the suspect objects to recording (Code E para 4). Again a decision to continue recording against the wishes of the suspect may be the subject of comment in court (Code E Note for Guidance 4G). This may be particularly relevant to the question of inferences to be drawn from failure to mention a fact on being questioned[95] where the police had insisted on tape recording an interview contrary to the wishes of the suspect. The action to be taken after recording is also detailed (Code E para 5).

A Practice Note has been issued on the preparation for proceedings in the Crown Court of tape recordings of police interviews.[96]

Videotapes

Code E does not define 'tape recording' but it is understood to refer to audio-taping rather than video-taping. It is understood that there are no current plans to introduce video-taping of police interviews nationally.[97]

The Judicial Committee of the Privy Council has held that if the police want to make a video recording of a confession which includes a reconstruction of the crime, they must give the accused a proper warning that participation is voluntary and the recording must be made as soon as possible after the confession. The accused must be given the opportunity to make and have recorded any comments on the film.[98]

---

with the affairs of the United Kingdom (which description specifically excludes Northern Ireland). Trials involving the tape recording of such interviews have been conducted, and it has been recommended that they should be included in the general tape recording provisions.

95 Under the Criminal Justice and Public Order Act 1994 s34. It could also be relevant to inferences under ss36 and 37.

96 [1989] 2 All ER 415.

97 Experiments have been conducted. See, for example, J Baldwin, 'Video Taping Police Interviews With Suspects: An Evaluation', Police Research Series: Paper 1 (Home Office, 1992). The Royal Commission on Criminal Justice was not convinced of the need for video-taping interviews. See its Report, Cm 2263 (HMSO 1993), esp p26.

98 *Li Shu-Ling v R* [1989] Crim LR 58, PC.

Identification

Vulnerable groups

References in this part of the chapter to the Code are to Code D: Code for the Identification of Persons By Police Officers.[99]

Code D provides that in the case of any procedure involving a suspect's consent, the consent of a person who is mentally disordered or handicapped is valid only if given in the presence of the appropriate adult (Code D para 1.11 and see above p210). Also any procedure involving such a person must take place only in the presence of the adult, but the adult must not be allowed to prompt any identification of a suspect by a witness (Code D para 1.14). Where any information must be given to a suspect it must be given in the presence of the appropriate adult (Code D para 1.13). If the suspect appears to be deaf or there is doubt about his or her hearing or speaking ability or ability to understand English, and the officer cannot establish effective communication, the information must be given through an interpreter. There are also special provisions concerning visually handicapped persons(Code D para 1.12).

In the case of juveniles, the above paragraph applies with the additional points that if the juvenile is under 14, the consent of a parent or guardian is sufficient in its own right and in the case of a juvenile in care consent may be given by the relevant authority or organisation. Parent or guardian has the same meaning as in s57 (see p208).[100] Note that where the appropriate adult is not a parent or guardian (or, where relevant, the care authority) s/he will not be able to give consent. Anyone who appears to be under the age of 17 must be treated as a juvenile (Code D para 1.4) and anyone who appears to be blind or seriously visually handicapped, deaf, unable to read, unable to speak or has difficulty orally because of a speech impediment must, unless there is clear evidence to the contrary, be treated as being vulnerable (Code D para 1.5). If an officer suspects, or is told in good faith, that a person is mentally disordered or handicapped the person must be treated as such (Code D para 1.3).

---

99 The title is somewhat odd, since Code D is concerned with identification procedures relating to all witnesses, not just police officers.
100 Code D para 1.11 and s65.

Fingerprints

The Act provides the police with power in certain circumstances to take fingerprints (the term includes palm prints (s65)) without consent and without a court order, and to use reasonable force to do so (see s117). Palm print is not defined in the Act but it was held in *R v Tottenham Justices ex p L (a minor)*[101] that its meaning is a question of fact in all cases. The Act does not affect police powers under the Immigration Act 1971 (see below p230) nor the Prevention of Terrorism (Temporary Provisions) Act 1989 (see below p268).

The police may take anyone's fingerprints with their consent, even their oral consent, provided that they are not at a police station when the consent is given. If they are at the police station at such a time, however, the consent must be in writing (s61). This means in practice there is no need, for instance, for the victims of burglaries who are often asked to provide fingerprints, to give written consent. The police must give reasons for taking the prints and inform the suspect that they will be destroyed in certain circumstances (see below p236) and of the right to witness their destruction. They must also inform the suspect that the fingerprints may be the subject of a speculative search (s61(7A) and Code D para 3.2A and see p236 below). This information must be given in the presence of the appropriate adult if relevant (Code D para 1.13). If the fingerprints were taken without consent or without 'appropriate consent' (see s65) where consent is required, then an action may be brought for assault and trespass to the person, and the fingerprints may not be admitted as evidence (see below chapters 11 and 13). There is nothing to prevent anyone withholding consent to fingerprints being taken until legal advice has been received, even if this right has been delayed under s58 (see above p202), unless the police have the power to take fingerprints without consent under s61.

Fingerprinting without consent

The first circumstance in which the police have power to take fingerprints without consent is where a person is detained (ie under arrest) at a police station and an officer of at least the rank of superintendent authorises it, in which case reasons must be given and recorded as soon as practicable afterwards, if relevant in the custody record (s61(3)(a) and (5), and Code D para 3). Such authorisation should be given only if the officer believes, on reasonable grounds (a court must later be satisfied that they were reasonable), that the person is

---

101 (1985) *Times* 11 November.

involved in a criminal offence[102] and that the fingerprints will tend to confirm or disprove the involvement (s61(4)). The offence for which the fingerprints are taken need not be the offence for which the suspect is detained. There is clearly no justification for taking fingerprints without consent on a routine basis and the necessity to record a reason should minimise this. If no fingerprints were found during the investigation there could be no grounds for fingerprinting under this provision. Any adviser challenging the admissibility of fingerprints should study the record carefully. If the authorisation was oral (eg, by telephone) it should be confirmed in writing as soon as practicable (s61(5)).

The second ground on which fingerprints may be taken without consent is where the suspect is detained at a police station and has been charged with a recordable offence (s27, and see Code D Note for Guidance 3A for definition) or informed that he or she will be reported for such an offence (that is, for the issue of a summons to be considered or where the institution of proceedings requires the consent of the Attorney-General or the DPP). In addition, the suspect's fingerprints must not have been taken earlier in the course of the investigation of that offence (s61(3)). Again reasons must be given and recorded for the taking of fingerprints without consent.

Finally, fingerprints may be taken without consent where a person has been convicted of a recordable offence (s61(6)). Section 27 (above p129) provides a power of arrest for fingerprinting, in limited circumstances, in the case of a person convicted of a recordable offence: it does not actually give any power to fingerprint. That power is provided by s61(6). Again reasons must be given and recorded.

Fingerprints taken from a person arrested on suspicion of being involved in a recordable offence (but not fingerprints taken in other circumstances) may be checked against other fingerprints held on police records or on behalf of the police (a speculative search) (s63A and see p236). A person whose fingerprints are taken at a police station must be informed that they may be the subject of a speculative search, and this must be recorded in the custody record as soon as practicable after the fingerprints have been taken (s61(7A) and Code D para 3.2A).

The safeguards relating to fingerprints contained in the 1984 Act do not apply to anyone detained under the Prevention of Terrorism (Temporary Provisions) Act 1989 s61(9)(b) (see also p268 below).

---

102 Not necessarily a recordable offence.

If force is used to take fingerprints, a record must be made of the circumstances and those present (Code D para 3.7).

Under the Immigration Act 1971 Sch 2 para 18(2) there is power for immigration officers, constables or prison officers to take all such steps as may be reasonably necessary for photographing, measuring or otherwise identifying a suspect, which includes fingerprinting. This power is preserved by the Act because it relates to the identifying of alleged illegal immigrants who could not otherwise, under the Act, be lawfully forced to give fingerprints (see Code D para 1.15).

Intimate samples

The police have power under the Act to take intimate samples from persons in police detention (see s118(2) and p150 above for the meaning of police detention), but consent or the appropriate consent (see s65 and p227) must be obtained and the action must be authorised (s62 and see below p232). These powers are in addition to their powers under the Road Traffic Act 1988 ss4–11 (see below p233). The Act distinguishes between powers in relation to intimate and non-intimate samples, which are defined in s65.

If a person is not in police detention an intimate sample may be taken (subject to the same requirements of consent and authorisation as set out above) if, in the course of investigation of an offence,[103] two or more non-intimate samples suitable for the same means of analysis have been taken which proved to be insufficient (s62(1A)). An insufficient sample is one that is insufficient with regard to quantity or quality (see s65(4) and Code D para 5.1A).[104] The requirement that the samples be suitable for the same means of analysis does not mean that they must be samples of the same type, merely that they are suitable to be subjected to the same scientific process. It would seem that the police have no power to take an intimate sample from a person not in police detention other than under s62(1A) for the purpose of confirming or disproving involvement in an offence, even if the person does consent. However, Code D Note for Guidance 5E confirms that an intimate sample could be taken outside of this

103 Note that the expression '*an* offence' as opposed to '*the* offence' is used, implying that the non-intimate sample may have been taken in respect of an offence other than that for which the sample is now required.
104 Note that para 5.1A also refers to a sample that has proved unsuitable, but it must mean unsuitable because of its quality and not unsuitable for a particular method of analysis; contrast the wording with s63A(4).

provision if the person consents where it is taken for elimination purposes.

In those circumstances where an intimate sample can be taken, it may be taken in a prison or other institution to which the Prison Act 1952 applies (s63A(3)). This would appear to be confined to the power under s62(1A), since the power under s62(1) is confined to persons in police detention.

By s63A(4) a person who is not in police detention nor held in custody by the police on the authority of a court may be required to attend a police station for a sample to be taken. The person must be so required within one month of the date of charge or conviction,[105] or from the date when the appropriate officer[106] is informed of the fact that the sample is not suitable for the same means of analysis or has proved insufficient. Such a requirement is only possible where the person has been charged with, reported for, or convicted of a recordable offence (see p229), and either no sample was taken during the investigation of that offence, or a sample was taken but was not suitable for the same method of analysis, or a sample was taken but was insufficient. If the person does not comply with the request, s/he may be arrested (see p131). Section 63A only gives a power to require a person to attend a police station (with arrest in default) and does not give extra powers to take intimate samples. Therefore, even where a person has been so required (or is arrested), an intimate sample can then only be taken if the conditions under s62(1) or s62(1A) are satisfied and consent or appropriate consent is given (see p227).[107]

An intimate sample is a sample of blood, semen or any other tissue fluid, urine or pubic hair, a dental impression or a swab taken from a person's body orifice other than the mouth. Neither sample nor swab is defined in the Act. A swab taken from any part of a person's body other than a body orifice (excluding the mouth) is a non-intimate sample, but owing to the definition of an intimate sample if it is a swab of blood, semen, other tissue fluid or urine, it should come within that definition, wherever it is deposited on the body.

105 It would seem to be a legislative oversight that there is no reference to a person being reported with a view to summons.
106 That is, the officer investigating the offence (where the person has not been convicted) or the officer in charge of the police station from which the investigation of the offence was conducted (where the person has been convicted) (s63A(8)).
107 Contrast the wording under s63A(4) with that used in s62(1A).

Authorisation

An intimate sample must not be taken without consent or appropriate consent (see above) which must be in writing (s62(1)(b), (1A)(b) and (4)). For the effect of failure to consent see s62(10) and below p233. Even if such consent is forthcoming the action must be authorised by an officer of at least the rank of superintendent, who should give authorisation only if there are reasonable grounds for suspecting the involvement of the person from whom the sample is to be taken in a recordable offence,[108] and for believing that the sample will tend to confirm or disprove involvement. Authorisation may be oral, but if it is, it should be confirmed in writing as soon as is practicable (s62(3)). The name and rank of the person authorising the taking of the sample, the grounds for giving the authorisation and the fact that the appropriate consent was given should be recorded as soon as practicable after the sample is taken and if the person is detained at a police station, these matters should be recorded in the custody record (s62(7) and (8 and Code D para 5.9)).

The person from whom the sample is to be taken should be informed of the fact of the authorisation, the grounds for the authorisation, including the nature of the offence of which the person is suspected and that in certain circumstances the sample will be destroyed. If the intimate sample is to be taken from a person at a police station, s/he must also be informed that it may be the subject of a speculative search (s62(7A) and Code D para 5.11A; see p236). This information must be given before the sample is taken (s62(7A)(b) and Code D paras 5.11A and 5.11B). If these requirements are not complied with, then the taking of the sample may be unlawful and the results inadmissible, and the relevant police officer or medical practitioner (see below) liable for assault, indecent or otherwise, or trespass to the person. Taking a sample in such a way may be held not to be in the execution of a police officer's duty. See further chapter 13.

Medical practitioner's role

If consent is given and the action authorised, samples or swabs of everything described in the definition of intimate sample except urine or a dental impression should be taken only by registered medical practitioners (s62(9)). If not, the action would be unlawful and the above consequences might apply. Dental impressions should be made only by a registered dentist (s62(9) and Code D para 5.3).

---

108 For meaning of 'recordable offence' see Code D Note for Guidance 3A.

Withholding of consent

There is a powerful sanction in the Act against a person who, without good cause, refuses to consent to an intimate sample being taken. In committal proceedings,[109] or in the trial itself, the court or jury may draw such inferences from the refusal as appear proper. What inference are proper will depend upon the circumstances.

Before being asked to provide an intimate sample or swab, the suspect must be warned that a refusal may have adverse consequences for him/her if the case comes to trial. The code provides a form of words and that a record must be made of the warning being given (Code D paras 5.2, 5.10 and Note for Guidance 5A). Suspects must also be reminded of their entitlement to free legal advice and the reminder noted in the custody record. If a person is voluntarily at a police station for a sample to be taken under s62(1A) (see p230), s/he must also be informed of his/her entitlement to legal advice (Code D para 5.2).[110]

Code D provides that if any clothing is removed from a person in circumstances likely to cause embarrassment, to obtain any samples, no person of the opposite sex who is not a medical practitioner should be present unless a juvenile, or mentally disordered or mentally handicapped person, specifically requests the presence of a particular adult of the opposite sex; nor should anyone whose presence is unnecessary. Clothes should be removed from a juvenile only in the presence of the appropriate adult, unless the juvenile signifies that it would be preferable for the adult to be absent and the latter agrees (Code D para 5.12).

The powers of the police in relation to the taking of blood and urine samples in connection with persons suspected of driving while under the influence of alcohol or drugs (see Road Traffic Act 1988 ss4–11) are unaffected by the Act (s62(11)).

109 Or transfer proceedings if and when they are introduced (s62(1)(a)(i) and Criminal Justice and Public Order Act 1994 Sch 4).
110 The section formerly provided that failure could amount to corroboration, but this was removed by the Criminal Justice and Public Order Act 1994, presumably to bring it in line with the general approach to corroboration in the 1994 Act. For a discussion of what may amount to 'good cause' and possible inferences, see E Cape, *Defending Suspects at Police Stations* (LAG, 2nd edition 1995) p171.

Non-intimate samples

The police have power to take non-intimate samples without consent provided certain conditions are satisfied. Non-intimate samples are defined as samples of hair (other than pubic hair),[111] samples taken from a nail or under a nail, a swab taken from any part of the body (including the mouth, but not other body orifices), saliva or a footprint or similar impression of any part of a person's body other than part of the hand (which is treated as a fingerprint (ss61 and 65). Swabs of blood, semen, urine, tissue fluid or saliva could be intimate samples (see p231). Where hair samples are taken for the purpose of DNA analysis (as opposed to, for example, making a visual match), the suspect must be allowed, within reason, to choose the part of the body from where the hairs are to be taken (Code D Note for Guidance 5C).

Consent and authorisation

The police do not have any powers to take non-intimate samples from anyone, whether or not they are in police detention (for definition see s118(2) and above p150), without the appropriate consent (see above p227) in writing unless the provisions of s63(3) and (4) apply (s63(1)). Code D previously provided that even if a person in detention consented, an inspector or above had to have reasonable grounds for believing that such a sample would tend to confirm or disprove the suspect's involvement in an offence. However, this requirement has been removed from the current Code D so that a person's written consent is, in itself, sufficient authority for a non-intimate sample to be taken (Code D para 5.4). A non-intimate sample may be taken without appropriate consent in three circumstances. First, a non-intimate sample may be taken if the person is in police detention, or is being held in police custody on the authority of a court, and an officer of at least the rank of superintendent authorises it. This should be done only if there are reasonable grounds for suspecting the involvement of the person from whom the sample is to be taken in a recordable offence (see p232 n108) and for believing that the sample will tend to confirm or disprove involvement (s63(3) and (4)). The authorisation must be made in the same way as in s62 (see p232) and the person involved must be given the same information before the sample is taken as the police are obliged to impart under s62. The name of the person who authorised the action must be recorded, together with the grounds for the

---

111 Hair (other than pubic hair) is non-intimate, whether it is cut or plucked (Code D para 5.11(b) and *R v Cooke* (1994) LS Gaz 7 October).

authorisation if relevant, in the custody record.

Second, a non-intimate sample may be taken if the person has been charged with a recordable offence or informed that s/he will be reported with a view to summons for such an offence, and either s/he has not had a non-intimate sample taken from him/her in the course of investigation of the offence, or a non-intimate sample was taken but either it was not suitable for the same means of analysis or, though it was suitable, it was insufficient (s63(3A)).[112] Third, a non-intimate sample may be taken if the person has been convicted of a recordable offence (s63(3B)). Note that no authorisation of a senior officer is required under s63(3A) or (3B).[112a]

The power to take non-intimate samples in prison establishments and the power to require a person to attend a police station in order for a sample to be taken, and the power of arrest in default, are the same as for intimate samples (see p231). However, on return to the police station, voluntarily or under arrest, the police powers to take non-intimate samples are extensive compared to intimate samples. Although the person would not then be in police detention for the purpose of s63(1), a non-intimate sample may be justified under s63(3A) or (3B) (see above).

The use of force

Reasonable force may be used if necessary to obtain non-intimate body samples, in circumstances where they can be obtained without consent (see s117). If force is used, a record must be made of the circumstances and those present (Code D para 5.9). As is the case when intimate samples are taken, no one of the opposite sex to the person from whom the sample is taken unless medically qualified should be present when clothes are removed in circumstances likely to cause embarrassment. No one else whose presence is unnecessary should be present (Code D para 5.12).

Withholding of consent

In the case of non-intimate samples there is no provision in the Act for the court to draw any adverse inference from the withholding of consent. The provision was inserted in s62 (intimate samples)

---

112 This is the same wording as used in s63A(4) (see p231). Note that the section refers to whether samples have been taken in the investigation of 'the' offence, that is, the one for which the person has been charged or reported. This may be contrasted with the power to take an intimate sample under s62(1A) (see p230).

112a See generally Home Office Circular 16/1995, *National DNA Database*.

specifically to make it more difficult for men suspected of rape to refuse their consent to intimate samples being taken. In most circumstances, as noted above, if consent is withheld the police may use reasonable force to obtain the sample.[112b]

Speculative searches

Fingerprints or samples, or the information derived from samples, taken under any power in PACE Part IV from a person arrested on suspicion of having committed a recordable offence may be checked against other fingerprints or samples or information derived from samples contained in records held by or on behalf of the police, or held in connection with or as a result of the investigation of an offence (s63A(1)). This is described as a 'speculative search'. Before fingerprints or a sample are taken from a person at a police station, the suspect must be informed that they may be used for a speculative search and a note of this made in the custody record (ss61(7A), 62(7A), and 63(8B), and Code D para 3.2A and 5.11A). Any speculative search should, of course, be conducted before the police are required to destroy the fingerprints or samples (see below). Any evidence obtained from a speculative search conducted after such time may be the subject of an application to exclude the evidence under s78 (see p300).

Destruction of fingerprints and samples

The police must destroy fingerprints or samples and all copies of either, taken from (a) persons who were suspected of involvement in crime and who have been cleared of that offence; (b) those who have neither been prosecuted nor cautioned; and (c) those who were not suspected of committing an offence (for instance, the victim of a burglary) (s64(1), (2) and (3), but see below). This must be done as soon as is practicable (a) after the conclusion of the proceedings, (b) after the relevant decision has been taken or (c) after they have fulfilled the purpose for which they were taken, respectively. When fingerprints are destroyed, access to the relevant computer data should be made impossible as soon as practicable. Any person to

---

112bIt may also be possible for inferences to be drawn at trial under the Criminal Justice and Public Order Act 1994 where a person refused to account for the presence of a sample, since it is likely to amount to an 'object, substance or mark' within the meaning of s36.

whose fingerprints the data relates may ask for a certificate that this duty has been performed and is entitled to such a certificate from the responsible chief officer within three months of the day of asking (s64(5)). Proceedings are taken to be concluded for this purpose if they are discontinued (s64(4)). Fingerprints and samples taken under the Immigration Act 1971 Sch 2 or from anyone detained under the Prevention of Terrorism (Temporary Provisions) Act 1989 may be retained, however. (s64 (7)).

If anyone asks to witness the destruction of his/her fingerprints and any copies, s/he must be allowed to do so, if the request is made within five days of the accused being cleared or informed of non-prosecution (s64(6) and Code D para 3.1 and 3.4). There is no such right to witness the destruction of samples, however. Where fingerprints are taken under the powers conferred by PACE, the person should have been informed that they would be destroyed in the above circumstances and that there is a right to witness that destruction (Code D para 3.1). The current Code D has omitted the requirement to inform a person from whom a sample is to be taken that it will be destroyed if the conditions are fulfilled.

The provisions regarding destruction of samples are subject to two exceptions inserted by the Criminal Justice and Public Order Act 1994 s57(3). First, samples taken from a person which are required to be destroyed by the above provisions need not be destroyed if they were taken for the purpose of investigation of the same offence for which another person, from whom a sample was also taken has been convicted. This provision deals with the technical difficulty of separating samples in certain circumstances. In order to protect the person who has not been convicted (and whose sample should otherwise have been destroyed), the information derived from that sample cannot be used in evidence against that person or for the purposes of any criminal investigation (s64(3A), Code D para 5.8A and Note for Guidance 5F). Second, similar restrictions are also placed on the use of information from samples which should have been (or presumably, have in fact been) destroyed under s64(1), (2) or (3) (see above).

Identification by witness

The Code of Practice for the Identification of Persons by Police Officers (Code D) governs such matters as the holding of identification parades, group identifications, video identifications, confrontations, the taking of photographs and the viewing of photographs by witnesses.

Photographs of suspects

Unlike fingerprints, PACE does not deal with photographs of suspects, but Code D provides that an arrested person may be photographed without written consent only if the circumstances in Code D para 4.2 apply. Even in those circumstances the police may not use force to take the photograph and if they do so may be guilty of an assault (Code D para 4.3). If a photograph is taken and the person is neither cautioned nor convicted, provided that the person in question does not have a previous conviction for a recordable offence,[113] the photograph and all copies and negatives must be destroyed in the suspect's presence or a certificate confirming their destruction should be provided if this is requested within five days of the above circumstances (Code D para 4.4). The suspect should be told of this right when the photograph is taken. The suspect must also be warned that if s/he significantly alters his/her appearance between the taking of the photograph and any attempt to conduct an identification procedure, this fact may be given in evidence if the case comes to trial (Code D para 4.1).

Detailed provisions governing the showing of photographs to witnesses are contained in Code D Annex D.

Under the Public Order Act 1986 s35 a court making an exclusion order which excludes offenders from football grounds on their conviction of an offence connected with football, may also make an order that the defendant should be photographed. The order can be made only if the prosecution applies for it.

If a photograph of a suspect is taken without consent in circumstances where consent should have been obtained, it is unlikely that a civil action will lie (see *Bernstein v Skyviews and General*)[114] although the police may be liable to disciplinary proceedings for breaching the code.

Since the possession by the police of a photograph of a suspect almost invariably means that the suspect has a criminal record, the fact that a witness has identified the accused by photograph should not be referred to in court by the prosecution unless, for example, the accused had refused to co-operate by failing to make a statement or refusing to participate in an identity parade, so that only photographic identification underlies their case. The defence should be informed that photographs have been shown to witnesses and they

113 See n108 p232 above.
114 [1977] 2 All ER 902.

should decide whether or not reference should be made to it (*R v Lamb*).[115] In such circumstances the *Turnbull* warning should normally be given.[116]

Identification parades

An identification parade may be held if the officer in charge of the investigation considers it useful and if the suspect consents. An identification parade must be held where identification is in dispute and the suspect consents unless the identification officer[117] considers that it would not be practicable to assemble enough sufficiently similar people, or the officer in charge of the investigation considers that a group or video identification would be more satisfactory (Code D para 2.3). Further, an alternative form of identification may be conducted if a suspect significantly alters his/her appearance before the conduct of a parade (Code D para 2.15). Identification is in dispute not only where the suspect denies that s/he was present, but also if s/he admits presence but denies involvement.[118] However, it has been held that Code D does not apply where the suspect is identified in the street shortly after the alleged incident,[119] or where there has been a subsequent accidental meeting between the witness and the suspect.[120] Code D para 2.17 enables the police to take a witness to a particular neighbourhood to see whether s/he can identify the person seen on an earlier occasion, but it is not open to the police to contrive an 'accidental' meeting in order to circumvent Code D.[121] Although it is not referred to in Code D, it would seem that the power to hold a parade applies after charge as well as before charge.[122] A number of cases have confirmed that a parade *must* be held where the conditions are satisfied.[123] However, these cases were decided under previous versions of Code D and it can be seen from the above that the police now have greater discretion to hold alternative forms of identification, even where a suspect has consented to, or requested, a parade.

115 [1980] Crim LR 433, CA.
116 *R v Maynard* (1979) 69 Cr App R 309, CA.
117 A uniformed officer of at least the rank of inspector who is not involved with the investigation (Code D para 2.2).
118 *R v Hope, Limburn and Bleasdale* [1994] Crim LR 118.
119 *R v Kelly* [1992] Crim LR 181. See also *R v Roger* [1993] Crim LR 386.
120 *R v Long* [1991] Crim LR 453.
121 *R v Nagah* [1991] Crim LR 55.
122 See *R v Joseph* [1994] Crim LR 48, where this seems to have been assumed without being specifically considered.
123 See, for example, *R v Gaynor* [1988] Crim LR 242 and *R v Conway* [1990] Crim LR 402.

Whether a parade is practicable may depend on the unusual appearance of the suspect or some other reason (Code D para 2.3). It was held in *R v Britton and Richards*[124] that the decision regarding practicability must be made on reasonable grounds, and the officer must take all reasonable steps to investigate the possibility of holding a parade before moving to another method of identification (although a group or video identification can now be held if they are more satisfactory, even if a parade would have been practicable). In *Britton and Richards*, it was held that a defence solicitor's offer to find people to stand on the parade should have been accepted.[125] If the police do act reasonably in determining whether a parade is practicable, it is unlikely that a court will exclude the identification evidence so obtained.[126]

Before a parade is held the police are required to supply the suspect or his solicitor with details of the first description of the suspect given by any witnesses who are to attend the parade. They should also be allowed to look at any material released to the media by the police for the purposes of recognising or tracing a suspect provided it is practicable to do so and this would not cause unreasonable delay (Code D Annex A para 2A). In addition, the identification officer must explain to the suspect (and give him/her written notice) about various rights, including the right to free legal advice (see Code D para 2.15).

The conduct of identification parades is governed by Code D Annex A, which sets out detailed provisions designed to ensure that a parade is conducted fairly. It includes provisions directed at preventing contamination of a witness by other witnesses or by police officers involved in the investigation. Immediately before viewing the parade, witnesses must be told that the person they previously saw may, or may not, be on the parade and that if they cannot make a positive identification, they should say so. The witness must then be asked to look[127] at each member of the parade at least twice before making any identification (Code D Annex A para 14). A colour photograph

---

124 [1989] Crim LR 144. See also *R v Gaynor*, n123, *R v Knowles* [1994] Crim LR 217, and *R v Penny* (1991) 94 Cr App R 345.

125 The case of *R v Thorne* [1981] Crim LR 702 can be distinguished because the parade had already been formed.

126 See *Tomkinson v DPP* [1995] Crim LR 60.

127 Previously, witness were required to walk up and down the parade at least twice, but this has been replaced in the current version of Code D apparently to cater for certain purpose-built identification suites that did not enable the witness to do this. See *R v Quinn* [1995] Crim LR 56.

or video film must now be taken of all identification parades, but must be destroyed or wiped clean at the end of the proceedings unless the suspect is convicted or is cautioned (Code D Annex A paras 19 and 20).

Although the purpose of identification parades is to see whether a witness can made a visual identification, the identification officer may, at the request of a suspect, ask members of a parade to speak. However, before doing so, the witness must be asked if s/he can make an identification on the basis of appearance only. The witness must also be reminded that the people on the parade have been chosen on the basis of physical appearance (Code D Annex A para 17.)

Group identification

A group identification may be held if identification is in dispute and the suspect consents to it, or refuses to stand on an identification parade, or if the investigating officer[128] considers that it is more satisfactory than a parade (Code D para 2.7). If it is practicable, a group identification can be held without the consent of the suspect, and may be conducted covertly (Code D para 2.7 and 2.8). It is unclear whether (but unlikely that) force could be used to require a suspect to co-operate with a group identification.[129]

Before a group identification is conducted, the suspect or his/her solicitor must be given the same information and supplied with the same documentation as for a parade (see above). A group identification may take a variety of forms, either inside or outside a police station. Where it is held is a matter for the identification officer, although normally it should not be held in a police station unless this is necessary on grounds of safety, security or practicability (Code D Annex E paras 3 and 36).

The conduct of a group identification is governed by detailed provisions contained in Code D Annex E, which distinguishes between moving and static groups. Code D Annex E para 1 provides that, as far as possible, group identifications should be conducted according to the same principles and procedures as identification parades.

---

128 As opposed to the identification officer (see n117).
129 The power to use reasonable force granted by s117 is restricted to powers granted by PACE, and identification procedures are not included in the Act.

Video identification

A video identification may be conducted where identification is in dispute and the investigating officer[130] considers that in the circumstances this would be the most satisfactory procedure (Code D para 2.10). As the technology becomes more widely available, it is likely that video identification will largely replace other forms of identification procedure. The suspect must be asked whether s/he consents, but if s/he does not, a video identification can proceed provided it is still practicable. Therefore, the police can override the wishes of a suspect who would prefer another type of identification, or does not wish any kind of identification procedure to be conducted, provided that the police have, or can obtain, suitable video film of the suspect. The suspect and the other people on the video must be filmed, as far as possible, in the same position and under identical conditions (Code D Annex B para 4).

The conduct of a video identification is governed by Code D Annex B. Before a video identification is conducted the suspect or his/her solicitor must be given the same information and supplied with the same documentation as for an identification parade (see p240). Many of the provisions are similar to those for parades, although for obvious reasons the suspect must not be present when the video is shown to witnesses, although their lawyer or some other representative may be (Code D Annex B para 8).

Confrontation

A confrontation may be held in a case where there is disputed identification, and no other form of identification has been arranged or is practicable (Code D para 2.13). Further, it was held in *R v Miller* [131] that if a suspect, in the presence of his/her solicitor, insists on a confrontation, then another form of identification procedure need not be held. Code D does not state whether practicability is to be decided by the investigating officer or the identification officer. Evidence of identification obtained in a confrontation 'engineered' by the police where another form of identification should have been held has been excluded.[132] It has also been held that a confrontation should not be held simply because the witness is a police officer.[133]

The conduct of a confrontation is governed by Code D Annex C.

---

130   As opposed to the identification officer (see n 117).
131   (1991) 23 March, unreported.
132   *R v Nagah* [1991] Crim LR 55.
133   *R v Samms, Elliot and Bartley* [1991] Crim LR 197.

It must be conducted by an identification officer[134] and no officer involved in the investigation must take part. Thus in *R v Ryan*[135] it was held to be a breach of the Code where an investigating officer accompanied the victim to the confrontation. The suspect does not have to be given the information that is required to be given before other forms of identification by Code D para 2.15 (see p240). However, the suspect or his/her solicitor must be given details of the original description given by any witness who is to attend the confrontation and must be allowed to view any material released to the press for the purpose of recognising or tracing the suspect (Code D Annex C para 2A).

134 See n117.
135 [1992] Crim LR 187.

CHAPTER 8

Police powers under the prevention of terrorism legislation

The Prevention of Terrorism (Temporary Provisions) Act 1989 replaces similar (but not identical) legislation of 1974, 1976 and 1984. Throughout this chapter the Prevention of Terrorism (Temporary Provisions) Act 1989 is referred to as the PTA, whereas 'the 1984 Act' refers to the Police and Criminal Evidence Act 1984.

Offences created by the PTA

Brief descriptions of the offences in England and Wales created by the PTA are given below. They are divided into either-way offences (which may be tried summarily by a magistrates' court or on indictment in the Crown Court) and summary offences (which must be tried in the magistrates' court). The maximum penalty on summary conviction of an either-way offence is six months' imprisonment and a level 5 fine. The maximum penalty on conviction on indictment is an unlimited fine and the number of years' imprisonment indicated in the table on p245. The maximum penalty for the summary offences is set out on p246. Proceedings (except for the Sch 5 offence) may only be instituted with the consent of the Attorney-General (s19(1)).

The s3 summary offence is committed by any person who in a public place wears any item of dress or wears, carries or displays any article in such a way or in such circumstances as to arouse reasonable apprehension of being a member or supporter of a proscribed organisation.

Either-way offences

Section	Offence	Penalty
2(1)(a)	Belonging or professing to belong to a proscribed organisation	10 years
2(1)(b)	Soliciting or inviting support for a proscribed organisation other than support with money or other property	10 years
2(1)(c)	Being involved in the arrangement of, or addressing, a meeting to support or to be addressed by a member or professed member of a proscribed organsation	10 years
8(1)	Failure to comply with an exclusion order	5 years
8(2)(a)	Facilitating the entry of an excluded person	5 years
8(2)(b)	Knowingly harbouring an excluded person	5 years
9(1)	Soliciting or receiving money or other property intending or having reasonable cause to suspect use in connection with acts of terrorism	14 years
9(2)	Making or arranging to be made available money or other property knowing or having reasonable cause to suspect use in connection with acts of terrorism	14 years
10(1)	Soliciting, making available, accepting or arranging to be made available money or other property for the benefit of a proscribed organisation	14 years
11(1)	Facilitating retention or control of terrorist funds	14 years
16A	Possession of articles for suspected terrorist purposes	10 years
16B	Unlawful collection etc of information	10 years
17(2)(a)	Knowingly and without reasonable excuse making any disclosure likely to prejudice a terrorist investigation where an application for a search warrant or order has been granted or is pending	5 years

Either-way offences – cont.

Section	Offence	Penalty
17(2)(b)	Falsifying, concealing, destroying or disposing of, or causing or permitting such in respect of material which is or is likely to be relevant to a terrorist investigation	5 years
18	Failing without reasonable excuse to disclose as soon as reasonably practicable information knowing or believing it might be of material assistance in preventing an act of terrorism connected with Northern Ireland or in securing the apprehension, prosecution or conviction of a person involved in such	5 years
18A	Failure without reasonable excuse to disclose knowledge or suspicion of offences under ss9–11 (other than privileged information)	5 years
Sch 7 para 6(4)	Making a statement knowing it to be false or misleading in a material particular or recklessly making a statement which is so, in purported compliance with an order of a circuit judge	2 years

Summary offences

Section	Offence	Penalty
3	Display of support in public	6 months and/or level 5 fine
13A(6)(a)	Failing to stop or to stop a vehicle when required to do so by a constable under s13A	6 months and/or level 5 fine
13A(6)(b)	Wilfully obstructing a constable in the exercise of powers under s13A	6 months and/or level 5 fine
Sch 5 para 11	Contravention of a Sch 5 prohibition, duty or requirement	3 months and/or level 4 fine

Offences of financial assistance generally

The offences under ss9 and 11 apply to all acts of terrorism connected with the affairs of Northern Ireland or of any other description except those connected solely with the affairs of the United Kingdom or any part of the United Kingdom other than Northern Ireland, provided that if the act is done outside the United Kingdom it constitutes an offence triable in the United Kingdom (ss9(3), (4), and 11(3)). This provision limits the application of the offences so that, for example, they cannot be used in connection with Welsh nationalism, or the animal liberation movement. Sections 11 and 12 also apply to the resources of a proscribed organisation.

There are statutory defences for a person who enters into or is otherwise concerned in any such transaction or arrangement as is mentioned in ss9, 10 or 11. These are:

- (for some of the offences) lack of knowledge or reasonable cause for suspicion (s9(5)(b), s10(2), s11(2));

- acting with the express consent of a constable (s12(2));

- disclosing to a constable, on his/her own initiative and as soon as is reasonable, any suspicion or belief relating to terrorist funds, and not contravening an order of constable forbidding involvement (s12(2));

- (for some of the offences) proof of intention to make such disclosure and reasonable excuse for failure to do so (s12(3)).

These statutory defences are clearly designed to facilitate and legitimise infiltration, entrapment and agents provocateurs.

The meaning of terrorism under the PTA

Many of the powers of the PTA, including powers of search, detention and arrest, depend upon there being an anticipated or actual act of terrorism. 'Terrorism' is the use of violence for political ends, including for the purpose of putting the public or any section of the public in fear (s20(1)). 'Violence', 'fear' and 'political' are not further defined and are treated as ordinary words to be interpreted by the magistrates or jury. Violence could include a trivial assault, and need not involve weapons or explosives. A police officer exercising a power which is dependent on the suspicion of terrorism (for instance arrest under s14(1)(b), see below) must have reasonable grounds to suspect that the act involved is an act of terrorism as defined by the PTA.

The phrase 'terrorist funds' is used in the definition of the s11 offences. This means (s11(3), (4)):

a) funds which may be applied or used for the commission of, or in furtherance of or in connection with, acts of terrorism to which s9 applies (see above, 'offences of financial assistance generally');
b) the proceeds of the commission of such acts of terrorism, or of activities engaged in, in furtherance of or in connection with such acts;
c) the resources of a proscribed organisation, including any money or other property which is, or is to be applied or made available, for the benefit of a proscribed organisation.

The offences under ss16A and 16B were inserted into the 1989 Act by the Criminal Justice and Public Order Act 1994 s82, came into force on 3 January 1995 and are subject to the same process of lapse or renewal as the rest of the 1989 Act.[1] In each case the acts of terrorism to which the offence applies are acts of terrorism connected with the affairs of Northern Ireland or of any other description except those connected solely with the affairs of the United Kingdom or any part of the United Kingdom except Northern Ireland (s16A(2), s16B(2)).

The s17 offence depends on there being a 'terrorist investigation'. This means (s17(1)): investigation into the commission, preparation or instigation of acts of terrorism to which s14 applies (see below), or any other act which appears to have been done in furtherance of or in connection with such acts, or into the resources of a proscribed organisation, or into whether there are grounds for proscribing an organisation.

Proscribed organisations

Proscribed organisations are specified in PTA Sch 1 and are the Irish Republican Army (IRA) and the Irish National Liberation Army (INLA), which include 'any organisation passing under' the same name (s1(1)).

---

1 For a further discussion of these offences see Card and Ward, *The Criminal Justice and Public Order Act 1994* Jordans 1994 at pp130–133.

The Secretary of State may by statutory instrument remove an organisation from the schedule (s1(2)(b)) or add 'any organisation that appears to him to be concerned in, or in promoting or encouraging, terrorism occurring in the United Kingdom and connected with the affairs of Northern Ireland' (s1(2)). For the purposes of the offences in ss10, 11 and 13, proscribed organisations include organisations proscribed in Northern Ireland under the Northern Ireland (Emergency Provisions) Act 1991 s28 (PTA s10(3)).

Exclusion orders

The appropriate Secretary of State is empowered to exclude certain persons from Great Britain (s5), Northern Ireland (s6) or the whole of the United Kingdom (s7). These powers may be exercised in such a way as appears to the Secretary of State expedient to prevent acts of terrorism connected with the affairs of Northern Ireland (s4). The order may be made if the Secretary of State is satisfied that any person is or has been concerned in the commission, preparation or instigation of such acts of terrorism, or is attempting or may attempt to enter the relevant area with a view to being so concerned. The decision to make an exclusion order is not immune from judicial review but the Secretary of State has a very wide discretion and is not obliged to give reasons for making the order because that might involve the disclosure of sensitive intelligence information which the courts would regard as being contrary to the public interest.[2] The order prohibits the person from being in the appropriate area, and the s8 offences relate to such orders. A British citizen may not be excluded from the whole of the United Kingdom (s7(4)) nor from a part of the United Kingdom if the person is and has for the last three years been ordinarily resident in that part (s5(4) and s6(4)). Schedules 2 and 3 deal with powers of detention pending the execution of the exclusion order.

2 *R v Secretary of State for Home Department ex p Gallagher* (1994) *Times* 16 February, CA; *R v Secretary of State for Home Department ex p Adams* [1995] All ER (EC) 177, QBD. But see *R v Secretary of State for Home Department ex p McQuillan* [1995] 4 All ER 400, QBD.

Stop and search under the PTA

Police powers of stop and seach without arrest under Pt I of the 1984 Act are available in connection with offences under the PTA as they are for other offences (see chapter 2), but further powers are provided by the PTA (s13A, as inserted by Criminal Justice and Public Order Act 1994 s81(1), s15(3) and Sch 5 para 4(2)). The safeguards in and the provisions of ss2 and 3 of the 1984 Act and Code of Practice A apply to the powers of stop and search under the PTA.

Written authorisation under s13A

This new power is for constables in uniform to stop and/or search vehicles, their drivers or passengers, and to stop pedestrians and search anything carried by them, for articles of a kind which could be used for a purpose connected with the commission, preparation or instigation of acts of terrorism connected with the affairs of Northern Ireland or of any other description except acts connected solely with the affairs of the United Kingdom or any part of the United Kingdom other than Northern Ireland (s13A(2) and (3)).

The power is only exercisable when it appears to a very senior police officer that it is expedient to authorise its exercise in order to prevent acts of terrorism within the above description and an authorisation is issued (s13A(1)).[3] Its exercise is subject to Code of Practice A.[4] It is an additional power and does not derogate from any other power (s13A(11)).

The authorisation may be issued by any police officer of or above the rank of commander in the Metropolitan Police District or City of London, or assistant chief constable for any other police area (s13A(1)). The sole ground for issue is that it appears to the officer expedient to issue the authorisation in order to prevent acts of terrorism. There is no requirement for reasonable belief or suspected imminence of such acts.

The period of the authorisation may not exceed 28 days (s13A(1)) but should be the minimum period that the authorising officer considers necessary to prevent or try to prevent or deal with the risk of terrorism.[5] The authorisation may be renewed for further periods not exceeding 28 days (s13A(8)).

3 For an analysis of this provision see Card and Ward, *The Criminal Justice and Public Order Act 1994* (Jordans 1994) pp20–22.
4 Code of Practice A para 1.5(c).
5 Code of Practice A para 1.8A and Note for Guidance 1F.

The authorisation must be in writing and signed by the authorising officer and must specify the period during which and any specified locality in which the powers under it are exercisable. Alternatively it may apply to any place within the area (s13A(1), (10)).

It is for the authorising officer to determine the geographical area in which the use of the powers is to be authorised and the officer should take into account factors such as the nature and venue of the anticipated incident, the numbers of people who may be in the immediate vicinity of any possible incident, and their access to surrounding areas. The officer should not set a wider area than that he believes necessary for the purpose of preventing terrorism.[6]

It should be noted that there is no power under s13A to search a pedestrian, only to search anything carried by that pedestrian. Any search of the pedestrian must be authorised under some other power, although the use of some other power might be appropriate to search the pedestrian if anything suspect is found as a result of the search under the s13A power.[7] Similar issues about the meaning of pedestrian arise as in the power under s60 of the Criminal Justice and Public Order Act 1994 (see above pp42–43). The power to stop vehicles applies with any necessary modifications to ships and aircraft (s13A(5)). The meaning of vehicle is further defined in s20(1) of the 1989 Act so as to include hovercraft and trains and their carriages.

The power may be exercised whether or not the constable suspects or has any grounds for suspecting that the person or vehicle is carrying such articles, and the constable may make any search that he thinks fit (s13A(4)). However, such stops and searches are subject to ss2 and 3 of the 1984 Act (pp28–35 above), dealing with information to be given, the nature of the search, and record keeping. They are also subject to the provisions of Code of Practice A (except where the Code deals with reasonable grounds for suspicion). In particular, the Code aims at restricting the degree of embarrassment that may be experienced, reserving force as a last resort, and limiting the nature of any search in public (see above pp28–30). On general principles, the nature of the search must be limited to that appropriate to search for the relevant articles.

A person who fails to stop or to stop a vehicle when required to do so by a constable in the exercise of powers under s13A, or wilfully obstructs a constable in the exercise of those powers, commits an offence and is liable on summary conviction to imprisonment for a

6 Code of Practice A Note for Guidance 1G.
7 Code of Practice A para 3.5A.

term not exceeding six months or to fine not exceeding level 5 or to both (s13A(6)(7)).

Where a vehicle is stopped by a constable under s13A (whether or not a search takes place) the driver is entitled to obtain a written statement that the vehicle was stopped under that section if an application for such a statement is made within twelve months of the stop (s 13A(9)). A similar right is conferred on a pedestrian who is stopped under s13A (s13A(9)). These rights are in addition to those conferred by s3 of the 1984 Act (see above pp33–35).

Stop and search under s15

Where a constable has power to arrest a person under the PTA s14 (see below p261), there is also power to stop and search a person without making an arrest, in order to ascertain whether that person possesses any document or article which may constitute evidence of liability to arrest (s15(3)). Such a search may be carried out only by a person of the same sex as the person being searched (s15(4)). This power does not extend to cases where the offence suspected is one under ss3, 13A, 17 or 18 or Sch 7.

There is no requirement for the constable to have reasonable grounds to suspect the presence of the items which may be searched for, although the constable must have reasonable grounds for suspecting that the person is liable to arrest (for instance, that a person is guilty of an offence under ss2, 8, 9, 10 or 11 of the Act).

Unlike the power of stop and search under the 1984 Act, a stop and search under s15(3) of the PTA may be carried out anywhere and is not limited to public places.

Examination under Sch 5

The power under Sch 5 para 4(2) may be exercised only in respect of a person who has arrived in, or is seeking to leave, Great Britain or Northern Ireland by ship or aircraft. There is a power to examine (ie question) such persons to determine whether they appear to be concerned in the commission, preparation or instigation of acts of terrorism (except those connected solely with the United Kingdom other than Northern Ireland) or whether they are subject to an exclusion order, or whether there are grounds for suspecting that they have committed offences under s8 of the PTA (Sch 5 para 2). This power is exercisable by examining officers. An examining officer who examines any person under this power may, for the purpose of determining whether a person comes within the categories listed above, search that person and his or her baggage, as well as any ship or aircraft and anything on board it or taken off or about to be taken aboard (Sch 5 para 4(2)). A search of a person may be carried out only by a person of the same sex (para 4(5)) but may be carried out by a person who is not an examining officer but has been authorised to do so by an examining officer acting in accordance with instructions from the Secretary of State (paras 4(7) and 1(4)). Again, there is no requirement for reasonable grounds for suspicion before the Sch 5 power is exercised.

Where a person has been arrested for an offence, the ordinary powers of search are available (see chapter 5). When a person has been arrested under PTA s14 for any reason other than the commission of any offence under the PTA (see below p262), there is a further power of search by a person of the same sex to ascertain whether he or she possesses any document or other article which may constitute evidence of liability to arrest (s15(4), (5)). This power applies when there are reasonable grounds to suspect involvement in terrorism or subjection to an exclusion order.

Detention and examination at ports of entry

The PTA s16 and Sch 5 provide powers to examine persons arriving in or leaving Great Britain or Northern Ireland and for connected purposes. The exercise of such powers is subject to supervision and review in accordance with PTA Sch 3 (s16(2) and see below).

There is also provision for controls on the movement of ships and aircraft between Great Britain and the Republic of Ireland, Northern Ireland, and the Channel Islands or Isle of Man (see s20) (s16(3), Sch 5 paras 8–10, Sch 6). In addition, the Secretary of State has power to make further provisions by statutory instrument with regard to the above travellers (s16(4), (5)).

Powers are given to examining officers. In England and Wales these are all constables, immigration officers and customs and excise officers acting as immigration officers (PTA Sch 5 para 1).

An examining officer may examine anyone who has arrived in or is seeking to leave Great Britain by ship or aircraft, or by the tunnel system[8] but only to discover whether:

---

8 That is, by the Channel Tunnel by virtue of powers in PTA s20(1) and the
   Channel Tunnel Act 1987. Also included are those who arrive as transit
   passengers, crew members and other people not seeking to enter Great Britain.

254 *Police Powers / Chapter 8*

a) a person appears to be or to have been concerned in the commission, preparation, or instigation of acts of terrorism (except those connected solely with the affairs of the United Kingdom other than Northern Irish affairs); or
b) a person is subject to an exclusion order; or
c) there are grounds for suspecting the person of committing an offence under the PTA s8 (exclusion orders) (Sch 5 para 2).

The examination need not be based on reasonable grounds for suspicion, but must be for one of the purposes indicated. The examination power is not available to see whether a person has committed any other offence, under the PTA or otherwise, although of course constables can exercise other powers for this purpose.

Those examined are under a duty to furnish all such information required, to produce a passport or other similar document, and to tell the examining officer whether they are carrying any other document of a description specified by the officer and to produce it if required (Sch 5 para 3). Failure to do so amounts to a summary offence (Sch 5 para 11) These provisions constitute an exception to the common law right to silence.[9] The examining officer also has extensive powers of search in relation to a person being examined (Sch 5 para 3 and see p273).

Detention for examination under Sch 5

An examination can be carried out without detention, although a person may be detained for examination by virtue of Sch 5 para 6 (see below). If they are examined without being detained, the examination cannot normally exceed 12 hours. However, if the examining officer has reasonable grounds for suspecting that the person examined is or has been concerned in the commission, preparation or instigation of acts of terrorism, the period of examination may be extended to 24 hours, provided written notice is given to the person (Sch 5 para 2(4)).

The period of examination is therefore limited, but the 24-hour period may be extended if a person is detained. There are three

---

9 Failure to co-operate could not lead to inferences under the Criminal Justice and Public Order Act 1994 ss34 or 36 since the person has not been arrested, and is unlikely to have been cautioned. For a critical analysis of the implementation of these and other PTA powers, see P Hillyard, *Suspect Community*, (Pluto Press, 1993).

grounds on which a person may be detained. The first of these is 'pending conclusion of his examination' (Sch 5 para 6(1)(a)). Since the 24-hour limit in para 2(4) is subject to para 6, and para 6 allows longer periods of detention (and, presumably, examination) it is difficult to see what the 24-hour limit achieves.

The other grounds for detention are that the matter is pending consideration by the Secretary of State whether to make an exclusion order against the person (Sch 5 para 6 (1)(b)), or pending a decision by the DPP or Attorney-General whether to institute proceedings against that person for an offence (Sch 5 para 6(1)(c)). Such detention on the authority of an examining officer may not exceed 48 hours from the time when the examination first began (Sch 5 para 6(2)). The Secretary of State may extend this 48-hour period, up to a maximum of five further days, so that a person can be detained for up to a maximum of seven days from when the examination first began (Sch 5 para 6(3)). There is no statutory restriction on the discretion of the Secretary of State to make such an extension except that it may be made only for the purposes of examination or the consideration of whether to make an exclusion order. Presumably the usual rules on ministerial discretion apply (see chapter 1).

Powers of search of persons examined under these provisions are discussed above (p252), and there are also powers to retain relevant documents for seven days generally, and for as long as necessary pending a deportation or exclusion decision or for use as evidence (Sch 5 para 4(4)).

Detention pending removal

Where an exclusion order has been made, the person to be excluded may be detained pending removal (Sch 2 para 7(1)). Such detention may take place following the seven days' maximum allowed for examination and there is no statutory limit on its duration.

Search of premises and seizure of property

Search for persons

A justice of the peace who is satisfied that there are reasonable grounds for suspecting that a person whom a constable believes to be liable to arrest under s14(1)(b) (see below p261) is to be found on any premises may grant a search warrant. This will authorise the constable to enter the premises for the purpose of searching for and arresting that person (s15(1)). A justice of the peace may issue a warrant on the same basis in the case of a person wanted under Sch 2 para 7(2) (see p263) (Sch 2 para 8(1)) and under Sch 5 para 6(4) (Sch 5 para 7(1)) (see below p263).

Search for evidence (Sch 7)

Justices of the peace have power to issue warrants and circuit judges can issue orders and warrants in relation to material which is likely to be of substantial value to a terrorist investigation. The procedures are set out in Sch 7. Such applications must be authorised by a constable of at least the rank of superintendent (Code B para 2.4). A 'terrorist investigation' is defined in s17 as an investigation into:

a) the commission, preparation or instigation of acts of terrorism to which s14 (below p261) applies; or

b) any other act which appears to have been done in furtherance of or in connection with such acts of terrorism, including any act which appears to constitute an offence under PTA ss2, 9, 10, 11, 18 or 18A or Northern Ireland (Emergency Provisions) Act 1991 ss28, 53, 54 or 54A; or

c) the resources of a proscribed organisation (see above) or a proscribed organisation for the purposes of the 1991 Act s28; or

d) whether there are grounds justifying the making of an order under PTA s1(2)(a) (above p249) or the 1991 Act s28(3).

Material other than excluded or special procedure material

A justice of the peace may, on an application made by a constable, issue a warrant authorising a search for material other than that which is excluded, special procedure or legally privileged. These terms have the same meaning as in the 1984 Act ss10–14 (see above pp56–67). If the justice of the peace is satisfied that a terrorist investigation is being carried out, then the grounds for justifying the issue of the warrant are the same as those for issuing a warrant for search for evidence of a serious arrestable offence under the 1984 Act s8 (see above p53) (Sch 7 para 2).

Warrants issued under this paragraph authorise a constable to enter and search the premises specified in the warrant and seize anything found there (this would include excluded and special procedure material), other than items which are legally privileged, if there are reasonable grounds for believing that it is:

a) likely to be of substantial value to the investigation (whether by itself or together with other material); and
b) necessary to seize it in order to prevent it being concealed, lost, damaged, altered or destroyed.

The police also have power to search any person found on the premises and to seize any property found on the person if the conditions above are applicable (para 2(3)). Any search of a person must be by a constable of the same sex as the person searched (para 10(2)).

'Excluded' and 'special procedure' material

On an application made by a constable, a circuit judge may make an order in relation to particular material or material of a particular description, being material which consists of or includes excluded material or special procedure material (para 3 as amended). A judge must be satisfied that the material does not include legally privileged material and that a terrorist investigation is being carried out and there are reasonable grounds for believing that the material is likely to be of substantial value, either by itself or with other material, to the investigation. The judge must also be satisfied that there are reasonable grounds for believing it is in the public interest that the material should be produced or access given to it, having regard to the benefit likely to accrue to the investigation if the material is obtained and to the circumstances in which the material is held (para 3(5)).

The order will be that a person who appears to the judge to have the material in his/her possession, custody or power shall produce it to a constable for him or her to take away or shall give a constable access to it, within seven days of the date of the order, unless it appears to the judge that a different period would be appropriate (paras 3(2) and (4)). If the material is not in that person's possession, custody or power and will not be, within the specified period, the order may require the person to state to the best of their knowledge and belief where it is (para 3(2)).

An order may be made in relation to material which is not yet in existence or not yet available to the person concerned but is expected to be so within twenty-eight days of the date of the order. An order in relation to such material shall require that person to notify a named constable as soon as possible after the material comes into existence or becomes available to that person (para 3(3)). An order may, on the application of a constable, order any person who appears to the constable to be entitled to grant entry to the premises, to permit the constable entry to obtain access to the material (para 3(6)). No sanction for breach of the order is provided but in *DPP v Channel Four Television Co Ltd and Box Productions*[10] the respondents were held to be in contempt of court and fined. It is also possible for a constable to obtain a warrant in some circumstances (see below).

It should be noted that unlike applications for similar orders under the 1984 Act the applications here are ex parte. The recipient of the order should have seven days (see above) in which to make the material available and in that time may make a written application to the court for the circuit judge to vary or discharge the order (see para 4 and Crown Court Rules which at the time of writing have not been made). In the absence of Crown Court Rules the Divisional Court has given guidance on the quantity of information which should be provided to the recipient of the order.[11] If the judge decides to make an order then directions should be given as to what information should be served with it and it would normally be a written statement from the constable. The information should be as full as possible, bearing in mind security. If the judge considers that it is inappropriate for any information to be served other than that contained in the order then a decision should be made whether it should be served in the event of an application to discharge or vary it. Unless a circuit judge directs otherwise on grounds of urgency, the applicant must, not less than forty-eight hours before making the application, send a copy of it and all relevant details of it to the constable who originally applied for the order or any other constable in the same police station (para 4(2)(b)). The application to discharge or vary the order should, where possible, be heard by the same judge who heard the ex parte application.[12]

Where the order relates to information contained in a computer, the information must be produced in a form in which it is visible and legible and can be taken away, if relevant (para 4(4)).

Orders under this paragraph have effect notwithstanding any obligations as to secrecy or other restrictions on the disclosure of information imposed by statute or otherwise, but do not confer any right to

10 (1992) *Guardian* 12 August. The respondents refused to disclose their source of information in order to protect both the source and their researcher from serious personal danger.
11 *R v Crown Court at Middlesex Guildhall ex p Salinger and Another* [1993] 2 All ER 310.
12 Ibid.

production of or access to legally privileged items. Orders may be made against government departments (para 4(5) and (6) as amended).[13]

Searches for excluded or special procedure material

In some cases, which are similar to those in the 1984 Act, a circuit judge may issue a warrant authorising a search for special procedure or excluded material. This could be done where either an order (as above) has not been complied with or the conditions in which an order could be made prevail, but it would not be appropriate to make an order for one of a number of reasons – for instance, that the investigation might be seriously prejudiced unless a constable could secure immediate access to the material (para 5(3)).

Warrants issued under these provisions authorise the same searches and seizure as warrants issued under Sch 7 para 2 (above).

Urgent cases

A police officer of at least the rank of superintendent who has reasonable grounds for believing that the case is one of great emergency and that in the interests of the state immediate action is necessary, may authorise by written order any search which could have been authorised by warrant issued under Sch 7 paras 2 and 5. Such an order may not authorise a search for items subject to legal privilege. The officer may also require, by notice, any person specified therein to provide an explanation of any material seized in pursuance of such an order (see further below). A person who, without reasonable excuse, fails to comply with such a notice is guilty of an offence (para 7(5)). Para 6(2)-(5) (below) is applicable to such a notice.

Particulars of any case in which an order under this paragraph is made must be notified as soon as may be to the Secretary of State (para 7(2)).

Application of the 1984 Act and the Code of Practice

Sections 15 and 16 of the 1984 Act (relating to the issue and execution of warrants) are applicable to warrants issued under the PTA (see s15(1)). Code of Practice B for the searching of premises by police officers is also applicable.

---

13 Amended by Criminal Justice and Public Order Act 1994 s83.

General powers of seizure and provisions on access, copying and retention

In addition to the particular powers of seizure granted by Sch 7, the police have the additional wide powers of seizure conferred by the 1984 Act s19 (see above p103). The provisions of ss21 and 22 on copying, access to and retention of seized material are also applicable (see above p107). For the purposes of those sections, terrorist investigations are treated as investigations of or in connection with an offence and material produced in pursuance of an order under Sch 7 para 3 is treated as if it were material seized by a constable (Sch 7 para 10).

Explanation of seized or produced material under Sch 7

On an application by a constable, a circuit judge may order any specified person to provide an explanation of any material seized in pursuance of a warrant under para 2 or 5 or produced or made available to a constable under para 3. No one shall be required, however, to disclose any information which could be withheld on grounds of legal professional privilege in proceedings in the High Court. An important exception is that a lawyer may be required to furnish the name and address of a client (para 6(2)).

A statement made by a person in response to such a requirement may be used in evidence against the person only on a prosecution for an offence under para 6(4) (see below) or on a prosecution for some other offence where, in giving evidence, the person makes an inconsistent statement (para 6(3)).

It is an offence knowingly or recklessly to make a statement under these provisions which is false or misleading (para 6.4). There is no sanction for failure to make a statement but again this is presumably contempt. Orders can be varied and discharged under this paragraph in the same way as they can under para 3 (see above) and can also be made against a government department.

Offence of disclosing information

It is an offence under s17(2), as amended,[14] for a person to disclose information or any other matter which is likely to prejudice a terrorist investigation (see above p248) or to falsify, conceal or destroy, inter alia, material which is likely to be relevant to an investigation. Liabil-

14 Amended by Criminal Justice Act 1993 s50.

ity for such an offence exists if the person knows or has reasonable cause to know that a constable is acting or is proposing to act in connection with a terrorist investigation.[15] It is a defence to prove that the person did not know and had no reasonable cause to suspect that the disclosure was likely to prejudice the investigation or to prove that there was lawful authority or reasonable excuse for making the disclosure.

Professional legal advisers who disclose such information in the course of advising their clients or in contemplation of, or in connection with, legal proceedings and for the purpose of those proceedings are exempt from liability, so long as the information is not disclosed with a view to furthering any criminal purpose (s17(2)(c) and (d)).

Arrest under the PTA

There are several different categories of arrest in connection with the provisions of the PTA.

Arrestable offences

The law on arrestable offences is dealt with in chapter 5. All of the indictable offences created by the PTA, with the exception of the Sch 7 offence (see above p246) are arrestable offences by virtue of carrying a maximum penalty of at least five years' imprisonment. Such offences are also capable of being serious arrestable offences (see above pp5–8) but do not automatically come within this category.

The PTA s14(1)(a) empowers a constable to arrest without warrant a person whom the constable has reasonable grounds for suspecting to be guilty of an offence under ss2, 8, 9, 10 or 11 of that Act. This power overlaps with, and seems to add nothing to, the power of arrest under 1984 Act s24(6) but has a consequential effect on the length of detention. In fact the powers of arrest under the 1984 Act are wider and are preserved by PTA s14(7).

No separate power of arrest is created by the PTA in respect of the other arrestable offences under PTA ss17 and 18.

---

15 s17 as amended contains further offences relating to disclosure of information, falsification and concealment.

Non-arrestable offences

The offences under PTA ss3 and 13A and Schs 5 and 7 are not arrestable offences and are not capable of being serious arrestable offences. The only power of arrest in respect of them is contained in the 1984 Act s25 (see chapter 5), unless the situation comes within the categories discussed below.

Suspicion of terrorism

A constable may arrest without warrant a person whom he or she has reasonable grounds for suspecting to be or to have been concerned in the preparation or instigation of acts of terrorism connected with the affairs of Northern Ireland or any other act of terrorism except those connected solely with the affairs of the United Kingdom or a part of the United Kingdom other than Northern Ireland (PTA s14(1)(b), (2)).

There need not be any suspicion in relation to a particular offence and the arrest is not for an offence but, in practice, for questioning and investigation. The suspicion must be based on reasonable grounds, but this can relate to the demeanour, background or whereabouts of the suspect, or can be founded on information received or items found in a search.

A person arrested on this basis is not arrested for an offence and therefore the 1984 Act Pt IV does not apply (see chapter 5). Instead the position is governed by PTA Sch 3.

Person subject to an exclusion order

A constable may arrest without warrant a person whom he or she has reasonable grounds for suspecting to be subject to an exclusion order excluding that person from the United Kingdom or Great Britain if the arrest is made in Great Britain (s14(1)(c), (3)(a)). There is a parallel provision in relation to arrest in Northern Ireland (s14(3)(b)).

The suspicion must be that an order has actually been made, not that it has been applied for, ought to be made, might be made or will be made.

Again, this is not an arrest for an offence and the comments made under the previous heading apply here.

Arrest by an examining officer

As seen above (pp244–245), a person who is examined under Sch 5 para 2 may be detained under para 6. A person liable to be detained under para 7 may be arrested without warrant by an examining officer (Sch 5 para 6(4)).

The schedule does not specify the reason for or purpose of such arrest and there are a number of possible interpretations of this provision:

a) that arrest is for the purpose of detention and examination;
b) that arrest may be for any purpose at all but, whatever the purpose, is exercisable by an examining officer and not only by a constable, and can always be without warrant;
c) that arrest may be for the matters specified on pp261–262 above, but may be carried out without warrant and by any examining officer.

Detention pending removal

A person who is subject to removal because of an exclusion order may be detained pending directions and removal and such a person may be arrested without warrant by an examining officer (Sch 2 para 7(2)).

Detention after arrest

Where a person has been arrested for an offence under ss17 or 18 or Sch 7, or for a summary PTA offence, the position is governed by the 1984 Act Pt IV (see chapter 5).

However, the provisions of the 1984 Act Pt IV do not apply where the arrest is under PTA s14, whether for an offence or otherwise.[16] Thus it is important to know whether the arrest is under s14 or some other power, such as the 1984 Act s24.

If the arrest is under PTA s14, then the arrested person may be detained for up to 48 hours following arrest (PTA s14(4)) but this period may be extended in any particular case by the Secretary of State by further periods not exceeding five days in all (PTA s14(5)). Thus the maximum period of detention is seven days from the time of arrest. This contrasts with the detention clock under the 1984 Act

16 1984 Act s51(b) as amended by PTA Sch 8 para 6(4).

which begins to run in most cases on arrival at a police station (see p162).

A similar provision under the 1984 predecessor to the PTA was considered by the European Court of Human Rights, which ruled that detention for four days and six hours or more under this provision breached the European Convention on Human Rights.[17] The UK government derogated from the Convention in this respect, and thus no action has been taken to bring the position in line with article 5 of the Convention.

Constraints on s14 detention powers

The exercise of the s14 detention powers is subject to supervision in accordance with PTA Sch 3 (s14(6)).

Schedule 3 provides for periodic reviews of detention under the various provisions of the PTA. The reviews are to be carried out as soon as practicable after the beginning of the detention, and at subsequent intervals of not more than 12 hours by an officer who has not been directly involved in the matter (Sch 3 paras 1, 2 and 3). A review within the first 24 hours must be by an officer of at least the rank of inspector and a subsequent review by an officer of at least the rank of superintendent (Sch 3 para 4). There are provisions for postponement in certain circumstances (Sch 3 para 5) and for representations by the detained person and any solicitor acting (Sch 3 para 6), as well as for written records (Sch 3 para 8), and the resolution of disputes between lower ranking review officers and superior officers (Sch 3 para 9). However, no review may take place after application has been made to the Secretary of State for extended detention under s14(5) or the parallel provision in Sch 5 para 6(3) (Sch 3 para 3).

On review, the review officer shall authorise the continued detention of the person only in the following circumstances:

a) Where the person is detained pending removal under Sch 2 para 7, and the review officer is satisfied that steps for giving directions for removal or for removing the person in pursuance of the directions, are being taken diligently and expeditiously (Sch 3 para 1(3)).

b) Where the person is being examined without detention under Sch 5 para 2(4), and the review officer is satisfied that the enquiries

---

17 *Brogan v UK* (1989) 11 EHRR 117, ECHR.

necessary to complete the examination are being carried out diligently and expeditiously (Sch 3 para 2(2)).

c) Where the person is detained under s14 (see above) or Sch 5 para 6 (detention for examination) and:

 i) detention is necessary to obtain or preserve evidence –
  – relating to offences by any person under the PTA,
  – indicating the person's own involvement in acts of terrorism, or
  – indicating that the person is subject to an exclusion order; or
 ii) detention is pending consideration of –
  – an exclusion order, or
  – a deportation order, or
  – prosecution (Sch 3 para 3(3), (4)).

The continued detention must be *necessary* for the above purposes. This must mean that the purposes cannot be fulfilled without the detention. The review officer must also be satisfied that the investigation or consideration is being proceeded with, diligently and expeditiously.

In such cases, no procedure is specified for charge and being brought before the court. However, at the end of the authorised period of detention, the person will have to be released or (having been charged) brought before the court, or have been made the subject of an exclusion order. In the last case, the person may be detained further, pending the giving of directions for removal and pending removal. The authority for such detention must be given by the Secretary of State (unless the person was examined by an examining officer and either made the subject of an order or found to be subject to an order already, in which case the examining officer may authorise the continued detention) (Sch 2 para 7(1)).

Treatment of detainees

Where a person is detained by the police the provisions of the Code of Practice on Detention, Treatment and Questioning (Code C) govern the detainee's treatment and breaches of it may have the consequences described on p4 above. This category includes a person who has been detained at a police station following examination at a port under Sch 5 of the Act and those detained under PTA s14 (Code C para 1.11). Where a person is detained under Sch 5 by examining officers who are not police officers and not at a police station, how-

ever, the officers need only 'have regard' to the relevant provisions
(1984 Act s67(9)). They will not be liable to disciplinary proceedings
but the sanction of possible inadmissibility of evidence obtained in
breach of Code C is applicable (1984 Act s67(11)).

Searches

A person who has been arrested under the PTA, whether for an
offence or under s14 or by an examining officer who is a constable
under Sch 5 para 6 (see above p252 and p263) and is taken to a police
station and is detained there or elsewhere in the charge of a constable
is 'in police detention' (1984 Act s118, as amended by the PTA). In
addition to being subject to the general powers of search contained
in the 1984 Act s54 (see p188), such a person may also be the subject
of an intimate search and seizure under s55 provided the normal
conditions are satisfied (see p192). If a person has not been arrested
s/he cannot be made the subject of an intimate search since s/he is
not in 'police detention'.

A person who has been arrested under s14 may be searched by the
police for documents or other articles which may be evidence that
the person is liable to arrest (s15(4)). This subsection applies whether
or not the suspect is in police detention within 1984 Act s118 as
amended. Such a search may be conducted only by a constable of the
same sex as the suspect (s15(5)). It is unclear whether s15(4) enables a
constable to conduct an intimate search. The 1984 Act s53 abolished
powers of intimate search that existed before the Act, but the PTA
was passed subsequently and makes no mention of intimate search.

Right to have someone informed of detention

The 1984 Act provides that a person who has been arrested and is
being held in custody in a police station or other premises is entitled,
subject to provision for delay in certain cases, to have someone
informed as soon as practicable of the arrest and detention. The Act
does not specify that the arrest must be for an offence and so all
arrests under the PTA trigger this provision. There would be a problem in connection with those people detained under PTA Sch 5
(powers at ports and borders) (see above p253) if they have not been
technically arrested; but the 1984 Act provides that for the purposes
of s56 (as amended) a person detained under the PTA is deemed to
have been arrested (s56(10)). However, the right under s56 would not

apply to a person being examined without being detained under Sch 5 para 2 (see p254).

In the case of a person detained by the police under the PTA s14(1), Sch 2 or 5, the right to have someone informed of the arrest and detention may be delayed for up to 48 hours (1984 Act s56(11)). The delay is permitted, however, only if an officer of at least the rank of superintendent authorises it orally or in writing (if authorised orally it must be confirmed in writing as soon as practicable) (s56(2) and (4)). An officer may authorise delay only if there are reasonable grounds for believing that telling the named person of the arrest will:

a) lead to interference with, or harm to, evidence connected with a serious arrestable offence or interference with, or physical injury to, other persons (offences under ss2, 8, 9, 10 or 11 and attempts or conspiracies to commit those offences are always serious arrestable offences for this purpose and for the same purpose in 1984 Act s58); or

b) lead to the alerting of other persons suspected of having committed such an offence but not yet arrested for it; or

c) hinder the recovery of any property obtained as a result of such an offence; or

d) lead to interference with the gathering of information about the commission, preparation or instigation of acts of terrorism; or

e) by alerting any person, make it more difficult –
   to prevent an act of terrorism; or
   – to secure the apprehension, prosecution or conviction of any person in connection with the commission, preparation or instigation of an act of terrorism (1984 Act s56(5) and (11)).

If delay is authorised, the detained person should be told the reason for it and if detained at a police station, the reason must be noted on the custody record (1984 Act s56(6)).

A child or young person detained under the PTA has the additional rights contained in 1984 Act s57 as if in police detention for any other reason (see pp207).

Access to legal advice

A person 'detained' under the PTA is treated as an arrested person (as above) for the purpose of triggering the provisions in the 1984 Act relating to access to legal advice, whether or not there has been a technical arrest (1984 Act s58(12)). Access can be delayed for the same reasons, in the same way, and for the same length of time, as the right to have someone informed of arrest and detention (see above).

A person detained under the PTA has the same right to obtain legal advice, subject to delay, as any other person in police detention except that an officer of the appropriate rank may direct that the consultation with a solicitor must take place in the sight and hearing of a qualified officer of the uniformed branch of the force of which the officer giving the direction is a member. A 'qualified officer' must be of at least the rank of inspector and, in the opinion of the officer giving the direction, unconnected with the case. The officer giving such a direction must be of at least the rank of commander or assistant chief constable. A direction can be given for any of the reasons for which access to legal advice can be delayed (see above), but once the reason ceases to subsist the direction should cease to have effect (1984 Act s58(13)-(18)).

Duties of review officer

Where the review officer authorises the continued detention of a person who has not yet exercised his or her rights under 1984 Act s56 or 58, the officer is under a duty to inform that person of those rights and if the exercise of either right is being delayed, that that is the case.

Where a review of detention is being carried out under Sch 3 para 1 or 3 (see above) at a time when either of the above rights is being delayed, the review officer must consider whether the reason or reasons why the delay was authorised continue to subsist. A review officer who did not authorise delay originally, and considers that the reason or reasons for the delay no longer exist, must inform the authorising officer of that opinion (Sch 3 para 7).

Identification

Where a person is detained under s14, Sch 2 or Sch 5 any constable, prison officer or examining officer or any other person authorised by the Secretary of State may take all such steps as may be reasonably necessary for photographing, measuring or otherwise identifying the detainee (s15(9), Sch 2 para 8(5) and Sch 5 para 7(5)).

Fingerprints

Where a person is detained under s14, Sch 2 or Sch 5, the fingerprinting provisions of the 1984 Act apply with certain modifications (1984

Act s61(9)(b) and PTA s15(10) and Sch 5 para 7(6)). Where the person is detained under s14, an officer may authorise fingerprinting only if satisfied that it is necessary to do so in order to assist in determining:

a) whether that person is or has been concerned in the commission, preparation or instigation of acts of terrorism to which s14 applies; or

b) whether the person is subject to an exclusion order under the Act;

or if the officer has reasonable grounds for suspecting that person's involvement in an offence under any of the provisions mentioned in s14(1)(a) (p261) and for believing that fingerprints will tend to confirm or disprove involvement (PTA s15(10)).

The test in the latter case for suspicion is purely objective and therefore may be more easily challenged in court than in cases (a) and (b).

Where a person is detained under Sch 5 an officer may authorise fingerprinting if satisfied that it is necessary to do so in order to assist in determining:

a) whether that person is or has been concerned in the commission, preparation or instigation of acts of terrorism to which Sch 5 para 2 applies (see above p252);

b) whether the person is subject to an exclusion order; or

c) whether there are grounds for suspecting that the person has committed an offence under s8 of the Act (see above p245) (Sch 5 para 7(6)).

A person detained under these provisions could also be required (if relevant) to have his/her fingerprints taken under the general power that applies where a person has been charged with or reported for a recordable offence (1984 Act s61(3)(a) as applied by PTA s14(10) and Sch 5 para 7(6)).

The provisions for the destruction of fingerprints contained in 1984 Act s64 are inapplicable to the PTA (1984 Act s64(7)).

Samples

The powers to take intimate and non-intimate samples in the 1984 Act are applied to persons detained under PTA s14 and Sch 5 with certain modifications (1984 Act ss62(12) and 63(10)[18] and PTA s15(11),

---

18 Note that two subsections (10) were, inadvertently, inserted into s63 by the Criminal Justice and Public Order Act 1994. The s63(10) referred to here is that inserted by Sch 10 para 62 of the 1994 Act.

(12), (13) and (14) and Sch 5 para 7(6A), (6B), (6C) and (6D)). The meaning of intimate and non-intimate samples is the same as under the 1984 Act (PTA s14(12) and (14) and Sch 5 para 7(6B) and (6D)). Arguably, the limitations on the taking of intimate and non-intimate samples contained in the 1984 Act do not apply to a person detained under the PTA Sch 2 since the general effect of ss62(12) and 63(10) is to provide that the sections do not apply to persons arrested or detained under the PTA except as specifically provided. However, it is likely that the intention was that samples should not be taken where a person is detained under Sch 2.

An intimate sample may be taken from a person arrested or detained under s14 if the person consents and authorisation is given by a superintendent or above, who must be satisfied that it is necessary in order to assist in determining:

a) whether the person is or has been concerned in the commission, preparation or instigation of acts of terrorism to which s14 applies; or

b) whether the person is subject to an exclusion order under the PTA; or

c) whether the person has been involved in an offence under any of the provisions mentioned in s14(1)(a) (see p261) if the officer has reasonable grounds for suspecting this and for believing that an intimate sample will tend to confirm or disprove that involvement (s15(11)).

Where the person is detained under Sch 5, authorisation may be given if (a) or (b) above apply, or if the officer is satisfied that taking an intimate sample is necessary to assist in determining whether there are grounds for suspecting that the person has committed an offence under PTA s8 (see p245) (Sch 5 para 7(6A)).

A non-intimate sample may be taken from a person detained under s14 in the same circumstances as under the 1984 Act s63 except that where authorisation by a superintendent or above is required, it can only be given if the officer is satisfied about the same matters as for intimate samples under s15(11) (see above) (s15(13)). Where the person is detained under Sch 5, a non-intimate sample may be taken in the same circumstances as under the 1984 Act s63 except that where authorisation by a superintendent or above is required, it can only be given if the officer is satisfied about the same matters as for intimate samples under Sch 5 para 7(6A) (see above) (Sch 5 para 7(6C)).

Application of Code D (identification)
With the exception of the taking of body samples and fingerprints from persons detained under PTA s14 or Sch 5, the code has no effect on the general powers of identification described on p268 (see Code D paras 1.15 and 1.16).

CHAPTER 9

Policing powers of customs and excise officers

General

Customs and excise officers exercise special policing powers under specific legislation, principally the Customs and Excise Management Act 1979, to which the section references in this chapter refer unless otherwise indicated.

The Commissioners of Customs and Excise are appointed by the Sovereign and may commission officers and others to discharge duties in relation to any of the Commissioners' responsibilities (s6(3)). Any officer acting under the authority of the Commissioners may do anything that the Commissioners are required or authorised to do (s8(1)(b)). It is the duty of every constable[1] (and every member of the armed forces or coastguard) to assist in the enforcement of the law relating to the Commissioners' responsibilities (s11).

For the purposes of the Drug Trafficking Act 1994, a customs and excise officer is a constable.[2]

It is an offence to obstruct or assault a person engaged in such duties (s16(1)). This is an arrestable offence under 1984 Act s24(2)(a) (as are all offences for which a person may be arrested under the Customs and Excise Acts) although the maximum penalty is two years' imprisonment (s16(2)). Section 16(3) provides that any person committing or aiding an offence under this section 'may be arrested'. This, and similar provisions in the Act, do not specify who may do the arresting and in what circumstances. This is dealt with below.

---

1 See chapter 1 for meaning of constable.
2 Drug Trafficking Act 1994 s63.

Applicability of the 1984 Act

The Treasury may, by order, apply any provision of the 1984 Act (subject to specified modifications) relating to investigation or detention by police, to those activities when carried out by customs and excise officers in pursuance of matters statutorily assigned to the responsibility of the Commissioners (1984 Act s114(2)). This was achieved by the Police and Criminal Evidence Act 1984 (Application to Customs and Excise) Order 1985 ('the 1985 Order').[3] In addition, customs and excise officers must have regard to any relevant provision of the Codes of Practice concerning their duty to investigate offences (1984 Act s67(9)).[4]

Stop and search without arrest

Any officer or constable or member of the armed forces or coastguard may stop and search a vehicle or vessel where there are reasonable grounds to suspect that it may be carrying any goods on which duty has not been paid, or which are being unlawfully removed to or from any place, or which are otherwise liable to forfeiture. It is an offence if the person in charge of the vehicle or vessel refuses to stop or to permit it to be searched (s163). The powers under this provision may be exercised anywhere and by a wide range of people.

However, only a customs and excise officer may exercise the power under s164 to stop and search persons. A constable would have to use the powers discussed in chapter 2. The s164 power may be exercised in respect of any person who is on board or has landed from any ship or aircraft; or is entering or about to leave the United Kingdom or a free zone or any wharf or transit shed; or is within the dock area of a port or at a customs and excise airport or in a wharf or transit shed; or is in Northern Ireland and travelling from or to any place on or beyond the land boundary within the Republic of Ireland (s164(4)).

The s164 power may be exercised only when there are reasonable grounds to suspect that such a person is carrying any article on which duty has not been paid or which is being unlawfully imported or exported (s164(1)). Such a person who has not been arrested, may be detained for so long as is necessary for the exercise of the powers

---

3 SI No 1800, as amended by SI No 439 of 1987.
4 See, eg, *R v Okafor* [1994] 3 All ER 741 and *R v Weerdersteyn* [1995] Crim LR 238.

of search (see below).

Section 164(2), (3) and (3A) govern the conduct of the search and apply whether or not the person has been arrested. They are discussed below.

The 1985 Order does not apply the safeguards in 1984 Act ss2 and 3 to the s164 search power, but officers must have regard to the Code of Practice A on stop and search (1984 Act s67(9)) which does apply to such a search.

An officer may use reasonable force if necessary in the exercise of the power of search (1985 Order article 11).

Arrest

Since offences under the Customs and Excise Acts are all arrestable offences, constables have powers of arrest under the 1984 Act s24, as discussed in chapter 3 above. Customs and excise officers, however, count as 'any person' for the purposes of s24 and therefore have more restricted powers of arrest. However, customs and excise officers have a specific power of arrest under the 1979 Act s138 (where 'officer' means a customs and excise officer):

> (1)   Any person who has committed, or whom there are reasonable grounds to suspect of having committed, any offence for which he is liable to be arrested under the customs and excise Acts may be arrested by any officer . . . or any member of Her Majesty's armed forces or coastguard at any time within 20 years from the date of the commission of the offence.
>
> (2)   Where it was not practicable to arrest any person so liable at the time of the commission of the offence, or where any such person having been then or subsequently arrested for that offence has escaped, he may be arrested by any officer . . . or any member of Her Majesty's armed forces or coastguard at any time and may be proceeded against in like manner as if the offence had been committed at the date when he was finally arrested.

The 20-year limitation period applies in relation to offences committed after 29 July 1988.[5] The previous limitation period was three years. However, the power in s138(2) deprives this limitation of much practical effect; it will apply only where it was practicable to arrest someone who was not in fact arrested.

A person who has been charged with a drug trafficking offence[6]

5 Finance Act 1988 s11.
6 As defined in the Drug Trafficking Act 1994 s1(3).

or with possession of controlled drugs[7] and is under a duty to surrender into customs detention (see below) having been released on bail in criminal proceedings, may be arrested by any customs and excise officer if that officer has reasonable grounds for believing that that person is not likely to surrender to custody.[8] This is a power not available to the police and seems to subvert the decision of the court to grant bail – although the person must be brought before a justice of the peace for the area in which the arrest took place, as soon as practicable and in any event within 24 hours of the arrest.[9] In calculating the period of 24 hours no account is taken of Christmas Day, Good Friday or any Sunday.[10]

Where any person who is a member of the crew of any ship in Her Majesty's employment or service is arrested by an officer for an offence under the Customs and Excise Acts, the commanding officer of the ship shall, if so required by the arresting officer, keep that person secured on board that ship until he or she can be brought before a court and shall then deliver him or her up to the proper officer.[11]

If anybody is arrested under s138(1) or under 1984 Act s24 for a Customs and Excise Acts offence by someone who is not a customs and excise officer, the person making the arrest must give notice of the arrest to an officer at the nearest convenient customs and excise office (s138(4)). This would apply to arrests under s138(1) by a member of the armed forces or a coastguard, and to s24 arrests by constables or civilians. It is unclear whether a failure to give such notice would render the continued detention unlawful.

The following provisions of the 1984 Act, which are discussed in chapter 5, apply to arrests made by customs and excise officers by virtue of the 1985 Order:

- information to be given on arrest (s28);
- procedure on voluntary attendance at a customs office or any other place with an officer (s29);
- procedure on arrest elsewhere than at a customs office (s30);
- liability to be arrested for a further offence (s31); and

---

7 Contrary to the Misuse of Drugs Act 1971 s5(2).
8 Criminal Justice Act 1988 s151(1).
9 Ibid s151(2).
10 Ibid s151(3).
11 Customs and Excise Management Act 1979 s138(3).

– search upon arrest subject to certain modifications discussed below (s32).

Detention and charge

Customs and excise officers have no power to charge a person with any offence, release a person on bail, nor to detain a person for an offence after being charged with that offence (1985 Order article 4). These are tasks to be carried out by the police. However, where a person aged at least 17 has been brought before a magistrates' court on a charge of possessing a controlled drug or a drug trafficking offence,[12] the court may commit that person to the custody of a customs officer for a period not exceeding 192 hours (ie, eight days) in any case where the court has power to remand.[13] This power is not available to the Crown Court, although there is nothing to stop magistrates making repeated remands into customs detention, and is designed for the convenience of customs investigators. There is a provision that 'nothing shall prevent a detained person from being transferred between customs detention and police detention' (1985 Order article 2(2)).

The detention time limits and procedures set out in 1984 Act ss34–37 and 39–44 and discussed in chapter 6 apply by virtue of the 1985 Order. If prisoners are transferred between customs and police detention, then it must be the cumulative period in detention which is relevant. Once the time comes to charge prisoners, this must be done by the police and there is no power to detain them in customs detention after charge. Thus in practice they will have to be in police detention by the time they are charged.

Personal searches before and after arrest

In addition to powers of search under the 1984 Act (see below) customs and excise officers have a specific power of search for prohibited goods under 1979 Act s164[14] (see above for the circumstances in which the search may be effected). There are three categories of search; these are 'rub-down', 'strip' and 'intimate' searches. An officer who considers such a search necessary or expedient must inform

12 See nn6 and 7 above.
13 Criminal Justice Act 1988 s152.
14 As amended by the Finance Act 1988 s10.

suspects of their rights under s164(3). Failure to do so may make the search unlawful (see further chapter 13 for possible remedies). The suspect's rights are that in the case of a 'rub-down' search, the suspect may require to be taken before a superior of the officer concerned and in the case of the other two categories, before a magistrate or a superior officer. The latter persons must then consider the grounds for suspicion and direct accordingly whether the suspect is to submit to the search.

A 'rub-down' search is any search which is neither an intimate nor a strip search. A 'strip search' is any search which is not an intimate search but which involves the removal of an article of clothing which:

a) is being worn (wholly or partly) on the trunk; and
b) is being so worn either next to the skin or next to an article of underwear.

An 'intimate search' is any search which involves a physical examination (that is, an examination which is more than simply a visual examination) of a person's body orifices (s164(5)).

'Rub-down' and 'strip' searches must be carried out by a person of the same sex as the suspect. Intimate searches must be carried out by a suitably qualified person, who is a registered medical practitioner or a registered nurse (s164(3A) and (5) as amended).

The Code of Practice for the detention, treatment and questioning of persons (Code C) is applicable (1984 Act s67(9)) (see chapter 7).[15] Officers are entitled to use reasonable force if necessary to carry out the searches (1985 Order article 11). Customs and excise officers have the search powers contained in 1984 Act ss54 and 55(1)(a) (see pp188–196, search for dangerous items) (1985 Order articles 3 and 9).

Access to legal advice and notification of detention

Suspects detained by customs and excise officers have the same rights of access and notification as suspects detained by the police.[16]

---

15 By virtue of 1985 Order (above n3).
16 See 1984 Act ss 56, 57 and 58 as amended by the Drug Trafficking Offences Act 1986 and the Criminal Justice Act 1988 (above pp196–209).

Identification

Customs and excise officers have the same powers to take intimate and non-intimate samples and the suspects have the same rights regarding destruction of samples, as in police investigations.[17]

Search of premises and seizure of property

Customs and excise officers have wide powers of entry and search both under the 1984 Act and other legislation. The 1979 Act, for instance, gives them powers, among others to:

a) board and search coasting ships (s72(3)); and

b) enter and search premises used for trading in dutiable goods for concealed pipes etc (s113 as amended)

In addition to such specific powers, officers also have the powers contained in ss8, 17(1)(b) and 18 of the 1984 Act but are subject to the restrictions contained in s9 (concerning special procedure, excluded and legally privileged material).[18] The latter section, if applied without modification would severely curtail customs and excise investigations. For that reason the 1985 Order retains their power to obtain search warrants from magistrates where the material sought has been acquired or created in the course of a trade, business or profession or for the purpose of any paid or unpaid office and which relates to an assigned matter as defined in 1979 Act s1.[19] There is no such saving for legally privileged material however,[20] and a warrant to search for such material should be unobtainable.

The power which the police have to enter and search premises occupied or controlled by a person under arrest for an arrestable offence (1984 Act s18) is modified in the case of customs and excise officers.[21] The effect is that they have power to enter and search premises under that section only where they are occupied or controlled by a person under arrest for an arrestable offence which relates to an assigned matter as defined in the 1979 Act. They may then search for evidence (other than legally privileged items) which relates to

---

17 See 1979 Act ss62, 63 and 64 as amended by the Criminal Justice Act 1988; Road Traffic (Consequential Provisions) Act 1988 and the Criminal Justice and Public Order Act 1994, above pp230–237.

18 See pp56–67 above.

19 Article 6.

20 As defined in the 1984 Act s10 (see above p56).

21 1985 Order article 7.

that offence or some other arrestable offence which is connected with or similar to that offence.

General power of seizure

In addition to their specific powers of seizure contained in the 1979 Act (corresponding to their search powers), customs and excise officers now have the wide power of seizure contained in 1984 Act s19.[22] They are thus now permitted to retain articles found during a lawful search which are evidence of *any* offence and to retain items seized by others. This power of seizure extends, as in the case of the police, to computerised information.[23] The provisions of the 1984 Act on access to and copying of property which has been seized are also applicable, but not where the property was seized as liable to forfeiture under the customs and excise legislation.[24] Their powers to retain property are as in 1984 Act s22. The owner of the property may have more problems however than if the property were retained by the police. The Police (Property) Act 1897, under which an accused person can recover property held by the police, is inapplicable, although it would be open to the owner of the property to bring a civil action for its return. Customs officers are protected from paying costs or damages and from punishment in any civil or criminal proceedings brought against them where property has been seized as liable to forfeiture under the customs and excise legislation and either the court has granted a certificate that there were reasonable grounds for the seizure, or the court is so satisfied (1979 Act s144).

The Code of Practice for the search of premises and seizure of property (Code B) is of course applicable to the exercise of these powers. Again officers are entitled to use reasonable force if necessary to put their powers into effect (1985 Order article 11).

22 1985 Order articles 3 and 5.
23 Ibid articles 3 and 5 and 1984 Act s20.
24 Ibid article 5(3) and 1984 Act s21.

CHAPTER 10

Further police powers

Interception of communications

General

It is a criminal offence, punishable with up to two years' imprisonment, to intercept intentionally a communication being transmitted by post or a public telecommunications system, except under a warrant for interception, with the consent of the receiver or sender, or for certain testing purposes (Interception of Communications Act 1985 s1). The offence would be committed by the person carrying out the interception. However, a police officer or anybody else who instigated the interception could be guilty of aiding and abetting, incitement, or conspiracy.

Any prosecution must have the consent of the Director of Public Prosecutions (s1(4)).

Interference with wireless telegraphy is lawful if it is authorised by a warrant issued by the Secretary of State under the Intelligence Services Act 1994 s5. This interference is governed by the same provisions as warrants under that section to enter onto or interfere with property (see p98–100 above).

A cordless telephone which is operated through a base unit which is connected to a public telecommunications system is not part of that public system but is a private system connected to the public system. The same is true of a police station payphone where the calls are routed through the police station switchboard and, presumably, of other calls on telephones which are routed through a switchboard such as in a hotel. In none of these circumstances is interception an offence under s1 of the 1985 Act.[1]

R v Effik [1994] 3 All ER 458 HL; *R v Ahmed and Others* [1995] Crim LR 246, CA; and see commentary in latter report by Professor J C Smith.

Warrants for interception

Warrants are issued by a Secretary of State after taking into account whether the information required could reasonably be acquired by other means, and on considering that it is necessary for one of three purposes (s2(2)).

This is a subjective discretion on the part of the Secretary of State. It is likely that the courts would be prepared to consider an application for judicial review of the issue of a warrant if there were evidence that the Secretary of State had acted with an improper motive or deliberately flouted the provisions of the Act, but it is not likely that the courts would be prepared to review the Secretary of State's view of what was reasonable.[2] Nevertheless, the issue of a warrant could not be considered 'necessary' unless there were no other reasonable means of achieving the same ends.

The three permitted purposes under s2(2) are:

a) in the interests of national security
b) for the purpose of preventing or detecting serious crime; or
c) for the purpose of safeguarding the economic well-being of the United Kingdom.

A warrant may not be considered necessary under (c) unless the information required relates to the acts or intentions of persons outside the British Islands (s2(4)).

A warrant must be signed by the Secretary of State personally except in an urgent case, when it can be signed by an authorised official of at least the rank of Assistant Under Secretary (s4(1)). A warrant signed by the Secretary of State remains in force for two months, and any other warrant expires at the end of the second working day after the day of issue (s4(6)). The Secretary of State must cancel the warrant before expiry if he or she considers that it is no longer necessary (s4(4)) but may renew it before it expires if its continuation is considered necessary (s4(3)). Renewal must be on the personal signature of the Secretary of State (s4(5)).

Renewal is for two months if the warrant was issued under the urgency provision and has not since been renewed, for one month if it is issued under the serious crime purpose, and for six months in other cases (s4(6)).

2 *R v Secretary of State for Home Department ex p Ruddock* [1987] 2 All ER 518; *R v Director of GCHQ ex p Hodges* (1988) *Independent* 21 July.

Applications for a warrant may be made by anybody but in practice they are made by the police (including special branches), customs and excise, the security service (MI5) and the intelligence agencies (including MI6). A warrant may be issued by any Secretary of State, but in practice they are issued by the Home and Foreign Secretaries, and the Secretaries of State for Scotland and Northern Ireland.

Several types of warrant may be issued:

a) To intercept telecommunications sent or received outside the British Isles, or such communications as it is necessary to intercept in order to intercept the above, if the Secretary of State certifies the descriptions of the intercepted material it is considered necessary to examine (s3(2)). Such a warrant may not specify an address in the British Isles unless this is necessary to prevent or detect terrorism, and then only for a period of three months (s3(3)).

b) To intercept communications to or from specified addresses likely to be used for communications to or from one particular specified person (s3(1)(a)(i)).

c) To intercept communications to or from specified addresses likely to be used for communications to or from one particular set of specified premises (s3(1)(a)(ii)).

There are detailed provisions for restricting access to material obtained by the interception (s6).

The Act does not define 'national security' or 'economic well-being' and the applicability of these phrases is within the discretion of the Secretary of State.

Serious crime

'Serious crime' means conduct which, in the United Kingdom, would constitute one or more offences and:

- involves the use of violence; or
- results in substantial financial gain; or
- is conduct by a large number of persons in pursuit of a common purpose; or
- is an offence for which a person aged 21 or over, without previous convictions, could reasonably expect to be sentenced to imprisonment for a term of three years or more (s10(3)).

It is clear that, apart from the final category, the crime need not be very serious at all. It could include minor criminal damage ('the use of violence'), or a march or demonstration (conduct by a large number of persons committing the offence of obstructing the highway).

Exclusion of evidence

In any court or tribunal proceedings there must be no evidence nor cross-examination which tends to suggest that a warrant has been or is to be issued to, or an offence of interception has been committed by, any person holding office under the Crown (this includes the police and security services), or the Post Office and persons engaged in its business, or any person engaged in the running of or operating a public telecommunication system (s9).

This exclusion does not apply to:

– prosecutions for interception or official secrets offences, or for attempting, conspiring, aiding, abetting, counselling or procuring, such offences;
– prosecutions for perjury or contempt of court in relation to proceedings for the above;
– proceedings before the tribunal established by s7 (see below);
– proceedings for unfair dismissal in relation to an unlawful interception (s9(3)).
– cases involving a private telephone system (see above p280); and
– an interception made outside the United Kingdom.[3]

The defence cannot compel disclosure of intercepts but the prosecution may chose to make disclosure, and the contents of the intercepts are admissible provided that s9 is complied with. Material that is not admissible under s9 should nevertheless be disclosed to prosecution counsel.[4]

3 *R v Governor of Belmarsh Prison and Another ex p Martin* [1995] 2 All ER 548, QBD.
4 *R v Preston and Others* [1993] 4 All ER 638, HL. See also Adam Tomkins, 'Intercepted Evidence: Now You Hear Me, Now You Don't' (1994) 57 MLR 941–954.

The Tribunal and Commissioner

Section 7 of the Act establishes a tribunal to investigate complaints of interception. The Tribunal can make one of two findings:

a) that there has been a contravention of the provisions of ss2–5 of the Act (s7(4)); or

b) that there has not been such a contravention (s7(7)).

Thus the Tribunal will not deal with allegations of interception where it is alleged that there is no warrant at all, such as interception by a private detective; this would be a matter for criminal investigation by the police.[5]

Where the Tribunal dismisses the complaint, it will not say whether it is because a warrant has not been issued or because it has been issued in accordance with the Act. If a warrant has been issued in breach of the Act, apart from having a duty to notify the applicant and the Prime Minister, the Tribunal may quash the warrant, direct the destruction of intercepted material, and direct the Secretary of State to pay compensation to the applicant (s7(4) and (5)).

The Act establishes a commissioner to review the way in which the Secretary of State issues warrants, to receive reports from the tribunal, and to report to the Prime Minister on these matters (s8). On 31 December 1994, 336 warrants for the interception of telecommunications and 60 for the interception of letters issued by the Home Secretary or by the Secretary of State for Scotland were in force.[6] The number of warrants issued by the Foreign Secretary or the Secretary of State for Northern Ireland is not published.[7]

Confiscation of the proceeds of crime

The prosecution has power to apply to the courts for confiscation orders in respect of certain offences under the Criminal Justice Act 1988, the Drug Trafficking Act 1994 and the Prevention of Terrorism (Temporary Provisions) Act 1989. The powers under each Act are described separately below. Part VI of the Criminal Justice Act 1988 is substantially amended by the Proceeds of Crime Act 1995 with effect from 1 November 1995. The revised powers only apply to people convicted of an offence committed on or after that date (s16(5)).

---

5 *Interception of Communications Act 1985: Guidance to the Police* Home Office, 8 April 1986, paras 12–14.

6 Report of the Commissioner for 1994, Cm 2828 Annex.

7 Cm 108 para 8.

Criminal Justice Act 1988

The Crown Court has powers to make a confiscation order, in addition to dealing with a case in any other way, if a person is found guilty of any indictable offence (other than a drug trafficking offence[8] or an offence under Pt III of the PTA, which both have their own confiscation regimes, described below) or an offence contained in Sch 4 to the 1988 Act. Magistrates' courts also have confiscation powers in relation to the latter. Schedule 4 lists summary offences relating to sex establishments; the supplying of video recordings of unclassified work; possession of such recordings with intent to supply and the use of unlicensed premises for an exhibition which requires a licence (s71). Where the prosecutor has given written notice, the court *must* make an order if satisfied that the accused has benefited from any relevant conduct. Where the prosecution has not given written notice, it *may* do so (s71(1), (1A) and (1B)).

A person benefits from an offence if property is obtained as a result of or in connection with its commission and the benefit is the value of the property (s71(4)). Where a person has derived a pecuniary advantage in the same circumstances, it is the sum equal to the value of the pecuniary advantage which counts (s71(5)). Pecuniary advantage is not defined. The order must be equal to the benefit in respect of which it is made or the amount appearing to the court to be the amount that might be realised at the time the order is made (s71(6)).

Generally, 'any relevant conduct' means, and therefore any order would be limited to the benefit from, the commission of any indictable or Sch 4 offence of which the accused has been convicted or which has been taken into consideration (s72(1D)). However, where s/he has been convicted of two or more such offences, at that time or within the previous six years, the court can make an order covering the value of property held by the accused at the time of conviction (or date of any later determination) or which has passed through his/her hands in the previous six years (s72AA). By s72AA(4), the court may assume that all such property resulted from the commission of offences. It is for the accused to satisfy the court that the assumptions are incorrect or that the order would lead to serious risk of injustice (s72AA(5)).

The court may subsequently review a decision not to make an order (s74A).

The standard of proof required to establish whether a convicted defendant has benefited financially from the offence or some other

8 Defined by the Drug Trafficking Act 1994 s1.

related or qualifying offence is defined by s71(7A) (inserted by the Criminal Justice Act 1993) as the civil standard, that is, the balance of probabilities, but subject to the assumptions noted below.

When considering whether to make an order and the extent of that order, the court may take into account any information about a potential claim by way of civil proceedings by a victim of the offence (s72(1C)).

The prosecution must and the defence may submit documents to the court for consideration in determining the amount of the order. These, of course, may be disputed. The defendant may be required by the court to indicate to what extent each allegation is accepted and if not accepted, to indicate matters which are proposed to be relied on. If the defendant fails to comply with this requirement for a particular allegation, acceptance is deemed to have taken place, except where allegations have been disputed or it is alleged that the defendant has benefited from an offence or that property was obtained as a result of or in connection with the commission of an offence. If the defendant submits a statement, then likewise the prosecution may accept certain allegations and the acceptance will be treated as conclusive of those matters. In the case of the prosecutor, however, non-response is not binding. Allegations may be accepted or matters indicated for the purpose of the section either orally or in writing. The section does not specify any time limits (ss73(1)-(5) and 73A).

The court may issue a certificate giving an opinion as to the matters concerned and must do so if satisfied that the amount which might be realised at the time the order is made is less than the assessed value of the defendant's benefit (s73(6)). It may also revise its assessment later (s74C).

Disclosure of information

Where a person discloses to a constable either a suspicion or belief that any property has been obtained as a result of or in connection with an offence listed above, or derives from property so obtained, or any matter on which a suspicion or belief is based, the disclosure shall not be treated as a breach of any restriction upon the disclosure of information imposed by contract (s98).

Treatment and questioning of defendants

Notification of arrest and access to legal advice may be delayed by the police where the offence is one in respect of which a confiscation order may be made and granting the rights above would hinder the recovery of property (s99, amending Police and Criminal Evidence Act 1984 ss56 and 58: see above pp203 and 206).

Enforcement

The courts have power to enforce confiscation orders (s75) and the High Court has power to make restraint and charging orders to prevent defendants circumventing the orders (ss76–78). Restraint and charging orders may be made prior to the commencement of proceedings (s76(2)). Imprisonment in default does not expunge the obligation to pay (s75(5A)).

Drug Trafficking Act 1994

The Crown Court has very similar powers in relation to drug trafficking offences (as defined by the Drug Trafficking Act 1994 s1) as are described above. As under the revised 1988 Act, the court can make an order of its own volition (Drug Trafficking Act 1994 s2). There is a provision preventing evidence turned up in confiscation proceedings from being used against the defendant in subsequent criminal charges (s11(11)). However, this protection is limited to an acceptance by the defendant of any payment or reward under the provisions of s11 only.[9]

Notification of arrest and access to legal advice may be delayed where investigations into the defendant's financial affairs are taking place (Police and Criminal Evidence Act 1984 ss56 and 58, as amended: see above pp203 and 206).

Prevention of Terrorism (Temporary Provisions) Act 1989

By virtue of PTA s13, a Crown Court or a magistrates' court has power to make a forfeiture order in respect of certain funds when a person is found guilty of an offence under PTA ss9, 10 or 11 (see p247 above). The operation of the order, and of complementary restraint orders preventing dealing in the relevant property, is governed by Sch 4 of the Act. Police powers to investigate offences under PTA ss9, 10 and 11 are described in detail in chapter 8.

---

9 For a critical review of this, see S. Whitehead, 'Disclosure Dilemma', (1995) LS Gaz 28 June.

CHAPTER 11

The exclusion of confessions and other evidence

Whether the police have exceeded their powers may be relevant to the admissibility of evidence in a criminal trial.

Confessions as evidence

Evidence from another person that the defendant had admitted an offence would be hearsay. Hearsay evidence is normally inadmissible, but evidence of a defendant's confession has always been allowed to be given as a special exception provided certain conditions are met.[1]

The 1984 Act defines the circumstances in which confession evidence is admissible, but reference must still be made to some of the old law and cases because the Act gives the courts a discretion to exclude evidence which is technically admissible.[2]

The Act states the general rule that a confession made by an accused person may be given in evidence in so far as it is relevant to any matter in issue in the proceedings and is not excluded by the court (s76(1)). 'Confession' is defined as including any statement wholly or partly adverse to the person who made it, whether to a person in authority or not and whether in words or otherwise (s82(1)).[3]

However, this is not an exhaustive definition and the courts could

---

1 See generally Cross on Evidence (Butterworths, 8th edn 1995).
2 S82(3). See eg, *Callis v Gunn* [1964] 1 QB 495 and *Ibrahim v R* [1914] AC 599.
3 See JC Smith, 'Exculpatory Statements and Confessions' [1995] Crim LR 280–285 for a discussion on the meaning and applicability of this definition. Peter Mirfield discusses possible side-effects of the Criminal Justice and Public Order Act 1994 at [1995] Crim LR 617–624.

find something else to be a confession even if not within this definition. This includes a confession made by way of a videotaped re-enactment of the offence.[4] A failure expressly to deny the offence is not a confession, and a failure to deny that incriminating fingerprints are those of the accused is not an admission that they are.[5] However, under the provisions of the Criminal Justice and Public Order Act 1994 ss34–39 certain inferences may be drawn from the silence of an accused person.

It is clear that the admission can be made to anybody, not just to a police officer.

When confessions *must* be excluded

Introduction

The 1984 Act lays down two broad grounds on which a confession must be excluded:[6] unreliability (s76(2)(b)) and oppression (s76(2)(a)).[7] The Act also governs the procedure by which admissibility is determined.

The issue arises when the prosecution proposes to give in evidence a confession made by an accused person. (This means that the Act is not concerned with the situation where the defence wishes to put a confession in evidence, for instance in mitigation, or to show some other fact.) A purely exculpatory statement is not a confession for these purposes, even if it is damaging to the defence because it contains obvious lies and prevarications.[8]

Admissibility must be dealt with before the confession is actually given in evidence. In a jury trial this means that the judge will deal with the matter in the absence of the jury. If the rules in s76 have been breached, then the jury will never hear the confession and will not be prejudiced by it. This procedure (known as the 'voir dire' or a trial within trial) must be followed, even if the defence does not wish

4 *Li Shu-Ling v R* [1989] AC 270.
5 *Chappell v DPP* (1988) 89 Cr App R 82.
6 See Ian Dennis, 'Miscarriages of Justice and the Law of Confessions: Evidentiary Issues and Solutions' [1993] Public Law 291–313 for a useful background analysis.
7 A co-defendant may cross-examine an accused on an inadmissible confession: *Lui Mei Lin v R* [1989] 2 WLR 175; *R v Rowson* [1986] QB 174, CA. See article by Keith Vaughan at (1989) 86 LS Gaz 8 November pp23–24.
8 *R v Sat-Bhambra* (1988) 88 Cr App R 55, CA. Cf *R v Ismail* [1990] Crim LR 109, CA. See also the article by JC Smith referred to in note 3 above.

to have the issue dealt with as a preliminary matter.[9] The defence is not obliged to put its case to prosecution witnesses at this stage.[10] If the judge rules that the confession is admissible, s76 ceases to have effect, the defence cannot challenge its admissibility before the jury, and the judge cannot reverse the ruling at a later stage. The jury can take the defence representations into account in its own deliberations and, if it has heard a confession which the judge has become unhappy about, the judge can take such steps as are necessary to prevent injustice, eg, by giving the jury a direction to disregard the confession or to give it reduced weight.[11]

Magistrates' courts

Different problems are presented in a summary trial, since the magistrate(s) hearing the representations as to admissibility will also be deciding the merits of the case. Generally, the High Court discourages magistrates from holding a trial within a trial.[12] However, if the defence makes a s76 representation before the close of the prosecution case, the *Liverpool* case[13] rules that the magistrate(s) must hold a trial within a trial to decide the admissibility of the confession, and must rule on it before the close of the prosecution case. Again, this does not preclude the defence from challenging the evidential value of the confession at any later stage. Nevertheless, the *Liverpool* case held that the prosecution is not required to call the same evidence twice (as might happen in a jury trial if the judge admits the confession after a trial within a trial) and thereby provide the opportunity for two cross-examinations. Irrespective of the kind of proceedings, 'representation' appears to mean some formal or explicit statement. It does not cover a suggestion in cross-exmination that the confession was obtained improperly.[14]

In *Re Walters*, Watkins LJ in the Divisional Court said he would 'assume that it was obligatory' in extradition proceedings for the magistrate to consider an application to exclude a confession from

---

9　*R v Sat-Bhambra* n8.
10　*R v Millard* [1987] Crim LR 196 does not seem to have been overruled by *R v Sat-Bhambra* on this particular point. See also *R v Manji* [1990] Crim LR 512, CA.
11　*R v Sat-Bhambra* n8. The Court of Appeal said that the rule in *R v Watson* ((1980) 70 Cr App R 273) does not survive the 1984 Act.
12　*F (An Infant) v Chief Constable of Kent ex p Margate Juvenile Court* [1982] Crim LR 682.
13　*R v Liverpool Juvenile Court ex p R* [1987] 2 All ER 668; [1987] 3 WLR 224.
14　Ibid.

evidence when it was obtained after access to a solicitor was delayed.[15]

Procedure

When the prosecution proposes to give confession evidence and the defence represents to the court that the evidence might have been obtained in consequence of oppression or unreliable circumstances, the evidence must not be given unless the prosecution proves that it was not so obtained (s76(2)). Even if no such representation is made, the court can, of its own motion, require such proof from the prosecution (s76(3)). The defence need not bring any evidence to support its representation; the fact of the representation is sufficient to invoke these provisions. Where the defendant's legal representative fails to make representations in circumstances such that evidence might well have been excluded, that does not of itself provide grounds for a successful appeal unless 'all promptings of reason and good sense point the other way' from the course adopted by the defence at the trial.[16]

Trial within a trial

The matter will have to be proved at a trial within a trial, at which witnesses may be called in the usual fashion. The prosecution must prove beyond reasonable doubt that the confession was not obtained by oppression nor in unreliable circumstances. Proof beyond reasonable doubt has been described in this way by Lord Denning:

> It need not reach certainty but it must carry a high degree of probability. Proof beyond reasonable doubt does not mean proof beyond the shadow of doubt . . . [nor] fanciful possibilities to deflect the course of justice. If the evidence is so strong . . . as to leave only a remote possibility . . . the case is proved beyond reasonable doubt, but nothing short of that will suffice.[17]

If the prosecution does not meet this requirement, then the confession may not be put in evidence (s76(2)). This is so even if the confession is true (s76(2)). At the trial within a trial it is not permissible for the prosecution to ask the accused about the truth of the confession, nor for the prosecution to refer at the substantive trial to

15 Ie under s58(8) of the 1984 Act. On the facts, *Re Walters* [1987] Crim LR 577 held that the delay was fair, reasonable and lawful but the court did not consider the detailed requirements prescribed in *R v Samuel* [1988] 2 All ER 135, CA.

16 *R v O'Reilly* [1994] Crim LR 943, CA; *R v Clinton* [1993] 2 All ER 998, CA.

17 *Miller v Ministry of Pensions* [1947] 2 All ER 372 at 373–374.

evidence given by the accused at the trial within a trial. The accused may give evidence at the trial within a trial without having to give evidence at the substantive trial.[18]

In the absence of mental disability, mental illness, or a personality order so severe as to amount to mental disorder, the court should not admit at the trial within a trial the evidence of an expert witness to the effect that the defendant was of dull normal intelligence and very suggestible. These are matters of human nature and behaviour within the competence of the judge or jury.[19]

If the confession was obtained by oppression or in unreliable circumstances, the fact that its contents can be corroborated will not prevent its exclusion from evidence, although the corroboration may still be given in evidence.

Of course, even if a confession is ruled to be admissible, it is always open to the jury (or the magistrates) to disbelieve its truth as a question of fact, and for this purpose the same issues can be raised on the question of the truth of the confession as were raised on the question of admissiblity.[20]

Chapter 7 deals with the provisions of the 1984 Act and codes relating to the questioning and treatment of people in police detention and references to the Code of Practice are to Code C, discussed there.

Oppression

The prosecution must prove that the confession was not obtained by oppression of the person who made it. Oppression includes, but is not limited to, torture, inhuman or degrading treatment, and the use or threat of violence not amounting to torture (s76(8)). An action which does not come within this concept might nevertheless amount to unreliable circumstances (pp294ff) or lead to the exclusion of the confession at the discretion of the court. The oppression must be of the person who made the confession, although threats to another person could constitute torture or inhuman or degrading treatment of the person making the confession. The oppression must have led to the obtaining of the confession.[21] For example, if a suspect con-

---

18 *Wong Kam-Ming v R* [1979] 1 All ER 939, PC; *R v Brophy* [1981] 2 All ER 705, HL; *R v Davis* [1990] Crim LR 860, CA; *Lam Chi-Ming and Others v R* [1991] 3 All ER 172, PC; *R v Cox* [1991] Crim LR 276, CA.

19 *R v Heaton* [1993] Crim LR 593, CA; *R v Turner* (1975) 60 Cr App R 80, CA.

20 *R v McCarthy* [1980] Crim LR 306, CA.

21 *R v Parker* [1995] Crim LR 233, CA.

fessed freely and was then assaulted, the confession would not be excluded under s76.

In *R v Fulling*,[22] the Court of Appeal held that oppression meant the exercise of authority or power in a burdensome, harsh or wrongful manner, or unjust or cruel treatment, or the imposition of unreasonable or unjust burdens, in circumstances which would almost always entail some impropriety on the part of the interrogator.[23] It did not include a female suspect being told by the police in the middle of an interrogation that her male lover had been having an affair for the previous three years with another woman who had been arrested in connection with the same matter and was in the next cell. It is interesting that at first instance, Ognall J had said that 'the word oppression means something above and beyond that which is inherently oppressive in police custody and must import some impropriety'. Remarkably, in view of the fundamental changes made to criminal procedure, the Court of Appeal held that the 1984 Act was a codifying statute and that its words should be given their natural meaning uninfluenced by any considerations derived from the previous state of the law.

In one case where the trial took place under the old law, but where the appeal was heard after the 1984 Act came into force, the Court of Appeal (applying the old law) said that if the police deliberately asked questions of a person suffering from paranoid schizophrenia with the intention of producing a disordered state of mind, that would amount to oppression. However, the mere fact that questions triggered off hallucinations or flights of fancy would not amount to oppression.[24] The court did not discuss whether the evidence could be excluded under s76(2)(b) or s82(3) of the Act.[25]

The absence of a solicitor during an interview would not usually amount to oppression, but the Crown Court has excluded, on grounds of oppression, a confession made during a three-hour interview which commenced after the suspect had been unlawfully detained for six hours.[26] Thus, oppression is not limited in meaning to torture or inhuman or degrading treatment, and it is for the court to

---

22 [1987] 2 All ER 65, CA.
23 See also *R v Heron* (1993) 1 November (unreported) discussed at (1994) 91 LS Gaz 20.
24 *R v Miller* [1986] 3 All ER 119, CA.
25 See commentary at [1986] Crim LR 550.
26 *R v Davison* [1988] Crim LR 442.

decide whether a particular set of circumstances amounts to oppression.

Rude and discourteous behaviour or aggressive and hostile questioning by an interviewing officer would not of itself amount to oppression.[27] However, in another case,[28] the Court of Appeal was in no doubt that there was oppression where a defendant, on the borderline of mental disability, had denied the offence over 300 times and had been subject to hectoring and bullying questioning. The court was 'horrified' that this had happened and commented that short of physical violence it was hard to conceive of a more hostile and intimidating approach. The court of Appeal has also quashed the conviction for manslaughter of a 16-year-old defendant where an interview in which he was instructed to answer questions after nine denials was excluded at the trial, but an interview eight days later had not been excluded. The court found that the second interview was, in the circumstances, tainted by the first, although that would not inevitably be so in all cases.[29] In another case the trial judge found that there was oppression where there was a combination of a hectoring manner by an interviewing officer with misrepresentations by the officer in the case.[30]

Torture

The Criminal Justice Act 1988 s134 creates an offence of torture by or on behalf of a public official and defines torture as the intentional infliction of severe pain or suffering on another, whether physical or mental and whether caused by an act or an omission.

Decisions under the European Convention on Human Rights have said that torture is deliberate inhuman treatment causing very serious and cruel suffering, and inhuman treatment can embrace intense physical and mental suffering and causing acute psychiatric disturbance as well as actual bodily injury.[31] Degrading treatment is such

---

27 *R v Emmerson* (1990) 92 Cr App R 99, CA; *R v L* [1994] Crim LR 839, CA; *R v Weeks* [1995] Crim LR 52, CA.

28 *R v Paris, Abdullahi and Miller* (1993) 97 Cr App R 99, CA. For a journalistic account of this case and its background see John Wiliams, *Bloody Valentine, A Killing in Cardiff* (HarperCollins 1995).

29 *R v Glaves* [1993] Crim LR 685, CA; see also *R v Conway* [1994] Crim LR 839.

30 *R v Beales* [1991] Crim LR 118, Crown Court.

31 *Ireland v UK* (1978) 2 EHRR 25 para 167.

as grossly humiliates a person before others, or drives a person to act against will or conscience.[32]

Appendix 7 sets out the definition of torture adopted by the United Nations.[33]

Unreliability

A confession must be excluded once the issue has been raised (even if no evidence of unreliability is brought by the defence), unless the prosecution proves that it was not obtained in consequence of anything said or done which was likely, in the circumstances existing at the time, to render it unreliable (s76(2)(b)).

Here the court has a wider discretion than in the case of oppression, and must decide whether the circumstances were likely to render the confession unreliable. The unreliability must result from things said or done by someone other than the accused.[34] If things are said or done which should not be (for example because they are unlawful), but which do not render the confession unreliable, then the confession is not excluded under s76, although it might be excluded under the court's general discretion (see below).

The Act gives no further guidance on what things said or done might render the confession unreliable,[35] but it is clear that there need be no impropriety on the part of an interrogator for a confession to be excluded on this ground.[36]

Clearly there is no real limit to the types of circumstances which might render a confession unreliable and defence advocates should always consider this point when deciding whether to challenge a confession and how to cross-examine at the trial within a trial.

Lord Lane CJ has suggested that the circumstances might include 'questioning which by its nature, duration or other attendant circumstances (including the fact of custody) excites hopes (such as the hope of release) or fears, or so affects the mind of the subject that his will

---

32 Greek case Yearbook 12 at 186; *Tyrer v UK* (1978) 2 EHRR 1; *Campbell and Cosans v UK* (1982) 4 EHRR 293.

33 For the full text and background see Ian Brownlie, ed. *Basic Documents on Human Rights* (Clarendon Press Oxford, 3rd edn 1992). The European Convention against Torture is reproduced on pp383–390 of the same volume.

34 *R v Crampton* [1991] Crim LR 277, CA; *R v Goldenberg* [1988] Crim LR 678; but cf *R v Doolan* [1988] Crim LR 747, CA.

35 For possible examples based on the old law, see the first edition of this book at pp149–150.

36 *R v Fulling* [1987] 2 All ER 65, CA at 70.

crumbles and he speaks when otherwise he would have stayed silent.'[37]

In one case the Court of Appeal quashed a conviction where the trial judge had treated negotiations over obtaining bail and making a confession as being similar to negotiating a contract.[38] Deception by the police might also be a ground for exclusion under this provision.[39]

Breaches of the Codes of Practice

The 1984 Act s67(11) allows the Code of Practice to be considered in determining the question of admissibility, and s67(9) requires police officers to have regard to the code.

The Court of Appeal has emphasised that:

> . . . the mere fact that there has been a breach of the Codes of Practice does not of itself mean that evidence has to be rejected. It is no part of the duty of the court to rule a statement inadmissible simply in order to punish the police for failure to observe the Codes of Practice.[40]

In that case, however, there were 'flagrant and serious breaches' of Code C relating to an interview of an educationally subnormal man who was emotionally unstable and whom the police told that their real purpose was to get psychiatric help rather than bring him to court. The Court of Appeal quashed the conviction because the confession should have been excluded under s76(2)(b).

A technical breach of the Codes will not be excluded if it does not prejudice the fairness of the proceedings,[41] but the combined effect of several breaches might lead to the exclusion of an admission.[42]

Other examples of the Court of Appeal finding that breaches of the code have, in the particular circumstances of the cases, rendered a confession unreliable, are where there was no caution, contemporaneous note of interview or record of the times of interview[43] and where there was questioning after the accused was charged but a

---

37 The words of Lord MacDermott at 21 CLP 10 quoted by Edmund Davies LJ in *R v Prager* [1972] 1 All ER 1114 at 1119, cited by Lord Lane CJ in *R v Fulling* [1987] 2 All ER 65, CA at 68.
38 *R v Barry* (1991) 95 Cr App R 384, CA, cf *R v Howden-Simpson* [1991] Crim LR 49, CA.
39 *R v Blake and Others* [1991] Crim LR 119, Crown Court.
40 Per Lord Lane CJ in *R v Delaney* [1989] Crim LR 139, CA. For commercial investigators see *R v Twaites* (1990) *Times* 16 April.
41 *R v Marsh* [1991] Crim LR 455, CA.
42 *R v Chung* [1991] Crim LR 622, CA.
43 *R v Doolan* [1988] Crim LR 747, CA.

failure to record the questions and answers.[44] In both cases the appeal was dismissed because there was ample evidence on which to convict apart from the confession, and it was queried whether the confession was made as a result of things said or done by another.[45] In one case, the Crown Court excluded a confession under this provision when a drug addict was interviewed in the absence of a solicitor after having been in custody for 18 hours without any rest at all (Code C requires a continuous period of at least 8 hours' rest, free from questioning, in any period of 24 hours).[46]

The test in s76(2)(b) is whether the particular person is more likely to make an unreliable confession as a result of anything said or done. Considerations might include the fact that the person is of low intelligence, as where a woman confessed to murder having heard her lover confess to the same murder and possibly motivated by a desire to protect him,[47] and where a 42-year-old man had a mental age of eight.[48] Other relevant factors might include age, the effect of medication, mental illness and hypoglycaemia.[49]

Where the prosecution depends wholly upon confession, a defendant suffers from significant mental disability and the confession itself is unconvincing, the judge should withdraw the case from the jury.[50] The mental condition of the defendant at the time of the interview is one of the circumstances to be considered by the trial judge on a submission under s76(2). A decision about this should be based on the medical evidence rather than the trial judge's own assessment. The issue is not solely whether the defendant's IQ is above an arbitrary figure.[51]

44 *R v Waters* [1989] Crim LR 62, CA.
45 See the commentary by D Birch in Crim LR on *Delaney, Doolan* and *Waters*.
46 *R v Trussler* [1988] Crim LR 446, and see Code C para 12.2.
47 *R v Harvey* [1988] Crim LR 241; and see *R v Delaney* n40. See also *R v Williams* [1979] Crim LR 47; *R v Westlake* [1979] Crim LR 652; *R v Platt* [1981] Crim LR 622.
48 *R v Everett* [1988] Crim LR 826. See also *R v Dutton Independent* 5 December.
49 See the cases cited in the first edition of this book at p150. Now see also *R v McGovern* [1991] Crim LR 124, CA, *R v Morse and Others* [1991] Crim LR 195, Crown Court; *R v Ward* [1993] 2 All ER 577, CA and *R v Kenny* [1994] Crim LR 284, CA; but cf *R v McKenzie* (1992) 92 Cr App R 98, CA and *R v W and Another* [1994] Crim LR 130, CA.
50 *R v Mckenzie* (1993) 96 Cr App R 98, CA; *R v Wood* [1994] Crim LR 222, CA; *R v Bailey* [1995] Crim LR 723, CA.
51 *R v Silcott, Braithwaite and Raghip* (1992) *Times* 9 December, CA. For a journalistic account of this case and its background see David Rose, *A Climate of Fear, The Murder of PC Blakelock and the Case of the Tottenham Three* (Bloomsbury 1992).

The test is not whether the confession is actually unreliable but whether the circumstances are likely to render it unreliable.[52]

Effect of exclusion

If any fact is discovered as a result of a confession which has been excluded under s76, that fact may still be given in evidence although the confession cannot be given, and the prosecution is not allowed to say that the fact was discovered as the result of a statement by the accused, although the defence may give evidence of this (s76(4)–(6)). Thus, if a defendant tells the police that stolen goods are hidden somewhere, and gives this information as a result of physical violence, the goods themselves can be produced and evidence given as to where they were found and any fingerprints on them, but not as to how the police came to look for them in that particular place. Although such facts are admissible as a matter of law, they may be excluded in pursuance of the court's discretion (see below).

If a confession is relevant in showing that the defendant speaks or writes in a particular way, so much of the confession as is necessary to prove that this is so, may be given in evidence even if the confession was obtained by oppression or in unreliable circumstances (s76(4)(b)). Again, the court can exclude such evidence in pursuance of its discretion (see below).

Confessions by mentally handicapped persons

As indicated above, the fact that a suspect is mentally handicapped might be relevant in regarding a confession as having been made in circumstances likely to render it unreliable, or as a factor leading the court to exercise its discretion to exclude the evidence (see below).

In addition, in certain circumstances, when a confession made by a mentally handicapped person is admitted in evidence (that is, where the court has already decided that the confession was not obtained as a result of oppression or in unreliable circumstances), the court must warn the jury, or a magistrates' court must take into account, that

52 *R v Everett* n48. The Court of Appeal has decided that the unreliability rule does not apply to Board of Trade Inspectors conducting an investigation under the Companies Act 1985 s432 (*R v Seelig and Another* [1991] 4 All ER 429, CA) but the European Commission of Human Rights has found that this rule breaches the Convention (*Saunders v United Kingdom*, Application 19187/91, (1994) *Independent* 30 September.

there is a special need for caution before convicting the accused in reliance on the confession. The court must explain that the need for caution arises because of the circumstances in which s77 applies (s77(1) and (2)).

However, the Act says nothing about those who are mentally disordered, although the Code of Practice treats both categories (and children) in the same way.[53] *R v Miller*[54] was decided in 1986 but concerned a pre-Act case. The defence argued that the police questioning had triggered off a schizophrenic episode. A psychiatrist gave evidence that the length and style of questioning would have produced a state in which the confession would reflect delusions and hallucinations rather than reality. The Court of Appeal upheld the refusal of the judge to exclude the confession because it was not obtained by oppression. It is very difficult to see how such a confession could now survive the unreliability rule in s76.[55]

Section 77 applies where:

a) the case depends wholly or substantially on a confession made by the accused; and

b) the court is satisfied that the accused is mentally handicapped; and

c) the confession was not made in the presence of an independent person.

The section does not apply unless the prosecution case is substantially less strong without the confession.[56] Mentally handicapped is defined in s77(3). It is for the court to decide whether a person comes into this category, although it might well be guided by expert evidence. An independent person is someone who is not a police officer nor employed for nor engaged on police purposes (such as a special constable, police cadet or civilian employed by the police)(s77(3)). Thus such a person might be a solicitor, friend or relative of the accused, social worker, or even a stranger off the street.

The Code of Practice emphasises the importance of mentally handicapped people (and those who are mentally disordered or juvenile) being interviewed in the presence of a third party except in the

---

53 Code C paras 10.6, 11.14 Annexes C and E and Note for Guidance 1G. For further discussion see Philip W H Fennell 'Mentally Disordered Suspects in the Criminal Justice System' (1994) 21 JLS 57–71 and Judith M Laing 'The Mentally Disordered Suspect at the Police Station' [1995] Crim LR 371–381.

54 [1986] 3 All ER 119, CA.

55 See *R v Moss* (1990) 91 Cr App R 371, CA.

56 *R v Campbell* [1995] Crim LR 157, CA

case of urgency[57] and of course a breach of this requirement might render the circumstances unreliable or oppressive. In particular, the independent person might consider that legal advice should be taken, and is there to advise as well as to facilitate communication.[58]

The Act does not specify the consequences if a court fails to give the necessary warning to the jury. However, this is 'an essential part of a fair summing-up' and its omission might lead to the quashing of any conviction.[59]

In cases where the defendant is significantly mentally handicapped and the prosecution would not have a case in the absence of the defendant's confessions, the judge is required to give a full and proper statement of the case against the confession being accepted by the jury as true and accurate and to place before the jury all points made on the defendant's behalf. This might include pointing out that the experience of the courts has shown that people with significant mental handicaps do make false confessions for a variety of reasons.[60]

Code C emphasises the importance of the police obtaining, where possible, corroboration of any facts admitted by a mentally handicapped person.[61] This goes beyond the requirements of the Act but is obviously good practice.

Discretionary exclusion of any evidence

Residual discretion

Section 82(3) of the 1984 Act operates to preserve any discretion to exclude evidence existing prior to the 1984 Act. It applies to any evidence, including but not limited to confessions. Before the 1984 Act there was a general discretion to exclude evidence to ensure a fair trial.[62] This was interpreted quite restrictively, however, so that by the time the Act was passed, the only basis on which a court could exclude evidence other than that obtained from the accused was if its prejudicial effect outweighed its probative value. But the court's discretion to exclude evidence obtained from the accused was fairly

---

57 See n53.
58 Code C Annex E.
59 *R v Lamont* [1989] Crim LR 813, CA.
60 *R v Bailey* [1995] Crim LR 723, CA.
61 Code C Note for Guidance 11B.
62 *Selvey v DPP* [1968] 2 All ER 497, HL and *Myers v DPP* [1964] 2 All ER 881, HL.

wide.[63] Within these limits, the courts retain the discretion to exclude any evidence which is not excluded by virtue of s76 or s78.

These powers are separate from and in addition to the power of the court to deal with abuse of process by the prosecution.[64]

Statutory discretion to exclude any evidence

Section 78 gives discretion to the court to refuse to allow evidence on which the prosecution proposes to rely to be given if it appears to the court that, having regard to all circumstances, including the circumstances in which the evidence was obtained, the admission of the evidence would have such an adverse effect on the fairness of the proceedings that the court ought not to admit it.

This provision applies to all evidence, including evidence of confessions.[65] However, if a confession is obtained by oppression or in unreliable circumstances, or if evidence is required to be excluded by some other rule of law, it must be excluded and there is no discretion not to exclude it (s78(2)).

The discretion is very wide, and is not limited to illegally or unlawfully obtained evidence, nor to 'prejudicial effect' (which seems to be a narrower concept than 'adverse effect'). There need be no improper conduct on the part of the police or anyone else, and there is no requirement that anything in particular be said or done.[66] Although the general rule is that illegally obtained evidence is admissible as a matter of law, s78 provides a discretion to exclude it.

As far as confessions are concerned, s78 will, for example, allow the exclusion of a confession which was made in circumstances not quite qualifying as oppressive or unreliable, if the oppression took place but did not lead to the confession being made, or because of the particular characteristics of the defendant, such as deafness.[67]

Section 78 does not require that the evidence in question be subject

---

63 *R v Sang* [1979] 2 All ER 1222, HL.
64 *R v Bow Street Metropolitan Stipendiary Magistrate ex p DPP* (1992) 95 Cr App R 9, CA; *R v Horseferry Road Magistrates' Court ex p Bennett* [1994] AC 42, HL; *R v Croydon Justices ex p Dean* [1994] 3 WLR 198, QBD; *Attorney-General's Reference (No 1 of 1990)* [1992] QB 630; *R v Wellingborough Justices ex p Francois* (1994) *Times* 1 July; *Attorney-General of Trinidad and Tobago v Philip* [1994] 1 WLR 1134, PC.
65 *R v Mason* [1987] 3 All ER 481, CA. *R v Manji* [1990] Crim LR 512, CA.
66 *R v Brine* [1992] Crim LR 122, CA.
67 *R v Clarke* [1989] Crim LR 892, CA.

to a preliminary ruling in the same way as under s76. The procedure is within the discretion of the court, but it seems that if a prosecution could not possibly succeed without the disputed evidence, then the question of admissibility should be decided as a preliminary issue in the magistrates' court,[68] and in jury trials the judge should usually hear arguments on admissibility in the absence of the jury. A trial within a trial will not generally be held when a point is taken under s78 on the admissibility of identification evidence.[69]

Once evidence has been given or admitted, then s78 no longer operates, but if the court then decides that it should not have been admitted, the discretion to stop the trial or take other steps necessary to prevent injustice is preserved by s82(3).[70]

The court always has the discretion to raise a s78 issue of its own motion during the trial, but if no objection is taken by defending counsel to evidence which is in principle admissible, it is not for the judge to seek to repair the situation in the summing up ex post facto and direct the jury to exclude it.[71]

Where prosecution evidence has been excluded, any attempt by the defence to cross-examine on issues that were part of the excluded evidence might be disallowed[72] or might lead to the excluded evidence being allowed back in.[73]

The Court of Appeal has declined to lay down general guidelines on s78 because 'circumstances vary infinitely' but certain patterns are emerging from the cases, although the way in which the judge's discretion is exercised in any particular case is not binding in any other case.[74]

---

68 Vel v Owen (Chief Constable of North Wales) [1987] Crim LR 496 and Carlisle v DPP (1987) unreported CO/1361/87 (Lexis transcript). Cf Halawa v Federation Against Copyright Theft [1995] Crim LR 409, QBD.

69 R v Beveridge [1987] Crim LR 401, CA (identification parades); R v Fleming (1987) 131 SJ 972; (1987) Independent 2 June. The proper procedure is set out in R v Turnbull [1977] QB 224 at 229.

70 R v Hassan [1995] Crim LR 404, CA; R v Vernon [1988] Crim LR 445, CA.

71 R v Oroegbu, unreported but digested at (1988) Independent 8 August.

72 R v Campbell [1993] Crim LR 47, CA.

73 R v Allen [1992] Crim LR 297, CA.

74 R v Grannell (1989) Times 16 August, CA; R v Samuel [1988] 2 All ER 135, CA. For a survey of the way in which individual judges exercise their discretion under s78 see Mary Hunter 'Judicial Discretion: Section 78 in Practice' [1994] Crim LR 558–565.

Confessions and s78

Breach of Code C

A statement or confession made by a suspect after a breach of the 1984 Act or the Codes of Practice, can be ruled inadmissible under s78 but is not necessarily ruled out. Each case has to be determined on its own facts.[75] The Court of Appeal has pointed out that in considering admissibility of evidence in such cases it is important not to be diverted from considering the statutory language by examining other decisions of the court, often on different facts.[76] Breaches of the Act or Codes, whether or not substantial and whether or not done in bad faith, have to be judged against the overall fairness of the proceedings.[77] Even if there are substantial breaches of the Code such that evidence should be excluded, the case against the defendant on the basis of other evidence might be so strong that a conviction will be upheld.[78] Technical breaches of the Code alone will not usually justify exclusion and Bingham LJ has said:[79]

> ... these provisions should not become so highly technical and sophisticated in their construction and application than no police officer, however well-intentioned and diligent, could reasonably be expected to comply with them ... police officers confronted with unexpected situations, and doing their best to be fair and to comply with the Codes [should] not fall foul on some technicality of authority or construction.

In most cases, however, a failure to caution will be regarded as a significant and substantial breach of the code, leading to exclusion of the confession.[80]

Confessions allegedly made in interviews which are not recorded in accordance with Code C (see pp212–215) might well be excluded. 'Significant and substantial' breaches of the 'verballing' provisions of Code C will fall foul of s78.[81] Lord Lane CJ has pointed out that 'the importance of the rules relating to contemporaneous noting of

---

75 *R v Parris* [1989] Crim LR 214, CA. See also *R v Abdullah* (1990) 31 January, unreported, CA; and *R v Manji* [1990] Crim LR 512, CA.

76 *R v Oliphant* [1992] Crim LR 40, CA.

77 *R v Kerawalla* [1991] Crim LR 451, CA; *R v Oni* [1992] Crim LR 183, CA; *R v Okafor* [1994] 3 All ER 741, CA.

78 *R v Sparks* [1991] Crim LR 128, CA; *R v Oransaye* [1993] Crim LR 772, CA.

79 *R v Marsh* [1991] Crim LR 456, CA, quoted in commentary by D J Birch.

80 *R v Weerdesteyn* [1995] Crim LR 239, CA, *R v Hunt* [1992] Crim LR 582, CA, *R v Pall* [1992] Crim LR 126, CA, *R v Sparks* [1991] Crim LR 128, CA, cf *R v O'Shea* [1993] Crim LR 950, CA, *R v Oni* [1992] Crim LR 183, CA, *R v Hoyte* [1994] Crim LR 215, CA.

81 *R v Keenan* [1989] 3 All ER 598, CA.

interviews can scarcely be overemphasised'. In *R v Canale* the Court of Appeal said that interviews should have been excluded under s78 when the police had flagrantly and deliberately breached Code C and shown a 'cynical disregard of the rules'.[82]

Confessions have also been excluded under s78 when, in breach of Code C, suspects have not been told of their rights to have legal advice before being interviewed[83] and where a suspect's own solicitors were unavailable and she agreed to be interviewed without legal advice. This occurred when she had not been told of the availability of a duty solicitor and the officer knew that the duty solicitor was on the way, in connection with another case, but had told the suspect that if she wanted to wait for a solicitor she would be held overnight.[84] However, in *R v Hughes* the Court of Appeal held that there was no breach of the code and that s78 did not apply where a suspect confessed, after being told in good faith that there was no duty solicitor available and agreeing to be interviewed on his own.[85] The difference might well be the presence or absence of good faith on the part of the police[86] although in other cases[87] the mere existence of 'serious and substantial breaches' sufficed to justify exclusion. The Court of Appeal has ruled that a confession should have been excluded after the police advised a person whose native language was not English that it was normal to conduct interviews without a solicitor being present.[88]

---

82 *R v Canale* [1990] 2 All ER 187, CA. See also *R v Scott* [1991] Crim LR 56, CA; *R v Joseph* [1993] Crim LR 206, CA; but cf *R v Gillard and Barrett* [1991] Crim LR 280, CA; *R v White* [1991] Crim LR 779, CA.

83 *R v Absolam* [1988] Crim LR 748 and *R v Williams (Violet)* [1989] Crim LR 66. See also *R v Delroy Fogah* [1989] Crim LR 141 concerning questioning a juvenile in the street in the absence of an appropriate adult. This was followed in *R v Grier* (1989) April *Legal Action* 14. In *R v Sanusi* [1992] Crim LR 43, CA a conviction was quashed because customs officers had interviewed a man from abroad who had no previous convictions and had not informed him of his rights. The Court of Appeal pointed out that a breach of the codes does not lead to automatic exclusion but here there were serious and substantial breaches as there was no good reason to think that the man was familiar with the rights of a suspect when faced with a police interview. See also *R v Neill* [1994] Crim LR 441, CA, where there was no opportunity to take legal advice between the first and second interviews.

84 *R v Vernon* [1988] Crim LR 445.

85 *R v Hughes* [1988] Crim LR 519.

86 As indicated in *R v Alladice* [1988] Crim LR 608. See also *R v Younis and Ahmed* [1990] Crim LR 425, CA.

87 Eg, in *R v Absolam* [1988] Crim LR 743.

88 *R v Beycan* [1990] Crim LR 185, CA.

Denial of access to a solicitor

A person who is in police detention is entitled on request to consult a solicitor privately at any time (1984 Act s58(1)). There are procedural requirements and provision for an officer of at least the rank of superintendent (or authorised to act as such) to delay access to a solicitor for up to 36 hours in the case of a serious arrestable offence (s58(6)). The grounds on which access may be delayed are limited to those set out in s58(3).[89]

The courts have been quick to exclude confessions obtained after access was delayed or denied in breach of s58.[90] In particular, s58(8)(b) allows delay to be authorised if obtaining advice from a solicitor 'will lead to the alerting of other persons suspected of having committed such an offence but not yet arrested for it'. In *R v Samuel*, the Court of Appeal has firmly declared that the right of a person detained by the police to have access to a solicitor is a fundamental right of the citizen, and a decision to delay access under s58(8)(b) must be based on very specific grounds relating to a particular solicitor, and would apply very rarely. A confession obtained, following denial of access to a solicitor, should be excluded when these strict requirements have not been satisfied.[91]

Alternatively, such a confession might be excluded under the provisions of s76 (see above pp289ff).[92] However, the confession might not be excluded at all if the circumstances of the particular defendant mean that there is no real unfairness. In *R v Alladice*[93] the appellant said that he was able to cope with the interviews, understood the caution and alleged that the admissions had not been made at all, and in *R v Dunford* a defendant with a criminal record had experience of the procedure and was aware of his rights.[94]

The Court of Appeal has declined to lay down guidelines as to when a court should admit a statement made in a foreign country

---

89 See pp196–200 above.
90 Eg, *R v Paul Deacon* [1987] Crim LR 404; *R v Eric Smith* [1987] Crim LR 579; *R v Cochrane* [1988] Crim LR 449; *R v Walsh* [1989] Crim LR 822; *R v Parris* [1989] Crim LR 214, CA; but cf the extradition case of *Re Walters* [1987] Crim LR 577 and *R v Matthews* [1990] Crim LR 190.
91 *R v Samuel* [1988] 2 All ER 135, CA. See also *R v Franklin* [1994] *Times* 16 June and Code C and chapter 7.
92 *R v McGovern* [1991] Crim LR 124, CA.
93 [1988] Crim LR 603.
94 Any solicitor who had been present could have been called as a witness (as in *R v Dunn* [1990] Crim LR 572) as to whether the admissions had been made. *R v Dunford* is reported at [1991] Crim LR 370.

according to rules which might not coincide with the provisions of the 1984 Act, and upheld the admissibility of a statement made to a Belgian customs officer in the absence of a caution or advice that the suspect could have a lawyer present.[95]

After 36 hours (or at any earlier stage where s58(8) ceases to apply) the suspect must be told 'in specific, easily understandable terms that . . . he could notify someone or have access to a solicitor' and a confession obtained subsequently might well be excluded if this has not been done.[96]

Confession obtained by deceit

Evidence of a confession can be excluded even if the defendant has legal advice. In *R v Mason*,[97] the Court of Appeal rejected a prosecution argument that s78 did not apply to confessions. Holding that the purpose of s78 was not to discipline the police but to ensure a fair trial, the Court nevertheless quashed a conviction based on a confession obtained by deceiving both the defendant and his solicitor. The police had questioned the defendant about an offence of arson and falsely told him and his solicitor that they had found near the scene a fragment of a bottle which had contained inflammable liquid and on which his fingerprint had been found. He then confessed to being involved. In fact the police had no evidence at all against the defendant except that the victim was the father of a girl who had been pregnant by him and there had been bad feeling between them. Watkins LJ said:

> . . . we hope never again to hear of deceit such as this being practised on an accused person, and more particularly possibly on a solicitor whose duty it is to advise him, unfettered by false information from the police.

In one case the Crown Court excluded the record of telephone conversations with the suspect instigated at police suggestion by the victim of an alleged rape[98] and in more dramatic and widely reported recent cases, evidence has been excluded after male suspects were befriended by undercover female police officers for the very purpose

---

95 *R v Konscol* [1993] Crim LR 950, CA. In that case there was no suggestion that the interview had not been conducted fairly according to Belgian law, and there was no dishonesty or bullying by the police. Would the Court of Appeal have ruled differently otherwise?

96 *R v Cochrane* (above). *R v Mary Quayson* [1989] Crim LR 218.

97 [1987] 3 All ER 481, CA. See also *R v Woodall* [1989] Crim LR 288; *R v Blake and Others* [1991] Crim LR 119, Crown Court.

98 *R v H* [1987] Crim LR 47, Crown Court.

of inducing the suspects to confide in them.[99] However, in a series of cases the courts have admitted evidence in secretly taped conversations obtained by subterfuge.[100]

One Crown Court judge excluded confessions after they had been made in the absence of any solicitor by a group of people who believed that they were helping the police as witnesses and did not appreciate that they were themselves in danger of being charged, although they had been arrested and cautioned and some had been placed in the cells. In this case they seem to have deceived themselves.[101]

Informal confessions

Informal confessions, especially when not made to police officers, can cause problems. A confession made by a prisoner to a prison officer while specifically seeking assistance in making a legal aid application might well be excluded under s78.[102] However, a statement on non-medical matters made to a psychiatrist who was trying to determine the defendant's mental state was held to be admissible.[103]

The effect of curtailing the right to silence

Limitations on the traditional rights to silence have been introduced by the Criminal Justice and Public Order Act 1994 ss34 to 39. It is too soon to say what effect these changes will have on the operation of s78.[104] However, it is quite possible that the courts will place greater emphasis on the importance of the revised caution and the right to legal advice, so that suspects are not left in the position where they do not say what they should be saying because they have not been properly advised of the significance of the new procedures.

99 *R v Hall* (1994) 11 March, Leeds Crown Court and *R v Stagg* (1994) 14 September, both unreported but discussed in 'Watching the Detectives' by Michael Doherty at (1994) 144 NLJ 1525–6.

100 *R v Jelen and Katz* (1990) 90 Cr App R 456, CA; *R v Maclean and Kosten* [1993] Crim LR 687, CA; *R v Khan* [1994] 4 All ER 427, CA; *R v Bailey and Another* [1993] 3 All ER 513, CA; *R v Cadette* [1995] Crim LR 229, CA.

101 *R v Williams* [1991] Crim LR 708, Crown Court.

102 *R v Umoh* [1987] Crim LR 258, CA, where the appeal was dismissed on the facts.

103 *R v McDonald* [1991] Crim LR 122, CA. See also *R v Sparks* [1991] Crim LR 128, CA.

104 See, eg, the discussions by Ian Dennis 'The Criminal Justice and Public Order Act 1994: The Evidence Provisions' [1995] Crim LR 4–18, by Helen Fenwick 'Curtailing the Right to Silence, Access to Legal Advice and Section 78' [1995] Crim LR 132–136 and by Rosemary Pattenden, 'Inferences from Silence' [1995] Crim LR 602.

Exclusion of evidence other than confessions

Evidence of identification

Procedures for identification are governed by common law and by Code of Practice D and are discussed in more detail on pp227–243 above. Evidence of identification can be excluded under s78, for example when there is no ground to apply the similar fact or striking similarity rule,[105] but a breach of the code will not inevitably lead to exclusion.[106] However, judges must draw the attention of juries to breaches of the code where identification is in issue[107] and a clear breach and 'complete flouting' of the code will lead to exclusion.[108] The code does not deal with voice identification and the courts will not use s78 to enforce analogous procedures.[109]

Guilty plea of co-defendant

In R v O'Connor[110] the appellant had been convicted of conspiracy to obtain property by deception, after evidence had been given of the guilty plea of an alleged co-conspirator to a count which named Mr O'Connor. The Court of Appeal accepted that this was tantamount to introducing a statement made by a co-accused in the absence of the defendant, which is hearsay evidence, and should have been excluded, notwithstanding provisions for proof of other convictions in the 1984 Act. Nevertheless, evidence of the guilty plea of a co-defendant will not be excluded under s78 if it is not evidence which implicates the defendant.[111]

Road traffic cases

In Jit Singh Matto v DPP,[112] the Divisional Court said that evidence of a positive breath test should have been excluded when it followed police officers deliberately and with bad faith exceeding their powers

---

105 R v Johnson [1995] Crim LR 53, CA.
106 R v Penny [1992] Crim LR 184, CA.
107 R v Quinn [1995] Crim LR 56, CA; R v Conway (1990) 91 Cr App R 143, CA; R v Brown [1991] Crim LR 368, CA, R v Graham [1994] Crim LR 212, CA; but cf R v Middlebrook [1994] Crim LR 357, CA.
108 R v Nagah [1991] Crim LR 55, CA. See also R v Samms, Elliot and Bartley [1991] Crim LR 197; but cf R v Taylor [Leroy] [1991] Crim LR 541, CA.
109 R v Deenik [1992] Crim LR 578, CA. See also R v Robb (1991) 93 Cr App R 161, CA.
110 [1987] Crim LR 260, CA; (1986) 85 Cr App R 298, followed in R v Curry [1988] Crim LR 527, CA. See also R v Mattison [1990] Crim LR 117, CA.
111 R v Robertson, R v Golder [1987] 3 All ER 231; R v Lunnon [1988] Crim LR 456, CA; R v Bennett [1988] Crim LR 686, CA.
112 [1987] Crim LR 641. See also Hudson v DPP [1992] RTR 27, QBD.

by trespassing on private property. However, in *DPP v Billington and Others* the Divisional Court ruled that waiting to consult a solicitor does not provide a reasonable excuse for failing to provide a specimen, nor do breaches of the Code of Practice. Section 78 could not be used to exclude the evidence of failure to provide a specimen, even where the defendant had been denied access to a solicitor who was in the police station at the time.[113]

An arrested person does not have a reasonable excuse for failing to provide a specimen because he first wishes to consult the codes.[114]

The absence of bad faith does not mean that the court cannot exclude evidence in these matters under s78.[115]

Exclusion of other evidence

In *R v O'Laughlin and McLaughlin*,[116] s78 was activated by a Central Criminal Court judge in an explosives jury trial to exclude from evidence the depositions of prosecution witnesses given in the court below, when those witnesses had left the country and refused to return to give evidence.

The courts have the power to exclude any kind of evidence under s78 and in one case excluded evidence of two searches made in breach of 1984 Act s2(3) and of Code A.[117] However, the courts are reluctant to exclude scientific or technical evidence.[118]

Entrapment

The leading pre-1984 Act case on the exclusion of unlawfully obtained evidence, *R v Sang*,[119] concerned entrapment – evidence obtained as a result of the activities of an agent provocateur. The House of Lords quite categorically ruled that there was no discretion to exclude such evidence. Thus there is no discretion to be preserved by s82(3).

In a decision on two cases where defendants solicited undercover police officers posing as contract killers to kill the defendants' spouses, the Court of Appeal has affirmed that s78 has not altered

---

113 [1988] 1 All ER 435.
114 *DPP v Whalley* [1991] Crim LR 211, QBD, *DPP v Cornell* [1990] RTR 254, QBD.
115 *DPP v McGladrigan* [1991] Crim LR 851, QBD.
116 [1988] 3 All ER 431.
117 *R v Fennelley* [1989] Crim LR 142.
118 *R v Cooke* [1995] Crim LR 497, CA; *DPP v British Telecommunications PLC* [1991] Crim LR 532, QBD.
119 [1979] 2 All ER 1222, HL.

the substantive rule that entrapment or use of an agent provocateur does not by itself afford a defence in law[120] However, in those cases the Court of Appeal ruled that the judge could exclude the evidence of an agent provocateur or informer under s78, depending on all the circumstances. The judges should take account of whether the defendant was being enticed to commit an offence that he would not otherwise commit, the nature of the entrapment, whether the offence was carried out or only attempted, the degree of activity or passivity of the police officer or other agent provocateur, the accuracy of the record, and whether the officer had abused his role in order to act as an interviewer.[121]

The Divisional Court has ruled that it was wrong to exclude the evidence of a purchase by plain clothes police officers of individual cans of alcohol from a shop licensed to sell it by the case[122] or the purchase of a category 18-video film by an 11-year-old boy sent into a shop by a trading standards officer.[123] It also upheld the convictions of defendants who removed dummy cartons of cigarettes from a van deliberately left insecure and unattended but under close observation by the police in a busy shopping area.[124] The Court of Appeal upheld a decision to admit evidence from police officers who set up a second-hand jewellery shop to enable them to trace burglars and handlers by enticing them to sell the stolen items to the shop.[125]

However, if the undercover operative uses his position to give evidence of conversations which are not recorded and in circum-

120 *R v Smurthwaite, R v Gill* [1994] 1 All ER 898, CA. See also *R v Harwood* [1989] Crim LR 285, CA, *R v Gill and Ranuana* [1989] Crim LR 358, CA, *R v Edwards* [1991] Crim LR 45, CA, *R v Latif and Shahzad* [1994] Crim LR 750, CA, *R v Pattemore* [1994] Crim LR 836, CA, *R v Morley, R v Hutton* [1994] Crim LR 919, CA, *R v Farooq, R v Ramzan* [1995] Crim LR 169, CA. The use of entrapment can be grounds for mitigation of sentence: *R v Mackey and Shaw* [1992] Crim LR 602, CA.

121 For discussion of these issues see Sybil Sharpe 'Covert Police Operations and the Discretionary Exclusion of Evidence' [1994] Crim LR 793–804, Geoffrey Robertson, 'Entrapment Evidence: Manna From Heaven, or Fruit of the Poisoned Tree?' [1994] Crim LR 805–816, and Helen Power, 'Entrapment and Gay Rights' (1993) 143 NLJ 47–49, 63. Sybil Sharpe suggests that electronic eavesdropping circumvents the protections in Code C and argues for a new code of practice to govern these activities. For the admissibilty of intercepted telephone calls, see p283 above and Adam Tomkins 'Intercepted Evidence: Now You Hear Me, Now you Don't' (1994) 57 MLR 941–954.

122 *DPP v Marshall* [1988] 3 All ER 683, QBD.

123 *London Borough of Ealing v Woolworths PLC* [1995] Crim LR 58, QBD.

124 *Williams and Another v DPP* [1993] 3 All ER 365, QBD

125 *R v Christou* [1992] 4 All ER 559, CA.

stances which amount to an avoidance of the safeguards in Code C, whether or not this was deliberate, such evidence should be excluded.[126]

In extradition cases, if the methods of obtaining prosecution evidence are legitimate under English law, such as entrapment, the fact that evidence had been obtained unlawfully according to foreign or international law will not lead to the exclusion of the evidence.[127]

---

126 *R v Bryce* [1992] 4 All ER 567, CA. See also the cases of *Hall* and *Stagg* referred to on p307 above.
127 *R v Governor of Pentonville Prison ex p Chinoy* [1992] 1 All ER 317, QBD. For the application of the European Convention on Human Rights, eg, *Ludi v Switzerland*, Decision 15 June 1992, (1992) *Guardian* 15 July.

CHAPTER 12

Police complaints procedures

The procedures for dealing with complaints about police conduct and for disciplinary proceedings are described in the 1984 Act Pt IX, as amended by the Police and Magistrates' Courts Act 1994 and accompanying regulations. The 1994 Act has made major changes to the 1984 legislation; for instance, a chief officer *must* send a report to the DPP where the investigation indicates that a police officer may have committed a criminal offence: there is no choice. At the date of writing the regulations referred to in this chapter are in force but a new set is expected to be in operation in early 1996 including a new discipline code. Otherwise the scheme described is the revised one.

A complaint may be made by or on behalf of a member of the public. Thus MPs, citizens advice bureaux or even the Police Complaints Authority (PCA) (see below) may make a complaint on behalf of another, provided they have written consent (s84(4)). If a complaint cannot be resolved informally (see below) it must be investigated. The investigation will be carried out by the police, but in some cases will be supervised by the PCA which was established by the 1984 Act.[1] There is nothing to prevent anyone sending a complaint direct to the PCA which will, in most cases, then refer it to the appropriate authority.

Complaints about the conduct of senior officers are treated differently and this procedure is described below under a separate heading.

Complaints about the way in which the chief officer exercises functions of direction and control are excluded from the police com-

1 The Authority's address is 10 Great George Street, London SW1P 3AE (Tel: 0171 273 6450). For a fuller account of police complaints procedures see Harrison and Cragg, *Police Misconduct* (Legal Action Group, 2nd edition 1995).

plaints procedure, as these are matters for the relevant police authority (s84(5)). However, this exclusion would not apply, for example, to a complaint that a chief officer had acted from a corrupt or unlawful motive, as that would not be a question of policy. If a complaint relates wholly or partly to conduct which is or has been the subject of criminal or disciplinary proceedings, the complaints procedure cannot be used (s84(6)).

The chief officer may delegate any of the functions or duties in relation to complaints to an assistant chief constable in the case of a provincial police force or to an assistant commissioner or deputy assistant commissioner in the metropolitan police force.[2] In the case of informal resolution, delegation must be to an officer of at least the rank of chief inspector. The chief officer may not however delegate any functions or duties to any officer who has carried out an investigative role in a complaint and tried to resolve it informally.

Decisions before investigation

The chief officer has a duty to take any steps which appear to be desirable for the purpose of obtaining or preserving evidence relating to the conduct forming the subject of the complaint (s84(1)). For example, immediate searches or observations may be necessary or the parties in an alleged assault case may need to be examined.

The chief officer must then determine which is the 'appropriate authority' in relation to the officer against whom the complaint has been made. This determination is based on the rank of the officer concerned: if the officer is 'senior', that is an officer holding a rank above superintendent, then the complaint, or if it was an oral complaint, written particulars of it, must be sent to the relevant police authority. The person by or on behalf of whom the complaint was made should be notified that this has been done. If the complaint concerns the conduct of an officer of lower rank, the chief officer is the 'appropriate authority' in relation to that officer. In the case of a metropolitan police officer of any rank, the Metropolitan Police Commissioner is the 'appropriate authority' (s84).

If the chief officer is the 'appropriate authority', the complaint must first be recorded and a decision must be taken as to its suitability for informal resolution. The chief officer may appoint an officer from the force to assist in this decision.

2 Police (Complaints) (General) Regulations 1985 SI No 520 reg 13.

Where either the complainant or the officer against whom the complaint has been made requests in writing a copy of the complaint, then a copy must be supplied, unless the appropriate authority is of the opinion that compliance with the request might prejudice any criminal investigation or proceedings pending or would be contrary to the public interest and the Secretary of State agrees.[3] The importance of these provisions is considered on p320 below.

Informal resolution

A complaint is suitable for informal resolution only if the member of the public concerned gives consent and the chief officer is satisfied that the conduct complained of, even if proved, would not justify criminal or disciplinary proceedings (s85(10)). There is clearly an element of discretion in the decision – almost all instances of police misconduct may constitute a technical breach of the Police Discipline Code, but the chief officer must assess the conduct and decide whether disciplinary proceedings would be justified. The chief officer may appoint an officer from the force to attempt informal resolution (s85(4)). The subject of the complaint need not consent to informal resolution. Complaints about certain conduct (for example a complaint alleging that police conduct resulted in death), must be referred to the PCA which is then obliged to supervise an investigation (see below). The PCA may require any complaint not otherwise referred to it to be referred, and may supervise the investigation of any complaint at all if it considers that it is in the public interest to do so. None of these categories of complaint may be resolved informally.[4]

The officer seeking to resolve the complaint must, as soon as practicable, seek the views of the complainant and officer concerned and take any other steps which appear appropriate. Records must be kept of the results of this procedure and the complainant is entitled to a copy on request within three months of the date on which resolution of the complaint was achieved or, as is the case, abandoned.[5] If the complainant is unhappy with the outcome, it is the policy of the police and the PCA that the complaint should be formally investigated.[6]

---

3 Complaints (General) Regulations (n2 above) reg 9.
4 Police (Complaints) (Informal Resolution) Regulations 1985 SI No 671 reg 3.
5 Ibid reg 4.
6 See *PCA: The First Ten Years* (Appendix) published by the PCA, June 1995 and confirmed by the PCA.

Investigation of complaints

Generally

If the chief officer decides that a complaint is unsuitable for informal resolution or if it appears, after attempts have been made to resolve the matter informally, that such resolution is impossible or that the complaint is for any other reason unsuitable, the complaint must be investigated formally (s85(3) and (5)). A complaint may be unsuitable for informal resolution if, for instance, it emerges that disciplinary charges should be preferred after all. In some cases the investigation will be supervised by the PCA (see below). The chief officer may appoint an officer from any force to carry out the investigations and a chief officer must comply with a request to supply an officer to another force to conduct an investigation. The officer appointed should not have been involved in any attempts at informal resolution of the complaint. The investigating officer should submit a report on the investigation to the chief officer, unless the investigation is being supervised by the PCA (s85(9)).

Where the PCA is of the opinion that the complaint is vexatious, oppressive or otherwise an abuse of the complaints procedures, and where the complainant has delayed making a complaint for more than 12 months and either that no good reason for the delay has been shown or that injustice would be likely to be caused by the delay, it may dispense with an investigation. Similarly, if the complaint is anonymous, the appropriate authority, with the consent of the PCA, can also dispense with an investigation.[7]

Supervision by the Police Complaints Authority

A chief officer is obliged to submit certain complaints to the PCA, which is under a duty to supervise the investigation of them (ss87(1) and 89(1)). The complaints to be submitted are any which allege that the conduct complained of resulted in the death of or serious injury to some other person (s87(1)). 'Serious injury' means a fracture, damage to an internal organ, impairment of bodily function, a deep cut or a deep laceration (s87(4)). Complaints which must also be referred are those which, if substantiated, would amount to conduct which is:

---

7 Police (Dispensation from Requirement to Investigate Complaints) Regulations 1985 SI No 672 (as amended).

a)   an assault occasioning actual bodily harm;
b)   an offence under Prevention of Corruption Act 1906 s1; or
c)   a serious arrestable offence (see above p5).[8]

In addition, the chief officer may refer any other complaint to the PCA (s87(1)(b)) and similarly it may require the submission of any complaint to it for consideration (s87(2)). The PCA is under a duty, in addition to its duty to supervise specific complaints under s89(1), to supervise the investigation of any complaint if it considers that it is desirable in the public interest to do so. The Authority must notify the chief officer of its determination whether or not to supervise the investigation or any complaints which it has 'called in' or of any which have been referred to it and which it is not mandatory for it to supervise (s89(3)).

Where the PCA is to supervise an investigation, it may insist that the appointment of the officer who is to conduct the investigation be subject to its prior approval. If so, the chief officer must submit the name of the proposed officer to the PCA and must not make the appointment unless the Authority gives notice that it approves. If an appointment has already been made and the PCA is dissatisfied with the appointment, the chief officer must select a different officer and notify the Authority of its proposed appointment. The PCA may veto the appointment (s89(4)(b)). The Authority may additionally impose other requirements on the investigation and any police officers concerned must comply with such requirements (s89(5)).[9] A member of the Authority is entitled to be present at interviews of police officers subject to investigation.[10]

At the end of an investigation which has been supervised by the PCA, the investigating officer must submit a report to the Authority and send a copy to the chief officer (s89(6)). The PCA must consider the report and then submit a statement to the chief officer, and also send a copy of the statement to the officer whose conduct has been investigated and to the person who made the complaint or on whose behalf the complaint was made 'if it is practicable to do so' (s89(8) and (9)). The PCA's statement should say whether or not the investigation was carried out to its satisfaction and specify any respect in which it was not so conducted. It should also deal with any other matters the Authority considers should be brought to the attention of the chief officer, the complainant or the officer under investigation,

---

8   Police (Complaints) (Mandatory Referrals etc) Regulations 1985 SI No 673.
9   Ibid.
10   *R v PCA ex p Thompson* (1989) *Times* 24 October.

or any other matters it considers should be dealt with in the public interest (s89(10) and Police (Complaints) (General) Regulations 1985). The Authority has power to issue separate statements on the criminal and disciplinary aspects of an investigation. This may be necessary, for instance, where it is desirable to proceed at once with criminal charges against a police officer and where the disciplinary enquiry may be clearly separate from the criminal investigation.

The chief officer should not bring disciplinary or criminal proceedings against an officer before receiving the statement from the PCA. The DPP should bring criminal proceedings only in 'exceptional circumstances' (s89(12)-(14)). The general prohibition is clearly to ensure that the PCA's statement on the effectiveness of the investigation is not pre-empted.

Proceedings after the investigation

Decisions to be taken by chief officer

On receipt of a report from the investigating officer, the chief officer has to take action under s90. This applies even where the investigation was supervised by the PCA.

The chief officer must first determine whether the report indicates that a criminal offence may have been committed by a member of the police force. If the chief officer determines that it does not, then, in certain cases prescribed by regulations, the PCA must still be sent a memorandum to that effect accompanied by (if the investigation was not supervised by the Authority) a copy or record of the complaint and a copy of the report of the investigation (s90(9) as amended). The memorandum must state whether the chief officer has brought (or proposes to bring) disciplinary proceedings and if not, reasons must be given.[11]

A chief officer who determines that the report indicates that a criminal offence may have been committed by a police officer must send a copy of the report to the DPP (s90(4) as amended).

When the DPP has dealt with the question of criminal proceedings, then, in certain cases prescribed by regulations, the chief officer must submit a memorandum and other documents as referred to above.

11 False statements made by police officers at a trial of a convicted defendant may be the subject of disciplinary proceedings: *R v. Metropolitan Police Disciplinary Tribunal, ex p PCA* (1992) *Independent* 29 April.

The Police Complaints Authority and disciplinary proceedings

When the chief officer has performed the duties described above, the PCA will have in its possession a copy of every complaint (except those resolved by informal resolution, in which case the Authority will only have received a copy if it asked for one (see above)), a report of the investigation and a memorandum concerning disciplinary proceedings.

On receipt of a memorandum, stating that the chief officer has not brought disciplinary proceedings and does not propose to do so, the PCA may *recommend* proceedings. If, after such a recommendation and consultation with the PCA, the chief officer is still unwilling to prefer charges, the Authority may *direct* the chief officer to bring disciplinary proceedings and it must provide the chief officer with reasons for doing so. The chief officer must then bring the proceedings indicated in the memorandum or directed by the PCA and such proceedings cannot be discontinued without leave of the PCA. The PCA can withdraw a direction, however.

The chief officer has to provide the PCA with any information it needs to make decisions under these provisions and also must advise the PCA of any action taken in response to a recommendation or a direction from it (s93 as amended).

When acting under this section the PCA must have regard to any guidance given to it by the Secretary of State, particularly in cases where criminal proceedings are involved (s105(4) as amended).

Treatment of complaints against senior officers

The police authority for the force's area is primarily responsible for dealing with complaints against senior officers, that is officers holding a rank above that of superintendent. In the case of the metropolitan police, however, responsibility lies with the Metropolitan Police Commissioner (s84(4)). Both the police authority and the Commissioner are the respective disciplinary authorities and are referred to in the Act as the 'appropriate authority'.

When a complaint is either sent directly to the appropriate authority or referred by a chief officer, the authority must record it (s86(1)). The appropriate authority has considerable discretion concerning the method of dealing with the complaint. There is no system of informal resolution referred to in the Act in relation to complaints against senior officers, but if the appropriate authority is satisfied that the conduct complained of would not justify a criminal or disciplinary charge even if proved, it may deal with the complaint as it considers appropriate. It is therefore not simply a decision whether there is suffcient evidence to bring a charge, but rather whether such a charge should be brought in the light of all the facts. The authority does not have to refer the matter to the DPP, or, except as mentioned below, to the PCA. In contrast to the system for informal resolution of complaints against less senior officers, the complainant does not have any right of veto over this use of the PCA's discretion, but this was thought unnecessary in the light of the independence of the appropriate authority (except in London).

If the appropriate authority is not satisfied that the conduct complained of would not justify disciplinary or criminal charges the complaint must be investigated (s86(1)). It may appoint an officer from its force or another force who must be of at least the same rank as the officer whose conduct is being investigated (s86(3) and (5)). A chief officer of another force who is asked to provide an officer for this purpose is obliged to comply with the request (s86(4)). The investigating officer must submit a report to the appropriate authority unless it is supervised by the PCA (s86(6)).

The PCA has exactly the same role in relation to the supervision of the investigation of complaints against senior officers as it has in relation to complaints against other officers. As in those cases some referrals to the PCA are mandatory and others discretionary. The Authority has a reserve power to supervise the investigation of other complaints if it considers such supervision desirable in the public interest and may require the submission of any complaint for its consideration. Complaints being informally resolved by the appropriate authority may therefore come within the PCA's jurisdiction. The requirements with regard to the investigating officer's report and the Authority's statement are also exactly the same.

On receiving the report of an investigation into a complaint against a senior officer the appropriate authority must send a copy of the report to the DPP unless it is satisfied, from the report, that no criminal offence has been committed (s90(1)). The PCA does not have a disciplinary role in relation to senior officers and so the matter rests in the hands of the police authority thereafter.

'Double jeopardy'

A police officer will no longer be protected against 'double jeopardy'. Therefore disciplinary proceedings may be brought against an officer even where there have been criminal proceedings arising from the same incident, whether the officer was convicted or not.[12]

Restrictions on disclosure of information

Any statements made by any person during informal resolution of a complaint, or attempts at such resolution, are inadmissible in any subsequent criminal, civil or disciplinary proceedings (s104(3)). The purpose of this rule is to encourage informal resolution; it was thought that without this rule, participants would be unduly cautious. The restriction on admissibility does not apply, however, where the statement in question relates to something other than the matter which is the subject of an informal resolution. An example would be where, if during the attempted resolution of what appears to be a relatively trivial matter, the officer or complainant admitted a serious offence (s104(4)).

All documents[13] created during the investigation of a complaint are prima facie available for discovery and use in court.[14] The House of Lords in *R v Chief Constable of the West Midlands Police ex p Wiley*[15] declared that public interest immunity did not attach to such documents and statements as a class.[16] There may, however, be public interest immunity for a narrower class of documents created in the investigation, for instance documents identifying informers and investigating officers' reports. Lord Woolf held that before granting any such class-based immunity there must be 'clear and compelling evidence that it is necessary'.[17] The question of reports compiled by investigating officers attracting immunity was left open in *Wiley* but

12 PACE s104(1) and (2) was repealed by Police and Magistrates' Courts Act 1994 s37.
13 With the exception of the report of the investigating officer (see below n18).
14 A complainant has no legal right to receive copies of documents emanating from an officer's appeal against dismissal: *R v Secretary of State for Home Dept ex p Goswell* (1994) *Times* 31 December.
15 [1994] 3 All ER 420; see also Harrison and Cragg, 'Police Complaints and Public Interest Immunity' (1994) 144 NLJ 1064.
16 Overruling *Neilson v Laugharne* [1981] 1 All ER 829, *Hehir v Commissioner of Police of the Metropolis* [1982] 2 All ER 335 and *Makanjuola v Commissioner of Police of the Metropolis* [1992] 3 All ER 617.
17 In *ex p Wiley* [1994] 3 All ER 420 at 446 h-j

has now been settled in *Taylor v Anderton*.[18] The Court of Appeal held that they are a class which is entitled to public interest immunity. As a result their disclosure will only be ordered where the public interest in disclosure outweighs that of preserving their confidentiality.

Despite the restriction of immunity on a class basis, there may still be immunity for a particular document because of its contents. Any claim for immunity is for the court, not an individual litigant, to decide, balancing the competing public interests for and against disclosure. The status of documents should be determined in the proceedings in which they are relevant, rather than in separate proceedings. This is because the balance of public interest may vary during proceedings and a document may lose immunity during the course of a hearing as its significance increases.[19] Also, contrary to what was said in the lower courts, any immunity recognised is from disclosure and not from the contents being used, except in exceptional circumstances.[20] If immunity is granted to material, the legal adviser to the party in possession of the material should do everything possible to assist the court and other party to mitigate any disadvantage which results from material not being disclosed.[21]

The decision in *Wiley* makes it crucial for lawyers pursuing civil actions on behalf of their clients to consider very carefully the documents which may become available through the investigation of a complaint.

In a civil action for damages against the police, the courts will not order disclosure of certificates of conviction and adjudications of guilt in police disciplinary proceedings merely on the ground that they might support a 'similar facts' line of enquiry or evidence.[22]

There is a risk of libel proceedings by the aggrieved police officer if a complaint is not upheld.

A police officer is entitled to a copy of the complaint (as is the complainant) if the request is made in writing. The appropriate authority may refuse the request if of the opinion that compliance might

---

18 *Taylor v Anderton (Police Complaints Authority Intervening)* [1995] 2 All ER 417, CA. See also *O'Sullivan v Commissioner of Police of the Metropolis* (1995) *Times* 3 July, where the initial report sent by the police to the CPS (Form 151) was held to belong to a class of documents to which public interest immunity attached.
19 *Wiley* [1994] 3 All ER 420 at 447 b-d.
20 Ibid per Lord Woolf at 447 e.
21 Ibid at 447 f-g.
22 *Thorpe v Chief Constable of Greater Manchester Police* (1989) *Independent* 31 March, CA.

prejudice any criminal investigation or proceedings pending or would be contrary to the public interest and the Secretary of State is of the same opinion.[23] This regulation clearly facilitates the bringing of a defamation action by a police officer. It may be possible to attack the appropriate authority's discretion in supplying the complaint on administrative law principles.

It is an offence for any past or present member, officer, or servant of the PCA to disclose any information received in connection with any of its functions. Any person found guilty of such an offence is liable on summary conviction to a fine not exceeding level 5 on the standard scale. There are several exceptions where disclosure is permitted: to the Secretary of State, to a member, officer, or servant of the PCA or, so far as may be necessary for the proper discharge of the Authority's functions, to other persons; or for the purposes of any civil, criminal or disciplinary proceedings or in the form of a summary or other general statement made by the PCA which does not identify the person from whom the information was received or any person to whom it relates (s98).

Disciplinary proceedings

Police officers of the rank of superintendent or below may not be demoted, dismissed or required to resign as a result of disciplinary proceedings unless they have had the opportunity of legal representation (there is no need for them to be legally represented). Legal aid is not available for this, but in practice the Police Federation will probably pay the costs. If the accused officer is not given the opportunity to be legally represented (and therefore is not liable to the most severe penalties) or does not exercise the option, representation may only be by another police officer (s102 as amended).

Composition of the Police Complaints Authority

The PCA consists of a chair appointed by Her Majesty and at least eight other members appointed by the Secretary of State, two of whom may be appointed deputy chairs. Members may be appointed on a full- or part-time basis. No person who is or has been a constable in any part of the United Kingdom is eligible for appointment to the PCA (Sch 4).

23 Police (Copies of Complaints) Regulations 1977 SI No 579.

Information and reports on the complaints system

It is part of every police authority's duty with respect to the maintenance of an efficient and effective police force to keep itself informed about the operation of the complaints system. Inspectors of constabulary have the same duty (s95 as amended).

The PCA must report each year on the discharge of its functions and must send a copy of each annual report and any statistical information referred to in it to the police authorities. This annual report must contain a statement of any guidance issued to the PCA by the Secretary of State under s105 (see above). This will ensure that the guidance is published (see below).

The PCA must comply with any request by the Secretary of State to report on matters relating to its functions as specified, and may carry out research for these purposes. The PCA may also report to the Secretary of State on any matters relating to the complaints procedure about which it is particularly concerned and must send a copy of any such report to the chief officer of the force concerned and to the police authority.

Every report of the PCA described above must be laid before Parliament and published (s97 as amended).

Constabularies not maintained by police authorities

The PCA is empowered (with approval of the Home Secretary) to make arrangements for the exercise of its functions in relation to constabularies maintained by bodies other than police authorities. For instance the Ministry of Defence police and the UK Atomic Energy Authority Constabulary are subject to the PCA.

Arrangements for members of the community to express views on policing

The Act states that police authorities for each force area are under a duty, in consultation with their chief constables, to make arrangements for obtaining the views of the communities in the force area on policing and for obtaining their co-operation with the police in preventing crime in the area. The Act does not specify what form the arrangements should take, so they may be different in each area, and in fact need not be identical in all parts of the area.

In the metropolitan police district, the Home Secretary issues guidance on such arrangements to the Commissioner who should make arrangements after taking account of such guidance. The Commissioner must make separate arrangements for each local borough, district, or part of a district within the metropolitan police district and in each case must consult with the appropriate council. The arrangements may be different for each part of a district or borough. In the City of London the Common Council must issue guidance to the Commissioner of Police for the City about the arrangements to be made and the Commissioner must take account of the guidance.

The person or body which is under a duty to make the arrangements must keep them under review and the Home Secretary has the power to require reports to be submitted on the arrangements. In the light of such reports, the relevant person or body may be required to review the arrangements. Consultation with the appropriate persons must take place where arrangements are reviewed, in the same way as when the arrangements were originally made (s106).

CHAPTER 13

Remedies

Unlawfulness of police action and conduct of defence

The lawfulness of police action may be relevant to defending a prosecution in two ways. First, an unlawful action on behalf of the police may render prosecution evidence inadmissible and second, such action may provide the defendant with a defence to the charge.

Making the evidence inadmissible

The prosecution evidence may be rendered inadmissible by the unlawful act of a police officer. Grounds for the exclusion of evidence are considered in detail in chapter 11 above.

A defendant who gives evidence may be asked about his/her previous convictions or bad character if the nature or conduct of the defence is such as to involve imputations on the character of the prosecutor or witnesses for the prosecution.[1] Thus, if the facts of the arrest or other allegedly unlawful action are in dispute, or the allegation of illegality involves attacking the character of prosecution witnesses, a defendant with previous convictions is at risk of having those convictions raised in cross-examination.[2]

Providing a defence to the charge

A person is entitled to use reasonable force to resist an unlawful arrest or search. The concept of reasonable force is discussed below. Physical resistance offered to the police may result in a charge of

1 Criminal Evidence Act 1898 s1(f).
2 *R v Powell* [1986] 1 All ER 193.

assault, and then the fact that the assault was no more than a reasonable defence against unlawful police action would secure an acquittal. In particular, there might be a prosecution for assaulting or obstructing a constable in the execution of his or her duty, contrary to the Police Act 1964 s51(1) or (3). Whether or not police officers are acting in the execution of their duty is a complex question. In the leading case of *R v Waterfield*[3] the Court of Criminal Appeal said that if the conduct of the police fell within their general duty to prevent crime and bring offenders to justice, then provided it was lawful, it would be within the protection of the statute. If the officers exceed their powers, the protection is lost, for instance if they search someone without giving reasons.[4]

In order to establish guilt under s51 it is not necessary for the prosecution to prove either that the defendant knew the victim was a police officer or that he was acting in the execution of his duty.[5] If, however, the defendant mistakenly thought that the police officer was an ordinary citizen who was assaulting him, then it may be possible to argue, following the decision in *Blackburn v Bowering*[6] that there is no offence. The force used, however, must be reasonable in the circumstances.[7]

Recovery of property held by the police

A person whose property is being held by the police can take the usual civil proceedings, for instance for trespass to goods, in the county court or High Court for its recovery and damages for any loss (for example to income from a business) caused by the police holding the property. However, such proceedings are likely to be expensive, the return of the property will not be ordered if it is still being

3 [1964] 1 QB 164.
4 *Brazil v Chief Constable of Surrey* (1983) 77 Cr App R237.
5 *R v Fennell* [1971] 1 QB 428.
6 [1994] 3 All ER 380. The Court of Appeal accepted the argument that *R v Gladstone Williams* (1984) 78 Cr App R 276 was applicable, so that a person is entitled to use reasonable force in the circumstances *as s/he perceives them to be*. It follows that there is no assault if such a plea is successful. See further Fairweather and Levy, 'Assaults on the Police: A Case of Mistaken Identity' [1994] Crim LR 817.
7 In *R v Scarlett* [1993] 4 All ER 629 the court appeared to hold that if the defendant believed the degree of force used to be reasonable in the circumstances then it was irrelevant if in fact it was excessive. The law has now been clarified in *R v Owino* [1995] Crim LR 743 so that a person may use such force as is (objectively) reasonable in the circumstances as he perceives them.

lawfully held and damages will not be awarded during any period for which the property was lawfully held. (See chapter 4 for the powers of the police to hold property belonging to others.)

A much simpler and cheaper remedy is provided by the Police (Property) Act 1897. On the application of either the police or a person claiming the property, a magistrates' court may order its delivery to the person appearing to be entitled to it. Often applications are made by third parties whose property has found its way into the possession of the police during investigation of a suspected offence. Such an order confers absolute title to the property subject to the rights of any other person to take legal proceedings against any person in possession of the property within six months from the date of the order.[8]

The 1897 Act procedure should not be used where there is difficulty in determining the real owner, for example where ownership is disputed or there are tricky questions of title. In such cases the civil process should be used.

The 1897 Act does not specify the method of making an application, and it is open to courts to adopt a simple procedure of filling in a form of application with copies served on interested parties, or to proceed in a more formal way by complaint and summons.[9]

The Act is inapplicable where property has been seized by customs and excise officers. There is no appeal against the merits of a magistrates' court's decision under the 1897 Act, although the lawfulness of the decision can be challenged by judicial review (see p339).

The Magistrates' Courts Act 1980 s48 empowers magistrates to order the return of property found and carried on an arrested person. It is inapplicable though when property has been taken from premises on or after arrest by customs and excise officers or, it seems, the police.[10]

Private prosecutions

In theory anyone may commence a private prosecution. In the context of the 1984 Act and unlawful police conduct, the most likely prosecutions will be for assault, indecent assault, criminal damage, entering premises by violence and false imprisonment. There is no legal aid,

8 *Irving v National Provincial Bank Ltd* [1962] 2 QB 73.
9 *R v Uxbridge Justices ex p Commissioner of Police for the Metropolis* [1981] QB 829.
10 *R v Southampton Magistrates' Court ex p Newman* [1988] 3 All ER 669.

however, for a private prosecution and it is likely, particularly in the Crown Court, that the private prosecutor will have to be legally represented.[11] If the prosecutor lacked reasonable and probable cause for instigating the prosecution and has a wrongful and improper motive, then s/he may be sued by the defendant for malicious prosecution.[12] The use of private prosecutions is subject to the powers of the Crown Prosecution Service and Attorney-General to intervene, and the discretion of magistrates to refuse to issue a summons.

In most cases the conduct which constitutes a crime will also amount to a civil tort and usually the victim of unlawful police behaviour will be better advised to take civil proceedings (see below p332) than to embark on a private criminal prosecution.

Offences

The offences referred to above are described very briefly below; for further information see Smith and Hogan's *Criminal Law*.[13]

Assault

If the police use excessive force in the exercise of their powers or use force where it is unnecessary, they may be liable to prosecution for either a common assault or a more serious assault under the Offences Against the Person Act 1861. Liability will depend on the degree of harm inflicted and the mens rea of the police officer.

Indecent assault

A prosecution for indecent assault is most likely to arise from the wrongful conduct of personal searches, either prior to arrest or afterwards. Under the Sexual Offences Act 1956 as amended by the Sexual Offences Act 1985 it is an offence punishable with ten years' imprisonment to commit an indecent assault on a man or a woman. A woman may be guilty of an indecent assault on a man and possibly of an indecent assault on another woman.[14]

11 Since the Courts and Legal Services Act 1990 a private prosecutor may be granted a right of audience in the Crown Court, but it is at the court's discretion. See *R v Southwark Crown Court ex p Tawfick* [1995] Crim LR 658 for an example of a situation where the right of audience was denied.

12 It has been held that where the prosecutor is an unreliable witness and is obsessive about the case, this is not sufficient reason to justify a court's decision that the proceedings are an abuse of process: *R v Durham Stipendiary Magistrate ex p Davies* (1993) *Times* 25 May.

13 Butterworths, 7th edn 1992.

14 *R v Hare* [1934] 1 KB 354.

Criminal damage

A police officer who either intentionally or recklessly damages property belonging to another without lawful excuse, for instance during the search of premises or while retaining property, may be prosecuted for criminal damage under the Criminal Damage Act 1971 s1(1) and may be liable to imprisonment for up to 10 years. There must be damage, but it need be only slight.[15]

Violent entry to premises

By virtue of the Criminal Law Act 1977 s6(1) it is a summary offence punishable with six months' imprisonment and/or a fine to use or threaten violence, without lawful authority, for the purpose of securing any entry into premises. There must be someone present on the premises at the time, who is opposed to the entry which the violence is intended to secure, and the person using or threatening the violence must know that. Actual entry is not required; the offence is complete as soon as violence is used or threatened.

False imprisonment

Like assault, false imprisonment is both a criminal offence and a tort (see below). The civil action is much more common. 'Imprisonment' probably includes the term 'arrest'.[16] There is no need for anyone to be physically detained but the victim must know of the constraint.[17] It appears that a constable cannot rely on the Constables' Protection Act 1750 as a defence to criminal prosecution where the arrest takes place under a defective warrant. The officer would, however, probably lack mens rea.[18]

Conduct of private prosecutions and the role of the DPP and Attorney-General[19]

Private prosecutions are usually commenced by laying an information and obtaining a summons. The magistrates or their clerk will, in practice, scrutinise the information much more carefully than they would when an information is laid by the police and take care to

15 *Gayford v Chouler* [1898] 1 QB 316.
16 *R v Rahman* (1985) 81 Cr App R 349.
17 *Alderson v Booth* [1969] 2 QB 216.
18 See Smith and Hogan (above n13) p435.
19 For a recent review of the problems relating to private prosecutions see E Saunders 'Private prosecutions by the Victims of Violent Crime' (1995) 145 NLJ 1423.

ensure the propriety of the prosecution and technical correctness of the summons. In some cases the consent of the Attorney-General, the DPP or other official person or body is required. A magistrate should not issue a summons until such consent has been obtained; such action would result in any conviction being quashed.

Another important limitation on the right of the individual to prosecute, is the power of the Attorney-General and the DPP to terminate proceedings. The Attorney-General can enter a nolle prosequi at any stage when proceedings for a trial on indictment are pending or in progress; this puts an end to the proceedings and the power is not subject to control by the courts. The DPP can take over the conduct of any proceedings (Prosecution of Offences Act 1985 s6(2)) and may take over a case with a view to offering no evidence, provided that this action is not manifestly unreasonable, so that the accused is acquitted. The safeguard against the abuse of this power by the DPP is that the Attorney-General superintends the DPP's duties (Prosecution of Offences Act 1985 s3) and is answerable to Parliament.

Compensation for criminal loss or injury

Power of the criminal courts to award compensation

The Powers of Criminal Courts Act 1973 s35(1) as amended provides that where any person is convicted of any offence, summary or indictable, the court may make an order requiring compensation to be paid for any personal injury, loss or damage resulting from that offence, or any other offence taken into consideration. Compensation can only be awarded for offences charged in an indictment or information unless there is an overall count covering total losses, or where the offences have been taken into consideration.[20]

There is no limit on the compensation which the Crown Court may award, but the magistrates' courts are limited to £5,000 for each offence for which the defendant is convicted. Compensation for offences taken into consideration is limited to an aggregate maximum of £5,000 for each offence of which the defendant is actually convicted. Therefore, if someone is guilty of nine offences involving nine victims but is charged with only one offence, the nine victims can be awarded only £5,000 between them.

20 *R v Crutchley* [1994] Crim LR 309.

It is now important, where the claim is worth less than £1,000 to claim compensation from the criminal courts, as this is below the Criminal Injuries Compensation Board's minimum figure (see below). When assessing the amount of compensation payable, the court will consider evidence as to the liability to compensation and also representations from the parties. The courts are hesitant about awarding compensation for personal injuries because of the complexities of assessment. The sentencer may, however, obtain guidance from the amounts paid by the Criminal injuries Compensation Board in similar cases and the Magistrates' Association also sets out guidance, for example:

Graze:	Some pain for a few days and depending on size	up to £50
Bruise:	Depending on size	up to £75
Loss of tooth:	Depending on position of tooth and age of victim	£250-£1,000

By virtue of the Criminal Justice Act 1988 the courts may now make an order payable to the same persons as those specified under Fatal Accidents Act 1976 s1A. The sum cannot exceed the final award for bereavement. A major limiting factor is that, by virtue of the 1973 Act s35(4) the court should have regard to the defendant's means and although under the Criminal Justice Act 1982 the court may make a compensation order rather than impose a fine or custodial sentence, the means are very often inadequate.

Compensation is usually applied for, although it can be ordered by a court of its own motion. The court is obliged to find reasons for not making a compensation order and this should ensure that it is considered in every case.[21]

The victim's rights to bring a civil action for compensation are unaffected by the award of a compensation order and an action could be commenced for the amount by which the loss exceeds the award. Again the defendant's ability to pay is clearly very relevant.

21 Powers of Criminal Courts Act 1973 s35(1), as amended by the Criminal Justice Act 1988 s104.

Compensation from the Criminal Injuries Compensation Board

Compensation from the Criminal Injuries Compensation Board[22] is funded by the State, and it is in cases where the defendant cannot afford compensation (or cannot be traced) that this scheme becomes indispensable. The Board, can award compensation even if the offender has not been caught.

Compensation may be claimed only where the value of the injury is at least £1,000 which is why it is important to claim compensation from the courts where the claim would be for less than this figure and there is a realistic prospect of an award being enforced against the assailant.

In most cases a claim is decided without a hearing. There is no legal aid available for an application and a successful applicant will not have costs reimbursed by the Board. An applicant who is dissatisfied with the decision may request a hearing before two Board members. It is possible to apply to the Divisional Court for judicial review of the Board's decisions. Compensation is assessed on the same principles as for a civil action for damages. There are some differences – for example, there can be no award for aggravated damages. Awards are always reduced by any amount obtained from any other source, such as sick pay, insurance or compensation orders.

In order to obtain compensation the applicant must show, on the balance of probabilities, that a personal injury has been suffered, which is directly attributable to a 'crime of violence' or that the applicant was a dependent of a person who died as a result of such an offence. 'Personal injury' includes shock and other psychiatric injuries.[23]

The Board has power to refuse an award or award less than it would otherwise have awarded in the following circumstances (apart

---

22 The Board was established as a non-statutory body. The Criminal Justice Act 1988, when implemented, would convert it into a statutory body. The scheme was not implemented, but in 1990 the non-statutory scheme was amended to incorporate some of the changes introduced by the 1988 Act. In 1994 the government introduced a tariff scheme which meant that compensation was no longer determined on the extent of individual injuries. This scheme was declared unlawful by the House of Lords (*R v Secretary of State for the Home Department ex p Fire Brigades Union and Others* [1995] 2 All ER 244) and the 1990 scheme is still in operation. The Criminal Injuries Compensation Act 1995 received royal assent on 8 November 1995 and it is thought that the CICB will be replaced by a statutory authority in 1996.

23 See, eg, *R v CICB ex p Johnson* (1994) *Times* 11 August.

from its general discretion):

a) the applicant has not taken, without delay, all reasonable steps to inform the police, or any other authority considered by the Board to be appropriate to the purpose, of the circumstances of the injury and to co-operate with the police or other authority in bringing the offender to justice;[24]

b) the applicant has failed to give all reasonable assistance to the Board or other authority in connection with the application.

The Board may also reduce an award because of the claimant's criminal convictions or unlawful conduct, even if unrelated to the application.[25] In the past the scheme has been plagued by severe delays in processing applications.

Civil actions against the police[26]

If any police officer enters property, examines or removes goods without legal authority, carries out an unlawful arrest or uses unlawful force on anyone, or embarks on a prosecution for a motive other than the pursuit of justice, it is open to the victim of such conduct to bring a civil action against the police. By virtue of the Police Act 1964 s48, the chief officer is liable for torts committed by constables under his direction or control in their performance or purported performance of their functions. Any damages are of course awarded out of police funds. This vicarious liability makes civil proceedings easier where it is difficult to identify the individual officer concerned. Such actions usually carry the right to trial by jury (see below). If there has been a prosecution as a result of the police conduct, it is advisable not to bring civil proceedings until it has been completed. It is obviously helpful if the plaintiff has been acquitted in criminal proceedings, but it is not essential. If a police officer has been successfully prosecuted, the Civil Evidence Act 1968 s11 allows the conviction to be adduced in evidence.

24 In *R v CICB ex p S* (1995) *Independent* 28 March the High Court held that the Board must appraise the reasons for delay before reducing the award.

25 In *R v CICB ex p Gambles* (1994) *Times* 5 January the High Court held, however, that if the Board decides that the applicant's conduct made a full award inappropriate, it must state to what extent the conduct impacted on the appropriateness of an award.

26 See further Harrison and Cragg, *Police Misconduct* (Legal Action Group, 3rd edition 1995), Winfield and Jolowicz on Tort (Sweet and Maxwell, 14th edn 1994) and Sime, *A Practical Approach to Civil Procedure* (Blackstone Press, 1994).

Despite the recent change in attitude by the courts to the law relating to public interest immunity (see chapter 12 for an analysis of the law in relation to police complaints), the High Court has held, following *Taylor v Anderton (Police Complaints Authority Intervening)*[27] that the initial report (Form 151) sent by the police to the CPS, following an investigation into a suspected criminal offence, belongs to a class of documents to which public interest immunity may attach.[28]

Causes of action

False imprisonment

This tort consists of the infliction of bodily restraint which is not expressly or impliedly authorised by law. It therefore includes wrongful arrest, which is not a separate tort. There need not be any physical contact at all for there to be imprisonment.[29] Where a plaintiff consents to a defendant's order, there is no liability for this tort, but there is obviously a fine line between consent and submission. Where a plaintiff consents to an activity because there appears to be no alternative, this is surely not a valid consent. Therefore where a person agrees to accompany a police officer to a police station the tort will have been committed if the request was made in such a way as to lead the plaintiff to believe there was no choice.[30] A lawful arrest is not false imprisonment and therefore an arrest in pursuance of a valid arrest warrant cannot constitute this tort[31] although there could still be an action for malicious prosecution (see below). Similarly a lawful arrest does not become unlawful because excessive force is used in effecting it (although there may be grounds for an action for battery, see below).[32] Where the arrest is without a warrant, the question will usually be whether the officer held a reasonable belief that the plaintiff had committed, was committing or was about to commit an offence, either arrestable or for which a relevant statute gives a power of arrest.[33]

27 [1995] 2 All ER 420.
28 *O'Sullivan v Commissioner of Police of the Metropolis* (1995) *Times* 3 July.
29 *Meering v Grahame-White Aviation Co Ltd* (1919) 122 LT 44.
30 See *Myers Stores Ltd v Soo* [1991] 2 UR 597.
31 *Sewell v National Telephone Co Ltd* [1907] 1 KB 557.
32 *Simpson v Chief Constable of South Yorkshire Police* (1991) *Times* 14 March.
33 Even though magistrates have made a finding of fact in criminal proceedings that an arresting officer did not apprehend a breach of the peace, this does not prevent a chief officer from alleging in civil proceedings that an arrest was lawful: *Nawrot v Chief Constable of Hampshire Police* (1992) *Independent* 7 January.

If a police officer has acted with some irrelevant consideration in mind or for an improper purpose, however, there may be liability.[34] A person who provides information to the police who thereafter effect an arrest, where the informant has not instigated or procured the arrest, cannot be liable.[35] It is not necessary for a person unlawfully detained to prove knowledge of the unlawful detention nor to prove harm resulting from the detention.[36] Where detention is lawful but conditions are poor or deteriorate, the appropriate action is not for false imprisonment, but it may be in negligence.[37]

Where the unlawful detention is continuing, the plaintiff may seek a writ of habeas corpus (see below). Such a person may also use self-help to escape, including reasonable force. However if what appears to be an unlawful detention is in fact lawful owing to the existence of reasonable suspicion that an offence has been committed by the plaintiff, for instance, the plaintiff may subsequently be held liable in tort for battery.[38]

Assault

An assault is an act of the defendant which causes the plaintiff reasonably to apprehend the infliction of a battery on him or herself by the defendant. Battery is the intentional and direct application of force to another person. 'Assault' is frequently used to describe both actions. Police officers are entitled to use reasonable force if necessary in the exercise of their powers under the 1984 Act (s117 and see above p188) but anything in excess of such force may be deemed to be an assault. A plaintiff who has been convicted of an offence arising from the same incident is not barred from bringing a civil claim against the police for assault.[39]

Intimidation

A person who causes another to act, or refrain from acting, either to

34 *Plange v Chief Constable of South Humberside Police* (1992) *Independent* 17 April.
35 *Davidson v Chief Constable of North Wales Police and Another* (1993) *Times* 26 April. But see also *Martin v Watson* [1995] 3 All ER 559, HL (malicious informant liable where facts solely within his knowledge).
36 *Murray v Ministry of Defence* [1988] 2 All ER 521. In such a case damages will usually be nominal only.
37 *R v Deputy Governor of Parkhurst Prison ex p Hague* [1991] 3 WLR 340.
38 This is the case even though the criminal law may recognise a defence on the existence of a mistaken belief: see *R v Gladstone Williams* (1984) 78 Cr App R 276 (above p325).
39 *Simpson v Chief Constable of South Yorkshire Police* (above n32).

his/her own detriment or the detriment of a third party, as a result of threatening an unlawful act commits the tort of intimidation. This may be relevant where the police induce a confession after making threats.

Trespass to land

Where the police enter land or property without lawful authority (consent, a warrant or other written authority or statutory authority) they may be liable for trespass. This would be the case if they searched further into a building than they had authority to do. Trespass is actionable per se; there is no need for any damage to be caused. Only a person in possession can sue; if premises are occupied by tenants, they, rather than the landlord, have a right of action.[40] The slightest entry without consent will be sufficent for an action to lie, as will remaining after licence to do so has been revoked.

If a search warrant is defective, the occupier of premises is entitled to refuse entry.[41] A police officer who acts in good faith when applying for a warrant and executes it in accordance with the 1984 Act s16 (above p81) is immune from legal action by the occupier. The occupier's remedy, if any, is against the issuing authority (see below p339). However, where the police have not acted lawfully in obtaining or executing a warrant, substantial damages may be awarded for the unlawful search and any unlawful seizures.[42]

Wrongful interference with goods

The law on this subject is complex and a brief outline only will be given here.

Essentially there are two torts: trespass to goods and conversion. Trespass to goods is wrongful interference with them. Despite the fact that trespass to land is actionable without evidence of damage, it is unclear whether damage is required for this action. An action may lie against the police for handling goods or documents when they lack lawful authority to do so. The plaintiff will be successful only if in possession of the goods at the time of the alleged trespass. The action is appropriate where the police have wrongfully seized property.

Conversion is an interference with the plaintiff's rights over goods and is most likely to be committed, in the context of police powers, by unlawful retention of goods.

40 *Cooper v Crabtree* (1882) 20 Ch D 589.
41 *Syce v Harrison* [1980] Crim LR 649.
42 See for instance: *R v Reading Justices and Others ex p South West Meat Ltd* [1992] Crim LR 672. (above p83).

Replevin is a form of interlocutory relief, whereby goods alleged to have been wrongfully taken are restored to the plaintiff pending an action for wrongful interference, in some cases subject to conditions. It may be a useful remedy to secure documents or goods being unlawfully held by the police.

Malicious prosecution or process

In order for an action in this tort to be successful it is essential for the plaintiff to prove that the prosecution was brought without reasonable or probable cause and also that the prosecution was brought maliciously.[43]

It is also necessary for the plaintiff to prove damage. This may be damage to reputation (for instance by imprisonment of the plaintiff); to financial position; or to physical security. A police officer will commit this tort by deliberately supplying a magistrate with false information to secure the issue of a warrant for search or arrest.[44] A person who, by making a false complaint, procures the institution of criminal proceedings, even where it is the police who make the final decision to proceed, may also be liable.[45] The prosecution must have been determined in the plaintiff's favour, either as a result of magistrates refusing to commit for trial, by an acquittal or a successful appeal.[46]

A person who, maliciously and without reasonable or probable cause, institutes the initial process of criminal investigation, without there being a prosecution, for instance merely obtaining a search warrant or an arrest warrant, may be liable for malicious process.[47]

Defamation of character

Defamation is the publication of a statement which reflects on the reputation and tends to lower a person in the estimation of members of society generally or tends to make them shun or avoid the person. An action for defamation was brought when a store detective ques-

---

43 See now *Martin v Watson* [1995] 3 All ER 559, HL and a useful article, Simister, 'With Malice Aforethought' (1995) LS Gaz 27 September p24.

44 *Elsee v Smith* (1882) 2 Chit 304.

45 *Martin v Watson* (above n43).

46 *Herniman v Smith* [1938] AC 305. A defendant who has agreed to be bound over is not necessarily precluded from suing the police for malicious prosecution: *Hourihane v Metropolitan Police Commissioner* (1995) *Independent* 18 January.

47 *Ray v Prior* [1971] AC 470.

tioned a woman and searched her handbag outside a shop in full view of the public. In the event the action was settled out of court and the store paid her £1,500 damages for defamation.[48]

Breach of statutory duty

The Police and Criminal Evidence Act 1984 imposes many obligations on the police, for instance to supply reasons or to record information. The Act does not state what are the consequences, if any, of failure to carry out these obligations. The remedy of an action for breach of statutory duty is probably not available, however, where the statute imposing the duty grants a remedy.[49] The 1984 Act establishes an elaborate structure for dealing with complaints and this may therefore preclude the action.

It has been held in the House of Lords,[50] that an action for breach of statutory duty is unsustainable where the duty is of a procedural nature designed to protect, in this case, a police officer's position in any future proceedings. These points may be relevant in connection with an action for breach of statutory duty where some duties in the 1984 Act have not been performed in accordance with the statute.

Breach of confidence

The law on breach of confidence is a complex amalgam of contract, tort and equity. There is some support for the view that this is an independent head of liability in tort.[51] An action for breach of confidence may be relevant in the context of disclosure of confidential information (see above chapter 3). It has been held that disclosure of a photograph may, in some cases, be actionable as a breach of confidence, but where the police make reasonable use of a photograph of a suspect taken at a police station, they have a public interest defence to any action taken against them.[52]

Misfeasance in public office

A claim for damages under this head of liability may be made if a public officer causes damage by acting maliciously, or knowingly

---

48 See news item, *Times* 16 November 1984.
49 See Sanders, 'Rights, Remedies and PACE' [1988] Crim LR 802.
50 *Calveley and Others v Chief Constable of Merseyside Police and Others* [1989] 1 All ER 1025.
51 See, eg, *Seager v Copydex Ltd* [1967] 1 WLR 923.
52 *Hellewell v Chief Constable of Derbyshire* (1994) *Times* 13 January.

does something for which there is no authority. Occasionally this may be the only cause of action available.[53]

Choice of court

Any action which includes a claim for 'personal injuries' must be commenced in the county court unless the value of the action is £50,000 or more. However, an action including a claim for damages for false imprisonment or malicious prosecution may be commenced in the High Court even though the value of the action is less than £50,000. If the value of the action is less than £25,000, it will be transferred to the county court. Even if an action commences in the county court, however, it may still be transferred to the High Court if it is important and suitable. This covers false imprisonment and malicious prosecution cases against the police.

In an action for false imprisonment or malicious prosecution there is a limited right to trial by jury. In an action for assault or wrongful interference with goods the court has a discretion whether to order trial by jury. The jury comprises 12 in the High Court and eight in the county court with no challenges permitted except for cause. Majority decisions of 10:2 or 7:1 are effective, or any other majority with the consent of the parties.

Damages

Where there is a jury, it determines the amount of damages. It is possible to obtain not only ordinary and special damages (for instance, in the case of wrongful imprisonment, for loss of liberty, humiliation and loss of earnings) but aggravated damages (to compensate the plaintiff for particular outrage to the emotions) and exemplary damages. Some recent examples are below:

a) Damages for assault, false imprisonment and malicious prosecution (arrest in undignified manner in public and detained for four hours for failure to display a road tax disc), £25,000; (Report: *Independent*, 12 October 1993);

b) Damages for 'distressing and humiliating' strip searches of two teenage girls: £12,000 and £9,000 each (out-of-court-settlement) (Report: *Independent*, 26 November 1994);

---

53 For instance, in *Gray v Metropolitan Police Commissioner* (1991) 1 March (unreported), Westminster County Court, the plaintiff sued a police officer who failed to arrest people who were assaulting him.

c) Damages for assault and oppressive, arbitrary or unconstitutional
    action (attempting to extract a confession by suffocation): compen-
    satory: £2,500; aggravated: £7,500; exemplary £40,000 (*Treada-
    way v Chief Constable of West Midlands* (1994) *Independent*, 23
    September).

Civil liability of the judiciary

A circuit judge who acts judicially and in good faith is immune from
suit and police officers who carry out the judge's instructions are
similarly immune.[54]

Magistrates do not enjoy the same immunity. A magistrate will
not be liable with respect to any matter within his or her jurisdiction.
The protection is withdrawn for acts done outside or in excess of
jurisdiction.[55] Magistrates who act wrongly may also face an order
for costs.[56]

Judicial review

Judicial review is a procedure under the Supreme Court Act 1971 s31
and RSC Order 53 whereby the High Court is asked to review the
legality of the actions of an inferior tribunal or a public authority.
The High Court can compel a public body to perform its duty (by an
order of mandamus), quash a decision (by an order of certiorari),
compel a party to act or refrain from acting in a particular way (by
an order of prohibition or an injunction) or make a declaration
stating the rights of the parties. In addition, the court can award
damages if they are claimed.[57]

The court will be prepared to intervene if the action involved is
unlawful or is an improper or unreasonable use of discretion. One
commentator has pointed out that short of interfering with primary
legislation, 'there are now no outer limits to judicial review, no other
executive function shielded from its jurisdiction'.[58] However, it will

---

54 Eg, *Sirros v Moore* [1975] QB 118. See also Constables Protection Act 1750.
55 See Justices of the Peace Act 1979, as amended.
56 See eg, *R v Newcastle-under-Lyme Justices ex p Massey* [1995] 1 All ER 120.
57 See Supperstone and Goudie: *Judicial Review* (Butterworths, 1992).
58 Michael Beloff, 'Judicial Review – 2001: A Prophetic Odyssey' (1995) 58 MLR
    143,146 .

not substitute its own views on an issue for the reasonable decision of any other body.[59]

The remedies are discretionary on the part of the court, which may therefore withhold them if it thinks fit, for example if the conduct of the applicant has been unmeritorious or unreasonable.

In the context of the 1984 Act, judicial review could be used, for example, to prevent the continuation of a road block, to compel the return of seized items and copies, and to restrain the use of information gleaned from them (by injunction); to quash the issue of a search warrant (certiorari); to prevent the Police Complaints Authority from taking action (prohibition); or to compel the chief officer of police to act in a particular way (mandamus). However, the courts are reluctant to interfere with the lawful exercise of police discretion.[60]

If the release of someone being detained unlawfully is required, then the appropriate remedy is habeas corpus (below).

A careful decision must be made on whether to seek judicial review or take ordinary civil proceedings. The basis on which this decision should be taken is discussed on pp350–352.

The court can grant an interim injunction to control the position pending full argument and a final decision.

Habeas corpus[61]

Habeas corpus is a writ issued by the High Court, theoretically requiring the production of someone who has been detained, and proof of the legality of the detention. An application is made to the High Court by, or on behalf of, someone detained, supported by an affidavit setting out the facts, under RSC Order 54. The application may be made and granted ex parte (that is, without notice to the other parties) but if so made will usually be adjourned for argument by both sides. This frequently leads to delay which severely limits the usefulness of the remedy. If the court is satisfied that the detention is unlawful, the writ will be issued. In practice this will contain an order for release if such an order is requested in the application.

59 *Council of Civil Service Unions v Minister for the Civil Service* [1984] 3 All ER 935, HL.
60 See Clayton and Tomlinson, *Civil Actions Against the Police* (Sweet and Maxwell, 1992) chapter 13.
61 See Atkin's Court Forms 2nd edition Volume 31 247 – 255, 373 – 381 (Butterworths 1993).

The court has no discretion to refuse habeas corpus if the detention is unlawful.[62] If the application is refused, repeated applications may not be made on the same grounds unless supported by fresh evidence which could not reasonably have been put forward previously.[63]

The right to apply for habeas corpus is preserved in the 1984 Act (s51(d)) but will not usually be relevant in the case of someone detained by the police. However, if the initial arrest was unlawful or if a person is being detained without being formally arrested or charged, or in breach of the requirements of Pt IV of the Act (chapter 6) an application for habeas corpus will still be the appropriate remedy. A solicitor, friend or relative of the detained person may apply for the writ. The habeas corpus procedure can be used to review only the legality of detention, not the wisdom of the decision to detain.[64]

The affidavit should specify the parties to whom the writ is directed. These will usually be the appropriate chief officer of police, the custody officer and the officer in charge of the case.[65]

Sometimes the mere threat of an application might secure the release of a person whom the police know they are holding unlawfully. This will be the case especially where the alleged offence is relatively minor and the officer is of junior rank. But when the police officer is less easily impressed, the usefulness of habeas corpus is, in practice, extremely limited by the courts' practice of adjourning applications for 24 hours to enable the police to present their case. This means that unlawful detention is allowed to continue, usually for long enough to enable the police to achieve their objective. Although the introduction of statutory regulation of detention for questioning by the 1984 Act may have reduced the extent to which the police detain people unlawfully, nothing in the Act repairs this defect in the habeas corpus procedure.

---

62 *Azam v Secretary of State for the Home Department* [1974] AC 18, HL at 32.
63 *R v Governor of Pentonville Prison ex p Tarling* [1979] 1 WLR 1417 and Administration of Justice Act 1960 s14(2).
64 This aspect has been criticised by the European Court of Human Rights, see p345 below.
65 See further T Gifford and P O'Connor 'Habeas Corpus' (1979) *LAG Bulletin* 182-184; Wade, *Administrative Law* (Oxford, 6th edn, 1988) pp617–624; R Sharpe, *Habeas Corpus* (Oxford, 2nd edn, 1989).

Compensation for miscarriages of justice

When a person has been convicted of and sentenced for a criminal offence and subsequently the conviction is reversed or a free pardon is granted because a newly discovered fact shows beyond reasonable doubt that there has been a miscarriage of justice, the Secretary of State is obliged to pay compensation on application, provided non-disclosure of the fact was not attributable to the person convicted. The amount is determined by an assessor appointed by the Secretary of State.[66]

There is no appeal against a refusal of compensation,[67] but it would be subject to judicial review on grounds of illegality, impropriety or unreasonableness (see pp339–340 and pp350–352).

In the context of this book, this provision might be relevant if a wrongful conviction occurs as a result of improper police behaviour.[68]

European Convention on Human Rights

The Convention

The European Convention on Human Rights is an international treaty which has been signed by several European countries to provide guidance for the protection of rights of individuals within the legal traditions of Western Europe.

The Convention is not part of English law and cannot be directly enforced in the courts of this country. However, as a treaty which has been signed by the United Kingdom, it can be used by the courts in some cases to assist in the interpretation and implementation of English law.[69]

The Convention was signed and is administered under the auspices of the Council of Europe. This has no direct connection with the European Union or European Community, although the Convention can be seen as part of the 'fabric' of Community law and relevant to its implementation.[70]

---

66 Criminal Justice Act 1988 s133.
67 Ibid s133(3).
68 See, eg, C Price and J Caplan *The Confait Confessions* (Marion Boyars, 1977).
69 *Brind and Others v Secretary of State for Home Department* [1991] 1 All ER 720, HL.
70 Michael Beloff, 'Judicial Review – 2001: A Prophetic Odyssey' (1995) 58 MLR 143, 152; Grief, 'The Domestic Impact of the ECHR Mediated through Community Law' [1991] Public Law 555.

There is a Commission of Human Rights consisting of part-time commissioners, and a Court of Human Rights, composed of full-time judges. Both of these bodies sit at Strasbourg (France) and act as independent international bodies, not as representatives of the member states. The whole system is supervised by the Council of Ministers, which consists of a senior member of the government of each country involved and which has certain duties under the Convention. Plans to streamline the procedure, by bypassing the Commission, with cases going direct to an enlarged court, have been approved but the date of implementation is uncertain.

The Convention sets out in its articles and protocols the various rights which are protected, and the exceptions to such protection. Most of the provisions are in vague, general terms, and are interpreted and applied in each case by the Commission (and in some cases by the Court).

Article 3 of the Convention provides that

No one shall be subjected to torture or inhuman or degrading treatment or punishment.

Intimate searches carried out under the 1984 Act could contravene this provision, the meaning of which has also been discussed on p292–294 in relation to the admissibility of confessions.[71]

The following articles are of particular relevance to police powers:

Article 5
1.   Everyone has the right to liberty and security of person. No one shall be deprived of his liberty save in the following cases and in accordance with a procedure prescribed by law:
a)   the lawful detention of a person after conviction by a competent court;
b)   the lawful arrest or detention of a person for non-compliance with the lawful order of a court or in order to secure the fulfilment of any obligation prescribed by law;
c)   the lawful arrest or detention of a person effected for the purpose of bringing him before the competent legal authority on reasonable suspicion of having committed an offence or when it is reasonably considered necessary to prevent his committing an offence or fleeing after having done so;
d)   the detention of a minor by lawful order for the purpose of educational supervision or his lawful detention for the purpose of bringing him before the competent legal authority;

---

71 See also *Tyrer v UK* (1978) 2 EHRR 1; cf *McFeeley v UK* (1980) 3 EHRR 161.

e) the lawful detention of persons for the prevention of the spreading of infectious disease, or persons of unsound mind, alcoholics or drug addicts, or vagrants;

f) the lawful arrest or detention of a person to prevent his effecting an unauthorised entry into the country or of a person against whom action is being taken with a view to deportation or extradition.

2. Everyone who is arrested shall be informed promptly, in a language which he understands, of the reasons for his arrest and of any charge against him.

3. Everyone arrested or detained in accordance with the provisions of paragraph 1(c) of this Article shall be brought promptly before a judge or other officer authorised by law to exercise judicial power and shall be entitled to trial within a reasonable time or to release pending trial. Release may be conditioned by guarantees to appear for trial.

4. Everyone who is deprived of his liberty by arrest or detention shall be entitled to take proceedings by which the lawfulness of his detention shall be decided speedily by a court and his release ordered if the detention is not lawful.

5. Everyone who has been the victim of arrest or detention in contravention of the provisions of this Article shall have an enforceable right to compensation.

Article 6

1. In the determination of his civil rights and obligations or of any criminal charge against him, everyone is entitled to a fair and public hearing within a reasonable time by an independent and impartial tribunal established by law. Judgement shall be pronounced publicly but the press and public may be excluded from all or part of the trial in the interests of morals, public order or national security in a democratic society where the interests of juveniles or the protection of the private life of the parties so require, or to the extent strictly necessary in the opinion of the court in special circumstances where publicity would prejudice the interests of justice.

2. Everyone charged with a criminal offence shall be presumed innocent until proved guilty according to the law.

3. Everyone charged with a criminal offence has the following minimum rights:

a) to be informed promptly, in a language which he understands and in detail, of the nature and the cause of the accusation against him;

b) to have adequate time and facilities for the preparation of his defence;

c) to defend himself in person through legal assistance of his own choosing or, if he has not sufficient means to pay for legal assistance, to be given it free when the interests of justice so require;

d)   to examine or have examined witnesses against him and to obtain the attendance and examination of witnesses on his behalf under the same conditions as witnesses against him;

e)   to have the free assistance of an interpreter if he cannot understand or speak the language used in court.

Article 7

1.   No one shall be held guilty of any criminal offence on account of any act or omission which did not constitute a criminal offence under national or international law at the time when it was committed. Nor shall a heavier penalty be imposed than the one that was applicable at the time the criminal offence was committed.

2.   This Article shall not prejudice the trial and punishment of any person for any act or omission which, at the time when it was committed, was criminal according to the general principles of law recognized by civilized nations.

Article 8

1.   Everyone has the right to respect for his private and family life, his home and his correspondence.

2.   There shall be no interference by a public authority with the exercise of this right except such as is in accordance with the law and is necessary in a democratic society in the interests of national security, public safety or the economic well-being of the country, for the prevention of disorder or crime, for the protection of health or morals, or for the protection of the rights and freedoms of others.

The issue of the compatability with the Convention of many of the provisions discussed in this book has yet to be fully explored, although lawyers and pressure groups are taking increasingly more interest in this avenue of redress.[72]

It is possible to use the Convention procedure to examine the adequacy of remedies in English law. For example, two cases have held that in certain circumstances habeas corpus is an insufficient remedy to accord with the right to liberty guaranteed by article 5.[73] A delay in taking an arrested person to the police station or the court, for instance, could contravene article 5(4) and a search of premises could contravene article 8, although they might be perfectly lawful under English law. Detention of a person under the prevention of terrorism legislation in police custody for four days and six hours

---

72 See, eg, Hamilton, Leach and Wadham, 'The Criminal Justice and Public Order Act 1994 and the ECHR' June 1995 *Legal Action* 14 – 16.

73 *Ireland v UK* (1980) 4 EHRR 264 and *X v UK* (1981) 4 EHRR 188.

without appearing before a judge or magistrate was held by the Court to have breached the Convention (see p264).[74]

Complaints under the Convention can only be brought against a government. The applicant must show either that the state or its agencies has breached his/her rights, or that the government has failed to secure such rights under the Convention.

Before a complaint can be accepted, the complainant must do all that is possible within the United Kingdom to put the matter right. This may mean going to court or a tribunal but does not include a political or discretionary remedy (eg, taking a case to an ombudsman). Once all of these 'domestic remedies' have been 'exhausted' the complaint under the Convention must be brought within six months.

Complaints to the Commission

A complainant, whose rights under the Convention have been violated, can write directly to the Commission. Although it might be advisable to do so with the help of a lawyer or a human rights organisation, a complainant can act in person. The complaint should be sent to:

Secretary of the European Commission for Human Rights
Council of Europe
67075 Strasbourg Cedex
France

(from whom further details and copies of the Convention and decisions made under it may be obtained).

The complaint should include the following details:

- the complainant's name, age, address, nationality and occupation;
- the name and address of any person or organisation representing the complainant;
- the name of the government against which the complaint is made;
- the object of the application and the Articles of the Convention which have allegedly been broken;
- a statement of the facts of the case;
- the reason why the facts of the case amount to denial of the complainant's rights under the Convention; and
- details of the steps taken to exhaust domestic remedies.

---

74 *Brogan v UK* (1989) 11 EHRR 117. Cf *Application No 12323/86 v UK* (1988) 85 LS Gaz 14 December p34.

Copies of any relevant documents should be enclosed.

Admissibility of applications

The Commission will have to decide whether the application is admissible (that is, whether it falls within its terms of reference). It might request further information, or ask the relevant government to comment on whether the application should be admitted. The complainant will be able to make further comments on any comments made by that government. The Commission can hold a hearing of the case at this stage but that is unusual and admissibility will usually be decided on the papers.

The Commission will declare the case inadmissible if any of the following apply:

- the application is anonymous;
- the time limit has expired;
- domestic remedies have not been exhausted;
- the situation has already been dealt with by the Commission or some other international process; or
- the application is inconsistent with the Convention or is an abuse of the right to complain or is 'manifestly ill-founded'. (The majority of applications are in fact rejected under this provision).

If the application is declared inadmissible there is no appeal.

The decision

If the application has been declared admissible, the complainant and the government will be asked to present written observations on the merits of the case. The Commission will then usually hold a hearing at Strasbourg. The Commission will reach a provisional opinion and then try to reach a friendly settlement between the complainant and the government.

If a friendly settlement (that is, a negotiated agreement) is reached, the Commission will publish a brief report about the case.

If no such settlement is reached, the Commission will draw up a full report and decide whether there has been a breach of the Convention. During the next three months the Commission or the government can refer the case to the Court of Human Rights for a hearing. The complainant cannot refer the case to the Court directly, but if the case goes to the Court, he or she will be allowed to have a representative appear before it. However, the main parties will be the Commission and the government. It is quite rare for cases to be referred to the Court.

Any decision by the Court is binding on the government and if it is ignored the offending country can be expelled by the Council of Ministers from the Council of Europe. The Court can award financial compensation for any breach of rights.

If the case does not go to the Court, the Commission will present a full report to the Council of Ministers, which will have to decide whether the Convention has been breached and what measures the government concerned should take.

If the government loses the case, it might be obliged to change the law of its own country as well as compensating the complainant or reversing the original decision.[75]

Legal aid

The English legal aid system does not cover work done under the Convention, but legal aid can be obtained from the Commission to cover lawyers' fees and expenses of preparing the case and conducting any hearing. An application for legal aid can be made to the Commission once the application has been declared admissible or the government has made written observations on admissibility.

Choice of remedy

The remedies discussed in this chapter and elsewhere in this work are obviously not mutually exclusive in most cases, but care must be taken in deciding which remedy to pursue.

Many unlawful police actions will amount to an assault or some other criminal offence, and every person has the right to use reasonable force in defence of self or another or to prevent a criminal offence.[76] However, although in theory an action such as an unlawful arrest or an unlawful search may be resisted by reasonable force, in practice a suspect will not know whether the police officer in fact has the power to take the action. If the exercise of the power depends on the existence of reasonable grounds, which is an objective test to be

---

75 Eg, the passage of the Interception of Communications Act 1985 resulting from the adverse decision in the Malone case, *Malone v UK* (1985) 7 EHRR 14.

76 Criminal Law Act 1967 s3.

determined subsequently by the court, a person will be in difficulty knowing whether the use of physical resistance would be upheld by a court. If an arrest is in fact lawful, a person who believes honestly but wrongly that it is not lawful might have no right to resist or intervene (but see above p324). A person who uses more than reasonable force will be committing offences of assault and/or obstruction of a police officer. Thus, although there might be a right to physical resistance, in most cases the best advice might be to submit under protest and to seek some other remedy subsequently.

Habeas corpus is in theory a speedy remedy compared to other courses of action, and, when it is appropriate, should be considered as the first recourse. It should be noted that applying for or obtaining release under habeas corpus does not preclude subsequent civil or criminal proceedings. Similarly an application under the Police (Property) Act 1897 would not preclude subsequent civil proceedings for damages for trespass.

Criminal or civil proceedings?

Many instances of unlawful police behaviour might give rise to both criminal and civil liability. If police officers are prosecuted and convicted, the victim of the police behaviour might receive compensation from the court and claim compensation from the Criminal Injuries Compensation Board. If the victim's aim is the punishment of guilty police officers, a successful prosecution might be more satisfying than any other remedy, but this is mitigated by the uncertainty of the outcome of the trial given that guilt must be proved beyond reasonable doubt.

Certainly, if the prosecuting authorities decline to prosecute, a private prosecution will rarely be advisable. The cost would fall on the prosecutor, there is no legal aid available for prosecutors (except to respond to an appeal from the magistrates' court to the Crown Court), and in many cases the defendant police officer will have the right to elect trial by jury, which will prove very expensive to the prosecutor (who may not be given permission to appear in person to prosecute at the Crown Court and may have to instruct solicitors and counsel). It is possible for prosecutors to be awarded costs from public funds, but such an order is considered at the end of the trial and, even if made, might not meet the full cost.

Thus, prosecution in the criminal courts is not a course that should be undertaken lightly. Civil proceedings will almost invariably prove the best course. They can be brought in person without the need to instruct lawyers (although it might be wise to do so), and the case need only be proven on the balance of probabilities. Legal aid, subject to means, is available to sue in civil courts except in minor cases. Proceedings can be kept in the speedier and less expensive county court if the amount of damages claimed is not too high. Finally, damages awarded in the High Court (especially if there is a jury) might be considerably more substantial than compensation awarded as a result of criminal proceedings.

Judicial review

However, if civil proceedings are contemplated to establish that a decision of an authority infringed rights under public law, the judicial review procedure must be used rather than the ordinary civil action.[77]

The disadvantages to the applicant of using the judicial review procedure are that:

a) the limitation period is three months, extendable by the court for good cause, compared with three or six years for a civil action;
b) the court must be asked for leave to apply for review and may impose conditions as to costs;
c) an application for leave to apply must be supported by reasons and affidavits although there will have been no discovery (disclosure) of documents;
d) discovery, interrogatories and cross-examination are permitted only with leave; and
e) damages are seldom awarded.

These conditions do not apply to ordinary civil actions.

It will not always be easy to decide whether the right to be protected is a public law or private law right. If the claim is for damages only, for example as a result of an unlawful arrest or search, this is a private law issue which raises no particular public law questions and should be brought in an ordinary civil action. However, if the claim is for the infringement of a public law right by a public law body exercising a public function, especially if a decision is challenged, the claim must proceed by judicial review. Examples might be to compel a chief officer of police to act in a particular way or to quash the issue of a warrant. However, the case-law is still developing and it is not clear what procedure should be used for

77 *O'Reilly v Mackman* [1982] 3 All ER 1124, HL. See further Wade, op cit n65 pp678–680.

example to stop a road-block. Where the position is unclear, the best course is to proceed by way of judicial review because the court will be able to consider the question of jurisdiction while considering whether to give leave, and on judicial review the court can proceed as if the matter were an ordinary civil action, although the reverse is not the case.

Locus standi

A further issue is that of locus standi (the right to bring proceedings). Generally speaking, to bring a civil action, an applicant must have a personal interest in the matter, although the courts have not always been consistent in their decisions as to what is a sufficient personal interest. In the context of the 1984 Act, the question will arise only in the case of a local authority or community group wishing to bring proceedings. A local authority has a general right to take any legal proceedings in its own name if it considers it expedient for the promotion or protection of the interests of the inhabitants of its area.[78] It is unlikely that this right would apply in the case of a private law action such as a police assault on an individual, but it would certainly apply to the judicial review procedure.

Whether a community group has locus standi for judicial review will depend on the substance of the action. If the matter directly affects local residents generally and the group represents local residents, it might well have locus standi,[79] but it will not if the matter is confidential between the people affected.[80]

If an individual or organisation does not have locus standi in a situation involving the public interest, it might still be possible to claim a declaration or injunction (though not other remedies) by way of a relator action. This is where the Attorney-General agrees to the case being brought in his or her name. However, the costs are borne by the person actually bringing the action, who in practice decides too on the conduct of the case. This procedure can also be used to enforce the criminal law through proceedings for an injunction. The Attorney-General might be reluctant to consent if this involves chal-

---

78 Local Government Act 1972 s222.
79 *Covent Garden Community Association Ltd v Greater London Council* [1981] JPL 183. See also *R v Secretary of State for Social Services ex parte Greater London Council* (1984) *Times* 16 August.
80 *IRC v National Federation of Self Employed and Small Businesses* [1981] 2 All ER 93, HL.

lenging the activities of a government department, and the refusal to consent is not open to legal challenge.[81]

Police complaints procedure

There remains the issue of whether the police complaints procedure should be invoked in conjunction with other remedies. A person prosecuted by the police who complains at the trial of police misconduct may be cross-examined by the prosecution about a failure to lodge a formal complaint, but, if this failure was due to solicitors' advice, based on the ineffectiveness of the complaints procedure, that should be a satisfactory answer.

It might be unwise to make a complaint if the complainant is defending a criminal prosecution and does not wish to disclose to the police the details of the defence case in advance of the trial. In such a situation, a letter could be sent stating that a complaint will be made at the conclusion of proceedings, but without giving details. A similar approach may also be advisable where a person also wishes to pursue a civil action against the police. The decision in *Neilson v Laugharne*,[82] that statements made in connection with the investigation of a complaint were subject to public interest immunity and therefore unavailable to the plaintiff, has been overruled by *R v Chief Constable of West Midlands Police ex p Wiley*.[83] However, the interests of the plaintiff may still be compromised by a complaint, since the police can use such documents, including the complainant's statement, in the preparation of their defence to the civil proceedings. A tactic suggested by Harrison and Cragg[84] is to postpone co-operation with investigation of the complaint until exchange of witness statements. This would avoid the police having the advantage of advance details of the plaintiff's case.

The remedies under the European Convention on Human Rights can be pursued only after all domestic remedies have been exhausted. Lack of legal aid and failure to comply with time limits for proceedings provide no excuse for failing to exhaust domestic remedies.

---

81 *Attorney-General v Harris* [1961] 1 QB 74, CA; *Gouriet v Union of Post Office Workers* [1978] AC 435, HL; Wade, op cit n65, pp603–612.
82 [1981] QB 736.
83 [1995] 1 AC 274.
84 J Harrison and S Cragg, *Police Misconduct: Legal Remedies* (Legal Action Group, 3rd edition 1995) p202.

Police and Criminal Evidence Act 1984

PART I
POWERS TO STOP AND SEARCH

1. (1) A constable may exercise any power conferred by this section—

(a) in any place to which at the time when he proposes to exercise the power the public or any section of the public has access, on payment or otherwise, as of right or by virtue of express or implied permission; or

(b) in any other place to which people have ready access at the time when he proposes to exercise the power but which is not a dwelling.

(2) Subject to subsection (3) to (5) below, a constable—

(a) may search—

(i) any person or vehicle;

(ii) anything which is in or on a vehicle,

for stolen or prohibited articles or any article to which subsection (8A) below applies; and

(b) may detain a person or vehicle for the purpose of such a search.

(3) This section does not give a constable power to search a person or vehicle or anything in or on a vehicle unless he has reasonable grounds for suspecting that he will find stolen or prohibited articles or any article to which subsection (8A) below applies.

(4) If a person is in a garden or yard occupied with and used for the purposes of a dwelling or on other land so occupied and used, a constable may not search him in the exercise of the power conferred by this section unless the constable has reasonable grounds for believing—

(a) that he does not reside in the dwelling; and

(b) that he is not in the place in question with the express or implied permission of the person who resides in the dwelling.

(5) If a vehicle is in a garden or yard occupied with and used for the purposes of a dwelling or on other land so occupied and used, a constable may not search the vehicle or anything in or on it in the exercise of the power conferred by this section unless he has reasonable grounds for believing—

(a) that the person in charge of the vehicle does not reside in the dwelling; and (*b*) that the vehicle is not in the place in question with the express or implied permission of a person who resides in the dwelling.

(6) If in the course of such a search a constable discovers an article which he has reasonable grounds for suspecting to be a stolen or prohibited article or an article to which subsection (8A) below applies, he may seize it.

(7) An article is prohibited for the purposes of this Part of this Act if it is—

(*a*) an offensive weapon; or

(*b*) an article—

(i) made or adapted for use in the course of or in connection with an offence to which this sub-paragraph applies; or

(ii) intended by the person having it with him for such use by him or by the other person.

(8) The offences to which subsection (7)(*b*)(i) above applies are—

(*a*) burglary;

(*b*) theft;

(*c*) offences under section 12 of the Theft Act 1968 (taking motor vehicle or other conveyance without authority); and

(*d*) offences under section 15 of that Act (obtaining property by deception).

(8A) This subsection applies to any article in relation to which a person has committed, or is committing or is going to commit an offence under section 139 of the Criminal Justice Act 1988.

(9) In this Part of this Act "offensive weapon" means any article—

(*a*) made or adapted for use for causing injury to persons; or

(*b*) intended by the person having it with him for such use by him or by some other person.

2. (1) A constable who detains a person or vehicle in the exercise—

(*a*) of the power conferred by section 1 above; or

(*b*) of any other power—

(i) to search a person without first arresting him; or

(ii) to search a vehicle without making an arrest,

need not conduct a search if it appears to him subsequently—

(i) that no search is required; or

(ii) that a search is impracticable.

(2) If a constable contemplates a search, other than a search of an unattended vehicle, in the exercise—

(*a*) of the power conferred by section 1 above; or

(*b*) of any other power, except the power conferred by section 6 below and the power conferred by section 27(2) of the Aviation Security Act 1982—

(i) to search a person without first arresting him; or

(ii) to search a vehicle without making an arrest,

it shall be his duty, subject to subsection (4) below, to take reasonable steps before he commences the search to bring to the attention of the appropriate person—

(i) if the constable is not in uniform, documentary evidence that he is a constable; and

(ii) whether he is in uniform or not, the matters specified in subsection (3) below;

and the constable shall not commence the search until he has performed that duty.

(3) The matters referred to in subsection (2)(ii) above are—

(*a*) the constable's name and the name of the police station to which he is attached;

(*b*) the object of the proposed search;

(*c*) the constable's grounds for proposing to make it; and

(*d*) the effect of section 3(7) or (8) below, as may be appropriate.

(4) A constable need not bring the effect of section 3(7) or (8) below to the attention of the appropriate person if it appears to the constable that it will not be practicable to make the record in section 3(1) below.

(5) In this section "the appropriate person" means—

(*a*) if the constable proposes to search a person, that person; and

(*b*) if he proposes to search a vehicle, or anything in or on a vehicle, the person in charge of the vehicle.

(6) On completing a search of an unattended vehicle or anything in or on such a vehicle in the exercise of any such power as is mentioned in subsection (2) above a constable shall leave a notice—

(*a*) stating that he has searched it;

(*b*) giving the name of the police station to which he is attached;

(*c*) stating that an application for compensation for any damage caused by the search may be made to that police station; and

(*d*) stating the effect of section 3(8) below.

(7) The constable shall leave the notice inside the vehicle unless it is not reasonably practicable to do so without damaging the vehicle.

(8) The time for which a person or vehicle may be detained for the purposes of such a search is such time as is reasonably required to permit a search to be carried out either at the place where the person or vehicle was first detained or nearby.

(9) Neither the power conferred by section 1 above nor any other power to detain and search a person without first arresting him or to detain and search a vehicle without making an arrest is to be construed—

(*a*) as authorising a constable to require a person to remove any of his clothing in public other than an outer coat, jacket or gloves; or

(*b*) as authorising a constable not in uniform to stop a vehicle.

(10) This section and section 1 above apply to vessels, aircraft and hovercraft as they apply to vehicles.

3. (1) Where a constable has carried out a search in the exercise of any such power as is mentioned in section 2(1) above, other than a search—

(*a*) under section 6 below; or

(*b*) under section 27(2) of the Aviation Security Act 1982,

he shall make a record of it in writing unless it is not practicable to do so.

(2) If—

(*a*) a constable is required by subsection (1) above to make a record of a search; but

(*b*) it is not practicable to make the record on the spot,

he shall make it as soon as practicable after the completion of the search.

(3) The record of a search of a person shall include a note of his name, if the constable knows it, but a constable may not detain a person to find out his name.

(4) If a constable does not know the name of a person whom he has searched, the record of the search shall include a note otherwise describing that person.

(5) The record of a search of a vehicle shall include a note describing the vehicle.

(6) The record of a search of a person or a vehicle—

(*a*) shall state—

(i) the object of the search;

(ii) the grounds for making it;

(iii) the date and time it was made;

(iv) the place where it was made;

(v) whether anything, and if so what, was found;

(vi) whether any, and if so what, injury to a person or damage to property appears to the constable to have resulted from the search; and

(b) shall identify the constable making it.

(7) If a constable who conducted a search of a person made a record of it, the person who was searched shall be entitled to a copy of the record if he asks for one before the end of the period specified in subsection (9) below.

(8) If—

(a) the owner of a vehicle which has been searched or the person who was in charge of the vehicle at the time when it was searched asks for a copy of the record of the search before the end of the period specified in subsection (9) below; and

(b) the constable who conducted the search made a record of it,

the person who made the request shall be entitled to a copy.

(9) The period mentioned in subsections (7) and (8) above is the period of 12 months beginning with the date on which the search was made.

(10) The requirements imposed by this section with regard to records of searches of vehicles shall apply also to records of searches of vessels, aircraft and hovercraft.

4. (1) This section shall have effect in relation to the conduct of road checks by police officers for the purpose of ascertaining whether a vehicle is carrying—

(a) a person who has committed an offence other than a road traffic offence or a vehicle excise offence;

(b) a person who is a witness to such an offence;

(c) a person intending to commit such an offence; or

(d) a person who is unlawfully at large.

(2) For the purposes of this section a road check consists of the exercise in a locality of the power conferred by section 163 of the Road Traffic Act 1988 in such a way as to stop during the period for which its exercise in that way in that locality continues all vehicles or vehicles selected by any criterion.

(3) Subject to subsection (5) below, there may only be such a road check if a police officer of the rank of superintendent or above authorises it in writing.

(4) An officer may only authorise a road check under subsection (3) above—

(a) for the purpose specified in subsection (1)(a) above, if he has reasonable grounds—

(i) for believing that the offence is a serious arrestable offence; and

(ii) for suspecting that the person is, or is about to be, in the locality in which vehicles would be stopped if the road check were authorised;

(b) for the purpose specified in subsection (1)(b) above, if he has reasonable grounds for believing that the offence is a serious arrestable offence;

(c) for the purpose specified in subsection (1)(b) above, if he has reasonable grounds—

(i) for believing that the offence would be a serious arrestable offence; and

(ii) for suspecting that the person is, or is about to be, in the locality in which vehicles would be stopped if the road check were authorised;

(d) for the purpose specified in subsection (1)(d) above, if he has reasonable grounds for suspecting that the person is, or is about to be, in that locality.

(5) An officer below the rank of superintendent may authorise such a road check if it appears to him that it is required as a matter of urgency for one of the purposes specified in subsection (1) above.

(6) If an authorisation is given under subsection (5) above, it shall be the duty of the officer who gives it—
  (a) to make a written record of the time at which he gives it; and
  (b) to cause an officer of the rank of superintendent or above to be informed that it has been given.

(7) The duties imposed by subsection (6) above shall be performed as soon as it is practicable to do so.

(8) An officer to whom a report is made under subsection (6) above may, in writing, authorise the road check to continue.

(9) If such an officer considers that the road check should not continue, he shall record in writing—
  (a) the fact that it took place; and
  (b) the purpose for which it took place.

(10) An officer giving an authorisation under this section shall specify the locality in which vehicles are to be stopped.

(11) An officer giving an authorisation under this section, other than an authorisation under subsection (5) above—
  (a) shall specify a period, not exceeding seven days, during which the road check may continue; and
  (b) may direct that the road check—
      (i) shall be continuous; or
      (ii) shall be conducted at specified times,
      during that period.

(12) If it appears to an officer of the rank of superintendent or above that a road check ought to continue beyond the period for which it has been authorised he may, from time to time, in writing specify a further period, not exceeding seven days, during which it may continue.

(13) Every written authorisation shall specify—
  (a) the name of the officer giving it;
  (b) the purpose of the road check; and
  (c) the locality in which vehicles are to be stopped.

(14) The duties to specify the purposes of a road check imposed by subsections (9) and (13) above include duties to specify any relevant serious arrestable offence.

(15) Where a vehicle is stopped in a road check, the person in charge of the vehicle at the time when it is stopped shall be entitled to obtain a written statement of the purpose of the road check if he applies for such a statement not later than the end of the period of twelve months from the day on which the vehicle was stopped.

(16) Nothing in this section affects the exercise by police officers of any power to stop vehicles for purposes other than those specified in subsection (1) above.

5. (1) Every annual report—
  (a) under section 12 of the Police Act 1964; or
  (b) made by the Commissioner of Police of the Metropolis, shall contain information—
      (i) about searches recorded under section 3 above which have been carried

out in the area to which the report relates during the period to which it relates; and

(ii) about road checks authorised in that area during that period under section 4 above.

(2) The information about searches shall not include information about specific searches but shall include—

(a) the total numbers of searches in each month during the period to which the report relates—

  (i) for stolen articles;

  (ii) for offensive weapons; and

  (iii) for other prohibited articles;

(b) the total number of persons arrested in each such month in consequence of searches of each of the descriptions specified in paragraph (a)(i) to (iii) above.

(3) The information about road checks shall include information—

(a) about the reason for authorising each road check; and

(b) about the result of each of them.

6. (1) A constable employed by statutory undertakers may stop, detain and search any vehicle before it leaves a goods area included in the premises of the statutory undertakers.

(2) In this section "goods area" means any area used wholly or mainly for the storage or handling of goods.

(3) For the purposes of section 6 of the Public Stores Act 1875, any person appointed under the Special Constables Act 1923 to be a special constable within any premises which are in the possession or under the control of British Nuclear Fuels Limited shall be deemed to be a constable deputed by a public department and any goods and chattels belonging to or in the possession of British Nuclear Fuels Limited shall be deemed to be Her Majesty's Stores.

(4) In the application of subsection (3) above to Northern Ireland, for the reference to the Special Constables Act 1923 there shall be substituted a reference to paragraph 1(2) of Schedule 2 to the Emergency Laws (Miscellaneous Provisions) Act 1947.

7. (1) The following enactments shall cease to have effect—

(a) section 8 of the Vagrancy Act 1824;

(b) section 66 of the Metropolitian Police Act 1839;

(c) section 11 of the Canals (Offences) Act 1840;

(d) section 19 of the Pedlars Act 1871;

(e) section 33 of the County of Merseyside Act 1980; and

(f) section 42 of the West Midlands County Council Act 1980.

(2) There shall also cease to have effect—

(a) so much of any enactment contained in an Act passed before 1974, other than—

  (i) an enactment contained in a public general Act; or

  (ii) an enactment relating to statutory undertakers,

  as confers power on a constable to search for stolen or unlawfully obtained goods; and

(b) so much of any enactment relating to statutory undertakers as provides that such a power shall not be exercisable after the end of a specified period.

(3) In this part of this Act "statutory undertakers" means persons authorised by any enactment to carry on any railway, light railway, road transport, water transport, canal, inland navigation, dock or harbour undertaking.

PART II
POWERS OF ENTRY, SEARCH AND SEIZURE

Search warrants

8. (1) If on an application made by a constable a justice of the peace is satisfied that there are reasonable grounds for believing—
   (a) that a serious arrestable offence has been committed; and
   (b) that there is material on premises specified in the application which is likely to be of substantial value (whether by itself or together with other material) to the investigation of the offence; and
   (c) that the material is likely to be relevant evidence; and
   (d) that it does not consist of or include items subject to legal privilege, excluded material or special procedure material; and
   (e) that any of the conditions specified in subsection (3) below applies,
he may issue a warrant authorising a constable to enter and search the premises.

(2) A constable may seize and retain anything for which a search has been authorised under subsection (1) above.

(3) The conditions mentioned in subsection (1)(e) above are—
   (a) that it is not practicable to communicate with any person entitled to grant entry to the premises;
   (b) that it is practicable to communicate with a person entitled to grant entry to the premises but it is not practicable to communicate with any person entitled to grant access to the evidence;
   (c) that entry to the premises will not be granted unless a warrant is produced;
   (d) that the purpose of a search may be frustrated or seriously prejudiced unless a constable arriving at the premises can secure immediate entry to them.

(4) In this Act "relevant evidence", in relation to an offence, means anything that would be admissible in evidence at a trial for the offence.

(5) The power to issue a warrant conferred by this section is in addition to any such power otherwise conferred.

9. (1) A constable may obtain access to excluded material or special procedure material for the purposes of a criminal investigation by making an application under Schedule 1 below and in accordance with that Schedule.

(2) Any Act (including a local Act) passed before this Act under which a search of premises for the purposes of a criminal investigation could be authorised by the issue of a warrant to a constable shall cease to have effect so far as it relates to the authorisation of searches—
   (a) for items subject to legal privilege; or
   (b) for excluded material; or
   (c) for special procedure material consisting of documents or records other than documents.

10. (1) Subject to subsection (2) below, in this Act "items subject to legal privilege" means—
   (a) communications between a professional legal adviser and his client or any

person representing his client made in connection with the giving of legal advice to the client;

(b) communications between a professional legal adviser and his client or any person representing his client or between such an adviser or his client or any such representative and any other person made in connection with or in contemplation of legal proceedings and for the purposes of such proceedings; and

(c) items enclosed with or referred to in such communications and made—
  (i) in connection with the giving of legal advice; or
  (ii) in connection with or in contemplation of legal proceedings and for the purposes of such proceedings,

when they are in the possession of a person who is entitled to possession of them.

(2) Items held with the intention of furthering a criminal purpose are not items subject to legal privilege.

11. (1) Subject to the following provisions of this section, in this Act "excluded material" means—

(a) personal records which a person has acquired or created in the course of any trade, business, profession or other occupation or for the purposes of any paid or unpaid office and which he holds in confidence;

(b) human tissue or tissue fluid which has been taken for the purposes of diagnosis or medical treatment and which a person holds in confidence;

(c) journalistic material which a person holds in confidence and which consists—
  (i) of documents; or
  (ii) of records other than documents.

(2) A person holds material other than journalistic material in confidence for the purposes of this section if he holds it subject—

(a) to an express or implied undertaking to hold it in confidence; or

(b) to a restriction on disclosure or an obligation of secrecy contained in any enactment, including an enactment contained in an Act passed after this Act.

(3) A person holds journalistic material in confidence for the purposes of this section if—

(a) he holds it subject to such an undertaking, restriction or obligation; and

(b) it has been continuously held (by one or more persons) subject to such an undertaking, restriction or obligation since it was first acquired or created for the purposes of journalism.

12. In this Part of this Act "personal records" means documentary and other records concerning an individual (whether living or dead) who can be identified from them and relating—

(a) to his physical or mental health;

(b) to spiritual counselling or assistance given or to be given to him; or

(c) to counselling or assistance given or to be given to him, for the purposes of his personal welfare, by any voluntary organisation or by any individual who—
  (i) by reason of his office or occupation has responsibilities for his personal welfare; or
  (ii) by reason of an order of a court has responsibilities for his supervision.

13. (1) Subject to subsection (2) below, in this Act "journalistic material" means material acquired or created for the purposes of journalism.

(2) Material is only journalistic material for the purposes of this Act if it is in the possession of a person who acquired or created it for the purposes of journalism.

(3) A person who receives material from someone who intends that the recipient shall use it for the purposes of journalism is to be taken to have acquired it for those purposes.

14. (1) In this Act "special procedure material" means—
(*a*) material to which subsection (2) below applies; and
(*b*) journalistic material, other than excluded material.

(2) Subject to the following provisions of this section, this subsection applies to material, other than items subject to legal privilege and excluded material, in the possession of a person who—
    (*a*) acquired or created it in the course of any trade, business, profession or other occupation or for the purpose of any paid or unpaid office; and
    (*b*) holds it subject—
        (i) to an express or implied undertaking to hold it in confidence; or
        (ii) to a restriction or obligation such as is mentioned in section 11(2)(*b*) above.

(3) Where material is acquired—
    (*a*) by an employee from his employer and in the course of his employment; or
    (*b*) by a company from an associated company,
it is only special procedure material if it was special procedure material immediately before the acquisition.

(4) Where material is created by an employee in the course of his employment, it is only special procedure material if it would have been special procedure material had his employer created it.

(5) Where material is created by a company on behalf of an associated company, it is only special procedure material if it would have been special procedure material had the associated company created it.

(6) A company is to be treated as another's associated company for the purposes of this section if it would be so treated under section 416 of the Income and Corporation Taxes Act 1988.

15. (1) This section and section 16 below have effect in relation to the issue to constables under any enactment, including an enactment contained in an Act passed after this Act, or warrants to enter and search premises; and an entry on or search of premises under a warrant is unlawful unless it complies with this section and section 16 below.

(2) Where a constable applies for any such warrant, it shall be his duty—
    (*a*) to state—
        (i) the ground on which he makes the application; and
        (ii) the enactment under which the warrant would be issued;
    (*b*) to specify the premises which it is desired to enter and search; and
    (*c*) to identify, so far as is practicable, the articles or persons to be sought.

(3) An application for such a warrant shall be made ex parte and supported by an information in writing.

(4) The constable shall answer on oath any question that the justice of the peace or judge hearing the application asks him.

(5) A warrant shall authorise an entry on one occasion only.

(6) A warrant—

(a) shall specify—

    (i) the name of the person who applies for it;

    (ii) the date on which it is issued;

    (iii) the enactment under which it is issued; and

    (iv) the premises to be searched; and

(b) shall identify, so far as is practicable, the articles or persons to be sought.

(7) Two copies shall be made of a warrant.

(8) The copies shall be clearly certified as copies.

16. (1) A warrant to enter and search premises may be executed by any constable.

(2) Such a warrant may authorise persons to accompany any constable who is executing it.

(3) Entry and search under a warrant must be within one month from the date of its issue.

(4) Entry and search under a warrant must be at a reasonable hour unless it appears to the constable executing it that the purpose of a search may be frustrated on an entry at a reasonable hour.

(5) Where the occupier of premises which are to be entered and searched is present at the time when a constable seeks to execute a warrant to enter and search them, the constable—

(a) shall identify himself to the occupier and, if not in uniform, shall produce to him documentary evidence that he is a constable;

(b) shall produce the warrant to him; and

(c) shall supply him with a copy of it.

(6) Where—

(a) the occupier of such premises is not present at the time when a constable seeks to execute such a warrant; but

(b) some other person who appears to the constable to be in charge of the premises is present,

subsection (5) above shall have effect as if any reference to the occupier were a reference to that other person.

(7) If there is no person present who appears to the constable to be in charge of the premises, he shall leave a copy of the warrant in a prominent place on the premises.

(8) A search under a warrant may only be a search to the extent required for the purpose for which the warrant was issued.

(9) A constable executing a warrant shall make an endorsement on it stating—

(a) whether the articles or persons sought were found; and

(b) whether any articles were seized, other than articles which were sought.

(10) A warrant which—

(a) has been executed; or

(b) has not been executed within the time authorised for its execution,

shall be returned—

    (i) if it was issued by a justice of the peace, to the clerk to the justices for the petty sessions area for which he acts; and

    (ii) if it was issued by a judge, to the appropriate officer of the court from which he issued it.

(11) A warrant which is returned under subsection (10) above shall be retained for 12 months from its return—

(a) by the clerk to the justices, if it was returned under paragraph (i) of that subsection; and

(b) by the appropriate officer, if it was returned under paragraph (ii).

(12) If during the period for which a warrant is to be retained the occupier of the premises to which it relates asks to inspect it, he shall be allowed to do so.

Entry and search without search warrant

17. (1) Subject to the following provisions of this section, and without prejudice to any other enactment, a constable may enter and search any premises for the purpose—

(a) of executing—

(i) a warrant of arrect issued in connection with or arising out of criminal proceedings; or

(ii) a warrant of commitment issued under section 76 of the Magistrates' Courts Act 1980;

(b) of arresting a person for an arrestable offence;

(c) of arresting a person for an offence under—

(i) section 1 (prohibition of uniforms in connection with political objects), of the Public Order Act 1936;

(ii) any enactment contained in sections 6 to 8 or 10 of the Criminal Law Act 1977 (offences relating to entering and remaining on property);

(iii) section 4 of the Public Order Act 1986 (fear or provocation of violence);

(iv) section 76 of the Criminal Justice and Public Order Act 1994 (failure to comply with interim possession order);

(d) of recapturing a person who is unlawfully at large and whom he is pursuing; or

(e) of saving life or limb or preventing serious damage to property.

(2) Except for the purpose specified in paragraph (e) of subsection (1) above, the powers of entry and search conferred by this section—

(a) are only exercisable if the constable has reasonable grounds for believing that the person whom he is seeking is on the premises; and

(b) are limited, in relation to premises consisting of two or more separate dwellings, to powers to enter and search—

(i) any parts of the premises which the occupiers of any dwelling comprised in the premises use in common with the occupiers of any other such dwelling; and

(ii) any such dwelling in which the constable has reasonable grounds for believing that the person whom he is seeking may be.

(3) The powers of entry and search conferred by this section are only exercisable for the purposes specified in subsection (1)(c)(ii) or (iv) above by a constable in uniform.

(4) The power of search conferred by this section is only a power to search to the extent that is reasonably required for the purpose for which the power of entry is exercised.

(5) Subject to subsection (6) below, all the rules of common law under which a constable has power to enter premises without a warrant are hereby abolished.

(6) Nothing in subsection (5) above affects any power of entry to deal with or prevent a breach of the peace.

18. (1) Subject to the following provisions of this section, a constable may enter and search any premises occupied or controlled by a person who is under arrest for an arrestable offence, if he has reasonable grounds for suspecting that there is on the premises evidence, other than items subject to legal privilege, that relates—

(*a*) to that offence; or

(*b*) to some other arrestable offence which is connected with or similar to that offence.

(2) A constable may seize and retain anything for which he may search under subsection (1) above.

(3) The power to search conferred by subsection (1) above is only a power to search to the extent that is reasonably required for the purpose of discovering such evidence.

(4) Subject to subsection (5) below, the powers conferred by this section may not be exercised unless an officer of the rank of inspector or above has authorised them in writing.

(5) A constable may conduct a search under subsection (1) above—

(*a*) before taking the person to a police station; and

(*b*) without obtaining an authorisation under subsection (4) above,

if the presence of that person at a place other than a police station is necessary for the effective investigation of the offence.

(6) If a constable conducts a search by virtue of subsection (5) above, he shall inform an officer of the rank of inspector or above that he has made the search as soon as practicable after he has made it.

(7) An officer who—

(*a*) authorises a search; or

(*b*) is informed of a search under subsection (6) above, shall make a record in writing—

(i) of the grounds for the search; and

(ii) of the nature of the evidence that was sought.

(8) If the person who was in occupation or control of the premises at the time of the search is in police detention at the time the record is to be made, the officer shall make the record as part of his custody record.

Seizure etc

19. (1) The powers conferred by subsections (2), (3) and (4) below are exercisable by a constable who is lawfully on any premises.

(2) The constable may seize anything which is on the premises if he has reasonable grounds for believing—

(*a*) that it has been obtained in consequence of the commission of an offence; and

(*b*) that it is necessary to seize it in order to prevent it being concealed, lost, damaged, altered or destroyed.

(3) The constable may seize anything which is on the premises if he has reasonable grounds for believing—

(*a*) that it is evidence in relation to an offence which he is investigating or any other offence; and

(*b*) that it is necessary to seize it in order to prevent the evidence being concealed, lost, altered or destroyed.

(4) The constable may require any information which is contained in a computer and is accessible from the premises to be produced in a form in which it can be

taken away and in which it is visible and legible if he has reasonable grounds for believing—

(a) that—

(i) it is evidence in relation to an offence which he is investigating or any other offence; or

(ii) it has been obtained in consequence of the commission of an offence; and

(b) that it is necessary to do so in order to prevent it being concealed, lost, tampered with or destroyed.

(5) The powers conferred by this section are in addition to any power otherwise conferred.

(6) No power of seizure conferred on a constable under any enactment (including an enactment contained in an Act passed after this Act) is to be taken to authorise the seizure of an item which the constable exercising the power has reasonable grounds for believing to be subject to legal privilege.

20. (1) Every power of seizure which is conferred by an enactment to which this section applies on a constable who has entered premises in the exercise of a power conferred by an enactment shall be construed as including a power to require any information contained in a computer and accessible from the premises to be produced in a form in which it can be taken away and in which it is visible and legible.

(2) This section applies—

(a) to any enactment contained in an Act passed before this Act;

(b) to sections 8 and 18 above;

(c) to paragraph 13 of Schedule 1 to this Act; and

(d) to any enactment contained in an Act passed after this Act.

21. (1) A constable who seizes anything in the exercise of a power conferred by any enactment, including an enactment contained in an Act passed after this Act, shall, if so requested by a person showing himself—

(a) to be the occupier of premises on which it was seized; or

(b) to have had custody or control of it immediately before the seizure,

provide that person with a record of what he seized.

(2) The officer shall provide the record within a reasonable time from the making of the request for it.

(3) Subject to subsection (8) below, if a request for permission to be granted access to anything which—

(a) has been seized by a constable; and

(b) is retained by the police for the purpose of investigating an offence,

is made to the officer in charge of the investigation by a person who had custody or control of the thing immediately before it was so seized or by someone acting on behalf of such a person, the officer shall allow the person who made the request to access it under the supervision of a constable.

(4) Subject to subsection (8) below, if a request for a photograph or copy of any such thing is made to the officer in charge of the investigation by a person who had custody or control of the thing immediately before it was so seized, or by someone acting on behalf of such a person, the officer shall—

(a) allow the person who made the request access to it under the supervision of a constable for the purpose of photographing or copying it; or

(b) photograph or copy it, or cause it to be photographed or copied.

(5) A constable may also photograph or copy, or have photographed or copied, anything which he has power to seize, without a request being made under subsection (4) above.

(6) Where anything is photographed or copied under subsection (4)(b) above, the photograph or copy shall be supplied to the person who made the request.

(7) The photograph or copy shall be so supplied within a reasonable time from the making of the request.

(8) There is no duty under this section to grant access to, or to supply a photograph or copy of, anything if the officer in charge of the investigation for the purposes of which it was seized has reasonable grounds for believing that to do so would prejudice—

(a) that investigation;

(b) the investigation of an offence other than the offence for the purposes of investigation which the thing was seized; or

(c) any criminal proceedings which may be brought as a result of—
   (i) the investigation of which he is in charge; or
   (ii) any such investigation as is mentioned in paragraph (b) above.

22. (1) Subject to subsection (4) below, anything which has been seized by a constable or taken away by a constable following a requirement made by virtue of section 19 or 20 above may be retained so long as is necessary in all the circumstances.

(2) Without prejudice to the generality of subsection (1) above—

(a) anything seized for the purposes of a criminal investigation may be retained, except as provided by subsection (4) below—
   (i) for use as evidence at a trial for an offence; or
   (ii) for forensic examination or for investigation in connection with an offence; and

(b) anything may be retained in order to establish its lawful owner, where there are reasonable grounds for believing that it has been obtained in consequence of the commission of an offence.

(3) Nothing seized on the ground that it may be used—

(a) to cause physical injury to any person;

(b) to damage property;

(c) to interfere with evidence; or

(d) to assist in escape from police detention or lawful custody,

may be retained when the person from whom it was seized is no longer in police detention or the custody of a court or is in the custody of a court but has been released on bail.

(4) Nothing may be retained for either of the purposes mentioned in subsection (2)(a) above if a photograph or copy would be sufficient for that purpose.

(5) Nothing in this section affects any power of a court to make an order under section 1 of the Police (Property) Act 1897.

Supplementary

23. In this Act—

"premises' includes any place and, in particular, includes—

(a) any vehicle, vessel, aircraft or hovercraft;

(b) any offshore installation; and

(*c*) any tent or movable structure; and
"offshore installation" has the meaning given to it by section 1 of the Mineral Workings (Offshore Installations) Act 1971.

PART III
ARREST

24. (1) The powers of summary arrest conferred by the following subsections shall apply—
   (*a*) to offences for which the sentence is fixed by law;
   (*b*) to offences for which a person of 21 years of age or over (not previously convicted) may be sentenced to imprisonment for a term of five years (or might be so sentenced but for the restrictions imposed by section 33 of the Magistrates' Courts Act 1980); and
   (*c*) to the offences to which subsection (2) below applies,
and in this Act "arrestable offence" means any such offence,
   (2) The offences to which this subsection applies are—
   (*a*) offences for which a person may be arrested under the customs and excise Acts, as defined in section 1(1) of the Customs and Excise Management Act 1979;
   (*b*) offences under the Official Secrets Act 1920 that are not arrestable offences by virtue of the term of imprisonment for which a person may be sentenced in respect of them;
   (*bb*) offences under any provision of the Official Secrets Act 1989 except section 8(1), (4) or (5);
   (*c*) offences under section 22 (causing prostitution of women) or 23 (procuration of girl under 21) of the Sexual Offences Act 1956;
   (*d*) offences under section 12(1) (taking motor vehicle or other conveyance without authority etc) or 25(1) (going equipped for stealing, etc) of the Theft Act 1968; and
   (*e*) any offence under the Football (Offences) Act 1991;
   (*f*) an offence under section 2 of the Obscene Publications Act 1959 (publication of obscene matter);
   (*g*) an offence under section 1 of the Protection of Children Act 1978 (indecent photographs and pseudo-photographs of children);
   (*h*) an offence under section 166 of the Criminal Justice and Public Order Act 1994 (sale of tickets for designated football matches by unauthorised persons);
   (*i*) an offence under section 19 of the Public Order Act 1986 (publishing, etc material intended or likely to stir up racial hatred);
   (*j*) an offence under section 167 of the Criminal Justice and Public Order Act 1994 (touting for hire car services).
   (3) Without prejudice to section 2 of the Criminal Attempts Act 1981, the powers of summary arrest conferred by the following subsections shall also apply to the offences of—
   (*a*) conspiring to commit any of the offences mentioned in subsection (2) above;
   (*b*) attempting to commit any such offence other than an offence under section 12(1) of the Theft Act 1968;
   (*c*) inciting, aiding, abetting, counselling or procuring the commission of any such offence;

and such offences are also arrestable offences for the purposes of this act.

(4) Any person may arrest without a warrant—

(a) anyone who is in the act of committing an arrestable offence;

(b) anyone whom he has reasonable grounds for suspecting to be committing such an offence.

(5) Where an arrestable offence has been committed, any person may arrest without a warrant—

(a) anyone who is guilty of the offence;

(b) anyone whom he has reasonable grounds for suspecting to be guilty of it.

(6) Where a constable has reasonable grounds for suspecting that an arrestable offence has been committed, he may arrest without a warrant anyone whom he has reasonable grounds for suspecting to be guilty of the offence.

(7) A constable may arrest without a warrant—

(a) anyone who is about to commit an arrestable offence;

(b) anyone whom he has reasonable grounds for suspecting to be about to commit an arrestable offence.

25. (1) Where a constable has reasonable grounds for suspecting that any offence which is not an arrestable offence has been committed or attempted, or is being committed or attempted, he may arrest the relevant person if it appears to him that service of a summons is impracticable or inappropriate because any of the general arrest conditions are satisfied.

(2) In this section "the relevant person" means any person whom the constable has reasonable grounds to suspect of having committed or having attempted to commit the offence or of being in the course of committing or attempting to commit it.

(3) The general arrest conditions are—

(a) that the name of the relevant person is unknown to, and cannot be readily ascertained by, the constable;

(b) that the constable has reasonable grounds for doubting whether a name furnished by the relevant person as his name is his real name;

(c) that—

(i) the relevant person has failed to furnish a satisfactory address for service; or

(ii) the constable has reasonable grounds for doubting whether an address furnished by the relevant person is a satisfactory address for service;

(d) that the constable has reasonable grounds for believing that arrest is necessary to prevent the relevant person—

(i) causing physical injury to himself or any other person;

(ii) suffering physical injury;

(iii) causing loss of or damage to property;

(iv) committing an offence against public decency; or

(v) causing an unlawful obstruction of the highway;

(e) that the constable has reasonable grounds for believing that arrest is necessary to protect a child or other vulnerable person from the relevant person.

(4) For the purposes of subsection (3) above an address is a satisfactory address for service if it appears to the constable—

(a) that the relevant person will be at it for a sufficiently long period for it to be possible to serve him with a summons; or (*b*) that some other person specified by the relevant person will accept service of a summons for the relevant person at it.

(5) Nothing in subsection (3)(*d*) above authorises the arrest of a person under subparagaph (iv) of that paragraph except where members of the public going about their normal business cannot reasonably be expected to avoid the person to be arrested.

(6) This section shall not prejudice any power of arrest conferred apart from this section.

26. (1) Subject to subsection (2) below, so much of any Act (including a local Act) passed before this Act as enables a constable—

(*a*) to arrest a person for an offence without a warrant; or

(*b*) to arrest a person otherwise than for an offence without a warrant or an order of a court,

shall cease to have effect.

(2) Nothing in subsection (1) above affects the enactments specified in Schedule 2 to this Act.

27. (1) If a person—

(*a*) has been convicted of a recordable offence;

(*b*) has not at any time been in police detention for the offence; and

(*c*) has not had his fingerprints taken—

(i) in the course of the investigation of the offence by the police; or

(ii) since the conviction,

any constable may at any time not later than one month after the date of the conviction require him to attend a police station in order that his fingerprints may be taken.

(2) A requirement under subsection (1) above—

(*a*) shall give the person a period of at least 7 days within which he must so attend; and

(*b*) may direct him to so attend at a specified time of day or between specified times of day.

(3) Any constable may arrest without warrant a person who has failed to comply with a requirement under subsection (1) above.

(4) The Secretary of State may by regulations make provision for recording in national police records convictions for such offences as are specified in the regulations.

(5) Regulations under this section shall be made by statutory instrument and shall be subject to annulment in pursuance of a resolution of either House of Parliament.

28. (1) Subject to subsection (5) below, where a person is arrested, otherwise than by being informed that he is under arrest, the arrest is not lawful unless the person arrested is informed that he is under arrest as soon as is practicable after his arrest.

(2) Where a person is arrested by a constable, subsection (1) above applies regardless of whether the fact of the arrest is obvious.

(3) Subject to subsection (5) below, no arrest is lawful unless the person arrested is informed of the ground for the arrest at the time of, or as soon as is practicable after, the arrest.

(4) Where a person is arrested by a constable, subsection (3) above applies regardless of whether the ground for the arrest is obvious.

(5) Nothing in this section is to be taken to require a person to be informed—

(a) that he is under arrest; or

(b) of the ground for the arrest,

if it was not reasonably practicable for him to be so informed by reason of his having escaped from arrest before the information could be given.

29. Where for the purpose of assisting with an investigation a person attends voluntarily at a police station or at any other place where a constable is present or accompanies a constable to a police station or any such other place without having been arrested—

(a) he shall be entitled to leave at will unless he is placed under arrest;

(b) he shall be informed at once that he is under arrest if a decision is taken by a constable to prevent him from leaving at will.

30. (1) Subject to the following provisions of this section, where a person—

(a) is arrested by a constable for an offence; or

(b) is taken into custody by a constable after being arrested for an offence by a person other than a constable,

at any place other than a police station, he shall be taken to a police station by a constable as soon as practicable after the arrest.

(2) Subject to subsections (3) and (5) below, the police station to which an arrested person is taken under subsection (1) above shall be a designated police station.

(3) A constable to whom this subsection applies may take an arrested person to any police station unless it appears to the constable that it may be necessary to keep the arrested person in police detention for more than six hours.

(4) Subsection (3) above applies—

(a) to a constable who is working in a locality covered by a police station which is not a designated police station; and

(b) to a constable belonging to a body of constables maintained by an authority other than a police authority.

(5) Any constable may take an arrested person to any police station if—

(a) either of the following conditions is satisfied—

(i) the constable has arrested him without the assistance of any other constable and no other constable is available to assist him;

(ii) the constable has taken him into custody from a person other than a constable without the assistance of any other constable and no other constable is available to assist him; and

(b) it appears to the constable that he will be unable to take the arrested person to a designated police station without the arrested person injuring himself, the constable or some other person.

(6) If the first police station to which an arrested person is taken after his arrest is not a designated police station, he shall be taken to a designated police station not more than six hours after his arrival at the first police station unless he is released previously.

(7) A person arrested by a constable at a place other than a police station shall be released if a constable is satisfied, before the person arrested reaches a police station, that there are no grounds for keeping him under arrest.

(8) A constable who releases a person under subsection (7) above shall record the fact that he has done so.

(9) The constable shall make the record as soon as is practicable after the release.

(10) Nothing in subsection (1) above shall prevent a constable delaying taking a person who has been arrested to a police station if the presence of that person elsewhere is necessary in order to carry out such investigations as it is reasonable to carry out immediately.

(11) Where there is delay in taking a person who has been arrested to a police station after his arrest, the reasons for the delay shall be recorded when he first arrives at a police station.

(12) Nothing in subsection (1) above shall be taken to affect—

(a) paragraphs 16(3) or 18(1) of Schedule 2 to the Immigration Act 1971;

(b) section 34(1) of the Criminal Justice Act 1972; or

(c) section 15(6) and (9) of the Prevention of Terrorism (Temporary Provisions) Act 1989 and paragraphs 7(4) and 8(4) and (5) of Schedule 2 and paragraphs 6(6) and 7(4) and (5) of Schedule 5 to that Act.

(13) Nothing in subsection (10) above shall be taken to affect paragraph 18(3) of Schedule 2 to the Immigration Act 1971.

31. Where—

(a) a person—

(i) has been arrested for an offence; and

(ii) is at a police station in consequence of that arrest; and

(b) it appears to a constable that, if he were released from that arrest, he would be liable to arrest for some other offence,

he shall be arrested for that other offence.

32. (1) A constable may search an arrested person, in any case where the person to be searched has been arrested at a place other than a police station, if the constable has reasonable grounds for believing that the arrested person may present a danger to himself or others.

(2) Subject to subsections (3) to (5) below, a constable shall also have power in any such case—

(a) to search the arrested person for anything—

(i) which he might use to assist him to escape from lawful custody; or

(ii) which might be evidence relating to an offence; and

(b) to enter and search any premises in which he was when arrested or immediately before he was arrested for evidence relating to the offence for which he has been arrested.

(3) The power to search conferred by subsection (2) above is only a power to search to the extent that is reasonably required for the purpose of discovering any such thing or any such evidence.

(4) The powers conferred by this section to search a person are not to be construed as authorising a constable to require a person to remove any of his clothing in public other than an outer coat, jacket or gloves but they do authorise a search of a person's mouth.

(5) A constable may not search a person in the exercise of the power conferred by subsection (2)(a) above unless he has reasonable grounds for believing that the person to be searched may have concealed on him anything for which a search is permitted under that paragraph.

(6) A constable may not search premises in the exercise of the power conferred by subsection (2)(b) above unless he has reasonable grounds for believing that there is evidence for which a search is permitted under that paragraph on the premises.

(7) In so far as the power of search conferred by subsection (2)(b) above relates to premises consisting of two or more separate dwellings, it is limited to a power to search—

(a) any dwelling in which the arrest took place or in which the person arrested was immediately before his arrest; and

(b) any parts of the premises which the occupier of any such dwelling uses in common with the occupiers of any other dwellings comprised in the premises.

(8) A constable searching a person in the exercise of the power conferred by subsection (1) above may seize and retain anything he finds, if he has reasonable grounds for believing that the person searched might use it to cause physical injury to himself or to any other person.

(9) A constable searching a person in the exercise of the power conferred by subsection (2)(a) above may seize and retain anything he finds, other than an item subject to legal privilege, if he has reasonable grounds for believing—

(a) that he might use it to assist him to escape from lawful custody; or

(b) that it is evidence of an offence or has been obtained in consequence of the commission of an offence.

(10) Nothing in this section shall be taken to affect the power conferred by section 15(3), (4) and (5) of the Prevention of Terrorism (Temporary Provisions) Act 1989.

33. In section 125 of the Magistrates' Courts Act 1980—

(a) in subsection (3), for the words "arrest a person charged with an offence" there shall be substituted the words "which this subsection applies";

(b) the following subsection shall be added after that subsection—

"(4) The warrants to which subsection (3) above applies are—

(a) a warrant to arrest a person in connection with an offence;

(b) without prejudice to paragraph (a) above, a warrant under section 186(3) of the Army Act 1955, section 186(3) of the Air Force Act 1955, section 105(3) of the Naval Discipline Act 1957 or Schedule 5 to the Reserve Forces Act 1980 (desertion etc.);

(c) a warrant under—

(i) section 102 or 104 of the General Rate Act 1967 (insufficiency of distress);

(ii) section 18(4) of the Domestic Proceedings and Magistrates' Courts Act 1978 (protection of parties to marriage and children of family); and

(iii) section 55, 76, 93 and 97 above."

PART IV
DETENTION

Detention—conditions and duration

34. (1) A person arrested for an offence shall not be kept in police detention except in accordance with the provisions of this Part of this Act.

(2) Subject to subsection (3) below, if at any time a custody officer—

(a) becomes aware, in relation to any person in police detention, that the grounds for the detention of that person have ceased to apply; and (*b*) is not aware of any other grounds on which the continued detention of that person could be justified under the provisions of this Part of this Act,

it shall be the duty of the custody officer, subject to subsection (4) below, to order his immediate release from custody.

(3) No person in police detention shall be released except on the authority of a custody officer at the police station where his detention was authorised or, if it was authorised at more than one station, a custody officer at the station where it was last authorised.

(4) A person who appears to the custody officer to have been unlawfully at large when he was arrested is not to be released under subsection (2) above.

(5) A person whose release is ordered under subsection (2) above shall be released without bail unless it appears to the custody officer—

(*a*) that there is need for further investigation of any matter in connection with which he was detained at any time during the period of his detention; or

(*b*) that proceedings may be taken against him in respect of any such matter,

and, if it so appears, he shall be released on bail.

(6) For the purposes of this Part of this Act a person arrested under section 6(5) of the Road Traffic Act 1988 is arrested for an offence.

(7) For the purposes of this Part of this Act a person who returns to a police station to answer to bail or is arrested under section 46A below shall be treated as arrested for an offence and the offence in connection with which he was granted bail shall be deemed to be that offence.

35. (1) The chief officer of police for each police area shall designate the police stations in his area which, subject to section 30(3) and (5) above, are to be the stations in that area to be used for the purpose of detaining arrested persons.

(2) A chief officer's duty under subsection (1) above is to designate police stations appearing to him to provide enough accommodation for that purpose.

(3) Without prejudice to section 12 of the Interpretation Act 1978 (continuity of duties) a chief officer—

(*a*) may designate a station which was not previously designated; and

(*b*) may direct that a designation of a station previously made shall cease to operate.

(4) In this Act "designated police station" means a police station for the time being designated under this section.

36. (1) One or more custody officers shall be appointed for each designated police station.

(2) A custody officer for a designated police station shall be appointed—

(*a*) by the chief officer of police for the area in which the designated police station is situated; or

(*b*) by such other police officer as the chief officer of police for that area may direct.

(3) No officer may be appointed a custody officer unless he is of at least the rank of sergeant.

(4) An officer of any rank may perform the functions of a custody officer at a designated police station if a custody officer is not readily available to perform them.

(5) Subject to the following provisions of this section and to section 39(2) below, none of the functions of a custody officer in relation to a person shall be performed

by an officer who at the time when the function falls to be performed is involved in the investigation of an offence for which that person is in police detention at that time.

(6) Nothing in subsection (5) above is to be taken to prevent a custody officer—

(*a*) performing any function assigned to custody officers—

    (i) by this Act; or

    (ii) by a code of practice issued under this Act;

(*b*) carrying out the duty imposed on custody officers by section 39 below;

(*c*) doing anything in connection with the identification of a suspect; or

(*d*) doing anything under sections 7 and 8 of the Road Traffic Act 1988.

(7) Where an arrested person is taken to a police station which is not a designated police station, the functions in relation to him which at a designated police station would be the functions of a custody officer shall be performed—

(*a*) by an officer who is not involved in the investigation of an offence for which he is in police detention, if such an officer is readily available; and

(*b*) if no such officer is readily available, by the officer who took him to the station or any other officer.

(8) References to a custody officer in the following provisions of this Act include references to an officer other than a custody officer who is performing the functions of a custody officer by virtue of subsection (4) or (7) above.

(9) Where by virtue of subsection (7) above an officer of a force maintained by a police authority who took an arrested person to a police station is to perform the functions of a custody officer in relation to him, the officer shall inform an officer who—

(*a*) is attached to a designated police station; and

(*b*) is of at least the rank of inspector,

that he is to do so.

(10) The duty imposed by subsection (9) above shall be performed as soon as it is practicable to perform it.

37. (1) Where—

(*a*) a person is arrested for an offence—

    (i) without a warrant; or

    (ii) under a warrant not endorsed for bail,

(*b*) [*Repealed*.]

the custody officer at each police station where he is detained after his arrest shall determine whether he has before him sufficient evidence to charge that person with the offence for which he was arrested and may detain him at the police station for such period as is necessary to enable him to do so.

(2) If the custody officer determines that he does not have such evidence before him, the person arrested shall be released either on bail or without bail, unless the custody officer has reasonable grounds for believing that his detention without being charged is necessary to secure or preserve evidence relating to an offence for which he is under arrest or to obtain such evidence by questioning him.

(3) If the custody officer has reasonable grounds for so believing, he may authorise the person arrested to be kept in police detention.

(4) Where a custody officer authorises a person who has not been charged to be kept in police detention, he shall, as soon as is practicable, make a written record of the grounds for the detention.

(5) Subject to subsection (6) below, the written record shall be made in the

presence of the person arrested who shall at that time be informed by the custody officer of the grounds for his detention.

(6) Subsection (5) above shall not apply where the person arrested is, at the time when the written record is made—

(a) incapable of understanding what is said to him;

(b) violent or likely to become violent; or

(c) in urgent need of medical attention.

(7) Subject to section 41(7) below, if the custody officer determines that he has before him sufficient evidence to charge the person arrested with the offence for which he was arrested, the person arrested—

(a) shall be charged; or

(b) shall be released without charge, either on bail or without bail.

(8) Where—

(a) a person is released under subsection (7)(b) above; and

(b) at the time of his release a decision whether he should be prosecuted for the offence for which he was arrested has not been taken,

it shall be the duty of the custody officer so to inform him.

(9) If the person arrested is not in a fit state to be dealt with under subsection (7) above, he may be kept in police detention until he is.

(10) The duty imposed on the custody officer under subsection (1) above shall be carried out by him as soon as practicable after the person arrested arrives at the police station or, in the case of a person arrested at the police station, as soon as practicable after the arrest.

(11)–(14) [*Repealed.*]

(15) In this Part of this Act—

"arrested juvenile" means a person arrested with or without a warrant who appears to be under the age of 17;

"endorsed for bail" means endorsed with a direction for bail in accordance with section 117(2) of the Magistrates' Courts Act 1980.

38. (1) Where a person arrested for an offence otherwise than under a warrant endorsed for bail is charged with an offence, the custody officer shall, subject to section 25 of the Criminal Justice and Public Order Act 1994, order his release from police detention, either on bail or without bail, unless—

(a) if the person arrested is not an arrested juvenile—

(i) his name or address cannot be ascertained or the custody officer has reasonable grounds for doubting whether a name or address furnished by him as his name or address is his real name or address;

(ii) the custody officer has reasonable grounds for believing that the person arrested will fail to appear in court to answer to bail;

(iii) in the case of a person arrested for an imprisonable offence, the custody officer has reasonable grounds for believing that the detention of the person arrested is necessary to prevent him from committing an offence;

(iv) in the case of a person arrested for an offence which is not an imprisonable offence, the custody officer has reasonable grounds for believing that the detention of the person arrested is necessary to prevent him causing physical injury to any other person or from causing loss of or damage to property;

(v) the custody officer has reasonable grounds for believing that the detention of the person arrested is necessary to prevent him from interfering with the administration of justice or with the investigation of offences or of a particular offence; or

(vi) the custody officer has reasonable grounds for believing that the detention of the person arrested is necessary for his own protection;

(b) if he is an arrested juvenile—

(i) any of the requirements of paragraph (a) above is satisfied; or

(ii) the custody officer has reasonable grounds for believing that he ought to be detained in his own interests.

(2) If the release of a person arrested is not required by subsection (1) above, the custody officer may authorise him to be kept in police detention.

(2A) The custody officer, in taking the decisions required by subsection (1)(a) and (b) above (except (a)(i) and (vi) and (b)(ii)), shall have regard to the same considerations as those which a court is required to have regard to in taking the corresponding decisions under paragraph 2 of Part I of Schedule 1 to the Bail Act 1976.

(3) Where a custody officer authorises a person who has been charged to be kept in police detention, he shall, as soon as practicable, make a written record of the grounds for the detention.

(4) Subject to subsection (5) below, the written record shall be made in the presence of the person charged who shall at that time be informed by the custody officer of the grounds for his detention.

(5) Subsection (4) above shall not apply where the person charged is, at the time when the written record is made—

(a) incapable of understanding what is said to him;

(b) violent or likely to become violent; or

(c) in urgent need of medical attention.

(6) Where a custody officer authorises an arrested juvenile to be kept in police detention under subsection (1) above, the custody officer shall, unless he certifies—

(a) that, by reason of such circumstances as are specified in the certificate, it is impracticable for him to do so; or

(b) in the case of an arrested juvenile who has attained the age of 12 years, that no secure accommodation is available and that keeping him in other local authority accommodation would not be adequate to protect the public from serious harm from him,

secure that the arrested juvenile is moved to local authority accommodation.

(6A) In this section—

"local authority accommodation" means accommodation provided by or on behalf of a local authority (within the meaning of the Children Act 1989).

"secure accommodation" means accommodation provided for the purpose of restricting liberty;

"sexual offence" and "violent offence" have the same meanings as in Part I of the Criminal Justice Act 1991;

and any reference, in relation to an arrested juvenile charged with a violent or sexual offence, to protecting the public from serious harm from him shall be construed as a reference to protecting members of the public from death or serious personal injury, whether physical or psychological, occasioned by further such offences committed by him.

(6B) Where an arrested juvenile is moved to local authority accommodation under subsection (6) above, it shall be lawful for any person acting on behalf of the authority to detain him.

(7) A certificate made under subsection (6) above in respect of an arrested

juvenile shall be produced to the court before which he is first brought thereafter.

(7A) In this section "imprisonable offence" has the same meaning as in Schedule 1 to the Bail Act 1976.

(8) In this Part of this Act "local authority" has the same meaning as in the Children Act 1989.

39. (1) Subject to subsections (2) and (4) below, it shall be the duty of the custody officer at a police station to ensure—

(a) that all persons in police detention at that station are treated in accordance with this Act and any code of practice issued under it and relating to the treatment of persons in police detention; and

(b) that all matters relating to such persons which are required by this Act or by such codes of practice to be recorded are recorded in the custody records relating to such persons.

(2) If the custody officer, in accordance with any code of practice issued under this Act, transfers or permits the transfer of a person in police detention—

(a) to the custody of a police officer investigating an offence for which that person is in police detention; or

(b) to the custody of an officer who has charge of that person outside the police station,

the custody officer shall cease in relation to that person to be subject to the duty imposed on him by subsection (1)(a) above; and it shall be the duty of the officer to whom the transfer is made to ensure that he is treated in accordance with the provisions of this Act and of any such codes of practice as are mentioned in subsection (1) above.

(3) If the person detained is subsequently returned to the custody of the custody officer, it shall be the duty of the officer investigating the offence to report to the custody officer as to the manner in which this section and the codes of practice have been complied with while that person was in his custody.

(4) If an arrested juvenile is moved to local authority accommodation under section 38(6) above, the custody officer shall cease in relation to the person to be subject to the duty imposed on him by subsection (1) above.

(5) [*Repealed.*]

(6) Where—

(a) an officer of higher rank than the custody officer gives directions relating to a person in police detention; and

(b) the directions are at variance—

    (i) with any decision made or action taken by the custody officer in the performance of a duty imposed on him under this Part of this Act; or

    (ii) with any decision or action which would but for the directions have been made or taken by him in the performance of such a duty,

the custody officer shall refer the matter at once to an officer of the rank of superintendent or above who is responsible for the police station for which the custody officer is acting as custody officer.

40. (1) Reviews of the detention of each person in police detention in connection with the investigation of an offence shall be carried out periodically in accordance with the following provisions of this section—

(a) in the case of a person who has been arrested and charged, by the custody officer; and

(b) in the case of a person who has been arrested but not charged, by an officer of at least the rank of inspector who has not been directly involved in the investigation.

(2) The officer to whom it falls to carry out a review is referred to in this section as a "review officer".

(3) Subject to subsection (4) below—

(a) the first review shall be not later than six hours after the detention was first authorised;

(b) the second review shall be not later than nine hours after the first;

(c) subsequent reviews shall be at intervals of not more than nine hours.

(4) A review may be postponed—

(a) if, having regard to all the circumstances prevailing at the latest time for it specified in subsection (3) above, it is not practicable to carry out the review at that time;

(b) without prejudice to the generality of paragraph (a) above—

(i) if at that time the person in detention is being questioned by a police officer and the review officer is satisfied that an interruption of the questioning for the purpose of carrying out the review would prejudice the investigation in connection with which he is being questioned; or

(ii) if at that time no review officer is readily available.

(5) If a review is postponed under subsection (4) above it shall be carried out as soon as practicable after the latest time specified for it in subsection (3) above.

(6) If a review is carried out after postponement under subsection (4) above, the fact that it was so carried out shall not affect any requirement of this section as to the time at which any subsequent review is to be carried out.

(7) The review officer shall record the reasons for any postponement of a review in the custody record.

(8) Subject to subsection (9) below, where the person whose detention is under review has not been charged before the time of the review, section 37(1) to (6) above shall have effect in relation to him, but with the substitution—

(a) of references to the person whose detention is under review for references to the person arrested; and

(b) of references to the review officer for references to the custody officer.

(9) Where a person has been kept in police detention by virtue of section 37(9) above, section 37(1) to (6) shall not have effect in relation to him but it shall be the duty of the review officer to determine whether he is yet in a fit state.

(10) Where the person whose detention is under review has been charged before the time of the review, section 38(1) to (6) above shall have effect in relation to him, but with the substitution of references to the person whose detention is under review for references to the person arrested.

(11) Where—

(a) an officer of higher rank than the review officer gives directions relating to a person in police detention; and

(b) the directions are at variance—

(i) with any decision made or action taken by the review officer in the performance of a duty imposed on him under this Part of this Act; or

(ii) with any decision or action which would but for the directions have been made or taken by him in the performance of such a duty,

the review officer shall refer the matter at once to an officer of the rank of superintendent or above who is responsible for the police station for which the review officer is acting as review officer in connection with the detention.

(12) Before determining whether to authorise a person's continued detention the review officer shall give—

(*a*) that person (unless he is asleep); or

(*b*) any solicitor representing him who is available at the time of the review,

an opportunity to make representations to him about the detention.

(13) Subject to subsection (14) below, the person whose detention is under review or his solicitor may make representations under subsection (12) above either orally or in writing.

(14) The review officer may refuse to hear oral representations from the person whose detention is under review if he considers that he is unfit to make such representations by reason of his condition or behaviour.

41. (1) Subject to the following provisions of this section and to sections 42 and 43 below, a person shall not be kept in police detention for more than 24 hours without being charged.

(2) The time from which the period of detention of a person is to be calculated (in this Act referred to as "the relevant time")—

(*a*) in the case of a person to whom this paragraph applies, shall be—

   (i) the time at which that person arrives at the relevant police station; or

   (ii) the time 24 hours after the time of that person's arrest,

  whichever is the earlier;

(*b*) in the case of a person arrested outside England and Wales, shall be—

   (i) the time at which that person arrives at the first police station to which he is taken in the police area in England or Wales in which the offence for which he was arrested is being investigated; or

   (ii) the time 24 hours after the time of that person's entry into England and Wales,

  whichever is the earlier;

(*c*) in the case of a person who—

   (i) attends voluntarily at a police station; or

   (ii) accompanies a constable to a police station without having been arrested,

  and is arrested at the police station, the time of his arrest;

(*d*) in any other case, except where subsection (5) below applies, shall be the time at which the person arrested arrives at the first police station to which he is taken after his arrest.

(3) Subsection (2)(*a*) above applies to a person if—

(*a*) his arrest is sought in one police area in England and Wales;

(*b*) he is arrested in another police area; and

(*c*) he is not questioned in the area in which he is arrested in order to obtain evidence in relation to an offence for which he is arrested;

and in sub-paragraph (i) of that paragraph "the relevant police station" means the first police station to which he is taken in the police area in which his arrest was sought.

(4) Subsection (2) above shall have effect in relation to a person arrested under section 31 above as if every reference in it to his arrest or his being arrested were a reference to his arrest or his being arrested for the offence for which he was originally arrested.

(5) If—

(*a*) a person is in police detention in a police area in England and Wales ("the first area"); and
(*b*) his arrest for an offence is sought in some other police area in England and Wales ("the second area"); and
(*c*) he is taken to the second area for the purposes of investigating that offence, without being questioned in the first area in order to obtain evidence in relation to it,
the relevant time shall be—
  (i) the time 24 hours after he leaves the place where he is detained in the first area; or
  (ii) the time at which he arrives at the first police station to which he is taken in the second area,
whichever is the earlier.
(6) When a person who is in police detention is removed to hospital because he is in need of medical treatment, any time during which he is being questioned in hospital or on the way there or back by a police officer for the purpose of obtaining evidence relating to an offence shall be included in any period which falls to be calculated for the purposes of this Part of this Act, but any other time while he is in hospital or on his way there or back shall not be so included.
(7) Subject to subsection (8) below, a person who at the expiry of 24 hours after the relevant time is in police detention and has not been charged shall be released at that time either on bail or without bail.
(8) Subsection (7) above does not apply to a person whose detention for more than 24 hours after the relevant time has been authorised or is otherwise permitted in accordance with section 42 or 43 below.
(9) A person released under subsection (7) above shall not be re-arrested without a warrant for the offence for which he was previously arrested unless new evidence justifying a further arrest has come to light since his release; but this subsection does not prevent an arrest under section 46A below.

42. (1) Where a police officer of the rank of superintendent or above who is responsible for the police station at which a person is detained has reasonable grounds for believing that—
  (*a*) the detention of that person without charge is necessary to secure or preserve evidence relating to an offence for which he is under arrest or to obtain such evidence by questioning him;
  (*b*) an offence for which he is under arrest is a serious arrestable offence; and
  (*c*) the investigation is being conducted diligently and expeditiously,
he may authorise the keeping of that person in police detention for a period expiring at or before 36 hours after the relevant time.
(2) Where an officer such as is mentioned in subsection (1) above has authorised the keeping of a person in police detention for a period expiring less than 36 hours after the relevant time, such an officer may authorise the keeping of that person in police detention for a further period expiring not more than 36 hours after that time if the conditions specified in subsection (1) above are still satisfied when he gives the authorisation.
(3) If it is proposed to transfer a person in police detention to another police area, the officer determining whether or not to authorise keeping him in detention under subsection (1) above shall have regard to the distance and the time the journey would take.

(4) No authorisation under subsection (1) above shall be given in respect of any person—

(a) more than 24 hours after the relevant time; or

(b) before the second review of his detention under section 40 above has been carried out.

(5) Where an officer authorises the keeping of a person in police detention under subsection (1) above, it shall be his duty—

(a) to inform that person of the grounds for his continued detention; and

(b) to record the grounds in that person's custody record.

(6) Before determining whether to authorise the keeping of a person in detention under subsection (1) or (2) above, an officer shall give—

(a) that person; or

(b) any solicitor representing him who is available at the time when it falls to the officer to determine whether to give the authorisation,

an opportunity to make representations to him about the detention.

(7) Subject to subsection (8) below, the person in detention or his solicitor may make representations under subsection (6) above either orally or in writing.

(8) The officer to whom it falls to determine whether to give the authorisation may refuse to hear oral representations from the person in detention if he considers that he is unfit to make such representations by reason of his condition or behaviour.

(9) Where—

(a) an officer authorises the keeping of a person in detention under subsection (1) above; and

(b) at the time of the authorisation he has not yet exercised a right conferred on him by section 56 or 58 below,

the officer—

(i) shall inform him of that right;

(ii) shall decide whether he should be permitted to exercise it;

(iii) shall record the decision in his custody record; and

(iv) if the decision is to refuse to permit the exercise of the right, shall also record the grounds for the decision in that record.

(10) Where an officer has authorised the keeping of a person who has not been charged in detention under subsection (1) or (2) above, he shall be released from detention, either on bail or without bail, not later than 36 hours after the relevant time, unless—

(a) he has been charged with an offence; or

(b) his continued detention is authorised or otherwise permitted in accordance with section 43 below.

(11) A person released under subsection (10) above shall not be re-arrested without a warrant for the offence for which he was previously arrested unless new evidence justifying a further arrest has come to light since his release; but this subsection does not prevent an arrest under section 46A below.

43. (1) Where, on an application on oath made by a constable and supported by an information, a magistrates' court is satisfied that there are reasonable grounds for believing that the further detention of the person to whom the application relates is justified, it may issue a warrant of further detention authorising the keeping of that person in police detention.

(2) A court may not hear an application for a warrant of further detention unless the person to whom the application relates—

(*a*) has been furnished with a copy of the information; and

(*b*) has been brought before the court for the hearing.

(3) The person to whom the application relates shall be entitled to be legally represented at the hearing and, if he is not so represented but wishes to be so represented—

(*a*) the court shall adjourn the hearing to enable him to obtain representation; and

(*b*) he may be kept in police detention during the adjournment.

(4) A person's further detention is only justified for the purposes of this section or section 44 below if—

(*a*) his detention without charge is necessary to secure or preserve evidence relating to an offence for which he is under arrest or to obtain such evidence by questioning him;

(*b*) an offence for which he is under arrest is a serious arrestable offence; and

(*c*) the investigation is being conducted diligently and expeditiously.

(5) Subject to subsection (7) below, an application for a warrant of further detention may be made—

(*a*) at any time before the expiry of 36 hours after the relevant time; or

(*b*) in a case where—

(i) it is not practicable for the magistrates' court to which the application will be made to sit at the expiry of 36 hours after the relevant time; but

(ii) the court will sit during the 6 hours following the end of that period,

at any time before the expiry of the said 6 hours.

(6) In a case to which subsection (5)(*b*) above applies—

(*a*) the person to whom the application relates may be kept in police detention until the application is heard; and

(*b*) the custody officer shall make a note in that person's custody record—

(i) of the fact that he was kept in police detention for more than 36 hours after the relevant time; and

(ii) of the reason why he was so kept.

(7) If—

(*a*) an application for a warrant of further detention is made after the expiry of 36 hours after the relevant time; and

(*b*) it appears to the magistrates' court that it would have been reasonable for the police to make it before the expiry of that period,

the court shall dismiss the application.

(8) Where on an application such as is mentioned in subsection (1) above a magistrates' court is not satisfied that there are reasonable grounds for believing that the further detention of the person to whom the application relates is justified, it shall be its duty—

(*a*) to refuse the application; or

(*b*) to adjourn the hearing of it until a time not later than 36 hours after the relevant time.

(9) The person to whom the application relates may be kept in police detention during the adjournment.

(10) A warrant of further detention shall—

(*a*) state the time at which it is issued;

(*b*) authorise the keeping in police detention of the person to whom it relates for the period stated in it.

(11) Subject to subsection (12) below, the period stated in a warrant of further

detention shall be such period as the magistrates' court thinks fit, having regard to the evidence before it.

(12) The period shall not be longer than 36 hours.

(13) If it is proposed to transfer a person in police detention to a police area other than that in which he is detained when the application for a warrant of further detention is made, the court hearing the application shall have regard to the distance and the time the journey would take.

(14) Any information submitted in support of an application under this section shall state—

(a) the nature of the offence for which the person to whom the application relates has been arrested;

(b) the general nature of the evidence on which that person was arrested;

(c) what inquiries relating to the offence have been made by the police and what further inquiries are proposed by them;

(d) the reasons for believing the continued detention of that person to be necessary for the purposes of such further inquiries.

(15) Where an application under this section is refused, the person to whom the application relates shall forthwith be charged or, subject to subsection (16) below, released, either on bail or without bail.

(16) A person need not be released under subsection (15) above—

(a) before the expiry of 24 hours after the relevant time; or

(b) before the expiry of any longer period for which his continued detention is or has been authorised under section 42 above.

(17) Where an application under this section is refused, no further application shall be made under this section in respect of the person to whom the refusal relates, unless supported by evidence which has come to light since the refusal.

(18) Where a warrant of further detention is issued, the person to whom it relates shall be released from police detention, either on bail or without bail, upon or before the expiry of the warrant unless he is charged.

(19) A person released under subsection (18) above shall not be re-arrested without a warrant for the offence for which he was previously arrested unless new evidence justifying a further arrest has come to light since his release; but this subsection does not prevent an arrest under section 46A below.

44. (1) On an application made by a constable and supported by an information a magistrates' court may extend a warrant of further detention issued under section 43 above if it is satisfied that there are reasonable grounds for believing that the further detention of the person to whom the application relates is justified.

(2) Subject to subsection (3) below, the period for which a warrant of further detention may be extended shall be such period as the court thinks fit, having regard to the evidence before it.

(3) The period shall not—

(a) be longer than 36 hours; or

(b) end later than 96 hours after the relevant time.

(4) Where a warrant of further detention has been extended under subsection (1) above, or further extended under this subsection, for a period ending before 96 hours after the relevant time, on an application such as is mentioned in that subsection a magistrates' court may further extend the warrant if it is satisfied as there mentioned; and subsections (2) and (3) above apply to such further extensions as they apply to extensions under subsection (1) above.

(5) A warrant of further detention shall, if extended or further extended under this section, be endorsed with a note of the period of the extension.

(6) Subsections (2), (3) and (14) of section 43 above shall apply to an application made under this section as they apply to an application made under that section.

(7) Where an application under this section is refused, the person to whom the application relates shall forthwith be charged or, subject to subsection (8) below, released, either on bail or without bail.

(8) A person need not be released under subsection (7) above before the expiry of any period for which a warrant of further detention issued in relation to him has been extended or further extended on an earlier application made under this section.

45. (1) In sections 43 and 44 of this Act "magistrates' court" means a court consisting of two or more justices of the peace sitting otherwise than in open court.

(2) Any reference in this Part of this Act to a period of time or a time of day is to be treated as approximate only.

Detention—miscellaneous

46. (1) Where a person—

(a) is charged with an offence; and

(b) after being charged—

    (i) is kept in police detention; or

    (ii) is detained by a local authority in pursuance of arrangements made under section 38(6) above,

he shall be brought before a magistrates' court in accordance with the provisions of this section.

(2) If he is to be brought before a magistrates' court for the petty sessions area in which the police station at which he was charged is situated, he shall be brought before such a court as soon as is practicable and in any event not later than the first sitting after he is charged with the offence.

(3) If no magistrates' court for that area is due to sit either on the day on which he is charged or on the next day, the custody officer for the police station at which he was charged shall inform the clerk to the justices for the area that there is a person in the area to whom subsection (2) above applies.

(4) If the person charged is to be brought before a magistrates' court for a petty sessions area other than that in which the police station at which he was charged is situated, he shall be removed to that area as soon as is practicable and brought before such a court as soon as is practicable after his arrival in the area and in any event not later than the first sitting of a magistrates' court for that area after his arrival in the area.

(5) If no magistrates' court for that area is due to sit either on the day on which he arrives in the area or on the next day—

(a) he shall be taken to a police station in the area; and

(b) the custody officer at that station shall inform the clerk to the justices for the area that there is a person in the area to whom subsection (4) applies.

(6) Subject to subsection (8) below, where a clerk to the justices for a petty sessions area has been informed—

(a) under subsection (3) above that there is a person in the area to whom subsection (2) above applies; or

(b) under subsection (5) above that there is a person in the area to whom subsection (4) above applies, the clerk shall arrange for a magistrates' court to sit not later than the day next following the relevant day.

(7) In this section "the relevant day"—

(a) in relation to a person who is to be brought before a magistrates' court for the petty sessions area in which the police station at which he was charged is situated, means the day on which he was charged; and

(b) in relation to a person who is to be brought before a magistrates' court for any other petty sessions area, means the day on which he arrives in the area.

(8) Where the day next following the relevant day is Christmas Day, Good Friday or a Sunday, the duty of the clerk under subsection (6) above is a duty to arrange for a magistrates' court to sit not later than the first day after the relevant day which is not one of those days.

(9) Nothing in this section requires a person who is in hospital to be brought before a court if he is not well enough.

46A. (1) A constable may arrest without a warrant any person who, having been released on bail under this Part of this Act subject to a duty to attend at a police station, fails to attend at that police station at the time appointed for him to do so.

(2) A person who is arrested under this section shall be taken to the police station appointed as the place at which he is to surrender to custody as soon as practicable after the arrest.

(3) For the purposes of—

(a) section 30 above (subject to the obligation in subsection (2) above), and

(b) section 31 above,

an arrest under this section shall be treated as an arrest for an offence.

47. (1) Subject to subsection (2) below, a release on bail of a person under this Part of this Act shall be a release on bail granted in accordance with sections 3, 3A, 5 and 5A of the Bail Act 1976 as they apply to bail granted by a constable.

(1A) The normal powers to impose conditions of bail shall be available to him where a custody officer releases a person on bail under section 38(1) above (including that subsection as applied by section 40(10) above) but not in any other cases.

In this subsection, "the normal powers to impose conditions of bail" has the meaning given in section 3(6) of the Bail Act 1976.

(2) Nothing in the Bail Act 1976 shall prevent the re-arrest without warrant of a person released on bail subject to a duty to attend at a police station if new evidence justifying a further arrest has come to light since his release.

(3) Subject to subsection (4) below, in this Part of this Act references to "bail" are references to bail subject to a duty—

(a) to appear before a magistrates' court at such time and such place; or

(b) to attend at such police station at such time,

as the custody officer may appoint.

(4) Where a custody officer has granted bail to a person subject to a duty to appear at a police station, the custody officer may give notice in writing to that person that his attendance at the police station is not required.

(5) [*Repealed.*]

(6) Where a person who has granted bail and either has attended at the police station in accordance with the grant of bail or has been arrested under section 46A above is detained at a police station, any time during which he was in police

detention prior to being granted bail shall be included as part of any period which falls to be calculated under this Part of this Act.

(7) Where a person who was released on bail subject to a duty to attend at a police station is re-arrested, the provisions of this Part of this Act shall apply to him as they apply to a person arrested for the first time; but this subsection does not apply to a person who is arrested under section 46A above or has attended a police station in accordance with the grant of bail (and who accordingly is deemed by section 34(7) above to have been arrested for an offence).

(8) In the Magistrates' Courts Act 1980—

(*a*) the following section shall be substituted for section 43—

"43. (1) Where a person has been granted bail under the Police and Criminal Evidence Act 1984 subject to a duty to appear before a magistrates' court, the court before which he is to appear may appoint a later time as the time at which he is to appear and may enlarge the recognizances of any sureties for him at that time.

(2) The recognizance of any surety for any person granted bail subject to a duty to attend at a police station may be enforced as if it were conditioned for his appearance before a magistrates' court for the petty sessions area in which the police station named in the recognizance is situated."; and

(*b*) the following subsection shall be substituted for section 117(3)—

"(3) Where a warrant has been endorsed for bail under subsection (1) above—

(*a*) where the person arrested is to be released on bail on his entering into a recognizance without sureties, it shall not be necessary to take him to a police station, but if he is so taken, he shall be released from custody on his entering into the recognizance; and

(*b*) where he is to be released on his entering into a recognizance with sureties, he shall be taken to a police station on his arrest, and the custody officer there shall (subject to his approving any surety tendered in compliance with the endorsement) release him from custody as directed in the endorsement."

48. In section 128 of the Magistrates' Courts Act 1980—

(*a*) in subsection (7) for the words "custody of a constable" there shall be substituted the words "detention at a police station";

(*b*) after subsection (7) there shall be inserted the following subsection—

"(8) Where a person is committed to detention at a police station under subsection (7) above—

(*a*) he shall not be kept in such detention unless there is a need for him to be so detained for the purposes of inquiries into other offences;

(*b*) if kept in such detention, he shall be brought back before the magistrates' court which committed him as soon as that need ceases;

(*c*) he shall be treated as a person in police detention to whom the duties under section 39 of the Police and Criminal Evidence Act 1984 (responsibilities in relation to persons detained) relate;

(*d*) his detention shall be subject to periodic review at the times set out in section 40 of that Act (review of police detention).".

49. (1) In subsection (1) of section 67 of the Criminal Justice Act 1967 (computation of custodial sentences) for the words from "period", in the first place where it occurs, to "the offender" there shall be substituted the words "relevant period, but where he".

(2) The following subsection shall be inserted after that subsection—

"(1A) In subsection (1) above "relevant period" means—

(a) any period during which the offender was in police detention in connection with the offence for which the sentence was passed; or

(b) any period during which he was in custody—

(i) by reason only of having been committed to custody by an order of a court made in connection with any proceedings relating to that sentence or the offence for which it was passed or any proceedings from which those proceedings arose; or

(ii) by reason of his having been so committed and having been concurrently detained otherwise than by order of a court.".

(3) The following subsections shall be added after subsection (6) of that section—

"(7) A person is in police detention for the purposes of this section—

(a) at any time when he is in police detention for the purposes of the Police and Criminal Evidence Act 1984; and

(b) at any time when he is detained under section 12 of the Prevention of Terrorism (Temporary Provisions) Act 1984.

(8) No period of police detention shall be taken into account under this section unless it falls after the coming into force of section 49 of the Police and Criminal Evidence Act 1984."

50. (1) Each police force shall keep written records showing on an annual basis—

(a) the number of persons kept in police detention for more than 24 hours and subsequently released without charge;

(b) the number of applications for warrants of further detention and the results of the applications; and

(c) in relation to each warrant of further detention—

(i) the period of further detention authorised by it;

(ii) the period which the person named in it spent in police detention on its authority; and

(iii) whether he was charged or released without charge.

(2) Every annual report—

(a) under section 12 of the Police Act 1964; or

(b) made by the Commissioner of Police of the Metropolis,

shall contain information about the matters mentioned in subsection (1) above in respect of the period to which the report relates.

51. Nothing in this Part of this Act shall affect—

(a) the powers conferred on immigration officers by section 4 of and Schedule 2 to the Immigration Act 1971 (administrative provisions as to control on entry etc);

(b) the powers conferred by or by virtue of section 14 of the Prevention of Terrorism (Temporary Provisions) Act 1989 or Schedule 2 or 5 to that Act (powers of arrest and detention and control of entry and procedure for removal);

(c) any duty of a police officer under—

(i) section 129, 190 or 202 of the Army Act 1955 (duties of governors of prisons and others to receive prisoners, deserters, absentees and persons under escort);

(ii) section 129, 190 or 202 of the Air Force Act 1955 (duties of governors of prisons and others to receive prisoners, deserters, absentees and persons under escort);

(iii) section 107 of the Naval Discipline Act 1957 (duties of governors of civil prisons etc); or

(iv) paragraph 5 of Schedule 5 to the Reserve Forces Act 1980 (duties of governors of civil prisons); or

(d) any right of a person in police detention to apply for a writ of habeas corpus or other prerogative remedy.

52. [*Repealed.*]

PART V
QUESTIONING AND TREATMENT OF PERSONS BY POLICE

53. (1) Subject to subsection (2) below, there shall cease to have effect any Act (including a local Act) passed before this Act in so far as it authorises—

(a) any search by a constable of a person in police detention at a police station; or

(b) an intimate search of a person by a constable;

and any rule of common law which authorises a search such as is mentioned in paragraph (a) or (b) above is abolished.

(2) [*Repealed.*]

54. (1) The custody officer at a police station shall ascertain and record or cause to be recorded everything which a person has with him when he is—

(a) brought to the station after being arrested elsewhere or after being committed to custody by an order or sentence of a court; or

(b) arrested at the station or detained there, as a person falling within section 34(7), under section 37 above.

(2) In the case of an arrested person the record shall be made as part of his custody record.

(3) Subject to subsection (4) below, a custody officer may seize and retain any such thing or cause any such thing to be seized and retained.

(4) Clothes and personal effects may only be seized if the custody officer—

(a) believes that the person from whom they are seized may use them—

(i) to cause physical injury to himself or any other person;

(ii) to damage property;

(iii) to interfere with evidence; or

(iv) to assist him to escape; or

(b) has reasonable grounds for believing that they may be evidence relating to an offence.

(5) Where anything is seized, the person from whom it is seized shall be told the reason for the seizure unless he is—

(a) violent of likely to become violent; or

(b) incapable of understanding what is said to him.

(6) Subject to subsection (7) below, a person may be searched if the custody officer considers it necessary to enable him to carry out his duty under subsection (1) above and to the extent that the custody officer considers necessary for that purpose.

(6A) A person who is in custody at a police station or is in police detention otherwise than at a police station may at any time be searched in order to ascertain whether he has with him anything which he could use for any of the purposes specified in subsection (4)(*a*) above.

(6B) Subject to subsection (6C) below, a constable may seize and retain, or cause to be seized and retained, anything found on such a search.

(6C) A constable may only seize clothes and personal effects in the circumstances specified in subsection (4) above.

(7) An intimate search may not be conducted under this section.

(8) A search under this section shall be carried out by a constable.

(9) The constable carrying out a search shall be of the same sex as the person searched.

55. (1) Subject to the following provisions of this section, if an officer of at least the rank of superintendent has reasonable grounds for believing—

(*a*) that a person who has been arrested and is in police detention may have concealed on him anything which—
   (i) he could use to cause physical injury to himself or others; and
   (ii) he might so use while he is in police detention or in the custody of a court; or
(*b*) that such person—
   (i) may have a Class A drug concealed on him; and
   (ii) was in possession of it with the appropriate criminal intent before his arrest,

he may authorise an intimate search of that person.

(2) An officer may not authorise an intimate search of a person for anything unless he has reasonable grounds for believing that it cannot be found without his being intimately searched.

(3) An officer may give an authorisation under subsection (1) above orally or in writing but, if he gives it orally, he shall confirm it in writing as soon as is practicable.

(4) An intimate search which is only a drug offence search shall be by way of examination by a suitably qualified person.

(5) Except as provided by subsection (4) above, an intimate search shall be by way of examination by a suitably qualified person unless an officer of at least the rank of superintendent considers that this is not practicable.

(6) An intimate search which is not carried out as mentioned in subsection (5) above shall be carried out by a constable.

(7) A constable may not carry out an intimate search of a person of the opposite sex.

(8) No intimate search may be carried out except—

(*a*) at a police station;
(*b*) at a hospital;
(*c*) at a registered medical practitioner's surgery; or
(*d*) at some other place used for medical purposes.

(9) An intimate search which is only a drug offence search may not be carried out at a police station.

(10) If an intimate search of a person is carried out, the custody record relating to him shall state—

(*a*) which parts of his body were searched; and
(*b*) why they were searched.

(11) The information required to be recorded by subsection (10) above shall be recorded as soon as practicable after the completion of the search.

(12) The custody officer at a police station may seize and retain anything which is found on an intimate search of a person, or cause any such thing to be seized and retained—

(a) if he believes that the person from whom it is seized may use it—
  (i) to cause physical injury to himself or any other person;
  (ii) to damage property;
  (iii) to interfere with evidence; or
  (iv) to assist him to escape; or

(b) if he has reasonable grounds for believing that it may be evidence relating to an offence.

(13) Where anything is seized under this section, the person from whom it is seized shall be told the reason for the seizure unless he is—

(a) violent or likely to become violent; or

(b) incapable of understanding what is said to him.

(14) Every annual report—

(a) under section 12 of the Police Act 1964; or

(b) made by the Commissioner of Police of the Metropolis, shall contain information about searches under this section which have been carried out in the area to which the report relates during the period to which it relates.

(15) The information about such searches shall include!

(a) the total number of searches;

(b) the number of searches conduced by way of examination by a suitably qualified person;

(c) the number of searches not so conducted but conducted in the presence of such a person; and

(d) the result of the searches carried out.

(16) The information shall also include, as separate items—

(a) the total number of drug offence searches; and

(b) the result of those searches.

(17) In this section—

"the appropriate criminal intent" means an intent to commit an offence under—

  (a) section 5(3) of the Misuse of Drugs Act 1971 (possession of controlled drug with intent to supply to another); or

  (b) section 68(2) of the Customs and Excise Management Act 1979 (exportation etc with intent to evade a prohibition or restriction);

"Class A drug" has the meaning assigned to it by section 2(1)(b) of the Misuse of Drugs Act 1971;

"drug offence search" means an intimate search for a Class A drug which an officer has authorised by virtue of subsection (1)(b) above; and

"suitably qualified person" means—

  (a) a registered medical practitioner; or

  (b) a registered nurse.

56. (1) When a person has been arrested and is being held in custody in a police station or other premises, he shall be entitled, if he so requests, to have one friend or relative or other person who is known to him or who is likely to take an interest in his welfare told, as soon as is practicable except to the extent that delay is permitted by this section, that he has been arrested and is being detained there.

(2) Delay is only permitted—

(a) in the case of a person who is in police detention for a serious arrestable offence; and

(b) if an officer of at least the rank of superintendent authorises it.

(3) In any case the person in custody must be permitted to exercise the right conferred by subsection (1) above within 36 hours from the relevant time, as defined in section 41(2) above.

(4) An officer may give an authorisation under subsection (2) above orally or in writing but, if he gives it orally, he shall confirm it in writing as soon as is practicable.

(5) Subject to subsection (5A) below an officer may only authorise delay where he has reasonable grounds for believing that telling the named person of the arrest—

(a) will lead to interference with or harm to evidence connected with a serious arrestable offence or interference with or physical injury to other persons; or

(b) will lead to the alerting of other persons suspected of having committed such an offence but not yet arrested for it; or

(c) will hinder the recovery or any property obtained as a result of such an offence.

(5A) An officer may also authorise delay where the serious arrestable offence is a drug trafficking offence or an offence to which Part VI of the Criminal Justice Act 1988 applies (offences in respect of which confiscation orders under that Part may be made) and the officer has reasonable grounds for believing—

(a) where the offence is a drug trafficking offence, that the detained person has benefited from drug trafficking and that the revovery of the value of that person's proceeds of drug trafficking will be hindered by telling the named person of the arrest; and

(b) where the offence is one to which Part VI of the Criminal Justice Act 1988 applies, that the detained person has benefited from the offence and that the recovery of the value of the property obtained by that person from or in connection with the offence or of the pecuniary advantage derived by him from or in connection with it will be hindered by telling the named person of the arrest.

(6) If a delay is authorised—

(a) the detained person shall be told the reason for it; and

(b) the reason shall be noted on his custody record.

(7) The duties imposed by subsection (6) above shall be performed as soon as is practicable.

(8) The rights conferred by this section on a person detained at a police station or other premises are exercisable whenever he is transferred from one place to another; and this section applies to each subsequent occasion on which they are exercisable as it applies to the first such occasion.

(9) There may be no further delay in permitting the exercise of the right conferred by subsection (1) above once the reason for authorising delay ceases to subsist.

(10) In the foregoing provisions of this section references to a person who has been arrested include references to a person who has been detained under the terrorism provisions and "arrest" includes detention under those provisions.

(11) In its application to a person who has been arrested or detained under the terrorism provisions—

(a) subsection (2)(a) above shall have effect as if for the words "for a serious arrestable offence" there were substituted the words "under the terrorism provisions";

(b) subsection (3) above shall have effect as if for the words from "within" onwards there were substituted the words "before the end of the period beyond which he may no longer be detained without the authority of the Secretary of State"; and

(c) subsection (5) above shall have effect as if at the end there were added "or

(d) will lead to interference with the gathering of information about the commission, preparation or instigation of acts of terrorism; or

(e) by alerting any person, will make it more difficult—

(i) to prevent an act of terrorism; or

(ii) to secure the apprehension, prosecution or conviction of any person in connection with the commission, preparation or instigation of an act of terrorism."

57. The following subsections shall be substituted for section 34(2) of the Children and Young Persons Act 1933—

"(2) Where a child or young person is in police detention, such steps as are practicable shall be taken to ascertain the identity of a person responsible for his welfare.

(3) If it is practicable to ascertain the identity of a person responsible for the welfare of the child or young person, that person shall be informed, unless it is not practicable to do so—

(a) that the child or young person has been arrested;

(b) why he has been arrested; and

(c) where he is being detained.

(4) Where information falls to be given under subsection (3) above, it shall be given as soon as it is practicable to do so.

(5) For the purposes of this section the persons who may be responsible for the welfare of a child or young person are—

(a) his parent or guardian; or

(b) any other person who has for the time being assumed responsibility for his welfare.

(6) If it is practicable to give a person responsible for the welfare of the child or young person the information required by subsection (3) above, that person shall be given it as soon as it is practicable to do so.

(7) If it appears that at the time of his arrest a supervision order, as defined in section 11 of the Children and Young Persons Act 1969, is in force in respect of him, the person responsible for his supervision shall also be informed as described in subsection (3) above as soon as it is reasonably practicable to do so.

(8) The reference to a parent or guardian in subsection (5) above is—

(a) in the case of a child or young person in the care of a local authority, a reference to that authority; and

(b) in the case of a child or young person in the care of a voluntary organisation in which parental rights and duties with respect to him are vested by virtue of a resolution under section 64(1) of the Child Care Act 1980, a reference to that organisation.

(9) The rights conferred on a child or young person by subsections (2) to (8) above are in addition to his rights under section 56 of the Police and Criminal Evidence Act 1984.

(10) The reference in subsection (2) above to a child or young person who is in police detention includes a reference to a child or young person who has been detained under the terrorism provisions; and in subsection (3) above 'arrest' includes such detention.

(11) In subsection (10) above 'the terrorism provisions' has the meaning assigned to it by section 65 of the Police and Criminal Evidence Act 1984."

58. (1) A person arrested and held in custody in a police station or other premises shall be entitled, if he so requests, to consult a solicitor privately at any time.

(2) Subject to subsection (3) below, a request under subsection (1) above and the time at which it was made shall be recorded in the custody record.

(3) Such a request need not be recorded in the custody record of a person who makes it at a time while he is at a court after being charged with an offence.

(4) If a person makes such a request, he must be permitted to consult a solicitor as soon as is practicable except to the extent that delay is permitted by this section.

(5) In any case he must be permitted to consult a solicitor within 36 hours from the relevant time, as defined in section 41(2) above.

(6) Delay in compliance with a request is only permitted—

(*a*) in the case of a person who is in police detention for a serious arrestable offence; and

(*b*) if an officer of at least the rank of superintendent authorises it.

(7) An officer may give an authorisation under subsection (6) above orally or in writing but, if he gives it orally, he shall confirm it in writing as soon as is practicable.

(8) Subject to subsection (8A) below an officer may only authorise delay where he has reasonable grounds for believing that the exercise of the right conferred by subsection (1) above at the time when the person detained desires to exercise it—

(*a*) will lead to interference with or harm to evidence connected with a serious arrestable offence or interference with or physical injury to other persons; or

(*b*) will lead to the alerting of other persons suspected of having committed such an offence but not yet arrested for it; or

(*c*) will hinder the recovery of any property obtained as a result of such an offence.

(8A) An officer may also authorise delay where the serious arrestable offence is a drug trafficking offence or an offence to which Part VI of the Criminal Justice Act 1988 applies and the officer has reasonable grounds for believing—

(*a*) where the offence is a drug trafficking offence, that the detained person has benefited from drug trafficking and that the recovery of the value of that person's proceeds of drug trafficking will be hindered by the exercise of the right conferred by subsection (1) above; and

(*b*) where the offence is one to which Part VI of the Criminal Justice Act 1988 applies, that the detained person has benefited from the offence and that the recovery of the value of the property obtained by that person from or in connection with the offence or of the pecuniary advantage derived by him from or in connection with it will be hindered by the exercise of the right conferred by subsection (1) above.

(9) If delay is authorised—

(*a*) the detained person shall be told the reason for it; and

(*b*) the reason shall be noted on his custody record.

(10) The duties imposed by subsection (9) above shall be performed as soon as is practicable.

(11) There may be no further delay in permitting the exercise of the right conferred by subsection (1) above once the reason for authorising delay ceases to subsist.

(12) The reference in subsection (1) above to a person arrested includes a reference to a person who has been detained under the terrorism provisions.

(13) In the application of this section to a person who has been arrested or detained under the terrorism provisions—

   (a) subsection (5) above shall have effect as if for the words from 'within' onwards there were substituted the words 'before the end of the period beyond which he may no longer be detained without the authority of the Secretary of State';

   (b) subsection (6)(a) above shall have effect as if for the words 'for a serious arrestable offence' there were substituted the words 'under the terrorism provisions'; and

   (c) subsection (8) above shall have effect as if at the end there were added 'or

   (d) will lead to interference with the gathering of information about the commission, preparation or instigation of acts of terrorism; or

   (e) by alerting any person, will make it more difficult—

      (i) to prevent an act of terrorism; or

      (ii) to secure the apprehension, prosecution or conviction of any person in connection with the commission, preparation or instigation of an act of terrorism.'

(14) If an officer of appropriate rank has reasonable grounds for believing that, unless he gives a direction under subsection (15) below, the exercise by a person arrested or detained under the terrorism provisions of the right conferred by subsection (1) above will have any of the consequences specified in subsection (8) above (as it has effect by virtue of subsection (13) above), he may give a direction under that subsection.

(15) A direction under this subsection is a direction that a person desiring to exercise the right conferred by subsection (1) above may only consult a solicitor in the sight and hearing of a qualified officer of the uniformed branch of the force of which the officer giving the direction is a member.

(16) An officer is qualified for the purpose of subsection (15) above if—

   (a) he is of at least the rank of inspector; and

   (b) in the opinion of the officer giving the direction he has no connection with the case.

(17) An officer is of appropriate rank to give a direction under subsection (15) above if he is of at least the rank of Commander or Assistant Chief Constable.

(18) A direction under subsection (15) above shall cease to have effect once the reason for giving it ceases to subsist.

59. [*Repealed*.]

60. (1) It shall be the duty of the Secretary of State—

   (a) to issue a code of practice in connection with the tape-recording of interviews of persons suspected of the commission of criminal offences which are held by police officers at police stations; and

   (b) to make an order requiring the tape-recording of interviews of persons suspected of the commission of criminal offences, or of such descriptions of criminal offences as may be specified in the order, which are so held, in accordance with the code as it has effect for the time being.

(2) An order under subsection (1) above shall be made by statutory instrument and shall be subject to annulment in pursuance of a resolution of either House of Parliament.

61. (1) Except as provided by this section no person's fingerprints may be taken without the appropriate consent.

(2) Consent to the taking of a person's fingerprints must be in writing if it is given at a time when he is at a police station.

(3) The fingerprints of a person detained at a police station may be taken without the appropriate consent—

(a) if an officer of at least the rank of superintendent authorises them to be taken; or

(b) if—
  (i) he has been charged with a recordable offence or informed that he will be reported for such an offence; and
  (ii) he has not had his fingerprints taken in the course of the investigation of the offence by the police.

(4) An officer may only give an authorisation under subsection (3)(a) above if he has reasonable grounds—

(a) for suspecting the involvement of the person whose fingerprints are to be taken in a criminal offence; and

(b) for believing that his fingerprints will tend to confirm or disprove his involvement.

(5) An officer may give an authorisation under subsection (3)(a) above orally or in writing but, if he gives it orally, he shall confirm it in writing as soon as is practicable.

(6) Any person's fingerprints may be taken without the appropriate consent if he has been convicted of a recordable offence.

(7) In a case where by virtue of subsection (3) or (6) above a person's fingerprints are taken without the appropriate consent—

(a) he shall be told the reason before his fingerprints are taken; and

(b) the reason shall be recorded as soon as is practicable after the fingerprints are taken.

(7A) If a person's fingerprints are taken at a police station, whether with or without the appropriate consent—

(a) before the fingerprints are taken, an officer shall inform him that they may be the subject of a speculative search; and

(b) the fact that the person has been informed of this possibility shall be recorded as soon as is practicable after the fingerprints have been taken.

(8) If he is detained at a police station when the fingerprints are taken, the reason for taking them and, in the case falling within subsection (7A) above, the fact referred to in paragraph (b) of that subsection shall be recorded on his custody record.

(9) Nothing in this section—

(a) affects any power conferred by paragraph 18(2) of Schedule 2 to the Immigration Act 1971; or

(b) except as provided in section 15(10) of, and paragraph 7(6) of Schedule 5 to, the Prevention of Terrorism (Temporary Provisions) Act 1989, applies to a person arrested or detained under the terrorism provisions.

62. (1) An intimate sample may be taken from a person in police detention only—
   (a) if a police officer of at least the rank of superintendent authorises it to be taken; and
   (b) if the appropriate consent is given.

(1A) An intimate sample may be taken from a person who is not in police detention but from whom, in the course of the investigation of an offence two or more non-intimate samples suitable for the same means of analysis have been taken which have proved insufficient—
   (a) if a police officer of at least the rank of superintendent authorises it to be taken; and
   (b) if the appropriate consent is given.

(2) An officer may only give an authorisation under subsection (1) or (1A) above if he has reasonable grounds—
   (a) for suspecting the involvement of the person from whom the sample is to be taken in a recordable offence; and
   (b) for believing that the sample will tend to confirm or disprove his involvement.

(3) An officer may give an authorisation under subsection (1) or (1A) above orally or in writing but, if he gives it orally, he shall confirm it in writing as soon as is practicable.

(4) The appropriate consent must be given in writing.

(5) Where—
   (a) an authorisation has been given; and
   (b) it is proposed that an intimate sample shall be taken in pursuance of the authorisation,
an officer shall inform the person from whom the sample is to be taken—
   (i) of the giving of the authorisation; and
   (ii) of the grounds for giving it.

(6) The duty imposed by subsection (5)(ii) above includes a duty to state the nature of the offence in which it is suspected that the person from whom the sample is to be taken has been involved.

(7) If an intimate sample is taken from a person—
   (a) the authorisation by virtue of which it was taken;
   (b) the grounds for giving the authorisation; and
   (c) the fact that the appropriate consent was given,
shall be recorded as soon as is practicable after the sample is taken.

(7A) If an intimate sample is taken from a person at a police station—
   (a) before the sample is taken, an officer shall inform him that it may be the subject of a speculative search; and
   (b) the fact that the person has been informed of this possibility shall be recorded as soon as practicable after the sample has been taken.

(8) If an intimate sample is taken from a person detained at a police station, the matters required to be recorded by subsection (7) or (7A) above shall be recorded in his custody record.

(9) An intimate sample, other than a sample of urine or a dental impression, may only be taken from a person by a registered medical practitioner and a dental impression may only be taken by a registered dentist.

(10) Where the appropriate consent to the taking of an intimate sample from a person was refused without good cause, in any proceedings against that person for an offence—

(a) the court, in determining—
    (i) whether to grant an application for dismissal made by that person under section 6 of the Magistrates' Courts Act 1980 (application for dismissal of charge in course of proceedings with a view to transfer for trial); or
    (ii) whether there is a case to answer; and

(aa) a judge, in deciding whether to grant an application made by the accused under—
    (i) section 6 of the Criminal Justice Act 1987 (application for dismissal of charge of serious fraud in respect of which notice of transfer has been given under section 4 of that Act); or
    (ii) paragraph 5 of Schedule 6 to the Criminal Justice Act 1991 (application for dismissal of charge of violent or sexual offence involving child in respect of which notice of transfer has been given under section 53 of that Act); and

(b) the court or jury, in determining whether that person is guilty of the offence charged,

may draw such inferences from the refusal as appear proper.

(11) Nothing in this section affects sections 4 to 11 of the Road Traffic Act 1988.

(12) Nothing in this section, except as provided in section 15(11) and (12) of, and paragraph 7(6A) and (6B) of Schedule 5 to, the Prevention of Terrorism (Temporary Provisions) Act 1989, applies to a person arrested or detained under the terrorism provisions.

63. (1) Except as provided by this section, a non-intimate sample may not be taken from a person without the appropriate consent.

(2) Consent to the taking of a non-intimate sample must be given in writing.

(3) A non-intimate sample may be taken from a person without the appropriate consent if—

(a) he is in police detention or is being held in custody by the police on the authority of a court; and

(b) an officer of at least the rank of superintendent authorises it to be taken without the appropriate consent.

(3A) A non-intimate sample may be taken from a person (whether or not he falls within subsection (3)(a) above) without the appropriate consent if—

(a) he has been charged with a recordable offence or informed that he will be reported for such an offence; and

(b) either he has not had a non-intimate sample taken from him in the course of the investigation of the offence by the police or he has had a non-intimate sample taken from him but either it was not suitable for the same means of analysis or, though so suitable, the sample proved insufficient.

(3B) A non-intimate sample may be taken from a person without the appropriate consent if he has been convicted of a recordable offence.

(4) An officer may only give an authorisation under subsection (3) above if he has reasonable grounds—

(a) for suspecting the involvement of the person from whom the sample is to be taken in a recordable offence; and

(b) for believing that the sample will tend to confirm or disprove his involvement.

(5) An officer may give an authorisation under subsection (3) above orally or in writing but, if he gives it orally, he shall confirm it in writing as soon as is practicable.

(6) Where—

(a) an authorisation has been given; and

(b) it is proposed that a non-intimate sample shall be taken in pursuance of the authorisation,

an officer shall inform the person from whom the sample is to be taken—

(i) of the giving of the authorisation; and

(ii) of the grounds for giving it.

(7) The duty imposed by subsection (6)(ii) above includes a duty to state the nature of the offence in which it is suspected that the person from whom the sample is to be taken has been involved.

(8) If a non-intimate sample is taken from a person by virtue of subsection (3) above—

(a) the authorisation by virtue of which it was taken; and

(b) the grounds for giving the authorisation,

shall be recorded as soon as is practicable after the sample is taken.

(8A) In a case where by virtue of subsection (3A) or (3B) a sample is taken from a person without the appropriate consent—

(a) he shall be told the reason before the sample is taken; and

(b) the reason shall be recorded as soon as practicable after the sample is taken.

(8B) If a non-intimate sample is taken from a person at a police station, whether with or without the appropriate consent—

(a) before the sample is taken, an officer shall inform him that it may be the subject of a speculative search; and

(b) the fact that the person has been informed of this possibility shall be recorded as soon as practicable after the sample has been taken.

(9) If a non-intimate sample is taken from a person detained at a police station, the matters required to be recorded by subsection (8) or (8A) or (8B) above shall be recorded in his custody record.

(10)* Subsection (3B) above shall not apply to persons convicted before the date on which that subsection comes into force.

(10)* Nothing in this section, except as provided in section 15(13) and (14) of, and paragraphs 7(6C) and (6D) of Schedule 5 to, the Prevention of Terrorism (Temporary Provisions) Act 1989, applies to a person arrested or detained under the terrorism provisions.

  *Note that two subsections (10) have been inadvertently inserted into s63, the first by s55(6) and the second by Sch 10 para 62 of the Criminal Justice and Public Order Act 1994.

63A. (1) Fingerprints or samples or the information derived from samples taken under any power conferred by this Part of this Act from a person who has been arrested on suspicion of being involved in a recordable offence may be checked against other fingerprints or samples or the information derived from other samples contained in records held by or on behalf of the police or held in connection with or as a result of an investigation of an offence.

(2) Where a sample of hair other than pubic hair is to be taken the sample may

be taken either by cutting hairs or by plucking hairs with their roots so long as no more are plucked than the person taking the sample reasonably considers to be necessary for a sufficient sample.

(3) Where any power to take a sample is exercisable in relation to a person the sample may be taken in a prison or other institution to which the Prison Act 1952 applies.

(4) Any constable may, within the allowed period, require a person who is neither in police detention nor held in custody by the police on the authority of a court to attend a police station in order to have a sample taken where—

(a) the person has been charged with a recordable offence or informed that he will be reported for such an offence and either he has not had a sample taken from him in the course of the investigation of the offence by the police or he has had a sample so taken from him but either it was not suitable for the same means of analysis or, though so suitable, the sample proved insufficient; or

(b) the person has been convicted of a recordable offence and either he has not had a sample taken from him since the conviction or he has had a sample taken from him (before or after his conviction) but either it was not suitable for the same means of analysis or, though so suitable, the sample proved insufficient.

(5) The period allowed for requiring a person to attend a police station for the purpose specified in subsection (4) above is—

(a) in the case of a person falling within paragraph (a), one month beginning with the date of the charge or one month beginning with the date on which the appropriate officer is informed of the fact that the sample is not suitable for the same means of analysis or has proved insufficient, as the case may be;

(b) in the case of a person falling within paragraph (b), one month beginning with the date of the conviction or one month beginning with the date on which the appropriate officer is informed of the fact that the sample is not suitable for the same means of analysis or has proved insufficient, as the case may be.

(6) A requirement under subsection (4) above—

(a) shall give the person at least 7 days within which he must so attend; and

(b) may direct him to attend at a specified time of day or between specified times of day.

(7) Any constable may arrest without a warrant a person who has failed to comply with a requirement under subsection (4) above.

(8) In this section "the appropriate officer" is—

(a) in the case of a person falling within subsection (4)(a), the officer investigating the offence with which that person has been charged or as to which he was informed that he would be reported;

(b) in the case of a person falling within subsection (4)(b), the officer in charge of the police station from which the investigation of the offence of which he was convicted was conducted.

64. (1) If—

(a) fingerprints or samples are taken from a person in connection with the investigation of an offence; and

(b) he is cleared of that offence,

they must, except as provided in subsection (3A) below, be destroyed as soon as is practicable after the conclusion of the proceedings.

(2) If—

(a) fingerprints or samples are taken from a person in connection with such an investigation; and

(b) it is decided that he shall not be prosecuted for the offence and he has not admitted it and been dealt with by way of being cautioned by a constable,

they must, except as provided in subsection (3A) below, be destroyed as soon as is practicable after that decision is taken.

(3) If—

(a) fingerprints or samples are taken from a person in connection with the investigation of an offence; and

(b) that person is not suspected of having committed the offence,

they must, except as provided in subsection (3A) below, be destroyed as soon as they have fulfilled the purpose for which they were taken.

(3A) Samples which are required to be destroyed under subsection (1), (2) or (3) above need not be destroyed if they were taken for the purpose of the same investigation of an offence of which a person from whom one was taken has been convicted, but the information derived from the sample of any person entitled (apart from this subsection) to its destruction under subsection (1), (2) or (3) above shall not be used—

(a) in evidence against the person so entitled; or

(b) for the purposes of any investigation of an offence.

(3B) Where samples are required to be destroyed under subsections (1), (2) or (3) above, and subsection (3A) above does not apply, information derived from the sample of any person entitled to its destruction under subsection (1), (2) or (3) above shall not be used—

(a) in evidence against the person so entitled; or

(b) for the purposes of any investigation of an offence.

(4) Proceedings which are discontinued are to be treated as concluded for the purposes of this section.

(5) If fingerprints are destroyed—

(a) any copies of the fingerprints shall also be destroyed; and

(b) any chief officer of police controlling access to computer data relating to the fingerprints shall make access to the data impossible, as soon as it is practicable to do so.

(6) A person who asks to be allowed to witness the destruction of his fingerprints or copies of them shall have a right to witness it.

(6A) If—

(a) subsection (5)(b) above fails to be complied with; and

(b) the person to whose fingerprints the data relate asks for a certificate that it has been complied with,

such a certificate shall be issued to him, not later than the end of the period of three months beginning with the day on which he asks for it, by the responsible chief officer of police or a person authorised by him or on his behalf for the purposes of this section.

(6B) In this section—

"chief officer of police" means the chief officer of police for an area mentioned in Schedule 8 to the Police Act 1964; and

"the responsible chief officer of police" means the chief officer of police in whose area the computer data were put on to the computer.

(7) Nothing in this section—
(a) affects any power conferred by paragraph 18(2) of Schedule 2 to the Immigration Act 1971; or
(b) applies to a person arrested or detained under the terrorism provisions.

65. In this Part of this Act—
"appropriate consent" means—
(a) in relation to a person who has attained the age of 17 years, the consent of that person;
(b) in relation to a person who has not attained that age but has attained the age of 14 years, the consent of that person and his parent or guardian; and
(c) in relation to a person who has not attained the age of 14 years, the consent of his parent or guardian;
"drug trafficking" and "drug trafficking offence" have the same meaning as in the Drug Trafficking Act 1994;
"fingerprints" includes palm prints;
"intimate sample" means
(a) a sample of blood, semen or any other tissue fluid, urine or pubic hair;
(b) a dental impression;
(c) a swab taken from a person's body orifice other than the mouth;
"intimate search" means a search which consists of the physical examination of a person's body orifices other than the mouth;
"non-intimate sample" means—
(a) a sample of hair other than pubic hair;
(b) a sample taken from a nail or from under a nail;
(c) a swab taken from any part of a person's body including the mouth but not any other body orifice;
(d) saliva;
(e) a footprint or a similar impression of any part of a person's body other than a part of his hand.
"registered dentist" has the same meaning as in the Dentists Act 1984;
"speculative search", in relation to a person's fingerprints or samples, means such a check against other fingerprints or samples or against information derived from other samples as is referred to in section 63A(1) above;
"sufficient" and "insufficient", in relation to a sample, means sufficient or insufficient (in point of quantity or quality) for the purpose of enabling information to be produced by the means of analysis used or to be used in relation to the sample.
"the terrorism provisions" means section 14(1) of the Prevention of Terrorism (Temporary Provisions) Act 1989; and any provision of Schedule 2 or 5 to that Act conferring a power of arrest or detention; and
"terrorism" has the meaning assigned to it by section 20(1) of that Act,
references in this Part to any person's proceeds of drug trafficking are to be construed in accordance with the Drug Trafficking Act 1994.

PART VI
CODES OF PRACTICE—GENERAL

66. The Secretary of State shall issue codes of practice in connection with—
(a) the exercise by police officers of statutory powers—

  (i) to search a person without first arresting him; or
  (ii) to search a vehicle without making an arrest;
(b) the detention, treatment, questioning and identification of persons by police officers;
(c) searches of premises by police officers; and
(d) the seizure of property found by police officers on persons or premises.

67. (1) When the Secretary of State proposes to issue a code of practice to which this section applies, he shall prepare and publish a draft of that code, shall consider any representations made to him about the draft and may modify the draft accordingly.

(2) This section applies to a code of practice under section 60 or 66 above.

(3) The Secretary of State shall lay before both Houses of Parliament a draft of any code of practice prepared by him under this section.

(4) When the Secretary of State has laid the draft of a code before Parliament, he may bring the code into operation by order made by statutory instrument.

(5) No order under subsection (4) above shall have effect until approved by a resolution of each House of Parliament.

(6) An order bringing a code of practice into operation may contain such transitional provisions or savings as appear to the Secretary of State to be necessary or expedient in connection with the code of practice thereby brought into operation.

(7) The Secretary of State may from time to time revise the whole or any part of a code of practice to which this section applies and issue that revised code; and the foregoing provisions of this section shall apply (with appropriate modifications) to such a revised code as they apply to the first issue of a code.

(8) [*Repealed.*]

(9) Persons other than police officers who are charged with the duty of investigating offences or charging offenders shall in the discharge of that duty have regard to any relevant provision of such a code.

(10) A failure on the part—
(a) of a police officer to comply with any provision of such a code; or
(b) of any person other than a police officer who is charged with the duty of investigating offences or charging offenders to have regard to any relevant provision of such a code in the discharge of that duty,
shall not of itself render him liable to any criminal or civil proceedings.

(11) In all criminal and civil proceedings any such code shall be admissible in evidence, and if any provision of such a code appears to the court or tribunal conducting the proceedings to be relevant to any question arising in the proceedings, it shall be taken into account in determining that question.

(12) In this section "criminal proceedings" includes—
(a) proceedings in the United Kingdom or elsewhere before a court-martial constituted under the Army Act 1955, or the Air Force Act 1955, or the Naval Discipline Act 1957 or a disciplinary court constituted under section 50 of the said Act of 1957;
(b) proceedings before the Courts-Martial Appeal Court; and
(c) proceedings before a standing civilian court.

PART VII
DOCUMENTARY EVIDENCE IN CRIMINAL PROCEEDINGS

68. [*Repealed.*]

69. (1) In any proceedings, a statement in a document produced by a computer shall not be admissible as evidence of any fact stated therein unless it is shown—
 (*a*) that there are no reasonable grounds for believing that the statement is inaccurate because of improper use of the computer;
 (*b*) that at all material times the computer was operating properly, or if not, that any respect in which it was not operating properly or was out of operation was not such as to affect the production of the document or the accuracy of its contents; and
 (*c*) that any relevant conditions specified in rules of court under subsection (2) below are satisfied.

(2) Provision may be made by rules of court requiring that in any proceedings where it is desired to give a statement in evidence by virtue of this section such information concerning the statement as may be required by the rules shall be provided in such form and at such time as may be so required.

70. (1) Part I of Schedule 3 to this Act shall have effect for the purpose of supplementing section 68 above.

(2) Part II of that Schedule shall have effect for the purpose of supplementing section 69 above.

(3) Part III of that Schedule shall have effect for the purpose of supplementing both sections.

71. In any proceedings the contents of a document may (whether or not the document is still in existence) be proved by the production of an enlargement of a microfilm copy of that document or of the material part of it, authenticated in such manner as the court may approve.

72. (1) In this Part of this Act—
"copy" and "statement" have the same meanings as in Part I of the Civil Evidence Act 1968; and
"proceedings" means criminal proceedings, including—
 (*a*) proceedings in the United Kingdom or elsewhere before a court-martial constituted under the Army Act 1955 or the Air Force Act 1955;
 (*b*) proceedings in the United Kingdom or elsewhere before the Courts-Martial Appeal Court—
  (i) on an appeal from a court-martial so constituted or from a court-martial constituted under the Naval Discipline Act 1957; or
  (ii) on a reference under section 34 of the Courts-Martial (Appeals) Act 1968; and
 (*c*) proceedings before a Standing Civilian Court.

(2) Nothing in this Part of this Act shall prejudice any power of a court to exclude evidence (whether by preventing questions from being put or otherwise) at its discretion.

PART VIII
EVIDENCE IN CRIMINAL PROCEEDINGS—GENERAL

Convictions and acquittals

73. (1) Where in any proceedings the fact that a person has in the United Kingdom been convicted or acquitted of an offence otherwise than by a Service court is admissible in evidence, it may be proved by producing a certificate of conviction or, as the case may be, of acquittal relating to that offence, and proving that the person named in the certificate as having been convicted or acquitted of the offence is the person whose conviction or acquittal of the offence is to be proved.

(2) For the purposes of this section a certificate of conviction or of acquittal—

(a) shall, as regards a conviction or acquittal on indictment, consist of a certificate, signed by the clerk of the court where the conviction or acquittal took place, giving the substance and effect (omitting the formal parts) of the indictment and of the conviction or acquittal; and

(b) shall, as regards a conviction or acquittal on a summary trial, consist of a copy of the conviction or of the dismissal of the information, signed by the clerk of the court where the conviction or acquittal took place or by the clerk of the court, if any, to which a memorandum of the conviction or acquittal was sent;

and a document purporting to be a duly signed certificate of conviction or acquittal under this section shall be taken to be such a certificate unless the contrary is proved.

(3) References in this section to the clerk of a court include references to his deputy and to any other person having the custody of the court record.

(4) The method of proving a conviction or acquittal authorised by this section shall be in addition to and not to the exclusion of any other authorised manner of proving a conviction or acquittal.

74. (1) In any proceedings the fact that a person other than the accused has been convicted of an offence by or before any court in the United Kingdom or by a Service court outside the United Kingdom shall be admissible in evidence for the purpose of proving, where to do so is relevant to any issue in those proceedings, that that person committed that offence, whether or not any other evidence of his having committed that offence is given.

(2) In any proceedings in which by virtue of this section a person other than the accused is proved to have been convicted of an offence by or before any court in the United Kingdom or by a Service court outside the United Kingdom, he shall be taken to have committed that offence unless the contrary is proved.

(3) In any proceedings where evidence is admissible of the fact that the accused has committed an offence, in so far as that evidence is relevant to any matter in issue in the proceedings for a reason other than a tendency to show in the accused a disposition to commit the kind of offence with which he is charged, if the accused is proved to have been convicted of the offence—

(a) by or before any court in the United Kingdom; or

(b) by a Service court outside the United Kingdom,

he shall be taken to have committed that offence unless the contrary is proved.

(4) Nothing in this section shall prejudice—

(a) the admissibility in evidence of any conviction which would be admissible apart from this section; or

(b) the operation of any enactment whereby a conviction or a finding of fact in any proceedings is for the purposes of any other proceedings made conclusive evidence of any fact.

75. (1) Where evidence that a person has been convicted of an offence is admissible by virtue of section 74 above, then without prejudice to the reception of any other admissible evidence for the purpose of identifying the facts on which the conviction was based—

(a) the contents of any document which is admissible as evidence of the conviction; and

(b) the contents of the information, complaint, indictment or charge-sheet on which the person in question was convicted,

shall be admissible in evidence for that purpose.

(2) Where in any proceedings the contents of any document are admissible in evidence by virtue of subsection (1) above, a copy of that document, or of the material part of it, purporting to be certified or otherwise authenticated by or on behalf of the court or authority having custody of that document shall be admissible in evidence and shall be taken to be a true copy of that document or part unless the contrary is shown.

(3) Nothing in any of the following—

(a) section 13 of the Powers of Criminal Courts Act 1973 (under which a conviction leading to probation or discharge is to be disregarded except as mentioned in that section);

(b) section 392 of the Criminal Procedure (Scotland) Act 1975 (which makes similar provision in respect of convictions on indictment in Scotland); and

(c) section 8 of the Probation Act (Northern Ireland) 1950 (which corresponds to section 13 of the Powers of Criminal Courts Act 1973) or any legislation which is in force in Northern Ireland for the time being and corresponds to that section,

shall affect the operation of section 74 above; and for the purposes of that section any order made by a court of summary jurisdiction in Scotland under section 182 or section 183 of the said Act 1975 shall be treated as a conviction.

(4) Nothing in section 74 above shall be construed as rendering admissible in any proceedings evidence of any conviction other than a subsisting one.

Confessions

76. (1) In any proceedings a confession made by an accused person may be given in evidence against him in so far as it is relevant to any matter in issue in the proceedings and is not excluded by the court in pursuance of this section.

(2) If, in any proceedings where the prosecution proposes to give in evidence a confession made by an accused person, it is represented to the court that the confession was or may have been obtained—

(a) by oppression of the person who made it; or

(b) in consequence of anything said or done which was likely, in the circumstances existing at the time, to render unreliable any confession which might be made by him in consequence thereof,

the court shall not allow the confession to be given in evidence against him except in so far as the prosecution proves to the court beyond reasonable doubt that the confession (notwithstanding that it may be true) was not obtained as aforesaid.

(3) In any proceedings where the prosecution proposes to give in evidence a confession made by an accused person, the court may of its own motion require

the prosecution, as a condition of allowing it to do so, to prove that the confession was not obtained as mentioned in subsection (2) above.

(4) The fact that a confession is wholly or partly excluded in pursuance of this section shall not affect the admissibility in evidence—

(a) of any facts discovered as a result of the confession; or

(b) where the confession is relevant as showing that the accused speaks, writes or expresses himself in a particular way, of so much of the confession as is necessary to show that he does so.

(5) Evidence that a fact to which this subsection applies was discovered as a result of a statement made by an accused person shall not be admissible unless evidence of how it was discovered is given by him or on his behalf.

(6) Subsection (5) above applies—

(a) to any fact discovered as a result of a confession which is wholly excluded in pursuance of this section; and

(b) to any fact discovered as a result of a confession which is partly so excluded, if the fact is discovered as a result of the excluded part of the confession.

(7) Nothing in Part VII of this Act shall prejudice the admissibility of a confession made by an accused person.

(8) In this section "oppression" includes torture, inhuman or degrading treatment, and the use or threat of violence (whether or not amounting to torture).

77. (1) Without prejudice to the general duty of the court at a trial on indictment to direct the jury on any matter on which it appears to the court appropriate to do so, where at such a trial—

(a) the case against the accused depends wholly or substantially on a confession by him; and

(b) the court is satisfied—

(i) that he is mentally handicapped; and

(ii) that the confession was not made in the presence of an independent person,

the court shall warn the jury that there is special need for caution before convicting the accused in reliance on the confession, and shall explain that the need arises because of the circumstances mentioned in paragraphs (a) and (b) above.

(2) In any case where at the summary trial of a person for an offence it appears to the court that a warning under subsection (1) above would be required if the trial were on indictment, the court shall treat the case as one in which there is a special need for caution before convicting the accused on his confession.

(3) In this section—

"independent person" does not include a police officer or a person employed for, or engaged on, police purposes;

"mentally handicapped", in relation to a person, means that he is in a state of arrested or incomplete development of mind which includes significant impairment of intelligence and social functioning; and

"police purposes" has the meaning assigned to it by section 64 of the Police Act 1964.

Miscellaneous

78. (1) In any proceedings the court may refuse to allow evidence on which the prosecution proposes to rely to be given if it appears to the court that, having regard to all the circumstances, including the circumstances in which the evidence was obtained, the admission of the evidence would have such an adverse effect on

the fairness of the proceedings that the court ought not to admit it.

(2) Nothing in this section shall prejudice any rule of law requiring a court to exclude evidence.

79. If at the trial of any person for an offence—

   (a) the defence intends to call two or more witnesses to the facts of the case; and

   (b) those witnesses include the accused,

the accused shall be called before the other witness or witnesses unless the court in its discretion otherwise directs.

80. (1) In any proceedings the wife or husband of the accused shall be competent to give evidence—

   (a) subject to subsection (4) below, for the prosecution; and

   (b) on behalf of the accused or any person jointly charged with the accused.

(2) In any proceedings the wife or husband of the accused shall, subject to subsection (4) below, be compellable to give evidence on behalf of the accused.

(3) In any proceedings the wife or husband of the accused shall, subject to subsection (4) below, be compellable to give evidence for the prosecution or on behalf of any person jointly charged with the accused if and only if—

   (a) the offence charged involves an assault on, or injury or a threat of injury to, the wife or husband of the accused or a person who was at the material time under the age of 16; or

   (b) the offence charged is a sexual offence alleged to have been committed in respect of a person who was at the material time under that age; or

   (c) the offence charged consists of attempting or conspiring to commit, or of aiding, abetting, counselling, procuring or inciting the commission of, an offence falling within paragraph (a) or (b) above.

(4) Where a husband and wife are jointly charged with an offence neither spouse shall at the trial be competent or compellable by virtue of subsection (1)(a), (2) or (3) above to give evidence in respect of that offence unless that spouse is not, or is no longer, liable to be convicted of that offence at the trial as a result of pleading guilty or for any other reason.

(5) In any proceedings a person who has been but is no longer married to the accused shall be competent and compellable to give evidence as if that person and the accused had never been married.

(6) Where in any proceedings the age of any person at any time is material for the purposes of subsection (3) above, his age at the material time shall for the purposes of that provision be deemed to be or to have been that which appears to the court to be or to have been his age at that time.

(7) In subsection (3)(b) above "sexual offence" means an offence under the Sexual Offences Act 1956, the Indecency with Children Act 1960, the Sexual Offences Act 1967, section 54 of the Criminal Law Act 1977 or the Protection of Children Act 1978.

(8) The failure of the wife or husband of the accused to give evidence shall not be made the subject of any comment by the prosecution.

(9) Section 1(d) of the Criminal Evidence Act 1898 (communications between husband and wife) and section 43(1) of the Matrimonial Causes Act 1965 (evidence as to marital intercourse) shall cease to have effect.

81. (1) Crown Court Rules may make provision for—

   (a) requiring any party to proceedings before the court to disclose to the other party or parties any expert evidence which he proposes to adduce in the proceedings; and

(b) prohibiting a party who fails to comply in respect of any evidence with any requirement imposed by virtue of paragraph (a) above from adducing that evidence without the leave of the court.

(2) Crown Court Rules made by virtue of this section may specify the kinds of expert evidence to which they apply and may exempt facts or matters of any description specified in the rules.

PART VIII
SUPPLEMENTARY

82. (1) In this part of this Act—

"confession" includes any statement wholly or partly adverse to the person who made it, whether made to a person in authority or not and whether made in words or otherwise;

"court-martial" means a court-martial constituted under the Army Act 1955, the Air Force Act 1955 or the Naval Discipline Act 1957 or a disciplinary court constituted under section 50 of the said Act of 1957;

"proceedings" means criminal proceedings, including—

(a) proceedings in the United Kingdom or elsewhere before a court-martial constituted under the Army Act 1955 or the Air Force Act 1955;

(b) proceedings in the United Kingdom or elsewhere before the Courts-Martial Appeal Court—

(i) on an appeal from a court-martial so constituted or from a court-martial constituted under the Naval Discipline Act 1957; or

(ii) on a reference under section 34 of the Courts-Martial (Appeals) Act 1968; and

(c) proceedings before a Standing Civilian Court; and

"Service court" means a court-martial or a Standing Civilian Court.

(2) In this Part of this Act references to conviction before a Service court are references—

(a) as regards a court-martial constituted under the Army Act 1955 or the Air Force Act 1955, to a finding of guilty which is, or falls to be treated as, a finding of the court duly confirmed;

(b) as regards—

(i) a court-martial; or

(ii) a disciplinary court,

constituted under the Naval Discipline Act 1957, to a finding of guilty which is, or falls to be treated, as the finding of the court;

and "convicted" shall be construed accordingly.

(3) Nothing in this Part of this Act shall prejudice any power of a court to exclude evidence (whether by preventing questions from being put or otherwise) at its discretion.

PART IX
POLICE COMPLAINTS AND DISCIPLINE

The Police Complaints Authority

83. (1) There shall be an authority to be known as "the Police Complaints Authority" and in this part of this Act referred to as "the Authority."

(2) Schedule 4 to this Act shall have effect in relation to the Authority.

(3) The Police Complaints Board is hereby abolished.

Handling of complaints etc.

84. (1) Where a complaint is submitted to the chief officer of police for a police area, it shall be his duty to take any steps that appear to him to be desirable for the purpose of obtaining or preserving evidence relating to the conduct complained of.

(2) After performing the duties imposed on him by subsection (1) above, the chief officer shall determine whether he is the appropriate authority in relation to the officer against whom the complaint was made.

(3) If he determines that he is not the appropriate authority, it shall be his duty—

(a) to send the complaint or, if it was made orally, particulars of it, to the appropriate authority; and

(b) to give notice that he has done so to the person by or on whose behalf the complaint was made.

(4) In this part of this Act—

"complaint" means any complaint about the conduct of a police officer which is submitted—

(a) by a member of the public; or

(b) on behalf of a member of the public and with his written consent;

"the appropriate authority" means—

(a) in relation to an officer of the metropolitan police, the Commissioner of Police of the Metropolis; and

(b) in relation to an officer of any other police force—

(i) if he is a senior officer, the police authority for the force's area; and

(ii) if he is not a senior officer, the chief officer of the force;

"senior officer" means an officer holding a rank above the rank of superintendent;

"discliplinary proceedings" means proceedings identified as such by regulations under section 33 of the Police Act 1964.

(5) Nothing in this Part of the Act has effect in relation to a complaint in so far as it relates to the direction or control of a police force by the chief officer or the person performing the functions of the chief officer.

(6) If any conduct to which a complaint wholly or partly relates is or has been the subject of criminal or disciplinary proceedings, none of the provisions of this Part of this Act which relate to the recording and investigation of complaints have effect in relation to the complaint in so far as it relates to that conduct.

85. (1) If a chief officer determines that he is the appropriate authority in relation to an officer about whose conduct a complaint has been made and who is not a senior officer, he shall record it.

(2) After doing so he shall consider whether the complaint is suitable for informal resolution and may appoint an officer from his force to assist him.

(3) If it appears to the chief officer that the complaint is not suitable for informal resolution, he shall appoint an officer from his force or some other force to investigate it formally.

(4) If it appears to him that it is suitable for informal resolution, he shall seek to resolve it informally and may appoint an officer from his force to do so on his behalf.

(5) If it appears to the chief officer, after attempts have been made to resolve a complaint informally—

(a) that informal resolution of the complaint is impossible; or

(b) that the complaint is for any other reason not suitable for informal resolution,

he shall appoint an officer from his force or some other force to investigate it formally.

(6) An officer may not be appointed to investigate a complaint formally if he has previously been appointed to act in relation to it under subsection (4) above.

(7) If a chief officer requests the chief officer of some other force to provide an officer of his force for appointment under subsection (3) or (5) above, that chief officer shall provide an officer to be so appointed.

(8) [*Repealed by the Police and Magistrates' Court Act 1994 ss 44, 93, Sch 5, Pt II, para 25, Sch 9, Pt I.*]

(9) Unless the investigation is supervised by the Authority under section 89 below, the investigating officer shall submit his report on the investigation to the chief officer.

(10) A complaint is not suitable for informal resolution unless—

(a) the member of the public concerned gives his consent; and

(b) the chief officer is satisfied that the conduct complained of, even if proved, would not justify criminal or disciplinary proceedings.

86. (1) Where a complaint about the conduct of a senior officer—

(a) is submitted to the appropriate auithority; or

(b) is sent to the appropriate authority under section 84(3) above,

it shall be the appropriate authority's duty to record it and, subject to subsection (2) below, to investigate it.

(2) The appropriate authority may deal with the complaint according to the appropriate authority's discretion, if satisfied that the conduct complained of, even if proved, would not justify criminal or disciplinary proceedings.

(3) In any other case the appropriate authority shall appoint an officer from the appropriate authority's force or from some other force to investigate the complaint.

(4) A chief officer shall provide an officer to be appointed, if a request is made to him for one to be appointed under subsection (3) above.

(5) No officer may be appointed unless he is of at least the rank of the officer against whom the complaint is made.

(6) Unless an investigation under this section is supervised by the Authority under section 89 below, the investigating officer shall submit his report on it to the appropriate authority.

87. (1) The appropriate authority—

(a) shall refer to the Authority—

(i) any complaint alleging that the conduct complained of resulted in the death of or serious injury to some other person; and

(ii) any complaint of a description specified for the purposes of this section in regulations made by the Secretary of State; and

(b) may refer to the Authority any complaint which is not required to be refered to them.

(2) The Authority may require the submission to them for consideration of any complaint not referred to them by the appropriate authority; and it shall be the

appropriate authority's duty to comply with any such requirement not later than the end of a period specified in regulations made by the Secretary of State.

(3) Where a complaint falls to be referred to the Authority under subsection (1)(*a*) above, it shall be the appropriate authority's duty to refer it to them not later than the end of a period specified in such regulations.

(4) In this Part of this Act "serious injury" means a fracture, damage to an internal organ, impairment of bodily function, a deep cut or a deep laceration.

88. The appropriate authority may refer to the Authority any matter which—

(*a*) appears to the appropriate authority to indicate that an officer may have committed a criminal offence or behaved in a manner which would justify disciplinary proceedings; and

(*b*) is not the subject of a complaint,

if it appears to the appropriate authority that it ought to be referred by reason—

   (i) of its gravity; or

   (ii) of exceptional circumstances.

89. (1) The Authority shall supervise the investigation—

(*a*) of any complaint alleging that the conduct of a police officer resulted in the death of or serious injury to some other person; and

(*b*) of any other descriptions of complaint specified for the purposes of this section in regulations made by the Secretary of State.

(2) The Authority shall supervise the investigation—

(*a*) of any complaint the investigation of which they are not required to supervise under subsection (1) above; and

(*b*) of any matter referred to them under section 88 above,

if they consider that it is desirable in the public interest that they should supervise that investigation.

(3) Where the Authority have made a determination under this section, it shall be their duty to notify it to the appropriate authority.

(4) Where an investigation is to be supervised by the Authority they may require—

(*a*) that no appointment shall be made under section 85(3) or 86(3) above unless they have given notice to the appropriate authority that they approve the officer whom that authority propose to appoint or;

(*b*) if such an appointment has already been made and the Authority are not satisfied with the officer appointed, that—

   (i) the appropriate authority shall, as soon as is reasonably practicable, select another officer and notify the Authority that they propose to appoint him; and

   (ii) the appointment shall not be made unless the Authority give notice to the appropriate authority that they approve that officer.

(5) It shall be the duty of the Secretary of State by regulations to provide that the Authority shall have power, subject to any restrictions or conditions specified in the regulations, to impose requirements as to a particular investigation additional to any requirements imposed by virtue of subsection (4) above; and it shall be the duty of a police officer to comply with any requirement imposed on him by virtue of the regulations.

(6) At the end of an investigation which the Authority have supervised the investigating officer—

(*a*) shall submit a report on the investigation to the Authority; and

(*b*) shall send a copy to the appropriate authority.

(7) After considering a report submitted to them under subsection (6) above, the Authority shall submit an appropriate statement to the appropriate authority.

(8) If it is practicable to do so, the Authority, when submitting the appropriate statement under subsection (7) above, shall send a copy to the officer whose conduct has been investigated.

(9) If—

(*a*) the investigation related to a complaint; and

(*b*) it is practicable to do so,

the Authority shall also send a copy of the appropriate statement to the person by or on behalf of whom the complaint was made.

(10) In subsection (7) above "appropriate statement" means a statement—

(*a*) whether the investigation was or was not conducted to the Authority's satisfaction;

(*b*) specifying any respect in which it was not so conducted; and

(*c*) dealing with any such other matters as the Secretary of State may be regulations provide.

(11) The power to issue an appropriate statement includes power to issue separate statements in respect of the disciplinary and criminal aspects of an investigation.

(12) No discliplinary proceedings shall be brought before the appropriate statement is submitted to the appropriate authority.

(13) Subject to subsection (14) below, neither the appropriate authority nor the Director of Public Prosecutions shall bring criminal proceedings before the appropriate statement is submitted to the appropriate authority.

(14) The restriction imposed by subsection (13) above does not apply if it appears to the Director that there are exceptional circumstances which make it undesirable to wait for the submission of the appropriate statement.

90. (1) It shall be the duty of the appropriate authority, on receiving—

(*a*) a report concerning the conduct of a senior officer which is submitted to them under section 86(6) above; or

(*b*) a copy of a report concerning the conduct of a senior officer which is sent to them under section 89(6) above,

to send a copy of the report to the Director of Public Prosecutions unless the report satisfies them that no criminal offence has been committed.

(2) Nothing in the following provisions of this section or in sections 91 to 94 below has effect in relation to senior officers.

(3) On receiving—

(*a*) a report concerning the conduct of an officer who is not a senior officer which is submitted to him under section 85(9) above; or

(*b*) a copy of a report concerning the conduct of such an officer which is sent to him under section 89(6) above

it shall be the duty of a chief officer of police—

(i) to determine whether the report indicates that a criminal offence may have been committed by a member of the police force for his area.

(4) If the chief officer—

(*a*) determines that the report does indicate that a criminal offence may have been committed by a member of the police force for his area, he shall send a copy of the report to the Director of Public Prosecutions.

(5) In such cases as may be prescribed by regulations made by the Secretary of State, after the Director has dealt with the question of criminal proceedings, the chief officer shall send the Authority a memorandum, signed by him and stating whether he has brought (or proposes to bring) disciplinary proceedings in respect of the conduct which was the subject of the investigation and, if not, giving his reasons.

(6) [*Repealed by the Police and Magistrates' Court Act 1994 ss 35, 93, Sch 9, Pt I.*]

(7) In such cases as may be prescribed by regulations made by the Secretary of State, if the chief officer considers that the report does not indicate that a criminal offence may have been committed by a member of the police force for his area, he shall send the Authority a memorandum to that effect, signed by him and stating whether he has brought (or proposes to bring) disciplinary proceedings in respect of the conduct which was the subject of the investigation and, if not, giving his reasons.

(8) [*Repealed by the Police and Magistrates' Court Act 1994 ss 35, 93, Sch 9, Pt I.*]

(9) Where the investigation—

(a) related to conduct which was the subject of a complaint; and

(b) was not supervised by the Authority.

then, if the chief officer is required by virtue of regulations under subsection (5) or (7) above to send the Authority a memorandum, he shall at the same time send them a copy of the complaint, or of the record of the complaint, and a copy of the report of the investigation.

(10) Subject to section 93(6) below—

(a) if a chief officer's memorandum states that he proposes to bring disciplinary proceedings, it shall be his duty to bring and proceed with them; and

(b) if such a memorandum states that he has brought such proceedings, it shall be his duty to proceed with them.

91. [*Repealed by the Police and Magistrates' Court Act 1994 ss 44, 93, Sch 5, Pt II, para 28, Sch 9, Pt I.*]

92. [*Repealed by the Police and Magistrates' Court Act 1994 ss 37(b), 93, Sch 9, Pt. I*]

93. (1) Where a memorandum under section 90 above states that a chief officer of police has not brought disciplinary proceedings or does not propose to do so, the Authority may recommend him to bring such proceedings.

(2) Subject to subsection (6) below, a chief officer may not discontinue disciplinary proceedings that he has brought in accordance with a recommendation under subsection (1) above.

(3) If after the Authority has made a recommendation under this section and consulted the chief officer he is still unwilling to bring disciplinary proceedings, they may direct him to do so.

(4) Where the Authority gives a chief officer a direction under this section, they shall furnish him with a written statement of their reasons for doing so.

(5) Subject to subsection (6) below, it shall be the duty of a chief officer to comply with such a direction.

(6) The Authority may withdraw a direction under this section.

(7) A chief officer shall—

(a) advise the Authority of what action he has taken in response to a recommendation or direction under this section, and

(b) furnish the Authority with such other information as they may reasonably require for the purpose of discharging their functions under this section.

94. [*Repealed by the Police and Magistrates' Court Act 1994 ss 37(c), 93, Sch 9, Pt I.*]

95. Every police authority in carrying out their duty with respect to the maintenance of an efficient and effective police force, and inspectors of constabulary in carrying out their duties with respect to the efficiency and effectiveness of any police force, shall keep themselves informed as to the working of sections 84 to 93 above in relation to the force.

96. (1) An agreement for the establishment in relation to any body of constables maintained by an authority other than a police authority of procedures corresponding or similar to any of those established by or by virtue of this Part of this Act may, with the approval of the Secretary of State, be made between the Authority and the authority maintaining the body of constables.

(2) Where no such procedures are in force in relation to any body of constables, the Secretary of State may by order establish such procedures.

(3) An agreement under this section may at any time be varied or terminated with the approval of the Secretary of State.

(4) Before making an order under this section the Secretary of State shall consult—

(a) the Authority; and

(b) the authority maintaining the body of constables to whom the order would relate.

(5) The power to make orders under this section shall be exercisable by statutory instrument; and any statutory instrument containing such an order shall be subject to annulment in pursuance of a resolution of either House of Parliament.

(6) Nothing in any other enactment shall prevent an authority who maintain a body of constables from carrying into effect procedures established by virtue of this section.

(7) No such procedures shall have effect in relation to anything done by a constable outside England and Wales.

97. (1) The Authority shall, at the request of the Secretary of State, report to him on such matters relating generally to their functions as the Secretary of State may specify, and the Authority may for that purpose carry out research into any such matters.

(2) The Authority may make a report to the Secretary of State on any matters coming to their notice under this Part of this Act to which they consider that his attention should be drawn by reason of their gravity or of other exceptional circumstances; and the Authority shall send a copy of any such report to the police authority and to the chief officer of police of any police force which appears to the Authority to be concerned or, if the report concerns any such body of constables as is mentioned in section 96 above, to the authority maintaining it and the officer having the direction and the control of it.

(3) As soon as practicable after the end of each calendar year the Authority shall make to the Secretary of State a report on the discharge of their functions during that year.

(4) [*Repealed by the Police and Magistrates' Court Act 1994 ss 37(d), 93, Sch 9, Pt I.*]

(5) The Secretary of State shall lay before Parliament a copy of every report received by him under this section and shall cause every such report to be published.

(6) The Authority shall send to every police authority—

(a) a copy of every report made by the Authority under subsection (3) above; and

(b) any statistical or other general information which relates to the year dealt with by the report and to the area of that authority and which the Authority consider should be brought to the police authority's attention in connection with their functions under section 95 above.

98. (1) No information received by the Authority in connection with any of their functions under sections 84 to 97 above or regulations made by virtue of section 99 below shall be disclosed by any person who is or has been a member, officer or servant of the Authority except—

(a) to the Secretary of State or to a member, officer or servant of the Authority or, so far as may be necessary for the proper discharge of the functions of the Authority, to other persons;

(b) for the purposes of any criminal, civil or disciplinary proceedings; or

(c) in the form of a summary or other general statement made by the Authority which does not identify the person from whom the information was received or any person to whom it relates.

(2) Any person who discloses information in contravention of this section shall be guilty of an offence and liable on summary conviction to a fine of an amount not exceeding level 5 on the standard scale . . .

99. (1) The Secretery of State may make regulations as to the procedure to be followed under this Part of this Act.

(2) It shall be the duty of the Secretary of State to provide by regulations—

(a) that, subject to such exceptions as may be specified by the regulations, a chief officer of police shall furnish, in accordance with such procedure as may be so specified, a copy of, or of the record of, a complaint against a member of the police force for his area—

(i) to the person by or on behalf of whom the complaint was made; and

(ii) to the officer against whom it was made;

(b) procedures for the informal resolution of complaints of such descriptions as may be specified in the regulations, and for giving the person who made the complaint a record of the outcome of any such procedure if he applies for one within such period as the regulations may provide;

(c) procedures for giving a police officer against whom a complaint is made which falls to be resolved informally an opportunity to comment orally or in writing on the complaint;

(d) for cases in which any provision of this Part of this Act is not to apply where a complaint, other than a complaint which falls to be resolved by an informal procedure, is withdrawn or the complainant indicates that he does not wish any further steps to be taken;

(e) for enabling the Authority to dispense with any requirement of this Part of this Act;

(ea) for enabling the Authority to relinquish the supervision of the investigation of any complaint or other matter;

(f) procedures for the reference or submission of complaints or other matters to the Authority;

(g) for the time within which the Authority are to give a notification under section 89(3) above;

(h) that the Authority shall be supplied with such information or documents of such description as may be so specified in the regulations at such time or in such circumstances as may be so specified;

(j) that any action or decision of the Authority which they take in consequence of their receipt of a memorandum under section 90 above shall be notified if it is an action or decision of a description specified in the regulations, to the person concerned and that, in connection with such a notification, the Authority shall have power to furnish him with any relevant information;

(k) that chief officers of police shall have power to delegate any functions conferred on them by or by virtue of the foregoing provisions of this Part of this Act.

100. (1) Regulations under this Part of this Act may make different provision for different circumstances and may authorise the Secretary of State to make provision for any purposes specified in the regulations.

(2) Before making regulations under this Part of this Act, the Secretary of State shall furnish a draft of the regulations to the Police Advisory Board for England and Wales and take into consideration any representations made by that Board.

(3) Any power to make regulations under this Part of this Act shall be exercisable by statutory instrument.

(4) Subject to subsection (5) below, regulations under this Part of this Act shall be subject to annulment in pursuance of a resolution of either House of Parliament.

(5) Regulations to which this subsection applies shall not be made unless a draft of them has been approved by resolution of each House of Parliament.

(6) Subsection (5) above applies to regulations made by virtue—

(a) of section 90(5) or (7) above;

(b) of section 99(2)(b), (e) or (ea) above.

101. [*Repealed by the Police and Magistrates' Courts Act 1994 ss 37(e), 93, Sch 9, Pt I.*]

102. (1) A police officer of the rank of superintendent or below may not be dismissed, required to resign or reduced in rank by a decision taken in proceedings under regulations made in accordance with section 33(3)(a) of the Police Act 1964 unless he has been given an opportunity to elect to be legally represented at any hearing held in the course of those proceedings.

(2) Where an officer makes an election to which subsection (1) above refers, he may be represented at the hearing, at his option, either by counsel or by a solicitor.

(3) Except in a case where an officer of the rank of superintendent or below has been given an opportunity to elect to be legally represented and has so elected, he may be represented at the hearing only by another member of a police force.

(4) Regulations under section 33 of the Police Act 1964 shall specify—

(a) a procedure for notifying an officer of the effect of subsections (1) to (3) above, (*b*) when he is to be notified of the effect of those subsections (1) to (3) above,

(*c*) when he is to give notice whether he wishes to be legally represented at the hearing.

(5) If an officer—

(*a*) fails without reasonable cause to give notice in accordance with the regulations that he wishes to be legally represented; or

(*b*) gives notice in accordance with the regulations that he does not wish to be legally represented, he may be dismissed, required to resign or reduced in rank without his being legally represented.

(6) If an officer has given notice in accordance with the regulations that he wishes to be legally represented, the case against him may be represented by counsel or a solicitor whether or not he is actually so represented.

103. [*Repealed by the Police and Magistrates' Court Act 1994 s 93, Sch 9, Pt I.*]

General.

104. (1) [*Repealed by the Police and Magistrates' Court Act 1994 ss 37(f), 93, Sch 9, Pt I.*]

(2) [*Repealed by the Police and Magistrates' Court Act 1994 ss 37(f), 93, Sch 9, Pt I.*]

(3) Subject to subsection (4) below, no statement made by any person for the purpose of the informal resolution of a complaint shall be admissible in any subsequent criminal, civil or disciplinary proceedings.

(4) A statement is not rendered inadmissible by subsection (3) above if it consists of or includes an admission relating to a matter which does not fall to be resolved informally.

105. (1) The Secretary of State may issue guidance to police and authorities, to chief officers of police and to other police officers concerning the discharge of their functions—

(*a*) under this Part of this Act; and

(*b*) under regulations made under section 33 of the Police Act 1964 in relation to the matters mentioned in subsection (2)(*e*) of that section

and police authorities and police officers shall have regard to any such guidance in the discharge of their functions.

(2) Guidance may not be issued under subsection (1) above in relation to the handling of a particular case.

(3) A failure on the part of a police authority or a police officer to have regard to any guidance issued under subsection (1) above shall be admissible in evidence on any appeal from a decision taken in proceedings under regulations made in accordance with subsection (3) of section 33 of the Police Act 1964.

(4) In discharging their functions under section 93 above the Authority shall have regard to any guidance given to them by the Secretary of State with respect to such matters as are for the time being the subject of guidance under subsection (1) above, and shall have regard in particular, but without prejudice to the generality of this subsection, to any such guidance as to the principles to be applied in cases that involve any question of criminal proceedings.

(5) The report of the Authority under section 97(3) above shall contain a statement of any guidance given to the Authority under subsection (4) above during the year to which the report relates.

PART X
POLICE—GENERAL

106. (1) Arrangements shall be made in each police area for obtaining the views of people in that area about matters concerning the policing of the area and for obtaining their co-operation with the police in preventing crime in the area.

(2) Except as provided by subsections (3) to (7) below, arrangements for each police area shall be made by the police authority after consulting the chief constable as to the arrangements that would be appropriate.

(3) The Secretary of State shall issue guidance to the Commissioner of Police of the Metropolis concerning arrangements for the Metropolitan Police District; and the Commissioner shall make such arrangements after taking account of that guidance.

(4) The Commissioner shall make separate arrangements—

(a) for each London borough;

(b) for each district which falls wholly within the Metropolitan Police District; and

(c) for each part of a district which falls partly within that District.

(5) The Commissioner shall consult the council of each London borough as to the arrangements that would be appropriate for the borough.

(6) The Commissioner shall consult the council of each such district as is mentioned in subsection (4)(b) above as to the arrangements that would be appropriate for the district.

(7) The Commissioner shall consult the council of each such district as is mentioned in subsection (4)(c) above as to the arrangements that would be appropriate for the part of the district for which it falls to him to make arrangements.

(8) The Common Council of the City of London shall issue guidance to the Commissioner of Police for the City of London concerning arrangements for the City; and the Commissioner shall make such arrangements after taking account of that guidance.

(9) A body or person whose duty it is to make arrangements under this section shall review the arrangements so made from time to time.

(10) If it appears to the Secretary of State that arrangements in a police area are not adequate for the purposes set out in subsection (1) above, he may require the body or person whose duty it is to make arrangements in that area to submit a report to him concerning the arrangements.

(11) After considering the report the Secretary of State may require the body or person who submitted it to review the arrangements and submit a further report to him concerning them.

(12) A body or person whose duty it is to make arrangements shall be under the same duties to consult when reviewing arrangements as when making them.

107. (1) For the purpose of any provision of this Act or any other Act under which a power in respect of the investigation of offences or the treatment of persons in police custody is exercisable only by or with the authority of a police officer of at least the rank of superintendent, an officer of the rank of chief inspector shall be treated as holding the rank of superintendent if—

(a) he has been authorised by an officer holding a rank above the rank of superintendant to exercise the power or, as the case may be, to give his authority for its exercise, or (*b*) he is acting during the absence of an officer holding the rank of superintendant who has authorised him, for the duration of that absence, to exercise the power or, as the case may be, to give his authority for its exercise.

(2) For the purpose of any provision of this Act or any other Act under which such a power is exercisable only by or with the authority of an officer of at least the rank of insector, an officer of the rank of sergeant shall be treated as holding the rank of inspector if he has been authorised by an officer of at least the rank of superintendent to exercise the power or, as the case may be, to give his authority for its exercise.

108. (1) The office of deputy chief constable is hereby abolished.
(2) [*repealed*]
(3) [*repealed*]
(4)–(6) [*apply only to Scotland*]

109. In section 44 of the Police Act 1964—
(*a*) in subsection (1), for the word "and", in the last place where it occurs, there shall be substituted the words "affecting individuals, except as provided by subsection (1A) below, and questions of";
(*b*) the following subsections shall be inserted after that subsection—
"(1A) A Police Federation may represent a member of a police force at any disciplinary proceedings or on an appeal from any such proceedings.
(1B) Except on an appeal to the Secretary of State or as provided by section 102 of the Police and Criminal Evidence Act 1984, a member of a police force may only be represented under subsection (1A) above by another member of a police force."; and
(*c*) in subsection (3), after the word "Federations", in the first place where it occurs, there shall be inserted the words "or authorise the Federations to make rules concerning such matters relating to their constitution and proceedings as may be specified in the regulations."

110, 111. [*Apply only to Scotland*]

112. (1) An officer belonging to the metropolitan police force who is assigned to the protection of any person or property in Scotland shall in the discharge of that duty have the powers and privileges of a constable of a police force maintained under the Police (Scotland) Act 1967.
(2) An officer belonging to the metropolitan police force who is assigned to the protection of any person or property in Northern Ireland shall in the discharge of that duty have the powers and privileges of a constable of the Royal Ulster Constabulary.

PART XI
MISCELLANEOUS AND SUPPLEMENTARY

113. (1) The Secretary of State may by order direct that any provision of this Act which relates to investigations of offences conducted by police officers or to persons detained by the police shall apply, subject to such modifications as he may specify, to investigations of offences conducted under the Army Act 1955, the Air Force Act 1955 or the Naval Discipline Act 1957 or to persons under arrest under any of those Acts.

(2) Section 67(9) above shall not have effect in relation to investigations of offences conducted under the Army Act 1955, the Air Force Act 1955 or the Naval Discipline Act 1957.

(3) The Secretary of State shall issue a code of practice, or a number of such codes, for persons other than police officers who are concerned with enquiries into offences under the Army Act 1955, the Air Force Act 1955 or the Naval Discipline Act 1957.

(4) Without prejudice to the generality of subsection (3) above, a code issued under that subsection may contain provisions, in connection with enquiries into such offences, as to the following matters—

(a) the tape-recording of interviews;

(b) searches of persons and premises; and

(c) the seizure of things found on searches.

(5) If the Secretary of State lays before both Houses of Parliament a draft of a code of practice under this section, he may by order bring the code into operation.

(6) An order bringing a code of practice into operation may contain such transitional provisions or savings as appear to the Secretary of State to be necessary or expedient in connection with the code of practice thereby brought into operation.

(7) The Secretary of State may from time to time revise the whole or any part of a code of practice issued under this section and issue that revised code, and the foregoing provisions of this section shall apply (with appropriate modifications) to such a revised code as they apply to the first issue of a code.

(8) A failure on the part of any person to comply with any provision of a code of practice issued under this section shall not of itself render him liable to any criminal or civil proceedings except those to which this subsection applies.

(9) Subsection (8) above applies—

(a) to proceedings under any provision of the Army Act 1955 or the Air Force Act 1955 other than section 70; and

(b) to proceedings under any provision of the Naval Discipline Act 1957 other than section 42.

(10) In all criminal and civil proceedings any such code shall be admissible in evidence and if any provision of such a code appears to the court or tribunal conducting the proceedings to be relevant to any question arising in the proceedings it shall be taken into account in determining that question.

(11) In subsection (10) above "criminal proceedings" includes—

(a) proceedings in the United Kingdom or elsewhere before a court-martial constituted under the Army Act 1955, the Air Force Act 1955 or the Naval Discipline Act 1957 or a disciplinary court constituted under section 50 of the said Act of 1957;

(b) proceedings before the Courts-Martial Appeal Court; and

(c) proceedings before a Standing Civilian Court.

(12) Parts VII and VIII of this Act have effect for the purposes of proceedings—

(a) before a court-martial constituted under the Army Act 1955 or the Air Force Act 1955;

(b) before the Courts-Martial Appeal Court; and

(c) before a Standing Civilian Court,

subject to any modifications which the Secretary of State may by order specify.

(13) An order under this section shall be made by statutory instrument and shall be subject to annulment in pursuance of a resolution of either House of Parliament.

114. (1) "Arrested", "arresting", "arrest" and "to arrest" shall respectively be substituted for "detained", "detaining", "detention" and "to detain" wherever in the customs and excise Acts, as defined in section 1(1) of the Customs and Excise Management Act 1979, those words are used in relation to persons.

(2) The Treasury may by order direct—

(*a*) that any provision of this Act which relates to investigations of offences conducted by police officers or to persons detained by the police shall apply, subject to such modifications as the order may specify, to investigations conducted by officers of Customs and Excise of offences which relate to assigned matters, as defined in section 1 of the Customs and Excise Management Act 1979, or to persons detained by officers of Customs and Excise; and

(*b*) that, in relation to investigations of offences conducted by officers of Customs and Excise—

(i) this Act shall have effect as if the following section were inserted after section 14—

"14A. Material in the possession of a person who acquired or created it in the course of any trade, business, profession or other occupation or for the purpose of any paid or unpaid office and which relates to an assigned matter, as defined in section 1 of the Customs and Excise Management Act 1979, is neither excluded material nor special procedure material for the purposes of any enactment such as is mentioned in section 9(2) above."; and

(ii) section 55 above shall have effect as if it related only to things such as are mentioned in subsection (1)(*a*) of that section.

(3) Nothing in any order under subsection (2) above shall be taken to limit any powers exercisable under section 164 of the Customs and Excise Management Act 1979.

(4) In this section "officers of Customs and Excise" means officers commissioned by the Commissioners of Customs and Excise under section 6(3) of the Customs and Excise Management Act 1979.

(5) An order under this section shall be made by statutory instrument and shall be subject to annulment in pursuance of a resolution of either House of Parliament.

115. Any expenses of a Minister of the Crown incurred in consequence of the provisions of this Act, including any increase attributable to those provisions in sums payable under any other Act, shall be defrayed out of money provided by Parliament.

116. (1) This section has effect for determining whether an offence is a serious arrestable offence for the purposes of this Act.

(2) The following arrestable offences are always serious—

(*a*) an offence (whether at common law or under any enactment) specified in Part I of Schedule 5 to this Act;

(*aa*) [*Repealed.*]

(*b*) an offence under enactment specified in Part II of that Schedule; and

(*c*) any of the offences mentioned in paragraphs (*a*) to (*f*) of section 1(3) of the Drug Trafficking Act 1994.

(3) Subject to subsections (4) and (5) below, any other arrestable offence is serious only if its commission—

(*a*) has led to any of the consequences specified in subsection (6) below; or
(*b*) is intended or is likely to lead to any of those consequences.

(4) An arrestable offence which consists of making a threat is serious if carrying out the threat would be likely to lead to any of the consequences specified in subsection (6) below.

(5) An offence under section 2, 8, 9, 10 or 11 of the Prevention of Terrorism (Temporary Provisions) Act) 1989 is always a serious arrestable offence for the purposes of section 56 or 58 above, and an attempt or conspiracy to commit any such offence is also always a serious arrestable offence for those purposes.

(6) The consequences mentioned in subsections (3) and (4) above are—
(*a*) serious harm to the security of the State or to public order;
(*b*) serious interference with the administration of justice or with the investigation of offences or of a particular offence;
(*c*) the death of any person;
(*d*) serious injury to any person;
(*e*) substantial financial gain to any person; and
(*f*) serious financial loss to any person.

(7) Loss is serious for the purposes of this section if, having regard to all the circumstances, it is serious for the person who suffers it.

(8) In this section "injury" includes any disease and any impairment of a person's physical or mental condition.

117. Where any provision of this Act—
(*a*) confers a power on a constable; and
(*b*) does not provide that the power may only be exercised with the consent of some person, other than a police officer,
the officer may use reasonable force, if necessary, in the exercise of the power.

118. (1) In this Act—
"arrestable offence" has the meaning assigned to it by section 24 above;
"designated police station" has the meaning assigned to it by section 35 above; ·
"document" has the same meaning as in Part I of the Civil Evidence Act 1968;
"item subject to legal privilege" has the meaning assigned to it by section 10 above;
"parent of guardian" means—
(*a*) in the case of a child or young person in the care of a local authority, that authority;
(*b*) [*Repealed.*]
"premises" has the meaning assigned to it by section 23 above;
"recordable offence" means any offence to which regulations under section 27 above apply;
"vessel" includes any ship, boat, raft or other apparatus constructed or adapted for floating on water.

(2) A person is in police detention for the purposes of this Act if—
(*a*) he has been taken to a police station after being arrested for an offence or after being arrested under section 14 of the Prevention of Terrorism (Temporary Provisions) Act 1989 or under paragraph 6 of Schedule 5 to that Act by an examining officer who is a constable; or
(*b*) he is arrested at a police station after attending voluntarily at the station or accompanying a constable to it,

and is detained there or is detained elsewhere in the charge of a constable, except that a person who is at a court after being charged is not in police detention for those purposes.

SCHEDULES

SCHEDULE 1

Section 9

SPECIAL PROCEDURE

Making of orders by circuit judge

1. If on an application made by a constable a circuit judge is satisfied that one or other of the sets of access conditions is fulfilled, he may make an order under paragraph 4 below.

2. The first set of access conditions is fulfilled if—
    (*a*) there are reasonable grounds for believing—
        (i) that a serious arrestable offence has been committed;
        ii) that there is material which consists of special procedure material or includes special procedure material and does not also include excluded material on premises specified in the application;
        (iii) that the material is likely to be of substantial value (whether by itself or together with other material) to the investigation in connection with which the application is made; and
        (iv) that the material is likely to be relevant evidence;
    (*b*) other methods of obtaining the material—
        (i) have been tried without success; or
        (ii) have not been tried because it appeared that they were bound to fail; and
    (*c*) it is in the public interest, having regard—
        (i) to the benefit likely to accrue to the investigation if the material is obtained; and
        (ii) to the circumstances under which the person in possession of the material holds it,
    that the material should be produced or that access to it should be given.

3. The second set of access conditions is fulfilled if—
    (*a*) there are reasonable grounds for believing that there is material which consists of or includes excluded material or special procedure material on premises specified in the application;
    (*b*) but for section 9(2) above a search of the premises for that material could have been authorised by the issue of a warrant to a constable under an enactment other than this Schedule; and
    (*c*) the issue of such a warrant would have been appropriate.

4. An order under this paragraph is an order that the person who appears to the circuit judge to be in possession of the material to which the application relates shall—
    (*a*) produce it to a constable for him to take away; or
    (*b*) give a constable access to it,
not later than the end of the period of seven days from the date of the order or the end of such longer period as the order may specify.

5. Where the material consists of information contained in a computer—
    (*a*) an order under paragraph 4(*a*) above shall have effect as an order to produce

the material in a form in which it can be taken away and in which it is visible and legible; and

(b) an order under paragraph 4(*b*) above shall have effect as an order to give a constable access to the material in a form in which it is visible and legible.

6. For the purposes of sections 21 and 22 above material produced in pursuance of an order under paragraph 4(*a*) above shall be treated as if it were material seized by a constable.

Notices of applications for orders

7. An application for an order under paragraph 4 above shall be made inter partes.

8. Notice of an application for such an order may be served on a person either by delivering it to him or by leaving it at his proper address or by sending it by post to him in a registered letter or by the recorded delivery service.

9. Such a notice may be served—

(a) on a body corporate, by serving it on the body's secretary or clerk or other similar officer; and

(b) on a partnership, by serving it on one of the partners.

10. For the purposes of this Schedule, and of section 7 of the Interpretation Act 1978 in its application to this Schedule, the proper address of a person, in the case of secretary or clerk or other similar officer of a body corporate, shall be that of the registered or principal office of that body, in the case of a partner of a firm shall be that of the principal office of the firm, and in any other case shall be the last known address of the person to be served.

11. Where notice of an application for an order under paragraph 4 above has been served on a person, he shall not conceal, destroy, alter or dispose of the material to which the application relates except—

(a) with the leave of a judge; or

(b) with the written permission of a constable,

until—

(i) the application is dismissed or abandoned; or

(ii) he has complied with an order under paragraph 4 above made on the application.

Issue of warrants by circuit judge

12. If on an application made by a constable a circuit judge—

(a) is satisfied—

(i) that either set of access conditions is fulfilled; and

(ii) that any of the further conditions set out in paragraph 14 below is also fulfilled; or

(b) is satisfied—

(i) that the second set of access conditions is fulfilled; and

(ii) that an order under paragraph 4 above relating to the material has not been complied with,

he may issue a warrant authorising a constable to enter and search the premises.

13. A constable may seize and retain anything for which a search has been authorised under paragraph 12 above.

14. The further conditions mentioned in paragraph 12(*a*)(ii) above are—

(a) that it is not practicable to communicate with any person entitled to grant entry to the premises to which the application relates;

(*b*) that it is practicable to communicate with a person entitled to grant entry to the premises but it is not practicable to communicate with any person entitled to grant access to the material;

(*c*) that the material contains information which—
  (i) is subject to a restriction or obligation such as is mentioned in section 11(2)(*b*) above; and
  (ii) is likely to be disclosed in breach of it if a warrant is not issued;

(*d*) that service of notice of an application for an order under paragraph 4 above may seriously prejudice the investigation.

15. (1) If a person fails to comply with an order under paragraph 4 above, a circuit judge may deal with him as if he had committed a contempt of the Crown Court.

(2) Any enactment relating to contempt of the Crown Court shall have effect in relation to such a failure as if it were such a contempt.

Costs

16. The costs of any application under this Schedule and of anything done or to be done in pursuance of an order made under it shall be in the discretion of the judge.

SCHEDULE 2

Section 26

PRESERVED POWERS OF ARREST

1892 c 43	Section 17(2) of the Military Lands Act 1892.
1911 c 27	Section 12(1) of the Protection of Animals Act 1911.
1920 c 55	Section 2 of the Emergency Powers Act 1920.
1936 c 6	Section 7(3) of the Public Order Act 1936.
1952 c 52	Section 49 of the Prison Act 1952.
1952 c 67	Section 13 of the Visiting Forces Act 1952.
1955 c 18	Sections 186 and 190B of the Army Act 1955.
1955 c 19	Sections 186 and 190B of the Air Force Act 1955.
1957 c 53	Sections 104 and 105 of the Naval Discipline Act 1957.
1959 c 37	Section 1(3) of the Street Offences Act 1959.
1969 c 54	Section 32 of the Children and Young Persons Act 1969.
1971 c 77	Section 24(2) of the Immigration Act 1971 and paragraphs 17, 24 and 33 of Schedule 2 and paragraph 7 of Schedule 3 to that Act.
1976 c 63	Section 7 of the Bail Act 1976.
1977 c 45	Sections 6(6), 7(11), 8(4), 9(7) and 10(5) of the Criminal Law Act 1977.
1980 c 9	Schedule 5 to the Reserve Forces Act 1980.
1981 c 22	Sections 60(5) and 61(1) of the Animal Health Act 1981.
1983 c 2	Rule 36 in Schedule 1 to the Representation of the People Act 1983.
1983 c 20	Sections 18, 35(10), 36(8), 38(7), 136(1) and 138 of the Mental Health Act 1983.
1984 c 47	Section 5(5) of the Repatriation of Prisoners Act 1984.

SCHEDULE 3

Section 70

PROVISIONS SUPPLEMENTARY TO SECTIONS 68 AND 69

PART I
PROVISIONS SUPPLEMENTARY TO SECTION 68

1–7. [Repealed.]

PART II
PROVISIONS SUPPLEMENTARY TO SECTION 69

8. In any proceedings where it is desired to give a statement in evidence in accordance with section 69 above, a certificate—
  (a) identifying the document containing the statement and describing the manner in which it was produced;
  (b) giving such particulars of any device involved in the production of that document as may be appropriate for the purpose of showing that the document was produced by a computer;
  (c) dealing with any of the matters mentioned in subsection (1) of section 69 above; and
  (d) purporting to be signed by a person occupying a responsible position in relation to the operation of the computer,
shall be evidence of anything stated in it; and for the purposes of this paragraph it shall be sufficient for a matter to be stated to the best of the knowledge and belief of the person stating it.

9. Notwithstanding paragraph 8 above, a court may require oral evidence to be given of anything of which evidence could be given by a certificate under that paragraph.

10. Any person who in a certificate tendered under paragraph 8 above in a magistrates' court, the Crown Court or the Court of Appeal makes a statement which he knows to be false or does not believe to be true shall be guilty of an offence and liable—
  (a) on conviction on indictment to imprisonment for a term not exceeding two years or to a fine or to both;
  (b) on summary conviction to imprisonment for a term not exceeding six months or to a fine not exceeding the statutory maximum or to both.

11. In estimating the weight, if any, to be attached to a statement regard shall be had to all the circumstances from which any inference can reasonably be drawn as to the accuracy or otherwise of the statement and, in particular—
  (a) to the question whether or not the information which the information contained in the statement reproduces or is derived from was supplied to the relevant computer, or recorded for the purpose of being supplied to it, contemporaneously with the occurrence or existence of the facts dealt with in that information; and
  (b) to the question whether or not any person concerned with the supply of information to that computer, or with the operation of that computer or any equipment by means of which the document containing the statement was produced by it, had any incentive to conceal or misrepresent the facts.

12. For the purposes of paragraph 11 above information shall be taken to be supplied to a computer whether it is supplied directly or (with or without human intervention) by means of any appropriate equipment.

PART III
PROVISIONS SUPPLEMENTARY TO SECTIONS 68 AND 69

13. [*Repealed.*]

14. For the purpose of deciding whether or not a statement is so admissible the court may draw any reasonable inference—

   (*a*) from the circumstances in which the statement was made or otherwise came into being; or

   (*b*) from any other circumstances, including the form and contents of the document in which the statement is contained.

15. Provision may be made by rules of court for supplementing the provisions of section 68 or 69 above or this Schedule.

SCHEDULE 4

Section 82

THE POLICE COMPLAINTS AUTHORITY
PART I—GENERAL

Constitution of Authority

1. (1) The Police Complaints Authority shall consist of a chairman and not less than 8 other members.

   (2) The chairman shall be appointed by Her Majesty.

   (3) The other members shall be appointed by the Secretary of State.

   (4) The members of the Authority shall not include any person who is or has been a constable in any part of the United Kingdom.

   (5) Persons may be appointed as whole-time or part-time members of the Authority.

   (6) The Secretary of State may appoint not more than two of the members of the Authority to be deputy chairmen.

Incorporation and status of Authority

2. (1) The Authority shall be a body corporate.

   (2) It is hereby declared that the Authority are not to be regarded as the servant or agent of the Crown or as enjoying any status, privilege or immunity of the Crown; and the Authority's property shall not be regarded as property of or property held on behalf of the Crown.

Members

3. (1) Subject to the following provisions of this Schedule, a person shall hold an office to which he is appointed under paragraph 1(2), (3) or (6) above in accordance with the terms of his appointment.

   (2) A person shall not be appointed to such an office for more than 3 years at a time.

(3) A person may at any time resign such an office.

(4) The Secretary of State may at any time remove a person from such an office if satisfied that—

(a) he has without reasonable excuse failed to carry out his duties for a continuous period of 3 months beginning not earlier than 6 months before that time; or

(b) he has been convicted of a criminal offence; or

(c) he has become bankrupt or made an arrangement with his creditors; or

(d) he is incapacitated by physical or mental illness; or

(da) he has acted improperly in relation to his duties; or

(e) he is otherwise unable or unfit to perform his duties.

4. The Secretary of State may pay, or make such payments towards the provision of, such remuneration, pensions, allowances or gratuities to or in respect of persons appointed to office under paragraph 1(2), (3) or (6) above or any of them as, with the consent of the Treasury, he may determine.

5. Where a person ceases to hold such an office otherwise than on the expiry of his term of office, and it appears to the Secretary of State that there are special circumstances which make it right for that person to receive compensation, the Secretary of State may, with the consent of the Treasury, direct the Authority to make to the person a payment of such amount as, with the consent of the Treasury, the Secretary of State may determine.

Staff

6. The Authority may, after consultation with the Secretary of State, appoint such officers and servants as the Authority think fit, subject to the approval of the Treasury as to numbers and as to remuneration and other terms and conditions of service.

7. (1) Employment by the Authority shall be included among the kinds of employment to which a superannuation scheme under section 1 of the Superannuation Act 1972 can apply, and accordingly in Schedule 1 to that Act, at the end of the list of "Other Bodies" there shall be inserted—

"Police Complaints Authority".

(2) Where a person who is employed by the Authority and is by reference to that employment a participant in a scheme under section 1 of the said Act of 1972 is appointed to an office under paragraph 1(2), (3) or (6) above, the Treasury may determine that his service in that office shall be treated for the purposes of the scheme as service as an employee of the Authority; and his rights under the scheme shall not be affected by paragraph 4 above.

8. The Employers' Liability (Compulsory Insurance) Act 1969 shall not require insurance to be effected by the Authority.

Power of Authority to set up regional offices

9. (1) If it appears to the Authority that it is necessary to do so in order to discharge their duties efficiently, the Authority may, with the consent of the Secretary of State and the Treasury, set up a regional office in any place in England and Wales.

(2) The Authority may delegate any of their functions to a regional office.

Proceedings

10. (1) Subject to the provisions of this Act, the arrangements for the proceedings of the Authority (including the quorum for meetings) shall be such as the Authority may determine.

(2) The arrangements may, with the approval of the Secretary of State, provide for the discharge, under the general direction of the Authority, of any of the Authority's functions by a committee or by one or more of the members, officers or servants of the Authority.

11. The validity of any proceedings of the Authority shall not be affected—
(*a*) by any defect in the appointment
   (i) of the chairman; or
   (ii) (*repealed*)
   (iii) of any other member or
(*b*) by any vacancy
   (i) in the office of chairman; or
   (ii) among the other members.

Finance

12. The Secretary of State shall pay to the Authority expenses incurred or to be incurred by the Authority under paragraphs 5 and 6 above and, with the consent of the Treasury, shall pay to the Authority such sums as the Secretary of State thinks fit for enabling the Authority to meet other expenses.

13. (1) It shall be the duty of the Authority—
(*a*) to keep proper accounts and proper records in relation to the accounts;
(*b*) to prepare in respect of each financial year of the Authority a statement of accounts in such form as the Secretary of State may direct with the approval of the Treasury; and
(*c*) to send copies of the statement to the Secretary of State and the Comptroller and Auditor General before the end of the month of August next following the financial year to which the statement relates.

(2) The Comptroller and Auditor General shall examine, certify and report on each statement received by him in pursuance of this paragraph and shall lay copies of each statement and of his report before Parliament.

(3) The financial year of the Authority shall be the 12 months ending on 31st March.

Part II
Transitional

Information received by Police Complaints Board

14. (1) No information received by the Police Complaints Board in connection with any complaint shall be disclosed by any person who has been a member, officer or servant of the Board except—
(*a*) to the Secretary of State or to a member, officer or servant of the Authority or, so far as may be necessary for the proper discharge of the functions of the Authority, to other persons; or

(*b*) for the purposes of any criminal, civil or disciplinary proceedings.

(2) Any person who discloses information in contravention of this paragraph shall be guilty of an offence and liable on summary conviction to a fine of an amount not exceeding level 5 on the standard scale.

Property, rights and liabilities

15. (1) On the day on which section 83 above comes into operation all property, rights and liabilities which immediately before that day were property, rights and liabilities of the Police Complaints Board shall vest in the Authority by virtue of this paragraph and without further assurance.

(2) Section 12 of the Finance Act 1895 (which requires Acts to be stamped as conveyances on sale in certain cases) shall not apply to any transfer of property effected by this paragraph.

Proceedings

16. Proceedings in any court to which the Police Complaints Board is a party and which are pending immediately before the date on which section 83 above comes into operation may be continued on and after that day by the Authority.

Payments to former members of Police Complaints Board

17. Where a person—
  (*a*) ceases to be a member of the Police Complaints Board by reason of its abolition; and
  (*b*) does not become a member of the Authority,
the Secretary of State may, with the consent of the Treasury, make to the person a payment of such amount as, with the consent of the Treasury, the Secretary of State may determine.

General

18. Paragraphs 14 to 17 above are without prejudice to the generality of section 121(4) above.

SCHEDULE 5

Section 116

Serious Arrestable Offences
Part I
Offences Mentioned in Section 116(2)(*a*)

  1. Treason.
  2. Murder.
  3. Manslaughter.
  4. Rape.
  5. Kidnapping.
  6. Incest with a girl under the age of 13.
  7. Buggery with a person under the age of 16.
  8. Indecent assault which constitutes an act of gross indecency.

PART II
OFFENCES MENTIONED IN SECTION 116(2)(*b*)

Explosive Substances Act 1883 (*c* 3)
1. Section 2 (causing explosion likely to endanger life or property).

Sexual Offences Act 1956 (*c* 69)
2. Section 5 (intercourse with a girl under the age of 13).

Firearms Act 1968 (*c* 27)
3. Section 16 (possession of firearms with intent to injure).
4. Section 17(1) (use of firearms and imitation firearms to resist arrest).
5. Section 18 (carrying firearms with criminal intent).
6. [*Repealed.*]

Taking of Hostages Act 1982 (*c* 28)
7. Section 1 (hostage-taking).

Aviation Security Act 1982 (*c* 36)
8. Section 1 (hi-jacking).

Criminal Justice Act 1988 (*c* 33)
9. Section 134 (torture).

Road Traffic Act 1988 (*c* 52)
10. Section 1 (causing death by dangerous driving).
10A. Section 3A (causing death by careless driving when under the influence of drink or drugs).

Aviation and Maritime Security Act 1990 (*c* 31)
11. Section 1 (endangering safety at aerodromes).
12. Section 9 (hijacking of ships).
13. Section 10 (seizing or exercising control of fixed platforms).

Protection of Children Act 1978 (*c* 37)
14. Section 1 (indecent photographs and pseudo-photographs of children).

Obscene Publications Act 1959 (*c* 66)
15. Section 2 (publication of obscene matter).

Schedules 6 and 7 [*Not reproduced.*]

Codes of Practice

A

Publisher's note
This third edition of the Codes of Practice made under the Police and Criminal Evidence Act 1984 came into force on 10 April 1995. The new edition preserves the numbering scheme of the second (1991) edition. Where additional paragraphs have been inserted, they have been sub-numbered.

A   Code of Practice for the Exercise by Police Officers of Statutory Powers of Stop and Search

1 General

1.1 This code of practice must be readily available at all police stations for consultation by police officers, detained persons and members of the public.

1.2 The notes for guidance included are not provisions of this code, but are guidance to police officers and others about its application and interpretation. Provisions in the annexes to the code are provisions of this code.

1.3 This code governs the exercise by police officers of statutory powers to search a person without first arresting him or to search a vehicle without making an arrest. The main stop and search powers to which this code applies at the time the code was prepared are set out in *Annex A*, but that list should not be regarded as definitive.

1.4 This code does not apply to the following powers of stop and search:
   (i) Aviation Security Act 1982, s27(2);
   (ii) Police and Criminal Evidence Act 1984, s6(1) (which relates specifically to powers of constables employed by statutory undertakers on the premises of the statutory undertakers).

1.5 This code applies to stops and searches under powers:
(a) requiring reasonable grounds for suspicion that articles unlawfully obtained or possessed are being carried;

(b) authorised under section 60 of the Criminal Justice and Public Order Act 1994 based upon a reasonable belief that incidents involving serious violence may take place within a locality;

(c) authorised under section 13A of the Prevention of Terrorism (Temporary Provisions) Act 1989 as amended by section 81 of the Criminal Justice and Public Order Act 1994;

(d) exercised under paragraph 4(2) of Schedule 5 to the Prevention of Terrorism (Temporary Provisions) Act 1989.

[See *Note 1A*]

(a) Powers requiring reasonable suspicion
1.6 Whether a reasonable ground for suspicion exists will depend on the circumstances in each case, but there must be some objective basis for it. An officer will need to consider the nature of the article suspected of being carried in the context of other factors such as the time and the place, and the behaviour of the person concerned or those with him. Reasonable suspicion may exist, for example, where information has been received such as a description of an article being carried or of a suspected offender; a person is seen acting covertly or warily or attempting to hide something; or a person is carrying a certain type of article at an unusual time or in a place where a number of burglaries or thefts are known to have taken place recently. But the decision to stop and search must be based on all the facts which bear on the likelihood that an article of a certain kind will be found.

1.7 Reasonable suspicion can never be supported on the basis of personal factors alone. For example, a person's colour, age, hairstyle or manner of dress, or the fact that he is known to have a previous conviction for possession of an unlawful article, cannot be used alone or in combination with each other as the sole basis on which to search that person. Nor may it be founded on the basis of stereotyped images of certain persons or groups as more likely to be committing offences.

1.7A Where a police officer has reasonable grounds to suspect that a person is in innocent possession of a stolen or prohibited article or other item for which he is empowered to search, the power of stop and search exists notwithstanding that there would be no power of arrest. However every effort should be made to secure the person's co-operation in the production of the article before resorting to the use of force.

(b) Authorisation under section 60 of the Criminal Justice and Public Order Act 1994
1.8 Authority to exercise the powers of stop and search under section 60 of the Criminal Justice and Public Order Act 1994 may be given where it is reasonably believed that incidents involving serious violence may take place in a locality, and it is expedient to use these powers to prevent their occurrence. Authorisation should normally be given by an officer of the rank of superintendent or above, in writing, specifying the locality in which the powers may be exercised and the period of time for which they are in force. Authorisation may be given by an inspector or chief inspector if he reasonably believes that violence is imminent and no superintendent is available. In either case the period authorised shall be no longer than appears reasonably necessary to prevent, or try to prevent incidents of serious violence, and it may not exceed 24 hours. A superintendent or the

authorising officer may direct that the period shall be extended for a further six hours if violence has occurred or is suspected to have occurred and the continued use of the powers is considered necessary to prevent further violence. That direction must also be given in writing at the time or as soon as practicable afterwards. [See *Notes 1F and 1G*]

(c) Authorisation under section 13A of the Prevention of Terrorism (Temporary Provisions) Act 1989, as amended by section 81 of the Criminal Justice and Public Order Act 1994

1.8A Authority to exercise the powers of stop and search under section 13A of the Prevention of Terrorism (Temporary Provisions) Act 1989 may be given where it appears expedient to do so to prevent acts of terrorism. Authorisation must be given by an officer of the rank of assistant chief constable (or equivalent) or above, in writing, specifying where the powers may be exercised and the period of time for which they are to remain in force. The period authorised may not exceed 28 days. Further periods of up to 28 days may be authorised. [See *Notes 1F and 1G*]

Notes for Guidance

1A It is important to ensure that powers of stop and search are used responsibly by those who exercise them and those who authorise their use. An officer should bear in mind that he may be required to justify the authorisation or use of the powers to a senior officer and in court, and that misuse of the powers is likely to be harmful to the police effort in the long term and can lead to mistrust of the police by the community. Regardless of the power exercised, all police officers should be careful to ensure that the selection and treatment of those questioned or searched is based upon objective factors and not upon personal prejudice. It is also particularly important to ensure that any person searched is treated courteously and considerately.

1B This code does not affect the ability of an officer to speak to or question a person in the ordinary course of his duties (and in the absence of reasonable suspicion) without detaining him or exercising any element of compulsion. It is not the purpose of the code to prohibit such encounters between the police and the community with the co-operation of the person concerned and neither does it affect the principle that all citizens have a duty to help police officers to prevent crime and discover offenders.

1C [Not Used]

1D Nothing in this code affects
(a) the routine searching of persons entering sports grounds or other premises with their consent, or as a condition of entry; or
(b) the ability of an officer to search a person in the street with his consent where no search power exists. In these circumstances an officer should always make it clear that he is seeking the consent of the person concerned to the search being carried out by telling the person that he need not consent and that without his consent he will not be searched.

1E If an officer acts in an improper manner this will invalidate a voluntary search. Juveniles, people suffering from a mental handicap or mental disorder and others who appear not to be capable of giving an informed consent should not be subject to a voluntary search.

1F *It is for the authorising officer to determine the period of time during which the powers mentioned in paragraph 1.5(b) and (c) may be exercised. The officer should set the minimum period he considers necessary to deal with the risk of violence or terrorism. A direction to extend the period authorised under the powers mentioned in paragraph 1.5(b) may be given only once. Thereafter further use of the powers requires a new authorisation.*

1G *It is for the authorising officer to determine the geographical area in which the use of the powers are to be authorised. In doing so he may wish to take into account factors such as the nature and venue of the anticipated incident, the numbers of people who may be in the immediate area of any possible incident, their access to surrounding areas and the ancitipated level of violence. The officer should not set a geographical area which is wider than that he believes necessary for the purpose of preventing anticipated violence or terrorism.*

2 Action before a search is carried out

(a) Searches requiring reasonable suspicion

2.1 Where an officer has the reasonable grounds for suspicion necessary to exercise a power of stop and search he may detain the person concerned for the purposes of and with a view to searching him. There is no power to stop or detain a person against his will in order to find grounds for a search.

2.2 Before carrying out a search the officer may question the person about his behaviour or his presence in circumstances which gave rise to the suspicion, since he may have a satisfactory explanation which will make a search unnecessary. If, as a result of any questioning preparatory to a search, or other circumstances which come to the attention of the officer, there cease to be reasonable grounds for suspecting that an article is being carried of a kind for which there is a power of stop and search, no search may take place. [See *Note 2A*]

2.3 The reasonable grounds for suspicion which are necessary for the exercise of the initial power to detain may be confirmed or eliminated as a result of the questioning of a person detained for the purposes of a search (or such questioning may reveal reasonable grounds to suspect the possession of a different kind of unlawful article from that originally suspected); but the reasonable grounds for suspicion without which any search or detention for the purposes of a search is unlawful cannot be retrospectively provided by such questioning during his detention or by his refusal to answer any question put to him.

(b) All searches

2.4 Before any search of a detained person or attended vehicle takes place the officer must take reasonable steps to give the person to be searched or in charge of the vehicle the following information:

    (i) his name (except in the case of enquiries linked to the investigation of terrorism, in which case he shall give his warrant or other identification number) and the name of the police station to which he is attached;

(ii) the object of the search; and

(iii) his grounds or authorisation for undertaking it.

A

2.5 If the officer is not in uniform he must show his warrant card. In doing so in the case of enquiries linked to the investigation of terrorism, the officer need not reveal his name. Stops and searches under the powers mentioned in paragraphs 1.5 (b) and (c) may be undertaken only by a constable in uniform.

2.6 Unless it appears to the officer that it will not be practicable to make a record of the search, he must also inform the person to be searched (or the owner or person in charge of a vehicle that is to be searched, as the case may be) that he is entitled to a copy of the record of the search if he asks for it within a year. If the person wishes to have a copy and is not given one on the spot, he shall be advised to which police station he should apply.

2.7 If the person to be searched, or in charge of a vehicle to be searched, does not appear to understand what is being said, or there is any doubt about his ability to understand English, the officer must take reasonable steps to bring the information in paragraphs 2.4 and 2.6 to his attention. If the person is deaf or cannot understand English and has someone with him then the officer must try to establish whether that person can interpret or otherwise help him to give the required information.

Note for Guidance

2A In some circumstances preparatory questioning may be unnecessary, but in general a brief conversation or exchange will be desirable as a means of avoiding unsuccessful searches. Where a person is lawfully detained for the purpose of a search, but no search in the event takes place, the detention will not thereby have been rendered unlawful.

3 Conduct of the search

3.1 Every reasonable effort must be made to reduce to the minimum the embarrassment that a person being searched may experience.

3.2 The co-operation of the person to be searched shall be sought in every case, even if he initially objects to the search. A forcible search may be made only if it has been established that the person is unwilling to co-operate (e.g. by opening a bag) or resists. Although force may only be used as a last resort, reasonable force may be used if necessary to conduct a search or to detain a person or vehicle for the purposes of a search.

3.3 The length of time for which a person or vehicle may be detained will depend on the circumstances, but must in all circumstances be reasonable and not extend beyond the time taken for the search. Where the exercise of the power requires reasonable suspicion, the thoroughness and extent of a search must depend on what is suspected of being carried, and by whom. If the suspicion relates to a particular article which is seen to be slipped into a person's pocket, then, in the absence of other grounds for suspicion or an opportunity for the article to be moved elsewhere, the search must be confined to that pocket. In the case of a small article which can readily be concealed, such as a drug, and which might be concealed anywhere on the person, a more extensive search may be necessary. In the case of searches mentioned in paragraph 1.5(b), (c) and (d), which do not require reasonable grounds for suspicion, the officer may make any reasonable search to find what he is empowered to search for. [See *Note 3B*]

3.4 The search must be conducted at or nearby the place where the person or vehicle was first detained.

3.5 Searches in public must be restricted to superficial examination of outer clothing. There is no power to require a person to remove any clothing in public other than an outer coat, jacket or gloves. Where on reasonable grounds it is considered necessary to conduct a more thorough search (e.g. by requiring a person to take off a T-shirt or headgear), this shall be done out of public view for example, in a police van or police station if there is one nearby. Any search involving the removal of more than an outer coat, jacket, gloves, headgear or footwear may only be made by an officer of the same sex as the person searched and may not be made in the presence of anyone of the opposite sex unless the person being searched specifically requests it. [See *Note 3A*]

3.5A Where a pedestrian is stopped under section 13A of the Prevention of Terrorism (Temporary Provisions) Act 1989, a search may be made of anything carried by him. The pedestrian himself must not be searched under this power. This would not prevent a search being carried out under other powers if, in the course of a search of anything carried by the pedestrian, the police officer formed reasonable grounds for suspicion.

Notes for Guidance

3A A search in the street itself should be regarded as being in public for the purposes of paragraph 3.5 above, even though it may be empty at the time a search begins. Although there is no power to require a person to do so, there is nothing to prevent an officer from asking a person to voluntarily remove more than an outer coat, jacket or gloves in public.

3B As a search of a person in public should be superficial examination of outer clothing, such searches should be completed as soon as possible.

4 Action after a search is carried out

(a) General
4.1 An officer who has carried out a search must make a written record unless it is not practicable to do so, on account of the numbers to be searched or for some other operational reason, e.g. in situations involving public disorder.

4.2 The records must be completed as soon as practicable – on the spot unless circumstances (e.g. other immediate duties or very bad weather) make this impracticable.

4.3 The record must be made on the form provided for this purpose (the national search record).

4.4 In order to complete the search record the officer shall normally seek the name, address and date of birth of the person searched, but under the search procedures there is no obligation on a person to provide these details and no power to detain him if he is unwilling to do so.

4.5 The following information must always be included in the record of a search even if the person does not wish to identify himself or give his date of birth:

    (i) the name of the person searched, or (if he withholds it) a description of him;

    (ii) a note of the person's ethnic origin;

    (iii) when a vehicle is searched, a descripton of it, including its registration number; [See *Note 4B*]

    (iv) the object of the search;

    (v) the grounds for making it;

    (vi) the date and time it was made;

    (vii) the place where it was made;

    (viii) its results;

    (ix) a note of any injury or damage to property resulting from it;

    (x) the identity of the officer making it (except in the case of enquiries linked to the investigation of terrorism, in which case the record shall state the officer's warrant or other identification number and duty station). [See *Note 4A*]

4.6 A record is required for each person and each vehicle searched. However, if a person is in a vehicle and both are searched, and the object and grounds of the search are the same, only one record need be completed.

4.7 The record of the grounds for making a search must, briefly but informatively, explain the reason for suspecting the person concerned, whether by reference to his behaviour or other circumstances; or in the case of those searches mentioned in paragraph 1.5(b), (c) and (d) by stating the authority provided to carry out such a search.

4.7A The driver (but not any passengers) of a vehicle which is stopped in accordance with the powers mentioned in paragraphs 1.5(b) and (c) may obtain a written statement to that effect within twelve months from the day the vehicle was searched. A written statement may be similarly obtained by a pedestrian if he is stopped in accordance with the powers mentioned in paragraph 1.5(b) and (c) (see paragraph 2.6). The statement may form part of the national search record or be supplied on a separate document. [See *Note 4C*]

(b) Unattended vehicles

4.8 After searching an unattended vehicle, or anything in or on it, an officer must leave a notice in it (or on it, if things in or on it have been searched without opening it) recording the fact that it has been searched.

4.9 The notice shall include the name of the police station to which the officer concerned is attached and state where a copy of the record of the search may be obtained and where any application for compensation should be directed.

4.10 The vehicle must if practicable be left secure.

Notes for Guidance

4A *Where a search is conducted by more than one officer the identity of all the officers engaged in the search must be recorded on the search record.*

4B *Where a vehicle has not been allocated a registration number (e.g. a rally car or a trials motorbike) that part of the requirements under 4.5 (iii) does not apply.*

4C *In paragraph 4.7A, a written statement means a record that a person or vehicle was stopped under the powers contained in paragraph 1.5 (b) and (c) of this code.*

Annex A   Summary of main stop and search powers [See paragraph 1.3]

Power	Object of search	Extent of search	Where exercisable
Unlawful articles general			
1. Public Stores Act 1875, s6	HM Stores stolen or unlawfully obtained	Persons, vehicles and vessels	Anywhere where the constabulary powers are exercisable
2. Firearms Act 1968, s47	Firearms	Persons and vehicles	A public place, or anywhere in the case of reasonable suspicion of offences of carrying firearms with criminal intent or trespassing with firearms
3. Misuse of Drugs Act 1971, s23	Controlled drugs	Persons and vehicles	Anywhere
4. Customs and Excise Management Act 1979, s163	Goods: (a) on which duty has not been paid; (b) being unlawfully removed, imported or exported; (c) otherwise liable to forfeiture to HM Customs and Excise	Vehicles and vessels only	Anywhere
5. Aviation Security Act 1982, s27(1)	Stolen or unlawfully obtained goods	Airport employees and vehicles carrying airport employees or aircraft or any vehicle in a cargo area whether or not carrying an employee	Any designated airport

Annex A *Continued*

Power	Object of search	Extent of search	Where exercisable
Unlawful articles general			
6. Police and Criminal Evidence Act 1984, s1	Stolen goods; articles for use in certain Theft Act offences; offensive weapons, including bladed or sharply-pointed articles (except folding pocket knives with a bladed cutting edge not exceeding 3 inches)	Persons and vehicles	Where there is public access
Police and Criminal Evidence Act 1984, s6(3) (by a constable of the United Kingdom Atomic Energy Authority Constabulary in respect of property owned or controlled by British Nuclear Fuels plc)	HM Stores (in the form of goods and chattels belonging to British Nuclear Fuels plc)	Persons, vehicles and vessels	Anywhere where the constabulary powers are exercisable
7. Sporting events (Control of Alcohol etc.) Act 1985, s7	Intoxicating liquor	Persons, coaches and trains	Designated sports grounds or coaches and trains travelling to or from a designated sporting event
8. Crossbows Act 1987, s4	Crossbows or parts of crossbows (except with a draw weight of less than 1.4 kilograms)	Persons and vehicles	Anywhere except dwellings

Annex A *Continued*

Power	Object of search	Extent of search	Where exercisable
Evidence of game and wildlife offences			
9. Poaching Prevention Act 1862, s2	Game or poaching equipment	Persons and vehicles	A public place
10. Deer Acts 1963, s5 and 1980, s4	Evidence of offences under the Act	Persons and vehicles	Anywhere except dwellings
11. Conservation of Seals Act 1970, s4	Seals or hunting equipment	Vehicles only	Anywhere
12. Badgers Act 1973, s10	Evidence of offences under the Act	Persons and vehicles	Anywhere
13. Wildlife and Countryside Act 1981, s19	Evidence of wildlife offences	Persons and vehicles	Anywhere except dwellings
Other			
14. Prevention of Terrorism (Temporary Provisions) Act 1989, s15(3)	Evidence of liability to arrest under section 14 of the Act	Persons	Anywhere
15. Prevention of Terrorism (Temporary Provisions) Act 1989, s13A as amended by s81 of the Criminal Justice and Public Order Act 1994	Articles which could be used for a purpose connected with the commission, preparation or instigation of acts of terrorism	Persons and vehicles	Anywhere within the area of locality authorised under subsection (1)
16. Prevention of Terrorism (Temporary Provisions) Act 1989, paragraph 4.2 of Schedule 5	Anything relevant to determining if a person being examined falls within paragraph 2(a) to (c) of Schedule 5	Persons, vehicles, vessels, etc.	At designated ports and airports
17. Section 60 Criminal Justice and Public Order Act 1994	Offensive weapons or dangerous instruments to prevent incidents of serious violence	Persons and vehicles	Anywhere within a locality authorised under subsection (1)

B   Code of Practice for the Searching of Premises by Police Officers and the Seizure of Property Found by Police Officers on Persons or Premises

1 General

1.1 This code of practice must be readily available at all police stations for consultation by police officers, detained persons and members of the public.

1.2 The notes for guidance included are not provisions of this code, but are guidance to police officers and others about its application and interpretation.

1.3 This code applies to searches of premises:
(a)   undertaken for the purposes of an investigation into an alleged offence, with the occupier's consent, other than searches made in the following circumstances:
   – routine scenes of crime searches
   – calls to a fire or a burglary made by or on behalf of an occupier or searches following the activation of fire or burglar alarms
   – searches to which paragraph 4.4 applies
   – bomb threat calls;
(b)   under powers conferred by sections 17, 18 and 32 of the Police and Criminal Evidence Act 1984;
(c)   undertaken in pursuance of a search warrant issued in accordance with section 15 of, or Schedule 1 to the Police and Criminal Evidence Act 1984, or section 15 of, or Schedule 7 to the Prevention of Terrorism (Temporary Provisions) Act 1989.

'Premises' for the purpose of this code is defined in section 23 of the Police and Criminal Evidence Act 1984. It includes any place and, in particular, any vehicle, vessel, aircraft, hovercraft, tent or movable structure. It also includes any offshore installation as defined in section 1 of the Mineral Workings (Offshore Installations) Act 1971.

1.3A Any search of a person who has not been arrested which is carried out during a search of premises shall be carried out in accordance with Code A.

1.3B This code does not apply to the exercise of a statutory power to enter premises or to inspect goods, equipment or procedures if the exercise of that power is not dependent on the existence of grounds for suspecting that an offence may have been committed and the person exercising the power has no reasonable grounds for such suspicion.

2 Search warrants and production orders

(a) Action to be taken before an application is made
2.1 Where information is received which appears to justify an application, the officer concerned must take reasonable steps to check that the information is

accurate, recent and has not been provided maliciously or irresponsibly. An application may not be made on the basis of information from an anonymous source where corroboration has not bee sought. [See *Note 2A*]

2.2 The officer shall ascertain as specifically as is possible in the circumstances the nature of the articles concerned and their location.

2.3 The officer shall also make reasonable enquiries to establish what, if anything, is known about the likely occupier of the premises and the nature of the premises themselves; and whether they have been previously searched and if so how recently; and to obtain any other information relevant to the application.

2.4 No application for a search warrant may be made without the authority of an officer of at least the rank of inspector (or, in the case of urgency where no officer of this rank is readily available, the senior officer on duty). No application for a production order or warrant under Schedule 7 to the Prevention of Terrorism (Temporary Provisions) Act 1989, may be made without the authority of an officer of at least the rank of superintendent.

2.5 Except in a case of urgency, if there is reason to believe that a search might have an adverse effect on relations between the police and the community then the local police/community liaison officer shall be consulted before it takes place. In urgent cases, the local police/community liaison officer shall be informed of the search as soon as practicable after it has been made. [See *Note 2B*]

(b) Making an application
2.6 An application for a search warrant must be supported by an information in writing, specifying:
   (i) the enactment under which the application is made;
  (ii) the premises to be searched and the object of the search; and
  (iii) the grounds on which the application is made (including, where the purpose of the proposed search is to find evidence of an alleged offence, an indication of how the evidence relates to the investigation).

2.7 An application for a search warrant under paragraph 12(a) of Schedule 1 to the Police and Criminal Evidence Act 1984, or under Schedule 7 to the Prevention of Terrorism (Temporary Provisions) Act 1989, shall also, where appropriate, indicate why it is believed that service of notice of an application for a production order may seriously prejudice the investigation.

2.8 If an application is refused, no further application may be made for a warrant to search those premises unless supported by additional grounds.

Notes for Guidance
2A The identity of an informant need not be disclosed when making an application, but the officer concerned should be prepared to deal with any questions the magistrate or judge may have about the accuracy of previous information provided by that source or any other related matters.

2B The local police/community consultative group, where it exists, or its equiva-

lent, should be informed as soon as practicable after a search has taken place where there is reason to belive that it might have had an adverse effect on relations between the police and the community.

Entry without warrant

(a) Making an arrest etc

3.1 The conditions under which an officer may enter and search premises without a warrant are set out in section 17 of the Police and Criminal Evidence Act 1984.

(b) Search after arrest of premises in which arrest takes place or in which the arrested person was present immediately prior to arrest

3.2 The powers of an officer to search premises in which he has arrested a person or where the person was immediately before he was arrested are as set out in section 32 of the Police and Criminal Evidence Act 1984.

(c) Search after arrest of premises other than those in which arrest takes place

3.3 The specific powers of an officer to search premises occupied or controlled by a person who has been arrested for an arrestable offence are as set out in section 18 of the Police and Criminal Evidence Act 1984. They may not (unless subsection (5) of section 18 applies) be exercised unless an officer of the rank of inspector or above has given authority in writing. That authority shall (unless wholly impracticable) be given on the Notice of Powers and Rights (see paragraph 5.7(1)). The record of the search required by section 18(7) of the Act shall be made in the custody record, where there is one. In the case of enquiries linked to the investigation of terrorism, the authorising officer shall use his warrant or other identification number.

4 Search with consent

4.1 Subject to paragraph 4.4 below, if it is proposed to search premises with the consent of a person entitled to grant entry to the premises the consent must, if practicable, be given in writing on the Notice of Powers and Rights before the search takes place. The officer must make enquiries to satisfy himself that the person is in a position to give such consent. [See *Notes 4A and 4B* and paragraph 5.7 (i)]

4.2 Before seeking consent the officer in charge of the search shall state the purpose of the proposed search and inform the person concerned that he is not obliged to consent and that anything seized may be produced in evidence. If at the time the person is not suspected of an offence, the officer shall tell him so when stating the purpose of the search.

4.3 An officer cannot enter and search premises or continue to search premises under 4.1 above if the consent has been given under duress or is withdrawn before the search is completed.

4.4 It is unnecessary to seek consent under paragraphs 4.1 and 4.2 above where in the circumstances this would cause disproportionate inconvenience to the person concerned. [See *Note 4C*]

Notes for Guidance

4A *In the case of a lodging house or similar accommodation a search should not be made on the basis solely of the landlord's consent unless the tenant, lodger or occupier is unavailable and the matter is urgent.*

4B *Where it is intended to search premises under the authority of a warrant or a power of entry and search without warrant, and the co-operation of the occupier of the premises is obtained in accordance with paragraph 5.4 below, there is no additional requirement to obtain written consent as at paragraph 4.1 above.*

4C *Paragraph 4.4 is intended in particular to apply to circumstances where it is reasonable to assume that innocent occupiers would agree to, and expect that, police should take the proposed action. Examples are where a suspect has fled from the scene of a crime or to evade arrest and it is necessary quickly to check surrounding gardens and readily accessible places to see whether he is hiding; or where police have arrested someone in the night after a pursuit and it is necessary to make a brief check of gardens along the route of the pursuit to see whether stolen or incriminating articles have been discarded.*

5 Searching of premises: general considerations

(a) Time of searches

5.1 Searches made under warrant must be made within one calendar month from the date of issue of the warrant.

5.2 Searches must be made at a reasonable hour unless this might frustrate the purpose of the search. [See *Note 5A*]

5.3 A warrant authorises an entry on one occasion only.

(b) Entry other than with consent

5.4 The officer in charge shall first attempt to communicate with the occupier or any other person entitled to grant access to the premises by explaining the authority under which he seeks entry to the premises and ask the occupier to allow him to enter, unless:

   (i) the premises to be searched are known to be unoccupied;

   (ii) the occupier and any other person entitled to grant access are known to be absent; or

   (iii) there are reasonable grounds for believing that to alert the occupier or any other person entitled to grant access by attempting to communicate with him would frustrate the object of the search or endanger the officers concerned or other people.

5.5 Where the premises are occupied the officer shall identify himself (by warrant or other identification number in the case of inquiries linked to the investigation of terrorism) and, if not in uniform, show his warrant card (but in so doing in the case of enquiries linked to the investigation of terrorism, the officer need not reveal his name); and state the purpose of the search and the grounds for undertaking it, before a search begins, unless sub-paragraph 5.4 (iii) applies.

5.6 Reasonable force may be used if necessary to enter premises if the officer in charge is satisified that the premises are those specified in any warrant, or in exercise of the powers described in 3.1 to 3.3 above, and where:

   (i) the occupier or any other person entitled to grant access has refused a request to allow entry to his premises;

  (ii) it is impossible to communicate with the occupier or any other person entitled to grant access; or

 (iii) any of the provisions of 5.4 (i) to (iii) apply.

(c) Notice of Powers and Rights

5.7 If an officer conducts a search to which this code applies he shall, unless it is impracticable to do so, provide the occupier with a copy of a notice in a standard format:

   (i) specifying whether the search is made under warrant, or with consent, or in the exercise of the powers described in 3.1 to 3.3 above (the format of the notice shall provide for authority or consent to be indicated where appropriate – see 3.3 and 4.1 above);

  (ii) summarising the extent of the powers of search and seizure conferred in the Act;

 (iii) explaining the rights of the occupier, and of the owner of property seized in accordance with the provisions of 6.1 to 6.5 below, set out in the Act and in this code;

 (iv) explaining that compensation may be payable in appropriate cases for damages caused in entering and searching premises, and giving the address to which an application for compensation should be directed;

  (v) stating that a copy of this code is available to be consulted at any police station.

5.8 If the occupier is present, copies of the notice mentioned above, and of the warrant (if the search is made under warrant) shall if practicable be given to the occupier before the search begins, unless the officer in charge of the search reasonably believes that to do so would frustrate the object of the search or endanger the officers concerned or other people. If the occupier is not present, copies of the notice, and of the warrant where appropriate, shall be left in a prominent place on the premises or appropriate part of the premises and endorsed with the name of the officer in charge of the search (except in the case of enquiries linked to the investigation of terrorism, in which case the officer's warrant or other identification number shall be given), the name of the police station to which he is attached and the date and time of the search. The warrant itself shall be endorsed to show that this has been done.

(d) Conduct of searches

5.9 Premises may be searched only to the extent necessary to achieve the object of the search, having regard to the size and nature of whatever is sought. A search under warrant may not continue under the authority of that warrant once all the things specified in it have been found, or the officer in charge of the search is satisfied that they are not on the premises.

5.10 Searches must be conducted with due consideration for the property and privacy of the occupier of the premises searched, and with no more disturbance than necessary. Reasonable force may be used only where this is necessary because the co-operation of the occupier cannot be obtained or is insufficient for the purpose.

5.11 If the occupier wishes to ask a friend, neighbour or other person to witness the search then he must be allowed to do so, unless the officer in charge has reasonable grounds for believing that this would seriously hinder the investigation or endanger the officers concerned or other people. A search need not be unreasonably delayed for this purpose.

(e) Leaving premises
5.12 If premises have been entered by force the officer in charge shall before leaving them, satisfy himself that they are secure either by arranging for the occupier or his agent to be present or by any other appropriate means.

(f) Search under Schedule 1 to the Police and Criminal Evidence Act 1984
5.13 An officer of the rank of inspector or above shall take charge of and be present at any search made under a warrant issued under Schedule 1 to the Police and Criminal Evidence Act 1984 or under Schedule 7 to the Prevention of Terrorism (Temporary Provisions) Act 1989. He is responsible for ensuring that the search is conducted with discretion and in such a manner as to cause the least possible disruption to any business or other activities carried on in the premises.

5.14 After satisfying himself that material may not be taken from the premises without his knowledge, the officer in charge of the search shall ask for the documents or other records concerned to be produced. He may also, if he considers it to be necessary, ask to see the index to files held on the premises, if there is one; and the officers conducting the search may inspect any files which, according to the index, appear to contain any of the material sought. A more extensive search of the premises may be made only if the person responsible for them refuses to produce the material sought, or to allow access to the index; if it appears that the index is inaccurate or incomplete; or if for any other reason the officer in charge has reasonable grounds for believing that such a search is necessary in order to find the material sought. [See *Note 5B*]

Notes for Guidance

5A *In determining at what time to make a search, the officer in charge should have regard, among other considerations, to the time of day at which the occupier of the premises is likely to be present, and should not search at a time when he, or any other person on the premises, is likely to be asleep unless not doing so is likely to frustrate the purpose of the search.*

5B *In asking for documents to be produced in accordance with paragraph 5.14 above, officers should direct the request to a person in authority and with responsibility for the documents.*

5C *If the wrong premises are searched by mistake, everything possible should be done at the earliest opportunity to allay any sense of grievance. In appropriate cases assistance should be given to obtain compensation.*

6 Seizure and retention of property

(a) Seizure

6.1 Subject to paragraph 6.2 below, an officer who is searching any premises under any statutory power or with the consent of the occupier may seize:

(a) anything covered by a warrant; and

(b) anything which he has reasonable grounds for believing is evidence of an offence or has been obtained in consequence of the commission of an offence.

Items under (b) may only be seized where this is necessary to prevent their concealment, alteration, loss, damage or destruction.

6.2 No item may be seized which is subject to legal privilege (as defined in section 10 of the Police and Criminal Evidence Act 1984).

6.3 An officer who decides that it is not appropriate to seize property because of an explanation given by the person holding it, but who has reasonable grounds for believing that it has been obtained in consequence of the commission of an offence by some person, shall inform the holder of his suspicions and shall explain that, if he disposes of the property, he may be liable to civil or criminal proceedings.

6.4 An officer may photograph or copy, or have photographed or copied, any document or other article which he has power to seize in accordance with paragraph 6.1 above.

6.5 Where an officer considers that a computer may contain information which could be used in evidence, he may require the information to be produced in a form which can be taken away and in which it is visible and legible.

(b) Retention

6.6 Subject to paragraph 6.7 below, anything which has been seized in accordance with the above provisions may be retained only for as long as is necessary in the circumstances. It may be retained, among other purposes:

(i) for use as evidence at a trial for an offence;

(ii) for forensic examination or for other investigation in connection with an offence; or

(iii) where there are reasonable grounds for believing that it has been stolen or obtained by the commission of an offence, in order to establish its lawful owner.

6.7 Property shall not be retained in accordance with 6.6(i) and (ii) (i.e. for use as evidence or for the purposes of investigation) if a photograph or copy would suffice for those purposes.

(c) Rights of owners etc

6.8 If property is retained the person who had custody or control of it immediately prior to its seizure must on request be provided with a list or description of the property within a reasonable time.

6.9 He or his representative must be allowed supervised access to the property to examine it or have it photographed or copied, or must be provided with a photograph or copy, in either case within a reasonable time of any request and at his own expense, unless the officer in charge of an investigation has reasonable grounds for believing that this would prejudice the investigation of an offence or any criminal proceedings. In this case a record of the grounds must be made.

Note for Guidance

6A *Any person claiming property seized by the police may apply to a magistrates' court under the Police (Property) Act 1897 for its possession, and should, where appropriate, be advised of this procedure.*

7 Action to be taken after searches

7.1 Where premises have been searched in circumstances to which this code applies, other than in the circumstances covered by the exceptions to paragraph 1.3(a), the officer in charge of the search shall, on arrival at a police station, make or have made a record of the search. The record shall include:

   (i) the address of the premises searched;

   (ii) the date, time and duration of the search;

   (iii) the authority under which the search was made. Where the search was made in the exercise of a statutory power to search premises without warrant, the record shall include the power under which the search was made; and where the search was made under warrant, or with written consent, a copy of the warrant or consent shall be appended to the record or kept in a place identified in the record;

   (iv) the names of all the officers who conducted the search (except in the case of enquiries linked to the investigation of terrorism, in which case the record shall state the warrant or other identification number and duty station of each officer concerned);

   (v) the names of any people on the premises if they are known;

   (vi) either a list of any articles seized or a note of where such a list is kept and, if not covered by a warrant, the reason for their seizure;

   (vii) whether force was used, and, if so, the reason why it was used;

   (viii) details of any damage caused during the search, and the circumstances in which it was caused.

7.2 Where premises have been searched under warrant, the warrant shall be endorsed to show:

   (i) whether any articles specified in the warrant were found;

   (ii) whether any other articles were seized;

   (iii) the date and time at which it was executed;

   (iv) the names of the officers who executed it (except in the case of enquiries linked to the investigation of terrorism, in which case the warrant or other identification number and duty station of each officer concerned shall be shown);

   (v) whether a copy, together with a copy of the Notice of Powers and Rights was handed to the occupier; or whether it was endorsed as required by paragraph 5.8, and left on the premises together with the copy notice and, if so, where.

7.3 Any warrant which has been executed or which has not been executed within one calendar month of its issue shall be returned, if it was issued by a justice of the peace, to the clerk to the justices for the petty sessions area concerned or, if issued by a judge, to the appropriate officer of the court from which he issued it.

8 Search registers

8.1 A search register shall be maintained at each sub-divisional police station. All records which are required to be made by this code shall be made, copied, or referred to in the register.

C Code of Practice for the Detention, Treatment and Questioning of Persons by Police Officers

1 General

1.1 All persons in custody must be dealt with expeditiously, and released as soon as the need for detention has ceased to apply.

1.1A A custody officer is required to perform the functions specified in this code as soon as is practicable. A custody officer shall not be in breach of this code in the event of delay provided that the delay is justifiable and that every reasonable step is taken to prevent unnecessary delay. The custody record shall indicate where a delay has occurred and the reason why. [See Note 1H]

1.2 This code of practice must be readily available at all police stations for consultation by police officers, detained persons and members of the public.

1.3 The notes for guidance included are not provisions of this code, but are guidance to police officers and others about its application and interpretation. Provisions in the annexes to this code are provisions of this code.

1.4 If an officer has any suspicion, or is told in good faith, that a person of any age may be mentally disordered or mentally handicapped, or mentally incapable of understanding the significance of questions put to him or his replies, then that person shall be treated as a mentally disordered or mentally handicapped person for the purposes of this code. [See Note 1G]

1.5 If anyone appears to be under the age of 17 then he shall be treated as a juvenile for the purposes of this code in the absence of clear evidence to show that he is older.

1.6 If a person appears to be blind or seriously visually handicapped, deaf, unable to read, unable to speak or has difficulty orally because of a speech impediment, he shall be treated as such for the purposes of this code in the absence of clear evidence to the contrary.

1.7 In this code 'the appropriate adult' means:
(a) in the case of a juvenile:
    (i) his parent of guardian (or, if he is in care, the care authority or voluntary organisation. The term 'in care' is used in this code to cover all cases in which a juvenile is 'looked after' by a local authority under the terms of the Children Act 1989);
    (ii) a social worker;
    (iii) failing either of the above, another responsible adult aged 18 or over who is not a police officer or employed by the police.
(b) in the case of a person who is mentally disordered or mentally handicapped:
    (i) a relative, guardian or other person responsible for his care or custody;
    (ii) someone who has experience of dealing with mentally disordered or

455

mentally handicapped people but who is not a police officer or employed by the police (such as an approved social worker as defined by the Mental Health Act 1983 or a specialist social worker); or

(iii) failing either of the above, some other responsible adult aged 18 or over who is not a police officer or employed by the police.

[See *Note 1E*]

1.8 Whenever this code requires a person to be given certain information he does not have to be given it if he is incapable at the time of understanding what is said to him or is violent or likely to become violent or is in urgent need of medical attention, but he must be given it as soon as practicable.

1.9 Any reference to a custody officer in this code includes an officer who is performing the functions of a custody officer.

1.10 Subject to paragraph 1.12, this code applies to people who are in custody at police stations in England and Wales whether or not they have been arrested for an offence and to those who have been removed to a police station as a place of safety under sections 135 and 136 of the Mental Health Act 1983. Section 15 (reviews and extensions of detention) however applies solely to people in police detention, for example those who have been brought to a police station under arrest for an offence or have been arrested at a police station for an offence after attending there voluntarily.

1.11 People in police custody include anyone taken to a police station after being arrested under section 14 of the Prevention of Terrorism (Temporary Provisions) Act 1989 or under paragraph 6 of Schedule 5 to that Act by an examining officer who is a constable.

1.12 This code does not apply to the following groups of people in custody:

(i) people who have been arrested by officers from a police force in Scotland exercising their powers of detention under section 137(2) of the Criminal Justice and Public Order Act 1994 (Cross Border powers of arrest etc);

(ii) people arrested under section 3(5) of the Asylum and Immigration Appeals Act 1993 for the purpose of having their fingerprints taken;

(iii) people who have been served a notice advising them of their detention under powers contained in the Immigration Act 1971;

(iv) convicted or remanded prisoners held in police cells on behalf of the Prison Service under the Imprisonment (Temporary Provisions) Act 1980);

but the provisions on conditions of detention and treatment in sections 8 and 9 of this code must be considered as the minimum standards of treatment for such detainees.

Notes for Guidance

1A Although certain sections of this code (e.g. section 9 – treatment of detained persons) apply specifically to people in custody at police stations, those there voluntarily to assist with an investigation should be treated with no less consideration (e.g. offered refreshments at appropriate times) and enjoy an absolute right to obtain legal advice or communicate with anyone outside the police station.

1B *This code does not affect the principle that all citizens have a duty to help police officers to prevent crime and discover offenders. This is a civic rather than a legal duty; but when a police officer is trying to discover whether, or by whom, an offence has been committed he is entitled to question any person from whom he thinks useful information can be obtained, subject to the restrictions imposed by this code. A person's declaration that he is unwilling to reply does not alter this entitlement.*

1C *A person, including a parent or guardian, should not be an appropriate adult if he is suspected of involvement in the offence in question, is the victim, is a witness, is involved in the investigation or has received admissions prior to attending to act as the appropriate adult. If the parent of a juvenile is estranged from the juvenile, he should not be asked to act as the appropriate adult if the juvenile expressly and specifically objects to his presence.*

C

1D *If a juvenile admits an offence to or in the presence of a social worker other than during the time that the social worker is acting as the appropriate adult for that juvenile, another social worker should be the appropriate adult in the interest of fairness.*

1E *In the case of people who are mentally disordered or mentally handicapped, it may in certain circumstances be more satisfactory for all concerned if the appropriate adult is someone who has experience or training in their care rather than a relative lacking such qualifications. But if the person himself prefers a relative to a better qualified stranger or objects to a particular person as the appropriate adult, his wishes should if practicable be respected.*

1EE *A person should always be given an opportunity, when an appropriate adult is called to the police station, to consult privately with a solicitor in the absence of the appropriate adult if they wish to do so.*

1F *A solicitor or lay visitor who is present at the police station in that capacity may not act as the appropriate adult.*

1G *The generic term 'mental disorder' is used throughout this code. 'Mental disorder' is defined in section 1(2) of the Mental Health Act 1983 as 'mental illness, arrested or incomplete development of mind, psychopathic disorder and any other disorder or disability of mind'. It should be noted that 'mental disorder' is different from 'mental handicap' although the two are dealt with similarly throughout this code. Where the custody officer has any doubt as to the mental state or capacity of a person detained an appropriate adult should be called.*

1H *Paragraph 1.1A is intended to cover the kinds of delays which may occur in the processing of detained persons because, for example, a large number of suspects are brought into the police station simultaneously to be placed in custody, or interview rooms are all being used, or where there are difficulties in contacting an appropriate adult, solicitor or interpreter.*

1I *It is important that the custody officer reminds the appropriate adult and the detained person of the right to legal advice and records any reasons for waiving it in accordance with section 6 of this code.*

2 Custody records

2.1 A separate custody record must be opened as soon as practicable for each person who is brought to a police station under arrest or is arrested at the police station having attended there voluntarily. All information which has to be recorded under this code must be recorded as soon as practicable in the custody record unless otherwise specified. Any audio or video recording made in the custody area is not part of the custody record.

2.2 In the case of any action requiring the authority of an officer of a specified rank, his name and rank must be noted in the custody record. The recording of names does not apply to officers dealing with people detained under the Prevention of Terrorism (Temporary Provisions) Act 1989. Instead the record shall state the warrant or other identification number and duty station of such officers.

2.3 The custody officer is responsible for the accuracy and completeness of the custody record and for ensuring that the record or a copy of the record accompanies a detained person if he is transferred to another police station. The record shall show the time of and reason for transfer and the time a person is released from detention.

2.4 A solicitor or appropriate adult must be permitted to consult the custody record of a person detained as soon as practicable after their arrival at the police station. When a person leaves police detention or is taken before a court, he or his legal representative or his appropriate adult shall be supplied on request with a copy of the custody record as soon as practicable. This entitlement lasts for 12 months after his release.

2.5 The person who has been detained, the appropriate adult, or the legal representative shall be permitted to inspect the original custody record after the person has left the police station provided they give reasonable notice of their request. A note of any such inspection shall be made in the custody record.

2.6 All entries in custody records must be timed and signed by the maker. In the case of a record entered on a computer this shall be timed and contain the operator's identification. Warrant or other identification numbers shall be used rather than names in the case of detention under the Prevention of Terrorism (Temporary Provisions) Act 1989.

2.7 The fact and time of any refusal by a person to sign a custody record when asked to do so in accordance with the provisions of this code must itself be recorded.

3 Initial action

(a) Detained persons: normal procedure
3.1 When a person is brought to a police station under arrest or is arrested at the police station having attended there voluntarily, the custody officer must tell him clearly of the following rights and of the fact that they are continuing rights which may be exercised at any stage during the period in custody.

(i) the right to have someone informed of his arrest in accordance with section 5 below;
(ii) the right to consult privately with a solicitor and the fact that independent legal advice is available free of charge; and
(iii) the right to consult these codes of practice. [See *Note 3E*]

3.2 In addition the custody officer must give the person a written notice setting out the above three rights, the right to a copy of the custody record in accordance with paragraph 2.4 above and the caution in the terms prescribed in section 10 below. The notice must also explain the arrangements for obtaining legal advice. The custody officer must also give the person an additional written notice briefly setting out his entitlements while in custody. [See *Notes 3A and 3B*] The custody officer shall ask the person to sign the custody record to acknowledge receipt of these notices and any refusal to sign must be recorded on the custody record.

3.3 A citizen of an independent Commonwealth country or a national of a foreign country (including the Republic of Ireland) must be informed as soon as practicable of his rights of communication with his High Commission, Embassy or Consulate. [See *Section 7*]

3.4 The custody officer shall note on the custody record any comment the person may make in relation to the arresting officer's account but shall not invite comment. If the custody officer authorises a person's detention he must inform him of the grounds as soon as practicable and in any case before that person is then questioned about any offence. The custody officer shall note any comment the person may make in respect of the decision to detain him but, again, shall not invite comment. The custody officer shall not put specific questions to the person regarding his involvement in any offence, nor in respect of any comments he may make in response to the arresting officer's account or the decision to place him in detention. Such an exchange is likely to constitute an interview as defined by paragraph 11.1A and would require the associated safeguards included in section 11. [See also paragraph 11.13 in respect of unsolicited comments.]

3.5 The custody officer shall ask the detained person whether at this time he would like legal advice (see paragraph 6.5). The person shall be asked to sign the custody record to confirm his decision. The custody officer is responsible for ensuring that in confirming any decision the person signs in the correct place.

3.5A If video cameras are installed in the custody area, notices which indicate that cameras are in use shall be prominently displayed. Any request by a detained person or other person to have video cameras switched off shall be refused.

(b) Detained persons: special groups
3.6 If the person appears to be deaf or there is doubt about his hearing or speaking ability or ability to understand English, and the custody officer cannot establish effective communication, the custody officer must as soon as practicable call an interpreter to ask him to provide the information required above. [See *Section 13*]

3.7 If the person is a juvenile, the custody officer must, if it is practicable, ascertain the identity of a person responsible for his welfare. That person may be his parent or guardian (or, if he is in care, the care authority or voluntary organisation) or any other person who has, for the time being, assumed responsibility for his welfare. That person must be informed as soon as practicable that the juvenile has been arrested, why he has been arrested and where he is detained. This right is in addition to the juvenile's right in section 5 of the code not to be held incommunicado. [See Note 3C]

3.8 In the case of a juvenile who is known to be subject to a supervision order, reasonable steps must also be taken to notify the person supervising him.

3.9 If the person is a juvenile, is mentally handicapped or appears to be suffering from a mental disorder, then the custody officer must, as soon as practicable, inform the appropriate adult (who in the case of a juvenile may or may not be a person responsible for his welfare, in accordance with paragraph 3.7 above) of the grounds for his detention and his whereabouts and ask the adult to come to the police station to see the person.

3.10 It is imperative that a mentally disordered or mentally handicapped person who has been detained under section 136 of the Mental Health Act 1983 shall be assessed as soon as possible. If that assessment is to take place at the police station, an approved social worker and a registered medical practitioner shall be called to the police station as soon as possible in order to interview and examine the person. Once the person has been interviewed and examined and suitable arrangements have been made for his treatment or care, he can no longer be detained under section 136. The person should not be released until he has been seen by both the approved social worker and the registered medical practitioner.

3.11 If the appropriate adult is already at the police station, then the provisions of paragraphs 3.1 to 3.5 above must be complied with in his presence. If the appropriate adult is not at the police station when the provisions of paragraphs 3.1 to 3.5 above are complied with, then these provisions must be complied with again in the presence of the appropriate adult once that person arrives.

3.12 The person shall be advised by the custody officer that the appropriate adult (where applicable) is there to assist and advise him and that he can consult privately with the appropriate adult at any time.

3.13 If, having been informed of the right to legal advice under paragraph 3.11 above, either the appropriate adult or the person detained wishes legal advice to be taken, then the provisions of section 6 of this code apply. [See Note 3G]

3.14 If the person is blind or seriously visually handicapped or is unable to read, the custody officer shall ensure that his solicitor, relative, the appropriate adult or some other person likely to take an interest in him (and not involved in the investigation) is available to help in checking any documentation. Where this code requires written consent or signification then the person who is assisting may be asked to sign instead if the detained person so wishes. [See Note 3F]

(c) Persons attending a police station voluntarily

3.15 Any person attending a police station voluntarily for the purpose of assisting with an investigation may leave at will unless placed under arrest. If it is decided that he should not be allowed to leave then he must be informed at once that he is under arrest and brought before the custody officer, who is responsible for ensuring that he is notified of his rights in the same way as other detained persons. If he is not placed under arrest but is cautioned in accordance with section 10 below, the officer who gives the caution must at the same time inform him that he is not under arrest, that he is not obliged to remain at the police station but if he remains at the police station he may obtain free and independent legal advice if he wishes. The officer shall point out that the right to legal advice includes the right to speak with a solicitor on the telephone and ask him if he wishes to do so.

3.16 If a person who is attending the police station voluntarily (in accordance with paragraph 3.15) asks about his entitlement to legal advice, he shall be given a copy of the notice explaining the arrangements for obtaining legal advice. [See paragraph 3.2]

(d) Documentation

3.17 The grounds for a person's detention shall be recorded, in his presence if practicable.

3.18 Action taken under paragraphs 3.6 to 3.14 shall be recorded.

Notes for Guidance

3A The notice of entitlements is intended to provide detained persons with brief details of their entitlements over and above the statutory rights which are set out in the notice of rights. The notice of entitlements should list the entitlements contained in this code, including visits and contact with outside parties (including special provisions for Commonwealth citizens and foreign nationals), reasonable standards of physical comfort, adequate food and drink, access to toilets and washing facilities, clothing, medical attention, and exercise where practicable. It should also mention the provisions relating to the conduct of interviews, the circumstances in which an appropriate adult should be available to assist the detained person and his statutory rights to make representation whenever the period of his detention is reviewed.

3B In addition to the notices in English, translations should be available in Welsh, the main ethnic minority languages and the principal European languages whenever they are likely to be helpful.

3C If the juvenile is in the care of a local authority or voluntary organisation but is living with his parents or other adults responsible for his welfare then, although there is no legal obligation on the police to inform them, they as well as the authority or organisation should normally be contacted unless suspected of involvement in the offence concerned. Even if a juvenile in care is not living with his parents, consideration should be given to informing them as well.

3D Most local authority Social Services Departments can supply a list of interpreters who have the necessary skills and experience to interpret for deaf people at police interviews. The local Community Relations Council may be able to provide similar information in cases where the person concerned does not understand English. [See section 13]

3E The right to consult the codes of practice under paragraph 3.1 above does not entitle the person concerned to delay unreasonably any necessary investigative or administrative action while he does so. Procedures requiring the provision of breath, blood or urine specimens under the terms of the Road Traffic Act 1988 need not be delayed.

3F Blind or seriously visually handicapped people may be unwilling to sign police documents. The alternative of their representative signing on their behalf seeks to protect the interests of both police and detained people.

3G The purpose of paragraph 3.13 is to protect the rights of a juvenile, mentally disordered or mentally handicapped person who may not understand the significance of what is being said to him. If such a person wishes to exercise the right to legal advice the appropriate action should be taken straightaway and not delayed until the appropriate adult arrives.

4 Detained persons' property

(a) Action
4.1 The custody officer is responsible for:
(a) ascertaining:
  (i) what property a detained person has with him when he comes to the police station (whether on arrest, re-detention on answering to bail, commitment to prison custody on the order or sentence of a court, lodgement at the police station with a view to his production in court from such custody, arrival at a police station on transfer from detention at another police station or from hospital or on detention under section 135 or 136 of the Mental Health Act 1983);
  ii) what property he might have acquired for unlawful or harmful purpose while in custody;
(b) the safekeeping of any property which is taken from him and which remains at the police station.
To these ends the custody officer may search him or authorise his being searched to the extent that he considers necessary (provided that a search of intimate parts of the body or involving the removal of more than outer clothing may be made only in accordance with *Annex A* to this code). A search may be only carried out by an officer of the same sex as the person searched. [See *Note 4A*]

4.2 A detained person may retain clothing and personal effects at his own risk unless the custody officer considers that he may use them to cause harm to himself or others, interfere with evidence, damage property or effect an escape or they are needed as evidence. In this event the custody officer may withhold such articles as he considers necessary. If he does so he must tell the person why.

4.3 Personal effects are those items which a person may lawfully need or use or refer to while in detention but do not include cash and other items of value.

(b) Documentation

4.4 The custody officer is responsible for recording all property brought to the police station which a detained person had with him, or had taken from him on arrest. The detained person shall be allowed to check and sign the record of property as correct. Any refusal to sign shall be recorded.

4.5 If a detained person is not allowed to keep any article of clothing or personal effects the reason must be recorded.

Notes for Guidance

4A Section 54(1) of PACE and paragraph 4.1 require a detained person to be searched where it is clear that the custody officer will have continuing duties in relation to that person or where that person's behaviour or offence makes an inventory appropriate. They do not require every detained person to be searched. Where, for example, it is clear that a person will only be detained for a short period and is not to be placed in a cell, the custody officer may decide not to search him. In such a case the custody record will be endorsed 'not searched', paragraph 4.4 will not apply, and the person will be invited to sign the entry. Where the person detained refuses to sign, the custody officer will be obliged to ascertain what property he has on him in accordance with paragraph 4.1.

4B Paragraph 4.4 does not require the custody officer to record on the custody record property in the possession of the person on arrest, if by virtue of its nature, quantity or size, it is not practicable to remove it to the police station.

4C Paragraph 4.4 above is not to be taken as requiring that items of clothing worn by the person be recorded unless withheld by the custody officer in accordance with paragraph 4.2.

5 Right not to be held incommunicado

(a) Action

5.1 Any person arrested and held in custody at a police station or other premises may on request have one person known to him or who is likely to take an interest in his welfare informed at public expense of his whereabouts as soon as practicable. If the person cannot be contacted the person who has made the request may choose up to two alternatives. If they too cannot be contacted the person in charge of detention or of the investigation has discretion to allow further attempts until the information has been conveyed. [See *Notes 5C and 5D*]

5.2 The exercise of the above right in respect of each of the persons nominated may be delayed only in accordance with *Annex B* to this code.

5.3 The above right may be exercised on each occasion that a person is taken to another police station.

5.4 The person may receive visits at the custody officer's discretion. [See *Note 5B*]

5.5 Where an enquiry as to the whereabouts of the person is made by a friend, relative or person with an interest in his welfare, this information shall be given, if he agrees and if *Annex B* does not apply. [See *Note 5D*]

5.6 Subject to the following condition, the person shall be supplied with writing materials on request and allowed to speak on the telephone for a reasonable time to one person. [See *Notes 5A and 5E*] Where an officer of the rank of Inspector or above considers that the sending of a letter or the making of a telephone call may result in:

(a) any of the consequences set out in the first and second paragraphs of *Annex B* and the person is detained in connection with an arrestable or a serious arrestable offence, for which purpose, any reference to a serious arrestable offence in *Annex B* includes an arrestable offence; or

(b) either of the consequences set out in paragraph 8 of *Annex B* and the person is detained under the Prevention of Terrorism (Temporary Provisions) Act 1989;

that officer can deny or delay the exercise of either or both these privileges. However, nothing in this section permits the restriction or denial of the rights set out in paragraphs 5.1 and 6.1.

5.7 Before any letter or message is sent, or telephone call made, the person shall be informed that what he says in any letter, call or message (other than in the case of a communication to a solicitor) may be read or listened to as appropriate and may be given in evidence. A telephone call may be terminated if it is being abused. The costs can be at public expense at the discretion of the custody officer.

(b) Documentation
5.8 A record must be kept of:
(a) any request made under this section and the action taken on it;
(b) any letters, messages or telephone calls made or received or visits received; and
(c) any refusal on the part of the person to have information about himself or his whereabouts given to an outside enquirer. The person must be asked to countersign the record accordingly and any refusal to sign shall be recorded.

Notes for Guidance
5A *An interpreter may make a telehone call or write a letter on a person's behalf.*

5B *In the exercise of his discretion the custody officer should allow visits where possible in the light of the availability of sufficient manpower to supervise a visit and any possible hindrance to the investigation.*

5C *If the person does not know of anyone to contact for advice or support or cannot contact a friend or relative, the custody officer should bear in mind any local voluntary bodies or other organisations who might be able to offer help in such cases. But if it is specifically legal advice that is wanted, then paragraph 6.1 below will apply.*

5D *In some circumstances it may not be appropriate to use the telephone to disclose information under paragraphs 5.1 and 5.5 above.*

5E *The telephone call at paragraph 5.6 is in addition to any communication under paragraphs 5.1 and 6.1.*

6 Right to legal advice

(a) Action

6.1 Subject to the provisos in Annex B all people in police detention must be informed that they may at any time consult and communicate privately, whether in person, in writing or by telephone with a solicitor, and that independent legal advice is available free of charge from the duty solicitor. [See paragraph 3.1 and *Note 6B* and *Note 6J*]

6.2 [Not Used]

6.3 A poster advertising the right to have legal advice must be prominently displayed in the charging area of every police station. [See *Note 6H*]

6.4 No police officer shall at any time do or say anything with the intention of dissuading a person in detention from obtaining legal advice.

6.5 The exercise of the right of access to legal advice may be delayed only in accordance with *Annex B* to this code. Whenever legal advice is requested (and unless *Annex B* applies) the custody officer must act without delay to secure the provision of such advice to the person concerned. If, on being informed or reminded of the right to legal advice, the person declines to speak to a solicitor in person, the officer shall point out that the right to legal advice includes the right to speak with a solicitor on the telephone and ask him if he wishes to do so. If the person continues to waive his right to legal advice, the officer shall ask him the reasons for doing so, and any reasons shall be recorded on the custody or the interview record as appropriate. Reminders of the right to legal advice must be given in accordance with paragraphs 3.5, 11.2, 15.3, 16.4 and 16.5 of this code and paragraphs 2.15(ii) and 5.2 of Code D. Once it is clear that a person neither wishes to speak to a solicitor in person nor by telephone he should cease to be asked his reasons. [See *Note 6K*]

6.6 A person who wants legal advice may not be interviewed or continue to be interviewed until he has received it unless:
(a) *Annex B* applies; or
(b) an officer of the rank of superintendent or above has reasonable grounds for believing that:
    (i) delay will involve an immediate risk of harm to persons or serious loss of, or damage to, property; or
    (ii) where a solicitor, including a duty solicitor, has been contacted and has agreed to attend, awaiting his arrival would cause unreasonable delay to the process of investigation; or
(c) the solicitor nominated by the person, or selected by him from a list:
    (i) cannot be contacted; or
    ii) has previously indicated that he does not wish to be contacted; or
    (iii) having been contacted, has declined to attend;
    and the person has been advised of the Duty Solicitor Scheme but has declined to ask for the duty solicitor, or the duty solicitor is unavailable. (In these circumstances the interview may be started or continued without further delay provided that an officer of the rank of Inspector or above has given agreement

for the interview to proceed in those circumstances – see *Note 6B*).
(d) the person who wanted legal advice changes his mind.

In these circumstances the interview may be started or continued without further delay provided that the person has given his agreement in writing or on tape to being interviewed without receiving legal advice and that an officer of the rank of inspector or above, having inquired into the person's reasons for his change of mind, has given authority for the interview to proceed. Confirmation of the person's agreement, his change of mind, his reasons where given and the name of the authorising officer shall be recorded in the taped or written interview record at the beginning or recommencement of interview. [See *Note 6I*]

6.7 Where 6.6(b)(i) applies, once sufficient information to avert the risk has been obtained, questioning must cease until the person has received legal advice unless 6.6(a), (b)(ii), (c) or (d) apply.

6.8 Where a person has been permitted to consult a solicitor and the solicitor is available (i.e. present at the station or on his way to the station or easily contactable by telephone) at the time the interview begins or is in progress, the solicitor must be allowed to be present while he is interviewed.

6.9 The solicitor may only be required to leave the interview if his conduct is such that the investigating officer is unable properly to put questions to the suspect. [See *Notes 6D* and *6E*]

6.10 If the investigating officer considers that a solicitor is acting in such a way, he will stop the interview and consult an officer not below the rank of superintendent, if one is readily available, and otherwise an officer not below the rank of inspector who is not connected with the investigation. After speaking to the solicitor, the officer who has been consulted will decide whether or not the interview should continue in the presence of that solicitor. If he decides that it should not, the suspect will be given the opportunity to consult another solicitor before the interview continues and that solicitor will be given an opportunity to be present at the interview.

6.11 The removal of a solicitor from an interview is a serious step and, if it occurs, the officer of superintendent rank or above who took the decision will consider whether the incident should be reported to the Law Society. If the decision to remove the solicitor has been taken by an officer below the rank of superintendent, the facts must be reported to an officer of superintendent rank or above who will similarly consider whether a report to the Law Society would be appropriate. Where the solicitor concerned is a duty solicitor, the report should be both to the Law Society and to the Legal Aid Board.

6.12 In Codes of Practice issued under the Police and Criminal Evidence Act 1984, 'solicitor' means a solicitor who holds a current practising certificate, a trainee solicitor, a duty solicitor representative or an accredited representative included on the register of representatives maintained by the Legal Aid Board. If a solicitor wishes to send a non-accredited or probationary representative to provide advice on his behalf, then that person shall be admitted to the police station for this purpose unless an officer of the rank of inspector or above considers that such a visit will hinder the investigation of crime and directs otherwise. (Hindering the investigation of a crime does not include giving proper legal advice to a detained person in accordance with *Note* 6D.) Once admitted to the police station, the provisions of paragraphs 6.6 to 6.10 apply.

6.13 In exercising his discretion under paragraph 6.12, the officer should take into account in particular whether the identity and status of the non-accredited or probationary representative have been satisfactorily established; whether he is of suitable character to provide legal advice (a person with a criminal record is unlikely to be suitable unless the conviction was for a minor offence and is not of recent date); and any other matters in any written letter of authorisation provided by the solicitor on whose behalf the person is attending the police station. [See *Note* 6F]

6.14 If the inspector refuses access to a non-accredited or probationary representative or a decision is taken that such a person should not be permitted to remain at an interview, he must forthwith notify a solicitor on whose behalf the non-accredited or probationary representative was to have acted or was acting, and give him an opportunity to make alternative arrangements. The detained person must also be informed and the custody record noted.

6.15 If a solicitor arrives at the station to see a particular person, that person must (unless *Annex B* applies) be informed of the solicitor's arrival whether or not he is being interviewed and asked whether he would like to see him. This applies even if the person concerned has already declined legal advice or having requested it, subsequently agreed to be interviewed without having received advice. The solicitor's attendance and the detained person's decision must be noted in the custody record.

(b) Documentation
6.16 Any request for legal advice and the action taken on it shall be recorded.

6.17 If a person has asked for legal advice and an interview is begun in the absence of a solicitor or his representative (or the solicitor or his representative has been required to leave an interview), a record shall be made in the interview record.

Notes for Guidance
6A In considering whether paragraph 6.6(b) applies, the officer should where practicable ask the solicitor for an estimate of the time that he is likely to take in coming to the station, and relate this information to the time for which detention is permitted, the time of day (i.e. whether the period of rest required by paragraph 12.2 is imminent) and the requirements of other investigations in progress. If the solicitor says that he is on his way to the station or that he will set off immediately, it will not normally be appropriate to begin an interview before he arrives. If it appears that it will be necessary to begin an interview before the solicitor's arrival he should be given an indication of how long the police would be able to wait before paragraph 6.6(b) applies so that he has an opportunity to make arrangements for legal advice to be provided by someone else.

6B A person who asks for legal advice should be given an opportunity to consult a specific solicitor or another solicitor from that solicitor's firm or the duty solicitor. If advice is not available by these means, or he does not wish to consult the duty solicitor, the person should be given an opportunity to choose a solicitor from a list of those willing to provide legal advice. If this solicitor is unavailable, he may choose up two alternatives. If these attempts to secure legal advice are unsuccessful, the custody officer has discretion to allow further attempts until a solicitor has been contacted and agrees to provide legal advice. Apart from carrying out his duties under Note 6B, a police officer must not advise the suspect about any particular firm of solicitors.

6C [Not Used]

6D A detained person has a right to free legal advice and to be represented by a solicitor. The solicitor's only role in the police station is to protect and advance the legal rights of his client. On occasions this may require the solicitor to give advice which has the effect of his client avoiding giving evidence which strengthens a prosecution case. The solicitor may intervene in order to seek clarification or to challenge an improper question to his client or the manner in which it is put, or to advise his client not to reply to particular questions, or if he wishes to give his client further legal advice. Paragraph 6.9 will only apply if the solicitor's approach or conduct prevents or unreasonably obstructs proper questions being put to the suspect or his response being recorded. Examples of unacceptable conduct include answering questions on a suspect's behalf or providing written replies for him to quote.

6E In a case where an officer takes the decision to exclude a solicitor, he must be in a position to satisfy the court that the decision was properly made. In order to do this he may need to witness what is happening himself.

6F If an officer of at least the rank of inspector considers that a particular solicitor or firm of solicitors is persistently sending non-accredited or probationary representatives who are unsuited to provide legal advice, he should inform an officer of at least the rank of superintendent, who may wish to take the matter up with the Law Society.

6G Subject to the constraints of Annex B, a solicitor may advise more than one client in an investigation if he wishes. Any question of a conflict of interest is for the solicitor under his professional code of conduct. If, however, waiting for a solicitor to give advice to one client may lead to unreasonable delay to the interview with another, the provisions of paragraph 6.6(b) may apply.

6H In addition to a poster in English advertising the right to legal advice, a poster or posters containing translations into Welsh, the main ethnic minority languages and the principal European languages should be displayed wherever they are likely to be helpful and it is practicable to do so.

6I Paragraph 6.6(d) requires the authorisation of an officer of the rank of inspector or above, to the continuation of an interview, where a person who wanted legal advice changes his mind. It is permissible for such authorisation to be given over the telephone, if the authorising officer is able to satisfy himself as to the reason for *the person's change of mind and is satisfied that it is proper to continue the interview in those circumstances.*

6J Where a person chooses to speak to a solicitor on the telephone, he should be allowed to do so in private unless this is impractical because of the design and layout of the custody area or the location of telephones.

6K A person is not obliged to give reasons for declining legal advice and should not be pressed if he does not wish to do so.

7 Citizens of Independent Commonwealth countries or foreign nationals

(a) Action
7.1 Any citizen of an independent Commonwealth country or a national of a foreign country (including the Republic of Ireland) may communicate at any time with his High Commission, Embassy or Consulate. He must be informed of this right as soon as practicable. He must also be informed as soon as practicable of his right, upon request to have his High Commission, Embassy or Consulate told of his whereabouts and the grounds for his detention. Such a request should be acted upon as soon as practicable.

7.2 If a person is detained who is a citizen of an independent Commonwealth or foreign country with which a bilateral consular convention or agreement is in force requiring notification of arrest, the appropriate High Commission, Embassy or Consulate shall be informed as soon as practicable, subject to paragraph 7.4 below. The countries to which this applies as at 1 January 1995 are listed in *Annex F*.

7.3 Consular officers may visit one of their nationals who is in police detention to talk to him and, if required, to arrange for legal advice. Such visits shall take place out of the hearing of a police officer.

7.4 Notwithstanding the provisions of consular conventions, where the person is a political refugee (whether for reasons of race, nationality, political opinion or religion) or is seeking political asylum, a consular officer shall not be informed of the arrest of one of his nationals or given access or information about him except at the person's express request.

(b) Documentation
7.5 A record shall be made when a person is informed of his rights under this section and of any communications with a High Commission, Embassy or Consulate.

Note for Guidance
7A *The exercise of the rights in this section may not be interfered with even though* Annex B *applies.*

8 Conditions of Detention

(a) Action
8.1 So far as is practicable, not more than one person shall be detained in each cell.

8.2 Cells in use must be adequately heated, cleaned and ventilated. They must be adequately lit, subject to such dimming as is compatible with safety and security to allow people detained overnight to sleep. No additional restraints shall be used within a locked cell unless absolutely necessary, and then only suitable handcuffs. In the case of a mentally handicapped or mentally disordered person, particular care must be taken when deciding whether to use handcuffs. [See Annex E paragraph 13]

8.3 Blankets, mattresses, pillows and other bedding supplied shall be of a reasonable standard and in a clean and sanitary condition. [See Note 8B]

8.4 Access to toilet and washing facilities must be provided.

8.5 If it is necessary to remove a person's clothes for the purposes of investigation, for hygiene or health reasons or for cleaning, replacement clothing of a reasonable standard of comfort and cleanliness shall be provided. A person may not be interviewed unless adequate clothing has been offered to him.

8.6 At least two light meals and one main meal shall be offered in any period of 24 hours. [See Note 8C] Drinks should be provided at meal times and upon reasonable request between meal times. Whenever necessary, advice shall be sought from the police surgeon on medical and dietary matters. As far as practicable, meals provided shall offer a varied diet and meet any special dietary needs or religious beliefs that the person may have; he may also have meals supplied by his family or friends at his or their own expense. [See Note 8B]

8.7 Brief outdoor exercise shall be offered daily if practicable.

8.8 A juvenile shall not be placed in a police cell unless no other secure accommodation is available and the custody officer considers that it is not practicable to supervise him if he is not placed in a cell or the custody officer considers that a cell provides more comfortable accommodation than other secure accommodation in the police station. He may not be placed in a cell with a detained adult.

8.9 Reasonable force may be used if necessary for the following purposes:
  (i) to secure compliance with reasonable instructions, including instructions given in pursuance of the provisions of a code of practice; or
  (ii) to prevent escape, injury, damage to property or the destruction of evidence.

8.10 People detained shall be visited every hour, and those who are drunk, at least every half hour. A person who is drunk shall be roused and spoken to on each visit. [See Note 8A] Should the custody officer feel in any way concerned about the person's condition, for example because he fails to respond adequately when roused, then the officer shall arrange for medical treatment in accordance with paragraph 9.2 of this code.

(b) Documentation
8.11 A record must be kept of replacement clothing and meals offered.

8.12 If a juvenile is placed in a cell, the reason must be recorded.

Notes for Guidance

8A *Whenever possible juveniles and other people at risk should be visited more frequently.*

8B *The provisions in paragraphs 8.3 and 8.6 respectively regarding bedding and a varied diet are of particular importance in the case of a person detained under the Prevention of Terrorism (Temporary Provisions) Act 1989, immigration detainees and others who are likely to be detained for an extended period.*

8C *Meals should so far as practicable be offered at recognised meal times.*

9 Treatment of Detained Persons

(a) General

9.1 If a complaint is made by or on behalf of a detained person about his treatment since his arrest, or it comes to the notice of any officer that he may have been treated improperly, a report must be made as soon as practicable to an officer of the rank of inspector or above who is not connected with the investigation. If the matter concerns a possible assault or the possibility of the unnecessary or unreasonable use of force then the police surgeon must also be called as soon as practicable.

(b) Medical Treatment

9.2 The custody officer must immediately call the police surgeon (or, in urgent cases, – for example, where a person does not show signs of sensibility or awareness, – must send the person to hospital or call the nearest available medical practitioner) if a person brought to a police station or already detained there:

(a) appears to be suffering from physical illness or a mental disorder; or
(b) is injured; or
(c) [Not Used]
(d) fails to respond normally to questions or conversation (other than through drunkenness alone); or
(e) otherwise appears to need medical attention.

This applies even if the person makes no request for medical attention and whether or not he has already had medical treatment elsewhere (unless brought to the police station direct from hospital). It is not intended that the contents of this paragraph should delay the transfer of a person to a place of safety under section 136 of the Mental Healt Act 1983 where that is applicable. Where an assessment under that Act is to take place at the police station, the custody officer has discretion not to call the police surgeon so long as he believes that the assessment by a registered medical practitioner can be undertaken without undue delay. [See *Note 9A*]

9.3 If it appears to the custody officer, or he is told, that a person brought to the police station under arrest may be suffering from an infectious disease of any significance he must take steps to isolate the person and his property until he has obtained medical directions as to where the person should be taken, whether fumigation should take place and what precautions should be taken by officers who have been or will be in contact with him.

9.4 If a detained person requests a medical examination the police surgeon must be called as soon as practicable. He may in addition be examined by a medical practitioner of his own choice at his own expense.

9.5 If a person is required to take or apply any medication in compliance with medical directions, but prescribed before the person's detention, the custody officer should consult the police surgeon prior to the use of the medication. The custody officer is responsible for the safekeeping of any medication and for ensuring that the person is given the opportunity to take or apply medication which the police surgeon has approved. However no police officer may administer medicines which are also controlled drugs subject to the Misuse of Drugs Act 1971 for this purpose. A person may administer a controlled drug to himself only under the personal supervision of the police surgeon. The requirement for personal supervision will have been satisfied if the custody officer consults the police surgeon (this may be done by telephone) and both the police surgeon and the custody officer are satisfied that, in all the circumstances, self administration of the controlled drug will not expose the detained person, police officers or anyone to the risk of harm or injury. If so satisfied, the police surgeon may authorise the custody officer to permit the detained person to administer the controlled drug. If the custody officer is in any doubt, the police surgeon should be asked to attend. Such consultation should be noted in the custody record.

9.6 If a detained person has in his possession or claims to need medication relating to a heart condition, diabetes, epilepsy or a condition of comparable potential seriousness then, even though paragraph 9.2 may not apply, the advice of the police surgeon must be obtained.

(c) Documentation
9.7 A record must be made of any arrangements made for an examination by a police surgeon under paragraph 9.1 above and of any complaint reported under that paragraph together with any relevant remarks by the custody officer.

9.8 A record must be kept of any request for a medical examination under paragraph 9.4, of the arrangements for any examinations made, and of any medical directions to the police.

9.9 Subject to the requirements of section 4 above the custody record shall include not only a record of all medication that a detained person has in his possession on arrival at the police station but also a note of any such medication he claims he needs but does not have with him.

Notes for Guidance
9A The need to call a police surgeon need not apply to minor ailments or injuries which do not need attention. However, all such ailments or injuries must be recorded in the custody record and any doubt must be resolved in favour of calling the police surgeon.

9B *It is important to remember that a person who appears to be drunk or behaving abnormally may be suffering from illness or the effects of drugs or may have sustained injury (particularly head injury) which is not apparent, and that someone needing or addicted to certain drugs may experience harmful effects within a short time of being deprived of their supply. Police should therefore always call the police surgeon when in any doubt, and act with all due speed.*

9C *If a medical practitioner does not record his clinical findings in the custody record, the record must show where they are recorded.*

10 Cautions

(a) When a caution must be given

10.1 A person whom there are grounds to suspect of an offence must be cautioned before any questions about it (or further questions if it is his answers to previous questions which provide the grounds for suspicion) are put to him regarding his involvement or suspected involvement in that offence if his answers or his silence (i.e. failure or refusal to answer a question or to answer satisfactorily) may be given in evidence to a court in a prosecution. He therefore need not be cautioned if questions are put for other purposes, for example, solely to establish his identity or his ownership of any vehicle or to obtain information in accordance with any relevant statutory requirement (see paragraph 10.5C) or in furtherance of the proper and effective conduct of a search, (for example to determine the need to search in the exercise of powers to stop and search or to seek cooperation while carrying out a search) or to seek verification of a written record in accordance with paragraph 11.13.

10.2 Whenever a person who is not under arrest is initially cautioned or is reminded that he is under caution (see paragraph 10.5) he must at the same time be told that he is not under arrest and is not obliged to remain with the officer (see paragraph 3.15).

10.3 A person must be cautioned upon arrest for an offence unless:
(a) it is impracticable to do so by reason of his condition or behaviour at the time; or
(b) he has already been cautioned immediately prior to arrest in accordance with paragraph 10.1 above.

(b) Action: general

10.4 The caution shall be in the following terms:
"You do not have to say anything But it may harm your defence if you do not mention when questioned something which you later rely on in court. Anything you do say may be given in evidence."
Minor deviations do not constitute a breach of this requirement provided that the sense of the caution is preserved. [See *Note 10C*]

10.5 When there is a break in questioning under caution the interviewing officer must ensure that the person being questioned is aware that he remains under caution. If there is any doubt the caution shall be given again in full when the interview resumes. [See *Note 10A*]

Special warnings under sections 36 and 37 of the Criminal Justice and Public Order Act 1994

10.5A When a suspect who is interviewed after arrest fails or refuses to answer certain questions, or to answer them satisfactorily, after due warning, a court or jury may draw such inferences as appear proper under sections 36 and 37 of the Criminal Justice and Public Order Act 1994. This applies when:

(a) a suspect is arrested by a constable and there is found on his person, or in or on his clothing or footwear, or otherwise in his possession, or in the place where he was arrested, any objects, marks or substances, or marks on such objects, and the person fails or refuses to account for the objects, marks or substances found; or

(b) an arrested person was found by a constable at a place at or about the time the offence for which he was arrested, is alleged to have been committed, and the person fails or refuses to account for his presence at that place.

10.5B For an inference to be drawn from a suspect's failure or refusal to answer a question about one of these matters or to answer it satisfactorily, the interviewing officer must first tell him in ordinary language:

(a) what offence he is investigating;

(b) what fact he is asking the suspect to account for;

(c) that he believes this fact may be due to the suspect's taking part in the commission of the offence in question;

(d) that a court may draw a proper inference if he fails or refuses to account for the fact about which he is being questioned;

(e) that a record is being made of the interview and that it may be given in evidence if he is brought to trial.

10.5C Where, despite the fact that a person has been cautioned, failure to co-operate may have an effect on his immediate treatment, he should be informed of any relevant consequences and that they are not affected by the caution. Examples are when his refusal to provide his name and address when charged may render him liable to detention, or when his refusal to provide particulars and information in accordance with a statutory requirement, for example, under the Road Traffic Act 1988, may amount to an offence or may make him liable to arrest.

(c) Juveniles, the mentally disordered and the mentally handicapped

10.6 If a juvenile or a person who is mentally disordered or mentally handicapped is cautioned in the absence of the appropriate adult, the caution must be repeated in the adult's presence.

(d) Documentation

10.7 A record shall be made when a caution is given under this section, either in the officer's pocket book or in the interview record as appropriate.

Notes for Guidance

10A In considering whether or not to caution again after a break the officer should bear in mind that he may have to satisfy a court that the person understood that he was still under caution when the interview resumed.

10B [Not Used]

10C *If it appears that a person does not understand what the caution means, the officer who has given it should go on to explain it in his own words.*

10D *[Not Used]*

11 Interviews: general

(a) Action

11.1A An interview is the questioning of a person regarding his involvement or suspected involvement in a criminal offence or offences which, by virtue of paragraph 10.1 of Code C, is required to be carried out under caution. Procedures undertaken under section 7 of the Road Traffic Act 1988 do not constitute interviewing for the purpose of this code.

11.1 Following a decision to arrest a suspect he must not be interviewed about the relevant offence except at a police station or other authorised place of detention unless the consequent delay would be likely:

(a) to lead to interference with or harm to evidence connected with an offence or interference with or physical harm to other people; or
(b) to lead to the alerting of other people suspected of having committed an offence but not yet arrested for it; or
(c) to hinder the recovery of property obtained in consequence of the commission of an offence.

Interviewing in any of these circumstances shall cease once the relevant risk has been averted or the necessary questions have been put in order to attempt to avert that risk.

11.2 Immediately prior to the commencement or re-commencement of any interview at a police station or other authorised place of detention, the interviewing officer shall remind the suspect of his entitlement to free legal advice and that the interview can be delayed for him to obtain legal advice (unless the exceptions in paragraph 6.6 or *Annex C* apply). It is the responsibility of the interviewing officer to ensure that all such reminders are noted in the record of interview.

11.2A At the beginning of an interview carried out in a police station, the interviewing officer, after cautioning the suspect, shall put to him any significant statement or silence which occurred before his arrival at the police station, and shall ask him whether he confirms or denies that earlier statement or silence and whether he wishes to add anything. A "significant" statement or silence is one which appears capable of being used in evidence against the suspect, in particular a direct admission of guilt, or failure or refusal to answer a question or to answer it satisfactorily, which might give rise to an inference under Part III of the Criminal Justice and Public Order Act 1994.

11.3 No police officer may try to obtain answers to questions or to elicit a statement by the use of oppression. Except as provided for in paragraph 10.5C, no police officer shall indicate, except in answer to a direct question, what action will be taken on the part of the police if the person being interviewed answers questions, makes a statement or refuses to do either. If the person asks the officer directly what action will be taken in the event of his answering questions, making a statement or refusing to do either, then the officer may inform the person what action the police propose to take in that event provided that action is itself proper and warranted.

11.4 As soon as a police officer who is making enquiries of any person about an offence believes that a prosecution should be brought against him and that there is sufficient evidence for it to succeed, he shall ask the person if he has anything further to say. If the person indicates that he has nothing more to say the officer shall without delay cease to question him about that offence. This should not, however, be taken to prevent officers in revenue cases or acting under the confiscation provisions of the Criminal Justice Act 1988 or the Drug Trafficking Offences Act 1986 from inviting suspects to complete a formal question and answer record after the interview is concluded.

(b) Interview records
11.5
(a) An accurate record must be made of each interview with a person suspected of an offence, whether or not the interview takes place at a police station.
(b) The record must state the place of the interview, the time it begins and ends, the time the record is made (if different), any breaks in the interview and the names of all those present; and must be made on the forms provided for this purpose or in the officer's pocket book or in accordance with the code of practice for the tape-recording of police interviews with suspects (Code E).
(c) The record must be made during the course of the interview, unless in the investigating officer's view this would not be practicable or would interfere with conduct of the interview, and must constitute either a verbatim record of what has been said or, failing this, an account of the interview which adequately and accurately summarises it.

11.6 The requirement to record the names of all those present at any interview does not apply to police officers interviewing people detained under the Prevention of Terrorism (Temporary Provisions) Act 1989. Instead the record shall state the warrant or other identification number and duty station of such officers.

11.7 If an interview record is not made during the course of the interview it must be made as soon as practicable after its completion.

11.8 Written interview records must be timed and signed by the maker.

11.9 If an interview record is not completed in the course of the interview the reason must be recorded in the officer's pocket book.

11.10 Unless it is impracticable, the person interviewed shall be given the opportunity to read the interview record and to sign it as correct or to indicate the respects in which he considers it inaccurate. If the interview is tape-recorded the arrangements set out in Code E apply. If the person concerned cannot read or refuses to read the record or to sign it, the senior officer present shall read it to him and ask him whether he would like to sign it as correct (or make his mark) or to indicate the respects in which he considers it inaccurate. The police officer shall then certify on the interview record itself what has occurred. [See Note 11D]

11.11 If the appropriate adult or the person's solicitor is present during the interview, he shall also be given an opportunity to read and sign the interview record (or any written statement taken down by a police officer).

11.12 Any refusal by a person to sign an interview record when asked to do so in accordance with the provisions of the code must itself be recorded.

11.13 A written record shall also be made of any comments made by a suspected person, including unsolicited comments, which are outside the context of an interview but which might be relevant to the offence. Any such record must be timed and signed by the maker. Where practicable the person shall be given the opportunity to read that record and to sign it as correct or to indicate the respects in which he considers it inaccurate. Any refusal to sign shall be recorded. [See *Note 11D*]

(c) Juveniles, mentally disordered people and mentally handicapped people
11.14 A juvenile or a person who is mentally disordered or mentally handicapped, whether suspected or not, must not be interviewed or asked to provide or sign a written statement in the absence of the appropriate adult unless paragraph 11.1 or *Annex C* applies.

11.15 Juveniles may only be interviewed at their places of education in exceptional circumstances and then only where the principal or his nominee agrees. Every effort should be made to notify both the parent(s) or other person responsible for the juvenile's welfare and the appropriate adult (if this is a different person) that the police want to interview the juvenile and reasonable time should be allowed to enable the appropriate adult to be present at the interview. Where awaiting the appropriate adult would cause unreasonable delay and unless the interviewee is suspected of an offence against the educational establishment, the principal or his nominee can act as the appropriate adult for the purposes of the interview.

11.16 Where the appropriate adult is present at an interview, he shall be informed that he is not expected to act simply as an observer; and also that the purposes of his presence are, first, to advise the person being questioned and to observe whether or not the interview is being conducted properly and fairly, and secondly, to facilitate communication with the person being interviewed.

Notes for Guidance
11A [Not Used]

11B It is important to bear in mind that, although juveniles or people who are mentally disordered or mentally handicapped are often capable of providing reliable evidence, they may, without knowing or wishing to do so, be particularly prone in certain circumstances to provide information which is unreliable, misleading or self-incriminating. Special care should therefore always be exercised in questioning such a person, and the appropriate adult should be involved, if there is any doubt about a person's age, mental state or capacity. Because of the risk of unreliable evidence it is also important to obtain corroboration of any facts admitted whenever possible.

11C *It is preferable that a juvenile is not arrested at his place of education unless this is unavoidable. Where a juvenile is arrested at his place of education, the principal or his nominee must be informed.*

11D *When a suspect agrees to read records of interviews and of other comments and to sign them as correct, he should be asked to endorse the record with words such as "I agree that this is a correct record of what was said" and add his signature. Where the suspect does not agree with the record, the officer should record the details of any disagreement and then ask the suspect to read these details and then sign them to the effect that they accurately reflect his disagreement. Any refusal to sign when asked to do so shall be recorded.*

12 Interviews in police stations

(a) Action

12.1 If a police officer wishes to interview, or conduct enquiries which require the presence of a detained person, the custody officer is responsible for deciding whether to deliver him into his custody.

12.2 In any period of 24 hours a detained person must be allowed a continuous period of at least 8 hours for rest, free from questioning, travel or any interruption by police officers in connection with the investigation concerned. This period should normally be at night. The period of rest may not be interrupted or delayed, except at the request of the person, his appropriate adult or his legal representative, unless there are reasonable grounds for believing that it would:
> (i) involve a risk of harm to people or serious loss of, or damage to, property; or
> (ii) delay unnecessarily the person's release from custody; or
> (iii) otherwise prejudice the outcome of the investigation.

If a person is arrested at a police station after going there voluntarily, the period of 24 hours runs from the time of his arrest and not the time of arrival at the police station. Any action which is required to be taken in accordance with section 8 of this code, or in accordance with medical advice or at the request of the detained person, his appropriate adult or his legal representative, does not constitute an interruption to the rest period such that a fresh period must be allowed.

12.3 A detained person may not be supplied with intoxicating liquor except on medical directions. No person, who is unfit through drink or drugs to the extent that he is unable to appreciate the significance of questions put to him and his answers, may be questioned about an alleged offence in that condition except in accordance with *Annex C*. [See *Note 12B*]

12.4 As far as practicable interviews shall take place in interview rooms which must be adequately heated, lit and ventilated.

12.5 People being questioned or making statements shall not be required to stand.

12.6 Before the commencement of an interview each interviewing officer shall identify himself and any other officers present by name and rank to the person being interviewed, except in the case of people detained under the Prevention of

Terrorism (Temporary Provisions) Act 1989 when each officer shall identify himself by his warrant or other identification number and rank rather than his name.

12.7 Breaks from interviewing shall be made at recognised meal times. Short breaks for refreshment shall also be provided at intervals of approximately two hours, subject to the interviewing officer's discretion to delay a break if there are reasonable grounds for believing that it would:
  (i)   involve a risk of harm to people or serious loss of, or damage to property;
  (ii) delay unnecessarily the person's release from custody; or
  (iii) otherwise prejudice the outcome of the investigation.
[See *Note 12C*]

12.8 If in the course of the interview a complaint is made by the person being questioned or on his behalf concerning the provisions of this code then the interviewing officer shall:
  (i)   record it in the interview record; and
  (ii) inform the custody officer, who is then responsible for dealing with it in accordance with section 9 of this code.

(b) Documentation
12.9 A record must be made of the time at which a detained person is not in the custody of the custody officer, and why; and of the reason for any refusal to deliver him out of that custody.

12.10 A record must be made of any intoxicating liquor supplied to a detained person, in accordance with paragraph 12.3 above.

12.11 Any decision to delay a break in an interview must be recorded, with grounds, in the interview record.

12.12 All written statements made at police stations under caution shall be written on the forms provided for the purpose.

12.13 All written statements made under caution shall be taken in accordance with *Annex D* to this code.

Notes for Guidance
12A If the interview has been contemporaneously recorded and the record signed by the person interviewed in accordance with paragraph 11.10 above, or has been tape recorded, it is normally unnecessary to ask for a written statement. Statements under caution should normally be taken in these circumstances only at the person's express wish. An officer may, however, ask him whether or not he wants to make such a statement.

12B The police surgeon can give advice about whether or not a person is fit to be interviewed in accordance with paragraph 12.3 above.

12C Meal breaks should normally last at least 45 minutes and shorter breaks after two hours should last at least 15 minutes. If the interviewing officer delays a break in accordance with paragraph 12.7 of this code and prolongs the interview, a longer break should then be provided. If there is a short interview, and a subsequent short interview is contemplated, the length of the break may be reduced if there are reasonable grounds to believe that this is necessary to avoid any of the consequences in paragraph 12.7 (i) to (iii).

13 Interpreters

(a) General

13.1 Information on obtaining the services of a suitably qualified interpreter for the deaf or for people who do not understand English is given in *Note for Guidance 3D*.

(b) Foreign languages

13.2 Except in accordance with paragraph 11.1 or unless Annex C applies, a person must not be interviewed in the absence of a person capable of acting as interpreter if:

(a)   he has difficulty in understanding English;
(b)   the interviewing officer cannot speak the person's own language; and
(c)   the person wishes an interpreter to be present.

13.3 The interviewing officer shall ensure that the interpreter makes a note of the interview at the time in the language of the person being interviewed for use in the event of his being called to give evidence, and certifies its accuracy. He shall allow sufficient time for the interpreter to make a note of each question and answer after each has been put or given and interpreted. The person shall be given an opportunity to read it or have it read to him and sign it as correct or to indicate the respects in which he considers it inaccurate. If the interview is tape-recorded the arrangements set out in Code E apply.

13.4 In the case of a person making a statement in a language other than English:

(a)   the interpreter shall take down the statement in the language in which it is made;
(b)   the person making the statement shall be invited to sign it; and
(c)   an official English translation shall be made in due course.

(c) Deaf people and people with a speech handicap

13.5 If a person appears to be deaf or there is doubt about his hearing or speaking ability, he must not be interviewed in the absence of an interpreter unless he agrees in writing to be interviewed without one or paragraph 11.1 or *Annex C* applies.

13.6 An interpreter shall also be called if a juvenile is interviewed and the parent or guardian present as the appropriate adult appears to be deaf or there is doubt about his hearing or speaking ability, unless he agrees in writing that the interview should proceed without one or paragraph 11.1 or *Annex C* applies.

13.7 The interviewing officer shall ensure that the interpreter is given an opportunity to read the record of the interview and to certify its accuracy in the event of his being called to give evidence.

(d) Additional rules for detained persons
13.8 All reasonable attempts should be made to make clear to the detained person that interpreters will be provided at public expense.

13.9 Where paragraph 6.1 applies and the person concerned cannot communicate with the solicitor, whether because of language, hearing or speech difficulties, an interpreter must be called. The interpreter may not be a police officer when interpretation is needed for the purposes of obtaining legal advice. In all other cases a police officer may only interpret if he first obtains the detained person's (or the appropriate adult's) agreement in writing or if the interview is tape-recorded in accordance with Code E.

13.10 When a person is charged with an offence who appears to be deaf or there is doubt about his hearing or speaking ability or ability to understand English, and the custody officer cannot establish effective communication, arrangements must be made for an interpreter to explain as soon as practicable the offence concerned and any other information given by the custody officer.

(e) Documentation
13.11 Action taken to call an interpreter under this section and any agreement to be interviewed in the absence of an interpreter must be recorded.

Note for Guidance
13A If the interpreter is needed as a prosecution witness at the person's trial, a second interpreter must act as the court interpreter.

14 Questioning: special restrictions

14.1 If a person has been arrested by one police force on behalf of another and the lawful period of detention in respect of that offence has not yet commenced in accordance with section 41 of the Police and Criminal Evidence Act 1984 no questions may be put to him about the offence while he is in transit between the forces except in order to clarify any voluntary statement made by him.

14.2 If a person is in police detention at a hospital he may not be questioned without the agreement of a responsible doctor. [See *Note 14A*]

Note for Guidance
14A If questioning takes place at a hospital under paragraph 14.2 (or on the way to or from a hospital) the period concerned counts towards the total period of detention permitted.

15 Reviews and extensions of detention

(a) Action
15.1 The review officer is responsible under section 40 of the Police and Criminal Evidence Act 1984 (or, in terrorist cases, under Schedule 3 to the Prevention of Terrorism (Temporary Provisions) Act 1989) for determining whether or not a person's detention continues to be necessary. In reaching a decision he shall provide an opportunity to the detained person himself to make representations (unless he is unfit to do so because of his condition or behaviour) or to his solicitor

or to the appropriate adult if available at the time. Other people having an interest in the person's welfare may make representations at the review officer's discretion.

15.2 The same people may make representations to the officer determining whether further detention should be authorised under section 42 of the Act or under Schedule 3 to the 1989 Act. [See *Note 15A*]

15.2A After hearing any representations, the review officer or officer determining whether further detention should be authorised shall note any comment the person may make if the decision is to keep him in detention. The officer shall not put specific questions to the suspect regarding his involvement in any offence, nor in respect of any comments he may make in response to the decision to keep him in detention. Such an exchange is likely to constitute an interview as defined by paragraph 11.1A and would require the associated safeguards included in section 11. [See also paragraph 11.13]

(b) Documentation
15.3 Before conducting a review the review officer must ensure that the detained person is reminded of his entitlement to free legal advice (see paragraph 6.5). It is the responsibility of the review officer to ensure that all such reminders are noted in the custody record.

15.4 The grounds for and extent of any delay in conducting a review shall be recorded.

15.5 Any written representations shall be retained.

15.6 A record shall be made as soon as practicable of the outcome of each review and application for a warrant of further detention or its extension.

Notes for Guidance
15A If the detained person is likely to be asleep at the latest time when a review of detention or an authorisation of continued detention may take place, the appropriate officer should bring it forward so that the detained person may make representations without being woken up.

15B An application for a warrant of further detention or its extension should be made between 10am and 9pm, and if possible during normal court hours. It will not be practicable to arrange for a court to sit specially outside the hours of 10am to 9pm. If it appears possible that a special sitting may be needed (either at a weekend, Bank/Public Holiday or on a weekday outside normal court hours but between 10am and 9pm) then the clerk to the justices should be given notice and informed of this possibility, while the court is sitting if possible.

15C If in the circumstances the only practicable way of conducting a review is over the telephone then this is permissible, provided that the requirements of section 40 of the Police and Criminal Evidence Act 1984 or of Schedule 3 to the Prevention of Terrorism (Temporary Provisions) Act 1989 are observed. However, a review to decide whether to authorise a person's continued detention under section 42 of the 1984 Act must be done in person rather than over the telephone.

16 Charging of detained persons

(a) Action

16.1 When an officer considers that there is sufficient evidence to prosecute a detained person, and that there is sufficient evidence for a prosecution to succeed, and that the person has said all that he wishes to say about the offence, he shall without delay (and subject to the following qualification) bring him before the custody officer who shall then be responsible for considering whether or not he should be charged. When a person is detained in respect of more than one offence it is permissible to delay bringing him before the custody officer until the above conditions are satisfied in respect of all the offences (but see paragraph 11.4). Any resulting action shall be taken in the presence of the appropriate adult if the person is a juvenile or mentally disordered or mentally handicapped.

16.2 When a detained person is charged with or informed that he may be prosecuted for an offence he shall be cautioned in the following terms:

> "You do not have to say anything. But it may harm your defence if you do not mention now something which you later rely on in court. Anything you do say may be given in evidence."

16.3 At the time a person is charged he shall be given a written notice showing particulars of the offence with which he is charged and including the name of the officer in the case (in terrorist cases, the officer's warrant or other identification number instead), his police station and the reference number for the case. So far as possible the particulars of the charge shall be stated in simple terms, but they shall also show the precise offence in law with which he is charged. The notice shall begin with the following words:

> "You are charged with the offence(s) shown below. You do not have to say anything. But it may harm your defence if you do not mention now something which you later rely on in court. Anything you do say may be given in evidence."

If the person is a juvenile or is mentally disordered or mentally handicapped the notice shall be given to the appropriate adult.

16.4 If, at any time after a person has been charged with or informed that he may be prosecuted for an offence, a police officer wishes to bring to the notice of that person any written statement made by another person or the content of an interview with another person, he shall hand to that person a true copy of any such written statement or bring to his attention the content of the interview record, but shall say or do nothing to invite any reply or comment save to warn him that he does not have to say anything but that anything he does say may be given in evidence and to remind him of his right to legal advice in accordance with paragraph 6.5 above. If the person cannot read then the officer may read it to him. If the person is a juvenile or mentally disordered or mentally handicapped the copy shall also be given to, or the interview record brought to the attention of, the appropriate adult.

16.5 Questions relating to an offence may not be put to a person after he has been charged with that offence, or informed that he may be prosecuted for it, unless they are necessary for the purpose of preventing or minimising harm or loss to some other person or to the public or for clearing up an ambiguity in a previous answer or statement, or where it is in the interests of justice that the person should have put to him and have an opportunity to comment on information concerning the offence which has come to light since he was charged or informed that he might be prosecuted. Before any such questions are put to him, he shall be warned that he does not have to say anything but that anything he does say may be given in evidence and reminded of his right to legal advice in accordance with paragraph 6.5 above. [See *Note 16A*]

16.6   Where a juvenile is charged with an offence and the custody officer authorises his continued detention he must try to make arrangements for the juvenile to be taken into care of a local authority to be detained pending appearance in court unless he certifies that it is impracticable to do so, or, in the case of a juvenile of at least 12 years of age, no secure accommodation is available and there is a risk to the public of serious harm from that juvenile, in accordance with section 38(6) of the Police and Criminal Evidence Act 1984, as amended by section 59 of the Criminal Justice Act 1991 and section 24 of the Criminal Justice and Public Order Act 1994. [See *Note 16B*]

(b) Documentation
16.7   A record shall be made of anything a detained person says when charged.

16.8   Any questions put after charge and answers given relating to the offence shall be contemporaneously recorded in full on the forms provided and the record signed by that person or, if he refuses, by the interviewing officer and any third parties present. If the questions are tape-recorded the arrangements set out in Code E apply.

16.9   If it is not practicable to make arrangements for the transfer of a juvenile into local authority care in accordance with paragraph 16.6 above the custody officer must record the reasons and make out a certificate to be produced before the court together with the juvenile.

Notes for Guidance
16A   The service of the Notice of Intended Prosecution under sections 1 and 2 of the Road Traffic Offenders Act 1988 does not amount to informing a person that he may be prosecuted for an offence and so does not preclude further questioning in relation to that offence.

16B   Except as provided for in 16.6 above, neither a juvenile's behaviour nor the nature of the offence with which he is charged provides grounds for the custody officer to decide that it is impracticable to seek to arrange for his transfer to the care of the local authority. Similarly, the lack of secure local authority accommodation shall not make it impracticable for the custody officer to transfer him. The availability of secure accommodation is only a factor in relation to a juvenile aged 12 or over when the local authority accommodation would not be adequate to protect the public from serious harm from the juvenile. The obligation to transfer a juvenile to local authority accommodation applies as much to a juvenile charged during the daytime as it does to a juvenile to be held overnight, subject to a requirement to bring the juvenile before a court under section 46 of the Police and Criminal Evidence Act 1984.

ANNEX A

Intimate and Strip Searches [see paragraph 4.1]

(A) Intimate search

1. An "intimate search" is a search which consists of the physical examination of a person's body orifices other than the mouth.

[a] *Action*

2. Body orifices other than the mouth may be searched only if an officer of the rank of superintendent or above has reasonable grounds for believing:

(a) that an article which could cause physical injury to the detained person or others at the police station has been concealed; or

(b) that the person has concealed a Class A drug which he intended to supply to another or to export; and

(c) that in either case an intimate search is the only practicable means of removing it.

The reasons why an intimate search is considered necessary shall be explained to the person before the search takes place.

3. An intimate search may only be carried out by a registered medical practitioner or registered nurse, unless an officer of at least the rank of superintendent considers that this is not practicable and the search is to take place under sub-paragraph 2(a) above.

4. An intimate search under sub-paragraph 2(a) above may take place only at a hospital, surgery, other medical premises or police station. A search under sub-paragraph 2(b) may take place only at a hospital, surgery or other medical premises.

5. An intimate search at a police station of a juvenile or a mentally disordered or mentally handicapped person may take place only in the presence of an appropriate adult of the same sex (unless the person specifically requests the presence of a particular adult of the opposite sex who is readily available). In the case of a juvenile the search may take place in the absence of the appropriate adult only if the juvenile signifies in the presence of the appropriate adult that he prefers the search to be done in his absence and the appropriate adult agrees. A record shall be made of the juvenile's decision and signed by the appropriate adult.

6. Where an intimate search under sub-paragraph 2(a) above is carried out by a police officer, the officer must be of the same sex as the person searched. Subject to paragraph 5 above, no person of the opposite sex who is not a medical practitioner or nurse shall be present, nor shall anyone whose presence is unnecessary but a minimum of two people, other than the person searched, must be present during the search. The search shall be conducted with proper regard to the sensitivity and vulnerability of the person in these circumstances.

[b] *Documentation*

7. In the case of an intimate search the custody officer shall as soon as practicable

record which parts of the person's body were searched, who carried out the search, who was present, the reasons for the search and its result.

8. If an intimate search is carried out by a police officer, the reason why it was impracticable for a suitably qualified person to conduct it must be recorded.

(B) Strip search
9. A strip search is a search involving the removal of more than outer clothing.

[a] Action
10. A strip search may take place only if it is considered necessary to remove an article which a person would not be allowed to keep, and the officer reasonably considers that the person might have concealed such an article. Strip searches shall not be routinely carried out where there is no reason to consider that articles have been concealed.

The conduct of strip searches
11. The following procedures shall be observed when strip searches are conducted:
(a) a police officer carrying out a strip search must be of the same sex as the person searched;
(b) the search shall take place in an area where the person being searched cannot be seen by anyone who does not need to be present, nor by a member of the opposite sex (except an appropriate adult who has been specifically requested by the person being searched);
(c) except in cases of urgency, where there is a risk of serious harm to the person detained or to others, whenever a strip search involves exposure of intimate parts of the body, there must be at least two people present other than the person searched, and if the search is of a juvenile or a mentally disordered or mentally handicapped person, one of the people must be the appropriate adult. Except in urgent cases as above, a search of a juvenile may take place in the absence of the appropriate adult only if the juvenile signifies in the presence of the appropriate adult that he prefers the search to be done in his absence and the appropriate adult agrees. A record shall be made of the juvenile's decision and signed by the appropriate adult. The presence of more than two people, other than an appropriate adult, shall be permitted only in the most exceptional circumstances;
(d) the search shall be conducted with proper regard to the sensitivity and vulnerability of the person in these circumstances and every reasonable effort shall be made to secure the person's co-operation and minimise embarrassment. People who are searched should not normally be required to have all their clothes removed at the same time, for example, a man shall be allowed to put on his shirt before removing his trousers, and a woman shall be allowed to put on her blouse and upper garments before further clothing is removed;
(e) where necessary to assist the search, the person may be required to hold his or her arms in the air or to stand with his or her legs apart and to bend forward so that a visual examination may be made of the genital and anal areas provided that no physical contact is made with any body orifice;
(f) if, during a search, articles are found, the person shall be asked to hand them over. If articles are found within any body orifice other than the mouth, and the person refuses to hand them over, their removal would constitute an

intimate search, which must be carried out in accordance with the provisions of Part A of this Annex;

(g) a strip search shall be conducted as quickly as possible, and the person searched allowed to dress as soon as the procedure is complete.

[*b*] *Documentation*
12. A record shall be made on the custody record of a strip search including the reason it was considered necessary to undertake it, those present and any result.

ANNEX B

Delay in Notifying Arrest or Allowing Access to Legal Advice

(A) Persons detained under the Police and Criminal Evidence Act 1984
(*a*) *Action*
1. The rights set out in sections 5 or 6 of the code or both may be delayed if the person is in police detention in connection with a serious arrestable offence, has not yet been charged with an offence and an officer of the rank of superintendent or above has reasonable grounds for believing that the exercise of either right:

   (i) will lead to interference with or harm to evidence connected with a serious arrestable offence or interference with or physical injury to other people; or
   (ii) will lead to the alerting of other people suspected of having committed such an offence but not yet arrested for it; or
   (iii) will hinder the recovery of property obtained as a result of such an offence.
[See *Note B3*]

2. These rights may also be delayed where the serious arrestable offence is either:
   (i) a drug trafficking offence and the officer has reasonable grounds for believing that the detained person has benefited from drug trafficking, and that the recovery of the value of that person's proceeds of drug trafficking will be hindered by the exercise of either right; or
   (ii) an offence to which Part VI of the Criminal Justice Act 1988 (covering confiscation orders) applies and the officer has reasonable grounds for believing that the detained person has benefited from the offence, and that the recovery of the value of the property obtained by that person from or in connection with the offence, or if the pecuniary advantage derived by him from or in connection with it, will be hindered by the exercise of either right.

3. Access to a solicitor may not be delayed on the grounds that he might advise the person not to answer any questions or that the solicitor was initially asked to attend the police station by someone else, provided that the person himself then wishes to see the solicitor. In the latter case the detained person must be told that the solicitor has come to the police station at another person's request, and must be asked to sign the custody record to signify whether or not he wishes to see the solicitor.

4. These rights may be delayed only for as long as is necessary and, subject to paragraph 9 below, in no case beyond 36 hours after the relevant time as defined in section 41 of the Police and Criminal Evidence Act 1984. If the above grounds cease

to apply within this time, the person must as soon as practicable be asked if he wishes to exercise either right, the custody record must be noted accordingly, and action must be taken in accordance with the relevant section of the code.

5. A detained person must be permitted to consult a solicitor for a reasonable time before any court hearing.

(b) Documentation
6. The grounds for action under this Annex shall be recorded and the person informed of them as soon as practicable.

7. Any reply given by a person under paragraphs 4 or 9 must be recorded and the person asked to endorse the record in relation to whether he wishes to receive legal advice at this point.

(B) Persons detained under the Prevention of Terrorism (Temporary Provisions) Act 1989
(a) Action
8. The rights set out in sections 5 or 6 of this code or both may be delayed if paragraph 1 above applies or if an officer of the rank of superintendent or above has reasonable grounds for believing that the exercise of either right:
(a) will lead to interference with the gathering of information about the commission, preparation or instigation of acts of terrorism; or
(b) by alerting any person, will make it more difficult to prevent an act of terrorism or to secure the apprehension, prosecution or conviction of any person in connection with the commission, preparation or instigation of an act of terrorism.

9. These rights may be delayed only for as long as is necessary and in no case beyond 48 hours from the time of arrest. If the above grounds cease to apply within this time, the person must as soon as practicable be asked if he wishes to exercise either right, the custody record must be noted accordingly, and action must be taken in accordance with the relevant section of this code.

10. Paragraphs 3 and 5 above apply.

(b) Documentation
11. Paragraphs 6 and 7 above apply.

Notes for Guidance
B1 Even if Annex B applies in the case of a juvenile, or a person who is mentally disordered or mentally handicapped, action to inform the appropriate adult (and the person responsible for a juvenile's welfare, if that is a different person) must nevertheless be taken in accordance with paragraphs 3.7 and 3.9 of this code.

B2 In the case of Commonwealth citizens and foreign nationals see Note 7A.

B3 Police detention is defined in section 118(2) of the Police and Criminal Evidence Act 1984.

B4 The effect of paragraph 1 above is that the officer may authorise delaying access to a specific solicitor only if he has reasonable grounds to believe that specific solicitor will, inadvertently or otherwise, pass on a message from the detained person or act in some other way which will lead to any of the three results in paragraph 1 coming about. In these circumstances the officer should offer the detained person access to a solicitor [who is not the specific solicitor referred to above) on the Duty Solicitor Scheme.

B5 The fact that the grounds for delaying notification of arrest under paragrah 1 above may be satisfied does not automatically mean that the grounds for delaying access to legal advice will also be satisfied.

ANNEX C

Vulnerable Suspects: Urgent Interviews at Police Stations

1. When an interview is to take place in a police station or other authorised place of detention, if, and only if, an officer of the rank of superintendent or above considers that delay will lead to the consequences set out in paragraph 11.1 (a) to (c) of this Code:

(a) a person heavily under the influence of drink or drugs may be interviewed in that state; or

(b) a juvenile or a person who is mentally disordered or mentally handicapped may be interviewed in the absence of the appropriate adult; or

(c) a person who has difficulty in understanding English or who has a hearing disability may be interviewed in the absence of an interpreter.

2. Questioning in these circumstances may not continue once sufficient information to avert the immediate risk has been obtained.

3. A record shall be made of the grounds for any decision to interview a person under paragraph 1 above.

Note for Guidance

C1 The special groups referred to in this Annex are all particularly vulnerable. The provisions of the Annex, which override safeguards designed to protect them and to minimise the risk of interviews producing unreliable evidence, should be applied only in exceptional cases of need.

ANNEX D

Written Statements under Caution [see paragraph 12.13]

(a) Written by a person under caution

1. A person shall always be invited to write down himself what he wants to say.

2. Where the person wishes to write it himself, he shall be asked to write out and sign, before writing what he wants to say, the following:

> "I make this statement of my own free will. I understand that I do not have to say anything but that it may harm my defence if I do not mention when questioned something which I later rely on in court. This statement may be given in evidence."

3. Any person writing his own statement shall be allowed to do so without any prompting except that a police officer may indicate to him which matters are material or question any ambiguity in the statement.

(b) Written by a police officer

4. If a person says that he would like someone to write it for him, a police officer shall write the statement, but, before starting, he must ask him to sign, or make his mark, to the following:

> "I, ..., wish to make a statement. I want someone to write down what I say. I understand that I do not have to say anything but that it may harm my defence if I do not mention when questioned something which I later rely on in court. This statement may be given in evidence."

5. Where a police officer writes the statement, he must take down the exact words spoken by the person making it and he must not edit or paraphrase it. Any questions that are necessary (e.g. to make it more intelligible) and the answers given must be recorded contemporaneously on the statement form.

6. When the writing of a statement by a police officer is finished the person making it shall be asked to read it and to make any corrections, alterations or additions he wishes. When he has finished reading it he shall be asked to write and sign or make his mark on the following certificate at the end of the statement:

> "I have read the above statement, and I have been able to correct, alter or add anything I wish. The statement is true. I have made it of my own free will."

7. If the person making the statement cannot read, or refuses to read it, or to write the above mentioned certificate at the end of it or to sign it, the senior police officer present shall read it to him and ask him whether he would like to correct, alter or add anything and to put his signature or make his mark at the end. The police officer shall then certify on the statement itself what has occurred.

ANNEX E

Summary of Provisions Relating to Mentally Disordered and Mentally Handicapped People

1. If an officer has any suspicion, or is told in good faith, that a person of any age may be mentally disorderd or mentally handicapped, or mentally incapable of understanding the significance of questions put to him or his replies, then that person shall be treated as mentally disordered or mentally handicapped for the purposes of this code. [See paragraph 1.4]

2. In the case of a person who is mentally disordered or mentally handicapped, "the appropriate adult" means:
(a) a relative, guardian or some other person responsible for his care or custody;
(b) someone who has experience of dealing with mentally disordered or mentally handicapped people but is not a police officer or employed by the police; or
(c) failing either of the above, some other responsible adult aged 18 or over who is not a police officer or employed by the police.
[See paragraph 1.7(b)]

3. If the custody officer authorises the detention of a person who is mentally handicapped or appears to be suffering from a mental disorder he must as soon as practicable inform the appropriate adult of the grounds for the person's detention and his whereabouts, and ask the adult to come to the police station to see the person. If the appropriate adult is already at the police station when information is given as required in paragraphs 3.1 to 3.5 the information must be given to the detained person in the appropriate adult's presence. If the appropriate adult is not at the police station when the provisions of 3.1 to 3.5 are complied with then these provisions must be complied with again in the presence of the appropriate adult once that person arrives. [See paragraphs 3.9 and 3.11]

4. If the appropriate adult, having been informed of the right to legal advice, considers that legal advice should be taken, the provisions of section 6 of the code apply as if the mentally disordered or mentally handicapped person had requested access to legal advice. [See paragraph 3.13 and *Note E2*]

5. If a person brought to a police station appears to be suffering from mental disorder or is incoherent other than through drunkenness alone, or if a detained person subsequently appears to be mentally disordered, the custody officer must immediately call the police surgeon or, in urgent cases, send the person to hospital or call the nearest available medical practitioner. It is not intended that these provisions should delay the transfer of a person to a place of safety under section 136 of the Mental Health Act 1983 where that is applicable. Where an assessment under that Act is to take place at the police station, the custody officer has discretion not to call the police surgeon so long as he believes that the assessment by a registered medical practitioner can be undertaken without undue delay. [See paragaph 9.2]

6. It is imperative that a mentally disordered or mentally handicapped person who has been detained under section 136 of the Mental Health Act 1983 should be assessed as soon as possible. If that assessment is to take place at the police station, an approved social worker and a registered medical practitioner shall be called to the police station as soon as possible in order to interview and examine the person. Once the person has been interviewed and examined and suitable arrangements have been made for his treatment or care, he can no longer be detained under section 136. The person shall not be released until he has been seen by both the approved social worker and the registered medical practitioner. [See paragraph 3.10]

7. If a mentally disordered or mentally handicapped person is cautioned in the absence of the appropriate adult, the caution must be repeated in the appropriate adult's presence. [See paragraph 10.6]

8. A mentally disordered or mentally handicapped person must not be interviewed or asked to provide or sign a written statement in the absence of the appropriate adult unless the provisions of paragraph 11.1 or *Annex C* of this code apply. Questioning in these circumstances may not continue in the absence of the appropriate adult once sufficient information to avert the risk has been obtained. A record shall be made of the grounds for any decision to begin an interview in these circumstances. [See paragraphs 11.1 and 11.14 and *Annex C*]

9. Where the appropriate adult is present at an interview, he shall be informed that he is not expected to act simply as an observer; and also that the purposes of his presence are, first, to advise the person being interviewed and to observe whether or not the interview is being conducted properly and fairly, and, secondly, to facilitate communication with the person being interviewed. [See paragraph 11.16]

10. If the detention of a mentally disordered or mentally handicapped person is reviewed by a review officer or a superintendent, the appropriate adult must, if available at the time, be given an opportunity to make representations to the officer about the need for continuing detention. [See paragraphs 15.1 and 15.2]

11. If the custody officer charges a mentally disordered or mentally handicapped person with an offence or takes such other action as is appropriate when there is sufficient evidence for a prosecution this must be done in the presence of the appropriate adult. The written notice embodying any charge must be given to the appropriate adult. [See paragraphs 16.1 to 16.3]

12. An intimate or strip search of a mentally disordered or mentally handicapped person may take place only in the presence of the appropriate adult of the same sex, unless the person specifically requests the presence of a particular adult of the opposite sex. A strip search may take place in the absence of an appropriate adult only in cases of urgency where there is a risk of serious harm to the person detained or to others. [See *Annex A*, paragraphs 5 and 11(c)]

13. Particular care must be taken when deciding whether to use handcuffs to restrain a mentally disordered or mentally handicapped person in a locked cell. [See paragraph 8.2]

Notes for Guidance

E1 In the case of mentally disordered or mentally handicapped people, it may in certain circumstances be more satisfactory for all concerned if the appropriate adult is someone who has experience or training in their care rather than a relative lacking such qualifications. But if the person himself prefers a relative to a better qualified stranger or objects to a particular person as the appropriate adult, his wishes should if practicable be respected. [See Note 1E]

E2 The purpose of the provision at paragraph 3.13 is to protect the rights of a mentally disordered or mentally handicapped person who does not understand the significance of what is being said to him. If the person wishes to exercise the right to legal advice, the appropriate action should be taken and not delayed until the appropriate adult arrives. [See Note 3G] A mentally disordered or mentally handicapped person should always be given an opportunity, when an appropriate adult is called to the police station, to consult privately with a solicitor in the absence of the appropriate adult if he wishes to do so. [See Note 1EE]

E3 It is important to bear in mind that although mentally disordered or mentally handicapped people are often capable of providing reliable evidence, they may, without knowing or wishing to do so, be particularly prone in certain circumstances to provide information which is unreliable, misleading or self-incriminating. Special care should therefore always be exercised in questioning such a person, and the appropriate adult involved, if there is any doubt about a person's mental state or capacity. Because of the risk of unreliable evidence, it is important to obtain corroboration of any facts admitted whenever possible. [See Note 11B]

E4 Because of the risks referred to in Note E3, which the presence of the appropriate adult is intended to minimise, officers of superintendent rank or above should exercise their discretion to authorise the commencement of an interview in the adult's absence only in exceptional cases, where it is necessary to avert an immediate risk of serious harm. [See paragraph 11.1 and Annex C and Note C1]

ANNEX F

Countries with which Bilateral Consular Conventions or Agreements Requiring Notification of the Arrest and Detention of their Nationals are in Force as at 1 January 1995

Armenia	Denmark	Mexico	Tajikistan
Austria	Egypt	Moldova	Turkmenistan
Azerbaijan	France	Mongolia	Ukraine
Belarus	Georgia	Norway	USA
Belgium	German Federal	Poland	Uzbekistan
Bosnia-Hercegovina	Republic	Romania	Yugoslavia
Bulgaria	Greece	Russia	
China*	Hungary	Slovak Republic	
Croatia	Kazakhstan	Slovenia	
Cuba	Kyrgyzstan	Spain	
Czech Republic	Macedonia	Sweden	

*Police are required to inform Chinese officials of arrest/detention in the Manchester consular district only. This comprises Derbyshire, Durham, Greater Manchester, Lancashire, Merseyside, North, South and West Yorkshire, and Tyne and Wear.

D   Code of Practice for the Identification of Persons by Police Officers

1 General

1.1 This code of practice must be readily available at all police stations for consultation by police officers, detained persons and members of the public.

1.2 The notes for guidance included are not provisions of this code, but are guidance to police officers and others about its application and interpretation. Provisions in the Annexes to the code are provisions of this code.

1.3 If an officer has any suspicion, or is told in good faith, that a person of any age may be mentally disordered or mentally handicapped, or mentally incapable of understanding the significance of questions put to him or his replies, then that person shall be treated as a mentally disordered or mentally handicapped person for the purposes of this code.

1.4 If anyone appears to be under the age of 17 then he shall be treated as a juvenile for the purposes of this code in the absence of clear evidence to show that he is older.

1.5 If a person appears to be blind or seriously visually handicapped, deaf, unable to read, unable to speak or has difficulty orally because of a speech impediment, he shall be treated as such for the purposes of this code in the absence of clear evidence to the contrary.

1.6 In this code the term "appropriate adult" has the same meaning as in paragraph 1.7 of Code C, and the term "solicitor" has the same meaning as in paragraph 6.12 of Code C.

1.7 Any reference to a custody officer in this code includes an officer who is performing the functions of a custody officer.

1.8 Where a record is made under this code of any action requiring the authority of an officer of a specified rank, his name (except in the case of enquiries linked to the investigation of terrorism, in which case the officer's warrant or other identification number shall be given) and rank must be included in the record.

1.9 All records must be timed and signed by the maker. Warrant or other identification numbers shall be used rather than names in the case of detention under the Prevention of Terrorism (Temporary Provisions) Act 1989.

1.10 In the case of a detained person records are to be made in his custody record unless otherwise specified.

1.11 In the case of any procedure requiring a person's consent, the consent of a person who is mentally disordered or mentally handicapped is only valid if given in the presence of the appropriate adult; and in the case of a juvenile the consent of his parent or guardian is required as well as his own (unless he is under 14, in which case the consent of his parent or guardian is sufficient in its own right). [See *Note 1E*]

1.12 In the case of a person who is blind or seriously visually handicapped or unable to read, the custody officer shall ensure that his solicitor, relative, the appropriate adult or some other person likely to take an interest in him (and not involved in the investigation) is available to help in checking any documentation. Where this code requires written consent or signification, then the person who is assisting may be asked to sign instead if the detained person so wishes. [See *Note 1F*]

1.13 In the case of any procedure requiring information to be given to or sought from a suspect, it must be given or sought in the presence of the appropriate adult if the suspect is mentally disordered, mentally handicapped or a juvenile. If the appropriate adult is not present when the information is first given or sought, the procedure must be repeated in his presence when he arrives. If the suspect appears to be deaf or there is doubt about his hearing or speaking ability or ability to understand English, and the officer cannot establish effective communication, the information must be given or sought through an interpreter.

1.14 Any procedure in this code involving the participation of a person (whether as a suspect or a witness) who is mentally disordered, mentally handicapped or a juvenile must take place in the presence of the appropriate adult; but the adult must not be allowed to prompt any identification of a suspect by a witness.

1.15 Subject to paragraph 1.16 below, nothing in this code affects any procedure under:
    (i) sections 4 to 11 of the Road Traffic Act 1988 or sections 15 and 16 of the Road Traffic Offenders Act 1988; or
   (ii) paragraph 18 of Schedule 2 to the Immigration Act 1971; or
  (iii) the Prevention of Terrorism (Temporary Provisions) Act 1989, section 15(9), paragraph 8(5) of Schedule 2, and paragraph 7(5) of Schedule 5.

1.16 Notwithstanding paragraph 1.15, the provisions of section 3 below on the taking of fingerprints, and of section 5 below on the taking of body samples, do apply to people detained under section 14 of, or paragraph 6 of Schedule 5 to, the Prevention of Terrorism (Temporary Provisions) Act 1989. (In the case of fingerprints, section 61 of PACE is modified by section 15(10) of, and paragraph 7(6) of Schedule 5 to, the 1989 Act.) In the case of samples, sections 62 and 63 of PACE are modified by section 15(11) of and paragraph 7(6A) of Schedule 5 to the 1989 Act. The effect of both of these modifications is to allow fingerprints and samples to be taken in terrorist cases to help determine whether a person is or has been involved in terrorism, as well as where there are reasonable grounds for suspecting that person's involvement in a particular offence. There is, however, no statutory requirement (and, therefore, no requirement under paragraph 3.4 below) to destroy fingerprints or body samples taken in terrorist cases, no requirement to tell the people from whom these were taken that they will be destroyed, and no statutory requirement to offer such people an opportunity to witness the destruction of their fingerprints.

1.17 In this code, references to photographs, negatives and copies include reference to images stored or reproduced through any medium.

1.18 This code does not apply to those groups of people listed in paragraph 1.12 of Code C.

Notes for Guidance

1A A person, including a parent or guardian, should not be the appropriate adult if he is suspected of involvement in the offence, is the victim, is a witness, is involved in the investigation or has received admissions prior to attending to act as the appropriate adult. If the parent of a juvenile is estranged from the juvenile, he should not be asked to act as the appropriate adult if the juvenile expressly and specifically objects to his presence.

1B If a juvenile admits an offence to, or in the presence of, a social worker other than during the time that the social worker is acting as the appropriate adult for that juvenile, another social worker should be the appropriate adult in the interest of fairness.

1C In the case of people who are mentally disordered or mentally handicapped, it may in certain circumstances be more satisfactory for all concerned if the appropriate adult is someone who has experience or training in their care rather than a relative lacking such qualifications. But if the person himself prefers a relative to a better-qualified stranger, or objects to a particular person as the appropriate adult, his wishes should if practicable be respected.

1D A solicitor or lay visitor who is present at the station in that capacity may not act as the appropriate adult.

1E For the purposes of paragraph 1.11 above, the consent required to be given by a parent or guardian may be given, in the case of a juvenile in the care of a local authority or voluntary organisation, by that authority or organisation.

1F People who are blind, seriously visually handicapped or unable to read may be unwilling to sign police documents. The alternative of their representative signing on their behalf seeks to protect the interests of both police and suspects.

1G Further guidance about fingerprints and body samples is given in Home Office circulars.

1H The generic term "mental disorder" is used throughout this code. "Mental disorder" is defined in section 1(2) of the Mental Health Act 1983 as "mental illness, arrested or incomplete development of mind, psychopathic disorder and any other disorder or disability of mind." It should be noted that "mental disorder" is different from "mental handicap" although the two are dealt with similarly throughout this code. Where the custody officer has any doubt as to the mental state or capacity of a person detained an appropriate adult should be called.

2 Identification by witnesses

2.0 A record shall be made of the description of the suspect as first given by a potential witness. This must be done before the witness takes part in the forms of identification listed in paragraph 2.1 or *Annex D* of this code. The record may be made or kept in any form provided that details of the description as first given by the witness can accurately be produced from it in a written form which can be provided to the suspect or his solicitor in accordance with this code. A copy shall be provided to the suspect or his solicitor before any procedures under paragraph 2.1 of this code are carried out. [See *Notes 2D and 2E*]

(a) Cases where the suspect is known
2.1 In a case which involves disputed identification evidence, and where the identity of the suspect is known to the police and he is available (See *Note 2D*), the methods of identification by witnesses which may be used are:
   (i) a parade;
   (ii) a group identification;
   (iii) a video film;
   (iv) a confrontation.

2.2 The arrangements for, and conduct of, these types of identification shall be the responsibility of an officer in uniform not below the rank of inspector who is not involved with the investigation ("the identification officer"). No officer involved with the investigation of the case against the suspect may take any part in these procedures.

Identification Parade
2.3 Whenever a suspect disputes an identification, an identification parade shall be held if the suspect consents unless paragraphs 2.4 or 2.7 or 2.10 apply. A parade may also be held if the officer in charge of the investigation considers that it would be useful, and the suspect consents.

2.4 A parade need not be held if the identification officer considers that, whether by reason of the unusual appearance of the suspect or for some other reason, it would not be practicable to assemble sufficient people who resembled him to make a parade fair.

2.5 Any parade must be carried out in accordance with *Annex A*. A video recording or colour photograph shall be taken of the parade.

2.6 If a suspect refuses or, having agreed, fails to attend an identification parade or the holding of a parade is impracticable, arrangements must if practicable be made to allow the witnesses an opportunity of seeing him in a group identification, a video identification, or a confrontation (see below).

Group Identification
2.7 A group identification takes place where the suspect is viewed by a witness amongst an informal group of people. The procedure may take place with the consent and co-operation of a suspect or covertly where a suspect has refused to co-operate with an identification parade or a group identification or has failed to

attend. A group identification may also be arranged if the officer in charge of the investigation considers, whether because of fear on the part of the witness or for some other reason, that it is, in the circumstances, more satisfactory than a parade.

2.8 The suspect should be asked for his consent to a group identification and advised in accordance with paragrahs 2.15 and 2.16 of this code. However, where consent is refused the identification officer has the discretion to proceed with a group identification if it is practicable to do so.

2.9 A group identification shall be carried out in accordance with *Annex E*. A video recording or colour photograph shall be taken of the group identification in accordance with *Annex E*.

Video Film Identification

2.10 The identification officer may show a witness a video film of a suspect if the investigating officer considers, whether because of the refusal of the suspect to take part in an identification parade or group identification or other reasons, that this would in the circumstances be the most satisfactory course of action.

2.11 The suspect should be asked for his consent to a video identification and advised in accordance with paragraphs 2.15 and 2.16. However, where such consent is refused the identification officer has the discretion to proceed with a video identification if it is practicable to do so.

2.12 A video identification must be carried out in accordance with *Annex B*.

Confrontation

2.13 If neither a parade, a group identification nor a video identification procedure is arranged, the suspect may be confronted by the witness. Such a confrontation does not require the suspect's consent, but may not take place unless none of the other procedures are practicable.

2.14 A confrontation must be carried out in accordance with *Annex C*.

Notice to Suspect

2.15 Before a parade takes place or a group identification or video identification is arranged, the identification officer shall explain to the suspect:

    (i)   the purposes of the parade or group identification or video identification;

   (ii)   that he is entitled to free legal advice (see paragraph 6.5 of Code C);

  (iii)   the procedures for holding it (including his right to have a solicitor or friend present);

  (iv)   where appropriate the special arrangements for juveniles;

   (v)   where appropriate the special arrangements for mentally disordered and mentally handicapped people;

  (vi)   that he does not have to take part in a parade, or co-operate in a group identification, or with the making of a video film and, if it is proposed to hold a group identification or video identification, his entitlement to a parade if this can practically be arranged;

 (vii)   if he does not consent to take part in a parade or co-operate in a group identification or with the making of a video film, his refusal may be given in evidence in any subsequent trial and police may proceed covertly without his consent or make other arrangements to test whether a witness identifies him;

(vii)a that if he should significantly alter his appearance between the taking of any photograph at the time of his arrest or after charge and any attempt to hold an identification procedure, this may be given in evidence if the case comes to trial; and the officer may then consider other forms of identification;

(vii)b that a video or photograph may be taken of him when he attends for any identification procedure;

(viii) whether the witness had been shown photographs, photofit, identikit or similar pictures by the police during the investigation before the identity of the suspect became known; [See *Note 2B*]

(ix) that if he changes his appearance before a parade it may not be practicable to arrange one on the day in question or subsequently and, because of his change of appearance, the identification officer may then consider alternative methods of identification;

(x) that he or his solicitor will be provided with details of the description of the suspect as first given by any witnesses who are to attend the parade, group identification, video identification or confrontation.

2.16 This information must also be contained in a written notice which must be handed to the suspect. The identification officer shall give the suspect a reasonable opportunity to read the notice, after which he shall be asked to sign a second copy of the notice to indicate whether or not he is willing to take part in the parade or group identification or co-operate with the making of a video film. The signed copy shall be retained by the identification officer.

(b) Cases where the identity of the suspect is not known
2.17 A police officer may take a witness to a particular neighbourhood or place to see whether he can identify the person whom he said he saw on the relevant occasion. Before doing so, where practicable a record shall be made of any description given by the witness of the suspect. Care should be taken not to direct the witness's attention to any individual.

2.18 A witness must not be shown photographs, photofit, identikit or similar pictures if the identity of the suspect is known to the police and he is available to stand on an identification parade. If the identity of the suspect is not known, the showing of such pictures to a witness must be done in accordance with *Annex D*. [See paragraph 2.15 (viii) and *Note 2D*]

(c) Documentation
2.19 The identification officer shall make a record of the parade, group identification or video identification on the forms provided.

2.20 If the identification officer considers that it is not practicable to hold a parade, he shall tell the suspect why and record the reason.

2.21 A record shall be made of a person's refusal to co-operate in a parade, group identification or video identification.

(d) Showing films and photographs of incidents

2.21A Nothing in this code inhibits an investigating officer from showing a video film or photographs of an incident to the public at large through the national, or local media, or to the police officers, for the purposes of recognition and tracing suspects. However when such material is shown to potential witnesses (including police officers [see *Note 2A*] for the purpose of obtaining identification evidence, it shall be shown on an individual basis so as to avoid any possibility of collusion, and the showing shall, as far as possible, follow the principles for Video Film Identification (see paragraph 2.10) or Identification by Photographs (see paragraph 2.18) as appropriate).

2.21B Where such a broadcast or publication is made a copy of the material released by the police to the media for the purposes of recognising or tracing the suspect shall be kept and the suspect or his solicitor should be allowed to view such material before any procedures under paragraph 2.1 of this Code are carried out [see *Notes 2D* and *2E*] provided it is practicable to do so and would not unreasonably delay the investigation. Each witness who is involved in the procedure shall be asked by the investigating officer after they have taken part whether they have seen any broadcast or published films or photographs relating to the offence and their replies shall be recorded.

Notes for Guidance

2A *Except for the provisions of Annex D paragraph 1, a police officer who is a witness for the purposes of this part of the code is subject to the same principles and procedures as a civilian witness.*

2B *Where a witness attending an identification parade has previously been shown photographs or photofit, identikit or similar pictures, it is the responsibility of the officer in charge of the investigation to make the identification officer aware that this is the case.*

2C *[Not Used]*

2D *References in this section to a suspect being "known" means there is sufficient information known to the police to justify the arrest of a particular person for suspected involvement in the offence. A suspect being "available" means that he is immediately available to take part in the procedure or he will become available within a reasonably short time.*

2E *Where it is proposed to show photographs to a witness in accordance with Annex D, it is the responsibility of the officer in charge of the investigation to confirm to the officer responsible for supervising and directing the showing that the first description of the suspect given by that witness has been recorded. If this description has not been recorded, the procedure under Annex D must be postponed. [See Annex D paragraph 1A]*

3 Identification by fingerprints

(a) Action

3.1 A person's fingerprints may be taken only with his consent or if paragraph 3.2 applies. If he is at a police station consent must be in writing. In either case the person must be informed of the reason before they are taken and that they will be destroyed as soon as practicable if paragraph 3.4 applies. He must be told that he may witness their destruction if he asks to do so within five days of being cleared or informed that he will not be prosecuted.

3.2 Powers to take fingerprints without consent from any person over the age of ten years are provided by sections 27 and 61 of the Police and Criminal Evidence Act 1984. These provide that fingerprints may be taken without consent:

(a) from a person detained at a police station if an officer of at least the rank of superintendent has reasonable grounds for suspecting that the fingerprints will tend to confirm or disprove his involvement in a criminal offence and the officer authorises the fingerprints to be taken;

(b) from a person detained at a police station who has been charged with a recordable offence or informed that he will be reported for such an offence and he has not previously had his fingerprints taken in relation to that offence;

(c) from a person convicted of a recordable offence. Section 27 of the Police and Criminal Evidence Act 1984 provides power to require such a person to attend a police station for the purposes of having his fingerprints taken if he has not been in police detention for the offence nor had his fingerprints taken in the course of the investigation of the offence or since conviction.

Reasonable force may be used if necessary to take a person's fingerprints without his consent.

3.2A A person whose fingerprints are to be taken with or without consent shall be informed beforehand that his prints may be subject of a speculative search against other fingerprints. [See *Note 3B*]

3.3 [Not Used]

3.4 The fingerprints of a person and all copies of them taken in that case must be destroyed as soon as practicable if:
(a) he is prosecuted for the offence concerned and cleared; or
(b) he is not prosecuted (unless he admits the offence and is cautioned for it).
An opportunity of witnessing the destruction must be given to him if he wishes and if, in accordance with paragraph 3.1, he applies within five days of being cleared or informed that he will not be prosecuted.

3.5 When fingerprints are destroyed, access to relevant computer data shall be made impossible as soon as it is practicable to do so.

3.6 References to fingerprints include palm prints.

(b) Documentation

3.7 A record must be made as soon as possible of the reason for taking a person's fingerprints without consent and of their destruction. If force is used a record shall be made of the circumstances and those present.

3.8 A record shall be made when a person has been informed under the terms of paragraph 3.2A that his fingerprints may be subject of a speculative search.

Notes for Guidance

3A References to recordable offences in this code relate to those offences for which convictions may be recorded in national police records. (See section 27(4) of the Police and Criminal Evidence Act 1984.) The recordable offences to which this code applies at the time when the code was prepared, are any offences which carry a sentence of imprisonment on conviction (irrespective of the period, or the age of the offender or actual sentence passed) and non-imprisonable offences under section 1 of the Street Offences Act 1959 (loitering or soliciting for purposes of prostitution), section 43 of the Telecommunications Act 1984 (improper use of public telecommunications system), section 25 of the Road Traffic Act 1988 (tampering with motor vehicles), section 1 of the Malicious Communications Act 1988 (sending letters etc with intent to cause distress or anxiety) and section 139(1) of the Criminal Justice Act 1988 (having article with a blade or point in a public place).

3B A speculative search means that a check may be made against other fingerprints contained in records held by or on behalf of the police or held in connection with or as a result of an investigation of an offence.

4 Photographs

(a) Action
4.1 The photograph of a person who has been arrested may be taken at a police station only with his written consent or if paragraph 4.2 applies. In either case he must be informed of the reason for taking it and that the photograph will be destroyed if paragraph 4.4 applies. He must be told that if he should significantly alter his appearance between the taking of the photograph and any attempt to hold an identification procedure this may be given in evidence if the case comes to trial. He must be told that he may witness the destruction of the photograph or be provided with a certificate confirming its destruction if he applies within five days of being cleared or informed that he will not be prosecuted.

4.2 The photograph of a person who has been arrested may be taken without consent if:
   (i) he is arrested at the same time as other people, or at a time when it is likely that other people will be arrested, and a photograph is necessary to establish who was arrested, at what time and at what place; or
   (ii) he has been charged with, or reported for a recordable offence and has not yet been released or brought before a court [see *Note 3A*]; or
   (iii) he is convicted of such an offence and his photograph is not already on record as a result of (i) or (ii). There is no power of arrest to take a photograph in pursuance of this provision which applies only where the person is in custody as a result of the exercise of another power (e.g. arrest for fingerprinting under section 27 of the Police and Criminal

Evidence Act 1984); or
(iv) an officer of at least the rank of superintendent authorises it, having reasonable grounds for suspecting the involvement of the person in a criminal offence and where there is identification evidence in relation to that offence.

4.3 Force may not be used to take a photograph.

4.4 Where a person's photograph has been taken in accordance with this section, the photograph, negatives and all copies taken in that particular case must be destroyed if:
(a) he is prosecuted for the offence and cleared unless he has a previous conviction for a recordable offence; or
(b) he has been charged but not prosecuted (unless he admits the offence and is cautioned for it or he has a previous conviction for a recordable offence).
An opportunity of witnessing the destruction or a certificate confirming the destruction must be given to him if he so requests, provided that, in accordance with paragraph 4.1, he applies within five days of being cleared or informed that he will not be prosecuted. [See *Note 4B*]

(b) Documentation
4.5 A record must be made as soon as possible of the reason for taking a person's photograph under this section without consent and of the destruction of any photographs.

Notes for Guidance
4A *The admissibility and value of identification evidence may be compromised if a potential witness in an identification procedure views any photographs of the suspect otherwise than in accordance with the provisions of this code.*

4B *This paragraph is not intended to require the destruction of copies of a police gazette in cases where, for example, a remand prisoner has escaped from custody, or a person in custody is suspected of having committed offences in other force areas, and a photograph of the person concerned is circulated in a police gazette for information.*

5 Identification by body samples and impressions

(a) Action
Intimate samples
5.1 Intimate samples may be taken from a person in police detention only:
(i) if an officer of the rank of superintendent or above has reasonable grounds to believe that such an impression or sample will tend to confirm or disprove the suspect's involvement in a recordable offence and gives authorisation for a sample to be taken; and
(ii) with the suspect's written consent.

5.1A Where two or more non-intimate samples have been taken from a person in the course of an investigation of an offence and the samples have proved unsuitable or insufficient for a particular form of analysis and that person is not in police detention, an intimate sample may be taken from him if a police officer of at least the rank of superintendent authorises it to be taken, and the person concerned gives his written consent. [See Note 5B and Note 5E]

5.2 Before a person is asked to provide an intimate sample he must be warned that if he refuses without good cause, his refusal may harm his case if it comes to trial. [See Note 5A] If he is in police detention and not legally represented, he must also be reminded of his entitlement to have free legal advice (see paragraph 6.5 of Code C) and the reminder must be noted in the custody record. If paragraph 5.1A above applies and the person is attending a police station voluntarily, the officer shall explain the entitlement to free legal advice as provided for in accordance with paragraph 3.15 of Code C.

5.3 Except for samples of urine, intimate samples or dental impressions may be taken only by a registered medical or dental practitioner as appropriate.

Non-intimate samples
5.4 A non-intimate sample may be taken from a detained person only with his written consent or if paragraph 5.5 applies.

5.5 A non-intimate sample may be taken from a person without consent in accordance with the provisions of section 63 of the Police and Criminal Evidence Act 1984, as amended by section 55 of the Criminal Justice and Public Order Act 1994. The principal circumstances provided for are as follows:
  (i) if an officer of the rank of superintendent or above has reasonable grounds to believe that the sample will tend to confirm or disprove the person's involvement in a recordable offence and gives authorisation for a sample to be taken; or
  (ii) where the person has been charged with a recordable offence or informed that he will be reported for such an offence; and he has not had a non-intimate sample taken from him in the course of the investigation or if he has had a sample taken from him, it has proved unsuitable or insufficient for the same form of analysis [See Note 5B]; or
  (iii) if the person has been convicted of a recordable offence after the date on which this code comes into effect. Section 63A of the Police and Criminal Evidence Act 1984, as amended by section 56 of the Criminal Justice and Public Order Act 1994, described the circumstances in which a constable may require a person convicted of a recordable offence to attend a police station in order that a non-intimate sample may be taken.

5.6 Where paragraph 5.5 applies, reasonable force may be used if necessary to take non-intimate samples.

(b) Destruction
5.7 [Not Used]

5.8 Except in accordance with paragraph 5.8A below, where a sample or impression has been taken in accordance with this section it must be destroyed as soon as practicable if:
(a) the suspect is prosecuted for the offence concerned and cleared; or

(b) he is not prosecuted (unless he admits the offence and is cautioned for it).

5.8A In accordance with section 64 of the Police and Criminal Evidence Act 1984 as amended by section 57 of the Criminal Justice and Public Order Act 1994 samples need not be destroyed if they were taken for the purpose of an investigation of an offence for which someone has been convicted, and from whom a sample was also taken. [See *Note 5F*]

(c) Documentation
5.9 A record must be made as soon as practicable of the reasons for taking a sample or impression and of its destruction. If force is used, a record shall be made of the circumstances and those present. If written consent is given to the taking of a sample or impression, the fact must be recorded in writing.

5.10 A record must be made of the giving of a warning required by paragraph 5.2 above. A record shall be made of the fact that a person has been informed under the terms of paragraph 5.11A below that samples may be subject of a speculative search.

(d) General
5.11 The terms intimate and non-intimate samples are defined in section 65 of the Police and Criminal Evidence Act 1984, as amended by section 58 of the Criminal Justice and Public Order Act 1994, as follows:
(a) "intimate sample" means a dental impression or a sample of blood, semen or any other tissue fluid, urine, or pubic hair, or a swab taken from a person's body orifice other than the mouth;
(b) "non-intimate sample" means:
    (i) a sample of hair (other than pubic hair) which includes hair plucked with the root [See *Note 5C*];
    (ii) a sample taken from a nail or from under a nail;
    (iii) a swab taken from any part of a person's body including the mouth but not any other body orifice;
    (iv) saliva;
    (v) a footprint or similar impression of any part of a person's body other than a part of his hand.

5.11A A person from whom an intimate or non-intimate sample is to be taken shall be informed beforehand that any sample taken may be the subject of a speculative search. [See *Note 5D*]

5.11B The suspect must be informed, before an intimate or non-intimate sample is taken, of the grounds on which the relevant authority has been given, including where appropriate the nature of the suspected offence.

5.12 Where clothing needs to be removed in circumstances likely to cause embarrassment to the person, no person of the opposite sex who is not a medical practitioner or nurse shall be present, (unless in the case of a juvenile or a mentally disordered or mentally handicapped person, that person specifically requests the presence of an appropriate adult of the opposite sex who is readily available) nor shall anyone whose presence is unnecessary. However, in the case of a juvenile this is subject to the overriding proviso that such a removal of clothing may take place in the absence of the appropriate adult only if the person signifies in the presence of the appropriate adult that he prefers his absence and the appropriate adult agrees.

Notes for Guidance

5A *In warning a person who is asked to provide an intimate sample in accordance with paragraph 5.2, the following form of words may be used:*

> "*You do not have to [provide this sample] [allow this swab or impression to be taken], but I must warn you that if you refuse without good cause, your refusal may harm your case if it comes to trial.*"

5B *An insufficient sample is one which is not sufficient either in quantity or quality for the purpose of enabling information to be provided for the purpose of a particular form of analysis such as DNA analysis. An unsuitable sample is one which, by its nature, is not suitable for a particular form of analysis.*

5C *Where hair samples are taken for the purpose of DNA analysis (rather than for other purposes such as making a visual match) the suspect should be permitted a reasonable choice as to what part of the body he wishes the hairs to be taken from. When hairs are plucked they should be plucked individually unless the suspect prefers otherwise and no more should be plucked than the person taking them reasonably considers necessary for a sufficient sample.*

5D *A speculative search means that a check may be made against other samples and information derived from other samples contained in records or held by or on behalf of the police or held in connection with or as a result of an investigation of an offence.*

5E *Nothing in paragraph 5.1A prevents intimate samples being taken for elimination purposes with the consent of the person concerned but the provisions of paragraph 1.11, relating to the role of the appropriate adult, should be applied.*

5F *The provisions for the retention of samples in 5.8A allow for all samples in a case to be available for any subsequent miscarriage of justice investigation. But such samples – and the information derived from them – may not be used in the investigation of any offence or in evidence against the person who would otherwise be entitled to their destruction.*

ANNEX A

Identification Parades

(a) *General*
1. A suspect must be given a reasonable opportunity to have a solicitor or friend present, and the identification officer shall ask him to indicate on a second copy of the notice whether or not he so wishes.

2. A parade may take place either in a normal room or in one equipped with a

screen permitting witnesses to see members of the parade without being seen. The procedures for the composition and conduct of the parade are the same in both cases, subject to paragraph 7 below (except that a parade involving a screen may take place only when the suspect's solicitor, friend, or appropriate adult is present or the parade is recorded on video).

2A. Before the parade takes place the suspect or his solicitor shall be provided with details of the first description of the suspect by any witnesses who are to attend the parade. The suspect or his solicitor should also be allowed to view any material released to the media by the police for the purpose of recognising or tracing the suspect, provided it is practicable to do so and would not unreasonably delay the investigation.

(b) Parades involving prison inmates
3. If an inmate is required for identification, and there are no security problems about his leaving the establishment, he may be asked to participate in a parade or video identification.

4. A parade may be held in a Prison Department establishment, but shall be conducted as far as practicable under normal parade rules. Members of the public shall make up the parade unless there are serious security or control objections to their admission to the establishment. In such cases, or if a group or video identification is arranged within the establishment, other inmates may participate. If an inmate is the suspect, he shall not be required to wear prison uniform for the parade unless the other people taking part are other inmates in uniform or are members of the public who are prepared to wear prison uniform for the occasion.

(c) Conduct for the parade
5. Immediately before the parade, the identification officer must remind the suspect of the procedures governing its conduct and caution him in the terms of paragraph 10.4 of Code C.

6. All unauthorised people must be excluded from the place where the parade is held.

7. Once the parade has been formed, everything afterwards in respect of it shall take place in the presence and hearing of the suspect and of any interpreter, solicitor, friend or appropriate adult who is present (unless the parade involves a screen, in which case everything said to or by any witness at the place where the parade is held must be said in the hearing and presence of the suspect's solicitor, friend or appropriate adult or be recorded on video).

8. The parade shall consist of at least eight people (in addition to the suspect) who so far as possible resemble the suspect in age, height, general appearance and position in life. One suspect only shall be included in a parade unless there are two suspects of roughly similar appearance in which case they may be paraded together with at least twelve other people. In no circumstances shall more than two suspects be included in one parade and where there are separate parades they shall be made up of different people.

9. Where all members of a similar group are possible suspects, separate parades shall be held for each member of the group unless there are two suspects of similar appearance when they may appear on the same parade with at least twelve other members of the group who are not suspects. Where police officers in uniform form an identification parade, any numerals or other identifying badges shall be concealed.

10. When the suspect is brought to the place where the parade is to be held, he shall be asked by the identification officer whether he has any objection to the arrangements for the parade or to any of the other participants in it. The suspect may obtain advice from his solicitor or friend, if present, before the parade proceeds. Where practicable, steps shall be taken to remove the grounds for objection. Where it is not practicable to do so, the officer shall explain to the suspect why his objections cannot be met.

11. The suspect may select his own position in the line. Where there is more than one witness, the identification officer must tell the suspect, after each witness has left the room, that he can if he wishes change position in the line. Each position in the line must be clearly numbered, whether by means of a numeral laid on the floor in front of each parade member or by other means.

12. The identification officer is responsible for ensuring that, before they attend the parade, witnesses are not able to:
  (i) communicate with each other about the case or overhear a witness who has already seen the parade;
  (ii) see any member of the parade;
  (iii) on that occasion see or be reminded of any photograph or description of the suspect or be given any other indication of his identity; or
  (iv) on that occasion, see the suspect either before or after the parade.

13. The officer conducting a witness to a parade must not discuss with him the composition of the parade, and in particular he must not disclose whether a previous witness has made any identification.

14. Witnesses shall be brought in one at a time. Immediately before the witness inspects the parade, the identification officer shall tell him that the person he saw may or may not be on the parade and if he cannot make a positive identification he should say so but that he should not make a decision before looking at each member of the parade at least twice. The officer shall then ask him to look at each member of the parade at least twice, taking as much care and time as he wishes. When the officer is satisfied that the witness has properly looked at each member of the parade, he shall ask him whether the person he himself saw on an earlier relevant occasion is on the parade.

15. The witness should make an identification by indicating the number of the person concerned.

16. If the witness makes an identification after the parade has ended the suspect and, if present, his solicitor, interpreter or friend shall be informed. Where this occurs, consideration should be given to allowing the witness a second opportunity to identify the suspect.

17. If a witness wishes to hear any parade member speak, adopt any specified posture or see him move, the identification officer shall first ask whether he can identify any persons on the parade on the basis of appearance only. When the request is to hear members of the parade speak, the witness shall be reminded that the participants in the parade have been chosen on the basis of physical appearance only. Members of the parade may then be asked to comply with the witness's request to hear them speak, to see them move or to adopt any specified posture.

17A. Where video films or photographs have been released to the media by the police for the purpose of recognising or tracing the suspect, the investigating officer shall ask each witness after the parade whether he has seen any broadcast or published films or photographs relating to the offence and shall record his reply.

18. When the last witness has left, the identification officer shall ask the suspect whether he wishes to make any comments on the conduct of the parade.

(d) Documentation
19. A colour photograph or a video film of the parade shall be taken. A copy of the photograph or video film shall be supplied on request to the suspect or his solicitor within a reasonable time.

20. The photograph or video film taken in accordance with paragraph 19 shall be destroyed or wiped clean at the conclusion of the proceedings unless the person concerned is convicted or admits the offence and is cautioned for it.

21. If the identification officer asks any person to leave a parade because he is interfering with its conduct the circumstances shall be recorded.

22. A record must be made of all those present at a parade whose names are known to the police.

23. If prison inmates make up a parade the circumstances must be recorded.

24. A record of the conduct of any parade must be made on the forms provided.

ANNEX B

Video Identification

(a) General
1. Where a video parade is to be arranged the following procedures must be followed.

2. Arranging, supervising and directing the making and showing of a video film to be used in a video identification must be the responsibility of an identification officer or identification officers who have no direct involvement with the relevant case.

3. The film must include the suspect and at least eight other people who so far as possible resemble the suspect in age, height, general appearance and position in

life. Only one suspect shall appear on any film unless there are two suspects of roughly similar appearance in which case they may be shown together with at least twelve other people.

4. The suspect and other people shall as far as possible be filmed in the same positions or carrying out the same activity and under identical conditions.

5. Provisions must be made for each person filmed to be identified by number.

6. If police officers are filmed, any numerals or other identifying badges must be concealed. If a prison inmate is filmed either as a suspect or not, then either all or none of the people filmed should be in prison uniform.

7. The suspect and his solicitor, friend, or appropriate adult must be given a reasonable opportunity to see the complete film before it is shown to witnesses. If he has a reasonable objection to the video film or any of its participants, steps shall, if practicable be taken to remove the grounds for objection. If this is not practicable the identification officer shall explain to the suspect and/or his representative why his objections cannot be met and record both the objection and the reason on the forms provided.

8. The suspect's solicitor, or where one is not instructed the suspect himself, where practicable shall be given reasonable notification of the time and place that it is intended to conduct the video identification in order that a representative may attend on behalf of the suspect. The suspect himself may not be present when the film is shown to the witness(es). In the absence of a person representing the suspect the viewing itself shall be recorded on video. No authorised people may be present.

8A. Before the video identification takes place the suspect or his solicitor shall be provided with details of the first description of the suspect by any witnesses who are to attend the parade. The suspect or his solicitor should also be allowed to view any material released to the media by the police for the purpose of recognising or tracing the suspect, provided it is practicable to do so and would not unreasonably delay the investigation.

(b) Conducting the video identification
9. The identification officer is responsible for ensuring that, before they see the film, witnesses are not able to communicate with each other about the case or overhear a witness who has seen the film. He must not discuss with the witness the composition of the film and must not disclose whether a previous witness has made any identification.

10. Only one witness may see the film at a time. Immediately before the video identification takes place the identification officer shall tell the witness that the person he saw may or may not be on the video film. The witness shall be advised that at any point he may ask to see a particular part of the tape again or to have a particular picture frozen for him to study. Furthermore, it should be pointed out that there is no limit on how many times he can view the whole tape or any part of it. However, he should be asked to refrain from making a positive identification or

saying that he cannot make a positive identification until he has seen the entire film at least twice.

11. Once the witness has seen the whole film at least twice and has indicated that he does not want to view it or any part of it again, the identification officer shall ask the witness to say whether the individual he saw in person on an earlier occasion has been shown on the film and, if so, to identify him by number. The identification officer will then show the film of the person identified again to confirm the identification with the witness.

12. The identification officer must take care not to direct the witness's attention to any one individual on the video film, or give any other indication of the suspect's identity. Where a witness has previously made an identification by photographs, or a photofit, identikit or similar picture has been made, the witness must not be reminded of such a photograph or picture once a suspect is available for identification by other means in accordance with this code. Neither must he be reminded of any description of the suspect.

12A. Where video films or photographs have been released to the media by the police for the purpose of recognising or tracing the suspect, the investigating officer shall ask each witness after the parade whether he has seen any broadcast or published films or photographs relating to the offence and shall record his reply.

(c) Tape security and destruction
13. It shall be the responsibility of the identification officer to ensure that all relevant tapes are kept securely and their movements accounted for. In particular, no officer involved in the investigation against the suspect shall be permitted to view the video film prior to it being shown to any witness.

14 Where a video film has been made in accordance with this section all copies of it must be destroyed if the suspect:
(a) is prosecuted for the offence and cleared; or
(b) is not prosecuted (unless he admits the offence and is cautioned for it).
An opportunity of witnessing the destruction must be given to him if he so requests within five days of being cleared or informed that he will not be prosecuted.

(d) Documentation
15. A record must be made of all those participating in or seeing the video whose names are known to the police.

16. A record of the conduct of the video identification must be made on the forms provided.

ANNEX C

Confrontation by a Witness

1. The identification officer is responsible for the conduct of any confrontation of a suspect by a witness.

2. Before the confrontation takes place, the identification officer must tell the witness that the person he saw may or may not be the person he is to confront and that if he cannot make a positive identification he should say so.

2A. Before the confrontation takes place, the suspect or his solicitor shall be provided with details of the first description of the suspect given by any witness who is to attend the confrontation. The suspect or his solicitor should also be allowed to view any material released by the police to the media for the purposes of recognising or tracing the suspect provided that it is practicable to do so and would not unreasonably delay the investigation.

3. The suspect shall be confronted independently by each witness, who shall be asked "Is this the person?" Confrontation must take place in the presence of the suspect's solicitor, interpreter or friend, unless this would cause unreasonable delay.

4. The confrontation should normally take place in the police station, either in a normal room or in one equipped with a screen permitting a witness to see the suspect without being seen. In both cases the procedures are the same except that a room equipped with a screen may be used only when the suspect's solicitor, friend or appropriate adult is present or the confrontation is recorded on video.

5. Where video films or photographs have been released to the media by the police for the purposes of recognising or tracing the suspect, the investigating officer shall ask each witness after the procedure whether he has seen any broadcast or published films or photographs relating to the offence and shall record his reply.

ANNEX D

Showing of Photographs

(a) Action
1. An officer of the rank of sergeant or above shall be responsible for supervising and directing the showing of photographs. The actual showing may be done by a constable or a civilian police employee.

1A. The officer must confirm that the first description of the suspect given by the witness has been recorded before the witness is shown the photographs. If he is unable to confirm that the description has been recorded, he shall postpone the showing.

2. Only one witness shall be shown photographs at any one time. He shall be given as much privacy as practicable and shall not be allowed to communicate with any other witness in the case.

3. The witness shall be shown not less than twelve photographs at a time, which shall, as far as possible, all be of a similar type.

4. When the witness is shown the photographs, he shall be told that the photograph of the person he saw may or may not be amongst them. He shall not be prompted

or guided in any way but shall be left to make any selection without help.

5. If a witness makes a positive identification from photographs, then, unless the person identified is otherwise eliminated from enquiries, other witnesses shall not be shown photographs. But both they and the witness who has made the identification shall be asked to attend an identification parade or group or video identification if practicable unless there is no dispute about the identification of the suspect.

6. Where the use of a photofit, identikit or similar picture has led to there being a suspect available who can be asked to appear on a parade, or participate in a group or video identification, the picture shall not be shown to other potential witnesses.

7. Where a witness attending an identification parade has previously been shown photographs or photofit, identikit or similar pictures (and it is the responsibility of the officer in charge of the investigation to make the identification officer aware that this is the case) then the suspect and his solicitor must be informed of this fact before the identity parade takes place.

8. None of the photograhs used shall be destroyed, whether or not an identification is made, since they may be required for production in court. The photographs shall be numbered and a separate photograph taken of the frame or part of the album from which the witness made an identification as an aid to reconstituting it.

(b) Documentation
9. Whether or not an identification is made, a record shall be kept of the showing of photographs and of any comment made by the witness.

ANNEX E

Group Identification

(a) General
1. The purpose of the provisions of this Annex is to ensure that as far as possible, group identifications follow the principles and procedures for identification parades so that the conditions are fair to the suspect in the way they test the witness's ability to make an identification.

2. Group identifications may take place either with the suspect's consent and co-operation or covertly without his consent.

3. The location of the group identification is a matter for the identification officer, although he may take into account any representations made by the suspect, appropriate adult, his solicitor or friend. The place where the group identification is held should be one where other people are either passing by, or waiting around informally, in groups such that the suspect is able to join them and be capable of being seen by the witness at the same time as others in the group. Examples include people leaving an escalator, pedestrians walking through a shopping centre, passengers on railway and bus stations waiting in queues or groups or where people are standing or sitting in groups in other public places.

4. If the group identification is to be held covertly, the choice of locations will be limited by the places where the suspect can be found and the number of other people present at that time. In these cases, suitable locations might be along regular routes travelled by the suspect, including buses or trains, or public places he frequents.

5. Although the number, age, sex, race and general description and style of clothing of other peole present at the location cannot be controlled by the identification officer, in selecting the location he must consider the general appearance and numbers of people likely to be present. In particular, he must reasonably expect that over the period the witness observes the group, he will be able to see, from time to time, a number of others (in addition to the suspect) whose appearance is broadly similar to that of the suspect.

6. A group identification need not be held if the identification officer believes that because of the unusual appearance of the suspect, none of the locations which it would be practicable to use satisfy the requirements of paragraph 5 necessary to make the identification fair.

7. Immediately after a group identification procedure has taken place (with or without the suspect's consent), a colour photograph or a video should be taken of the general scene, where this is practicable, so as to give a general impression of the scene and the number of people present. Alternatively, if it is practicable, the group identification may be video recorded.

8. If it is not practicable to take the photograph or video film in accordance with paragraph 7, a photograph or film of the scene should be taken later at a time determined by the identification officer, if he considers that it is practicable to do so.

9. An identification carried out in accordance with this code remains a group identification notwithstanding that at the time of being seen by the witness the suspect was on his own rather than in a group.

10. The identification officer need not be in uniform when conducting a group identification.

11. Before the group identification takes place the suspect or his solicitor should be provided with details of the first description of the suspect by any witnesses who are to attend the identification. The suspect or his solicitor should also be allowed to view any material released by the police to the media for the purposes of recognising or tracing the suspect provided that it is practicable to do so and would not unreasonably delay the investigation.

12. Where video films or photographs have been released to the media by the police for the purposes of recognising or tracing the suspect, the investigating officer shall ask each witness after the procedure whether he has seen any broadcast or published films or photographs relating to the offence and shall record his reply.

(b) Identification with the consent of the suspect
13. A suspect must be given a reasonable opportunity to have a solicitor or friend present. The identification officer shall ask him to indicate on a second copy of the notice whether or not he so wishes.

14. The witness, identification officer and suspect's solicitor, appropriate adult, friend or any interpreter for the witness, if present, may be concealed from the sight of the persons in the group which they are observing if the identification officer considers that this facilitates the conduct of the identification.

15. The officer conducting a witness to a group identification must not discuss with the witness the forthcoming group identification and in particular he must not disclose whether a previous witness has made any identification.

16. Anything said to or by the witness during the procedure regarding the identification should be said in the presence and hearing of the identificaiton officer and, if present, the suspect's solicitor, appropriate adult, friend or any interpreter for the witness.

17. The identification officer is responsible for ensuring that before they attend the group identification witnesses are not able to:
   (i) communicate with each other about the case or overhear a witness who has already been given an opportunity to see the suspect in the group;
   (ii) on that occasion see the suspect; or
   (iii) on that occasion see or be reminded of any photographs or description of the suspect or be given any other indication of his identity.

18. Witnesses shall be brought to the place where they are to observe the group one at a time. Immediately before the witness is asked to look at the group, the identification officer shall tell him that the person he saw may or may not be in the group and if he cannot make a positive identification he should say so. The witness shall then be asked to observe the group in which the suspect is to appear. The way in which the witness should do this will depend on whether the group is moving or stationary.

Moving group
19. When the group in which the suspect is to appear is moving, for example, leaving an escalator, the provisions of paragraphs 20 to 23 below should be followed.

20. If two or more suspects consent to a group identification, each should be the subject of separate identification procedures. These may however be conducted consecutively on the same occasion.

21. The identification officer shall tell the witness to observe the group and ask him to point out any person he thinks he saw on the earlier relevant occasion. When the witness makes such an indication the officer shall, if it is practicable, arrange for the witness to take a closer look at the person he has indicated and ask him whether he can make a positive identification. If this is not practicable, the officer shall ask the witness how sure he is that the person he has indicated is the relevant person.

22. The witness should continue to observe the group for the period which the identification officer reasonably believes is necessary in the circumstances for the witness to be able to make comparisons between the suspect and other persons of broadly similar appearance to the suspect in accordance with pargraph 5.

23. Once the identification officer has informed the witness in accordance with paragraph 20, the suspect should be allowed to take any position in the group he wishes.

Stationary groups
24. When the group in which the suspect is to appear is stationary, for example, people waiting in a queue, the provisions of paragraphs 25 to 28 below should be followed.

25. If two or more suspects consent to a group identification, each should be the subject of separate identification procedures unless they are of broadly similar appearance when they may appear in the same group. Where separate group identifications are held, the groups must be made up of different persons.

26. The suspect may take any position in the group he wishes. Where there is more than one witness, the identification officer must tell the suspect, out of the sight and hearing of any witness, that he can if he wishes change his position in the group.

27. The identification officer shall ask the witness to pass along or amongst the group and to look at each person in the group at least twice, taking as much care and time as is possible according to the circumstances, before making an identification. When he has done this, the officer shall ask him whether the person he saw on an earlier relevant occasion is in the group and to indicate any such person by whatever means the identification officer considers appropriate in the circumstances. If this is not practicable, the officer shall ask the witness to point out any person he thinks he saw on the earlier relevant occasion.

28. When the witness makes an indication in accordance with paragraph 27, the officer shall, if it is practicable, arrange for the witness to take a closer look at the person he has indicated and ask him whether he can make a positive identification. If this is not practicable, the officer shall ask the witness how sure he is that the person he has indicated is the relevant person.

All cases
29. If the suspect unreasonably delays joining the group, or having joined the group, deliberately conceals himself from the sight of the witness, the identification officer may treat this as a refusal to co-operate in a group identification.

30. If the witness identifies a person other than the suspect, an officer should inform that person what has happened and ask if they are prepared to give their name and address. There is no obligation upon any member of the public to give these details. There shall be no duty to record any details of any other member of the public present in the group or at the place where the procedure is conducted.

31. When the group identification has been completed, the identification officer shall ask the suspect whether he wishes to make any comments on the conduct of the procedure.

32. If he has not been previously informed the identification officer shall tell the suspect of any identifications made by the witnesses.

(c) Identification without suspect's consent
33. Group identifications held covertly without the suspect's consent should so far as is practicable follow the rules for conduct of group identification by consent.

34. A suspect has no right to have a solicitor, appropriate adult or friend present as the identification will, of necessity, take place without the knowledge of the suspect.

35. Any number of suspects may be identified at the same time.

(d) Identifications in police stations
36. Group identifications should only take place in police stations for reasons of safety, security, or because it is impracticable to hold them elsewhere.

37. The group identification may take place either in a room equipped with a screen permitting witnesses to see members of the group without being seen, or anywhere else in the police station that the identification officer considers appropriate.

38. Any of the additional safeguards applicable to identification parades should be followed if the identification officer considers it is practicable to do so in the circumstances.

(e) Identifications involving prison inmates
39. A group identification involving a prison inmate may only be arranged in the prison or at a police station.

40. Where a group identification takes place involving a prison inmate, whether in a prison or in a police station, the arrangements should follow those in paragraphs 36 to 38 of this Annex. If a group identification takes place within a prison other inmates may participate. If an inmate is the suspect he should not be required to wear prison uniform for the group identification unless the other persons taking part are wearing the same uniform.

(f) Documentation
41. Where a photograph or video film is taken in accordance with paragraph 7 or 8, a copy of the photograph or video film shall be supplied on request to the suspect or his solicitor within a reasonable time.

42. If the photograph or film includes the suspect, it shall be destroyed or wiped clean at the conclusion of the proceedings unless the person is convicted or admits the offence and is cautioned for it.

43. A record of the conduct of any group identification must be made on the forms provided. This shall include anything said by the witness or the suspect about any identifications or the conduct of the procedure and any reasons why it was not practicable to comply with any of the provisions of this code governing the conduct of group identifications.

E Code of Practice on Tape Recording of Interviews with Suspects

1 General

1.1 This code of practice must be readily available for consultation by police officers, detained persons and members of the public at every police station to which an order made under section 60(1)(b) of the Police and Criminal Evidence Act 1984 applies.

1.2 The notes for guidance included are not provisions of this code. They form guidance to police officers and others about its application and interpretation.

1.3 Nothing in this code shall be taken as detracting in any way from the requirements of the Code of Practice for the Detention, Treatment and Questioning of Persons by Police Officers (Code C). [See *Note 1A*]

1.4 This code does not apply to those groups of people listed in paragraph 1.12 of Code C.

1.5 In this code the term "appropriate adult" has the same meaning as in paragraph 1.7 of Code C; and the term "solicitor" has the same meaning as in paragraph 6.12 of Code C.

Note for Guidance
1A As in Code C, references to custody officers include those carrying out the functions of a custody officer.

2 Recording and the sealing of master tapes

2.1 Tape recording of interviews shall be carried out openly to instil confidence in its reliability as an impartial and accurate record of the interview. [See *Note 2A*]

2.2 One tape, referred to in this code as the master tape, will be sealed before it leaves the presence of the suspect. A second tape will be used as a working copy. The master tape is either one of the two tapes used in a twin deck machine or the only tape used in a single deck machine. The working copy is either the second tape used in a twin deck machine or a copy of the master tape made by a single deck machine. [See *Notes 2B and 2C*]

Notes for Guidance
Police officers will wish to arrange that, as far as possible, tape recording arrangements are unobtrusive. It must be clear to the suspect, however, that there is no opportunity to interfere with the tape recording equipment or the tapes.

2B The purpose of sealing the master tape before it leaves the presence of the suspect is to establish his confidence that the integrity of the tape is preserved. Where a single deck machine is used the working copy and the master tape must be made in the presence of the suspect and without the master tape having left his sight. The working copy shall be used for making further copies where the need arises. The recorder will normally be capable of recording voices and have a time coding or other security device.

2C *Throughout this code any reference to "tapes" shall be construed as "tape", as appropriate, where a single deck machine is used.*

3 Interviews to be tape recorded

3.1 Subject to paragraph 3.2 below, tape recording shall be used at police stations for any interview:

(a) with a person who has been cautioned in accordance with section 10 of Code C in respect of an indictable offence (including an offence triable either way) [see *Notes 3A and 3B*];

(b) which takes place as a result of a police officer exceptionally putting further questions to a suspect about an offence described in sub-paragraph (a) above after he has been charged with, or informed he may be prosecuted for, that offence [see *Note 3C*]; or

(c) in which a police officer wishes to bring to the notice of a person, after he has been charged with, or informed he may be prosecuted for an offence described in sub-paragraph (a) above, any written statement made by another person, or the content of an interview with another person [see *Note 3D*].

3.2 Tape recording is not required in respect of the following:

(a) an interview with a person arrested under section 14(1)(a) or Schedule 5 paragraph 6 of the Prevention of Terrorism (Temporary Provisions) Act 1989 or an interview with a person being questioned in respect of an offence where there are reasonable grounds for suspecting that it is connected to terrorism or was committed in furtherance of the objectives of an organisation engaged in terrorism. This sub-paragraph applies only where the terrorism is connected with the affairs of Northern Ireland or is terrorism of any other description except terrorism connected solely with the affairs of the United Kingdom or any part of the United Kingdom other than Northern Ireland. "Terrorism" has the meaning given by section 20(1) of the Prevention of Terrorism (Temporary Provisions) Act 1989 [see *Notes 3E, 3F, 3G and 3H*];

(b) an interview with a person suspected on reasonable grounds of an offence under section 1 of the Official Secrets Act 1911 [see *Note 3H*].

3.3 The custody officer may authorise the interviewing officer not to tape record the interview:

(a) where it is not reasonably practicable to do so because of failure of the equipment or the non-availability of a suitable interview room or recorder and the authorising officer considers on reasonable grounds that the interview should not be delayed until the failure has been rectified or a suitable room or recorder becomes available [see *Note 3J*]; or

(b) where it is clear from the outset that no prosecution will ensue.

In such cases the interview shall be recorded in writing and in accordance with section 11 of Code C. In all cases the custody officer shall make a note in specific terms of the reasons for not tape recording. [See *Note 3K*]

3.4 Where an interview takes place with a person voluntarily attending the police station and the police officer has grounds to believe that person has become a suspect (i.e. the point at which he should be cautioned in accordance with paragraph 10.1 of Code C) the continuation of the interview shall be tape recorded, unless the custody officer gives authority in accordance with the provisions of paragraph 3.3 above for the continuation of the interview not to be recorded.

3.5 The whole of each interview shall be tape recorded, including the taking and reading back of any statement.

Notes for Guidance

3A Nothing in this code is intended to preclude tape recording at police discretion of interviews at police stations with people cautioned in respect of offences not covered by paragraph 3.1, or responses made by interviewees after they have been charged with, or informed they may be prosecuted for, an offence, provided that this code is complied with.

3B Attention is drawn to the restrictions in paragraph 12.3 of Code C on the questioning of people unfit through drink or drugs to the extent that they are unable to appreciate the significance of questions put to them or of their answers.

3C Circumstances in which a suspect may be questioned about an offence after being charges with it are set out in paragraph 16.5 of Code C.

3D Procedures to be followed when a person's attention is drawn after charge to a statement made by another person are set out in paragraph 16.4 of Code C. One method of bringing the content of an interview with another person to the notice of a suspect may be to play him a tape recording of that interview.

3E Section 14(1)(a) of the Prevention of Terrorism (Temporary Provisions) Act 1989, permits the arrest without warrant of a person reasonably suspected to be guilty of an offence under section 2, 8, 9, 10 or 11 of the Act.

3F Section 20(1) of the Prevention of Terrorism (Temporary Provisions) Act 1989 says "terrorism means the use of violence for political ends, and includes any use of violence for the purpose of putting the public or any section of the public in fear".

3G It should be noted that the provisions of paragraph 3.2 apply only to those suspected of offences connected with terrorism connected with Northern Ireland, or with terrorism of any other description other than terrorism connected solely with the affairs of the United Kingdom or any part of the United Kingdom other than Northern Ireland, or offences committed in furtherance of such terrorism. Any interviews with those suspected of offences connected with terrorism of any other description or in furtherance of the objectives of an organisation engaged in such terrorism should be carried out in compliance with the rest of this code.

3H When it only becomes clear during the course of an interview which is being tape recorded that the interviewee may have committed an offence to which paragraph 3.2 applies the interviewing officer should turn off the tape recorder.

3J *Where practicable, priority should be given to tape recording interviews with people who are suspected of more serious offences.*

3K *A decision not to tape record an interview for any reason may be the subject of comment in court. The authorising officer should therefore be prepared to justify his decision in each case.*

4 The interview

(a) Commencement of interviews

4.1 When the suspect is brought into the interview room the police officer shall without delay, but in the sight of the suspect, load the tape recorder with clean tapes and set it to record. The tapes must be unwrapped or otherwise opened in the presence of the suspect. [See *Note 4A*]

4.2 The police officer shall then tell the suspect formally about the tape recording. He shall say:
(a) that the interview is being tape recorded;
(b) his name and rank and the name and rank of any other police officer present except in the case of enquiries linked to the investigation of terrorism where warrant or other identification numbers shall be stated rather than names;
(c) the name of the suspect and any other party present (e.g. a solicitor);
(d) the date, time of commencement and place of the interview; and
(e) that the suspect will be given a notice about what will happen to the tapes.
[See *Note 4B*]

4.3 The police officer shall then caution the suspect in the following terms:

> "You do not have to say anything. But it may harm your defence if you do not mention when questioned something which you later rely on in court. Anything you do say may be given in evidence."

Minor deviations do not constitute a breach of this requirement provided that the sense of the caution is preserved. [See *Note 4C*]

4.3A The police officer shall remind the suspect of his right to free and independent legal advice and that he can speak to a solicitor on the telephone in accordance with paragraph 6.5 of Code C.

4.3B The police officer shall then put to the suspect any significant statement of silence (i.e. failure or refusal to answer a question or to answer it satisfactorily) which occurred before the start of the tape-recorded interview, and shall ask him whether he confirms or denies that earlier statement or silence or whether he wishes to add anything. A "significant" statement or silence means one which appears capable of being used in evidence against the suspect, in particular a direct admission of guilt, or failure or refusal to answer a question or to answer it satisfactorily, which might give rise to an inference under Part III of the Criminal Justice and Public Order Act 1994.

Special warnings under sections 36 and 37 of the Criminal Justice and Public Order Act 1994

4.3C When a suspect who is interviewed after arrest fails or refuses to answer

certain questions, or to answer them satisfactorily, after due warning, a cou
jury may draw proper inference from this silence under sections 36 and 37
Criminal Justice and Public Order Act 1994. This applies when:
(a) a suspect is arrested by a constable and there is found on his person, or i or
   on his clothing or footwear, or otherwise in his possession, or in the place
   where he was arrested, any objects, marks or substances, or marks on such
   objects, and the person fails or refuses to account for the objects, marks or
   substances found; or
(b) an arrested person was found by a constable at a place at or about the time the
   offence for which he was arrested, is alleged to have been committed, and the
   person fails or refuses to account for his presence at that place.

4.3D For an inference to be drawn from a suspect's failure or refusal to answer a
question about one of these matters or to answer it satisfactorily, the interviewing
officer must first tell him in ordinary language:
(a) what offence he is investigating;
(b) what fact he is asking the suspect to account for;
(c) that he believes this fact may be due to the suspect's taking part in the
   commission of the offence in question;
(d) that a court may draw a proper inference from his silence if he fails or
   refuses to account for the fact about which he is being questioned;
(e) that a record is being made of the interview and may be given in evidence if he
   is brought to trial.

4.3E Where, despite the fact that a person has been cautioned, failure to co-
operate may have an effect on his immediate treatment, he should be informed of
any relevant consequences and that they are not affected by the caution. Examples
are when his refusal to provide his name and address when charged may render
him liable to detention, or when his refusal to provide particulars and information
in accordance with a statutory requirement, for example, under the Road Traffic
Act 1988, may amount to an offence or may make him liable to arrest.

(b) Interviews with the deaf
4.4 If the suspect is deaf or there is doubt about his hearing ability, the police
officer shall take a contemporaneous note of the interview in accordance with the
requirements of Code C, as well as tape record it in accordance with the provisions
of this code. [See *Notes 4E and 4F*]

(c) Objections and complaints by the suspect
4.5 If the suspect raises objections to the interview being tape recorded either at
the outset or during the interview or during a break in the interview, the police
officer shall explain the fact that the interview is being tape recorded and that the
provisions of this code require that the suspect's objections shall be recorded on
tape. When any objections have been recorded on tape or the suspect has refused to
have his objections recorded, the police office may turn off the recorder. In this
eventuality he shall say that he is turning off the recorder and give his reasons for
doing so and then turn it off. The police officer shall then make a written record of
the interview in accordance with section 11 of Code C. If, however, the police
officer reasonably considers that he may proceed to put questions to the suspect
with the tape recorder still on, he may do so. [See *Note 4G*]

4.6 If in the course of an interview a complaint is made by the person being questioned, or on his behalf, concerning the provisions of this code or of Code C, then the officer shall act in accordance with paragraph 12.8 of Code C. [See *Notes 4H and 4J*]

4.7 If the suspect indicates that he wishes to tell the police officer about matters not directly connected with the offence of which he is suspected and that he is unwilling for these matters to be recorded on tape, he shall be given the opportunity to tell the police officer about these matters after the conclusion of the formal interview.

(d) Changing tapes
4.8 When the recorder indicates that the tapes have only a short time left to run, the police officer shall tell the suspect that the tapes are coming to an end and round off that part of the interview. If the police officer wishes to continue the interview but does not already have a second set of tapes, he shall obtain a set. The suspect shall not be left unattended in the interview room. The police officer will remove the tapes from the tape recorder and insert the new tapes which shall be unwrapped or otherwise opened in the suspect's presence. The tape recorder shall then be set to record on the new tapes. Care must be taken, particularly when a number of sets of tapes have been used, to ensure that there is no confusion between the tapes. This may be done by marking the tapes with an identification number immediately they are removed from the tape recorder.

(e) Taking a break during interview
4.9 When a break is to be taken during the course of an interview and the interview room is to be vacated by the suspect, the fact that a break is to be taken, the reason for it and the time shall be recorded on tape. The tapes shall then be removed from the tape recorder and the procedures for the conclusion of an interview set out in paragraph 4.14 below followed.

4.10 When a break is to be a short one and both the suspect and a police officer are to remain in the interview room, the fact that a break is to be taken, the reasons for it and the time shall be recorded on tape. The tape recorder may be turned off; there is, however, no need to remove the tapes and when the interview is recommenced the tape recording shall be continued on the same tapes. The time at which the interview recommences shall be recorded on tape.

4.11 When there is a break in questioning under caution the interviewing officer must ensure that the person being questioned is aware that he remains under caution and of his right to legal advice. If there is any doubt the caution must be given again in full when the interview resumes. [See *Notes 4K and 4L*]

(f) Failure of recording equipment
4.12 If there is a failure of equipment which can be rectified quickly, for example by inserting new tapes, the appropriate procedures set out in paragraph 4.8 shall be followed, and when the recording is resumed the officer shall explain what has happened and record the time the interview recommences. If, however, it will not be possible to continue recording on that particular tape recorder and no replacement recorder or recorder in another interview room is readily available, the

interview may continue without being tape recorded. In such circumstances the procedures in paragrahs 3.3 above for seeking the authority of the custody officer will be followed. [See *Note 4M*]

(g) Removing tapes from the recorder
4.13 Where tapes are removed from the recorder in the course of an interview, they shall be retained and the procedures set out in paragraph 4.18 below followed.

(h) Conclusion of interview
4.14 At the conclusion of the interview, the suspect shall be offered the opportunity to clarify anything he has said and to add anything he may wish.

4.15 At the conclusion of the interview, including the taking and reading back of any written statement, the time shall be recorded and the tape recorder switched off. The master tape shall be sealed with a master tape label and treated as an exhibit in accordance with the force standing orders. The police officer shall sign the label and ask the suspect and any third party present to sign it also. If the suspect or third party refuses to sign the label, an officer of at least the rank of inspector, or if one is not available the custody officer, shall be called into the interview room and asked to sign it. In the case of enquiries linked to the investigation of terrorism, an officer who signs the label shall use his warrant or other identification number.

4.16 The suspect shall be handed a notice which explains the use which will be made of the tape recording and the arrangements for access to it and that a copy of the tape shall be supplied as soon as practicable if the person is charged or informed that he will be prosecuted.

Notes for Guidance
4A The police officer should attempt to estimate the likely length of the interview and ensure that the appropriate number of clean tapes and labels with which to seal the master copies are available in the interview room.

4B It will be helpful for the purpose of voice identification if the officer asks the suspect and any other people present to identify themselves.

4C If it appears that a person does not understand what the caution means, the officer who has given it should go on to explain it in his own words.

4D [Not Used]

4E This provision is intended to give the deaf equivalent rights of first hand access to the full interview record as other suspects.

4F The provisions of paragraphs 13.2, 13.5 and 13.9 of Code C on interpreters for the deaf or for interviews with suspects who have difficulty in understanding English continue to apply. In a tape recorded interview there is no requirement on the interviewing officer to ensure that the interpreter makes a separate note of interview as prescribed in section 13 of Code C.

4G The officer should bear in mind that a decision to continue recording against the wishes of the suspect may be the subject of comment in court.

4H Where the custody officer is called immediately to deal with the complaint, wherever possible the tape recorder should be left to run until the custody officer has entered the interview room and spoken to the person being interviewed. Continuation or termination of the interview should be at the discretion of the interviewing officer pending action by an inspector under paragraph 9.1 of Code C.

4I [Not Used]

4J Where the complaint is about a matter not connected with this code of practice or Code C, the decision to continue with the interview is at the discretion of the interviewing officer. Where the interviewing officer decides to continue with the interview the person being interviewed shall be told that the complaint will be brought to the attention of the custody officer at the conclusion of the interview. When the interview is concluded the interviewing officer must, as soon as practicable, inform the custody officer of the existence and nature of the complaint made.

4K In considering whether to caution again after a break, the officer should bear in mind that he may have to satisfy a court that the person understood that he was still under caution when the interview resumed.

4L The officer should bear in mind that it may be necessary to show to the court that nothing occurred during a break in an interview or between interviews which influenced the suspect's recorded evidence. The officer should consider, therefore, after a break in an interview or at the beginning of a subsequent interview summarising on tape the reason for the break and confirming this with the suspect.

4M If one of the tapes breaks during the interview it should be sealed as a master tape in the presence of the suspect and the interview resumed where it left off. The unbroken tape should be copied and the original sealed as a master tape in the suspect's presence, if necessary after the interview. If equipment for copying the unbroken tape is not readily available, both tapes should be sealed in the suspect's presence and the interview begun again. If the tape breaks when a single deck machine is being used and the machine is one where a broken tape cannot be copied on available equipment, the tape should be sealed as a master tape in the suspect's presence and the interview begun again.

5 After the interview

5.1 The police officer shall make a note in his notebook of the fact that the interview has taken place and has been recorded on tape, its time, duration and date and the identification number of the master tape.

5.2 Where no proceedings follow in respect of the person whose interview was recorded the tapes must nevertheless be kept securely in accordance with paragraph 6.1 and Note 6A.

Note for Guidance

5A Any written record of a tape recorded interview shall be made in accordance with national guidelines approved by the Secretary of State.

6 Tape security

6.1 The officer in charge of each police station at which interviews with suspects are recorded shall make arrangements for master tapes to be kept securely and their movements accounted for on the same basis as other material which may be used for evidential purposes, in accordance with force standing orders. [See *Note 6A*]

6.2 A police officer has no authority to break the seal on a master tape which is required for criminal proceedings. If it is necessary to gain access to the master tape, the police officer shall arrange for its seal to be broken in the presence of a representative of the Crown Prosecution Service. The defendant or his legal adviser shall be informed and given a reasonable opportunity to be present. If the defendant or his legal representative is present he shall be invited to reseal and sign the master tape. If either refuses or neither is present this shall be done by the representative of the Crown Prosecution Service. [See *Notes 6B and 6C*]

6.3 Where no criminal proceedings result it is the responsibility of the chief officer of police to establish arrangements for the breaking of the seal on the master tape, where this becomes necessary.

Notes for Guidance

6A This section is concerned with the security of the master tape which will have been sealed at the conclusion of the interview. Care should, however, be taken of working copies of tapes since their loss or destruction may lead unnecessarily to the need to have access to master tapes.

6B If the tape has been delivered to the crown court for their keeping after committal for trial the crown prosecutor will apply to the chief clerk of the crown court centre for the release of the tape for unsealing by the crown prosecutor.

6C Reference to the Crown Prosecution Service or to the crown prosecutor in this part of the code shall be taken to include any other body or person with statutory responsibility for prosecution for whom the police conduct any tape recorded interviews.

Prevention of Terrorism (Temporary Provisions) Act 1989

PART I
PROSCRIBED ORGANISATIONS

1 Proscribed organisations

(1) Any organisation for the time being specified in Schedule 1 to this Act is a proscribed organisation for the purposes of this Act; and any organisation which passes under a name mentioned in that Schedule shall be treated as proscribed whatever relationship (if any) it has to any other organisation of the same name.

(2) The Secretary of State may by order made by statutory instrument—

(*a*) add to Schedule 1 to this Act any organisation that appears to him to be concerned in, or in promoting or encouraging, terrorism occurring in the United Kingdom and connected with the affairs of Northern Ireland;

(*b*) remove an organisation from that Schedule.

(3) No order shall be made under this section unless—

(*a*) a draft of the order has been laid before and approved by a resolution of each House of Parliament; or

(*b*) it is declared in the order that it appears to the Secretary of State that by reason of urgency it is necessary to make the order without a draft having been so approved.

(4) An order under this section of which a draft has not been approved under subsection (3) above—

(*a*) shall be laid before Parliament; and

(*b*) shall cease to have effect at the end of the period of forty days beginning with the day on which it was made unless, before the end of that period, the order has been approved by a resolution of each House of Parliament, but without prejudice to anything previously done or to the making of a new order.

(5) In reckoning for the purposes of subsection (4) above any period of forty days, no account shall be taken of any period during which Parliament is dissolved or prorogued or during which both Houses are adjourned for more than four days.

(6) In this section "organisation" includes any association or combination of persons.

2 Membership, support and meetings

(1) Subject to subsection (3) below, a person is guilty of an offence if he—

(a) belongs or professes to belong to a proscribed organisation;

(b) solicits or invites support for a proscribed organisation other than support with money or other property; or

(c) arranges or assists in the arrangement or management of, or addresses, any meeting of three or more persons (whether or not it is a meeting to which the public are admitted) knowing that the meeting is—

  (i) to support a proscribed organisation;

  (ii) to further the activities of such an organisation; or

  (iii) to be addressed by a person belonging or professing to belong to such an organisation.

(2) A person guilty of an offence under subsection (1) above is liable—

(a) on conviction on indictment, to imprisonment for a term not exceeding ten years or a fine or both;

(b) on summary conviction, to imprisonment for a term not exceeding six months or a fine not exceeding the statutory maximum or both.

(3) A person belonging to a proscribed organisation is not guilty of an offence under this section by reason of belonging to the organisation if he shows—

(a) that he became a member when it was not a proscribed organisation under the current legislation; and

(b) that he has not since he became a member taken part in any of its activities at any time while it was a proscribed organisation under that legislation.

(4) In subsection (3) above "the current legislation", in relation to any time, means whichever of the following was in force at that time—

(a) the Prevention of Terrorism (Temporary Provisions) Act 1974;

(b) the Prevention of Terrorism (Temporary Provisions) Act 1976;

(c) the Prevention of Terrorism (Temporary Provisions) Act 1984; or

(d) this Act.

(5) The reference in subsection (3) above to a person becoming a member of an organisatin is a reference to the only or last occasion on which he became a member.

3 Display of support in public

(1) Any person who in a public place—

(a) wears any item of dress; or

(b) wears, carries or displays any article,

in such a way or in such circumstances as to arouse reasonable apprehension that he is a member or supporter of a proscribed organisation, is guilty of an offence and liable on summary conviction to imprisonment for a term not exceeding six months or a fine not exceeding level 5 on the standard scale or both.

(2) (*Applies to Scotland only.*)

(3) In this section "public place" includes any highway or, in Scotland, any road within the meaning of the Roads (Scotland) Act 1984 and any premises to which at the material time the public have, or are permitted to have, access, whether on payment or otherwise.

PART II
EXCLUSION ORDERS

4 Exclusion orders: general

(1) The Secretary of State may exercise the powers conferred on him by this Part of this Act in such a way as appears to him expedient to prevent acts of terrorism to which this Part of this Act applies.

(2) The acts of terrorism to which this Part of this Act applies are acts of terrorism connected with the affairs of Northern Ireland.

(3) An order under section 5, 6 or 7 below is referred to in this Act as an "exclusion order".

(4) Schedule 2 to this Act shall have effect with respect to the duration of exclusion orders, the giving of notices, the right to make representations, powers of removal and detention and other supplementary matters for this Part of this Act.

(5) The exercise of the detention powers conferred by that Schedule shall be subject to supervision in accordance with Schedule 3 to this Act.

5 Orders excluding persons from Great Britain

(1) If the Secretary of State is satisfied that any person—

(*a*) is or has been concerned in the commission, preparation or instigation of acts of terrorism to which this Part of this Act applies; or

(*b*) is attempting or may attempt to enter Great Britain with a view to being concerned in the commission, preparation or instigation of such acts of terrorism,

the Secretary of State may make an exclusion order against him.

(2) An exclusion order under this section is an order prohibiting a person from being in, or entering, Great Britain.

(3) In deciding whether to make an exclusion order under this section against a person who is ordinarily resident in Great Britain, the Secretary of State shall have regard to the question whether that person's connection with any country or territory outside Great Britain is such as to make it appropriate that such an order should be made.

(4) An exclusion order shall not be made under this section against a person who is a British citizen and who—

(*a*) is at the time ordinarily resident in Great Britain and has then been ordinarily resident in Great Britain throughout the last three years; or

(*b*) is at the time subject to an order under section 6 below.

6 Orders excluding persons from Northern Ireland

(1) If the Secretary of State is satisfied that any person—

(*a*) is or has been concerned in the commission, preparation or instigation of acts of terrorism to which this Part of this Act applies; or

(*b*) is attempting or may attempt to enter Northern Ireland with a view to being concerned in the commission, preparation or instigation of such acts of terrorism,

the Secretary of State may make an exclusion order against him.

(2) An exclusion order under this section is an order prohibiting a person from being in, or entering, Northern Ireland.

(3) In deciding whether to make an exclusion order under this section against a person who is ordinarily resident in Northern Ireland, the Secretary of State shall have regard to the question whether that person's connection with any country or territory outside Northern Ireland is such as to make it appropriate that such an order should be made.

(4) An exclusion order shall not be made under this section against a person who is a British citizen and who—

(*a*) is at the time ordinarily resident in Northern Ireland and has then been ordinarily resident in Northern Ireland throughout the last three years;

(*b*) is at the time subject to an order under section 5 above.

7 Orders excluding persons from the United Kingdom

(1) If the Secretary of State is satisfied that any person—

(*a*) is or has been concerned in the commission, preparation or instigation of acts of terrorism to which this Part of this Act applies; or

(*b*) is attempting or may attempt to enter Great Britain or Northern Ireland with a view to being concerned in the commission, preparation or instigation of such acts of terrorism,

the Secretary of State may make an exclusion order against him.

(2) An exclusion order under this section is an order prohibiting a person from being in, or entering, the United Kingdom.

(3) In deciding whether to make an exclusion order under this section against a person who is ordinarily resident in the United Kingdom, the Secretary of State shall have regard to the question whether that person's connection with any country or territory outside the United Kingdom is such as to make it appropriate that such an order should be made.

(4) An exclusion order shall not be made under this section against a person who is a British citizen.

8 Offences in respect of exclusion orders

(1) A person who is subject to an exclusion order is guilty of an offence if he fails to comply with the order at a time after he has been, or has become liable to be, removed under Schedule 2 to this Act.

(2) A person is guilty of an offence—

(*a*) if he is knowingly concerned in arrangements for securing or facilitating the entry into Great Britain, Northern Ireland or the United Kingdom of a person whom he knows, or has reasonable grounds for believing, to be an excluded person; or

(*b*) if he knowingly harbours such a person in Great Britain, Northern Ireland or the United Kingdom.

(3) In subsection (2) above "excluded person" means—

(*a*) in relation to Great Britain, a person subject to an exclusion order made under section 5 above who has been, or has become liable to be, removed from Great Britain under Schedule 2 to this Act;

(*b*) in relation to Northern Ireland, a person subject to an exclusion order made under section 6 above who has been, or has become liable to be, removed from Northern Ireland under that Schedule; and

(*c*) in relation to the United Kindgom, a person subject to an exclusion order made under section 7 who has been, or has become liable to be, removed from the United Kingdom under that Schedule.

(4) A person guilty of an offence under this section is liable—

(a) on conviction on indictment, to imprisonment for a term not exceeding five years or a fine or both;

(b) on summary conviction, to imprisonment for a term not exceeding six months or a fine not exceeding the statutory maximum or both.

PART III
FINANCIAL ASSISTANCE FOR TERRORISM

9 Contributions towards acts of terrorism

(1) A person is guilty of an offence if he—

(a) solicits or invites any other person to give, lend or otherwise make available, whether for consideration or not, any money or other property;

(b) receives or accepts from any other person, whether for consideration or not, any money or other property; or

(c) uses or has possession of, whether for consideration or not, any money or other property,

intending that it shall be applied or used for the commission of, or in furtherance of or in connection with, acts of terrorism to which this section applies or having reasonable cause to suspect that it may be so used or applied.

(2) A person is guilty of an offence if he—

(a) gives, lends or otherwise makes available to any other person, whether for consideration or not, any money or other property; or

(b) enters into or is otherwise concerned in an arrangement whereby money or other property is or is to be made available to another person,

knowing or having reasonable cause to suspect that it will or may be applied or used as mentioned in subsection (1) above.

(3) The acts of terrorism to which this section applies are—

(a) acts of terrorism connected with the affairs of Northern Ireland; and

(b) subject to subsection (4) below, acts of terrorism of any other description except acts connected solely with the affairs of the United Kingdom or any part of the United Kingdom other than Northern Ireland.

(4) Subsection (3)(b) above does not apply to an act done or to be done outside the United Kingdom unless it constitutes or would constitute an offence triable in the United Kingdom.

(5) In proceedings against a person for an offence under this section in relation to an act within subsection (3)(b) above done or to be done outside the United Kingdom—

(a) the prosecution need not prove that that person knew or had reasonable cause to suspect that the act constituted or would constitute such an offence as is mentioned in subsection (4) above; but

(b) it shall be a defence to prove that he did not know and had no reasonable cause to suspect that the facts were such that the act constituted or would constitute such an offence.

10 Contributions to resources of proscribed organisations

(1) A person is guilty of an offence if he—

(*a*) solicits or invites any other person to give, lend or otherwise make available, whether for consideration or not, any money or other property for the benefit of a proscribed organisation;

(*b*) gives, lends or otherwise makes available or receives or accepts or uses or has possession of, whether for consideration or not, any money or other property for the benefit of such an organisation; or

(*c*) enters into or is otherwise concerned in an arrangement whereby money or other property is or is to be made available for the benefit of such an organisation.

(2) In proceedings against a person for an offence under subsection (1)(*b*) above it is a defence to prove that he did not know and had no reasonable cause to suspect that the money or property was for the benefit of a proscribed organisation; and in proceedings against a person for an offence under subsection (1)(*c*) above it is a defence to prove that he did not know and had no reasonable cause to suspect that the arrangement related to a proscribed organisation.

(3) In this section and sections 11 and 13 below "proscribed organisation" includes a proscribed organisation for the purposes of section 28 of the Northern Ireland (Emergency Provisions) Act 1991.

11 Assisting in retention or control of terrorist funds

(1) A person is guilty of an offence if he enters into or is otherwise concerned in an arrangement whereby the retention or control by or on behalf of another person of terrorist funds is facilitated, whether by concealment, removal from the jurisdiction, transfer to nominees or otherwise.

(2) In proceedings against a person for an offence under this section it is a defence to prove that he did not know and had no reasonable cause to suspect that the arrangement related to terrorist funds.

(3) In this section and section 12 below "terrorist funds" means—

(*a*) funds which may be applied or used for the commission of, or in furtherance of or in connection with, acts of terrorism to which section 9 above applies;

(*b*) the proceeds of the commission of such acts of terrorism or of activities engaged in furtherance of or in connection with such acts; and

(*c*) the resources of a proscribed organisation.

(4) Paragraph (*b*) of subsection (3) includes any property which in whole or in part directly or indirectly represents such proceeds as are mentioned in that paragraph; and paragraph (*c*) of that subsection includes any money or other property which is or is to be applied or made available for the benefit of a proscribed organisation.

12 Disclosure of information about terrorist funds

(1) A person may notwithstanding any restriction on the disclosure of information imposed by statute or otherwise disclose to a constable a suspicion or belief that any money or other property is or is derived from terrorist funds or any matter on which such a suspicion or belief is based.

(2) A person who enters into or is otherwise concerned in any such transaction or arrangement as is mentioned in section 9, 10 or 11 above does not commit an

offence under that section if he is acting with the express consent of a constable or if—

(a) he discloses to a constable his suspicion or belief that the money or other property concerned is or is derived from terrorist funds or any matter on which such a suspicion or belief is based; and

(b) the disclosure is made after he enters into or otherwise becomes concerned in the transaction or arrangement in question but is made on his own initiative and as soon as it is reasonable for him to make it,

but paragraphs (a) and (b) above do not apply in a case where, having disclosed any such suspicion, belief or matter to a constable and having been forbidden by a constable to enter into or otherwise be concerned in the transaction or arrangement in question, he nevertheless does so.

(2A) For the purposes of subsection (2) above a person who uses or has possession of money or other property shall be taken to be concerned in a transaction or arrangement.

(3) In proceedings against a person for an offence under section 9(1)(b) or (c) or (2), 10(1)(b) or (c) or 11 above it is a defence to prove—

(a) that he intended to disclose to a constable such a suspicion, belief or matter as is mentioned in paragraph (a) of subsection (2) above; and

(b) that there is a reasonable excuse for his failure to make the disclosure as mentioned in paragraph (b) of that subsection.

(4) In the case of a person who was in employment at the relevant time, subsections (1) to (3) above shall have effect in relation to disclosures, and intended disclosures, to the appropriate person in accordance with the procedure established by his employer for the making of such disclosures as they have effect in relation to disclosures, and intended disclosures, to a constable.

(5) No constable or other person shall be guilty of an offence under section 9(1)(b) or (c) or (2) or 10(1)(b) or (c) above in respect of anything done by him in the course of acting in connection with the enforcement, or intended enforcement, of any provision of this Act, or of any other enactment relating to terrorism or the proceeds of or resources of terrorism.

(6) For the purposes of subsection (5) above, having possession of any property shall be taken to be doing an act in relation to it.

13 Penalties and forfeiture

(1) A person guilty of an offence under section 9, 10 or 11 above is liable—

(a) on conviction on indictment, to imprisonment for a term not exceeding fourteen years or a fine or both;

(b) on summary conviction, to imprisonment for a term not exceeding six months or a fine not exceeding the statutory maximum or both.

(2) Subject to the provisions of this section, the court by or before which a person is convicted of an offence under section 9(1) or (2)(a) above may order the forfeiture of any money or other property—

(a) which, at the time of the offence, he had in his possession or under his control; and

(b) which, at that time—

(i) in the case of an offence under subsection (1) of section 9, he intended should be applied or used, or had reasonable cause to suspect might be applied or used, as mentioned in that subsection;

(ii) in the case of an offence under subsection (2)(*a*) of that section, he knew or had reasonable cause to suspect would or might be applied or used as mentioned in subsection (1) of that section.

(3) Subject to the provisions of this section, the court by or before which a person is convicted of an offence under section 9(2)(*b*), 10(1)(*c*) or 11 above may order the forfeiture of the money or other property to which the arrangement in question related and which, in the case of an offence under section 9(2)(*b*), he knew or had reasonable cause to suspect would or might be applied or used as mentioned in section 9(1) above.

(4) Subject to the provisions of this section, the court by or before which a person is convicted of an offence under section 10(1)(*a*) or (*b*) above may order the forfeiture of any money or other property which, at the time of the offence, he had in his possession or under his control for the use or benefit of a proscribed organisation.

(5) The court shall not under this section make an order forfeiting any money or other property unless the court considers that the money or property may, unless forfeited, be applied or used as mentioned in section 9(1) above but the court may, in the absence of evidence to the contrary, assume that any money or property may be applied or used as there mentioned.

(6) Where a person other than the convicted person claims to be the owner of or otherwise interested in anything which can be forfeited by an order under this section, the court shall, before making such an order in respect of it, gave him an opportunity to be heard.

(7) (*Applies to Scotland only.*)

(8) Schedule 4 to this Act shall have effect in relation to orders under this section.

PART IV

ARREST, DETENTION AND CONTROL OF ENTRY

14 Arrest and detention of suspected persons

(1) Subject to subsection (2) below, a constable may arrest without warrant a person whom he has reasonable grounds for suspecting to be—
  (*a*) a person guilty of an offence under section 2, 8, 9, 10 or 11 above;
  (*b*) a person who is or has been concerned in the commission, preparation or instigation of acts of terrorism to which this section applies; or
  (*c*) a person subject to an exclusion order.

(2) The acts of terrorism to which this section applies are—
  (*a*) acts of terrorism connected with the affairs of Northern Ireland; and
  (*b*) acts of terrorism of any other description except acts connected solely with the affairs of the United Kingdom or any part of the United Kingdom other than Northern Ireland.

(3) The power of arrest conferred by subsection (1)(*c*) above is exercisable only—
  (*a*) in Great Britain if the exclusion order was made under section 5 above; and
  (*b*) in Northern Ireland if it was made under section 6 above.

(4) Subject to subsection (5) below, a person arrested under this section shall not be detained in right of the arrest for more than forty-eight hours after his arrest.

(5) The Secretary of State may, in any particular case, extend the period of

forty-eight hours mentioned in subsection (4) above by a period or periods specified by him, but any such further period or periods shall not exceed five days in all and if an application for such an extension is made the person detained shall as soon as practicable be given written notice of that fact and of the time when the application was made.

(6) The exercise of the detention powers conferred by this section shall be subject to supervision in accordance with Schedule 3 to this Act.

(7) The provisions of this section are without prejudice to any power of arrest exercisable apart from this section.

15 Provisions supplementary to s 14

(1) If a justice of the peace is satisfied that there are reasonable grounds for suspecting that a person whom a constable believes to be liable to arrest under section 14(1)(b) above is to be found on any premises he may grant a search warrant authorising any constable to enter those premises for the purpose of searching for and arresting that person.

(2) (*Applies to Scotland only.*)

(3) In any circumstances in which a constable has power under section 14 above to arrest a person, he may also, for the purpose of ascertaining whether he has in his possession any document or other article which may constitute evidence that he is a person liable to arrest, stop that person and search him.

(4) Where a constable has arrested a person under that section for any reason other than the commission of a criminal offence, he, or any other constable, may search him for the purpose of ascertaining whether he has in his possession any document or other article which may constitute evidence that he is a person liable to arrest.

(5) A search of a person under subsection (3) or (4) above may only be carried out by a person of the same sex.

(6) A person detained under section 14 above shall be deemed to be in legal custody at any time when he is so detained and may be detained in such a place as the Secretary of State may from time to time direct.

(7) The following provisions (requirement to bring accused person before the court after his arrest) shall not apply to a person detained in right of an arrest under section 14 above—

(a) (*Applies to Scotland only*);

(b) Article 47 of the Police and Criminal Evidence (Northern Ireland) Order 1989;

(c) section 50(3) of the Children and Young Persons Act (Northern Ireland) 1968.

(8) (*Applies to Scotland only.*)

(9) Where a person is detained under section 14 above, any constable or prison officer, or any other person authorised by the Secretary of State, may take all such steps as may be reasonably necessary for photographing, measuring or otherwise identifying him.

(10) Section 61(1) to (8) of the Police and Criminal Evidence Act 1984 (fingerprinting) shall apply to the taking of a person's fingerprints by a constable under subsection (9) above as if for subsection (4) there were substituted—

"(4) An officer may only give an authorisation under subsection (3)(a) above for the taking of a person's fingerprints if he is satisfied that it is necessary to do so in order to assist in determining—

(a) whether that person is or has been concerned in the commission, preparation or instigation of acts of terrorism to which section 14 of the Prevention of Terrorism (Temporary Provisions) Act 1989 applies; or

(b) whether he is subject to an exclusion order under that Act;

or if the officer has reasonable grounds for suspecting that person's involvement in an offence under any of the provisions mentioned in subsection (1)(a) of that section and for believing that his fingerprints will tend to confirm or disprove his involvement."

16 Port and border controls

(1) Schedule 5 to this Act shall have effect for conferring powers to examine persons arriving in or leaving Great Britain or Northern Ireland and for connected purposes.

(2) The exercise of the examination and detention powers conferred by paragraphs 2 and 6 of that Schedule shall be subject to supervision in accordance with Schedule 3 to this Act.

(3) The designated ports for the purposes of paragraph 8 of Schedule 5 to this Act shall be those specified in Schedule 6 to this Act but the Secretary of State may by order add any port to, or remove any port from, that Schedule.

(4) Without prejudice to the provisions of Schedule 5 to this Act with respect to persons who enter or leave Northern Ireland by land or who seek to do so, the Secretary of State may by order make such further provision with respect to those persons as appears to him to be expedient.

(5) The power to make orders under this section shall be exercisable by statutory instrument.

(6) An order under subsection (4) above may contain transitional provisions and savings and shall be subject to annulment in pursuance of a resolution of either House of Parliament

PART IVA
OFFENCES AGAINST PUBLIC SECURITY

16A Possession of articles for suspected terrorist purposes

(1) A person is guilty of an offence if he has any article in his possession in circumstances giving rise to a reasonable suspicion that the article is in his possession for a purpose connected with the commission, preparation or instigation of acts of terrorism to which this section applies.

(2) The acts of terrorism to which this section applies are—

(a) acts of terrorism connected with the affairs of Northern Ireland; and

(b) acts of terrorism of any other description except acts connected solely with the affairs of the United Kingdom or any part of the United Kingdom other than Northern Ireland.

(3) It is a defence for a person charged with an offence under this section to prove that at the time of the alleged offence the article in question was not in his possession for such a purpose as is mentioned in subsection (1) above.

(4) Where a person is charged with an offence under this section and it is proved that at the time of the alleged offence—

(a) he and that article were both present in any premises; or

(b) the article was in premises of which he was the occupier or which he habitually used otherwise than as a member of the public.

the court may accept the fact proved as sufficient evidence of his possessing that article at that time unless it is further proved that he did not at that time know of its presence in the premises in question, or, if he did know, that he had no control over it.

(5) A person guilty of an offence under this section is liable—

(a) on conviction on indictment, to imprisonment for a term not exceeding ten years or a fine or both;

(b) on summary conviction, to imprisonment for a term not exceeding six months or a fine not exceeding the statutory maximum or both.

(6) This section applies to vessels, aircraft and vehicles as it applies to premises.

16B Unlawful collection, etc. of information

(1) No person shall, without lawful authority or reasonable excuse (the proof of which lies on him)—

(a) collect or record any information which is of such a nature as is likely to be useful to terrorists in planning or carrying out any act of terrorism to which this section applies; or

(b) have in his possession any record or document containing any such information as is mentioned in paragraph (a) above.

(2) The acts of terrorism to which this section applies are—

(a) acts of terrorism connected with the affairs of Northern Ireland; and

(b) acts of terrorism of any other description except acts connected solely with the affairs of the United Kingdom or any part of the United Kingdom other than Northern Ireland.

(3) In subsection (1) above the reference to recording information includes a reference to recording it by means of photography or by any other means.

(4) Any person who contravenes this section is guilty of an offence and liable—

(a) on conviction on indictment, to imprisonment for a term not exceeding ten years or a fine or both;

(b) on summary conviction, to imprisonment for a term not exceeding six months or a fine not exceeding the statutory maximum or both.

(5) The court by or before which a person is convicted of an offence under this section may order the forfeiture of any record or document mentioned in subsection (1) above which is found in his possession.

PART V
INFORMATION, PROCEEDINGS AND INTERPRETATION

17 Investigation of terrorist activities

(1) Schedule 7 to this Act shall have effect for conferring powers to obtain information for the purposes of terrorist investigations, that is to say—

(a) investigations into—

(i) the commission, preparation or instigation of acts of terrorism to which section 14 above applies; or

(ii) any other act which appears to have been done in furtherance of or in connection with such acts of terrorism, including any act which appears to constitute an offence under section 2, 9, 10, 11, 18 or 18A of this Act or section 27, 28, 53, 54 or 54A of the Northern Ireland (Emergency Provisions) Act 1991; or

(iii) without prejudice to sub-paragraph (ii) above, the resources of a pro-scribed organisation within the meaning of this Act or a proscribed organisation for the purposes of section 28 of the said Act of 1991; and

(b) investigations into whether there are grounds justifying the making of an order under section 1(2)(a) above or section 28(3) of that Act.

(2) A person is guilty of an offence if, knowing or having reasonable cause to suspect that a constable is acting, or is proposing to act, in connection with a terrorist investigation which is being, or is about to be, conducted, he—

(a) discloses to any other person information or any other matter which is likely to prejudice the investigation or proposed investigation, or

(b) falsifies, conceals or destroys or otherwise disposes of, or causes or permits the falsification, concealment, destruction or disposal of, material which is likely to be relevant to the investigation, or proposed investigation.

(2A) A person is guilty of an offence if, knowing or having reasonable cause to suspect that a disclosure ("the disclosure") has been made to a constable under section 12, 18 or 18A of this Act or section 53, 54 or 54A of the Northern Ireland (Emergency Provisions) Act 1991, he—

(a) discloses to any other person information or any other matter which is likely to prejudice any investigation which might be conducted following the disclosure; or

(b) falsifies, conceals or destroys or otherwise disposes of, or causes or permits the falsification, concealment, destruction or disposal of, material which is or is likely to be relevant to any such investigation.

(2B) A person is guilty of an offence if, knowing or having reasonable cause to suspect that a disclosure ("the disclosure") of a kind mentioned in section 12(4) or 18A(5) of this Act or section 53(4A), 54(5D) or 54A(5) of the Act of 1991 has been made, he—

(a) discloses to any person information or any other matter which is likely to prejudice any investigation which might be conducted following the disclosure; or

(b) falsifies, conceals or destroys or otherwise disposes of, or causes or permits the falsification, concealment, destruction or disposal of, material which is or is likely to be relevant to any such investigation.

(2C) Nothing in subsections (2) to (2B) above makes it an offence for a professional legal adviser to disclose any information or other matter—

(a) to, or to a representative of, a client of his in connection with the giving by the adviser of legal advice to the client; or

(b) to any person—

(i) in contemplations of, or in connection with, legal proceedings; and

(ii) for the purpose of those proceedings.

(2D) Subsection (2C) above does not apply in relation to any information or other matter which is disclosed with a view to furthering any criminal purpose.

(2E) No constable or other person shall be guilty of an offence under this section in respect of anything done by him in the course of acting in connection with the enforcement, or intended enforcement, or any provision of this Act or of any other enactment relating to terrorism or the proceeds of or resources of terrorism.

(3) In proceedings against a person for an offence under subsection (2)(a) above it is a defence to prove—

(a) that he did not know and had no reasonable cause to suspect that the disclosure was likely to prejudice the investigation or proposed investigation; or

(b) that he had lawful authority or reasonable excuse for making the disclosure.

(3A) In proceedings against a person for an offence under subsection (2A)(a) or (2B)(a) above it is a defence to prove—

(a) that he did not know and had no reasonable cause to suspect that his disclosure was likely to prejudice the investigation in question; or

(b) that he had lawful authority or reasonable excuse for making his disclosure.

(4) In proceedings against a person for an offence under subsection (2)(b) above it is a defence to prove that he had no intention of concealing any information contained in the material in question from any person conducting, or likely to be conducting, the investigation or proposed investigation.

(4A) In proceedings against a person for an offence under subsection (2A)(b) or (2B)(b) above, it is a defence to prove that he had no intention of concealing any information contained in the material in question from any person who might carry out the investigation in question.

(5) A person guilty of an offence under subsectin (2) above is liable—

(a) on conviction on indictment, to imprisonment for a term not exceeding five years or a fine or both;

(b) on summary conviction, to imprisonment for a term not exceeding six months or a fine not exceeding the statutory maximum or both.

(6) For the purposes of subsection (1) above, as it applies in relation to any offence under section 18 or 18A below or section 54A of the Act of 1991, "act" includes omission.

18 Information about acts of terrorism

(1) A person is guilty of an offence if he has information which he knows or believes might be of material assistance—

(a) in preventing the commission by any other person of an act of terrorism connected with the affairs of Northern Ireland; or

(b) in securing the apprehension, prosecution or conviction of any other person for an offence involving the commission, preparation or instigation of such an act,

and fails without reasonable excuse to disclose that information as soon as reasonably practicable—

(i) in England and Wales, to a constable;

(ii) (applies to Scotland only); or

(iii) in Northern Ireland, to a constable or a member of Her Majesty's Forces.

(2) A person guilty of an offence under this section is liable—

(a) on conviction on indictment, to imprisonment for a term not exceeding five years or a fine or both;

(b) on summary conviction, to imprisonment for a term not exceeding six months or a fine not exceeding the statutory maximum or both.

(3) Proceedings for an offence under this section may be taken, and the offence may for the purposes of those proceedings be treated as having been committed, in

any place where the person to be charged is or has at any time been since he first knew or believed that the information might be of material assistance as mentioned in subsection (1) above.

18A Failure to disclose knowledge or suspicion of offences under sections 9 to 11

(1) A person is guilty of an offence if—

(a) he knows, or suspects, that another person is providing financial assistance for terrorism;

(b) the information, or other matter, on which that knowledge or suspicion is based came to his attention in the course of his trade, profession, business or employment; and

(c) he does not disclose the information or other matter to a constable as soon as is reasonably practicable after it comes to his attention.

(2) Subsection (1) above does not make it an offence for a professional legal adviser to fail to disclose any information or other matter which has come to him in privileged circumstances.

(3) It is a defence to a charge of committing an offence under this section that the person charged had a reasonable excuse for not disclosing the information or other matter in question.

(4) Where a person discloses to a constable—

(a) his suspicion or belief that another person is providing financial assistance for terrorism; or

(b) any information or other matter on which that suspicion or belief is based;

the disclosure shall not be treated as a breach of any restriction imposed by statute or otherwise.

(5) Without prejudice to subsection (3) or (4) above, in the case of a person who was in employment at the relevant time, it is a defence to a charge of committing an offence under this section that he disclosed the information or other matter in question to the appropriate person in accordance with the procedure established by his employer for the making of such disclosures.

(6) A disclosure to which subsection (5) above applies shall not be treated as a breach of any restriction imposed by statute or otherwise.

(7) In this section "providing financial assistance for terrorism" means doing any act which constitutes an offence under section 9, 10 or 11 above or, in the case of an act done otherwise than in the United Kingdom, which would constitute such an offence if done in the United Kingdom.

(8) For the purposes of subsection (7) above, having possession of any property shall be taken to be doing an act in relation to it.

(9) For the purposes of this section, any information or other matter comes to a professional legal adviser in privileged circumstances if it is communicated, or given, to him—

(a) by, or by a representative of, a client of his in connection with the giving by the adviser of legal advice to the client;

(b) by, or by a representative of, a person seeking legal advice from the adviser; or

(c) by any person—

(i) in contemplation of, or in connection with, legal proceedings; and

(ii) for the purpose of those proceedings.

(10) No information or other matter shall be treated as coming to a professional

legal adviser in privileged circumstances if it is communicated or given with a view to furthering any criminal purpose.

(11) A person guilty of an offence under this section shall be liable—

(a) on summary conviction, to imprisonment for a term not exceeding six months or a fine not exceeding the statutory maximum or to both; or

(b) on conviction on indictment, to imprisonment for a term not exceeding five years or a fine or to both.

19 Prosecutions and evidence

(1) Proceedings shall not be instituted—

(a) in England and Wales for an offence under section 2, 3, 8, 9, 10, 11, 17, 18 or 18A above or Schedule 7 to this Act except by or with the consent of the Attorney General; or

(b) in Northern Ireland for an offence under section 8, 9, 10, 11, 17, 18 or 18A above or Schedule 7 to this Act except by or with the consent of the Attorney General for Northern Ireland.

(2) Any document purporting to be an order, notice or direction made or given by the Secretary of State for the purposes of any provision of this Act and to be signed by him or on his behalf shall be received in evidence, and shall, until the contrary is proved, be deemed to be made or given by him.

(3) A document bearing a certificate purporting to be signed by or on behalf of the Secretary of State and stating that the document is a true copy of such an order, notice or direction shall, in any legal proceedings, be evidence, and in Scotland sufficient evidence, of the order, notice or direction.

19A Extension of certain offences to Crown servants and exemptions for regulators etc.

(1) The Secretary of State may by regulations provide that, in such circumstances as may be prescribed, sections 9 to 11, 17 and 18A above, shall apply to such persons in the public service of the Crown, or such categories of person in that service, as may be prescribed.

(2) Section 18A of this Act shall not apply to—

(a) any person designated by regulations made by the Secretary of State for the purpose of this paragraph; or

(b) in such circumstances as may be prescribed, any person who falls within such category of person as may be prescribed for the purpose of this paragraph.

(3) The Secretary of State may designate, for the purpose of paragraph (a) of subsection (2) above, any person appearing to him to be performing regulatory, supervisory, investigative or registration functions.

(4) The categories of person prescribed by the Secretary of State, for the purpose of paragraph (b) of subsection (2) above, shall be such categories of person connected with the performance by any designated person of regulatory, supervisory, investigative or registration functions as he considers it appropriate to prescribe.

(5) In this section—

"the Crown" includes the Crown in right of Her Majesty's Government in Northern Ireland; and "prescribed" means prescribed by regulations made by the Secretary of State.

(6) The power to make regulations under this section shall be exercisable by statutory instrument.

(7) Any such instrument shall be subject to annulment in pursuance of a resolution of either House of Parliament.

20 Interpretation

(1) In this Act—

"aircraft" includes hovercraft;
"captain" means master of a ship or commander of an aircraft;
"concessionaires" has the same meaning as in the Channel Tunnel Act 1987;
"examining officer" has the meaning given in paragraph 1 of Schedule 5 to this Act;
"exclusion order" has the meaning given by section 4(3) above but subject to section 25(3) below;
"the Islands" means the Channel Islands or the Isle of Man;
"port" includes airport and hoverport;
"premises" includes any place and in particular includes—

(a) any vehicle, vessel or aircraft;
(b) any offshore installation as defined in section 1 of the Mineral Workings (Offshore Installations) Act 1971; and
(c) any tent or moveable structure;

"property" includes property wherever situated and whether real or personal, heritable or moveable and things in action and other intangible or incorporeal property;
"ship" includes every description of vessel used in navigation;
"terrorism" means the use of violence for political ends, and includes any use of violence for the purpose of putting the public or any section of the public in fear;
"tunnel system" has the same meaning as in the Channel Tunnel Act 1987;
"vehicle" includes a train and carriages forming part of a train.

(2) A constable or examining officer may, if necessary, use reasonable force for the purpose of exercising any powers conferred on him under or by virtue of any provision of this Act other than paragraph 2 of Schedule 5; but this subsection is without prejudice to any provision of this Act, or of any instrument made under it, which implies that a person may use reasonable force in connection with that provision.

(3) The powers conferred by Part II and section 16 of, and Schedules 2 and 5 to, this Act shall be exercisable notwithstanding the rights conferred by section 1 of the Immigration Act 1971 (general principles regulating entry into and staying in the United Kingdom).

(4) Any reference in a provision of this Act to a person having been concerned in the commission, preparation or instigation of acts of terrorism shall be taken to be a reference to his having been so concerned at any time, whether before or after the passing of this Act.

21–24 [(*Pt VI*) *Repealed by the Northern Ireland (Emergency Provisions) Act 1991, s 70(4), Sch 8, Pt I.*]

PART VII
SUPPLEMENTARY

25 Consequential amendments, repeals and transitional provisions

(1) The enactments mentioned in Schedule 8 to this Act shall have effect with the amendments there specified, being amendments consequential on the provisions of this Act.

(2) The enactments mentioned in Part I of Schedule 9 to this Act are hereby repealed to the extent specified in the third column of that Schedule; and the Orders mentioned in Part II of that Schedule are hereby revoked.

(3) Any exclusion order in force under any provision of Part II of the Prevention of Terrorism (Temporary Provisions) Act 1984 ("the former Act") shall have effect as if made under the corresponding provision of Part II of this Act and references in this Act to an exclusion order shall be construed accordingly.

(4) Any person who immediately before 22nd March 1989 is being detained under provision of the former Act or of an order made under section 13 of that Act shall be treated as lawfully detained under the correspnding provision of this Act.

(5) Paragraph 2 of Schedule 5 to this Act shall not apply in relation to a person whose examination under any corresponding provision of an order made under section 13 of the former Act has begun but has not been concluded before the coming into force of that paragraph, and that provision shall continue to apply to him but any reference in this Act to examination under that paragraph shall include a reference to examination under that corresponding provision.

(6) The expiry of the former Act and its repeal by this Act shall not affect the operation of any Order in Council extending it to any of the Channel Islands or the Isle of Man; but any such Order may be revoked as if made under section 28(3) below and, notwithstanding anything contained in any such Order, shall continue in operation until revoked.

26 Expenses and receipts

There shall be paid out of money provided by Parliament—

(a) any expenses incurred under this Act by the Secretary of State or the Lord Advocate; and

(b) any increase attributable to this Act in the sums payable out of such money under any other Act;

and any sums received by the Secretary of State under this Act shall be paid into the Consolidated Fund.

27 Commencement and duration

(1) Subject to subsections (2), (3) and (4) below, this Act shall come into force on 22nd March 1989.

(2) (*repealed*)

(3) Schedule 3 and paragraphs 8 to 10, 18 to 20, 28 to 30 and 34 of Schedule 4 shall come into force on such day as the Secretary of State may appoint by an order made by statutory instrument; and different days may be appointed for different provisions and for England and Wales, for Scotland and for Northern Ireland.

(4) The repeal by Schedule 9 of paragraph 9 of Schedule 7 shall come into force on the coming into force of the Land Registration Act 1988.

(5) The provisions of Parts I to V of this Act and of subsection (6)(c) below shall remain in force until 22nd March 1990 and shall then expire unless continued in force by an order under subsection (6) below.

(6) The Secretary of State may by order made by statutory instrument provide—

(a) that all or any of those provisions which are for the time being in force (including any in force by virtue of an order under this paragraph or paragraph (c) below) shall continue in force for a period not exceeding twelve months from the coming into operation of the order;

(b) that all or any of those provisions which are for the time being in force shall cease to be in force; or

(c) that all or any of those provisions which are not for the time being in force shall come into force again and remain in force for a period not exceeding twelve months from the coming into operation of the order.

(7) No order shall be made under subsection (6) above unless—

(a) a draft of the order has been laid before and approved by a resolution of each House of Parliament; or

(b) it is declared in the order that it appears to the Secretary of State that by reason of urgency it is necessary to make the order without a draft having been so approved.

(8) An order under that subsection of which a draft has not been approved under section (7) above—

(a) shall be laid before Parliament; and

(b) shall cease to have effect at the end of the period of forty days beginning with the day on which it was made unless, before the end of that period, the order has been approved by a resolution of each House of Parliament, but without prejudice to anything previously done or to the making of a new order.

(9) In reckoning for the purposes of subsection (8) above the period of forty days no account shall be taken of any period during which Parliament is dissolved or prorogued or during which both Houses are adjourned for more than four days.

(10) In subsection (5) above the reference to Parts I to V of this Act does not include a reference to the provisions of Parts III and V so far as they have effect in Northern Ireland and relate to proscribed organisations for the purposes of section 28 of the Northern Ireland (Emergency Provisions) Act 1991 or offences or orders under that section.

(11) The provisions excluded by subsection (10) above from subsection (5) shall remain in force until 15th June 1992 and then expire but shall be—

(a) included in the provisions to which subsection (3) of section 69 of the said Act of 1991 applies (provisions that can be continued in force, repealed or revived by order); and

(b) treated as part of that Act for the purposes of subsection (9) of that section (repeal at end of five years).

(12) (*repealed*)

28 Short title and extent

(1) This Act may be cited as the Prevention of Terrorism (Temporary Provisions) Act 1989.

(2) This Act extends to the whole of the United Kingdom except that—

(a) Part I and section 15(1) do not extend to Northern Ireland and Part III of Schedule 4 and the repeal in Schedule 9 relating to the Explosives Act 1875 extend only to Northern Ireland;

(b) section 15(10), Part I of Schedule 4 and paragraph 7(6) of Schedule 5 extend only to England and Wales;

(c) *(applies to Scotland only)*;

(d) Part I of Schedule 7 extends only to England, Wales and Northern Ireland; and

(e) subject to paragraph (a) above, the amendments and repeals in Schedules 8 and 9 have the same extent as the enactments to which they refer.

(3) Her Majesty may by Order in Council direct that any of the provisions of this Act shall extend, with such exceptions, adaptations and modifications, if any, as may be specified in the Order, to any of the Channel Islands and the Isle of Man.

SCHEDULES

Schedule 1

(Section 1)
PROSCRIBED ORGANISATIONS

Irish Republican Army
Irish National Liberation Army

Schedule 2

(Section 4(4))
EXCLUSION ORDERS

Duration

1. (1) An exclusion order may be revoked at any time by a further order made by the Secretary of State.

(2) An exclusion order shall, unless revoked earlier, expire at the end of the period of three years beginning with the day on which it is made.

(3) The fact that an exclusion order against a person has been revoked or has expired shall not prevent the making of a further exclusion order against him.

Notice of making of order

2. (1) As soon as may be after the making of an exclusion order, notice of the making of the order shall be served on the person against whom it has been made; and the notice shall—

(a) set out the rights afforded to him by paragraph 3 below; and

(b) specify the manner in which those rights are to be exercised.

(2) Sub-paragraph (1) above shall not impose an obligation to take any steps to serve a notice on a person at a time when he is outside the United Kingdom.

(3) Where the person against whom an exclusion order is made is not for the time being detained by virtue of this Act, the notice of the making of the order may be served on him by posting it to him at his last known address.

Right to make representations

3. (1) If after being served with notice of the making of an exclusion order the person against whom it is made objects to the order he may—

(a) make representations in writing to the Secretary of State setting out the grounds of his objections; and

(b) include in those representations a request for a personal interview with the person or persons nominated by the Secretary of State under sub-paragraph (5) below.

(2) Subject to sub-paragraphs (3) and (4) below, a person against whom an exclusion order has been made must exercise the rights conferred by sub-paragraph (1) above within seven days of the service of the notice.

(3) Where before the end of that period—

(a) he has consented to his removal under paragraph 5 below from Great Britain, Northern Ireland or the United Kingdom, as the case may be; and

(b) he has been removed accordingly,

he may exercise the rights conferred by sub-paragraph (1) above within fourteen days of his removal.

(4) Where at the time when the notice of an exclusion order is served on a person he is in a part of the United Kingdom other than that from which the order excludes him he may exercise the rights conferred by sub-paragraph (1) above within fourteen days of the service of the notice.

(5) If a person exercises those rights within the period which they are required to be exercised by him, the matter shall be referred for the advice of one or more persons nominated by the Secretary of State.

(6) Where sub-paragraph (2) above applies, the person against whom the exclusion order has been made shall be granted a personal interview with the person or persons so nominated.

(7) Where sub-paragraph (3) or (4) above applies, the person against whom the exclusion order has been made shall be granted a personal interview with the person or persons so nominated if it appears to the Secretary of State that it is reasonably practicable to grant him such an interview in an appropriate country or territory within a reasonable period from the date on which he made his representations.

(8) In sub-paragraph (7) above "an appropriate country or territory" means—

(a) Northern Ireland or the Republic of Ireland if the exclusion order was made under section 5 of this Act;

(b) Great Britain or the Republic of Ireland if it was made under section 6 of this Act;

(c) the Republic of Ireland if it was made under section 7 of this Act.

(9) Where it appears to the Secretary of State that it is reasonably practicable to grant a personal interview in more than one appropriate country or territory he may grant the interview in whichever of them he thinks fit.

(10) It shall be for the Secretary of State to determine the place in any country or territory at which an interview under this paragraph is to be granted.

Reconsideration of exclusion order following representations

4. (1) Where the Secretary of State receives representations in respect of an exclusion order under paragraph 3 above he shall consider the matter as soon as reasonably practicable after receiving the representations and any report of an interview relating to the matter which has been granted under that paragraph.

(2) In reconsidering a matter under this paragraph the Secretary of State shall take into account everything which appears to him to be relevant and in particular—

(a) the representations relating to the matter made to him under paragraph 3 above;

(*b*) the advice of the person or persons to whom the matter was referred by him under that paragraph; and

(*c*) the report of any interview relating to the matter granted under that paragraph.

(3) The Secretary of State shall thereafter, if it is reasonably practicable to do so, give notice in writing to the person against whom the exclusion order has been made of any decision he takes as to whether or not to revoke the order.

Powers of removal

5. Where an exclusion order has been made against a person and notice of the making of the order has been served on him, the Secretary of State may have him removed from the relevant territory—

(*a*) if he consents;

(*b*) if the period mentioned in paragraph 3(2) above has expired and he has not made representations relating to the matter in accordance with that paragraph; or

(*c*) if he has made such representations but the Secretary of State has notified him that he has decided not to revoke the order.

Removal directions

6. (1) The Secretary of State may in accordance with the following provisions of this paragraph give directions for the removal from the relevant territory of any person subject to an exclusion order; but a person shall not be removed in pursuance of the directions until notice of the making of the order has been served on him and one of the conditions in paragraph 5(*a*), (*b*) and (*c*) above is fulfilled.

(2) Directions under this paragraph above may be—

(*a*) directions given to the captain of a ship or aircraft about to leave the relevant territory requiring him to remove the person in question from that territory in that ship or aircraft; or

(*b*) directions given to the owners or agents of any ship or aircraft requiring them to make arrangements for the removal from the relevant territory of the person in question in a ship or aircraft specified or indicated in the directions; or

(*c*) directions for the removal from the relevant territory of the person in question in accordance with arrangements to be made by the Secretary of State;

and any such directions shall specify the country or territory to which the person in question is to be removed.

(3) Directions under this paragraph may also be given for the removal of a person by land to the Republic of Ireland; and those directions may be—

(*a*) directions given to the driver or owner of any vehicle (being, in the case of a private vehicle, one in which that person arrived in Northern Ireland) requiring him to remove that person in question to the Republic of Ireland in a vehicle specified in the directions; or

(*b*) directions for the removal of the person in accordance with arrangements to be made by the Secretary of State.

(4) No directions under this paragraph shall be for the removal of a person to any country or territory other than one—

(*a*) of which the person in question is a national citizen;

(*b*) in which he obtained a passport or other document of identity; or

(c) to which there is reason to believe that he will be admitted;
and no such directions shall be given for the removal of a British citizen, a British
Dependent Territories citizen, a British Overseas citizen or a British National
(Overseas) to a country or territory outside the United Kingdom unless he is also a
national or citizen of, or has indicated that he is willing to be removed to, that
country or territory.

(5) Where—

(a) a person is found on examination under Schedule 5 to this Act to be subject
to an exclusion order; or

(b) an exclusion order is made against a person following such an examination,

the power to give directions for his removal under any provision of this paragraph
except sub-paragraphs (2)(c) and (3)(b) shall be exercisable by an examining officer
as well as by the Secretary of State; and where any such person has arrived in a
ship or aircraft (including arrival as a transit passenger, member of the crew or
other person not seeking to enter Great Britain or Northern Ireland) the countries or
territories to which he may be directed to be removed under sub-paragraph (2) above
include the country or territory in which he embarked on that ship or aircraft.

(6) A person in respect of whom directions are given under this paragraph may
be placed under the authority of the Secretary of State or an examining officer on
board any ship or aircraft or, as the case may be, in or on any vehicle in which he
is to be removed in accordance with the directions.

(7) The costs of complying with any directions under this paragraph shall be
defrayed by the Secretary of State.

(8) Any person who without reasonable excuse fails to comply with directions
given to him under this paragraph is guilty of an offence and liable on summary
conviction to imprisonment for a term not exceeding three months or a fine not
exceeding level 4 on the standard scale or both.

(9) In this paragraph "the relevant territory" means—

(a) in relation to a person subject to an exclusion order made under section 5 of
this Act, Great Britain;

(b) in relation to a person subject to an exclusion order made under section 6 of
this Act, Northern Ireland; and

(c) in relation to a person subject to an exclusion order made under section 7 of
this Act, the United Kingdom.

Detention pending removal

7. (1) A person in respect of whom directions for removal may be given under
paragraph 6 above may be detained pending the giving of such directions and
pending removal in pursuance of the directions under the authority of the Secretary
of State or, if the directions are to be or have been given by an examining officer,
of such an officer.

(2) A person liable to be detained under this paragraph may be arrested without
warrant by an examining officer.

(3) The captain of a ship or aircraft, if so required by an examining officer, shall
prevent any person placed on board the ship or aircraft under paragraph 6 above
from disembarking in the relevant territory or, before the directions for his removal have been fulfilled, elsewhere.

(4) Where under sub-paragraph (3) above the captain of a ship or aircraft is
required to prevent a person from disembarking he may for that purpose detain
him in custody on board the ship or aircraft.

(5) The captain of a ship or aircraft who fails to take reasonable steps to comply with a requirement imposed under sub-paragraph (3) above is guilty of an offence and liable on summary conviction to imprisonment for a term not exceeding six months or a fine not exceeding level 4 on the standard scale or both.

(6) A person may be removed from a vehicle for detention under this paragraph.

(7) In this paragraph "relevant territory" has the same meaning as in paragraph 6 above.

Detention: supplementary provisions

8. (1) If a justice of the peace is satisfied that there are reasonable grounds for suspecting that a person liable to be arrested under paragraph 7(2) above is to be found on any premises he may grant a search warrant authorising any constable to enter those premises for the purpose of searching for and arresting that person.

(2) (*Applies to Scotland only.*)

(3) In Northern Ireland an application for a warrant under sub-paragraph (1) above shall be made by a complaint on oath.

(4) A person detained under this Schedule shall be deemed to be in legal custody at any time when he is so detained and, if detained otherwise than on board a ship or aircraft, may be detained in such a place as the Secretary of State may from time to time direct.

(5) Where a person is detained under this Schedule, any examining officer, constable or prison officer, or any other person authorised by the Secretary of State, may take all such steps as may be reasonably necessary for photographing, measuring or otherwise identifying him.

(6) Any person detained under this Schedule may be taken in the custody of a constable or an examining officer, or of any person acting under the authority of an examining officer, to and from any place where his attendance is required for the purpose of establishing his nationality or citizenship or for making arrangements for his admission to a country or territory outside the United Kingdom or where he is required to be for any other purpose connected with the operation of this Act.

Exemption from exclusion orders

9. (1) When any question arises under this Act whether a person is exempted from the provisions of section 5, 6 or 7 of this Act it shall be for the person asserting that he is exempt to prove it.

(2) A person is not to be treated as ordinarily resident in Great Britain for the purposes of the exemption in section 5(4)(a) of this Act or in Northern Ireland for the purpose of the exemption in section 6(4)(a) of this Act at a time when he is there in breach of—

(a) an exclusion order; or

(b) the Immigration Act 1971 or any law for purposes similar to that Act in force in the United Kingdom after the passing of this Act.

(3) In each of these exemptions "the last three years" is to be taken as a period amounting in total to three years exclusive of any time during which the person claiming exemption was undergoing imprisonment or detention for a period of six months or more by virtue of a sentence passed for an offence on a conviction in the United Kingdom or in any of the Islands.

(4) In sub-paragraph (3) above—

(a) "sentence" includes any order made on conviction of an offence;

(b) two or more sentences for consecutive (or partly consecutive) terms shall be treated as a single sentence;

(c) a person shall be deemed to be detained by virtue of a sentence—
   (i) at any time when he is liable to imprisonment or detention by virtue of the sentence but is unlawfully ar large; and
   (ii) during any period of custody by which under any relevant enactment the term to be served under the sentence is reduced.

(5) In sub-paragraph (4)(c)(ii) above "relevant enactment" means section 67 of the Criminal Justice Act 1967 and any similar enactment which is for the time being or has (before or after the passing of this Act) been in force in any part of the United Kingdom or in any of the Islands.

Schedule 3

(Sections 4(5), 14(6) and 16(2))
SUPERVISION OF DETENTION AND EXAMINATION POWERS

Detention pending removal

1. (1) Where a person is detained under paragraph 7 of Schedule 2 to this Act under the authority of an examining officer his detention shall be periodically reviewed in accordance with this paragraph by a review officer and shall not continue unless that officer has authorised it to continue.

(2) The reviews shall be carried out as follows—

(a) the first review shall be as soon as practicable after the beginning of the detention;

(b) the subsequent reviews shall be at intervals of not more than twelve hours.

(3) On any such review the review officer shall authorise the continued detention of the person in question if, and only if, he is satisfied that steps for giving directions for his removal or for removing him in pursuance of the directions are being taken diligently and expeditiously.

Examination without detention

2. (1) Where a person has been required by a notice under paragraph 2(4) of Schedule 5 to this Act to submit to further examination but is not detained under paragraph 6 of that Schedule his further examination shall be reviewed by a review officer not later than twelve hours after the beginning of the examination and shall not continue unless that officer has authorised it to continue.

(2) The review officer shall authorise the examination to continue if, and only if, he is satisfied that the enquiries necessary to complete the examination are being carried out diligently and expeditiously.

Detention for examination or as suspected person

3. (1) Where a person is detained under section 14 of this Act or under paragraph 6 of Schedule 5 to this Act his detention shall be periodically reviewed in accordance with this paragraph by a review officer and shall not continue unless—

(a) that officer has authorised it to continue; or

(b) an application has been made to the Secretary of State for an extension of the period of detention under subsection (5) of that section or sub-paragraph (3) of that paragraph.

(2) The reviews shall be carried out as follows—

(a) the first review shall be as soon as practicable after the beginning of the detention; and

(b) the subsequent reviews shall be at intervals of not more than twelve hours;

and no review shall be carried out after such an application as is mentioned in sub-paragraph (1)(b) above has been made.

(3) Subject to sub-paragraph (4) below, on any such review the review officer shall authorise the continued detention of the person in question if, and only if, he is satisfied—

(a) that his continued detention is necessary in order to obtain (whether by questioning him or otherwise) or to preserve evidence which—

　(i) relates to an offence under section 2, 8, 9, 10 or 11 of this Act (in the case of detention under section 14) or under section 8 (in the case of detention under paragraph 6 of Schedule 5);

　(ii) indicates that he is or has been concerned in the commission, preparation or instigation of acts of terrorism to which section 14 of this Act applies; or

　(iii) indicates that he is subject to an exclusion order; and

(b) that the investigation in connection with which that person is detained is being conducted diligently and expeditiously.

(4) The review officer may also authorise the continued detention of the person in question—

(a) pending consideration of the question whether he is subject to an exclusion order;

(b) pending consideration by the Secretary of State whether to make an exclusion order against him or to serve him with notice of a decision to make a deportation order under the Immigration Act 1971;

(c) pending a decision by the Director of Public Prosecutions or Attorney General or, as the case may be, the Lord Advocate or the Director of Public Prosecutions or Attorney General for Northern Ireland whether proceedings for an offence should be instituted against him; or

(d) if he is satisfied as to the matters specified in sub-paragraph (5) below.

(5) The matters referred to in sub-paragraph (4)(d) above are—

(a) that the continued detention of the person in question is necesary—

　(i) pending a decision whether to apply to the Secretary of State for an exclusion order to be made in respect of him or for notice of a decision to make a deportation order under the Immigration Act 1971 to be served on him; or

　(ii) pending the making of such an application; and

(b) that consideration of that question is being undertaken, or preparation of the application is being proceeded with, diligently and expeditiously.

The review officer

4. The review officer shall be an officer who has not been directly involved in the matter in connection with which the person in question is detained or examined and—

(a) in the case of a review carried out within twenty-four hours of the beginning of that person's detention or in the case of a review under paragraph 2 above, shall be an officer of at least the rank of inspector;

(b) in the case of any other review, shall be an officer of at least the rank of superintendent.

Postponement of reviews

5. (1) A review may be postponed—

(a) if, having regard to all the circumstances prevailing at the latest time specified in paragraph 1(2), 2(2) or 3(2) above, it is not practicable to carry out the review at that time;

(b) without prejudice to the generality of paragraph (a) above—

(i) if at that time the person in detention or being examined is being questioned by a police officer or an examining officer and the review officer is satisfied that an interruption of the questioning for the purpose of carrying out the review would prejudice the investigation in connection with which the person is being detained or examined; or

(ii) if at that time no review officer is readily available.

(2) If a review is postponed under this paragraph it shall be carried out as soon as practicable after the latest time specified for it under the relevant provision mentioned in sub-paragraph (1)(a) above.

(3) If a review is carried out after postponement under this paragraph, the fact that it was so carried out shall not affect any requirement of this Schedule as to the time at which any subsequent review is to be carried out.

Representation about detention

6. (1) Before determining whether to authorise a person's continued detention the review officer shall give—

(a) that person (unless he is asleep); or

(b) any solicitor representing him who is available at the time of the review,

an opportunity to make representations to him about the detention.

(2) Subject to sub-paragraph (3) below, the person whose detention is under review or his solicitor may make representations under this paragraph either orally or in writing.

(3) The review officer may refuse to hear oral representations from the person whose detention is under review if he considers that he is unfit to make such representations by reason of his condition or behaviour.

Rights of detained persons

7. (1) Where the review officer authorises a person's continued detention and at that time that person has not yet exercised a right conferred on him by section 56 or 58 of the Police and Criminal Evidence Act 1984 (right of arrested person to have someone informed and to have access to legal advice) the review officer shall inform him of that right and, if its exercise is being delayed in accordance with the provisions of the section in question, that it is being so delayed.

(2) Where a review of a person's detention is carried out under paragraph 1 or 3 above at a time when his exercise of a right conferred by either of those sections is being delayed—

(a) the review officer shall consider whether the reason or reasons for which the delay was authorised continue to subsist; and

(b) if he is not himself the officer who authorised the delay and is of the opinion that the reason or reasons have ceased to subsist, he shall inform that officer of his opinion.

(3) (*Applies to Scotland only.*)

(4) In the application of this paragraph to Northern Ireland for the references to sections 56 and 58 of the said Act of 1984 there shall be substituted references to sections 44 and 45 of the Northern Ireland (Emergency Provisions) Act 1991.

Records of review

8. (1) The review officer carrying out a review under this Schedule shall make a written record of the outcome of the review, including, where the continued detention or examination of the person in question is authorised, the grounds for authorisation and, where a review is postponed, the reason for the postponement.

(2) The record required by this paragraph shall be made in the presence of the person detained or examined and, where his continued detention or examination is authorised, he shall at that time be told the grounds for the authorisation.

(3) Sub-paragraph (2) above shall not apply where the person detained or examined is, at the time when the written record is made—

(a) incapable of understanding what is said to him;

(b) violent or likely to become violent; or

(c) in urgent need of medical attention.

(4) Where the review officer informs a detained person of the matters mentioned in sub-paragraph (1) of paragraph 7 above he shall make a written record of the fact that he has done so.

(5) The review office shall also make a written record of his conclusion on the matter which he is required to consider under sub-paragraph (2)(a) of that paragraph, and, if he has taken action in accordance with sub-paragraph (2)(b) of that paragraph, of the fact that he has done so.

Intervention by superior officer

9. Where the review officer is of a rank lower than superintendent and—

(a) an officer of higher rank than the review officer gives directions relating to the person detained or examined; and

(b) the directions are at variance—

(i) with any decision made or action taken by the review officer in the performance of a duty imposed on him by this Schedule; or

(ii) with any decision or action which would but for the directions have been made or taken by him in the performance of that duty,

the review officer shall refer the matter at once to an officer of the rank of superintendent or above.

Schedule 4

(Section 13(8))
FORFEITURE ORDERS

PART I
ENGLAND AND WALES

Implementation of forfeiture orders

1. (1) Where a court in England and Wales makes an order under section 13(2), (3) or (4) of this Act (in this Part of this Schedule referred to as a "forfeiture order") it may make an order—

(a) requiring any money or other property to which the forfeiture order applies to be paid or handed over to the proper office or to a constable designated for the purpose by the chief officer of police of a police force specified in the order;

(b) directing any such property other than money or land to be sold or otherwise disposed of in such manner as the court may direct and the proceeds to be paid to the proper officer;

(c) appointing a receiver to take possession, subject to such conditions and exceptions as may be specified by the court, of any such property which is land, to realise it in such manner as the court may direct and to pay the proceeds to the proper officer;

(d) directing a specified part of any money, or of the proceeds of the sale, disposal or realisation of any property, to which the forfeiture order applies to be paid by the proper officer to or for a specified person falling within section 13(6) of this Act;

(e) making such other provision as appears to the court to be necessary for giving effect to the forfeiture order or to any order made by virtue of paragraph (a), (b), (c) or (d) above.

(2) A forfeiture order shall not come into force until (disregarding any power of a court to grant leave to appeal out of time) there is no further possibility of the order being set aside.

(3) Any balance in the hands of the proper officer after making any payment required under sub-paragraph (1)(d) above or paragraph 2 below shall be treated for the purposes of section 61 of the Justices of the Peace Act 1979 (application of fines etc.) as if it were a fine imposed by the magistrates' court.

(4) The proper officer shall, on the application of the prosecutor or defendant in the proceedings in which a forfeiture order is made, certify in writing the extent (if any) to which, at the date of the certificate, effect has been given to the order in respect of the money or other property to which it applies.

(5) In this paragraph "the proper officer" means, where the forfeiture order is made by a magistrates' court, the clerk of that court and, where the order is made by the Crown Court—

(a) the clerk of the magistrates' court by which the defendant was committed to the Crown Court; or

(b) if the proceedings were instituted by a bill of indictment preferred by virtue of section 2(2)(b) of the Administration of Justice (Miscellaneous Provisions) Act 1933, the clerk of the magistrates' court for the place where the trial took place;

and in this sub-paragraph references to the clerk of a magistrates' court shall be construed in accordance with section 141 of the Magistrates' Courts Act 1980 taking references to that Act as references to this Act.

(6) In this paragraph references to the proceeds of the sale, disposal or realisation of property are references to the proceeds after deduction of the costs of sale, disposal or realisation.

(7) This paragraph has effect to the exclusion of section 140 of the said Act of 1980.

2. (1) Where a receiver appointed under paragraph 1 above takes any action—

(a) in relation to property which is not subject to forfeiture, being action which he would be entitled to take if it were such property;

(b) believing, and having reasonable grounds for believing, that he is entitled to take that action in relation to that property, he shall not be liable to any person in respect of any loss or damage resulting from his action except in so far as the loss or damage is caused by his negligence.

(2) A receiver appointed under paragraph 1 above shall be entitled to be paid his remuneration and expenses out of the proceeds of the property realised by him or, if and so far as those proceeds are insufficient, by the prosecutor.

Restraint orders

3. (1) The High Court may in accordance with this paragraph by an order (referred to in this Part of this Schedule as a "restraint order") prohibit any person, subject to such conditions and exceptions as may be specified in the order, from dealing with any property liable to forfeiture, that is to say, any property in respect of which a forfeiture order has been made or in respect of which such an order could be made in the proceedings referred to in sub-paragraph (2) or (3) below.

(2) A restraint order may be made where—
(a) proceedings have been instituted against a defendant in England or Wales for an offence under Part III of this Act;
(b) the proceedings have not been concluded; and
(c) either a forfeiture order has been made or it appears to the court that there are reasonable grounds for thinking that a forfeiture order may be made in those proceedings.

(3) A restraint order may also be made where—
(a) the court is satisfied that, whether by the laying of an information or otherwise, a person is to be charged in England and Wales with an offence under Part III of this Act; and
(b) it appears to the court that a forfeiture order may be made in proceedings for the offence.

(4) In the application of the provisions of this Part of this Schedule at a time when a restraint order may be made by virtue of sub-paragraph (3) above references to the prosecutor shall be construed as references to the person who the High Court is satisfied is to have the conduct of the proposed proceedings.

(5) Where the court has made an order under this paragraph by virtue of sub-paragraph (3) above the court may discharge the order if proceedings in respect of the offence are not instituted (whether by the laying of an information or otherwise) within such time as the court considers reasonable.

(6) For the purposes of this paragraph, dealing with property includes, without prejudice to the generality of that expression—
(a) where a debt is owed to the person concerned, making a payment to any person in reduction of the amount of the debt; and
(b) removing the property from the jurisdiction of the High Court.

(7) In exercising the powers conferred by this paragraph the court shall not take account of any obligations of any person having an interest in the property subject to the restraint order which might frustrate the making of a forfeiture order.

(8) For the purposes of this paragraph proceedings for an offence are instituted—
(a) when a justice of the peace issues a summons or warrant under section 1 of the Magistrates' Courts Act 1980 in respect of that offence;
(b) when a person is charged with the offence after being taken into custody without a warrant;
(c) when a bill of indictment is preferred by virtue of section 2(2)(b) of the Administration of Justice (Miscellaneous Provisions) Act 1933;

and where the application of this sub-paragraph would result in there being more than one time for the institution of proceedings they shall be taken to be instituted at the earliest of those times.

(9) For the purposes of this paragraph and paragraph 4 below proceedings are concluded—

(a) when a forfeiture order has been made in those proceedings and effect has been given to it in respect of all the money or other property to which it applies; or

(b) when (disregarding any power of a court to grant leave to appeal out of time) there is no further possibility of a forfeiture order being made in the proceedings.

4. (1) A restraint order—

(a) may be made only on an application by the prosecutor;

(b) may be made on an ex parte application to a judge in chambers; and

(c) shall provide for notice to be given to persons affected by the order.

(2) A restraint order—

(a) may be discharged or varied in relation to any property; and

(b) shall be discharged when proceedings for the offence are concluded.

(3) An application for the discharge or variation of a restraint order may be made by any person affected by it.

5. (1) Where the High Court has made a restraint order a constable may for the puprose of preventing any property subject to the order being removed from the jurisdiction of the court seize that property.

(2) Property seized under this paragraph shall be dealt with in accordance with the court's directions.

6. (1) The Land Charges Act 1972 and the Land Registration Act 1925 shall apply—

(a) in relation to restraint orders as they apply in relation to orders affecting land made by the court for the purpose of enforcing judgments or recognizances; and

(b) in relation to applications for restraint orders as they apply in relation to other pending land actions.

(2) The prosecutor shall be treated for the purposes of section 57 of the Land Registration Act 1925 (inhibitions) as a person interested in relation to any registered land to which a restraint order or an application for such an order relates.

Compensation

7. (1) If proceedings are instituted against a person for an offence under Part III of this Act and either—

(a) the proceedings do not result in his conviction for any such offence; or

(b) where he is convicted of one or more such offences—

(i) the conviction or convictions concerned are quashed; or

(ii) he is pardoned by Her Majesty in respect of the conviction or convictions concerned,

the High Court may, on an application by a person who had an interest in any property which was subject to a forfeiture or restraint order made in or in relation to those proceedings, order compensation to be paid to the applicant if, having regard to all the circumstances, it considers it appropriate to do so.

(2) The High Court shall not order compensation to be paid in any case unless it is satisfied—

(*a*) that there is some serious default on the part of a person concerned in the investigation or prosecution of the offence concerned, being a person mentioned in sub-paragraph (5) below; and

(*b*) that the applicant has suffered loss in consequence of anything done in relation to the property by or in pursuance of an order under this Part of this Schedule.

(3) The court shall not order compensation to be paid in any case where it appears to it that the proceedings would have been instituted even if the serious default had not occurred.

(4) The amount of compensation to be paid under this paragraph shall be such as the High Court thinks just in all the circumstances of the case.

(5) Compensation payable under this paragraph shall be paid—

(*a*) where the person in default was or was acting as a member of a police force, out of the police fund out of which the expenses of that police force are met;

(*b*) where the person in default was a member of the Crown Prosecution Service or acting on behalf of the Service, by the Director of Public Prosecutions.

(6) Sub-paragraph (8) of paragraph 3 above applies for the purposes of this paragraph as it applies for the purposes of that paragraph.

Enforcement of orders made elsewhere in the British Islands

8. (1) In the following provisions of this Part of this Schedule—
"a Scottish order" means—

(*a*) an order made in Scotland under section 13(2), (3) or (4) of this Act ("a Scottish forfeiture order");

(*b*) an order made under paragraph 13 below ("a Scottish restraint order"); or

(*c*) an order made under any other provision of Part II of this Schedule in relation to a Scottish forfeiture or restraint order;
"a Northern Ireland" order means—

(*a*) an order made in Northern Ireland under section 13(2), (3) or (4) of this Act ("a Northern Ireland forfeiture order");

(*b*) an order made under paragraph 23 or 25A below ("a Northern Ireland restraint order"); or

(*c*) an order made under any other provision of Part III of this Schedule in relation to a Northern Ireland forfeiture or restraint order;
"an Islands order" means—

(*a*) an order made in any of the Islands under section 13(2), (3) or (4) of this Act as extended to that Island under section 28(3) of this Act ("an Islands forfeiture order");

(*b*) an order under paragraph 3 above as so extended ("an Islands restraint order"); or

(*c*) an order made under any other provision of this Part of this Schedule as so extended in relation to an Islands forfeiture or restraint order.

(2) In paragraphs (*a*), (*b*) and (*c*) of the definition of "an Islands order" the reference to a provision of this Act as extended to an Island under section 28(3) of this Act includes a reference to any other provision of the law of that Island for purposes corresponding to that provision.

9. (1) A Scottish order, Northern Ireland order or Islands order shall, subject to the provisions of this paragraph, have effect in the law of England and Wales but shall be enforced in England and Wales only in accordance with the provisions of

this paragraph and any provision made by rules of court as to the manner in which and the conditions subject to which such orders are to be enforced there.

(2) The High Court shall, on an application made to it in accordance with rules of court for registration of a Scottish order, Northern Ireland order, or Islands order, direct that the order shall, in accordance with such rules, be registered in that court.

(3) Rules of courts shall also make provision—

(a) for cancelling or varying the registration of a Scottish, Northern Ireland or Islands forfeiture order when effect has been given to it (whether in England and Wales or elsewhere) in respect of all or, as the case may be, part of the money or other property to which the order applies;

(b) for cancelling or varying the registration of a Scottish, Northern Ireland or Islands restraint order which has been discharged or varied by the court by which it was made.

(4) If a Scottish, Northern Ireland or Islands forfeiture order is registered under this paragraph the High Court shall have, in relation to that order, the same powers as a court has under paragraph 1(1) above in relation to a forfeiture order made by it (and paragraph 2 above applies accordingly) but any functions of the clerk of a magistrates' court shall be exercised by the appropriate officer of the High Court.

(5) After making any payment required by virtue of paragraph 1(1)(d) or 2 above, the balance of any sums received by the appropriate officer of the High Court by virtue of an order made under sub-paragraph (4) above shall be paid by him to the Secretary of State.

(6) Paragraphs 3(7), 5 and 6 above shall apply to a registered Scottish, Northern Ireland or Islands restraint order as they apply to a restraint order and the High Court shall have the like power to make an order under section 33 of the Supreme Court Act 1981 (extended power to order inspection of property etc) in relation to proceedings brought or likely to be brought for a Scottish, Northern Ireland or Islands restraint order as if those proceedings had been brought or were likely to be brought in the High Court.

(7) Without prejudice to the foregoing provisions, if a Scottish order, Northern Ireland order or Islands order is registered under this paragraph—

(a) the High Court shall have, in relation to its enforcement, the same power;

(b) proceedings for or with respect to its enforcement may be taken; and

(c) proceedings for or with respect to any contravention of such an order (whether before or after such registration) may be taken,

as if the order had originally been made in the High Court.

(8) The High Court may, additionally, for the purpose of—

(a) assisting the achievement in England and Wales of the purposes of a Scottish order, Northern Ireland order or Islands order; or

(b) assisting any receiver or other person directed by any such order to sell or otherwise dispose of property,

make such orders or do otherwise as seems to it appropriate.

(9) A document purporting to be a copy of a Scottish order, Northern Ireland order or Islands order and to be certified as such by a proper officer of the court by which it was made or purporting to be a certificate for purposes corresponding to those of paragraph 1(4) above and to be certified by a proper officer of the court concerned shall, in England and Wales, be received in evidence without further proof.

Enforcement of orders made in designated countries

10. (1) Her Majesty may by Order in Council make such provision as appears to Her Majesty to be appropriate for the purpose of enabling the enforcement in England and Wales of orders to which this paragraph applies.

(2) This paragraph applies to any order ("an external order") which is made in a country or territory designated for the purposes of this paragraph by the Order in Council and—

(*a*) provides for the forfeiture of terrorist funds within the meaning of section 11(3)(*a*) or (*b*) of this Act ("an external forfeiture order"); or

(*b*) makes provision prohibiting dealing with property which is subject to an external forfeiture order or in respect of which such an order could be made in proceedings which have been or are to be instituted in that country or territory ("an external restraint order").

(3) Without prejudice to the generality of subsection (1) above, an Order in Council under this paragraph may make provision for matters corresponding to those for which provision is made by, or can be made under, paragraph 9(1) to (8) above in relation to the orders to which that paragraph applies and for the proof of any matter relevant for the purposes of anything falling to be done in pursuance of the Order in Council.

(4) An Order in Council under this paragraph may also make such provision as appears to Her Majesty to be appropriate with respect to anything falling to be done on behalf of the United Kingdom in a designated country or territory in relation to proceedings in that country or territory for or in connection with the making of an external order.

(5) An Order under this paragraph may make different provision for different cases.

(6) No Order shall be made under this paragraph unless a draft of it has been laid before and approved by a resolution of each House of Parliament.

11–20. [*(Pt II) Apply to Scotland only.*]

21–30. [*(Pt III) Apply to Northern Ireland only.*]

PART IV

INSOLVENCY: UNITED KINGDOM PROVISIONS

Protection of creditors against forfeiture

31. (1) During the period of six months following the making of a forfeiture order no money which is subject to the order, or which represents any property subject to it, shall be finally disposed of under this Schedule.

(2) If, in the case where any money or other property is subject to a forfeiture order—

(*a*) the commencement of an insolvency occurs, or has occurred, in the course of any qualifying insolvency proceedings,

(*b*) any functions in relation to that property would (apart from the forfeiture order) be exercisable by an insolvency practitioner acting in those proceedings, and

(*c*) during the period of six months following the making of the forfeiture order any such insolvency practitioner gives written notice to the relevant officer of the matters referred to in paragraphs (*a*) and (*b*) above,

then sub-paragraph (3) below shall apply in relation to the property in question.

(3) Where this sub-paragraph applies then, subject to the following provisions of

this Part of this Schedule, the property in question or, if it has been sold, the proceeds of sale—

(a) shall cease to be subject to the forfeiture order and any ancillary order; and

(b) shall fall to be dealt with in the insolvency proceedings as if the forfeiture order had never been made.

(4) In any case where—

(a) sub-paragraph (3) above would, apart from this sub-paragraph, apply in relation to any property, but

(b) the relevant officer, or any person acting in pursuance of an ancillary order, has entered into a contract for the sale of that property or has incurred any other obligations in relation to it,

the sub-paragraph shall not take effect in relation to that property, or its proceeds of sale, unless and until those obligations have been discharged.

(5) Where in consequence of sub-paragraph (3) above any money or other property falls to be dealt with in insolvency proceedings, the Secretary of State shall be taken to be a creditor in those proceedings to the amount or value of that property but, notwithstanding any provision contained in or made under any other enactment—

(a) except in sequestration proceedings, his debt shall rank after the debts of all other creditors and shall not be paid until they have been paid in full with interest under section 189(2) or, as the case may be, section 328(4) of the 1986 Act or Article 25 of the Bankruptcy Amendment (Northern Ireland) Order 1980; and

(b) in sequestration proceedings, his debt shall rank after all the debts mentioned in section 51(1) of the Bankruptcy (Scotland) Act 1985 and shall not be paid until they have been paid in full.

(6) In any case where—

(a) by virtue of sub-paragraph (3) above any property ceases to be subject to a forfeiture order in consequence of the making of a bankruptcy order or an award of sequestration, and

(b) subsequently the bankruptcy order is annulled or the award of sequestraiton is recalled or reduced,

the property shall again become subject to the forfeiture order and, if aplicable, any ancillary orders.

(7) If any of the property referred to in sub-paragraph (6) above is money, or has been converted into money, then—

(a) the court which ordered the annulment, or which recalled or reduced the award of sequestration, shall make an order specifying, for the purposes of paragraph (b) below, property comprised in the estate of the bankrupt or debtor to the amount or value of the property in question; and

(b) the property so specified shall become subject to the forfeiture order, and any applicable ancillary orders, in place of the property in question.

(8) In this paragraph—

"the commencement of an insolvency" means—

(a) the making of a bankruptcy order;

(b) the date of sequestration of a person's estate, within the meaning of section 12(4) of the Bankruptcy (Scotland) Act 1985;

(c) in England and Wales, in the case of the insolvent estate of a deceased person, the making of an insolvency administration order;

(d) in the case of a company—

(i) the passing of a resolution for its winding up; or

(ii) the making of an order by the court for the winding up of the company where no such resolution has been passed;

"final disposal under this Schedule", in relation to any money, means—

(a) in England and Wales, its payment to the Secretary of State in accordance with paragraph 1(3) or 9(5) above;

(b) in Scotland, its payment to the proper officer in Exchequer under section 203 of the Criminal Procedure (Scotland) Act 1975;

(c) in Northern Ireland, its payment into, or its disposal for the benefit of, the Consolidated Fund in accordance with paragraph 21(3) or 29(5) above;

and "finally dispose" shall be construed accordingly.

Expenses incurred in connection with the forfeiture

32. (1) Where any money or other property would, apart from this paragraph, fall to be dealt with in accordance with paragraph 31(3) above, the relevant officer may—

(a) deduct from that money any allowable forfeiture expenses; or

(b) retain so much of that property as he considers necessary for the purpose of realising it and deducting any such expenses from the proceeds of realisation;

and paragraph 31(3) above shall apply only in relation to any balance remaining after making provision for those expenses.

(2) If any money or other property is delivered up in pursuance of paragraph 31(3) above and provision has not been made for any allowable forfeiture expenses, then—

(a) the person who incurred them shall have a claim to their value in the insolvency proceedings; and

(b) the expenses in question shall be treated for the purposes of the insolvency proceedings as if they were expenses of those proceedings.

(3) In this paragraph "allowable forfeiture expenses"—

(a) means any expenses incurred in relation to property subject to the forfeiture order—

(i) by the relevant officer;

(ii) by any receiver, administrator or other person appointed by the relevant officer; or

(iii) by any person appointed or directed to deal with any property by an order under paragraph 11(1) above; and

(b) includes any amount paid, or required to be paid, under paragraph 1(1)(d), 11(1)(c) or 21(1)(d) above.

Protection of insolvency practitioners

33. (1) In any case where—

(a) an insolvency practitioner seizes or disposes of any property in relation to which his functions are not exercisable because it is for the time being subject to a forfeiture or restraint order, and

(b) at the time of the seizure or disposal he believes and has reasonable grounds for believing that he is entitled (whether in pursuance of a court order or otherwise) to seize or dispose of that property,

he shall not be liable to any person in respect of any loss or damage resulting from the seizure or disposal except in so far as the loss or damage is caused by his negligence in so acting.

(2) An insolvency practitioner shall have a lien on the property mentioned in sub-paragraph (1) above or the proceeds of its sale—

(a) for such of his expenses as were incurred in connection with insolvency proceedings in relation to which the seizure or disposal purported to take place; and

(b) for so much of his remuneration as may reasonably be assigned for his acting in connection with those proceedings.

(3) Sub-paragraphs (1) and (2) above are without prejudice to the generality of any provision contained in the 1986 Act or the Bankruptcy (Scotland) Act 1985 or any other Act or the Bankruptcy Acts (Northern Ireland) 1857 to 1980 or the Companies (Northern Ireland) Order 1986.

(4) In this paragraph "insolvency practitioner", in any part of the United Kingdom, means a person acting as an insolvency practitioner in that or any other part of the United Kingdom; and for this purpose—

(a) any question whether a person is acting as an insolvency practitioner in England and Wales or in Scotland shall be determined in accordance with seciton 388 of the 1986 Act, except that—

(i) the reference in subsection (2)(a) to a permanent or interim trustee in a sequestration shall be taken to include a reference to a trustee in sequestration;

(ii) subsection (5) shall be disregarded; and

(iii) the expression shall also include the Official Receiver acting as receiver or manager of property; and

(b) a person acts as an insolvency practitioner in Northern Ireland if he acts as an Official Assignee, trustee, liquidator, receiver or manager of a company, provisional liquidator or a receiver or manager under section 68 of the Bankruptcy (Ireland) Amendment Act 1872.

Insolvency practitioners in the Islands and designated countries

34. (1) The Secretary of State may by order make provision for securing that an Islands or external insolvency practitioner has, with such modifications as may be specified in the order, the same rights under this Part of this Schedule in relation to property situated in any part of the United Kingdom as he would have if he were an insolvency practitioner in that or any other part of the United Kingdom.

(2) An order under this paragraph may make provision as to the manner in which, and the conditions subject to which, an Islands or external insolvency practitioner may exercise the rights conferred under sub-paragraph (1) above; and any such order may, in particular, make provision—

(a) for requiring him to obtain leave of a court as a condition of exercising any such rights; and

(b) for empowering a court granting any such leave to impose such conditions as it thinks fit.

(3) An order under this paragraph may make different provision for different cases.

(4) The power to make an order under this paragraph shall be exercisable by statutory instrument and, in relation to property situated in England and Wales, shall be so exercisable with the concurrence of the Lord Chancellor.

(5) A statutory instrument containing an order under this paragraph shall be subject to annulment in pursuance of a resolution of either House of Parliament.

(6) In this paragraph—

"Islands or external insolvency practitioner" means a person exercising under the insolvency law of a relevant country or territory functions corresponding to those exercised by insolvency practitioners under the insolvency law of any part of the United Kingdom;

"involvency law" has the meaning given by section 426(10) of the 1986 Act, except that the reference to a relevant country or territory shall be construed in accordance with this paragraph;

"relevant country or territory" means—

(a) any of the Channel Islands or the Isle of Man; or

(b) any country or territory designated as mentioned in paragraph 10, 20 or 30 above.

Interpretation of Part IV

35. (1) In this Part of this Schedule—

"the 1986 Act" means the Insolvency Act 1986;

"ancillary order" means any order made in connection with the forfeiture in question, other than the forfeiture order;

"forfeiture or restraint order" means a forfeiture or restraint order, as the case may be, of any of the descriptions referred to in Parts I to III of this Schedule;

"insolvency practitioner", except in paragraph 33 above, means a person acting in any qualifying insolvency proceedings in any part of the United Kindgom as—

(a) a liquidator of a company or partnership;

(b) a trustee in bankruptcy;

(c) an interim or permanent trustee in sequestration;

(d) an administrator of the insolvent estate of a deceased person;

(e) a receiver or manager of any property;

"qualifying insolvency proceedings" means—

(a) any proceedings under the 1986 Act or the Companies (Northern Ireland) Order 1986 for the winding up of a company or an unregistered company and includes any voluntary winding up of a company under Part IV of that Act or Part XX of that Order;

(b) any proceedings in England and Wales under or by virtue of section 420 of the 1986 Act for the winding up of an insolvent partnership;

(c) any proceedings in bankruptcy or, in Scotland, any sequestration proceedings;

(d) any proceedings in England and Wales under or by virtue of section 421 of the 1986 Act in relation to the insolvent estate of a deceased person;

"the relevant officer" means—

(a) in Scotland—

(i) where the forfeiture order in question is made by a court in Scotland, the clerk of that court;

(ii) in any other case, the Principal Clerk of Session and Justiciary;

(b) in any other part of the United Kingdom—

(i) where the forfeiture order in question is made by a court in that part, the proper officer within the meaning of paragraph 1 or, as the case may be, paragraph 21 above;

(ii) in any other case, the appropriate officer of the High Court.

(2) Any reference in this Part of this Schedule to the proceeds of the sale or

realisation of any property are references to those proceeds after deduction of the costs of sale or realisation.

Schedule 5
(Section 16(1), (3) and (4))

PORT AND BORDER CONTROL

Examining officers

1. (1) The following shall be examining officers for the purposes of this Act—
   (a) constables;
   (b) immigration officers appointed for the purposes of the Immigration Act 1971 under paragraph 1 of Schedule 2 to that Act; and
   (c) officers of customs and excise who are the subject of arrangements for their employment as immigration officers made under that paragraph by the Secretary of State.

   (2) In Northern Ireland members of Her Majesty's Forces may perform such functions conferred on examining officers as the Secretary of State may by order specify.

   (3) The power to make orders under sub-paragraph (2) above shall be exercisable by statutory instrument subject to annulment in pursuance of a resoluition of either House of Parliament.

   (4) Examining officers shall exercise their functions under this Act in accordance with such instructions as may from time to time be given to them by the Secretary of State.

Examination on arrival or departure

2. (1) Any person who has arrived in, or is seeking to leave, Great Britain or Northern Ireland, by ship or aircraft may be examined by an examining officer for the purpose of determining—
   (a) whether that person appears to be a person who is or has been concerned in the commission, preparation or instigation of acts of terrorism to which this paragraph applies; or
   (b) whether any such person is subject to an exclusion order; or
   (c) whether there are grounds for suspecting that any such person has committed an offence under section 8 of this Act.

   (2) This paragraph applies to—
   (a) acts of terrorism connected with the affairs of Northern Ireland; and
   (b) acts of terrorism or any other description except acts connected solely with the affairs of the United Kingdom or any part of the United Kingdom other than Northern Ireland.

   (3) An examining officer may—
   (a) examine any person who is entering or seeking to enter or leave Northern Ireland by land from, or to go to, the Republic of Ireland for the purpose of determining whether that person is such a person as is mentioned in any of paragraphs (a) to (c) of sub-paragraph (1) above;
   (b) examine any person found in Northern Ireland within a distance of one mile from the border with the Republic of Ireland for the purpose of ascertaining whether he is in the course of entering or leaving Northern Ireland by land;
   (c) examine any person entering Northern Ireland by train when he arrives at

the first place where the train is scheduled to stop for the purpose of allowing passengers to alight.

(4) The period of a person's examination under this paragraph shall not exceed twenty-four hours unless he is detained under paragraph 6 below, and may only exceed twelve hours if an examining officer—

(a) has reasonable grounds for suspecting that the person examined is or has been concerned in the commission, preparation or instigation of acts of terrorism to which this paragraph applies; and

(b) gives him a notice in writing requiring him to submit to further examination.

(5) In sub-paragraph (1) above the reference to arrival by ship or aircraft includes a reference to arrival as a transit passenger, member of the crew or other person not seeking to enter Great Britain or Northern Ireland.

Production of information and documents

3. (1) It shall be the duty of any person examined under paragraph 2 above to furnish to the person carrying out the examination all such information in his possession as that person may require for the purpose of his functions under that paragraph.

(2) A person on his examination under paragraph 2 above by an examining officer shall, if so required by the examining officer—

(a) produce either a valid passport with photograph or some other document satisfactorily establishing his identity and nationality or citizenship; and

(b) declare whether or not he is carrying or conveying documents of any relevant description specified by the examining officer, and produce any documents of that description which he is carrying or conveying.

(3) In sub-paragraph (2)(b) above "relevant description" means any description appearing to the examining officer to be relevant for the purposes of the examination.

Powers of search, etc.

4. (1) An examining officer may, for the purpose of satisfying himself whether there are persons he may wish to examine under paragraph 2 above, search any ship or aircraft and anything on board it or anything taken off or about to be taken aboard a ship or aircraft.

(2) An examining officer who examines any person under paragraph 2 above may, for the purpose of determining whether he is such a person as is mentioned in any of paragraphs (a) to (c) of sub-paragraph (1) of that paragraph, search that person and any baggage belonging to him or any ship or aircraft and anything on board it or anything taken off or about to be taken aboard a ship or aircraft.

(3) Without prejudice to sub-paragaphs (1) and (2) above, an examining officer who examines any person in Northern Ireland under paragraph 2 above may, for the purpose mentioned in sub-paragraph (2) above, search any vehicle and anything in or on it or anything taken out of or off it or about to be placed in or on it.

(4) An examining officer may detain for the purpose of examining it anything produced pursuant to paragraph 3(2)(b) above or found on a search under this paragraph for a period not exceeding seven days; and if on examination of anything so produced or found the examining officer is of the opinion that it may be needed—

(a) in connection with the taking of a decision by the Secretary of State as to whether or not to make an exclusion order or a deportation order under the Immigration Act 1971; or

(*b*) for use as evidence in criminal proceedings,
he may detain it until he is satisfied that it will not be so needed.

(5) A search of a person under this paragraph may only be carried out by a person of the same sex.

(6) An examining officer may board any ship or aircraft or enter any vehicle for the purpose of exercising any of his functions under this Act.

(7) Where an examining officer has power to search under this paragraph, he may, instead, authorise the search to be carried out on his behalf by a person who is not an examining officer.

(8) Where a person who is not an examining officer carries out a search in accordance with sub-paragraph (7) above, he may—

(*a*) for that purpose, board any ship or aircraft or enter any vehicle; and

(*b*) exercise the power of detaining articles conferred by sub-paragraph (4) above;

and he may, if necessary, use reasonable force for the purpose of carrying out his functions under this paragraph.

(9) In Scotland any person employed by a police authority for the assistance of constables under section 9 of the Police (Scotland) Act 1967 may perform any functions conferred on examining officers by this paragraph, and may, if necessary, use reasonable force for the purpose of performing those functions.

Landing, embarkation, entry and departure cards

5. (1) Subject to sub-paragraph (2) below, any person who disembarks from, or embarks on—

(*a*) a ship or aircraft in Great Britain which has come from, or is going to, the Republic of Ireland, Northern Ireland or any of the Islands; or

(*b*) a ship or aircraft in Northern Ireland which has come from, or is going to Great Britain, the Republic of Ireland or any of the Islands,

shall, if so required by an examining officer, complete and produce to that officer a landing or, as the case may be, and embarkation card in such form as the Secretary of State may direct, which, where the ship or aircraft is employed to carry passengers for reward, shall be supplied for the purpose to that person by the owners or agents of that ship or aircraft.

(2) Sub-paragraph (1) above shall not apply to a person disembarking from a ship or aircraft coming from the Republic of Ireland if that person is required to produce a landing card under any order for the time being in force under paragraph 5 of Schedule 2 to the Immigration Act 1971.

(3) Any person who may be examined under paragraph 2(3)(*a*) or (*c*) above shall, if so required by an examining officer, complete and produce to that officer an entry or, as the case may be, a departure card in such form as the Secretary of State may direct.

Detention pending examination etc.

6. (1) A person who is examined under this Schedule may be detained under the authority of an examining officer—

(*a*) pending conclusion of his examination;

(*b*) pending consideration by the Secretary of State whether to make an exclusion order against him; or

(*c*) pending a decision by the Director of Public Prosecutions or Attorney General or, as the case may be, the Lord Advocate or the Director of Public

Prosecutions or Attorney General for Northern Ireland whether proceedings for an offence should be instituted against him.

(2) Subject to sub-paragraph (3) below, a person shall not be detained under sub-paragraph (1) above for more than forty-eight hours from the time when he is first examined.

(3) The Secretary of State may, in any particular case, extend the period of forty-eight hours mentioned in sub-paragraph (2) above by a period or periods specified by him, but any such further period or periods shall not exceed five days in all and if an application for such an extension is made the person detained shall as soon as practicable be given written notice of the fact and of the time when the application was made.

(4) A person liable to be detained under this paragraph may be arrested without warrant by an examining officer.

(5) A person on board a ship or aircraft may, under the authority of an examining officer, be removed from the ship or aircraft for detention under this paragraph; but if an examining officer so requires, the captain of the ship or aircraft shall prevent from disembarking in the relevant territory any person who has arrived in the ship or aircraft if the examining officer notifies him either that the person is the subject of an exclusion order or that consideration is being given by the Secretary of State to the making of an exclusion order against that person.

(6) Where under sub-paragraph (5) above the captain of a ship or aircraft is required to prevent a person from disembarking he may for that purpose detain him in custody on board the ship or aircraft.

(7) A person may be removed from a vehicle for detention under this paragraph.

(8) In sub-paragraph (5) above "the relevant territory" has the same meaning as in paragrph 6 of Schedule 2 to this Act.

Detention: supplementary provisions

7. (1) If a justice of the peace is satisfied that there are reasonable grounds for suspecting that a person liable to be arrested under paragraph 6(4) above is to be found on any premises he may grant a search warrant authorising any constable to enter those premises for the purpose of searching for and arresting that person.

(2) In Scotland the power to issue a warrant under sub-paragraph (1) above shall be exercised by a sheriff or a justice of the peace, an application for such a warrant shall be supported by evidence on oath and a warrant shall not authorise a constable to enter any premises unless he is a constable for the police area in which they are situated.

(3) In Northern Ireland an application for a warrant under sub-paragraph (1) above shall be made by a complaint on oath.

(4) A person detained under this Schedule shall be deemed to be in legal custody at any time when he is so detained and, if detained otherwise than on board a ship or aircraft, may be detained in such a place as the Secretary of State may from time to time direct.

(5) Where a person is detained under this Schedule, any examining officer, constable or prison officer, or any other person authorised by the Secretary of State, may take all such steps as may be reasonably necessary for photographing, measuring or otherwise identifying him.

(6) Section 61(1) to (8) of the Police and Criminal Evidence Act 1984 (fingerprinting) shall apply to the taking of a person's fingerprints by a constable under sub-paragraph (5) above as if for subsection (4) there were substituted—

"(4) An officer may only give an authorisation under subsection (3)(*a*) above for the taking of a person's fingerprints if he is satisfied that it is necessary to do so in order to assist in determining—

(*a*) whether that person is or has been concerned in the commission, preparation or instigation of acts of terrorism to which paragraph 2 of Schedule 5 to the Prevention of Terrorism (Temporary Provisions) Act 1989 applies;

(*b*) whether he is subject to an exclusion order under that Act; or

(*c*) whether there are grounds for suspecting that he has committed an offence under section 8 of that Act."

(7) Any person detained under this Schedule may be taken in the custody of an examining officer, or of any person acting under the authority of such an officer, to and from any place where his attendance is required for the purpose of establishing his nationality or citizenship or for making arrangements for his admission to a country or territory outside the United Kingdom or where he is required to be for any other purpose connected with the operation of this Act.

Designated ports

8. (1) The owners or agents of a ship or aircraft employed to carry passengers for reward and coming to Great Britain from the Republic of Ireland, Northern Ireland or any of the Islands or going from Great Britain to any other of those places shall not, without the approval of an examining officer, arrange for the ship or aircraft to call at a port in Great Britain other than a designated port for the purpose of disembarking or embarking passengers.

(2) The captain of an aircraft not employed to carry passengers for reward and coming to Great Britain from the Republic of Ireland, Northern Ireland or any of the Islands or going from Great Britain to any other of those places shall not, without the approval of an examining officer, permit the aircraft to call at or leave a port in Great Britain other than a designated port.

(3) The owners or agents of a ship or aircraft employed to carry passengers for reward and coming to Northern Ireland from Great Britain, the Republic of Ireland or any of the Islands or going from Northern Ireland to any other of those places shall not, without the approval of an examining officer, arrange for the ship or aircraft to call at a port in Northern Ireland other than a designated port for the purpose of disembarking or embarking passengers.

(4) The captain of an aircraft not employed to carry passengers for reward and coming to Northern Ireland from Great Britain, the Republic of Ireland or any of the Islands or going from Northern Ireland to any other of those places shall not, without the approval of an examining officer, permit the aircraft to call at or leave a port in Northern Ireland other than a designated port.

Control areas

9. (1) The Secretary of State may from time to time give written notice to the owners or agents of any ships or aircraft designating control areas for the disembarkation or embarkation of passenters in any port in the United Kingdom and specifying the conditions and restrictions (if any) to be observed in any control area; and where by notice given to any owners or agents a control area is for the time being so designated at any port, the owners or agents shall take all reasonable steps to ensure that, in the case of their ships or aircraft, passengers do not disembark or, as the case may be, embark at the port outside the control area and that any conditions or restrictions notified to them are observed.

(2) The Secretary of State may also from time to time give to any persons concerned with the management of a port in the United Kingdom written notice designating control areas in the port and specifying facilities to be provided and conditions and restrictions to be observed in any control area; and any such person shall take all reasonable steps to secure that any facilities, conditions or restrictions notified to him are provided or observed.

Requirements with respect to embarkation and disembarkation of passengers and crew

10. (1) The captain of a ship or aircraft employed to carry passengers for reward arriving in Great Britain from the Republic of Ireland, Northern Ireland or any of the Island or arriving in Northern Ireland from Great Britain, the Republic of Ireland or any of the Islands—

(*a*) shall, except so far as he may be otherwise required to do so under paragraph 27(1) of Schedule 2 to the Immigration Act 1971, take such steps as may be necessary to secure that passengers on board and members of the crew do not disembark there unless either they have been examined by an examining officer or they disembark in accordance with arrangements approved by an examining officer; and

(*b*) where any examination of persons on board is to be carried out on the ship or aircraft, shall take such steps as may be necesary to secure that those to be examined are presented for the purpose in an orderly manner.

(2) The captain of a ship or aircraft employed to carry passengers for reward going from Great Britain to the Republic of Ireland, Northern Ireland or any of the Islands or going from Northern Ireland to Great Britain, the Republic of Ireland or any of the Islands shall take such steps as may be necessary to secure that—

(*a*) passengers and members of the crew do not embark except in accordance with arrangements approved by an examining officer; and

(*b*) if persons embarking are to be examined on board the ship or aircraft, they are presented for the purpose in an orderly manner.

(3) Sub-paragraphs (1) and (2) above apply also to aircraft not employed to carry passengers for reward.

(4) The captain of a ship or aircraft arriving in Great Britain from the Republic of Ireland, Northern Ireland or any of the Islands or arriving in Northern Ireland from Great Britain, the Republic of Ireland or any of the Islands shall, unless he is subject to the requirements of an order under paragraph 27(2) of Schedule 2 to the Immigration Act 1971 and subject to sub-paragraph (6) below, comply with the requirements of sub-paragraph (5) below with respect to the furnishing to the examining officer of the particulars of the passengers on and crew of the ship or aircraft.

(5) The requirements referred to in sub-paragrph (4) above are—

(*a*) in the case of a ship employed to carry passengers for reward or an aircraft, to furnish to the examining officer, as soon as reasonably practicable after the arrival of the ship or aircraft, a list of the names and of the dates and places of birth of all passengers and members of the crew arriving on the ship or aircraft; and

(*b*) in the case of a ship not employed to carry passengers for reward, to furnish to the examining officer, within twelve hours of the arrival of the ship, a list of the names, the dates and places of birth and the addresses of the destinations in Great Britain or Northern Ireland of all passengers and members of the crew arriving on the ship.

(6) An examining officer may dispense with all, or any, of the requirements of sub-paragraph (5) above either generally or in respect of such classes of persons as he may specify.

(7) Any passenger on a ship or aircraft shall furnish to the captain of the ship or aircraft, as the case may be, any information required by him for the purpose of complying with the provisions of sub-paragraph (5) above.

Offences

11. A person who knowingly contravenes any prohibition or fails to comply with any duty or requirement imposed by or under this Schedule is guilty of an offence and liable on summary conviction to imprisonment for a term not exceeding three months or a fine not exceeding level 4 on the standard scale or both.

Schedule 6
(Section 16(3))

DESIGNATED PORTS

PART I

GREAT BRITAIN

Seaports	Airports
Ardossan	Aberdeen
Cairnryan	Biggin Hill
Fishguard	Birmingham
Fleetwood	Blackpool
Heysham	Bournemouth (Hurn)
Holyhead	Bristol
Pembroke Dock	Cambridge
Plymouth	Cardiff
Port of Liverpool	Carlisle
Poole Harbour	Coventry
Portsmouth Continental Ferry	East Midlands
Port	Edinburgh
Southampton	Exeter
Stranraer	Glasgow
Swansea	Gloucester/Cheltenham (Staverton)
Torquay	Humberside
Weymouth	Leeds/Bradford
	Liverpool
	London-City
	London-Gatwick
	London-Heathrow
	Luton
	Lydd
	Manchester
	Manston
	Newcastle
	Norwich

Seaports	Airports
	Plymouth
	Prestwick
	Southampton
	Southend
	Stansted
	Teesside

PART II

NORTHERN IRELAND

Seaports	Airports
Belfast	Aldergrove
Larne	Sydenham
Warrenpoint	

Schedule 7
(Section 17)

TERRORIST INVESTIGATIONS

PART I

ENGLAND, WALES AND NORTHERN IRELAND

Interpretation

1. In this part of this Schedule a "terrorist investigation" means any investigation to which section 17(1) of this Act applies and "items subject to legal privilege", "excluded material" and "special procedure material" have the meanings given in sections 10 to 14 of the Police and Criminal Evidence Act 1984.

Search for material other than excluded or special procedure material

2. (1) A justice of the peace may, on an application made by a constable, issue a warrant under this paragraph if satisfied that a terrorist investigation is being carried out and that there are reasonable grounds for believing—

    (a) that there is material on premises specified in the application which is likely to be of substantial value (whether by itself or together with other material) to the investigation;

    (b) that the material does not consist of or include items subject to legal privilege, excluded material or special procedure material; and

    (c) that any of the conditions in sub-paragraph (2) below are fulfilled.

    (2) The conditions referred to in sub-paragraph (1)(c) above are—

    (a) that it is not practicable to communicate with any person entitled to grant entry to the premises;

    (b) that it is practicable to communicate with a person entitled to grant entry to the premises but it is not practicable to communicate with any person entitled to grant access to the material;

(c) that entry to the premises will not be granted unless a warrant is produced;

(d) that the purpose of a search may be frustrated or seriously prejudiced unless a constable arriving at the premises can secure immediate entry to them.

(3) A warrant under this paragraph shall authorise a constable to enter the premises specified in the warrant and to search the premises and any person found there and to seize and retain anything found there or on any such person, other than items subject to legal privilege, if he has reasonable grounds for believing—

(a) that it is likely to be of substantial value (whether by itself or together with other material) to the investigation; and

(b) that it is necessary to seize it in order to prevent it being concealed, lost, damaged, altered or destroyed.

(4) In Northern Ireland an application for a warrant under this paragraph shall be made by a complaint on oath.

Order for production of excluded or special procedure material

3. (1) A constable may, for the purposes of a terrorist investigation, apply to a Circuit judge for an order under sub-paragraph (2) below in relation to particular material or material of a particular description, being material consisting of or including excluded material or special procedure material.

(2) If on such an application the judge is satisfied that the material consists of or includes such material as is mentioned in sub-paragraph (1) above, that it does not include items subject to legal privilege and that the conditions in sub-paragraph (5) below are fulfilled, he may order a person who appears to him to have in his possession, custody or power any of the material to which the applications relates, to—

(a) produce it to a constable for him to take away; or

(b) give a constable access to it,

within such period as the order may specify and if the material is not in that person's possession, custody or power (and will not come into his possession, custody or power within that period) to state to the best of his knowledge and belief where it is.

(3) An order under sub-paragraph (2) above may relate to material of a particular description which is expected to come into existence or become available to the person concerned in the period of twenty-eight days beginning with the date of the order; and an order made in relation to such material shall require that person to notify a named constable as soon as possible after the material comes into existence or becomes available to that person.

(4) The period to be specified in an order under sub-paragraph (2) above shall be seven days from the date of the order or, in the case of an order made by virtue of sub-paragraph (3) above, from the notification to the constable unless it appears to the judge that a longer or shorter period would be appropriate in the particular circumstances of the application.

(5) The conditions referred to in sub-paragraph (2) above are—

(a) that a terrorist investigation is being carried out and that there are reasonable grounds for believing that the material is likely to be of substantial value (whether by itself or together with other material) to the investigation for the purposes of which the application is made; and

(b) that there are reasonable grounds for believing that it is in the public interest, having regard—

(i) to the benefit likely to accrue to the investigation if the material is obtained; and

(ii) to the circumstances under which the person has the material in his possession, custody or power,

that the material should be produced or that access to it should be given.

(6) Where the judge makes an order under sub-paragraph (2)(*b*) above in relation to material on any premises he may, on the application of a constable, order any person who appears to him to be entitled to grant entry to the premises to allow a constable to enter the premises to obtain access to the material.

(7) In Northern Ireland the power to make an order under this paragraph shall be exercised by a county court judge.

4. (1) Provision may be made by Crown Court Rules as to—

(*a*) the discharge and variation of orders under paragraph 3 above; and

(*b*) proceedings relating to such orders.

(2) The following provisions shall have effect pending the coming into force of Crown Court Rules under sub-paragraph (1) above—

(*a*) an order under paragraph 3 above may be discharged or varied by a Circuit judge on a written application made to the appropriate officer of the Crown Court by any person subject to the order;

(*b*) unless a Circuit judge otherwise directs on grounds of urgency, the applicant shall, not less than forty-eight hours before making the application, send a copy of it and a notice in writing of the time and place where the application is to be made to the constable on whose application the order to be discharged or varied was made or on any other constable serving in the same police station.

(3) An order of a Circuit judge under paragraph 3 above shall have effect as if it were an order of the Crown Court.

(4) Where the material to which an application under that paragraph relates consists of information contained in a computer—

(*a*) an order under sub-paragraph (2)(*a*) of that paragraph shall have effect as an order to produce the material in a form in which it can be taken away and in which it is visible and legible; and

(*b*) an order under sub-paragraph (2)(*b*) of that paragraph shall have effect as an order to give access to the material in a form in which it is visible and legible.

(5) An order under paragraph 3 above—

(*a*) shall not confer any right to production of, or access to, items subject to legal privilege;

(*b*) shall have effect notwithstanding any obligation as to secrecy or other restriction on the disclosure of information imposed by statute or otherwise.

(6) An order may be made under paragraph 3 above in relation to material in the possession, custody or power of a government department which is an authorised government department for the purposes of the Crown Proceedings Act 1947; and any such order (which shall be served as if the proceedings were civil proceedings against the department) may require any officer of the department, whether named in the order or not, who may for the time being have in his possession, custody or power the material concerned to comply with it.

(7) In the application of this paragraph to Northern Ireland for references to a Circuit judge there shall be substituted references to a county court judge and for

references to a government department or authorised government department there shall be substituted references to a Northern Ireland department or authorised Northern Ireland department.

Search for excluded or special procedure material

5. (1) A constable may apply to a Circuit judge for a warrant under this paragraph in relation to specified premises.

(2) On such an application the judge may issue a warrant under this paragraph if satisfied—

(a) that an order made under paragraph 3 above in relation to material on the premises has not been complied with; or

(b) that there are reasonable grounds for believing that there is on the premises material consisting of or including excluded material or special procedure material, that it does not include items subject to legal privilege and that the conditions in sub-paragraph (5) of that paragraph and the condition in sub-paragraph (3) below are fulfilled in respect of that material.

(3) The condition referred to in sub-paragraph (2)(b) above is that it would not be appropriate to make an order under paragraph 3 above in relation to the material because—

(a) it is not practicable to communicate with any person entitled to produce the material; or

(b) it is not practicable to communicate with any person entitled to grant access to the material or entitled to grant entry to the premises on which the material is situated; or

(c) the investigation for the purposes of which the application is made might be seriously prejudiced unless a constable could secure immediate access to the material.

(4) A warrant under this paragraph shall authorise a constable to enter the premises specified in the warrant and to search the premises and any person found there and to seize and retain anything found there or on any such person, other than items subject to legal privilege, if he has reasonable grounds for believing that it is likely to be of substantial value (whether by itself or together with other material) to the investigation for the purposes of which the application was made.

(5) In Northern Ireland the power to issue a warrant under this paragraph shall be exercised by a county court judge.

Explanation of seized or produced material

6. (1) A Circuit judge may, on an application made by a constable, order any person specified in the order to provide an explanation of any material seized in pursuance of a warrant under paragraph 2 or 5 above or produced or made available to a constable under paragraph 3 above.

(2) A person shall not under this paragraph be required to disclose any information which he would be entitled to refuse to disclose on grounds of legal professional privilege in proceedings in the High Court, except that a lawyer may be required to furnish the name and address of his client.

(3) A statement by a person in response to a requirement imposed by virtue of this paragraph may only be used in evidence against him—

(a) on a prosecution for an offence under sub-paragraph (4) below; or

(b) on a prosecution for some other offence where in giving evidence he makes a statement inconsistent with it.

(4) A person who, in purportd compliance with a requirement under this paragraph—

(*a*) makes a statement which he knows to be false or misleading in a material particular; or

(*b*) recklessly makes a statement which is false or misleading in a material particular,

is guilty of an offence.

(5) A person guilty of an offence under sub-paragraph (4) above is liable—

(*a*) on conviction on indictment, to imprisonment for a term not exceeding two years or a fine or both;

(*b*) on summary conviction, to imprisonment for a term not exceeding six months or a fine not exceeding the statutory maximum or both.

(6) In Northern Ireland the power to make an order under this paragraph shall be exercised by a county court judge.

(7) Paragraph 4(1), (2), (3) and (6) above shall apply to orders under this paragraph as they apply to orders under paragraph 3.

Ugent cases

7. (1) If a police officer of at least the rank of superintendent has reasonable grounds for believing that the case is one of great emergency and that in the interests of the State immediate action is necessary, he may by a written order signed by him give to any constable the authority which may be given by a search warrant under paragraph 2 or 5 above.

(2) Where an authority is given under this paragraph particulars of the case shall be notified as soon as may be to the Secretary of State.

(3) An order under this paragraph may not authorise a search for items subject to legal privilege.

(4) If such a police officer as is mentioned in sub-paragraph (1) above has reasonable grounds for believing that the case is such as is there mentioned he may by a notice in writing signed by him require any person specified in the notice to provide an explanation of any material seized in pursuance of an order under this paragraph.

(5) Any person who without reasonable excuse fails to comply with a notice under sub-paragraph (4) above is guilty of an offence and liable on summary conviction to imprisonment for a term not exceeding six months or a fine not exceeding level 5 on the standard scale or both.

(6) Sub-paragraphs (2) to (5) of paragraph 6 above shall apply to a requirement imposed under sub-paragraph (4) above as they apply to a requirement under that paragraph.

Orders by Secretary of State in relation to certain investigations

8. (1) This paragraph has effect in relation to a terrorist investigation concerning any act which appears to the Secretary of State to constitute an offence under Part III of this Act.

(2) Without prejudice to the foregoing provisions of this Part of this Schedule, the Secretary of State may by a written order signed by him or on his behalf give to any constable in Northern Ireland the authority which may be given by a search warrant under paragraph 2 or 5 above or impose on any person in Northern Ireland any such requirement as may be imposed by an order under paragraph 3 above if—

(a) he is satisfied as to the matters specified in those paragraphs respectively for the issue of a warrant by a justice of the peace or the making of an order by a county court judge; and

(b) it appears to him that the disclosure of information that would be necessary for an application under those provisions would be likely to prejudice the capability of members of the Royal Ulster Constabulary in relation to the investigation of offences under Part III of this Act or otherwise prejudice the safety of, or of persons in, Northern Ireland.

(3) A person who disobeys an order under this paragraph which corresponds to an order under paragraph 3 above (a "Secretary of State's production order") is liable—

(a) on conviction on indictment, to imprisonment for a term not exceeding two years or a fine or both;

(b) on summary conviction, to imprisonment for a term not exceeding six months or a fine not exceeding the statutory maximum or both.

(4) A Secretary of State's production order may be varied or revoked by the Secretary of State and references in paragraphs 4(4), (5) and (6) and 5 above to an order under paragraph 3 above shall include references to a Secretary of State's production order.

(5) The Secretary of State may by a written order signed by him or on his behalf require any person in Northern Ireland to provide an explanation of any material seized or produced in pursuance of an order under the foregoing provisions of this paragraph; and paragraphs 6(2) to (5) and 7(5) above shall apply to an order under this sub-paragraph as they apply to an order or notice under those paragraphs.

9. *(Repealed)*

Supplementary

10. (1) Any power of seizure conferred by this Schedule is without prejudice to the powers conferred by section 19 of the Police and Criminal Evidence Act 1984 and for the purposes of sections 21 and 22 of that Act (access to, and copying and retention of, seized material)—

(a) a terrorist investigation shall be treated as an investigation of or in connection with an offence; and

(b) material produced in pursuance of an order under paragraph 3 or 8 above shall be treated as if it were material seized by a constable.

(2) A search of a person under this Part of this Schedule may only be carried out by a person of the same sex.

(Part II: applies to Scotland only)

(Schedules 8 and 9: not reproduced)

The Police and Criminal Evidence Act 1984 (Application to Customs and Excise) Order 1985

SI No 1800

1. This Order may be cited as the Police and Criminal Evidence Act 1984 (Application to Customs and Excise) Order 1985 and shall come into operation on 1st January 1986.

2. (1) In this Order, unless the context otherwise requires—

"the Act" means the Police and Criminal Evidence Act 1984;

"assigned matter" has the meaning given to it by section 1 of the Customs and Excise Management Act 1979;

"the customs and excise Acts" has the meaning give to it by section 1 of the Customs and Excise Management Act 1979;

"customs office" means a place for the time being occupied by Her Majesty's Customs and Excise;

"officer" means a person commissioned by the Commissioners of Customs and Excise under section 6(3) of the Customs and Excise Management Act 1979.

(2) A person is in customs detention for the purpose of this Order if—

(a) he has been taken to a customs office after being arrested for an offence; or

(b) he is arrested at a customs office after attending voluntarily at the office or accompanying an officer to it,

and is detained there or is detained elsewhere in the charge of an officer, and nothing shall prevent a detained person from being transferred between customs detention and police detention.

3. (1) Subject to the modifications in paragraphs (2) and (3) of this article, in articles 4 to 11 below and in Schedule 2 to this Order, the provisions of the Act contained in Schedule 1 to this Order which relate to investigations of offences conducted by police officers or to persons detained by the police shall apply to investigations conducted by officers of Customs and Excise of offences which relate to assigned matters, and to persons detained by such officers.

(2) The Act shall have effect as if the words and phrases in Column 1 of Part 1 of Schedule 2 to this Order were replaced by the substitute words and phrases in Column 2 of that Part.

(3) Where in the Act any act or thing is to be done by a constable of a specified rank that act or thing shall be done by an officer of at least the grade specified in Column 2 of Part 2 of Schedule 2 to this Order, and the Act shall be interpreted as if the substituted grade were specified in the Act.

4. Nothing in the application of the Act to Customs and Excise shall be construed as conferring upon an officer any power—
(a) to charge a person with any offence;
(b) to release a person on bail;
(c) to detain a person for an offence after he has been charged with that offence.

5. (1) Where in the Act a constable is given power to seize and retain any thing found upon a lawful search of person or premises, an officer shall have the same power notwithstanding that the thing found is not evidence of an offence in relation to an assigned matter.

(2) Nothing in the application of the Act to Customs and Excise shall be construed to prevent any thing lawfully seized by a person under any enactment from being accepted and retained by an officer.

(3) Section 21 of the Act (access and copying) shall not apply to any thing seized as liable to forfeiture under the customs and excise Acts.

6. In its application by virtue of article 3 above the Act shall have effect as if the following section were inserted after section 14—

"14A. Material in the possession of a person who acquired or created it in the course of any trade, business, profession or other occupation or for the purpose of any paid or unpaid office and which relates to an assigned matter, as defined in section 1 of the Customs and Excise Management Act 1979, is neither excluded material nor special procedure material for the purposes of any enactment such as is mentioned in section 9(1) above."

7. Section 18(1) of the Act shall be modified as follows—

"18. (1) Subject to the following provisions of this section, an officer of Customs and Excise may enter and search any premises occupied or controlled by a person who is under arrest for any arrestable offence which relates to an assigned matter, as defined in section 1 of the Customs and Excise Management Act 1979, if he has reasonable grounds for suspecting that there is on the premises evidence, other than items subject to legal privilege, that relates—
(a) to that offence; or
(b) to some other arrestable offence which is connected with or similar to that offence.".

8. (1) The Commissioners of Customs and Excise shall keep on an annual basis the written records mentioned in subsection (1) of section 50 of the Act.

(2) The Annual Report of the Commissioners of Her Majesty's Customs and Excise shall contain information about the matters mentioned in subsection (1) of section 50 of the Act in respect of the period to which it relates.

9. (1) Section 55 of the Act shall have effect as if it related only to things such as are mentioned in subsection (1)(a) of that section.

(2) The Annual Report of the Commissioners of Her Majesty's Customs and

Excise shall contain the information mentioned in subsection (15) of section 55 of the Act about searches made under that section.

10. Section 77(3) of the Act shall be modified to the extent that the definition of "independent person" shall, in addition to the persons mentioned therein, also include an officer or any other person acting under the authority of the Commissioners of Customs and Excise.

11. Where any provision of the Act as applied to Customs and Excise—
(*a*) confers a power on an officer, and
(*b*) does not provide that the power may only be exercised with the consent of some person other than an officer,
the officer may use reasonable force, if necessary, in the exercise of the power.

Schedule 1
Provisions of the Act applied to Customs and Excise

(Article 3)

Section 8
Section 9 and Schedule 1
Section 15
Section 16
Section 17(1)(*b*), (2), (4)
Section 18 subject to the modification in article 7 hereof
Section 19
Section 20
Section 21 subject to the modifications in article 5 hereof
Section 22(1) to (4)
Section 28
Section 29
Section 30(1) to (4)(*a*) and (5) to (11)
Section 31
Section 32(1) to (9) subject to the modifications in article 5 hereof
Section 34(1) to (5)
Section 35
Section 36
Section 37
Section 39
Section 40
Section 41
Section 42
Section 43
Section 44
Section 50 subject to the modifications in article 8 hereof
Section 51(*d*)
Section 52
Section 54
Section 55 subject to the modifications in articles 5 and 9 hereof
Section 56(1) to (9)
Section 57(1) to (9)

Section 58(1) to (11)
Section 62
Section 63
Section 64(1) to (6)

Schedule 2 *(Article 3)*

PART 1

Substitution of equivalent words and phrases in the Act.
Where in the Act a word or phrase specified in Column 1 below is used, in the application of the Act to Customs and Excise, there shall be substituted the equivalent word or phrase in Column 2 below—

Column 1	Column 2
WORDS AND PHRASES USED IN THE ACT	SUBSTITUTED WORDS AND PHRASES
area	collection
chief officer	collector
constable	officer
designated police station	designated customs office
officer of a force maintained by a police authority	officer
police area	collection
police detention (except in section 118 and in section 39(1)(a) the second time the words occur)	customs detention
police force	HM Commissioners of Customs and Excise
police officer	officer
police station	customs office
rank	grade
station	customs office
the police	HM Customs and Excise

PART 2

Equivalent grades of officers
Where in the Act an act or thing is to be done by a constable of the rank specified in Column 1 below, that same act or thing shall, in the application of the Act to Customs and Excise, be done by an officer of at least the grade specified in Column 2 below—

Column 1	Column 2
RANK OF CONSTABLE	GRADE OF OFFICER
sergeant	executive officer
inspector	higher executive officer
superintendent	senior executive officer

Criminal Justice Act 1987

ss2 and 3

Director's investigation powers

2. (1) The power of the Director under this section shall be exercisable of his own motion or at the request of an authority entitled to make such a request, but only for the purposes of an investigation under section 1 above, in any case in which it appears to him that there is good reason to do so for the purpose of investigating the affairs, or any aspect of the affairs, of any person.

(1A) The authorities entitled to request the Director to exercise his powers under this section are—

(*a*) the Attorney-General of the Isle of Man, Jersey or Guernsey, acting under legislation corresponding to section 1 of this Act and having effect in the Island whose Attorney-General makes the request; and

(*b*) the Secretary of State acting under section 4(2A) of the Criminal Justice (International Co-operation) Act 1990, in response to a request received by him from an overseas court, tribunal or authority (an "overseas authority").

(1B) The Director shall not exercise his powers on a request from the Secretary of State acting in response to a request received from an overseas authority within subsection (1A)(*b*) above unless it appears to the Director on reasonable grounds that the offence in respect of which he has been requested to obtain evidence involves serious or comlex fraud.

(2) The Director may by notice in writing require the person whose affairs are to be investigated ("the person under investigation") or any other person whom he has reason to believe has relevant information to answer questions or otherwise furnish information with respect to any matter relevant to the investigation at a specified place and either at a specified time or forthwith.

(3) The Director may by notice in writing require the person under investigation or any other person to produce at such place as may be specified in the notice and either forthwith or at such time as may be so specified any specified documents which appear to the Director to relate to any matter relevant to the investigation or any documents of a specified description which appear to him to so relate; and—

(*a*) if any such documents are produced, the Director may—

(i) take copies or extracts from them;

    (ii) require the person producing them to provide an explanation of any of them;

  (b) if any such documents are not produced, the Director may require the person who was required to produce them to state, to the best of his knowledge and belief, where they are.

(4) Where, on information on oath laid by a member of the Serious Fraud Office, a justice of the peace is satisfied, in relation to any documents, that there are reasonable grounds for believing—

  (a) that—

    (i) a person has failed to comply with an obligation under this section to produce them;

    (ii) it is not practicable to serve a notice under subsection (3) above in relation to them; or

    (iii) the service of such a notice in relation to them might seriously prejudice the investigation; and

  (b) that they are on premises specified in the information,

he may issue such a warrant as is mentioned in subsection (5) below.

(5) The warrant referred to above is a warrant authorising any constable—

  (a) to enter (using such force as is reasonably necessary for the purpose) and search the premises, and

  (b) to take possession of any documents appearing to be documents of the description specified in the information or to take in relation to any documents so appearing any other steps which may appear to be necessary for preserving them and preventing interference with them.

(6) Unless it is not practicable in the circumstances, a constable executing a warrant issued under subsection (4) above shall be accompanied by an appropriate person.

(7) In subsection (6) above "appropriate person" means—

  (a) a member of the Serious Fraud Office; or

  (b) some person who is not a member of that Office but whom the Director has authorised to accompany the constable.

(8) A statement by a person in response to a requirement imposed by virtue of this section may only be used in evidence against him—

  (a) on a prosecution for an offence under subsection (14) below; or

  (b) on a prosecution for some other offence where in giving evidence he makes a statement inconsistent with it.

(8A) Any evidence obtained by the Director for use by an overseas authority shall be furnished by him to the Secretary of State for transmission to the overseas authority which requested it.

(8B) If in order to comply with the request of the overseas authority it is necessary for any evidence obtained by the Director to be accompanied by any certificate, affidavit or other verifying document, the Director shall also furnish for transmission such document of that nature as may be specified by the Secretary of State when asking the Director to obtain the evidence.

(8C) Where any evidence obtained by the Director for use by an overseas authority consists of a document the original or a copy shall be transmitted, and where it consits of any other article the article itself or a description, photograph or other representation of it shall be transmitted, as may be necesary in order to comply with the request of the overseas authority.

(9) A person shall not under this section be required to disclose any information

or produce any document which he would be entitled to refuse to disclose or produce on grounds of legal professional privilege in proceedings in the High Court, except that a lawyer may be required to furnish the name and address of his client.

(10) A person shall not under this section be required to disclose information or produce a document in respect of which he owes an obligation of confidence by virtue of carrying on any banking business unless—

(a) the person to whom the obligation of confidence is owed consents to the disclosure or production; or

(b) the Director has authorised the making of the requirement or, if it is impracticable for him to act personally, a member of the Serious Fraud Office designated by him for the purposes of this subsection has done so.

(11) Without prejudice to the power of the Director to assign functions to members of the Serious Fraud Office, the Director may authorise any competent investigator (other than a constable) who is not a member of that Office to exercise on his behalf all or any of the powers conferred by this section, but no such authority shall be granted except for the purpose of investigating the affairs, or any aspect of the affairs, of a person specified in the authority.

(12) No person shall be bound to comply with any requirement imposed by a person exercising powers by virtue of any authority granted under subsection (11) above unless he has, if required to do so, produced evidence of his authority.

(13) Any person who without reasonable excuse fails to comply with a requirement imposed on him under this section shall be guilty of an offence and liable on summary conviction to imprisonment for a term not exceeding six months or to a fine not exceeding level 5 on the standard scale or to both.

(14) A person who, in purported compliance with a requirement under this section—

(a) makes a statement which he knows to be false or misleading in a material particular, or

(b) recklessly makes a statement which is false or misleading in a material particular,

shall be guilty of an offence.

(15) A person guilty of an offence under subsection (14) above shall—

(a) on conviction on indictment, be liable to imprisonment for a term not exceeding two years or to a fine or to both; and

(b) on summary conviction, be liable to imprisonment for a term not exceeding six months or to a fine not exceeding the statutory maximum, or to both.

(16) Where any person—

(a) knows or suspects that an investigation by the police or the Serious Fraud Office into serious or complex fraud is being or is likely to be carried out; and

(b) falsifies, conceals, destroys or otherwise disposes of, or causes or permits the falsification, concealment, destruction or disposal of documents which he knows or suspects are or would be relevant to such an investigation,

he shall be guilty of an offence unless he proves that he had no intention of concealing the facts disclosed by the documents from persons carrying out such an investigation.

(17) A person guilty of an offence under subsection (16) above shall—

(a) on conviction on indictment, be liable to imprisonment for a term not exceeding 7 years or to a fine or to both; and

(b) on summary conviction, be liable to imprisonment for a term not exceeding 6 months or to a fine not exceeding the statutory maximum or to both.

(18) In this section, "documents" includes information recorded in any form and, in relation to information recorded otherwise than in legible form, references to its production include references to producing a copy of the information in legible form and "evidence" (in relation to subsections (1A)(*b*), (8A), (8B) and (8C) above) includes documents and other articles.

(19) In the application of this section to Scotland, the reference to a justice of the peace is to be construed as a reference to the sheriff; and in the application of this section to Northern Ireland, subsection (4) above shall have effect as if for the references to information there were substituted references to a complaint.

Disclosure of information

3. (1) Where any information subject to an obligation of secrecy under the Taxes Management Act 1970 has been disclosed by the Commissioners of Inland Revenue or an officer of those Commissioners to any member of the Serious Fraud Office for the purposes of any prosecution of an offence relating to inland revenue, that information may be disclosed by any member of the Serious Fraud Office—

(*a*) for the purposes of any prosecution of which that Office has the conduct;

(*b*) to any member of the Crown Prosecution Service for the purposes of any prosecution of an offence relating to inland revenue; and

(*c*) to the Director of Public Prosecutions for Nothern Ireland for the purposes of any prosecution of an offence relating to inland revenue,

but not otherwise.

(2) Where the Serious Fraud Office has the conduct of any prosecution of an offence which does not relate to inland revenue, the court may not prevent the prosecution from relying on any evidence under section 78 of the Police and Criminal Evidence Act 1984 (discretion to exclude unfair evidence) by reason only of the fact that the information concerned was disclosed by the Commissioners of Inland Revenue or an officer of those Commissioners for the purposes of any prosecution of an offence relating to inland revenue.

(3) Where any information is subject to an obligation of secrecy imposed by or under any enactment other than an enactment contained in the Taxes Management Act 1970, the obligation shall not have effect to prohibit the disclosure of that information to any person in his capacity as a member of the Serious Fraud Office but any information disclosed by virtue of this subsection may only be disclosed by a member of the Serious Fraud Office for the purposes of any prosecution in England and Wales, Northern Ireland or elsewhere and may only be disclosed by such a member if he is designated by the Director for the purposes of this subsection.

(4) Without prejudice to his power to enter into agreements apart from this subsection, the Director may enter into a written agreement for the supply of information to or by him subject, in either case, to an obligation not to disclose the information concerned otherwise than for a specified purpose.

(5) Subject to subsections (1) and (3) above and to any provision of an agreement for the supply of information which restricts the disclosure of the information supplied, information obtained by any person in his capacity as a member of the Serious Fraud Office may be disclosed by any member of that Office designated by the Director for the purposes of this subsection—

(*a*) to any government department or Northern Ireland department or other authority or body discharging its functions on behalf of the Crown (including the Crown in right of Her Majesty's Government in Northern Ireland);

(b) to any competent authority;

(c) for the purposes of any prosecution in England and Wales, Northern Ireland or elsewhere; and

(d) for the purposes of assisting any public or other authority for the time being designated for the purposes of this paragraph by an order made by the Secretary of State to discharge any functions which are specified in the order.

(6) The following are competent authorities for the purposes of subsection (5) above—

(a) an inspector appointed under Part XIV of the Companies Act 1985 or Part XV of the Companies (Northern Ireland) Ortder 1986;

(b) an Official Receiver;

(c) the Accountant in Bankruptcy;

(d) an Official Assignee;

(e) a person appointed to carry out an investigation under section 55 of the Building Societies Act 1986;

(f) a body administering a compensation scheme under section 54 of the Financial Services Act 1986;

(g) an inspector appointed under section 94 of that Act;

(h) a person exercising powers by virtue of section 106 of that Act;

(i) an inspector appointed under section 177 of that Act;

(j) a person appointed by the Bank of England under section 41 of the Banking Act 1987 to carry out an investigation and make a report;

(k) a person exercising powers by virtue of section 44(2) of the Insurance Companies Act 1982;

(l) any body having supervisory, regulatory or disciplinary functions in relation to any profession or any area of commercial activity; and

(m) any person or body having, under the law of any country or territory outside the United Kingdom, functions corresponding to any of the functions of any person or body mentioned in any of the foregoing paragraphs.

(7) An order under subsection (5)(d) above may impose conditions subject to which, and otherwise restrict the circumstances in which, information may be disclosed under that paragraph.

Statutory police powers to enter and search premises

The following list gives those powers to enter and search premises under warrant, and under other written authority, which are normally exercised by the police. The list is restricted to provisions in public general legislation. It should be noted that while in most cases the power of entry is connected with the search of premises for evidence relating to a criminal offence, in some cases the entry is to enable the police to search the premises for a person, or for some other purpose. The relevant powers to issue warrants are conferred on magistrates, except where otherwise mentioned. The list is not comprehensive.

For powers of search and seizure under the customs and excise legislation see chapter 9; under the prevention of terrorism legislation see chapter 8; under the Criminal Justice Act 1987 (serious fraud) see chapter 3 and under the Drug Trafficking Act 1994 see pp 94–96.

(a) Powers of entry and search under warrant

Provision	Circumstances in which warrant can be issued	Power	Notes
Animals (Scientific Procedures) Act 1986	Where there are reasonable grounds for believing an offence under the Act has been or is being committed at any place	To enter the place and search it and to require any person found there to give his name and address	
Betting, Gaming & Lotteries Act 1963 s 51	Where there is reasonable ground for suspecting that an offence under the Act is being, has been or is about to be committed on any premises	To enter the premises, search them, seize and remove anything likely to be evidence of an offence under the Act, and arrest and search any person reasonably believed to be committing or to have committed an offence under the Act	

Provision	Circumstances in which warrant can be issued	Power	Notes
Biological Weapons Act 1974 s 4	Where there is reasonable ground for suspecting that an offence under s 1 of the Act has been, or is about to be committed	To enter the premises, and to search them and any person found there; to inspect and copy or seize and detain any document found there or in possession of any person found there; and to inspect, seize and detain any equipment or substance so found, and to sample such substance	
Children Act 1989 s 48(9)	Where a person attempting to exercise powers under an emergency protection order has been prevented from doing so by being refused entry to the premises concerned or access to the child concerned; or that such a person is likely to be so prevented	To assist the person in the exercise of those powers	
s 102	Where a person attempting to exercise powers under any enactment referred to in s 102(6) has been prevented from doing so by being refused entry to the premises or access to the child; or that such a person is likely to be so prevented	To assist the person in the exercise of those powers	
Children and Young Persons Act 1933 s 40 (as amended)	Where there is reasonable cause to suspect that a child or young person has been or is being assaulted, ill-treated or neglected in a manner likely to cause him unnecessary suffering or injury to health, or that one of certain offences has been or is being committed in respect of the child or young person	To enter any place named in the warrant to search for such child or young person and, if it is found that the ill-treatment etc is or has been occurring in the manner aforesaid, to remove him to a place of safety	Warrant may include power to arrest any person accused of any offence in respect of the child or young person in question
Children and Young Persons Act 1969, s 32(2A) (as added by Children Act 1975 s 68)	Where there are reasonable grounds for believing that a child or young person is absent without proper authority from a place of safety, or a place where he is living in the care of a local authority, or a remand home, special reception centre etc and is in specified premises	To search the premises for the said person	
Children and Young Persons (Harmful Publications) Act 1955 s 3	Where a summons or warrant of arrest in respect of an offence under s 2 of the Act has been issued, and there is reasonable ground for believing that a person has in his possession or under his control copies of a harmful publication within the meaning of the Act, or any plate or film prepared for the purpose of printing copies of such a publication	To enter and search premises named in the warrant; to seize any harmful publication within the meaning of the Act, and any plate or film prepared for printing such a publication	Power of search and seizure can extend to any vehicle or stall used by the suspect for trade or business

Provision	Circumstances in which warrant can be issued	Power	Notes
Cinemas Act 1985 s 13	Where there is reasonable cause to believe certain exhibitions are to be given in premises licensed for certain events	To enter and inspect the premises with a view to seeing whether the relevant provisions are being complied with	
Coinage Offences Act 1936 s 11(3)	Where there is reasonable cause to suspect that any person has been concerned in counterfeiting any current coin; or has any counterfeit coin, or counterfeiting machine or material	To search the relevant premises and seize any counterfeit coin or counterfeiting instrument, machine or material	
Companies Act 1985 s 448 as substituted by Companies Act 1989 s 64	(1) Where there are reasonable grounds for believing that there are on any premises documents whose production has been required and which have not been produced (2) Where there are reasonable grounds for believing that an offence has been committed for which there is a minimum penalty of 2 years' imprisonment and there are documents on premises relating to the offence; that there is power to require the production of the documents and that there are reasonable grounds for believing that the documents would not be produced if required	To enter and search premises, to seize documents, to take copies and to require any person named in the warrant to provide an explanation of them	
Computer Misuse Act 1990 s 14	Where there are reasonable grounds for believing that an offence under s 1 is being or is about to be committed and that evidence of that is on the premises	To enter, search and seize evidence	
Criminal Damage Act 1971 s 6(1)	Where there is reasonable cause to believe that any person has anything which there is reasonable cause to believe has been used or is intended for use unlawfully to destroy or damage property belonging to another, or in such a way as to be likely to endanger the life of another	To enter and search the premises and to seize anything belived to have been so used or to be intended to be so used	
Criminal Justice Act 1988 s 93I (as inserted by Proceeds of Crime Act 1995)	Where an order under Criminal Justice Act 1988 s 93H has not been complied with or other sircumstances prevail	To enter, search and seize material relevant to making of confiscation order	
Criminal Justice (International Co-operation) Act 1990 s 7	Where there are reasonable grounds to suspect that there is evidence on premises relating to a criminal investigation overseas	To enter and search premises and seize evidence	
Dangerous Dogs Act 1991 s 5(2)	Where there are reasonable grounds for believing an offence under the Act is being or has been committed or that evidence is to be found on any premises	To enter, search and seize any dog or other evidence	

Provision	Circumstances in which warrant can be issued	Power	Notes
Dogs (Protection of Livestock) Act 1953 s 2A (Police and Criminal Evidence Act 1984 Sch VI para 7)	Where there are reasonable grounds for believing that an offence under this Act has been committed; and that the dog in respect of which the offence has been committed is on the premises specified in the application	To enter and search premises in order to identify the dog	
Emergency Laws (Re-enactments and Repeals) Act 1964 Sch 1 para 2	Where there are reasonable grounds for suspecting that there are on the premises any documents of which production has been required by virtue of para 1 of the Schedule, and which have not been produced	To enter and search premises and take possession of any documents appearing to be those required by virtue of para 1 of the Schedule; or to take any steps which may appear necessary for preserving them and preventing interference with them	
Explosives Act 1875 s 73 (as extended by the Explosive Substances Act 1883 s 8)	Where there is reasonable cause to believe that an offence has been or is being committed with respect to any explosive in any case etc	To enter and search the relevant premises; and take samples of any explosive, or ingredient of any explosive, or of any substance reasonably supposed to be an explosive or an ingredient of an explosive	
Financial Services Act 1986 s 199 as amended by Companies Act 1989 s 76	(1) Where there are reasonable grounds for believing that offences under this legislation or the Company Securities (Insider Dealing) Act 1985 have been committed and there are relevant documents on any premises (2) Where there are reasonable grounds for believing that there are documents on premises whose production has been required and which have not been produced	To enter and search premises and seize documents	
Firearms Act 1968 (as amended) s 46	Where there is reasonable ground for suspecting that an offence under the Act (with certain exceptions) has been, is being, or is about to be committed	To enter and search the premises or place, and to search every person found therein; to seize and detain any firearm or ammunition; and (if the premises are those of a registered firearms dealer) to examine any books relating to the business	
Forgery and Counterfeiting Act 1981 s 7	Where there are reasonable grounds for believing that a person has in his custody and control anything used to commit an offence under the Act	To enter, search for and seize any such item	
Gaming Act 1968 s 43(4) and (5)	Where there are reasonable grounds for suspecting that an offence under the Act is being, has been or is about to be committed	To enter and search premises and remove anything which may be required as evidence for the purpose of proceedings under the Act; and to arrest and search any person found on the premises who is reasonably believed to be committing or to have committed an offence under the Act	

Provision	Circumstances in which warrant can be issued	Power	Notes
Hop (Prevention of Frauds) Act 1866 s 10	Where there is good reason to believe that any hops, or bags or pockets in which they are contained are not marked as required in the Act and certain other Acts	To enter any premises where the relevant hops, bags or pockets may be, to search for them and any such article which is reasonably believed not to be marked as required	
Immigration Act 1971 Sch 2 para 17	Where there is reasonable ground for suspecting that a person liable to be arrested (for the purpose of examination or removal) under a provision of the Act is to be found on any premises	To enter the premises for the purpose of searching for and arresting the person	
Incitement to Disaffection Act 1934 s 2	Where there is reasonable ground for suspecting an offence under the Act and that evidence of the commission of such an offence is to be found at any premises or place	To enter the premises or place, to search it and every person found therein, and to seize anything which is reasonably believed to be evidence of an offence under the Act	Warrant may only be issued by a judge of the High Court on application by a police officer of rank no lower than inspector
Indecent Displays (Control) Act 1981 s 2	Where there are reasonable grounds for suspecting that an indecent display has been or is being held on any premises	To enter to seize any articles which a constable has reasonable grounds to believe to be or to contain indecent matter and to have been used in the commission of an offence under the Act	
Insurance Companies Act 1982 s 44 as amended by Companies Act 1989	See Companies Act 1985 s 448 above	See Companies Act 1985 s 448 above	
Licensing Act 1964 s 54	Where there is reasonable ground for cancelling in whole or in part a registration certificate held by a club, and that evidence of it is to be obtained at the club premises; or that intoxicating liquor is sold, supplied or kept by a club in contravention of the provisions of the Act	To enter and search the club premises and to seize any documents relating to the business of the club	
s 85	Where there is reasonable ground for believing that any premises are kept or habitually used for the holding of parties at which the provisions of s 84(1) of the Act (relating to parties organised for gain through the sale of liquor) are contravened	To enter and search the premises and to seize and remove any intoxicating liquor reasonably believed to be connected with a contravention of s 84(1) of the Act	
s 187	Where there is reasonable ground to believe that any intoxicating liquor is sold by retail, or exposed or kept for sale by retail at any place	To enter and search the place for intoxicating liquor; and to seize and remove any liquor reasonably supposed to be there for the purpose of unlawful sale, and any vessels containing such liquor	

Provision	Circumstances in which warrant can be issued	Power	Notes
Lotteries and Amusements Act 1976 s 19	Where there is reasonable ground for suspecting that an offence under the Act is being, has been or is about to be committed	To enter and search the premises and seize and remove any documents etc which may be required as evidence for the purpose of proceedings under the Act; and to arrest and search any person found on the premises who is reasonably believed to be committing or to have committed an offence under the Act	
Mental Health Act 1983 s 135(1)	Where there is reasonable cause to suspect that a person believed to be suffering from mental disorder has been or is being ill-treated or neglected or kept otherwise than under proper control, or, being unable to care for himself, is living alone	To enter the premises specified and, if thought fit, to remove the person to a place of safety	
s 135(2)	Where there is reasonable cause to believe that a patient in respect of whom there is authority to take to any place, or to take or re-take into custody, is to be found on premises, and that admission to such premises has been refused or such refusal is apprehended	To enter the premises and remove the patient	
Misuse of Drugs Act 1971 s 23(3)	Where there is reasonable ground for suspecting that any controlled drugs are unlawfully in the possession of a person on any premises, or that a document relating to a transaction which is or would be an offence under the Act is unlawfully in the possession of a person on any premises	To enter the premises, and search them and any person found therein, and to seize and detain drugs or documents in respect of which or in connection with which there is reasonable ground for suspecting that an offence under the Act has been committed	
Obscene Publications Act 1959 s 3	Where there is reasonable ground for suspecting that in any premises, stall or vehicle obscene articles are, or are from time to time, kept for publication for gain	To enter and search the premises, or to search the stall or vehicle and to seize and remove any araticles which there is reason to believe are obscene and to be kept for publication for gain. If such articles are seized other trade or business documents may be seized too.	
Offences Against the Person Act 1861 s 65	Where any gunpowder, other explosive, dangerous or noxious substance or thing or any machine, engine, instrument or thing is suspected to be made, kept, or carried for the purpose of being used for certain offences under the Act	To search any house, mill, magazine, storehouse, warehouse, shop, cellar, yard, wharf or other place, or any carriage, waggon, cart, ship, boat or vessel in which the gunpowder etc is suspected to be made, kept or carried and to seize and remove to a proper place the gunpowder etc and any receptacle in which it is contained	

Provision	Circumstances in which warrant can be issued	Power	Notes
Official Secrets Act 1911 s 9(1)	Where there is reasonable ground for suspecting that an offence under the Act or the 1989 Act, with the exception of s 8(1)(4) or (5) of that Act, has been or is about to be committed	To enter the premises specified and to search them and any person found therein, and to seize any sketch, plan, model, article, note, document etc, which is evidence of an offence under the Act having been or being about to be committed and with regard to which there is reasonable ground for suspecting that such an offence has been or is about to be committed.	
Public Order Act 1936 s 2(5)	Where there is reasonable ground for suspecting that an offence under the section (relating to the prohibition of quasi-military organisations) has been committed, and that evidence thereof is to be found at any place or premises	To enter and search the premises or place, and to search every person found there, and to seize anything which is reasonably suspected to be evidence of the commission of such an offence	Warrant may only be issued by a judge of the High Court on the application of a police officer of rank not lower than inspector
Public Order Act 1986 s 24	Where there are reasonable grounds to suspect a person is in possession of material in contravention of s 23 (racially inflammatory material)	To enter and search premises where it is suspected material is situated	
Public Stores Act 1875 s 12, as substituted by Theft Act 1968 Sch 2 Pt III	Where there is reasonable cause to believe that any person has any stores in respect of which an offence under s 5 of the Act has been committed	To search for and seize the stores	
Scrap Metal Dealers Act 1964 s 6(3)	Where admission to the place specified is reasonably required in order to secure compliance with the provisions of the Act, or to ascertain whether those provisions are being complied with	To enter the place	
Sexual Offences Act 1956 s 42	Where there is reasonable cause to suspect that any house or part of a house is used by a woman for prostitution and that a man residing in or frequenting the house is living wholly or partly on her earnings	To enter and search the house, and to arrest the man	
s 43	Where there is reasonable cause to suspect that a woman is detained in any place in order that she may have unlawful sexual intercourse, and that she is detained against her will, or is a defective, or is under 16, or if under 18 is detained against the will of her parent or guardian	To enter and search the premises specified and to remove the woman to a place of safety, and detain her there until she can be brought before a magistrate	

Provision	Circumstances in which warrant can be issued	Power	Notes
Theatres Act 1968 s 15(1)	Where there are reasonable grounds for suspecting that a performance of a play is to be given at the specified premises and that an offence under s 2, 5 or 6 of the Act is likely to be committed in respect of that performance, or that an offence under s 13 of the Act is being or will be committed in respect of the premises	If an offence under s 2, 5 or 6 is reasonably suspected, to enter and attend any relevant performance; if an offence under s 13 is reasonbly suspected, to inspect the premises	
Theft Act 1968 s 26(1) and (3)	Where there is reasonable cause to believe that any person has in his custody or possession or on his premises any stolen goods	To enter and search the specified premises, and seize any goods believed to be stolen goods	
Wildlife and Countryside Act 1981 s 19	Where there are reasonable grounds for suspecting that certain offences under the Act have been committed	To enter and search premises for the purpose of obtaining evidence	

(b) Powers of entry and search under other forms of written authority

Provision	From of authority	Circumstances in which authority can be issued	Power
Broadcasting Act 1990 s 196	Order of magistrate	Where there are reasonable grounds to believe a relevant offence has been commited	To copy material
Children and Young Persons Act 1933, s 28(1) (as extended by s 59 of the Education Act 1944)	Magistrate's order	Where there is reasonable cause to believe that certain provisions of the Act (in regard to the employment of children, or their performance in entertainments) are being contravened with respect to any person	To enter any place where the person is, or is believed to be, employed, taking part in a performance, or being trained, and to make enquiries with respect to that person. (Order valid only at reasonable times within 48 hours of its making)
Children Act 1989 s 50(3)(d)	Recovery order	Where a recovery order has been made under s 50	To enter premises and search for the child
Criminal Justice Act 1988 s 93H (inserted by Proeeds of Crime Act 1995)	Order of a judge	Where there is an investigation into whether someone has benefitted from a course of criminal conduct or the extent and whereabouts of the proceeds	To seize material
Criminal Libel Act 1819, s 1	Order of a judge	Where a person is convicted of composing, printing or publishing a blasphemous or seditious libel	To enter and search any house, building or any place whatsoever belonging to the person convicted, and of any person named as keeping copies of the libel for the use of the convicted person; and to carry away and detain any copies of the libel which are found

Provision	From of authority	Circumstances in which authority can be issued	Power
Explosives Act 1875 s 73 (as extended by the Explosive Substances Act 1883 s 8)	Written order by a police officer of at least superintendent rank	Where there is reasonable cause to believe that an offence has been or is being committed with respect to any explosive in any case etc and the delay in obtaining a magistrate's warrant (as above) would be likely to endanger life	To enter and search the relevant premises; and take samples of any explosive or ingredient of an explosive, or of any substance reasonably supposed to be an explosive or an ingredient of an explosive
Licensing Act 1964 s 45	Written authority of chief officer of police, or his designee	Where a club applies for the issue of a registration certificate in respect of any premises, and in the opinion of the chief officer of police there are special reasons making it necessary for the premises to be inspected for the proper discharge of his functions in relation to the registration of clubs	To enter and inspect the premises
Metropolitan Police Act 1839 s 47	Written order of Commissioner to superintendent of Metropolitan Police, with such constables as he shall think necessary		To enter any place in the Metropolitan Police District kept or used for bear-baiting, cock-fighting etc, and take into custody all persons found therein without lawful excuse
Official Secrets Act 1911 s 9(2)	Written order of a superintendent of police	Where there is reasonable ground for suspecting that an offence under the Act has been or is about to be committed and the case is one of great emergency, and immediate action is necessary in the interests of the State. (As to entry under warrant, where the case is not one of great emergency, see above)	To enter the premises specified and to search them and any person found therein, and to seize any sketch, plan, model, article, note, document etc, which is evidence of an offence under the Act having been or being about to be committed and with regard to which there is reasonable ground for suspecting that such an offence has been or is about to be committed
Safety of Sports Grounds Act 1975 s 11	Authority of a chief officer of police, the local authority, the building authority or the Secretary of State		On production, if required, of his authority, to enter a sports ground at any reasonable time, and make such inspection of it as he considers necessary for the purposes of this Act, and in particular to examine records of attendance and records relating to the maintenance of safety, and to copy such documents

(c) Statutory police powers to enter premises without warrant

The following list of provisions in public general legislation is in addition to those mentioned above. The list refers to premises and does not extend to powers to enter and search vehicles, ships etc, except where these are referred to in the same provision.

Provision	Power	Restrictions
Animal Health Act 1981 s 62	To enter and search any vessel, boat, aircraft or vehicle to arrest a person committing an offence under s 61 (introduction of rabies) and to seize any relevant animals	
Aviation Security Act 1982 s 13	To enter and search any part of an aerodrom or any aircraft, vehicle of goods, or any building or works in the aerodrome for any of the articles prohibited by s 4	
s 27	To search any aircraft or vehicle for stolen or unlawfully obtained goods	
Betting, Gaming and Lotteries Act 1963 s 10(4)	To enter any licensed betting office for the purpose of ascertaining whether the provisions of s 10(1) (relating to the conduct of licensed betting offices) are being complied with	
s 23	To enter any race track for the purpose of ascertaining whether the provisions of the relevant part of the Act (relating to betting) are being complied with	Entry may be made only "at all reasonable times"
Children and Young Persons Act 1933 s 12(4)	To enter any building in which the constable has reason to believe that an entertainment for children is being, or is about to be, provided, with a view to seeing whether the provisions of the section (relating to the safety of children at entertainments) are carried into effect	
s 28(2)	To enter any place where a person (to whom a licence under s 22 or 24 of the Act relates) is authorised by the licence to take part in an entertainment, or to be trained, and to make enquiries therein with respect to that person	
Cinemas Act 1985 s 13	Where the constable has reasonable grounds to believe that an offence under s 10(1) has been, is being or is about to be committed, to enter and search premises	
Criminal Justice and Public Order Act 1994 s 64	To enter land for purposes of dealing with raves under s 63	
Crossbows Act 1987 s 4	To enter any land other than a dwelling house to search a vehicle or anything in or on it for a crossbow, or part of one, in contravention of the Act	
Deer Act 1991	To enter any land (other than a dwelling house) to arrest for an offence and to search or examine any vehicle	
Explosives Act 1875 s 75	To enter, inspect and examine any wharf, ship etc of any carrier etc (where there is reasonable cause to suppose an explosive to be for the purpose of or in the course of conveyance) for the purpose of ascertaining whether the provisions of the Act relating to the conveyance of explosives are being complied with	Power exercisable by chief officer of police only; the work or business of the carrier etc should not be obstructed unnecessarily
Fire Services Act 1947 s 30(1)	To enter any premises or place in which a fire has or is reasonably believed to have broken out, or any premises or place which it is necessary to enter in order to extinguish a fire, or to protect the premises from acts done for fire fighting purposes, and to do all such things as may be deemed necessary for extinguishing the fire, or protecting the premises or for rescuing any person or property found therein.	

Provision	Power	Restrictions
Game laws (Amendment) Act 1960 s 2	Where there are reasonable grounds for suspecting that a person is committing an offence on any land under s 1 or s 9 of the Night Poaching Act 1828 or under s 30 or s 33 of the Game Act 1831 to enter on the land for the purpose of exercising the powers conferred on the constable	Power does not extend to land occupied by the Ministry of Defence etc
Gaming Act 1845 s 14	To enter any house, room or place where any public table or board is kept for playing at billiards, bagatelle, or any game of the like kind	
Gaming Act 1968 s 43(2)	To enter any premises in respect of which a licence under the Act is for the time being in force and to inspect the premises and any machine or other equipment and any book or document which the constable reasonably requires to inspect for the purpose of ascertaining whether a contravention of the Act, or the regulations made thereunder, is being, or has been committed. (Note: see also power of entry under warrant above)	Entry may be made only "at any reasonable times"
Hypnotism Act 1952 s 4	To enter any premises where any entertainment is held if he has reasonable cause to believe that any act is being or may be done in contravention of the Act	
Late Night Refreshment Houses Act 1969 s 10(1)	To enter a late night refreshment house licensed under the Act, and any premises belonging thereto	
Licensing Act 1964 s 186 (as substituted by the Licensing (Amendment) Act 1977 s 1)	To enter any licensed premises, a licensed canteen or premises for which a special hours certificate is in force, for the purpose of preventing or detecting the commission of an offence under the Act of 1964	The power may only be exercised within certain times as set out in the section
Misuse of Drugs Act 1971 s 23(1)	For the purpose of the execution of the Act, to enter the premises of a person carrying on business as a producer or supplier of any controlled drugs, and to demand the production of, and to inspect, any books or documents relating to dealings in such drugs and to inspect stocks of such drugs.	
Performing Animals (Regulation) Act 1925 s 3	To enter and inspect any premises in which any performing animals are being trained or exhibited or kept for training or exhibition and any animals found thereon; and to require any person whom there is reason to believe to be a trainer or exhibitor of performing animals to produce his certificate.	A constable exercising the power may not go on or behind the stage during a public performance. Entry may only be made "at all reasonable times"
Protection of Animals Act 1911 s 5(2)	To enter any knacker's yard for the purpose of examining whether there is or has been any contravention of or non-compliance with the Act	Entry may only be made "at any hour by day, or at any hour when business is or apparently is in progress or is usually carried on therein"
Road Traffic Act 1988 s 4(7)	To enter premises to arrest a person reasonably suspected to have been driving under the influence of drink or drugs	
Scrap Metal Dealers Act 1964 s 6(1)	To enter and inspect any place registered as a scrap metal store, or in connection with scrap metal dealings, and to require production of, and to inspect, any scrap metal kept there, and any book or receipt which the dealer is required to keep, and to take copies or extracts from any such book or receipt	Entry may only be made "at all reasonable times"

Provision	Power	Restrictions
Sporting Events (Control of Alcohol etc) Act 1985 s 7(1) as amended	To enter at any time during the period of a designated sporting event at any designated sports ground and to enter any part of the ground for the purpose of enforcing the provisions of the Act	
Theatres Act 1968 s 15(3)	To enter any premises in respect of which a licence under the Act is in force at which he has reason to believe that a performance of a play is being or is about to be given and to inspect them with a view to seeing whether the terms or conditions of the licence are being complied with	Entry may only be made "at all reasonable times". (Officers shall not if wearing uniform be required to produce any authority)
Wildlife and Countryside Act 1981 s 19	To enter land (but not a dwelling-house) if a constable suspects with reasonable cause that any person is committing an offence under the Act	

United Nations Convention against Torture and Other Cruel, Inhuman or Degrading Treatment or Punishment

(Resolution 39/46) Article 1

PART I

Article 1

1. For the purposes of this Convention, the term "torture" means any act by which severe pain or suffering, whether physical or mental, is intentionally inflicted on a person for such purposes as obtaining from him or a third person information or a confession, punishing him for an act he or a third person has committed or is suspected of having committed, or intimidating or coercing him or a third person, or for any reason based on discrimination of any kind, when such pain or suffering is inflicted by or at the instigation of or with the consent or acquiescence of a public official or other person acting in an official capacity. It does not include pain or suffering arising from, inherent in or incidental to lawful sanctions.

2. This article is without prejudice to any international instrument or national legislation which does or may contain provisions of wider application.

(Adopted 10 December 1984)

Children Act 1989 s46

Removal and accommodation of children by police in cases of emergency

46. (1) Where a constable has reasonable cause to believe that a child would otherwise be likely to suffer significant harm, he may—

(*a*) remove the child to suitable accommodation and keep him there; or

(*b*) take such steps as are reasonable to ensure that the child's removal from any hospital, or other place, in which he is then being accommodated is prevented.

(2) For the purposes of this Act, a child with respect to whom a constable has exercised his powers under this section is referred to as having been taken into police protection.

(3) As soon as is reasonably practicable after taking a child into police protection, the constable concerned shall—

(*a*) inform the local authority within whose area the child was found of the steps that have been, and are proposed to be, taken with respect to the child under this section and the reasons for taking them;

(*b*) give details to the authority within whose area the child is ordinarily resident ("the appropriate authority") of the place at which the child is being accommodated;

(*c*) inform the child (if he appears capable of understanding)—

 (i) of the steps that have been taken with respect to him under this section and of the reasons for taking them; and

 (ii) of the further steps that may be taken with respect to him under this section;

(*d*) take such steps as are reasonably practicable to discover the wishes and feelings of the child;

(*e*) secure that the case is inquired into by an officer designated for the purposes of this section by the chief officer of the police area concerned; and

(*f*) where the child was taken into police protection by being removed to accommodation which is not provided—

 (i) by or on behalf of a local authority; or

 (ii) as a refuge, in compliance with the requirements of section 51,

 secure that he is moved to accommodation which is so provided.

(4) As soon as is reasonably practicable after taking a child into police protection,

the constable concerned shall take such steps as are reasonably practicable to inform—

(a) the child's parents;

(b) every person who is not a parent of his but who has parental responsibility for him; and

(c) any other person with whom the child was living immediately before being taken into police protection,

of the steps that he has taken under this section with respect to the child, the reasons for taking them and the further steps that may be taken with respect to him under this section.

(5) On completing any inquiry under subsection (3)(e), the officer conducting it shall release the child from police protection unless he considers that there is still reasonable cause for believing that the child would be likely to suffer significant harm if released.

(6) No child may be kept in police protection for more than 72 hours.

(7) While a child is being kept in police protection, the designated officer may apply on behalf of the appropriate authority for an emergency protection order to be made under section 44 with respect to the child.

(8) An application may be made under subsection (7) whether or not the authority know of it or agree to its being made.

(9) While a child is being kept in police protection—

(a) neither the constable concerned nor the designated officer shall have parental responsibility for him; but

(b) the designated officer shall do what is reasonable in all the circumstances of the case for the purpose of safeguarding or promoting the child's welfare (having regard in particular to the length of the period during which the child will be so protected).

(10) Where a child has been taken into police protection, the designated officer shall allow—

(a) the child's parents;

(b) any person who is not a parent of the child but who has parental responsibility for him;

(c) any person with whom the child was living immediately before he was taken into police protection;

(d) any person in whose favour a contact order is in force with respect to the child;

(e) any person who is allowed to have contact with the child by virtue of an order under section 34; and

(f) any person acting on behalf of those persons,

to have such contact (if any) with the child as, in the opinion of the designated officer, is both reasonable and in the child's best interests.

(11) Where a child who has been taken into police protection is in accommodation provided by, or on behalf of, the appropriate authority, subsection (10) shall have effect as if it referred to the authority rather than to the designated officer.

Index